Introduction to Tibetan Buddhism

Introduction to Tibetan Buddhism

REVISED EDITION

by John Powers

Snow Lion Publications
ITHACA, NEW YORK • BOULDER, COLORADO

Snow Lion Publications
P.O. Box 6483 • Ithaca, NY 14851 USA
(607) 273-8519 • www.snowlionpub.com

 First edition 1995
Second edition 2007

Printed in Canada on acid-free recycled paper.
Designed and typeset by Gopa & Ted2, Inc.

Library of Congress Cataloging-in-Publication Data

Powers, John, 1957-
Introduction to Tibetan Buddhism / by John Powers. — Rev. ed.
p. cm.
Includes bibliographical references and indexes.
ISBN-13: 978-1-55939-282-2 (alk. paper)
ISBN-10: 1-55939-282-7 (alk. paper)
1. Buddhism—China—Tibet. 2. Tibet (China)—Religion. I. Title.

BQ7604.P69 2007
294.3'923—dc22

2007019309

Table of Contents

PART TWO: TIBETAN HISTORY AND CULTURE

Part Three: Tibetan Buddhist Doctrines and Practices

Part Four: The Orders of Tibetan Buddhism

To Terry and Leo

PREFACE

IN THE DECADE since the publication of the first edition of this book, a veritable flood of literature has appeared in Western languages on topics relating to Tibetan religion, history, and culture. At the same time, the availability of Tibetan texts that were either difficult to access or that had been presumed lost has increased. A number of groundbreaking studies by academics have appeared, and there is now a substantial library of treatises, videos, and CDs, as well as Internet-based resources by Tibetan masters describing aspects of their philosophical and meditative traditions, folk tales, traditional stories, biographies and autobiographies, and oral and written discourses on such topics as astrology, divination, and Vajrayāna.

The first edition was the result of years of study in university courses and libraries with primary texts, secondary works, oral instructions by lamas from the four major orders of Tibetan Buddhism (Nyingma, Kagyu, Sakya, and Géluk), as well as fieldwork in the Himalayan region. The goal of the first edition—and of the present one—was to meet the growing need for an introduction to Tibetan Buddhism written specifically for people with little or no previous exposure to the tradition.

This book is intended for an audience of undergraduates, Buddhist practitioners looking for an overview of the tradition, and readers with a general interest in the subject. It attempts to provide information regarding the history and practices of Tibetan Buddhism in a clear manner, without presuming previous knowledge of the subject, and also without assuming the supremacy (or inferiority) of any school or lineage. Its outline is not derived from any traditional organizing structure, and grows out of my own study of this tradition and my attempts to place its components in context and to make sense of the often conflicting claims and counterclaims of its exponents.

The tragedy of Tibet's invasion and annexation by the People's Republic of China in the 1950s has had a devastating effect on the people of Tibet and their rich traditional culture, but the rest of the world has benefited from the resulting diaspora, which has brought Tibetan lamas out of their monasteries and retreat huts and into universities and newly-established Buddhist centers. Now students can have access to them in ways that would have been impossible in traditional Tibet.

As a result of their exposure to teachings and teachers from this tradition, thousands of Westerners have become Tibetan Buddhists, and there is widespread interest even among nonconverts in the public lectures of such luminaries as the Dalai Lama, Sogyel Rinpoché, Pema Norbu Rinpoché, and Sakya Tridzin. Modern technology allows their words to be printed and disseminated all over the world, in print and electronic forms. Most major cities in North America, Europe, and Australia have at least one Buddhist center, and many have several representing various denominations. College courses on Buddhism in general and Tibetan Buddhism in particular are a common feature of contemporary curricula.

The present incarnation of this book incorporates a number of important new perspectives and theories. In addition, my own expanding knowledge of the subject has rendered some of my earlier conclusions questionable or outdated, but the possibility of writing a second edition provides a mechanism to revise and update my earlier work, one of the luxuries of modern word processing and publishing technology.

As with the first edition, the scope of this book is broad, encompassing history, philosophy, ritual, architecture, art, and a range of other subjects, but it still only scratches the surface of this ancient and rich culture. The first part of the book explores the Indian background in which Buddhism arose. It focuses on the figure of the Buddha, some important doctrines attributed to him, the practice and theory of Buddhist meditation, the main distinctions between the Mahāyāna and Hīnayāna schools, and the relation of Vajrayāna to other Mahāyāna systems. Part two is concerned with the history and culture of Tibet, and examines its early religious history, the present-day situation of Tibetan Buddhism, and some important aspects of the daily religious lives of Tibetan Buddhists. Part three looks at Vajrayāna and at the most influential teaching lineages of

Tibetan Buddhism, focusing on their histories, important figures, and distinctive practices.

Since beginning serious study of Tibetan Buddhism more than two decades ago, I have had the good fortune to receive oral instructions from some of the most prominent Western scholars of Buddhism as well as eminent and articulate exponents of each of the four orders of Tibetan Buddhism. Grant-giving agencies including the Australian Research Council, the American Philosophical Association, and the American Institute for Indian Studies have generously funded several years of fieldwork study in south India, the Himalayan region (including Ladakh, Zanskar, Sikkim, and Himachal Pradesh), Nepal, and various sites in northern India. I have received oral teachings, both in groups and in private, from scores of lamas, and have been allowed to witness and participate in a number of esoteric rituals. These experiences have provided the raw material for this book in both of its incarnations.

The scope of the project lies beyond the expertise of any researcher, and I would like to acknowledge my thanks to the many people who aided in the process of writing, editing, and correcting the various stages of the two editions. Sidney Piburn of Snow Lion Publications deserves credit for initiating the project and for his help throughout, as well as gently pressing me to get to work on the second edition. Joe Wilson's comments and corrections of the first section made me rethink some of my initial assumptions. Thanks are also due to William Magee for his careful reading of the manuscript and for his comments. Since beginning a teaching career, various versions of this work have been studied and critiqued by hundreds of students in the United States and Australia, and many of them have made invaluable comments and clarifications. In addition, they have helped me in adapting what I have seen and read to an audience of intelligent people with little or no background in the subject matter, and they have been perhaps my greatest resource in this process. Ronald Davidson's critique of the Sakya chapter significantly contributed to significant changes in the final version of the first edition, and I have greatly benefited from several of his conference presentations. I would also like to thank Paul Hackett for valuable information on sources. Sylvia Gretchen's contributions in proofreading the Nyingma chapter and suggesting corrections are deeply appreciated. A special debt of gratitude is owed to Jeffrey Hopkins, my graduate advisor, whose unstinting help and advice provided me with a paradigm for an academic mentor. My wife

Cindy has also made significant contributions to this project, both in terms of material support and through her help and encouragement. Her explanations of contemporary Western psychology and counseling techniques were very helpful in reaching an understanding of how they differ from Buddhist meditation practices.

A number of Tibetan scholars have contributed significantly to this book, among them the late Kensur Yéshé Thubten of Loseling Monastic College, with whom I studied in graduate school and during a year in India. Throughout my time in graduate school, Géshé Jambel Thardo patiently answered questions and provided oral instructions on a wide range of subjects, and much of my understanding of the Gélukpa scholastic system is due to him. Thanks are also due to Géshé Palden Dragpa of Tibet House in Delhi and Georges Dreyfus of Williams College, who initiated me into the subtleties of Tibetan oral debate and who patiently answered hundreds of questions during our graduate studies. While in India in 1988, many productive hours were spent discussing Buddhist philosophy with Professor Yéshé Thabkhé of the Central Institute of Higher Tibetan Studies. My sincere thanks to Ven. Samdhong Rinpoché, the current Kalon Tripa of the Tibetan exile government's legislative assembly and former Vice-Chancellor of the Central Institute, and to Géshé Ngawang Samten for allowing me to study there on several occasions and for making available the considerable resources of that wonderful institution.

Several Sakya lamas, including H.E. Chogyé Trichen Rinpoché and Lama Choedak Rinpoché, have generously shared their knowledge of the "triple vision" and "path and result" teachings over the past several years and helped me to understand their complexities. Khetsun Sangpo Rinpoché guided me and a small group of students through Mipam's exposition of the "great perfection" during a memorable summer, and Khamtrül Rinpoché provided months of instructions on the preliminary practices and the techniques of great perfection meditation during a fieldwork trip to Dharamsala in the 1990s. I would also like to thank H.H. the Dalai Lama for making time in his busy schedule to talk with me on several occasions and for the insights provided by his public lectures. Thanks are also due to Khenpo Könchog Gyeltsen for his many helpful talks on the Kagyu order and his making time to answer questions. I have also benefited from several invitations to lecture at the Kagyu E-wam Buddhist Institute in Melbourne, founded by Traleg Rinpoché, and from my informal discussions with him on various topics of Buddhist philosophy and practice.

The Tibetan lamas who are now teaching publicly and publishing works for a Western audience are well versed in their respective traditions, but are generally not trained to place them in a wider context in Tibet or the Buddhist world, nor do their backgrounds prepare them for comparing their orders' teachings and practices to those of other traditions. Much of Tibetan Buddhist literature is tinged with sectarian biases and broad (sometimes unfounded) generalizations about orders other than the one to which a particular teacher belongs, and the claims and counterclaims often prove confusing for those who have recently begun their study. In addition, traditional Tibetan mythology and hagiographical stories are often repeated by lamas who assume them to be veridical, and this creates conceptual difficulties for many Westerners, particularly those who have been exposed to modern science and skeptical philosophy. In a sense, this book is intended to explain Tibetan Buddhism to a foreign audience, one composed of people whose background and education resemble my own and who have encountered many of the same conceptual problems, questions, and gaps that I have during my ongoing engagement with Tibetan Buddhism and its exponents. This is a rich and diverse tradition, and I expect that there will be a number of future editions, each of which will reflect my deepening and expanding understanding of this subject, as well as changing perspectives and theories.

During the years I have studied Tibetan Buddhism and lived with Tibetans, it has become clear to me that this tradition is one of the richest shared legacies of humankind. It is my hope that this book will help make Tibetan Buddhism more accessible to interested students and that it will benefit sentient beings everywhere.

TECHNICAL NOTE

IN KEEPING with the introductory nature of this work, technical terms have been kept to a minimum. Some Tibetan words have been spelled phonetically and treated as English words, while others have been given English translations. The first occurrence of the most important technical terms is accompanied by an italicized transliteration in parentheses. All other terms, as well as names, places, and titles of texts are given in indexes, along with their transliterated spellings. The transliteration follows the system of Turrell Wylie, which he describes in his article, "A Standard System of Tibetan Transcription" (*Harvard Journal of Asiatic Studies*, 22, 1959, pp. 261–76).

Phonetic spellings of terms, names, and places have been adopted for the benefit of nonspecialists, who are often bewildered by the many unpronounced consonants found in Tibetan and by the subtleties of Tibetan pronunciation. Most words have been phoneticized in accordance with the dialect of Lhasa, the capital of Tibet and its cultural and religious center. Pronunciations of these words vary greatly in other parts of Tibet, but the central Tibetan pronunciation was chosen as the most commonly accepted standard. Some familiar terms have been rendered in accordance with their common spelling: for example, "Bön" and "Sakya." In this edition I have adopted umlauts and accent marks to facilitate pronunciation of some Tibetan sounds. Thus, the "ö" in *chö* (the Tibetan equivalent of the Sanskrit term *dharma*) is pronounced as in German, and the "é" in *rinpoché* is pronounced "ay." Many Tibetan teachers who teach and publish in the West have established transliterations of their names that are widely used (e.g., Lama Yeshe), and I have used these in this book instead of my own phonetic system.

Most of the quotations used in the text are taken from English language publications. In cases where none was available (or where I disagreed with a published translation) my own translations have been provided. The decision to use other translations was based on complaints from students who read early versions of the manuscript and noted that for nonspecialists it is often frustrating to read a pithy quote and not be able to read the original text in order to obtain further information or explore the context.

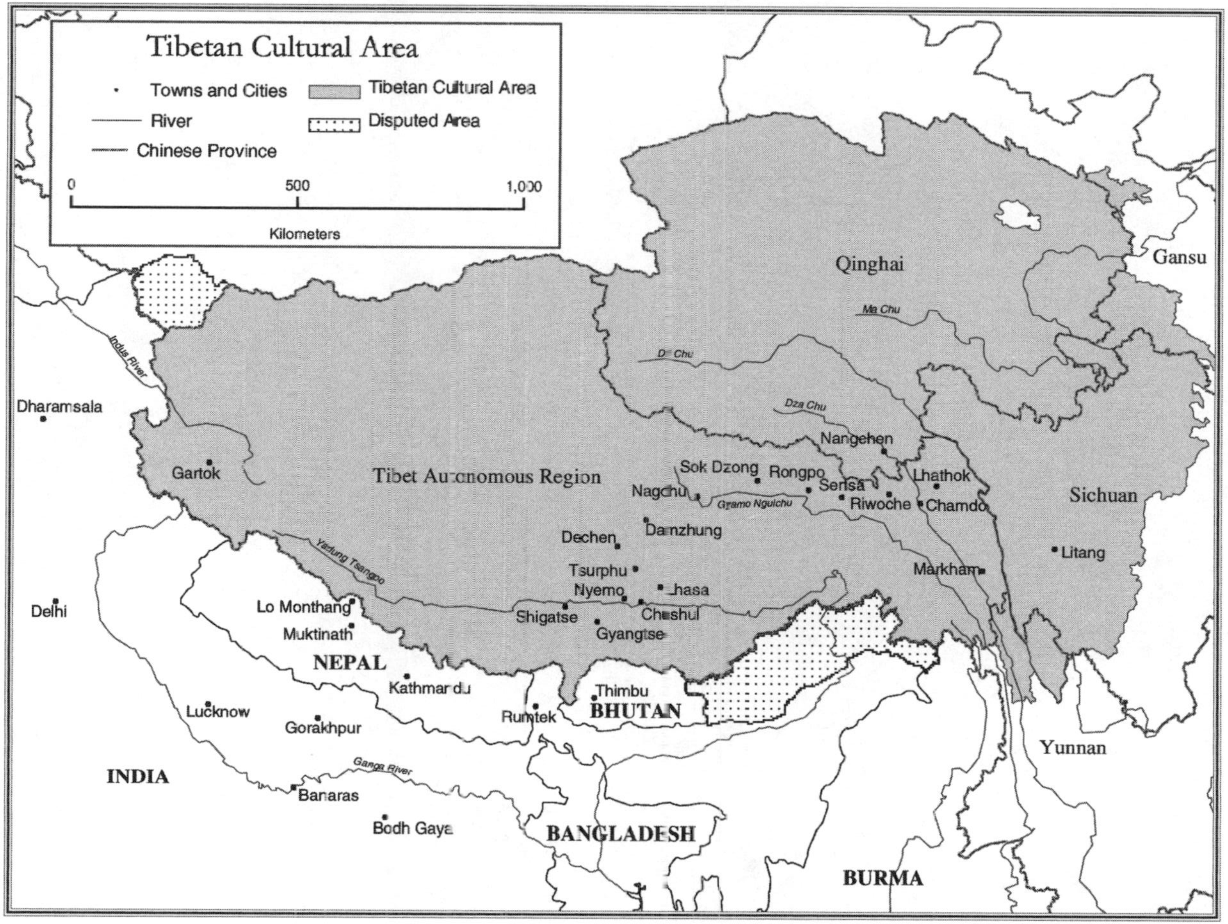

Created by Tsering Wangyal Shawa

Introduction

At dawn in Dharamsala, as the sun rises over the mountains, a number of people are already awake and walking on the path around the residence of the Dalai Lama, the spiritual leader of the Tibetan people. Dharamsala is a small town in the northern Indian state of Himachal Pradesh perched on the side of Mt. Dhauladhar in the foothills of the Himalayas, the world's highest mountains. Dharamsala today is the center of the Tibetan Buddhist exile community in India and the home of the Dalai Lama. Tenzin Gyatso, the fourteenth Dalai Lama, is considered by his followers to be a physical manifestation of Avalokiteśvara (*Chenrezi*), the buddha of compassion and patron deity of Tibet. Forced to flee his homeland in 1959 when the Chinese army forcibly annexed Tibet, he and many of his people have resettled in India, where they continue to look over the mountains, hoping someday to return to their homeland.

The harsh realities of diaspora and the tenuousness of their position in exile have not dimmed the reverence of the Tibetan people for the Dalai Lama, and the crowds that circumambulate his residence in Dharamsala are a testament to their respect for him. The individuals and groups walking the path are a cross-section of the Tibetan community: male and female, young and old, lay and monastic, and people from all levels of society. Some are on their way to work or to shop, and chose the route around the Dalai Lama's residence because they believe that circumambulating it brings merit, even if one only walks part of the way. Many of those on the path will make the circuit a number of times, and their trek will be an act of religious devotion.

Most carry prayer beads, used to mark the number of times they chant a mantra. The use of mantras is deeply rooted in Tibetan Buddhism. They are short prayers that are thought to subtly alter one's mind and make a connection with a particular buddha, or awakened being. Tibetan Buddhism has no gods in the Western sense of the term—the deities of Tibetan Buddhism are buddhas, literally "awakened ones," who in past lives were ordinary people, but who have transcended the ordinary through their meditations and realizations. When Tibetans chant a mantra associated with a particular buddha, they are not simply asking for the blessings and aid of the buddha—the final goal of the practice is to become buddhas themselves, since buddhas are sentient beings who have actualized the highest potential that we all possess.

The Tibetans walking around the Dalai Lama's palace often chant the mantra of Avalokiteśvara—*oṃ maṇi padme hūṃ*—a practice that pays tribute to the Dalai Lama as an incarnation of Avalokiteśvara and focuses their minds on the goal of eventually attaining his level of wisdom and compassion, the two primary qualities that buddhas embody. Many will stop along the path at *chödens* (*mchod rten, stūpa*),[1] small shrines that generally contain religious artifacts of some sort. Often the Tibetans will make prostrations toward the chödens or toward the Dalai Lama's residence. This is thought to bring great religious merit and, like the chanting of mantras, helps to orient one's mind to the goal of buddhahood.

One notable feature of this practice is its primary focus: other living beings. It is generally thought that if one performs religious actions solely for one's own benefit, the practices are ineffective and yield little or no merit. Since one is trying to attain buddhahood—and since buddhas are beings whose compassion extends to all living creatures—anyone who chants the mantra of the buddha of compassion or pays homage to the Dalai Lama seeking personal gain is thought to be profoundly misguided. Tibetans recognize this, and when asked will generally indicate that they offer the merit of their religious devotions for the benefit of all sentient beings.

All along the path are religious symbols, most of which are connected with Avalokiteśvara or his human manifestation, the Dalai Lama. There are several *maṇi* walls, which are piles of stones, each of which is inscribed with the mantra *oṃ maṇi padme hūṃ*. This literally means "*oṃ* in the jewel lotus *hūṃ*," although few of the Tibetans who chant the mantra would be aware of this. For most it is simply an invocation to the Dalai Lama and Avalokiteśvara that brings merit in both the present and future lives. In

Indian Buddhist scriptures, the mantra is related to the notion that beings born in the "pure land" of Sukhāvatī (Joyous Land) arise in jeweled lotuses rather than wombs, and the mantra probably originally expressed an aspiration for rebirth there. Avalokiteśvara is one of the principal figures of Sukhāvatī and is closely associated with Amitābha, the buddha who rules over it.[2]

The mantra has been interpreted in various ways, and Buddhist teachers commonly associate it with aspects of Buddhist thought and practice. The Dalai Lama, for example, relates it to the twin factors of method (skillfully adapting one's actions for the benefit of others) and wisdom (comprehending the true nature of reality) and the transformation of one's body, speech, and mind into those of a buddha.[3] A number of Tibetan teachers have connected each of the six syllables with the six "perfections" (*pha rol tu phyin pa, pāramitā*: generosity, ethics, patience, effort, concentration, and wisdom) in which those who are on the path to buddhahood train, while others relate them to the six realms of rebirth and escape from them.[4]

The lotus (*padma*) is an important symbol in Tibetan Buddhism and is commonly associated with the process of becoming a buddha. In Tibetan Buddhist iconography, buddhas are often seated on lotus thrones, indicating their transcendent state. A lotus is born in the muck and mud at the bottom of a swamp, but when it emerges on the surface of the water and opens its petals a beautiful flower appears, unstained by the mud from which it arose. Similarly, the compassion and wisdom of buddhas arise from the muck of the ordinary world, which is characterized by fighting, hatred, distrust, anxiety, and other negative emotions. These emotions tend to cause people to become self-centered and lead to suffering and harmful actions. But just as the world is the locus of destructive emotions, it is also the place in which we can become buddhas, perfected beings who have awakened from the sleep of ignorance and who perceive reality as it is, with absolute clarity and with profound compassion for suffering living beings.

Just as the lotus arises from the bottom of a swamp, so buddhas were formerly humans, immersed in the negative thoughts and actions in which all ordinary beings engage: the strife, wars, petty jealousies, and hatreds to which all humans, animals, and other creatures are subject. Through their meditative training, however, buddhas have transcended such things, and like lotuses have risen above their murky origins and look down on them unsullied by the mud and mire below. The symbolism may be extended still further, because buddhas do not simply escape the world and look down on others with pity or detached amusement; rather, like the lotus, which has roots that still connect it with the bottom of the swamp, buddhas continue to act in the world for the benefit of others, continually manifesting in various forms in order to help them, to make them aware of the reality of their situations, and to indicate the path to the awakening of buddhahood, which can free them from all suffering.

These symbols are operating in the minds of the Tibetans who make the circuit around the residence of the Dalai Lama, and advanced practitioners have been exposed to oral teachings that further deepen their appreciation for the potential implications of the mantra *oṃ maṇi padme hūṃ*. They perceive Avalokiteśvara (and his physical manifestation, the Dalai Lama) as the embodiment of their own highest aspirations, a person who through individual effort, compassionate activity, and diligent meditation has transcended the world, but who still continues to emanate physical manifestations for the benefit of others. The compassion of Avalokiteśvara is completely unstained by any ordinary emotions; he has no need for praise, does not seek the approval of others, and his actions are completely untouched by thoughts of personal gain. Rather, he exemplifies the highest and purest level of compassion, a compassion that is said to be inconceivable to ordinary beings. This indicates the multifaceted nature of the symbolism of the mantra that Tibetans chant as they circumambulate the residence of the Dalai Lama. As they walk, they try to keep this symbolism in mind, because the more one familiarizes oneself with something the more natural it becomes, and one increasingly thinks and acts accordingly.

This is a basic idea underlying the system of tantric meditation, which is considered by Tibetans to be the most effective means for attaining buddhahood. In this system, one tries to transform one's mind through meditation and through surrounding oneself with symbols that resonate with one's religious goals, that draw the mind toward thoughts of compassion, wisdom, altruism, ethical behavior, patience, and so on. The people on the path around the Dalai Lama's residence are making religious merit that is expected to pay dividends in the future, but on a deeper level they are trying to reorient their minds in the direction of greater and more spontaneous compassion, since ultimately they hope to attain the same level as Avalokiteśvara. As they catch glimpses of the residence of Avalokiteśvara's human manifestation, they aspire to become like him, and the *maṇi* walls, *chödens*, and rock faces carved with his mantra all serve to draw their attention to the task at hand, which is not just to ask some powerful deity for help, but to become deities themselves and work for the betterment of others.

One aspect of life in a Tibetan community that strikes most Westerners immediately is the pervasiveness of such symbolism. Everywhere one looks, Buddhist motifs stand out: there are walls of prayer wheels inscribed with mantras, and people who turn them are thought to be sending out prayers for the benefit of all sentient beings. Prayer flags with short mantras or invocations written on them flap in the wind, each movement betokening an aspiration to benefit others. Shrines of various sizes, as well as monasteries, monks, nuns, temples, and statues catch the eye everywhere, and many of the people one passes are engaged in activities associated with Buddhist practice: a woman on the way to the market is holding her prayer beads and softly chanting a mantra; a group of children is prostrating in front of a temple; and a line of people is moving slowly around a wall of prayer wheels, turning each one as they pass.

Wherever one looks, one perceives signs of activities that would be identified by most Westerners as "religious," but they are so deeply woven into the fabric of daily Tibetan life that it is difficult to single out a part of the tapestry that is purely "religious" or one that is only "secular." There is no clear distinction between religious and secular life in Tibetan societies, and "religion" is not compartmentalized into certain places and times as it tends to be in Western societies. Rather, Buddhism is the very lifeblood of the community, and its influence is seen in all aspects of daily life.

The Tibetan language does not even have a term with the same connotations as the English word *religion.* The closest is the word *chö (chos)*, which is a Tibetan translation of the Sanskrit word *dharma. Chö* has a wide range of possible meanings, and no English word comes close to expressing the associations it has for Tibetans. In its most common usage it refers to the teachings of Buddhism, which express the truth and outline a path to awakening. The path is a multifaceted one, and there are doctrines and practices to suit every sort of person. There is no one path that everyone must follow and no practices that are prescribed for every Buddhist. Rather, the dharma has something for everyone, and anyone can profit from some aspect of it.

Because of its multifaceted nature, however, there is no ultimate "truth" that can be put into words, nor is there one program of training that everyone can or must pursue. Tibetan Buddhism recognizes that people have differing capacities, attitudes, and predispositions, and the dharma can and should be adapted to these. Thus, there is no one church in which everyone should worship, no service that everyone must attend, no prayers that everyone must say, no text that everyone should treat as normative, and no one deity that everyone must worship. The dharma is extremely flexible, and if one finds that a particular practice leads to a diminishment of negative emotions, greater peace and happiness, and increased compassion and wisdom, this is dharma. The Dalai Lama even states that one may practice the dharma by following the teachings and practices of non-Buddhist traditions such as Christianity, Islam, Judaism, or Hinduism.[5] If one belongs to any of these traditions, and if one's religious practice leads to spiritual advancement, the Dalai Lama counsels that one should keep at it, since this is the goal of all religious paths.

In this sentiment he hearkens back to the historical Buddha, Śākyamuni, who was born in the fifth century B.C.E. in present-day Nepal. As he was about to die, the Buddha was questioned by some of his students, who were concerned that after the master's death people might begin propounding doctrines that had not been spoken by the Buddha himself and that these people might tell others that their doctrines were the actual words of the Buddha. In reply, the Buddha told them, "Whatever is well-spoken is the word of the Buddha."[6] In other words, if a particular teaching results in greater peace, compassion, and happiness, and if it leads to a lessening of negative emotions, then it can safely be adopted and practiced as dharma, no matter who originally propounded it.

This flexibility makes it difficult to write about Tibetan Buddhism. The tradition is a multilayered tapestry comprised of many different strands, and anyone hoping to write an introduction to it is faced with the daunting task of sorting through centuries of history, huge amounts of textual material, and multiple lineages of teaching and practice. The problem is compounded by the scope of Tibetan Buddhism, which is found throughout the Tibetan cultural area. This area includes the central Tibetan provinces of Ü and Tsang; large parts of western Tibetan plateau that have traditionally been autonomous; Amdo and Kham in the eastern regions which, although culturally Tibetan, speak distinctive dialects and have maintained their independence from the central provinces; the open plains of the Changtang, home of the Tibetan nomads; much of present-day

Mongolia; large expanses of central Asia; smaller enclaves in present-day Russia and parts of several republics of the former Soviet Union; much of the Himalayan region of northern India, including Ladakh, Zanskar, and Sikkim; and the neighboring countries of Nepal and Bhutan.

In addition, due to the diaspora of the Tibetan people brought about by the invasion and occupation of Tibet by China, today Tibetan religion and culture are being spread all over the world, and increasing numbers of people in the West consider themselves to be adherents of Tibetan Buddhism. Millions more have heard teachings or read books and articles by Tibetan teachers, with the result that Tibetan culture is attracting unprecedented attention outside of its homeland at the same time that it is being systematically eradicated in the land of its origin.

In the chapters that follow, some of the distinctive features of Tibetan Buddhism will be discussed. Some specialists will no doubt question my choice of subject matter, and it would be entirely possible to write an introductory study of Tibetan Buddhism that would be far different from this one. The choices of which topics to discuss and how much space to give them reflect my own orientation, which is primarily concerned with history, philosophy, and meditative practice. Many important elements of Tibetan culture, ethnographic studies, and historical issues have only been mentioned briefly, or even omitted completely. However, it is hoped that this book will serve its primary purpose, which is to draw students into the subject of Tibetan Buddhism and open up further avenues of exploration in this rich and multifaceted tradition.

Notes

1. Throughout this book technical terms are mostly consigned to the indexes at the end. Important ones are placed in parentheses, with the Tibetan term first, followed by a Sanskrit equivalent where appropriate.
2. The most detailed examination of this mantra to date is Alexander Studholme's *The Origins of Oṃ Maṇi Padme Hūṃ: A Study of the Kāraṇḍavyūha Sūtra* (Albany: State University of New York Press, 2002). He focuses on the *Kāraṇḍavyūha-sūtra*, the earliest known Indic text in which the mantra appears. In this work, the mantra is explicitly related to the jeweled lotuses of Sukhāvatī, but, as Studholme states, there have been numerous other interpretations. A number of early Orientalists, for example, construed *maṇipadme* as a vocative: "oṃ jewel lotus hūṃ!" The problem with this interpretation is that it would be a feminine vocative, and Avalokiteśvara is a male

buddha. I have also heard several Tibetan lamas translate it as "oṃ jewel in the lotus hūṃ," and equate this jewel with the compassion of Avalokiteśvara. This interpretation, while possible, is also not supported by the grammar, because *maṇi* is part of a compound, and not in the nominative case (*maṇiḥ*), as would be required for this reading to be valid. As Studholme argues, its meaning in the *Kāraṇḍavyūha-sūtra* and other Indic texts suggests that "oṃ in the jewel lotus hūṃ" is the most probable reading. But it should also be noted that Sanskrit mantras do not always have any literal meaning. Many do not adhere to the rules of classical Sanskrit grammar, and so their interpretation is often ambiguous. For example, the syllable *oṃ*—the most common opening syllable for mantras—has no literal meaning. It is often associated with the final nature of reality, as is *hūṃ,* but neither have any exact meaning, and so cannot be translated into other languages. The history of interpretation of this mantra is also discussed by Donald S. Lopez, Jr. (who sides with the Orientalists' reading of "oṃ jewel lotus hūṃ!") in *Prisoners of Shangri-La: Tibetan Buddhism and the West* (Chicago: University of Chicago Press, 1998), pp. 114–134.

3. Tenzin Gyatso, Dalai Lama XIV, "Oṃ Maṇi Padme Hūṃ," in *Kindness, Clarity, and Insight* (Ithaca: Snow Lion, 1984), p. 117.
4. See Studholme, p. 109.
5. See, for example, John Avedon, *An Interview with the Dalai Lama* (New York: Littlebird Publications, 1980), p. 14.
6. See *Aṅguttara-nikāya* IV.163; and George Bond, *The Word of the Buddha* (Colombo: M.D. Gunasena, 1982), p. 30ff.

Part One

The Indian Background

1. Buddhism in India

The Buddha

The passing of the founder of a religious tradition often leaves a void in the community because there is no longer the possibility of daily guidance and personal inspiration. A common response is to develop a biography and regularly recount the paradigmatic deeds of the founder, whose life story is presented as a model for emulation by the faithful. In the case of the early Buddhist community, the memory of the Buddha was preserved by his disciples, who passed on their recollections of his words and deeds to others who had never met him. After the Buddha's death, his followers began recounting his story in order to inspire others. As time passed, the legend was embellished and augmented, with the result that a rich and detailed mythology developed. This has become a shared cultural legacy for Buddhists. The story highlights important aspects of their tradition and serves as a paradigm for devout practitioners.

By the time Buddhism reached Tibet, the historical Buddha had faded into the mists of the distant past, and the religion's founder mainly functioned as an important shared symbol. This symbol was understood and interpreted differently by different schools of Buddhism, each of which appropriated it in accordance with its own ideas, presuppositions, and practices. For each school, the Buddha's life and teachings were represented in a way that validated and corroborated its own doctrines and its own understanding of the methods and goals of Buddhist thought and practice.

Theravāda Buddhists, for example, developed the idea of a Buddha who was very much a human teacher, with human limitations and with abilities within the range of human comprehension, and who died a human death at the end of a human lifespan.[1] The Mahāyāna schools, by contrast, viewed the Buddha as a transcendent and cosmic figure. Mahāyānists agree that the Buddha *appeared* in the world as a mere human being, but in reality he had surpassed even the great gods of India in his wisdom and power. Like all buddhas, he attained a state of omniscience, was not bound by time or the laws of physics, and, contrary to appearances, he did not *really* die, but instead only appeared to do so, and in fact he continues on today, manifesting when needed to those who require his help.

As the historical Buddha faded from memory, his followers began to embellish his story and to recast the shared legend of their founder in ways that reflected changing assumptions about the tradition. As is true of all living religions, Buddhism has never been fixed or static, but instead has continued to evolve and adapt to changing attitudes and circumstances, while its adherents strive to retain a perceived connection with the origins of the tradition. In addition, each community has modified the image of Buddha in ways that reflect its own assumptions, doctrines, and practices, with the result that the Buddha is represented quite differently in different parts of the world.[2]

For these reasons, a quest to discover the "historical Buddha" is not to be the goal of the present section. Others have attempted to locate the historical Buddha, with varying degrees of success, but since the aim of this book is to present the worldview of Tibetan Buddhism, the life of the Buddha will be presented from the perspective of how it was inherited, developed, and embellished by Tibetan Buddhists. Thus, I will not attempt to sort through mythological accounts of his life to determine which elements of his biographies reflect historical "truth." Whatever the facts of his life may have been, they are largely irrelevant to the task of explaining how the figure of Buddha appears to Tibetan Buddhists. His Tibetan followers inherited the Buddha through stories, and so in Tibetan Buddhism he is more important as a powerful shared symbol than as a historical personage.

This is how he will be presented in this section. The account of his life that follows is drawn from standard sources that continue to be popular throughout the cultural area influenced by Tibetan Buddhism.[3] Taken together, they encapsulate the aspects of this shared paradigm that reflect the core assumptions, values, and goals of Tibetan Buddhists. Who or what the "real" historical Buddha was or what he did will be left for others to discover.

The Buddha's Dates

Among Buddhist historians, there is a wide range of opinions concerning when the Buddha lived and died. These generally focus on the date of his death, referred to by traditional Buddhists as the "final nirvana" (*yongs su mya ngan las 'das pa, parinirvāṇa*). Buddhists believe that at the end of his life he completely transcended all mundane limitations and entered a state of perfect bliss and freedom from suffering, or nirvana, which is the result of successful meditative training. Like all other buddhas, or "awakened ones," he woke up from the sleep of ignorance in which most beings spend their lives, and after his awakening he remained in the world in order to share his insights with others who were still mired in ignorance and were suffering as a result.[4] After attaining buddhahood, he realized that all ordinary beings are enmeshed in a continual round of birth, death, and rebirth, and that each successive life is conditioned and determined by the actions of previous ones. Since ordinary beings tend to act selfishly, thinking of short-term personal gains rather than considering the future consequences of actions, their deeds create the causes of future unhappiness for themselves. After breaking this vicious cycle in his own life, the Buddha was so moved by compassion for others that he decided to remain in the world in order to help them find the truth. Those who did so could also become buddhas, or they could at least find a way to break the cycle of ignorance and attain nirvana.

According to traditional accounts, the man who would become the Buddha was born a prince in what is today southern Nepal. Traditional historians differ on the time of his birth and death. The earliest dating is by Sureśamati, who states that Buddha's final nirvana occurred in 2420 B.C.E. Atīśa, an Indian scholar who was instrumental in the transmission of Buddhism to Tibet, placed the final nirvana at 2136 B.C.E. There are numerous other proposed dates, but contemporary scholars tend to place the Buddha around the fifth century B.C.E.[5] The wide discrepancy in dates indicates one of the greatest difficulties facing historically inclined scholars of Buddhism: traditional Indian sources exhibit little concern with history as understood in contemporary Western circles, and often great figures are assigned to distant antiquity in order to enhance their status. Sometimes the tales of their lives are intertwined with those of other important personages, and accounts of meetings between luminaries of the past become a part of the shared narrative of people in various traditions. Even more problematic from the point of view of a modern historian, the lives of great figures in India are generally remembered for how they personified core myths and symbols. Thus, the sages of the past are venerated not primarily for their uniqueness and their innovative ideas and practices, but rather for how well their lives reflected shared paradigms in Indian culture.

The Buddha's Life and Lives

The term "buddha," as we have seen, is a title that means "awakened one" and is given to people who have overcome ignorance and transcended suffering, who have attained the highest level of awareness, and who then teach what they have realized to others. All schools of Buddhism recognize numerous beings who have attained the state of buddhahood, and all are said to have reached the same level of accomplishment. Thus the term "buddha" is used to refer to many different awakened beings, but when I discuss "the Buddha," I refer to the historical founder of the Buddhist tradition, a man who was born in southern Nepal, probably around the fifth century B.C.E., and who was named Siddhārtha Gautama at birth. He was born into a kṣatriya family[6] of the Śākya clan, and so when he became a prominent religious teacher he was widely known as "Śākyamuni," or "Sage of the Śākyas." His parents were the rulers of a small kingdom in the foothills of the Himalayas, and as an only child Siddhārtha was expected to inherit his father's throne.

According to traditional accounts of his life, his incarnation as Siddhārtha Gautama was the culmination of a long series of rebirths in which he had progressively advanced toward the state of buddhahood. Stories of his former lives are very popular among Buddhists in Tibet, and they indicate how he diligently applied himself to meditative practice, moral training, and the development of compassion, all the time motivated by a deep desire to help others. These stories of Siddhārtha's previous births, or *Jātakas,* provide a paradigm of the gradual path to awakening. In each life, the future Buddha demonstrated his mastery of one of the attributes that would someday constitute the matrix of qualities of his omniscient mind and compassionate personality.

An example is his previous life as the world-renouncing ascetic Kṣāntivādin ("Teacher of Patience"). As his name indicates, in this life he was committed to developing unshakable patience. One day, as he was sitting in a forest glade immersed in meditation, a test of his equanimity came to him in the form of the king who ruled the area. The king had entered the forest with his many courtesans, and they were cavorting together until the king fell into a drunken sleep. The courtesans became bored and began to wander around the grove until they encountered Kṣāntivādin. The story portrays them as superficially devoted to fleeting sensuous pleasures and heedless of the consequences of their actions, but when they came upon Kṣāntivādin they were immediately impressed with his saintly demeanor. Approaching him with the reverence due to a holy man, they asked him to instruct them, and he agreed, describing to them the dangers of sexual indulgence, the joys of the ascetic lifestyle, and the importance of patience. The women were entranced by his profound teachings and listened intently. They asked him what sort of meditation he practiced, and he informed them that he was cultivating the virtue of patience. They requested that he teach them, but during his discourse, the king—who had awoken with a hangover and was enraged that his retinue had abandoned him—strode into the circle, angrily demanding to know what the ascetic was preaching. Kṣāntivādin replied that he taught "the doctrine of patience," which means that one does not become angry "even when people abuse you or strike and revile you." The king decided to expose him as a fraud by testing his purported patience. He ordered his executioner to whip him with a branch of thorns one thousand times. Even though the flesh was ripped from him in chunks and he bled profusely, the ascetic never lost his equanimity. The king then ordered that his hands be cut off, and then his feet, expecting that Kṣāntivādin would become angry, but he forgave the king every atrocity. As he lay dying from his wounds, he told his tormenter that he bore him no ill will; he felt only compassion for this violent man, whose actions would bring him suffering in the future.

The king, realizing that Kṣāntivādin's patience was unshakable, lurched away from the scene of carnage, still overcome with anger and hatred. As he left the grove, the earth itself opened and swallowed him, drawing him down to the depths of hell, where he would suffer horribly for inflicting grave injuries on such a holy man. The king's subjects were concerned that Kṣāntivādin might hold them responsible for the king's actions, but the ascetic reassured them that he bore no ill-will either toward them or the king. He then taught them about the value of patience, and this discourse ends the story.

This fairly grisly tale contains a number of themes that are typical of the Jātakas. They are morality plays that provide Buddhists with paradigms of the highest level of development of the qualities toward which devout Buddhists should strive, such as altruism, ethics, patience, generosity, and compassion. In many of these stories, the future Buddha is placed in a situation that tests him to the utmost, and in each he is portrayed as performing acts of kindness that are extraordinary. For pious Buddhists who read the Jātakas, the narratives provide models that they should strive to emulate. The stories also indicate how far most readers are from approaching the level of goodness exhibited by the future Buddha (who is referred to as a *bodhisattva*, or "buddha in training"). This does not mean that Buddhists are encouraged to seek self-mutilation or extreme hardship, but rather that they are given a standard that is almost impossibly high, and they are encouraged to work toward attaining the degree of compassion, patience, love, and so on that the Buddha embodied in his previous incarnations.

The difficulty of living up to this paradigm is indicated in a tale of one of the Buddha's past incarnations in which he was born in the most torturous hell.[7] The narrative makes it clear that he had fallen into hell as a result of evil deeds, but even in this horrible place his compassion was manifested. At one time, he and another wretched hell-being were forced to pull a heavy cart, but as the future Buddha saw the suffering of his companion he felt empathy for him and decided to pull the cart himself, even though he knew that this act of kindness would enrage the demons that torture the denizens of hell. Despite the pain inflicted on him, the future Buddha persevered, and this act of genuine compassion served to define the course of his future lives. The generation of compassion is extremely difficult in our world, but it is unimaginably rare in the hells, in which beings are constantly beset with horrible sufferings and are so consumed by their own troubles that they are very unlikely even to think of others. Because he overcame these obstacles and helped another being to alleviate his torment, this act had tremendous power and served to establish him on the road to buddhahood.

Attainment of Buddhahood

After cultivating patience, compassion, and other good qualities to their highest degree, having overcome all mental afflictions, the future Buddha was reborn as the bodhisattva Śvetaketu in Tuṣita heaven (the final training ground for buddhas-to-be). In this celestial realm conditions are optimal for the attainment of perfect awakening, and those who are born there progress steadily toward the final goal of buddhahood. After his training in Tuṣita was complete, Śvetaketu began looking for the ideal life situation for his decisive incarnation as Śākyamuni. It is believed by Buddhists that those who have reached a high level of development can choose their own life situations, including their parents and the time and place of birth. According to the *Extensive Sport Sūtra* (a traditional account of Buddha's life), these decisions were not taken lightly, and the future Buddha searched far and wide for the best situation.[8]

Because of his exalted spiritual development, ordinary parents were unsuitable, and so he had to choose people of exceptional moral qualities. He eventually decided on a royal couple who possessed all the attributes required for the parents of a buddha. His father was a king named Śuddhodana, and his mother was named Māyādevī, and as he decided to take rebirth as their son, the man who would become known as Śākyamuni Buddha brought up the final curtain on his journey toward full awakening.

The Twelve Great Deeds of the Buddha

Traditional accounts of the Buddha's life agree that his exceptional deeds are innumerable, but the defining moments of his life are generally divided into twelve "great acts."[9] These are:

1. existence in Tuṣita heaven
2. descent from Tuṣita
3. entering the womb of his mother
4. birth as a prince
5. proficiency in the worldly arts
6. life in the palace
7. departure from home
8. practice of austerities
9. defeat of Māra
10. awakening
11. turning the wheel of doctrine
12. final nirvana.

These twelve deeds are not unique to Śākyamuni, but rather constitute the paradigmatic career followed by all buddhas in their final lifetimes.

Some Buddhist sources even state that Śākyamuni really became a buddha long before his final birth and that he manifested these twelve deeds as a way of instructing his followers. Together they provide a model for others to follow, beginning with the development of an attitude of renunciation toward worldly attachments, continuing through the practice of meditation, and ending with the result of successful meditative practice: complete eradication of all negative mental states and the development of perfect wisdom and compassion. The Buddha's qualities of wisdom and compassion are manifested in his decision to teach others and in the final instruction of his death, which serves to remind others of their mortality and the importance of dedication to religious practice.

It should be noted that according to Buddhists Śākyamuni was not the first buddha, nor will he be the last. He is considered to be one of innumerable buddhas, and according to the *Sūtra of the Fortunate Eon* he is the fourth in a series of one thousand awakened beings who will manifest as buddhas in the present age.[10] The buddhas who preceded Śākyamuni lived in the distant past, and no historical records of their lives survive; the next buddha has not yet been born. According to Buddhist sources, he will take birth at a time when the teachings of Buddhism have disappeared from the world. He will be named Maitreya, and he will reintroduce the *dharma* (Buddhist doctrine) and help to establish countless living beings on the path to awakening.

Entry into His Mother's Womb

Realizing that the time for his physical manifestation on earth had arrived, the future Buddha revealed his intention to his future mother in a dream. She saw a white elephant enter into her womb (an auspicious sign), after which she knew that she was pregnant. According to the *Extensive Sport Sūtra,*

> An elephant, white as snow or silver, entered her womb,
> With six perfect tusks, and beautiful feet,
> A finely formed trunk, and a rosy head;
> The most beautiful of elephants, with graceful gait,
> And a body immutable as a diamond.
> Completely absorbed in contemplation,
> She had never felt such bliss;

Never had she known such pleasure,
Both in body and in mind.[11]

Seven astrologers were called in to interpret the dream, and all agreed that it indicated that Māyādevī was carrying an exceptional child, one who would do great things. They told the delighted king that his son would grow up to be a mighty ruler if certain conditions were met. The most important of these was that the boy be kept ignorant of the harsh realities of life, such as suffering, disease, old age, and death. In particular, they cautioned the king to prevent his son from seeing four things, which are referred to by Buddhists as the "four sights": (1) a sick person, (2) an old person, (3) a corpse, and (4) a world-renouncing ascetic. The first three exemplify the sufferings of cyclic existence, which is full of pain. Beings who are caught up in the round of birth, death, and rebirth are subject to various torments and dissatisfactions, and they experience them helplessly as a result of their own actions.

The astrologers predicted that if the prince grew to maturity without being confronted by such difficulties, he would follow in his father's footsteps and rule his kingdom with benevolence and righteousness. They added, however,

If he abandons love, royalty, and home,
And leaves to wander as a monk,
Free from attachment, out of compassion for all the worlds,
He will become a buddha . . .
With the excellent nectar of immortality,
He will satisfy all beings.[12]

Śuddhodana resolved that his son would live a sheltered existence, free from any hints of the sorrows of the world. He would live in a palace, surrounded by the finest sensual delights, and thus would become immersed in all worldly pleasures and develop an attachment to the world that would overpower any inclination to renounce it.

The Birth

Traditional stories report that the term of pregnancy was ten months. During this time, Māyādevī experienced no discomfort, and many auspicious signs were seen by all the people of the kingdom. When the time for the child's birth approached, Māyādevī decided to travel to a grove named Lumbinī. There she gave birth standing up, and the child emerged from her right side, without touching her womb. His mother felt no pain, only pleasure. Immediately after being born, the baby took seven steps in each of the four cardinal directions, and where his feet touched the ground, lotuses sprang up. He turned and declared, "I am the leader of the world. I am the guide of the world. This is my final birth." Gods appeared in the sky and proclaimed his praises, and the earth rumbled. A great light radiated in all directions, and celestial music was heard all over the world.

Because of the auspicious signs surrounding his birth, the child was given the name Sarvārthasiddha, "He Who Accomplishes All Goals." He was later commonly referred to as Siddhārtha, which is a shortened version of Sarvārthasiddha.

Seven days later, his mother died, as is common for mothers of buddhas. She had attained an advanced degree of saintliness, and this is why she had been chosen to give birth to Siddhārtha. Her primary task for that life completed, she was reborn in Trāyatriṃśa heaven. According to the *Great Chronicle*,

> The mothers of all bodhisattvas die on the last of the seven days following their delivery of the supreme man . . . . While still dwelling in Tuṣita, the bodhisattva carefully searches for a mother whose karma is good. He says, "I will descend into the womb of a woman who has only seven nights and ten months of her life remaining."[13]

After the death of his mother, Siddhārtha was raised by his stepmother, Prajāpatī, who later became the first Buddhist nun.

Siddhārtha Becomes Skilled in Worldly Arts

As the young prince grew, he excelled in all his studies and in the arts of kings. He became proficient in archery, horse riding, wrestling, and other martial skills, and he was widely renowned for his great strength, exceptional physical beauty, and grace. During his early years, his father, remembering the prophecies he had received earlier, tried to keep his son immersed in worldly affairs and to provide him with constant entertainment.

In particular, the king kept his son from experiencing the "four sights," since these would make him aware of the unpleasant aspects of cyclic existence. All beings who remain within cyclic existence are subject to various sorts of sufferings, to sickness, old age, and death. Only those who renounce the beguiling appearances of the world, who pursue liberation through meditation, can escape these things. Siddhārtha's father realized that if his son came to understand the full existential import of the four sights he would see worldly life for what it is: a trap in which ignorant beings become so enmeshed that they even fail to recognize that they are trapped.

In order to assure that his son would follow in his footsteps, Śuddhodana ordered that only young, healthy people would surround the prince. Those who became ill were dismissed until they recovered, and when people died their corpses were removed before Siddhārtha could see them. World renouncers were not permitted inside the palace, and he was not allowed to venture outside, where his father would have less control.

In addition to these precautions, Śuddhodana surrounded his son with sensual pleasures and diversions. He was constantly entertained by musicians and actors, surrounded by young and beautiful women, and provided with athletic contests. The king reasoned that if his son developed attachment to such things he would be unlikely to renounce the world and forsake his royal heritage.

In order to insure his son's complete involvement in worldly life, he decided to arrange a marriage. Siddhārtha, however, had little enthusiasm for the idea, and he reflected that this would only serve to ensnare him in worldly life, which he already recognized was ultimately pointless. He thought to himself,

> I know the evils of desire are endless; they are the root of suffering, accompanied by regrets, struggles, and hostility; they are frightful, like poison ivy, like fire, like the blade of a sword. I have no taste or interest in the qualities of desire. I prefer to dwell in a forest, silent, with my mind calmed by the happiness of meditation and contemplation.[14]

Siddhārtha then recalled that all previous buddhas had taken wives and fathered sons in their final lives, and so he eventually consented to the idea, on the condition that his father locate a woman who was generous, intelligent, and free from laziness, greed, and pride. If such a woman could be found, Siddhārtha would agree to marry her.

The king sent his ministers to find a woman who met these criteria, and eventually one was found. Her name was Yaśodharā, the daughter of Daṇḍapāṇi.[15] When Śuddhodana asked Daṇḍapāṇi for permission to arrange a marriage, however, he was reluctant, since he had heard that Siddhārtha had spent his life in the palace surrounded by comfort and luxury. Daṇḍapāṇi doubted that the prince had developed the manly qualities required of a good *kṣatriya*, particularly martial skills and the strength of character needed to rule.

In order to assuage his doubts, Śuddhodana arranged a contest among the young men of the kingdom, confident that his son would win. The victor in the contest would receive Yaśodharā's hand in marriage. As expected, Siddhārtha defeated all his competitors in wrestling, and he also surpassed them in mathematics and linguistics. He was the finest horseman in the kingdom, his archery skills were legendary, and so he triumphed in every test. His doubts relieved, Daṇḍapāṇi happily gave his daughter in marriage to the young prince.

This union made Śuddhodana very happy, since it appeared to solidify his son's ties to the world. He was still concerned with the prophecies that he had received before Siddhārtha's birth, however, and he continued to surround his son with sensual pleasures and entertainments and to keep him inside the palace. Soon after the marriage, Siddhārtha and Yaśodharā conceived a son, further increasing the king's joy, since this provided a further connection with the world.

The Four Sights

Śuddhodana's plan had worked as intended for the early part of his son's life. Shortly after the marriage, however, Siddhārtha asked for permission to visit some gardens outside the city. Śuddhodana tried to talk him out of the idea, but eventually his son won him over, and he reluctantly agreed to let Siddhārtha ride to the gardens through Kapilavastu, the capital city of his kingdom.

Before the prince ventured out of the palace, Śuddhodana took precautions: he ordered his guards to clear the streets of all sick people, old people, corpses, and world renouncers. As Siddhārtha emerged from the palace in his royal chariot, the citizens of the city gathered in throngs to cheer their future king. Banners waved, parents held their children aloft to catch a glimpse of the prince, and all seemed well in Kapilavastu. The prince joyfully rode through the streets, basking in the adulation of his subjects, until the chariot was halted by an old man in its path. As Channa, the royal charioteer, reined in the horses, Siddhārtha asked,

> O charioteer, who is this man, feeble and helpless?
> His flesh and blood have dried up, he has but skin and sinews,
> His hair is white, his teeth scarce, his body meager,
> He walks painfully and reeling and leans upon a staff.[16]

Channa informed the prince that the man had grown old and that such afflictions were the inevitable result of age. He added,

> O prince, this is neither the property of his race, nor of his country only.
> With all the living beings, youth gives way to decrepitude
> Thy father and mother and the host of thy relatives likewise
> Cannot be delivered from the suffering of old age—
> No other way exists for living beings![17]

Siddhārtha expressed amazement that people who saw such sights every day failed to realize that this would be their lot. He remarked on the folly of those who are attached to their bodies and their petty concerns when all their youthful dreams would end up in the decrepitude of age. He was also deeply disturbed by the idea that his young, healthy physique would someday be reduced to the sad state of the man in front of him, and so Siddhārtha ordered Channa to return to the palace. All joy was gone from the prince's heart.

> O charioteer, what a great misfortune it is for weak and ignorant beings,
> Who, drunk with the pride of youth, do not see old age!
> Turn the chariot around; I will return home.
> Games and pleasures no longer matter to me,
> Since I will be the abode of old age![18]

Siddhārtha brooded on this event for a while, and his father redoubled his efforts to surround his son with worldly enjoyments, so that he might come to overlook the faults of cyclic existence, such as physical decay.

Siddhārtha, however, remained despondent in the knowledge that he would someday lose his youth and be struck down by the frailties of age.

After a few months, Siddhārtha decided that he should again try to go to the gardens outside the city, and again his father attempted to talk him out of the idea, but without success. As before, he ordered his guards to clear the streets of old and sick people, corpses, and world renouncers, but again the prince saw one of the "four sights," this time a sick person. He asked Channa,

> Charioteer, who is this man, his body so ravaged and weak,
> Covered with his own filth, with weakened faculties,
> Breathing with great difficulty, whose limbs have withered,
> Whose stomach is sunken, who suffers so terribly?[19]

Channa replied that the man was gravely ill, and that sickness strikes randomly and without warning, laying low the rich and the poor, the old and the young. Horrified, Siddhārtha exclaimed, "Then health is just the play of a dream!" He added that given the truth of things, no sane person could find joy in mundane pursuits, since at any time he or she could be plagued with illness. Again Siddhārtha returned to the palace in despair.

After a while Siddhārtha went out of the palace again, and this time the chariot was halted by a funeral procession. Wailing and lamenting, the people in the procession carried a man whose death had bereaved his relatives, wife, and children. When Siddhārtha asked Channa about the cause of their distress, he was told that the man was dead, and that death is the inevitable fate of all who live. At this point, the folly of worldly existence was fully revealed to Siddhārtha.

> Old age and disease are always followed by death.
> But even were there no old age, no sickness, and no death,
> Great suffering would still arise based on the five aggregates, the elements of existence.
> What more can one say?
> Let us return—I will think of liberation![20]

After a period of reflection, Siddhārtha again left the palace with Channa. This time, he noticed a world-renouncing ascetic standing apart from the crowd, aloof and calm, radiating peace and serenity. Channa told him,

> Lord, this man is one of those called mendicants *(bhikṣu)*.[21]
> Having abandoned the joys of desire, he has perfect and
> disciplined conduct.
> He has become a wandering monk who seeks inner peace.
> Without desire he wanders, without hate he wanders,
> Begging for alms.[22]

Siddhārtha was so impressed with the man's demeanor that he resolved to emulate him, to renounce the pleasures of the palace and his royal heritage and become a wandering mendicant seeking ultimate peace.

Shortly after this, his wife gave birth to a son, but so little did Siddhārtha care for worldly attachments that when asked to name the child, Siddhārtha said, "I will name him Rāhula (Fetter)." The king was understandably upset when he heard of these things, and he forbade his son to leave the palace. He offered his son anything he wished, but Siddhārtha replied,

> I seek four things,
> If you can give them to me, I will remain here,
> And you will always see me in this house; I will never leave.
> My lord, I wish that old age will never take hold of me;
> And that I will always have the glow of youth;
> That I will always be in perfect health
> And that illness will never afflict me;
> That my life will never end, and that there will be no death.[23]

His father, of course, was powerless to give Siddhārtha these things, and with deep regret he realized that his son was about to leave him. Still, he decided to do whatever he could to forestall Siddhārtha's departure. He posted guards at all the gates with strict instructions to prevent the prince from leaving the palace, and he told the women in his retinue to increase their efforts to entertain Siddhārtha. A grand party was planned in hopes that it would show the prince the folly of leaving his life of pleasure and opulence. Beautiful women dressed provocatively filled the royal residence, music played all night, sumptuous decorations and flowers filled the grounds; but at the end of the party, Siddhārtha remained awake, looking over the revelers sprawled on the floor. The flowers had begun to wilt, the decorations hung askew, and the women who had earlier looked so beautiful were now transformed in his eyes.

> He saw that some had torn clothing and disheveled hair; their ornaments and diadems lay on the floor . . . . Some had crossed their eyes while sleeping, and others were drooling. Some women snored, laughed, mumbled, coughed, or gritted their teeth. Some had their legs apart and their heads hung, while others had tried to cover their uneven features . . . . Struck by the sheer ugliness of the women thus transformed as they lay disheveled on the floor, the bodhisattva had the impression of a cemetery.[24]

Siddhārtha Leaves the Palace

Siddhārtha resolved to depart the palace that very night and pursue perfect awakening, which he saw as the only way to escape from cyclic existence. He now realized that worldly life is characterized by transitory pleasures, suffering, decay, sickness, old age, and death.

With a profound sense of revulsion for mundane affairs, he called Channa and told him to make ready his chariot, but Channa, unwilling to contravene the king's orders, attempted to talk Siddhārtha out of his resolution. The prince was adamant, however, and so finally the charioteer relented and drove Siddhārtha from the palace and into a life of renunciation.

Channa headed toward the forest, and when he reached it, Siddhārtha ordered him to halt. Dismounting from the chariot, he informed Channa of his resolution to pursue awakening in order to benefit others.

> In pursuit of the welfare of all that lives,
> I, having attained Enlightenment and the state
> Where there is no old age, illness, and death,
> Shall bring deliverance to the world.
> Such was the vow I made long before,
> And the time of fulfilling it has now come.[25]

With these words, Siddhārtha renounced his royal heritage, his wealth, friends, and family, and began a new life as a wandering ascetic. He left with no regrets and with a sense of renewed purpose and enthusiasm.

In search of instruction, he traveled to meet several renowned teachers, hoping that they could show him the way to attain awakening and overcome suffering. In Vaiśālī, he met Ārāḍa Kālāma, a famous meditation teacher, and asked him to share his wisdom. The master instructed Siddhārtha in his system of meditation, which culminates in the experience of an indescribably blissful state of consciousness. Siddhārtha quickly mastered his teacher's instructions and attained this state, which was later referred to in Buddhist meditation literature as the third "formless absorption."[26] Ārāḍa Kālāma was very impressed that his student was able to accomplish this so quickly. He offered to make Siddhārtha his chief disciple, but he refused the offer, because he realized that the blissful consciousness of the third formless absorption is merely a transitory experience, after which one must return to the realities of cyclic existence.

Leaving Ārāḍa, Siddhārtha traveled to meet the ascetic teacher Udraka Rāmaputra, who had discovered a meditative state that surpassed the third formless absorption. He taught the technique for attaining this to Siddhārtha, who soon excelled in his practice. Udraka was amazed that Siddhārtha had been able so quickly to attain the state that he had worked for many years to reach, and he offered to share leadership of his community of meditators with the young prodigy. Siddhārtha asked him if the consciousness he had attained (which Buddhist meditation literature refers to as the "fourth formless absorption") could lead to final eradication of suffering and a permanent condition of happiness. Udraka had to admit that it could not and that one must inevitably return to the world after experiencing it. Siddhārtha, realizing that this was not the solution to the problems of cyclic existence, decided to leave Udraka and seek his own path.

He subsequently joined five other seekers of liberation who were convinced that the path to awakening lay in severe asceticism and physical hardship. Siddhārtha and his five companions engaged in the most extreme asceticism imaginable and, according to traditional accounts, Siddhārtha became so accomplished in his self-denial that he was able to survive on one grain of rice per day. For six years he devoted himself single-mindedly to this regimen, but the result was that he became sickly and weak, and no closer to awakening.

Recognizing that his austerities were getting him nowhere, he decided to begin eating regularly, since if the body lacks strength one will not be able to engage in meditation effectively. Shortly after he made this resolution, a young woman named Rādhā saw Siddhārtha and offered him a sweet rice dish she had made. Siddhārtha accepted the offer, and as he ate he felt renewed vitality entering into his body and his mind becoming more alert. When his five companions saw him eating, however, they viewed this as a sign of weakness and concluded that Siddhārtha had fallen from the true path of asceticism. They decided to leave him behind, which did not bother Siddhārtha, since he knew that the time had come for him to complete the quest for awakening and that this could only be accomplished in solitude.

He proceeded to a place called the "Circle of Awakening" (near present-day Bodhgayā in the Indian state of Bihar), where countless buddhas had attained awakening in the past. When he reached this spot, he made a solemn vow that he would finally attain awakening or perish in the attempt.

He prepared a place to sit under a tree later referred to as the "Tree of Awakening" and sat in a posture of meditation. Rays of light poured forth from him, illuminating all worlds in all directions. Perceiving this overwhelming radiance, the demon Māra became alarmed, since he knew that this presaged the awakening of a buddha.

Māra in Buddhist mythology plays a role similar to that of Satan in Christianity: he tempts people to perform evil actions, which lead to their downfall. Unlike Satan, however, Māra primarily seduces people into ignorance, and not sin. Sin, in Buddhism, is a second-order problem, an outgrowth of ignorance. We only commit evil deeds because we fail to recognize that they inevitably rebound on us and cause suffering. More importantly, we think that selfish actions will result in personal happiness, but the only true satisfaction comes from the attainment of awakening. Māra's primary purpose is to blind people to these truths. The awakening of a buddha is the greatest tragedy for Māra, since buddhas not only escape Māra's clutches, but through their compassionate activity they teach others the path to nirvana, thus robbing Māra of countless victims.

Overwhelmed by terror and hatred of the incipient buddha, Māra rushed to the Circle of Awakening to stop Siddhārtha's ascension to buddhahood. With his screaming hordes of demons, Māra hurled missiles, rocks, and other objects at Siddhārtha, who was sitting calmly, absorbed in meditation. Through Siddhārtha's yogic power, everything Māra threw at him was transformed into flowers, which fell harmlessly to the ground.

Enraged at his failure even to gain Siddhārtha's attention, Māra then ordered his daughters to seduce him. These women are infinitely more attractive than any human woman, and they shamelessly flaunted their great beauty in front of Siddhārtha, but he was completely unmoved. With his yogic power, he transformed them into hideous hags, withered and ugly, and they were so overcome with fear and shame that they begged him to return them to their previous forms. He did so, and then ordered them to leave him, and they obeyed.

Māra, however, was not willing to concede defeat, and so he rallied his vast demon army for an all-out assault on Siddhārtha, who still had not moved from his place of meditation. During the attack, Siddhārtha remained motionless, but he showed Māra a vision of the inevitable outcome of the attack: his forces routed and in disarray, and Māra himself humbled before Siddhārtha. Māra was then shown a vision of his own old age and death, which so terrified him that he fled, together with all his host.

After defeating Māra, Siddhārtha returned to single-pointed meditation. He "initiated energy, undeterred, attended to self-possession, not distracted, calmed his body, not excited, and concentrated his thoughts, focused on one point."[27] Distancing his mind from all mundane attachments, he attained meditative states referred to in Buddhist meditation literature as the first and second concentrations. He then surpassed them, entering into the third and fourth concentrations, each of which surpasses those below it. These, however, are merely mundane meditative attainments, and they only lead to rebirth in a blissful state, and not to awakening. Those who attain this state must someday exhaust the karma that caused their happy rebirth and again return to the lower realms of cyclic existence, and so Buddhists traditionally have viewed them as a trap, since they only lead to a transitory period of happiness.

Siddhārtha pressed on in his meditation. During the first watch of the night, he realized that all things within cyclic existence are bound together by intersecting causal connections. He perceived how all beings are born, age, and pass away under the influence of their past karma, and he fully comprehended the operations of karma. At that time, he developed three of the distinctive powers of a buddha: the ability to create miraculous manifestations, the faculty of clairaudience, and supranormal perception that knows the thoughts of others.

During the second watch of the night, he acquired the three "knowledges" (*rig pa, vidyā*): he was able to know all of his previous births, he understood how beings transmigrate in accordance with their karma, and he comprehended the "four noble truths" which became the cornerstone of Buddhist thought and practice.

In the third watch, he understood the causes of suffering and realized how it can be eliminated. According to the *Vinaya* (the texts which outline the rules for Buddhist monks and nuns), during the night of his awakening, his future attendant Ānanda and his son Rāhula were born.[28]

At dawn he perfected his awareness and became a buddha, a being who has eliminated even the subtlest traces of ignorance, who has become omniscient and spontaneously, perfectly compassionate.

For several weeks, he remained in a transcendent state of meditative awareness. During this time, Māra again visited the Buddha, praising him for his attainments. Māra then told Buddha that what he had realized was beyond the comprehension of humans or gods and that no one would understand if he were to teach them. Reflecting on these words, Siddhārtha saw that they were mostly true, since the understanding of a buddha surpasses all mundane wisdom. He thought,

> I have secured the cognition of the Truth, profound,
> Free from defilement, illuminating, eternal, and like nectar.
> But, if I should demonstrate it to others, they will not understand.
> Therefore I shall abide in solitude in the forest.[29]

After thinking this, however, he recalled his former resolutions to work for the benefit of others, and he was moved by compassion for their sufferings. Then Brahmā, one of the gods of the Indian pantheon, appeared before him and begged the Buddha to teach others in order that they might free themselves from suffering. Buddha knew that most people would be utterly incapable of understanding the profundity of his instructions, but there would be some exceptional individuals who would hear him and develop true realization. For their benefit, Buddha decided to devote himself to teaching.

Still absorbed in profound meditation on the final nature of reality, he pondered where to begin his teaching career. He first thought of instructing his former teachers, Ārāḍa Kālāma and Udraka Rāmaputra, but his supranormal perception revealed that they had already died. He then decided to teach his five former companions, who were practicing austerities in the Deer Park in Sarnath (near modern-day Vārāṇasī). Arising from meditation, he began walking toward Sarnath, but when his former companions saw him in the distance they resolved not to speak with him, viewing him as a weakling who had been unable to endure the rigors of ascetic practices.

> The ascetic Gautama who has slackened (in his austerities), has eaten plentifully, and has neglected the removal (of all that is worldly), is now coming here. No one need rise up and present him the religious robes and the bowl.[30]

Despite their resolve, however, as he approached, his former companions were struck by the change in his demeanor: Siddhārtha radiated wisdom and serenity, and they were so overwhelmed that they felt compelled to ask him to teach them what he had realized. He agreed and, after immersing himself in meditation, he delivered his first sermon. This is referred to as *The Sūtra Turning the Wheel of Dharma* because in this discourse he set in motion a new cycle of teaching that would lead countless sentient beings to awakening.

After hearing this teaching, Kauṇḍinya (one of the five ascetics) grasped the meaning of Buddha's words, overcame attachment, desire, and ignorance, and became the first *arhat.* (An *arhat* is someone who will attain final nirvana at the end of the present life as a result of eliminating mental afflictions and attachment to the things of the world.) The five ascetics asked to be accepted by Buddha as his disciples, and thus began the *saṃgha*, the Buddhist monastic order.

After spending the rainy season in Sarnath with his first disciples, the Buddha began to travel, teaching anyone who asked. According to Buddhist tradition, he never attempted to formulate a philosophical system, but rather adapted his instructions to the needs and spiritual proclivities of every person and audience he encountered. Buddhists compare him to a skilled physician who prescribes the proper remedy for every ailment. As A.K. Warder has noted,

> It is most characteristic of the Buddha that he always adapts his talk to the person he is conversing with. His courtesy in argument results from this: it is certainly not his way to denounce the opinions and practices of another to his face and challenge him to justify them. His method rather is to seem to adopt the other's point of view and then by question and answer to improve on it until a position compatible with his own has been arrived at. Thus he leads his partner in discussion towards the truth as he has discovered it, but so that the partner seems himself to continue his own quest, in whatever form it had

taken, and to arrive at higher truths than he had previously been aware of, or more convincing moral ideas.[31]

This makes sense as spiritual therapy, but from a doctrinal standpoint it created difficulties for his later followers. The Buddhist canon contains a bewildering array of doctrines, discourses, and approaches, each of which was intended for a particular person or group. When the Buddha was alive, his followers could ask the master to reconcile contradictions or fill in the gaps, but after his death they had to sort through his teachings on their own and attempt to formulate a consistent presentation of his "real" thought. This task was further compounded by the fact that in several discourses the Buddha tells his audience that the teaching they are hearing represents his final thought, but what he tells them disagrees with what he told other audiences was his final thought. Even more confusingly, when asked near the end of his life how to distinguish between the "word of the Buddha" and spurious teachings that others might attribute to him after his death, he replied, "Whatever is well spoken is the word of the Buddha." In other words, if a particular teaching leads to virtuous action and to a decrease of suffering, and if it accords with reality, it may safely be adopted and practiced, no matter who originally propounded it.

Buddha's Teaching Career

As the Buddha traveled around India, his fame and following grew. People came from all over to listen to the holy man whose teachings pointed to a way out of suffering, a path to the final peace of nirvana. Traditional accounts indicate that thousands of people became monks, and many more became lay followers. After several years of preaching, he decided to visit Kapilavastu in order to bring the dharma to the people of the kingdom he had renounced.

Upon hearing that his son was coming, Śuddhodana sent messengers ahead to ask the Buddha to reconsider his career choice and return to his royal heritage. Every messenger who met the Buddha, however, lost all interest in worldly affairs and became a monk. Finally, Śuddhodana went in person to meet him as he walked toward Kapilavastu with a crowd of disciples. As he saw his son, he was so overcome by the splendor of his awakened demeanor that he gave up all thought of asking him to return to the throne, bowed at his feet, and asked the Buddha to teach him the dharma. Buddha agreed, and he instructed his father on the effects of previous actions. This discourse has been preserved in the Buddhist canon as *The Sūtra of the Meeting of Father and Son.* Later Śuddhodana himself became a monk and renounced the throne.

After Buddha's return to Kapilavastu, his stepmother Prajāpatī decided to renounce the world and follow her stepson, but at that time there was no order of nuns. She traveled to meet the Buddha, and arrived exhausted and covered with dust. Approaching the Buddha with reverence, she asked him to initiate an order of nuns for her and other women wishing to seek awakening, but he refused her request, advising her instead to pursue a virtuous life as a laywoman. Prajāpatī persisted, however, but again she was refused.

Unwilling to give up, she asked Ānanda to intercede for her, which he did, but the Buddha turned down his plea as well. Ānanda asked if the master refused to ordain women because they were incapable of attaining awakening, but the Buddha indicated that they were able to do so. He added, however, that if he were to ordain nuns, this would shorten the duration of the true dharma in the world. His response indicates that his refusal was not based on a denigration of the morals of women, their intelligence, or their spiritual capacities, but rather on an understanding of interpersonal and intrasexual relations. The monks who followed the Buddha at that time had no monastic institutions and were a group of wandering celibate male ascetics who had renounced the world and its attachments. The Buddha recognized that one of the strongest of these attachments is the desire for sexual intercourse, and that if he placed men and women in close proximity this would inevitably lead to conflicts and would tempt those of weak resolve. Finally, however, the Buddha relented, agreeing that if he were to ordain women as nuns some would attain nirvana as *arhatīs* (female arhats). For their benefit—and for women of future generations who would desire liberation—he created an order of nuns.

The Final Nirvana

Buddha continued to travel and to teach anyone who cared to listen. Many who heard him lost all interest in worldly affairs and decided to enter the monastic community, and others became lay followers. Traditional sources report that he continued to teach until the age of eighty, at which point he decided that his aims had been achieved and that it was time to pass beyond earthly existence. This is referred to as Buddha's "final nirvana" (*parinirvāṇa*), and the events leading up to it are described in some detail in a text entitled *The Discourse of the Great Final Nirvana.*[32] The text recounts the Buddha's travels and teachings in the last part of his life.

His decease was presaged by a serious illness. He suffered through it with great calm and equanimity, but his followers feared for his life. Ānanda, his personal attendant, requested that he leave some final instructions for the community of monks, in response to which Śākyamuni exerted his psychic power, and the disease diminished. He then replied to Ānanda,

> What does the community of monks expect of me, Ānanda? I have taught the doctrine without omission, without excluding anything. As to this, Ānanda, the Tathāgata [Buddha] is not a "closed-fisted teacher" with reference to the doctrine [i.e., he does not hold anything back]. If anyone should think that he should watch over the community of monks or that the community of monks should refer to him, then let him promulgate something about the community of monks. The Tathāgata does not think that he should watch over the community of monks or that the community of monks should refer to him . . . . Ānanda, I am now aged, old, an elder, my time has gone, I have arrived at the period of my life, which is eighty years. Just as an old cart is made to go by tying it together with bands, so I think that the Tathāgata's body is made to go by tying it together with bands. Ānanda, on an occasion when the Tathāgata by withdrawing his attention from all signs, by the cessation of some emotions, enters into the signless concentration of thought and stays in it, on that occasion the Tathāgata's body is made comfortable. Therefore, Ānanda . . . you should live with yourselves as islands, with yourselves as refuges, with no one else as refuge; with the doctrine as an island, with the doctrine as a refuge, with no one else as refuge.[33]

The next morning he dressed and went to the town of Vaiśālī for alms, after which he returned and spoke again to Ānanda about the "four bases of magical emanation," which are special powers gained by advanced meditators. He hinted to Ānanda that through these he could prolong his life, even for an eon, but his disciple failed to grasp the implication of his words. The text indicates that if Ānanda had seized this opportunity and asked the Buddha to remain, he would have done so. When Ānanda later realized his mistake, he implored the Buddha to remain longer, but Śākyamuni had already declared that he would enter final nirvana in three months, and since the prediction had been made the date was fixed. This event was marked by an earthquake, and the Buddha commented to Ānanda that whenever a buddha decides to give up his life forces the earth responds in this way.[34]

After this, Śākyamuni left Vaiśālī and continued to travel and give instructions. Shortly before his death he gathered his disciples and provided them with a set of guidelines concerning the authority of scriptures. He reminded them that they had all heard him teach the discourses (*mdo, sūtra*) and monastic discipline (*'dul ba, vinaya*); and added that after his death these should be their guides. New teachings, he said, should be compared with the sūtra and vinaya; if they are in accord with these sources, they may be adopted, but if not, they are not the word of the Buddha and should be rejected.

Shortly before his final nirvana, Buddha had a meal at the house of a lay follower named Cunda, after which he departed for Kuśinagara. When he reached a spot known as the Śāla Grove, he delivered final instructions to his disciples, and then he announced that the time of his final nirvana was at hand. The Buddha instructed his students to cremate his body and to build a reliquary monument (*stūpa*) for the remains. Although those who attended him were overcome by grief and tried to persuade him to remain longer, Buddha pointed out to them that he had taught them everything he could, holding nothing back. They possessed all they needed to attain liberation, and he advised them to rely on their own efforts. He told them that in the final analysis each person decides his or her own fate, and liberation is gained through personal effort, not through the intervention of another being. He then turned to Ānanda and said,

> It might be that you would think, Ānanda, that the teaching has lost its teacher, our teacher does not exist. You should not perceive things in this way. The doctrine and discipline that I have taught and described will be the teacher after me.[35]

He then told Ānanda that after his death it would be permissible for monks to abolish the minor rules of monastic discipline, but Ānanda neglected to ask him which these are. He again exhorted his followers to rely on the instructions he had already given them, and Ānanda informed him that none of the monks present had any doubts about the doctrine, the path or monastic discipline. The Buddha then delivered this final sermon to his disciples:

> Monks, all compounded things are subject to decay and disintegration. Work out your own salvations with diligence![36]

After speaking these words, the Buddha entered into progressively higher meditative states, until he completely transcended all worldly things and attained nirvana.

Epilogue

The First Council

After the master's death, the order he founded continued to grow and develop, but one result of the passing of the Buddha was the emergence of sects with differing interpretations of his teachings. In addition, there were groups with different versions of his discourses, and so shortly after the final nirvana some senior members of the community of monks decided to hold a council in order to recite the words of Buddha and decide on a definitive canon. This was viewed with some urgency by many members of the saṃgha, because several of Buddha's senior disciples had died, which meant that their first-hand knowledge of the master and their memories of his teachings had departed with them. In order to prevent further loss of the dharma, the greatest of those who had been present when the Buddha spoke and who were arhats were invited. The decision to exclude non-arhats was a practical one, based on the idea that since arhats have eliminated mental afflictions, their thoughts and memories are undisturbed by passion. This was understood to be an effective way of overcoming the problems of faulty memories and biased sectarianism.

This rule excluded Ānanda, who had not yet become an arhat, but whose position as Buddha's personal attendant had allowed him to be present for more teachings than anyone else. Fortunately, he attained arhathood just before the conference was convened, and thus was able to recount the teachings he had heard.

According to tradition, there were five hundred arhats at this council. They assembled at Rājagṛha, under the leadership of Mahākāśyapa, and began with a recitation of the sūtras by Ānanda. The assembly then agreed that he had remembered them correctly. The discourses on monastic discipline were recited by Upāli, who specialized in that subject. Once a sermon had been reported and corroborated, it was accepted as authoritative. This council began the process of developing a Buddhist canon.[37] The collections of sūtras and vinaya are referred to as "baskets" (*sde snod, piṭaka*). Later a third "basket," consisting of scholastic treatises (*chos mngon pa, abhidharma*) was added, and the standard Indian canon is commonly referred to as the "three baskets" (*sde snod gsum, tripiṭaka*).[38] The first basket—the sūtras—contains texts that were purported to have been spoken by Śākyamuni (or sometimes by his immediate disciples). The vinaya texts were mainly spoken by the Buddha in response to questions about matters of monastic discipline. He never set down a systematic rule for monks and nuns, preferring instead to decide disciplinary issues on a case-by-case basis. These texts generally focus on a question that is brought to him concerning the behavior of a certain person in the order, in response to which Śākyamuni declares a general edict for the community of monks. Abhidharma texts extrapolate from the sūtras and systematize the teachings and vocabulary in them.

In an oral culture like that of ancient India, people develop the ability to memorize prodigious amounts of material, and although the arhats had only heard Śākyamuni give a particular sermon one time, they were able to remember it. As A.K. Warder states, writing was generally confined to mundane matters, such as politics and commerce, but religious teachings were memorized, since this was assumed to be essential for understanding.[39]

The Importance of the Story of a "First Council"

Although traditional sources accept the story of the first council without question, several modern scholars have noted discrepancies in the details, and some even doubt that it occurred. Erich Frauwallner, for instance, contends that the story is a fiction invented in order to give the force of the Buddha's authority to a particular edition of the canon. He compares the creation of the legend of a council convened to decide scriptural authority to the attribution of Hindu texts to famous authorities of the past: "When the Upaniṣads place a text in the mouth of a famous teacher, this has the purpose of placing it under his authority." Frauwallner contends that the story of the first council was created by some Buddhists "in order to place their own holy tradition under a common authority, to which recourse could be made through a list of teachers on the Vedic model."[40]

The legend of the first council was also used by Buddhist traditionalists to stop the creation and propagation of new texts. If the Buddha is dead, and his immediate disciples have definitively reported his teachings, then there should be no possibility of new sūtras. The assertion that all the council participants were arhats is crucial, since it indicates they had attained a high level of purity and were free from bias. Their memories were presumably unhindered by mental afflictions, and so the canon they created should be regarded as definitive. This is indicated in Mahākāśyapa's final summary statement, in which he declares that the sūtras that had been recited constituted the whole of the Buddha's word, and that there are no others.

Although the traditional account is questioned by some contemporary scholars, it is reported in Buddhist histories, which agree that the council resulted in a compilation of the canon in five "collections" (referred to as *āgamas* in Sanskrit sources and *nikāyas* in Pali): (1) the *Lengthy Collection*, which in the Theravāda canon consists of thirty-four of Buddha's longest discourses; (2) the *Middle Length Collection*, which includes about 150 discourses of intermediate length; (3) the *Associated Collection*, in which sermons are collected according to their subject matter; (4) the *Enumerated Collection*, in which the teachings are arranged according to the numbers of the items discussed; and (5) the *Short Collection*, which contains texts not included in the other collections, some of which were considered to be of questionable authenticity.

Eventually the various schools of Buddhism developed canons, and surviving examples of these indicate that there were significant differences between the schools (although they also accepted many texts and doctrines in common).[41]

Whatever the historical status of the first council, the story is widely reported in Buddhist chronicles, and traditional Buddhists generally accept the conclusion that the canon was recited and codified by the five hundred arhats. As we will see in later sections, however, the process of canonization did not end with the first council, but continued for many centuries afterward. During this time, new texts were added, and older texts were modified, and so, according to Otto Franke,

> it may now be considered as safely established, that the books of the Canon *as a whole* are not authentic; that the Canon was not com-

> posed and compiled in one and the same period of time, but that different books came into being at different periods covering a considerable time; that the contents of each book were not collected, but were composed, each by a separate hand, with more or less reference to preexisting traditional materials; and that even the first two Piṭakas [the sūtra and vinaya] cannot possibly have been presented as finished before either the 'first' or the 'second' Council, even if these events took place at the intervals assigned to them.[42]

Following the death of the Buddha, the tradition he founded began to develop different schools, many of which compiled their own versions of the canon, and each of which had its own understanding of the doctrines he propounded and the path to liberation that he showed his followers. In the following sections we will examine some of the most important doctrines of Buddhism, particularly those that were influential in the development of Tibetan Buddhism.

Notes

1. Theravāda is predominant in Southeast Asia. It is the main school of Buddhism in Sri Lanka, Cambodia, Thailand, and Laos. It is a generally conservative tradition that has its scriptural basis in the Pāli canon, which it traces back to the historical Buddha. Mahāyāna, the other major tradition of Buddhism, believes that the Pāli treatises are only a portion of what the Buddha taught, and it emphasizes other texts written in Sanskrit (or a hybrid form of Sanskrit). These works are rejected by Theravāda as forgeries. Mahāyāna schools are predominant in East and Central Asia.
2. This process of reinterpreting the founder of a religion is not, of course, unique to Buddhism: a similar movement can be seen within Christian traditions, each of which tends to represent Jesus in its own image. Striking examples may be seen in portraits of Jesus; although he was born in the Middle East, images of Jesus in North America generally look like the people who drew them and have no Semitic features. I have seen Jesus pictures in Chinese Christian churches that have Chinese features, and a very Scandinavian-looking Jesus in a Swedish Lutheran church. More importantly, each tradition tends to represent the life and teachings of its founder in ways that reflect its values, presuppositions, and practices.
3. In this section, I mainly follow the account contained in the *Extensive Sport Sūtra* (*Lalitavistara-sūtra)* and the *Acts of the Buddha* (*Buddha-carita*), which are supplemented by other sources, particularly those contained in the Pāli *nikāyas* and the *Great History* (*Mahāvastu).* For an overview of sources on the Buddha's life, see Hajime Naka-

mura, *Indian Buddhism: A Survey with Bibliographical Notes* (Delhi: Motilal Banarsidass, 1987), pp. 130ff. See also André Bareau, *Recherches sur la biographie du Buddha dans les Sūtrapiṭaka et les Vinayapiṭaka anciens* (Paris: École Française d'Extrême-Orient, 1963–1995).

4. According to all schools of Buddhism, he was not the first buddha, nor will he be the last. In our era, he was preceded by six others (named, respectively, Vipaśyin, Śikhin, Viśvabhu, Krakucchanda, Kanakamuni, and Kāśyapa). He will be followed by another buddha, who will be named Maitreya.
5. There is a great deal of controversy on this issue, however. For a good overview of various proposed chronologies of the Buddha's life, see Nakamura, *Indian Buddhism*, pp. 12-15. Another important contribution is Richard Gombrich, "Dating the Buddha: A Red Herring Revealed," H. Bechert (ed.) *The Dating of the Historical Buddha. Part 2* (Göttingen: Vandendoeck & Ruprecht, 1992). This book contains several excellent articles on controversies relating to the Buddha's dates. Gombrich posits the dates of 404 B.C.E. for the Buddha's death.
6. *Kṣatriyas* are one of the four *varṇas*, or social groupings, of traditional Indian society. The others are: *brahmans*, whose primary duty is to perform sacrifices to the gods; *vaiśyas*, who are traditionally merchants and tradespeople; and *śūdras*, whose duty is to serve the upper *varṇas*, particularly *brahmans*. The *kṣatriyas* rank second in the hierarchy, after *brahmans*, and their traditional role was to be soldiers and rulers.
7. This story is recounted by Pudön (Bu ston rin chen grub, 1290–1364) in his *History of Buddhism* (tr. Eugene Obermiller, Heidelberg, 1931), p. 108. It is a clear indication that Buddhists revere Buddha for his attainment of buddhahood against the odds, which serves to inspire his followers to emulate his example. The fact that he was born in a hell is significant, because he began his career at the lowest point in cyclic existence, but through diligent practice was able to attain the summit of perfection as a buddha. His followers should draw the conclusion that buddhahood is not a state reserved for exceptional beings, but rather an ever-present possibility for everyone.
8. *The Voice of the Buddha* (tr. Gwendolyn Bays; Berkeley: Dharma Publishing, 1983, 2 vols.), pp. 37–43 describes the deliberation process.
9. See Pudön's *History of Buddhism*, pp. 133–34.
10. According to other sources, such as the *Wheel of Time Tantra* (*Kālacakra-tantra*), there were seven buddhas prior to Śākyamuni; and Maitreya, the future buddha, will be the eighth and last buddha of this era.
11. *The Lalita Vistara*, ed. Rajendralala Mitra (Calcutta: C.R. Lewis, Baptist Mission Press, 1877), pp. 63.
12. Ibid., p. 66.
13. *Mahāvastu Avadāna*, ed. Pradhagovinda Basak (Calcutta: Sanskrit College, 1963), p. 171.
14. *The Lalita Vistara*, p. 223.
15. There are numerous discrepancies regarding Siddhārtha's wife. In some sources she is referred to as Gopā, and in others it is asserted that he had more than one wife. In the *Mūlasārvastivāda-vinaya*, for example, he is said to have had three wives: Yaśodharā, Gopā, and Mṛgajā, as well as sixty thousand courtesans (see Taishō 1450, ch. 3, pp. 111c, 112c, 114b).
16. *History of Buddhism*, p. 23.
17. Ibid., p. 24.
18. *The Lalita Vistara*, p. 267.

19. Ibid., p. 268.
20. Ibid., p. 269.
21. This term literally means "mendicant" and was adopted by Buddhism as the term for a fully ordained monk.
22. *The Lalita Vistara*, p. 270.
23. Ibid., pp. 290–291.
24. Ibid., pp. 291–292.
25. *History of Buddhism*, vol. II, p. 29.
26. According to Buddhist meditation literature, there are four "formless absorptions," which are meditative states that follow the attainment of the four "concentrations." Both types of meditative states are discussed in the next chapter.
27. *History of Buddhism*, p. 35.
28. Since traditional sources agree that Siddhārtha had been practicing meditation for six years, this chronology requires that his wife carried Rāhula for that time. Theravāda tradition, however, holds that Rāhula was born before Siddhārtha left his home in Kapilavastu.
29. *History of Buddhism*, vol. II, p. 41.
30. Ibid., vol. II, p. 44.
31. A. K. Warder, *Indian Buddhism* (Delhi: Motilal Banarsidass, 1970), pp. 64–65.
32. This is found in the *Long Discourse Collection* (*Dīgha-nikaya*), tr. T.W. and C.A.F. Rhys Davids (London: Luzac & Co., 1959), pp. 78ff.
33. *Dīgha-nikāya*, ed. T.W. Rhys Davids (London: Luzac & Co., 1967), p. 108.
34. Earthquakes also occur when a future buddha descends into his mother's womb, when he is born, when he attains awakening, when he first turns the wheel of doctrine, and when he enters final nirvana.
35. *Dīgha-nikāya*, ed. T.W. Rhys Davids (London: Luzac & Co., 1967), p. 154.
36. *Discourse of the Great Final Nirvana* (*Mahāparinibbāna-sutta*) (*Dialogues of the Buddha*, tr. T.W. and C.A.F. Rhys Davids; London: Luzac & Co., 1959), p. 173.
37. For a survey of sources on Buddhist scriptures, see Nakamura, *Indian Buddhism*, pp. 22–56.
38. The composition of *abhidharma* treatises probably began several centuries after the first council, but, according to one tradition, the main *abhidharma* works were taught by the Buddha to his mother while he visited her in the Heaven of the Thirty-Three (Trāyastriṃśa), and then recited at the first council by Mahākāśyapa.
39. A.K. Warder, *Indian Buddhism*, p. 205.
40. Erich Frauwallner, *The Earliest Vinaya and the Beginnings of Buddhist Literature* (Rome: Serie Orientale Roma, vol. VIII, 1956), p. 63ff. See also Hermann Oldenberg's introduction to the *Vinaya Piṭaka* (London: Luzac & Co., 1964), vol. I, p. xi, which also questions the authenticity of the story of the first council.
41. See Lamotte, *History of Indian Buddhism*, pp. 517–49, and Warder, *Indian Buddhism*, pp. 11–13.
42. Otto Franke, "The Buddhist Councils at Rājagaha and Vesālī," *Journal of the Pāli Text Society* (1908), p. 2.

2. Some Important Buddhist Doctrines

Cyclic Existence

Karma and Rebirth

The previous section focused on how the life of the Buddha is understood by Tibetan Buddhists. The present section will examine some of the major doctrines that they attribute to him. This qualification is an important one, because there is a great deal of discussion among scholars concerning what the Buddha actually taught and which doctrines can legitimately be ascribed to him. Although many of the discourses that are accepted by Tibetans as being the words of Śākyamuni Buddha are of doubtful historical authenticity, there is, nevertheless, little debate within the tradition that their source is in fact the Buddha. Thus, for the purposes of the present study, the focus will be on what Tibetans believe the Buddha taught, and not on what modern historians would accept as authentic teachings.

Among the most basic and pervasive of these are discourses attributed to the Buddha concerning karma and rebirth. These ideas were already present in the culture in which he was born, and he accepted them in much the same way that his contemporaries did. According to Tibetan Buddhists, the Buddha taught that one's present life is only one in a beginningless series of incarnations, and each of these is determined by one's actions in previous lives. These actions are collectively referred to as *karma*.[1] This idea specifically refers to one's volitional actions, which may be good, bad, or neutral. The Buddhist concept of karma is similar to Newton's Third Law of Motion, which holds that for every action there is a concordant reaction. Similarly, in Buddhism, actions give rise to corresponding effects: good, bad, and neutral experiences are the direct results of good, bad, and neutral karma. This is presented as a universal law that has nothing to do with abstract ideas of justice, reward, or punishment. Every action produces a concordant reaction, and this occurs automatically. It does not require the control, intervention, or modification of any outside power, and as long as one remains within cyclic existence one performs actions (karma), and these inevitably produce concordant results.

> Karmas, therefore, are being made all the time. When one speaks with a good motivation, a friendly atmosphere is created as an immediate result; also, the action makes an imprint on the mind, inducing pleasure in the future. With a bad motivation, a hostile atmosphere is created immediately, and pain is induced for the speaker in the future. Buddha's teaching is that you are your own master; everything depends on yourself. This means that pleasure and pain arise from virtuous and nonvirtuous actions which come not from outside but from within yourself.[2]

As long as one fails to recognize the causally interconnected nature of karma and rebirth, one will continue to transmigrate helplessly in cyclic existence. As we have seen in the life of the Buddha, however, it is possible to break the vicious cycle and escape from the sufferings that repeated births bring. The cycle is driven by ignorance, and the key to liberation (*thar pa, mokṣa*) lies in overcoming ignorance. The Buddha is the paradigm of a person who has accomplished this, and so devout Buddhists strive to emulate his example. The first requirement is the development of dissatisfaction with cyclic existence. As long as one is basically comfortable within the cycle of rebirth, there is no possibility of release. One must develop a profound revulsion, looking back on one's beginningless lives with disgust and vowing to break the pattern by any means necessary. According to Lama Thubten Yeshe, this attitude

> indicates a deep, heartfelt decision definitely to emerge from the repeated frustrations and disappointments of ordinary life. Simply stated, renunciation is the feeling of being so completely fed up with our recurring problems that we are finally ready to turn away from

our attachments to this and that and begin searching for another way to make our life satisfying and meaningful.[3]

Next, one must emulate the Buddha's example and develop the positive moral qualities that he cultivated. This leads to mental peace and equanimity, which are necessary for successful meditation. Without mental calm, one's thoughts will be so agitated that meditation is impossible. Meditation is the key to overcoming ignorance, for through mental training one can develop insight into the true nature of reality, which acts as a counter-agent to ignorance. Successful attainment of insight allows one to transcend the influence of karma, to end ignorant engagement in actions that bind one to continued transmigration, and eventually to end the cycle altogether.

The Four Noble Truths

Buddhism holds that the problem is a cognitive one, and the solution lies in cognitive restructuring. Buddhism teaches that every creature has transmigrated helplessly since beginningless time under the influence of ignorance and that their lack of understanding has led to performance of actions that have created connections with cyclic existence. In order to break this pattern, we must reorient our thinking to accord with reality.

One of the greatest obstacles to this goal lies in the fact that worldly existence is full of traps that beguile the unwary and blind them to the harsh realities of cyclic existence. Life is full of suffering, aging, and death, but most of us overlook these and focus on momentary pleasures. Those who view the world in accordance with reality, however, understand that all who are born in it must inevitably suffer and die. This fact was recognized with full existential clarity by the Buddha on the night of his awakening, and he expressed it in a set of propositions that are referred to by Buddhists as the "four noble truths." These are: (1) the truth of suffering; (2) the truth of the origin of suffering; (3) the truth of the cessation of suffering; and (4) the truth of the eightfold path which overcomes suffering.

The truth of suffering holds that all of cyclic existence is inevitably connected with unpleasantness. It is important to note that the term translated here as "suffering" has a wide range of connotations. *Duḥkha*, or suffering, refers not only to physical pain, but also to emotional turmoil, discomfort, dissatisfaction, and sorrow. The truth of suffering is a recognition that these things are found in the lives of ordinary beings and that those who experience them consider them unpleasant.

It should be noted that Buddhism does not deny the presence of happiness in human life. What it does deny is that satisfaction can be permanent for those enmeshed in cyclic existence, which is characterized by constant change. Even when one finds happiness, it must inevitably end, only to be replaced by loss, longing, and sorrow. This state of affairs is considered to be unacceptable, and Buddhism teaches a path by which this unsatisfactory situation may be transcended.

Suffering is generally divided into three types: (1) the suffering of misery, which includes physical and mental pain; (2) the suffering of change, which includes all contaminated feelings of happiness (called sufferings because they are subject to change at any time, which leads to dissatisfaction); and (3) compositional suffering—the unpleasantness endemic to cyclic existence, in which sentient beings are prone to distress due to being under the influence of contaminated actions and afflictions.

The first type is easily identifiable and includes ordinary pains, such as headaches, physical injuries, and emotional torment. All beings naturally wish to be free from this type of suffering and to experience its opposite, which is physical and emotional pleasure.

The second type is more difficult to identify, since it includes things that ordinary beings mistakenly regard as pleasurable, such as buying a new car. Looking at a desirable car for the first time, most people view it as something that will bring satisfaction and happiness, not even considering the fact that all cars break down, often in inconvenient places. Moreover, they cost money for the initial purchase, for taxes, insurance, maintenance, gas, and so on, and from the moment they are driven out of the dealer's lot they begin their inevitable progress toward the junkyard. What at first is a gleaming high-performance machine begins to rust, leak oil, and require repairs, until finally it becomes unusable and has to be discarded. As the Dalai Lama points out,

> When you first get it, you are very happy, pleased, and satisfied but then as you use it, problems arise. If it were intrinsically pleasurable, no matter how much more you used this cause of satisfaction, your pleasure should increase correspondingly, but such does not happen. As you use it more and more, it begins to cause trouble. Therefore,

> such things are called sufferings of change; it is through change that their nature of suffering is displayed.[4]

Anything impermanent inevitably leads to discontent, since eventually it breaks down, leaving one with a sense of disappointment and loss.

The third type of suffering is the basis for the first two, since it refers to the fundamentally unsatisfactory nature of cyclic existence, which is so constituted that it entails dissatisfaction for all who are caught up in it. The Dalai Lama says that

> it is called pervasive compositional suffering since it pervades or applies to all types of transmigrating beings and is compositional in that it is the basis of present suffering and induces future suffering. There is no way of getting away from this type of suffering except by ending the continuum of rebirth.[5]

Transmigrating beings experience distress as a result of their previous negative actions, actions motivated by afflictive emotions (*nyon mongs, kleśa*). The primary afflictive emotions are ignorance, desire, and aversion. These motivate people to engage in counterproductive actions that inevitably rebound on them, and they also tend to produce concordant mental states, leading to a vicious cycle.

The cycle can only be broken through eliminating the underlying negative emotions. Although we have been caught in transmigration since beginningless time, it is possible for an individual to bring her own transmigration to an end. This is the focus of the *second noble truth*. Buddha recognized that suffering has a basis, and he identified this basis as desire motivated by ignorance. Beings suffer due to their afflicted desires, and the way to overcome suffering lies in eliminating them. In a discussion of the first two noble truths, Kalu Rinpoche indicates that Buddha

> taught these subjects extensively and in great detail, and it is important for us to understand them in order to recognize the limitations of our present situation. We have to understand our circumstances and know that, given the nature of cause and effect . . . we can look forward to nothing but suffering. We have to realize that we are enmeshed in the various factors of cause and effect, which lead first to one state of suffering and on that basis to another, and so on. When

> we have seen the inherent limitations of this situation, we can begin to consider getting out of it. We can begin to look for the possibility of transcending samsaric existence and all its attendant sufferings, limitations, and frustrations.[6]

Desire is divided into three types: (1) desire for pleasure, (2) desire for continued existence, and (3) desire for nonexistence. The first type is the result of contact with sense objects that one finds attractive, and it creates the seeds of future attachments. The second type is the common wish that one's existence will continue forever and the tendency to live as if this were the case, despite the overwhelming evidence that one will inevitably die. The third craving arises from the belief that everything comes to an end in death, and so it is wrong to find happiness in material things, or in the present life, since death is inevitable. Buddhist philosophy holds that all three kinds of desire are mistaken and that all must be overcome in order to find lasting happiness.

The third noble truth indicates that it is possible to bring suffering to an end through overcoming afflicted desire. Suffering depends on causes, and if one removes the causes, suffering will disappear. The problem is cognitive, and so the solution is also cognitive: we suffer due to false ideas about what is pleasurable, worthwhile, or desirable, and *the truth of the path* indicates a way to restructure one's cognitions in accordance with reality in order to bring suffering to an end.

The path is commonly referred to as the "noble eightfold path" because it is divided into: (1) correct view, (2) correct intention, (3) correct speech, (4) correct action, (5) correct livelihood, (6) correct effort, (7) correct mindfulness, and (8) correct meditative absorption.

The eightfold path outlines a course of practice aimed at overcoming suffering. The root of suffering is desire based on ignorance, and the primary concern of the path is overcoming this underlying cause of all cyclic existence. The parts of the path are commonly divided into three groups (called "the three trainings" because each represents a particular aspect of the training program of the path). The first two members of the eightfold path are grouped under the heading of "wisdom" (*shes rab, prajñā*), since they entail a fundamental cognitive reorientation that is necessary as an initial prerequisite for the path. The next three are classed as "ethics" (*tshul khrims, śīla*), because taken together they are concerned with training in moral actions and attitudes. Morality is a necessary prerequisite for progress on the Buddhist path, since a person with good morality is calm and self-assured. The last three are grouped under the heading of "meditative absorption" (*ting nge 'dzin, samādhi*), because they are concerned with developing concentration.

Correct view consists of both positive and negative aspects: on the positive side, correct view involves knowing certain key Buddhist concepts, such as the four truths and the operation of dependent arising, or understanding what actions lead to good and bad effects. It also entails eliminating wrong views, the most important and dangerous of which is the "view of true personhood" (*'jig tshogs la lta ba, satkāya-dṛṣṭi*), the conviction that the elements of the psychophysical personality constitute a truly existent person. Wrong views are to be avoided not merely because they are philosophically or logically untenable, but because they are conceptual manifestations of ignorance, desire, and aversion. Holding them leads to further desire, hatred, ignorance, and ultimately to further suffering.

Correct intention involves developing a proper orientation, that is, a mental attitude that aims at following the Buddhist path to awakening. In cultivating correct intention, a person decides what is ultimately important, what he or she will work at. In a Buddhist context, the ultimate goal is awakening, and a person who has correct intention will take this as the goal of religious activity. This decision is of fundamental importance, because in order to achieve something difficult (such as buddhahood) it is necessary to devote oneself to it single mindedly. A person with correct intention cultivates an attitude of renunciation of worldly things, avoids harming others, and engages in activities that are concordant with the goal.

A person with *correct speech* avoids abusive, coarse, and untruthful words, says what is correct and true, speaks gently and nonbelligerently. Since one's discourse is an outward manifestation of internal mental states, cultivating truthful and pleasant speech also leads to gradual development of concordant mental attitudes.

For monks and nuns, *correct action* involves keeping the rules of monastic discipline outlined in the system of "individual liberation" (*so sor thar pa, prātimokṣa*), and for laypeople it involves keeping the lay precepts of individual liberation, which forbid killing, stealing, lying, sexual misconduct, and ingesting intoxicants. These rules are not simply arbitrary strictures, and they have a practical basis: cultivating morality results in mental calm, and this calm is a prerequisite for later concentrations and advanced levels of consciousness. In order to attain the higher meditative states, one must overcome the mental troubles and disturbances that agitate the minds of ordinary beings and that impede their ability to concentrate. Correct action is mainly concerned with avoiding the physical expressions of negative mental attitudes.

Correct livelihood is also connected with moral training: it consists in avoiding occupations that result in breaking the precepts—professions that lead people to kill, lie, cheat, steal, or engage in sexual misconduct. Prohibited occupations include hunting, fishing, meat-selling, making weapons, prostitution, and other activities that involve people in evil deeds. These are to be avoided because they create negative mental states as well as bad karma, and this combination prevents a person from successfully practicing meditation.

The next three aspects of the path are concerned with meditation. A person who has cultivated the previous good qualities has created a foundation consisting of proper attitudes and actions. Based on morality and the calm mental states that it produces, a person has the prerequisites for pursuing the higher levels of meditative training. *Correct effort* involves properly orienting the mind toward the desired goal of liberation. In this practice, a yogi (*rnal 'byor pa*) overcomes negative feelings that inhibit equanimity and meditation, such as impatience, slothfulness, excessive pride, vengefulness, concern with unimportant things such as wealth, power, and so on. The yogi then focuses on the goal of liberation through concentrated meditative practice. This involves steady effort rather than spurts of enthusiastic activity.

Correct mindfulness is emphasized in Buddhist meditation manuals as being of fundamental importance in meditation. In order to attain liberation, one must initially develop awareness of what one is doing and why one is doing it. In addition, one must learn to control and regulate the mind. A person seeking liberation must move from his or her present state of confusion and random thoughts to one of clarity and mindfulness in which he or she is aware of mental processes and attitudes and, more importantly, is in control of them.

Correct concentration requires the previous steps. Without a focused mind that can fix itself calmly and one-pointedly on a single object without being distracted by laxity or excitement, one cannot properly enter into the concentrations, which are advanced meditative states in which one's attention is fully devoted to one's object of observation.

Taken together, the four noble truths constitute a summary of the Buddhist path. The truth of suffering indicates the basic problem that Buddhism proposes to overcome, and the truth of the origin of suffering shows the cause of the problem. The third truth holds that the negative elements of the human condition are not immutable, and the fourth truth indicates how a person may bring about a cognitive reorientation and transcend suffering.

Appearance and Reality

According to Buddhist meditation theory, the basic causes of suffering are cognitive in origin. We mentally create a vision of reality, but because of ignorance this vision is skewed and does not reflect things as they are. Some of our wrong ideas are harmless, but others lead to the creation of negative mental states, such as ignorance, desire, or hatred. One of the most dangerous of these mistaken concepts is the false notion of a self, which Buddhist meditation theory contends is innately present in all human beings. On a very basic level, every person believes in a self or soul that is uncreated, immortal, unchanging, and permanent. Contrary to some other religious systems, Buddhism denies the existence of such an entity and contends that in order to attain liberation one must eliminate the false belief in a self or soul.

There has been some disagreement among Western scholars of Buddhism concerning whether or not Śākyamuni Buddha really advocated this idea, but there is no debate among Tibetan scholars, who view the concept of no-self (*bdag med, anātman*) as a cornerstone of Buddhist thought and practice. In Tibetan meditation texts, belief in a self or soul is said to be based on a false imputation, and techniques to examine this notion in order to eradicate it are an important focus of meditation literature.

But if the concept is common to all human beings, where do we get it? And if it is mistaken, why is it so universally accepted? The answer, Buddhist texts suggest, is that although there is a basis for belief in a self, the imputation is still a false one. The basis for the imputation of self is the collection of elements that together constitute the psychophysical personality, which Buddhism divides into five "aggregates" (*phung po, skandha*): (1) form, (2) feelings, (3) discriminations, (4) compositional factors, and (5) consciousness.

These are the constituents of all impermanent phenomena and are the basis on which we impute the notions of "I" and "mine." Taken together, they are the components of the individual, but we mistakenly impute something more, an essence, a self or soul. When one analyzes this concept to locate its basis, however, all one finds are these five factors, none of which can constitute a self because they are constantly changing, whereas the self that sentient beings imagine is self-sufficient and enduring.

Form refers to phenomena that comprise the physical world, which includes the sense organs (eye, ear, nose, tongue, body, and mind) and their objects. These are material things composed of the four great elements: earth, water, fire, and air. *Feelings* are our sensations of things, and these are divided into three types: pleasant, unpleasant, and neutral. They result when the senses come into contact with objects. *Discriminations* are the differentiations we make regarding objects of perception as a result of contact. They cause us to discriminate between colors, sounds, smells, tastes, tangible objects, and mental images. *Consciousness* includes the six types of consciousnesses: eye, ear, nose, tongue, body, and mind. *Compositional factors* are volitional activities, both good and bad. Karma is included within compositional factors, since it directs the mind in particular directions, thus influencing the content of future mental states.

Taken together, these five aggregates constitute the sum total of the psychophysical personality, and Buddhist teachers claim that the totality of an individual is included within this group. Ordinary beings, however, impute something extra: an enduring, uncreated "self" that exists apart from and independently of these constituents, but this is nothing more than a label imputed to what are really constantly changing phenomena. This mistaken notion leads to grasping and attachment, which in turn result in harmful actions, and so the mistaken belief in a self is said to be one of the most powerful factors that keep ordinary beings enmeshed in cyclic existence. According to Lama Zopa,

> The door that leads us out of saṃsāra is the wisdom that realizes the emptiness of self-existence. This wisdom is the direct remedy for the ignorance which is both a cause and effect of clinging to the self, and which believes the self or 'I' to be inherently and independently existent . . . . We then become addicted to this phantom I and treasure it as if it were a most precious possession. Wisdom recognizes that such an autonomously existing I is totally nonexistent and thus, by wisdom, ignorance is destroyed. It is said in the Buddhist scriptures

> that to realize the correct view of emptiness, even for a moment, shakes the foundations of saṃsāra.[7]

This is not as easy as it might at first appear. The false conception of self is deeply ingrained, and every sentient being has cultivated it not only in the present lifetime, but for countless past lives. Since it has been reified and strengthened over such a long period, it is deeply embedded in our basic assumptions and consequently very difficult to dislodge. Because of its strength, it is not possible to eradicate the idea of self all at once through simply recognizing that the belief is untenable (although this is an important first step). One initially understands no-self conceptually, through a process of reasoning. The reasoning begins with a consideration of how the self appears to us—that is, as something that is autonomous, enduring, and independent of the psychophysical continuum.

The reasoning process begins with an analysis of whether or not the self can exist in the way that it appears. The meditator first determines that if there is a self, it must be either separate from or identical with the psychophysical aggregates. If it is different from them, then there is no connection between the self and the meditator, since they are different factualities. The self appears to consciousness as something enduring and autonomous, but all of us are impermanent and only exist due to causes and conditions that are external to ourselves. The only constant in human life is change, and all the constituents of the psychophysical personality are changing from moment to moment; thus the meditator should conclude that even if there were a self different from the aggregates, it would be unrelated to him, since an autonomous, enduring entity could have no conceivable relation with an impermanent being. The Dalai Lama concludes that

> if the self or the person exists independently, separate from the aggregates, then after mentally disintegrating the aggregates one should be able to point out a self or person existing independent of these aggregates—but one cannot. If the self or the person is a totally different and separate entity from the aggregates, then there should be no relation between the self and the aggregates at all.[8]

Having eliminated the possibility of a self that exists independently of the aggregates, one then considers the possibility that there might be a self which is the same as the aggregates. If there is such a self, it must be the same as at least one of them; but when one examines each in turn one realizes that they are all impermanent, changing from moment to moment, and there is no underlying unity or essence that remains throughout the ongoing process of change. The Dalai Lama points out that the idea of a self that is identical with the aggregates is untenable because

> if the self exists as single or totally one with the aggregates, then the contradiction arises that just as the aggregates are many, the self should also be multiple. Also, when this present life ceases at the time of death, the continuity of the self should also cease right then. And, if the self or the person is totally one with the aggregates, how can one have the natural feeling of the self being the master of these aggregates and the aggregates being the subjects and possessions of that self?[9]

The only conclusion that can legitimately be reached is that the self is a fiction, a mere label superimposed onto the constantly changing aggregates, a concept created and reified by the mind, but lacking any substantial reality. This reasoning process alone does not eliminate the idea, however; it merely weakens it. Because it is so deeply ingrained, the idea of self is only eliminated through repeated meditation on the reasonings of no-self, which enable the yogi to become progressively more familiar with the understanding that no self or essence exists. The Dalai Lama concludes that "when such a realization is maintained and reinforced through constant meditation and familiarization, you will be able to develop it into an intuitive or direct experience."[10]

Many Westerners reject this notion, contending that it would be a sort of cognitive suicide. The idea that the self (which is assumed even by people who reject religions that propound the idea) does not exist is profoundly disturbing to many non-Buddhists, but in Buddhist thought the denial of self is not seen as constituting a loss, but rather is viewed as a profoundly liberating insight. Since the innate idea of self implies an autonomous, unchanging essence, if such a thing were in fact the core of one's being, it would mean that change would be impossible, and one would be stuck being just what one is right now. Because there is no such self, however, we are constantly changing, and thus are open toward the future. One's nature is never fixed and determined, and so through engaging in Buddhist practice one can exert control over the process of change and progress in wisdom, compassion, patience, and other good qualities. One can even become a buddha, a fully awakened being who is completely liberated from all the frailties, sufferings, and limitations of ordinary beings. But this is only possible because there is no fixed and static self, no soul that exists self-sufficiently, separated from the ongoing process of change.

Such intellectual understanding is not enough by itself, however. Even when beginning meditators gain a conceptual grasp of the doctrine of emptiness, it does not weaken the strength of the appearances of inherent existence. People and things still appear to exist from their own side, independently of external causes and conditions. On a personal level, even when one intellectually recognizes that there is no basis for the mistaken concept of "I," this false idea still appears. As an analogy, a physicist might know that the table in front of her is mostly composed of space and that the matter of the table consists of infinitesimally tiny particles in a constant state of vibration, but the table still appears as a solid, hard object.

Because intellectual comprehension of a concept is not the same as fully grasping it, Buddhist texts make a distinction between three levels of understanding, which are called respectively "wisdom arisen from hearing," "wisdom arisen from thinking," and "wisdom arisen from meditating." The first type is the superficial understanding one gains from simply hearing someone else teaching something. It does not involve a great deal of analysis, but is primarily based on listening to someone and comprehending the meaning of the words. Wisdom arisen from thinking comes from pondering the significance of what one has heard and gaining a deeper understanding, although this is still only conceptual. Wisdom arisen from meditating occurs when one fully internalizes what one has learned and pondered, through apprehending with direct perception on a level that transcends merely conceptual realization.[11] At this level of awareness, one moves beyond dependence on the mere words of the teaching and perceives the truth directly.

Dependent Arising

Closely connected with the idea of no-self is the doctrine of dependent arising (*rten cing 'brel bar 'byung ba, pratītya-samutpāda*), which holds that all compounded phenomena arise due to causes and conditions external to themselves, remain in existence due to causes and conditions, and eventually pass away due to other causes and conditions. The classical formulation of this doctrine expresses it as follows: "Because this exists, that arises; because this is produced, that is produced."[12] The first line indicates that effects arise from conditions unalterably, and the second states that objects are produced from conditions that are themselves impermanent. This process is broken down into twelve steps, which are referred to as the "twelve limbs of dependent arising":

1. ignorance
2. action
3. consciousness
4. name and form
5. the six sources
6. contact
7. feeling
8. attachment
9. grasping
10. existence
11. birth
12. aging and death.

In this process, the primary factor is *ignorance*. This is not just an absence of knowledge, but is also a consciousness that perceives reality incorrectly. It motivates beings to engage in actions, but since the basis of the actions is mistaken, they lead to negative reactions. The most basic type of ignorance is the belief in an inherently existent self, which gives rise to thoughts of acquiring things for this self to possess.

In the context of the schema of the twelve links of dependent arising, *action* generally refers to a defining act that determines one's future rebirth. If this deed is meritorious, one will be reborn in one of the three good transmigrations—human, demi-god, or god. If it is a negative action, one will be reborn in one of the three lower transmigrations—animal, hungry ghost, or hell-being.

The defining action conditions one's *consciousness*, since each type of transmigration has a distinctive type of mind. (All are characterized by basic ignorance, however, and ignorant thoughts tend to perpetuate themselves.) At the beginning of a new life, one acquires a particular sort of cognition, and this is determined by one's past deeds. If one is born as a human, one

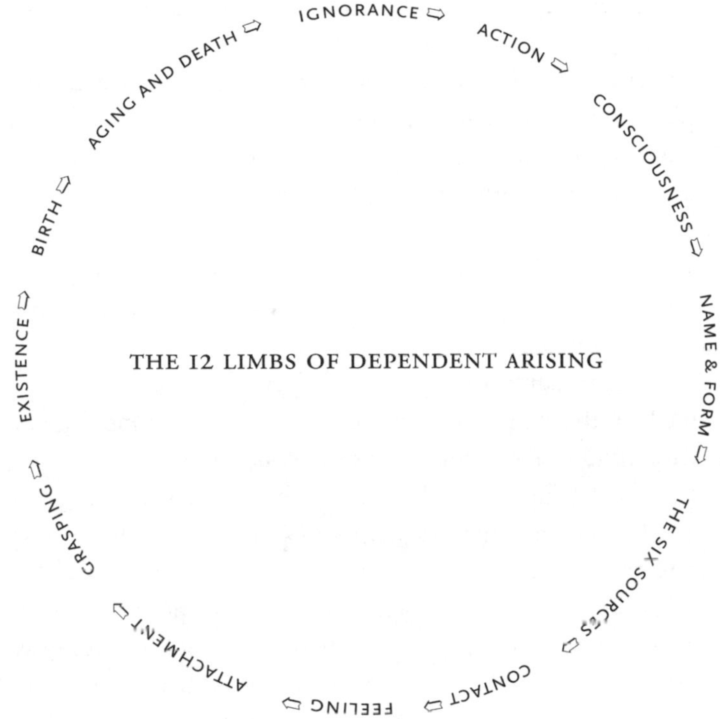

TABLE 1. THE TWELVE LIMBS OF DEPENDENT ARISING

will have a human consciousness, which will be conditioned by one's past deeds. Moreover, a human who engaged in acts of violence in a past life, for instance, will be predisposed toward violence in the present life, and unless he does something to reverse this trend, he will likely repeat the pattern in the present life, leading to negative karma and a lower rebirth.[13]

Consciousness conditions the next link, *name and form. Name* refers to the aggregates of feelings, discriminations, compositional factors, and consciousness. *Form* refers to the aggregate of form. Together these constitute the psychophysical personality, and this is conditioned by the predispositions that have been inherited from past lives. According to Kalu Rinpoche, these are influenced by the false sense of self, which all of us have cultivated since beginningless time.

> From this basic dualistic or discursive consciousness there arises the sense of self, of "I." At the same time, whatever forms are seen, what-

> ever sounds are heard—in short, whatever phenomena are experienced—are perceived as some version of "other." In this way there occurs a definite split into self and other. At this point, although there is no physical basis for consciousness, there is nevertheless a sense of embodiment, of identity coalescing. There is also the sense of naming things in the phenomenal world.[14]

The *six sources* are the sense powers of eye, ear, nose, tongue, body, and mind. As the form aggregate develops, these also mature, and the process is influenced by the previous four members. As the sense powers mature, one begins to have contact with external things, and this contact is also conditioned by the previous stages. *Contact* is the coming together of object, sense faculty, and consciousness. It conditions the next link, *feeling*, which has the function of discriminating some things as pleasant, some as unpleasant, and others as neutral in accordance with how they are distinguished in contact.

All of these are conditioned by ignorance, and so they are all mistaken with respect to their appearing objects. As one develops ideas of pleasure, pain, and neutrality, one begins to grasp at things that are pleasant and avoid things that are unpleasant. Thus one experiences *grasping* and *attachment*, the eighth and ninth links of the process.

These in turn create the basis for continued *existence*. Existence results from grasping and attachment: when one becomes attracted to the things of cyclic existence, one assures that in the future one will again be reborn in cyclic existence. This is a predisposition that began with ignorance, which in turn led to actions, and these led to contact and grasping.

All of these taken together constitute the link to future *birth*. Due to the force of previously generated desires, a being who is about to be reborn feels desire toward its future parents. If the being is to be reborn as a male, it will feel desire toward its future mother, and if it will be a female, it will feel desire toward its future father. Moreover, the type of being toward which it will be attracted is determined by the nature of its past karma. If its karma destines it for rebirth as a human, then it will be drawn toward human parents, and if it will be reborn as an animal, then it will seek out animal parents, and so forth. It will be attracted to a male and female who are about to copulate and who are appropriate for its future life situation. The completion of the process of rebirth occurs when the future father impregnates the future mother, and the being takes rebirth in the appropriate life situation. The moment of physical birth is the culmination of this process.

The final factor, *aging and death*, begins at the moment of birth. Everything that is born is moving toward death, and in each moment cells are dying and being replaced by new ones. Eventually the regeneration process begins to break down and one's physical condition degenerates. The inevitable result is death, and so Sogyal Rinpoche asks,

> What is our life but this dance of transient forms? Isn't everything always changing: the leaves on the trees in the park . . . the seasons, the weather, the time of day, the people passing you in the street? And what about us? Doesn't everything we have done in the past seem like a dream now? . . . The cells of our body are dying, the neurons in our brain are decaying, even the expression on our face is always changing, depending on our mood. What we call our basic character is only a "mindstream," nothing more.[15]

Most beings are beguiled by the transitory things of cyclic existence and seek to acquire those that are perceived as pleasant. They are blind to the inevitable results of such actions, which only bind them to continued rebirth and resultant sufferings. As we will see in the next section, the cycle can be broken, but it requires a profound restructuring of cognition through meditation.

Notes

1. The Tibetan term is *las*, which is pronounced "lay."
2. H.H. the Dalai Lama, *Kindness, Clarity, and Insight* (Ithaca: Snow Lion, 1984), pp. 26–27.
3. Lama Thubten Yeshe, *Introduction to Tantra* (Boston: Wisdom, 1987), p. 53.
4. *Kindness, Clarity, and Insight*, p. 23.
5. Ibid., p. 23.
6. Kalu Rinpoche, *The Dharma That Illuminates All Beings Like the Light of the Sun and the Moon* (Albany: State University of New York Press, 1986), pp. 28–29.
7. Lama Zopa Rinpoche, "Seeking the I," in *Wisdom Energy II* (London: Wisdom, 1979), p. 68.
8. H.H. the Dalai Lama, *Path to Bliss* (Ithaca: Snow Lion, 1991), p. 201.
9. Ibid., p. 201.
10. Ibid., pp. 201–202.

11. See, for example, Étienne Lamotte, *History of Indian Buddhism* (Louvain-la-Neuve: Université Catholique de Louvain, 1988), p. 46, and *Dīgha-nikāya,* III, p. 219.
12. See, for example, *Saṃyutta-nikāya* II, p. 65, and *Saṃdhinirmocana-sūtra* (Stog Palace edition), ch. 6, p. 40.
13. See Wonch'uk's commentary on the *Saṃdhinirmocana-sutra* (entitled *Saṃdhinirmocana-ṭīkā;* Sde dge edition), vol. *ti* [118], p. 505.4ff.
14. Kalu Rinpoche, *The Dharma,* p. 17.
15. Sogyal Rinpoche, *The Tibetan Book of Living and Dying* (San Francisco: Harper San Francisco, 1992), pp. 26-27.

3. Meditation

The Role of Meditation in Indian and Tibetan Buddhism

Tibetan Buddhism has many different schools and lineages, with a variety of practices and goals. All schools of Tibetan Buddhism agree, however, that the final goal of Mahāyāna practice is the attainment of buddhahood for the benefit of all other sentient beings. A buddha, as we saw in previous sections, is someone who has awakened from the sleep of ignorance in which others live, who has broken through the cognitive barriers that impede understanding and become omniscient through a long process of mental training.

The key factor in this process is meditation (*bsgom pa, bhāvanā*), a general term that encompasses a wide range of practices and goals. Some of these aim at pacifying the mind and quieting the mental confusion that afflicts ordinary beings. Other meditative practices are concerned with developing clear understanding of Buddhist tenets such as the four noble truths, impermanence, no-self, and so on, or with cultivating direct perception of the true nature of reality.

According to the Dalai Lama, "meditation is a *familiarization* of the mind with an object of meditation."[1] Sentient beings have lived since beginningless time, and in every lifetime we have accustomed ourselves to wrong ideas, which has led to suffering, death, and rebirth. Since this preconditioning is deeply ingrained, the meditational process used to break its power requires a great deal of effort and repeated familiarization of the mind with meditational objects—Buddhist concepts, doctrines, symbols (and sometimes objects or images with no Buddhist associations).

Most meditative practices aim at some form of cognitive restructuring. Since dissatisfaction arises from wrong ideas, the solution to the problem of suffering lies in changing these ideas, and this is accomplished through meditation. Suffering arises from actions based on afflictive mental states such as desire, ignorance, hatred, and so on, and many of the techniques of Tibetan meditation are designed to serve as counteragents to afflictions. For instance, a meditator who is particularly prone to anger might be instructed by a meditation teacher to cultivate feelings of love and compassion. Love and compassion are incompatible with anger, and so the more one trains in the former attitudes, the more one's tendency toward anger diminishes.

A person with strong desire might be instructed to consider the impermanence of all the phenomena of cyclic existence. No matter how much money or power one accumulates, one must eventually lose them, either sooner or later. Even the richest people cannot know with certainty that they will still have their money in a week, a month, or a year. And no amount of wealth can forestall death, which is the final end of the ambitions, desires, and concerns of this present life. Through contemplating these truths, one should experience a diminution of mundane desires and a corresponding interest in pursuing religious practice, which can lead to ultimate and lasting happiness.

Meditation on Death

In many cases, Buddhist meditators contemplate the basic realities of cyclic existence—such as suffering, impermanence, and death—but at other times meditators purposely visualize things that are not real but which have a therapeutic purpose. For example, practitioners with strong sexual desire will sometimes mentally imagine the whole world filled with skeletons. This serves to remind them that all living things inevitably die, and so there is no good reason to be attached to any of them or to seek one's happiness in sexual activity. Alternatively, meditators sometimes bring to mind people they find particularly attractive and then imagine what these people will look like as decaying corpses. They will picture the corpses in various stages of decomposition and will consider how repulsive corpses are to the living.[2] This meditation is sometimes done in burial grounds or cemeteries, since such places are said to be conducive to contemplation of death.

The outcome of this process should be a recognition that one's desire for particular individuals is only a result of deluded thinking, since there is nothing inherently attractive about anyone. If a particular person were inherently desirable, then he or she should be attractive to anyone at any time in any circumstance. That this is not the case is indicated by the fact that different societies (and different individuals) have varying standards of beauty: some consider thin bodies to be beautiful, while others view full figures as more appealing; some value light skin, while others prefer dark skin. Standards of shape and size of facial features vary between cultures, as do notions of ideal hair color and style. This variety indicates that there is no universal standard of beauty, and that one's ideas of physical attractiveness are largely a result of conditioning.

In addition, if a particular person's body were inherently attractive, then it should still be attractive as a decaying corpse. The fact that images of corpses induce feelings of revulsion and horror indicates that beauty is a transient and conditioned thing. If one considers these factors, one should conclude that there is no good reason to desire any one person more than others. Beauty is in the eye (and mind) of the beholder, and through changing one's attitudes it is possible to overcome afflicted attachment. This does not mean that one should go through life viewing people as decaying corpses and feeling disgust toward them; the purpose of the meditation is to develop an attitude of equanimity. Excessive revulsion is as much an affliction as excessive desire. Since humans are particularly susceptible to desire, however, some need to cultivate rather extreme antidotes in order to counteract it.[3] It is unlikely that most people will be able to overcome sensual desire completely, but through repeated familiarization with these visualizations it is often possible to diminish its force. The end result of this meditation should be an outlook that views all living beings as equal and that realizes that feelings of attraction and revulsion are transient results of afflicted mental states.

The Four Concentrations and the Four Formless Absorptions

Tibetan Buddhist meditation literature contains extensive discussions of meditative states that can be reached through specific trainings. Among these are the four concentrations (*bsam gtan, dhyāna*) and the four formless absorptions (*gzugs med kyi snyoms 'jug, ārūpya-samāpatti*), meditative trances that correspond to states of existence. These are shared by both Buddhist and Hindu schools. The four concentrations correspond to levels within the Form Realm, the second of the three levels of cyclic existence. One reaches the first concentration by overcoming the subtlest levels of attachment to the Desire Realm, the lowest level of cyclic existence and the one in which we exist.[4] In order to do this, the meditator views the Desire Realm as gross and the first concentration as subtle and seeks to attain it. By successfully attaining it, the meditator can achieve rebirth in this state, which is said to be endowed with joy and bliss. To reach the other three concentrations, the procedure is similar: The meditator views the lower concentration as gross and the higher one as subtle and seeks to attain it.[5]

In the first two concentrations joy and bliss are present, but in the third concentration joy is absent but bliss is present. One also develops meditative equanimity in the third concentration, which is strengthened in the fourth concentration to the point where bliss also disappears and is replaced with a pervasive equanimity. The reason why joy and bliss are progressively eliminated is that they interfere with mental stability. The Buddha describes this process as follows:

> Having become separated from sensual desire, having become separated from nonvirtuous qualities, a monk enters into and abides in the first concentration, in which there is conceptuality and analysis, which has joy and bliss, and which arises from separation from hindrances . . . . Due to diminishment of conceptuality and analysis, he enters into and abides in the second concentration, has internal tranquility and has one-pointed concentration of thought, devoid of conceptuality and analysis, but having joy and bliss . . . . Due to detachment from joy, the monk dwells in equanimity, has mindfulness and clear understanding, experiencing bliss in mind and body. . . . Through eliminating both pain and pleasure, and due to previous disappearance of sorrow and happiness, the monk enters into and abides in the fourth concentration, devoid of pain and pleasure, a state of equanimity and absolute purity of mindfulness.[6]

The four formless absorptions are meditative states that correspond to levels within the Formless Realm, which encompasses the highest regions within cyclic existence. One is reborn in one of these planes in dependence upon successfully cultivating the corresponding absorption. They are called "absorptions" because in them one's attention is withdrawn from external objects and the mind and mental factors are all equally focused on the meditative object. The four are: (1) the absorption of limitless space, (2) the absorption of limitless consciousness, (3) the absorption of nothingness, and (4) the peak of cyclic existence.

In the absorption of limitless space, the appearance of forms to the mind completely disappears, and the meditator perceives everything as uninterrupted space, without any obstruction or variety.

In the absorption of limitless consciousness, the meditator first views the preceding absorption as gross and then views the discrimination that consciousness is limitless as peaceful. This mainly involves stabilizing meditation, and in the absorption the meditator perceives everything as just pure, undifferentiated consciousness.

In the absorption of nothingness, even viewing everything as limitless consciousness appears as gross, and the meditator cultivates a mental state in which only nothingness appears to the mind. In his commentary on the *Compendium of the Mahayāna*, Vasubandhu states that this is a sphere of lucid consciousness in which beings are still caught up in cyclic existence.[7] It is more subtle than the preceding absorption, since there is no content at all, only undifferentiated nothingness. In the succeeding absorption, even this is left behind, and there is no coarse discrimination at all, only subtle discrimination. This is referred to as the "peak of cyclic existence," because it leads to rebirth at the highest level of the Formless Realm, a state in which beings have enormously long lifespans characterized by no hint of unpleasantness and only the subtlest of discriminations.

In a Buddhist context, however, this is still unsatisfactory, since one's lifespan eventually ends and one is again reborn in the lower realms of cyclic existence. One will again suffer, grow old, and die. Thus for Buddhists the final goal should be a supramundane path, one that leads out of cyclic existence altogether and which results in either the state of buddhahood or at least the more limited nirvana of an arhat or solitary realizer.[8]

Stabilizing and Analytical Meditation

The minds of ordinary beings are scattered and confused, beguiled by surface appearances and deluded by false ideas. Advanced Buddhist meditators, by contrast, are said to have calm and disciplined minds, and they are able to see through appearances to understand the transient and unsatisfactory nature of the phenomena of cyclic existence.

Buddhist meditation literature contains many descriptions of meditative trainings that lead to equanimity and insight. An important goal of these practices is the attainment of "a union of calm abiding and higher insight," in which one is able to remain focused on a meditative object for as long as one wishes and at the same time to analyze its final nature. In Tibetan Buddhist literature there are numerous presentations of the development of calm abiding (*zhi gnas, śamatha*) and higher insight (*lhag mthong, vipaśyanā*), which differ in some details of the process. The account that follows is based on that of the Gélukpa school (which follows Tsong Khapa's *Great Exposition of the Stages of the Path*), supplemented by material drawn from Kamalaśīla's *Stages of Meditation* and from the *Sūtra Explaining the Thought* (see table 2).

In Mahāyāna literature, calm abiding and higher insight are often declared to be essential to advanced meditative practice. In the *Sūtra Explaining the Thought*, for example, Buddha declares that "all of the many kinds of meditative stabilization . . . . that I have explained are included [within calm abiding and higher insight]."[9]

Calm abiding is so called because it is a state in which the mind remains fixed on an object of observation without wavering. Takpo Tashi Namgyal states that it is attained

> by fixing the mind upon any object so as to maintain it without distraction . . . by focusing the mind on an object and maintaining it in that state until finally it is channeled into one stream of attention and evenness.[10]

According to Geshe Lhundup Sopa, calm abiding is

> just a one-pointedness of mind (*cittaikāgratā*) on a meditative object (*ālambana*). Whatever the object may be . . . if the mind can remain upon its object one-pointedly, spontaneously and without effort (*nābhisaṃskāra*), and for as long a period of time as the meditator likes, it is approaching the attainment of meditative stabilization (*śamatha*).[11]

The Process of Developing Calm Abiding

There are six prerequisites for achieving calm abiding: (1) staying in an agreeable place, (2) having few desires, (3) knowing satisfaction, (4) not having many activities, (5) pure ethics, and (6) thoroughly abandoning thoughts of desire and so forth.

The meditator should find a place in which conditions are conducive to meditation. Such a place will be free from wars and political upheavals, commotion, evil people, dangers from wild animals, robbers, and the like, and will have the necessary prerequisites for life, particularly sufficient food and water. One should seek to diminish desire for material things and be content with what one has, and avoid excessive engagement in conversation, moving about, or other activities that interfere with the development of concentration. Cultivation of pure ethics and abandoning thoughts of desire are essential to the process, since a mind that is enmeshed in afflictive thoughts and sensual desires will be too distracted to develop the mental stability of calm abiding.

Calm abiding is characterized by the ability to fix one's attention on an internal object of observation for as long as one wishes, without being disturbed by mental fluctuation. According to Buddhist meditation literature, any object can be the basis for calm abiding, but meditators generally focus on objects that have soteriological value, such as the body of a buddha. Since one's ultimate goal is the attainment of buddhahood, this serves to orient the mind and purify mental obstructions.

The two primary obstacles to attainment of calm abiding are laxity (*bying ba, laya*) and excitement (*rgod pa, auddhatya*). The former is an internal dullness that diminishes mental clarity in meditative states. Excitement is

> a scattering of the mind to attributes of the Desire Realm experienced previously and an engagement in them with attachment. Excitement is a non-peacefulness of mind that involves desirous engagement in the pleasant; it has the function of preventing calm abiding.[12]

Laxity and excitement diminish one's ability to concentrate, and so it is essential to overcome them. This is accomplished through development of mindfulness, a quality that allows the mind to examine itself and to recognize incipient laxity or excitement. When they appear, meditators apply antidotes to counteract them. When laxity arises or is about to arise, one counteracts it by brightening or enlarging the object of observation. Excitement may be counteracted in a number of ways: contemplating death and impermanence, decreasing the size and brightness of the object of observation, or heightened concentration on another object, such as the breath.

The Nine Mental Abidings

Prior to development of actual calm abiding, meditators progressively cultivate nine levels of increasing concentration, called the nine "mental abidings": (1) setting the mind, (2) continuous setting, (3) resetting, (4) close setting, (5) disciplining, (6) pacifying, (7) thorough pacifying, (8) one-pointedness, and (9) setting in equipoise.

Setting the mind is a level of intermittent concentration which is often distracted by random thoughts. The meditator can only hold the object in mind for a brief while and is easily distracted. As she gains more familiarity with meditation, she is able to hold the mind on the object for longer periods of time; this is *continuous setting.*

During these first two stages, the main obstacles are laziness and forgetfulness. Laziness is a tendency to procrastinate or avoid practice of meditation. One desires to engage in other activities, such as sleep, mundane affairs, and so on. Forgetfulness refers to mental distraction due to forgetting virtuous objects because one instead focuses on afflicted objects. Due to this, one loses awareness of the object of observation and scatters one's attention to phenomena of desire. These tendencies are overcome through mindfulness and continued attention to the object of observation.

In *resetting,* the third mental abiding, when the mind leaves the meditative object it is forced back to it, and one is able to remain focused on the object for more time than one is distracted from it.

Close setting, the next mental abiding, arises when one develops mindfulness to the point that one is able to remain focused on the object of observation. One has developed powerful attention, and the mind no longer wanders randomly from the object without one's being aware of it. At this point, laxity and excitement are the major obstacles, and one cultivates the antidotes to them.

In *disciplining,* the fifth mental abiding, one develops a strong faculty of introspection, which represents a powerful counteragent to laxity. In this stage, the mind is constantly being observed by introspective mindfulness that is aware of the arising of laxity. When one recognizes incipient laxity, one moves to counteract it by heightening one's perception of the object, or one increases its brightness or size. This, however, adds to the danger of becoming overstimulated, and so, during *pacifying*, the sixth mental abiding, one "pacifies" the mind. This involves controlling it through contemplation of death, impermanence, the negative results of mental distraction, and the like, in order to counteract excitement. At this level, the meditator has powerful introspection and mindfulness and is aware of even small mental fluctuations. According to Geshe Gendün Lodrö,

> introspection has two functions. One, near the beginning of the process, is concerned with inspecting whether or not the mind is abiding on the object of observation; this causes the mind to remain on the object of observation. Later, introspection is more concerned with whether or not laxity or excitement has arisen; at this time, its function is to cause application of the appropriate antidote.[13]

In *thorough pacifying*, the seventh mental abiding, one cultivates the power of effort, through which one overcomes subtle levels of laxity and excitement. There is no longer any great danger that they will arise, but if they do the meditator is able to counteract them quickly. When one is able to hold the object of observation in mind for as long as one wishes, without being disturbed by laxity or excitement, one attains the eighth mental abiding, *one-pointedness*, which is so called because one's power of mindfulness is so strong that one's attention is fixed unwaveringly on the object.

In the ninth mental abiding, *setting in equipoise,* one can remain in meditative equipoise spontaneously, without effort.

> At this point one has achieved the power of familiarity; one is free from laxity and excitement, is able to set the mind continuously in meditative stabilization, and has subjective and objective clarity.[14]

Physical and Mental Pliancy

At the level of the ninth mental abiding, the meditator has become so familiar with meditative concentration that all traces of physical lethargy and mental scattering have been eliminated. As a result, one experiences the arising of a factor of clarity referred to as "pliancy" (*shin tu sbyangs pa, praśrabdhi*). It is defined as "a serviceability of mind and body such that the mind can be set on a virtuous object of observation as long as one likes; it has the function of removing all obstructions."[15] In the *Stages of Hearers*, Asaṅga states that "pliancy is supreme happiness and joy that is preceded by faith and clarity. Gradually making the mind joyful, pliancy [eliminates] the non-virtuous class of assumptions of bad states."[16]

The four types of pliancy are: (1) mental pliancy, (2) physical pliancy, (3) bliss of physical pliancy, and (4) bliss of mental pliancy. Mental pliancy is a cognitive factor that removes "assumptions of bad states," which are subtle traces of nonvirtuous propensities that are the results of former negative actions and attitudes. Mental pliancy is experienced as a lightness of mind, and it is the result of successful cultivation of meditative stabilization.[17]

A physical pliancy is "a special, light tangible object that removes physical tiredness and other unfavorable physical functionings."[18] Physical pliancies are the opposite of assumptions of bad states; they are physical factors generated by meditative stabilization. According to Geshe Gendün Lodrö,

> an assumption of a bad state is: a factor that cannot bear the mind's being aimed at its object of observation. The general meaning of a pliancy is: a factor of being able to take to mind, or a factor of facility with aiming the mind at an object of observation. That which causes the yogic practitioner to dislike aiming the mind at an object of observation is called the assumption of a bad state.[19]

With the arising of physical and mental pliancy, one also experiences a feeling of profound bliss, and one's body and mind feel light as wind. The bliss that accompanies the sense consciousnesses is referred to as "bliss of physical pliancy," and the bliss that is associated with mental consciousness is called "bliss of mental pliancy." These are connected with the removal of assumptions of bad states, which lead to heaviness of mind. According to Gendün Lodrö, due to the force of mental pliancy a subtle energy current called a "wind" courses through subtle channels in the body, giving rise to feelings of physical lightness, mental clarity, and great bliss.

Higher Insight

At this point one has overcome the assumptions of bad states, and one's mind and body are disciplined and serviceable. One has attained stability and equanimity due to pacifying the assumptions of bad states. As the initial euphoria of the bliss of mental pliancy fades, one's mind becomes fully pacified, and at this point one attains calm abiding, which Gélukpa scholars describe as "a non-fluctuating meditative stabilization conjoined with special pliancy."[20]

Calm abiding is held to be a necessary prerequisite for attainment of higher insight, but meditators must initially cultivate stabilizing meditation and analytical meditation separately. When one has first developed calm abiding, one is not able to remain in that state while performing analysis, and so one must alternate between calming and analytical meditation. Through repeated practice, however, one develops the ability to maintain the two types of meditation in equal portions at the same time.

When this is accomplished, one turns one's analysis on the object of observation and considers its nature. One recognizes that it—like all phenomena of cyclic existence—is empty of inherent existence. All phenomena lack a self; they are dependently arisen due to the force of causes and conditions other than themselves. Through repeatedly familiarizing oneself with this notion, one gradually weakens the force of the appearance of inherent existence and directly apprehends the emptiness of the object of observation.

This, however, is not higher insight. Higher insight occurs when one's analytical meditation itself generates mental stability and is conjoined with physical and mental pliancy. At this point one enters into a powerful meditative stabilization that is characterized by stability and the appearance of a wisdom consciousness that understands the nature of the object of observation. The combination of stability and analysis in a single consciousness serves as a powerful counteragent to afflictions and is a potent tool for developing the ability to perceive emptiness directly.

The Five Buddhist Paths

The Path of Accumulation

Buddhist meditation texts distinguish five stages of spiritual advancement that constitute the path to awakening followed by meditators: (1) the path

Table 2. Calming and Analytical Meditation

Meditative state	Pre-requisites	Stages	Signs of success	Counter-agents
Calm Abiding	1. Staying in an agreeable place 2. Having few desires 3. Knowing satisfaction 4. Few activities 5. Pure ethics 6. Abandoning thoughts of desire	Nine Mental Abidings: 1.Setting the mind 2. Continuous setting 3. Resetting 4. Close setting 5. Disciplining 6. Pacifying 7. Thorough pacifying 8. One-pointedness 9. Setting in equipoise	1. Ability to focus mind on object of observation for extended periods 2. Physical pliancy (at ninth mental abiding) 3. Mental pliancy (at ninth mental abiding)	1. Laxity 2. Excitement
Higher Insight	1. Calm abiding 2. Elimination of assumptions of bad states		1. Direct apprehension of emptiness 2. Stabilizing meditation generates physical and mental pliancy	1. Artificial conceptions of inherent existence 2. Innate conceptions of true existence
Union of Calm Abiding and Higher Insight			Maintaining calm abiding and direct perception of emptiness in a single mind	

of accumulation, (2) the path of preparation, (3) the path of seeing, (4) the path of meditation, and (5) the path of no more learning (see table 3).

The path of accumulation is so named because on this level one amasses the two "collections": the collection of merit and the collection of wisdom. The collection of merit consists of virtuous deeds and attitudes, which produce corresponding good karmic results and positive mental states. The collection of wisdom refers to cultivation of wisdom for the sake of all other sentient beings. One enters this path with the generation of the "mind of awakening" (*byang chub kyi sems, bodhicitta*) the altruistic intention to become awakened for the benefit of others. According to Sakya Pandita, the term "accumulation"

> denotes the dual accumulation of merit and gnosis, and path means the process of attending to the factors conducive to liberation. The disciples [i.e., hearers] meditate on the faults of the compulsive aggregates that make up the body, such as sickness, sores, and so on, while practitioners of the great vehicle cultivate antidotes for the compulsory nature of the aggregates by realizing their lack of inherent identity.[21]

On the path of accumulation one also cultivates the four establishments in mindfulness: mindfulness of (1) body, (2) feelings, (3) mind, and (4) phenomena;[22] the four abandonments: (1) abandonment of nonvirtuous phenomena already generated, (2) nongeneration of nonvirtuous phenomena not yet generated, (3) increasing of virtuous phenomena already generated, and (4) generation of virtuous phenomena not yet generated;[23] and the four bases of magical emanation: (1) aspiration, (2) effort, (3) mental attention, and (4) analytical meditative stabilization.[24]

The Path of Preparation

The path of preparation is attained when a meditator reaches the level of a union of calm abiding and higher insight with emptiness as the object of observation. On this path, one gradually eliminates conceptuality in one's understanding of suchness (the true nature of reality, which is equated with emptiness) in four stages: (1) heat, (2) peak, (3) patience, and (4) supreme mundane qualities. The heat stage is so called because it is a sign that the fire of nonconceptual understanding on the path of seeing will soon be produced; it is "the precursor of unconditioned gnosis [of the path of seeing], just as the warmth produced by rubbing two sticks together is the precursor of fire."[25] At this level the meditator attains a clear conceptual awareness of suchness in a meditative stabilization.

The peak stage marks a point at which the virtuous roots that have been cultivated previously will no longer decrease or be lost. One also attains a meditative stabilization focusing on suchness in which conceptual understanding increases. This is an intimation of unconditioned direct perception of emptiness, which occurs on the path of seeing.

At the level of patience the meditator develops familiarity with the concept of emptiness and overcomes fear with respect to it. This stage also marks a point at which one is no longer able to descend to the lower realms of rebirth (animals, hell beings, or hungry ghosts) through the force of afflicted actions and attitudes. (Bodhisattvas may choose to be reborn in these realms due to compassion, but they are no longer reborn in them powerlessly.) The meditator also attains a clear conceptual awareness of suchness and a meditative stabilization in which emptiness, the object of observation, is perceived as being distinct from the mind of the meditator.

During the path of preparation, meditators attain the highest worldly attributes and prepare to attain a supramundane path (the path of seeing). At this level, the cognizing subject no longer appears while one is in meditative stabilization. Prior to this, one had appearances of subject and object as distinct entities, but at the end of the path of preparation one is no longer able to ascertain subject or object. These factors do, however, still appear to the meditator, but she is no longer consciously perceiving them.

The Path of Seeing

The meditator continues contemplating emptiness, and with repeated training all appearances of subject and object disappear in emptiness. All thoughts of subject and object are overcome, and one perceives emptiness directly. This marks the beginning of the path of seeing, and at this point subject and object are undifferentiable, like water poured into water.

On the path of seeing meditators remove the artificial conceptions of inherent existence, those which are acquired through training and studying mistaken philosophical systems. However, one does not yet remove the innate misconceptions of inherent existence, which are the results of conditioning since beginningless time and are more difficult to overcome.

The path of seeing is divided into two parts: uninterrupted paths and paths of liberation. The former abandon artificial afflictions and are called "uninterrupted" because having attained them one immediately moves on to a path of liberation from these afflictions. The path of liberation is the state or condition of having overcome the artificial afflictions. On the path of seeing one contemplates the four noble truths and the meditating subjects that comprehend them, and one understands both as being empty of inherent existence. While in meditative equipoise, one perceives only emptiness, but when one emerges from meditation one again perceives everyday appearances, although they no longer are perceived as solid and real. Rather, like a magician viewing an illusion that he has created, a person on the path of seeing perceives conditioned appearances but knows them to be false.

Through repeated familiarization with emptiness, one is liberated from artificial innate conceptions with respect to the four noble truths and with respect to oneself, because one understands the emptiness of these concepts and of the consciousness that comprehends them. Sakya Pandita indicates that on the path of seeing one has

> unconditioned perceptions of the real nature of things for the first time. It is the initial occurrence of a mode of mental functioning unconditioned by mundane patterning and is thus the beginning of the "Superior" practice. It is not merely temporary suppression of such patterning, but elimination of their automatic readout in cognitive functioning.[26]

Bodhisattvas on the path of seeing have transcended the condition of "ordinary beings" and have reached the state of "superiors" (*'phags pa, ārya*) because they have attained a supramundane path due to perceiving emptiness directly. Ordinary beings only view afflicted and false appearances and do not have direct perceptual awareness of emptiness. Mahāyānists on the path of seeing also enter the first of the ten "bodhisattva levels," called "the very joyous."[27]

The Path of Meditation

During the path of seeing one removes the artificial or latent conceptions of inherent existence, but the subtler, innate traces of these conceptions remain and sometimes reassert themselves when one is not in meditative equipoise. During the path of meditation the subtlest traces are removed and will never reappear. This is because the mind is a clear and luminous entity, and when the adventitious conceptions of inherent existence are eliminated there is no longer any basis for their re-emergence within one's mental continuum.

> The cognitive patternings or conditionings eliminated by the transcendent meditation path are the innate patternings that produce concepts of personal ego and separate identities of phenomena, which in turn prevent pacification [of the subtlest negative mental functions].[28]

On the path of meditation, one continues to familiarize oneself with meditation on emptiness. Like the path of seeing, the path of meditation is divided into uninterrupted paths and paths of liberation. On an uninterrupted path, meditators overcome innate conceptions of inherent existence, and the subsequent path of liberation is a meditative equipoise in which one is free from these cognitions. Meditators on the path of meditation also attain advanced meditative states that are neither uninterrupted paths nor paths of liberation. Bodhisattvas cultivate the remaining nine bodhisattva levels on the path of meditation.

The Path of No More Learning

The final phase of this process is the path of no more learning, during which meditators eliminate the very subtlest vestiges of the conception of inherent existence, together with its seeds. The culmination of the path of no more learning for Hīnayānists is the attainment of arhathood or the state of a solitary realizer, and for bodhisattvas it is the attainment of buddhahood. Khenpo Könchog Gyaltsen explains that bodhisattvas

> attain buddhahood, and one's meditation is free from obstacles, saṃsāric actions and obscurations. The mind, having become completely stable, cannot be moved by conceptual thoughts. One experiences the one taste of all the Buddha's wisdom which pervades the suchness of phenomena. In this state one ceases the complete cause of suffering, and for this reason no longer experiences its effects.

Table 3. The Five Paths

The Five Paths	Attainments	Levels	Corresponding Bhūmis
Path of Preparation	1. Amassing collections of merit and wisdom 2. Cultivation of four establishments in mindfulness and four abandonments		
Path of Accumulation	Union of calm abiding and higher insight	1. Heat 2. Peak 3. Patience 4. Supreme mundane qualities	
Path of Seeing	1. Deepening perception of emptiness 2. Removal of artificial conceptions of inherent existence 3. Dualistic appearances are overcome	1. Uninterrupted paths 2. Paths of liberation	First bodhisattva bhūmi
Path of Meditation	Removal of latent conceptions of inherent existence	1. Uninterrupted paths 2. Paths of liberation	Bhūmis 9–10
Path of No More Learning	Removal of subtlest traces of conception of inherent existence	1. Bodhisattvas eliminate afflictive obstructions and 2. Obstructions to omniscience	Culminates in buddha-bhūmi

> Because there is no more to learn and practice, one enters into the state of beyond-saṃsāra and beyond-nirvāṇa called the Path of Complete Perfection.[29]

Hīnayānists attain this level upon successful cultivation of the "vajra-like meditative stabilization," supported by the fourth concentration. Bodhisattvas attain it on the tenth bodhisattva level, supported by the highest level of the fourth concentration. On the path of no more learning, bodhisattvas eliminate all the remaining traces of the afflictive obstructions and the obstructions to omniscience and reach their goal of attainment of buddhahood for the benefit of all living beings.

Notes

1. H.H. the Dalai Lama, *Kindness, Clarity, and Insight*, p. 183.
2. For a discussion of this meditation, see *Abhidharmakośa*, VI, tr. Louis de La Vallée Poussin (Paris: Institut Belge des Hautes Études Chinoises, 1971), pp. 148–153.
3. The realm of existence that humans inhabit is called the Desire Realm because the predominant factor in this realm is desire. In the other two realms of existence, the Form Realm and the Formless Realm, desire does not afflict the inhabitants as much.
4. See Lati Rinbochay and Denma Lochö Rinbochay, *Meditative States in Tibetan Buddhism* (London: Wisdom, 1983), pp. 115–116.
5. For further details, see *The Path of Purity (Buddhaghosa's Visuddhimagga)*, tr. Pe Maung Tin (London: Pāli Text Society, 1971), X.376ff., and *Le Compendium de la Super-Doctrine d'Asaṅga (Abhidharmasamuccaya)*, tr. Walpola Rahula (Paris: École Française d'Extrème-Orient, 1971), p. 112.
6. *Dīgha-nikāya*, ed. T.W. Rhys Davids, vol. I, p. 73–76. See also *Majjhima-nikāya* I, p. 21ff. and *Saṃyutta-nikāya* V, p. 318ff.
7. See *La Somme du Grand Véhicule d'Asaṅga (Mahāyānasaṃgraha)*, tr. Étienne Lamotte (Louvain: Université de Louvain, 1973), p. 62.
8. Solitary realizers (*rang sangs rgyas, pratyekabuddha*) follow a Hīnayāna path to personal nirvana and attain it in their final lives without receiving instruction from a buddha. Unlike buddhas, they do not devote the rest of their lives to teaching others. They are described in more detail in chapter 4, "Mahāyāna."
9. *Saṃdhinirmocana-sūtra* (*'Phags pa dgongs pa nges par 'grel pa'i mdo*): *The Tog Palace Edition of the Tibetan Kanjur* (Leh: Smanrtsis Shesrig Dpemzod, 1975–1978), vol. 63, p. 98.2.
10. Takpo Tashi Namgyal, *Mahāmudrā* (Boston: Shambhala, 1986), p. 27.
11. "*Śamathavipaśyanāyuganaddha*: The Two Leading Principles of Buddhist Meditation," in Minoru Kiyota, ed., *Mahāyāna Buddhist Meditation* (Honolulu: University Press of Hawaii, 1978), p. 48.
12. Jeffrey Hopkins, *Meditation on Emptiness* (London: Wisdom, 1983), p. 265.

13. Geshe Gendün Lodrö, *Walking Through Walls*, tr. Jeffrey Hopkins (Ithaca: Snow Lion, 1992), p. 187.
14. *Walking Through Walls*, p. 190.
15. *Meditation on Emptiness*, p. 252.
16. Asaṅga, *Stages of Hearers* (*Śrāvaka-bhūmi*: Otani Sde dge, *sems tsam* vol. 6, p. 117a.4–5; Karunesha Shukla, ed., *Śrāvakabhūmi* [Patna: K.P. Jayaswal, 1973], p. 320.3–5). See also Sde dge p. 147b.6–148a.4, a description of the means of achieving pliancy, which is connected with gaining mental one-pointedness (*rtse gcig pa*).
17. See *Walking Through Walls*, pp. 199–204.
18. Ibid., p. 205.
19. Ibid., pp. 205–206.
20. Ibid., p. 212.
21. Sakya Pandita, *Illuminations*, tr. Geshe Wangyal and Brian Cutillo (Novato, CA: Lotsawa, 1988), p. 82.
22. For further discussions of these, see: Venerable U Silananda, *The Four Foundations of Mindfulness*, (London: Wisdom, 1990); *Smṛtyopsthāna-sūtra* (*Middle Length Sayings [Majjhima-nikāya]* #10, tr. I.B. Horner (London: Luzac & Co., 1967), pp. 70ff. [=*Dīgha-nikāya* XXII]; Vasubandhu's *Treasury of Abhidharma (Abhidharmakośa*: tr. Louis de La Vallée Poussin; English tr. Leo Pruden; Berkeley: Asian Humanities Press, 1988), ch. 4 and ch. 6; and Asaṅga's *Compendium of Abhidharma* (*Le Compendium de la Super-Doctrine d'Asaṅga [Abhidharmasamuccaya]),* tr. Walpola Rahula), pp. 118, 169.
23. For further discussions of these, see: *Path of Purity*, ch. 21, p. 679; Vasubandhu's *Treasury of Abhidharma,* ch. 5, p. 283; Asaṅga's *Compendium of Abhidharma*, ch. 1.4; Edward Conze, *The Large Sūtra on Perfect Wisdom* (London, Luzac & Co., 1961), pp. 146–147; and Jeffrey Hopkins, *Compassion in Tibetan Buddhism* (London: Rider, 1980), p. 225.
24. For discussions of these, see *Treasury of Abhidharma*, ch. 6, pp. 281–285 and *Path of Purity*, ch. 12, p. 385.
25. *Illuminations*, p. 83.
26. Ibid., p. 85.
27. These are discussed in the next chapter.
28. *Illuminations*, p. 94.
29. Khenpo Könchog Gyaltsen, *In Search of the Stainless Ambrosia* (Ithaca: Snow Lion, 1988), pp. 98–99.

4. Mahāyāna

Origins

In the centuries following Śākyamuni's death, numerous schools and sub-schools arose, some of which were identified by points of doctrine or monastic discipline, and others by their association with particular regions. In addition, even after the death of the founder of the tradition, new texts continued to appear, many of which claimed to have been spoken by him. To make the situation even more confusing, older texts were being redacted, and new material was often added. In some cases, this textual development can be traced by examining the dated Chinese translations of a given work, which often indicate that as new ideas and models developed in India they were incorporated into existing texts.[1] Successive versions of a given text sometimes exhibit significant growth, as new ideas were incorporated into existing canonical sources in order to give them added validity. Since Buddhism has no centralized authority and no ecclesiastical body that oversees the purity of the doctrine and canon, the treatises and teachings of Buddhism were open to revision.

The problem of deciding which works and teachings were authentic was compounded by the fact that Śākyamuni left no clear instructions concerning how spurious texts were to be identified. When asked shortly before his death to provide guidelines for determining the true "word of the Buddha," he is reported to have answered, "Whatever is well spoken is the word of the Buddha."[2] In other words, if a particular teaching accords with Buddhist doctrines and norms, if it leads to diminishment of afflictions and toward nirvana, then it can be accepted as authoritative, no matter who originally spoke it. This left the door open for new texts and doctrines, and created innumerable difficulties in interpretation and practice; but on the positive side it allowed the Buddhist canon to remain fluid. Because of this, the body of authoritative writings was able to adapt and grow, incorporating religious insights from many quarters.

Perhaps the most historically and doctrinally significant development in the centuries following Śākyamuni's death was the movement that came to be known as *Mahāyāna* (*theg pa chen po, mahāyāna*), a term that literally means "Great Vehicle." The origins of this movement are obscure, and contemporary scholars have advanced a number of theories concerning when, where, and by whom it was developed.[3] It appears to have begun as an unorganized movement centered in local cults, each with its own texts and practices.[4] Distinctively Mahāyāna works apparently began to appear during the first or second century C.E., several hundred years after the death of Śākyamuni. Some of these were referred to as "sūtras," implying that they had been spoken by the Buddha, even though he had been dead for centuries.[5]

This discrepancy was noted by early Mahāyānists,[6] who explained that Śākyamuni gave these teachings to a select few followers during his lifetime, but that most of his disciples (referred to as "hearers") were unprepared for these advanced doctrines, and so the texts were hidden in the realm of *nāga*s (beings with serpentlike bodies and human heads who live under the water) until people arose in the world who were able to understand and explain them.[7] Early in the second century C.E., several qualified teachers were born, and the texts were returned to the world of humans. The most important of these teachers was Nāgārjuna, generally credited with being the main expositor of the "Middle Way School" (*dbu ma, madhyamaka*), which systematized the Mahāyāna teachings of emptiness and the path of the bodhisattva.

Some scholars believe that the origins of the Mahāyāna movement lie in the aftermath of the "second council" (held in Vaiśālī one hundred years after Śākyamuni's final nirvana, according to traditional accounts), when a group calling itself the "Great Assembly" (*phal chen pa, mahāsaṃghika*) split off from a minority group that referred to itself as the "Elders" (*gnas brtan pa, sthavira*).[8] Little is known with certainty about the Great Assembly, but available records indicate that its members viewed the Buddha in cosmic terms, as a being endowed with supernatural powers and faculties, in contrast with their more conservative rivals, who tended to emphasize the Buddha's humanity.

If they were in fact the precursors of Mahāyāna, however, it seems clear from their surviving writings (and from references to their doctrines in the writings of rival schools) that the members of the Great Assembly were distant relations, and there is no evidence that they espoused the doctrines and practices that came to be associated with the developed traditions of Mahāyāna that eventually found their way to Tibet. As Graeme MacQueen has noted, Mahāyāna constitutes a "religious revolution" that shares some doctrines and practices with its predecessors, but which differed from other Buddhist schools in significant ways.[9]

The earliest dated version of a text that can be confidently associated with Mahāyāna is a Chinese translation of the *Perfection of Wisdom in 8,000 Lines* by Lokakṣema, in the second century C.E. Although some of the doctrines and practices that are commonly associated with Mahāyāna are absent in this text,[10] other characteristically Mahāyāna concepts are expounded, particularly the ideal of the bodhisattva and the doctrine of emptiness. It should be noted that both of these terms (as well as many other important Mahāyāna concepts) are also found in non-Mahāyāna sources, but their treatment in Mahāyāna treatises is distinctive.

By the time Buddhism arrived in Tibet, Mahāyāna had become a well-defined religious movement that saw itself as separate from (and superior to) other forms of Buddhism. These it labeled as "Hīnayāna" (*theg pa dman pa, hīnayāna*), which literally means "Lesser (or Inferior) Vehicle." The following sections will examine some of the main ideas and images of the Mahāyāna Buddhism that entered Tibet.

The Perfection of Wisdom Literature

The earliest clearly Mahāyāna texts are the "Perfection of Wisdom" sūtras, which were probably composed during the first and second centuries C.E. Although they hold many terms and doctrines in common with earlier schools of Buddhism, they represent a major paradigm shift in the tradition. According to Graeme MacQueen, "as is often the case with revolutionaries, many of the terminological and conceptual resources available to them were in the tradition with which they were breaking," but these terms were often used in strikingly new ways.[11]

In these texts, the ideal of personal liberation is denounced, and the figure of the bodhisattva is valorized. The Perfection of Wisdom sūtras also discourse at length on the doctrine of emptiness (*stong pa nyid, śūnyatā*), which holds that all phenomena are empty of inherent existence and are merely collections of parts that arise due to causes and conditions. Thus they utterly lack any essence. These truths are only fully understood by those who develop the "perfection of wisdom" (*shes rab kyi pha rol tu phyin pa, prajñā-pāramitā*), which allows sages to free themselves from the shackles of false conceptuality and perceive reality as it is. The true nature of reality is referred to in these texts as "suchness" (*de bzhin nyid, tathatā*), which is described as ineffable and utterly beyond the realm of language or conceptual thought. It is associated with emptiness, and is only known by yogic adepts who transcend language and conceptuality. Such people enter into direct understanding of reality as it is, freed from the false imaginings of conceptually influenced consciousness.

Like the sermons contained in the Pāli canon, the Perfection of Wisdom sūtras generally begin with the standard opening line: "Thus have I heard at one time: the Bhagavan [Buddha] was dwelling in . . . ."[12] Many of the places where the discourses are situated are also mentioned in the Pāli texts, and Buddha's main disciples are often present (although in the Perfection of Wisdom texts they are commonly portrayed as being inferior in understanding to bodhisattvas).

There are many other divergences,[13] and among the more notable ones are the changes in the way the Buddha is presented. In the Perfection of Wisdom literature he becomes a cosmic figure whose wisdom surpasses that of all humans and gods, and his power allows him to transcend the ordinary laws of time and space. No longer a mortal human teacher, he generates bodies that pervade all of space, is omniscient (an attribute that Buddha denies in the Pāli canon) and, perhaps most strikingly, he declares that he never truly dies or enters a final nirvana. Rather, he only *appeared* to pass away for the benefit of his hearer disciples, who needed this graphic lesson in impermanence so that they would make greater effort in religious practice. Although they believed that Śākyamuni died and entered a final nirvana, he really continues to live in a "pure land," where advanced practitioners still visit him and receive his teachings.

In addition to these doctrinal changes, the Perfection of Wisdom sūtras differ stylistically from the Pāli sūtras (*sutta* in Pāli). For one thing, many of them are much longer than the Pāli texts, and the dialogue is strikingly different in tone and content.[14] Another change occurs in the cast of characters: in many of these texts bodhisattvas appear as interlocutors and teachers, and they are portrayed as vastly superior in understanding to the Hīnayānists. One exception to this is Subhūti, who is said in the Pāli canon to be the most advanced of Buddha's immediate disciples in understanding of emptiness.[15] Presumably because of this designation, in texts like the *Perfection of Wisdom in 8,000 Lines* he questions the Buddha on the subject of emptiness.

Perhaps the most striking change in these texts is found in the content of the discourses. In the Pāli texts Buddha presents his teachings as accurate descriptions of the true nature of reality, but in the Perfection of Wisdom literature the ultimate validity of these presentations is denied. Buddha tells his audience that his doctrines are mere words that only operate on the level of conceptuality. This is even true of the goals of the path, and he informs them that there is no truly existent nirvana, and no truly existent person who attains it. Thus in the *Diamond Sūtra* Buddha tells Subhūti,

> due to being established in the bodhisattva vehicle, one should give rise to the thought, 'As many sentient beings there are that are included among the realms of sentient beings . . . whatever realms of sentient beings can be conceived, all these should be brought by me to nirvana, to a final nirvana that is a realm of nirvana without remainder; but, although countless sentient beings have reached final nirvana, no sentient being whatsoever has reached final nirvana.' Why is this? Subhūti, if a discrimination of a sentient being arises in a bodhisattva, he should not be called a bodhisattva. Why is this? Subhūti, one who gives rise to the discrimination of such a self, the discrimination of a sentient being, the discrimination of a soul, or the discrimination of a person should not be called a bodhisattva.[16]

Even the term "bodhisattva" is merely a verbal designation lacking ultimate validity. Buddha's teachings are likewise mere words that at best indicate the direction of awakening, but do not describe reality as it truly is; this can only be understood by those who transcend words and concepts.

Mahāyāna Doctrines

The Bodhisattva

The figure of the bodhisattva is central to Mahāyāna. The Sanskrit term literally means "awakening (*bodhi*) being (*sattva*)," and it indicates that a bodhisattva is someone who is progressing toward the state of awakening of a buddha. The term was translated into Tibetan as *byang chub sems dpa'* (pronounced "jangchup semba"), which means "awakening (*byang chub*) hero (*sems dpa'*)," indicating that the bodhisattva is viewed by Tibetans as a noble and courageous figure. This reflects the fact that bodhisattvas are often depicted in Mahāyāna literature as mythic heroes, possessing supernatural powers and ceaselessly working for the benefit of others.

The bodhisattva is commonly contrasted with the Hīnayāna ideal of the *arhat* (*dgra bcom pa, arhat*), who seeks to escape from cyclic existence but is primarily concerned with personal liberation (see table 4). The bodhisattva, by contrast, seeks to establish all sentient beings in awakening and even takes on their karmic burdens. Mahāyāna texts indicate that bodhisattvas are able to transfer the sufferings and afflictions of others to themselves, and that they also give their own merit to others.

The purview of the bodhisattva's compassion is universal, since bodhisattvas seek the liberation of all beings, without exception and without distinctions. It is admitted in Mahāyāna literature that arhats also have compassion and that they teach others. Moreover, the accomplishments of arhats are impressive: they overcome the afflictive emotions, eliminate hatred, ignorance, and desire for the things of cyclic existence. They become dispassionate toward material possessions, care nothing for worldly fame and power, and because of this they transcend the mundane world. When they die, they pass beyond the world into a blissful state of nirvana in which there is no further rebirth, and no suffering. Despite these attainments, however, their path is denigrated by the Mahāyāna sūtras, which draw a sharp distinction between the "great compassion" (*snying rje chen po, mahākaruṇā*) of bodhisattvas and the limited compassion of arhats. Tsong Khapa, for instance, contends that

> there are low trainees who seek a low object of intention which is a low attainment solely for their own sake—the state of merely extinguishing the suffering of cyclic existence. There are supreme trainees who seek an elevated object of intention, the supreme attainment—the state of Buddhahood—for the sake of all sentient beings. Since there are these two types of trainees, low and high, the vehicles by which they go to their own state are called the Low Vehicle (Hīnayāna) and the Great Vehicle (Mahāyāna).[17]

Hīnayāna is divided by Mahāyāna exegetes into two paths: the path of "hearers" (*nyan thos, śrāvaka*) and the path of "solitary realizers" (*rang sangs rgyas, pratyeka-buddha*). The term "hearers" originally referred to the immediate disciples of Śākyamuni, who heard his words and practiced meditation in accordance with the literal meaning of his teachings. According to Mahāyānists, they believed that the teachings they heard were the only ones taught by Śākyamuni and that all other doctrines attributed to him (including Mahāyāna teachings) are spurious. Mahāyānists further contend that Śākyamuni propounded doctrines that surpassed his Hīnayāna teachings, but hearers were not permitted to listen to them because their cognitive capacities were inferior to those for whom he presented his Mahāyāna lectures. Although they criticize Hīnayāna on these grounds, Mahāyānists also contend that Hīnayāna paths are valid ways of making spiritual progress and that they were taught for certain people who are primarily interested in personal liberation and not in working for the salvation of others.

Hearers seek liberation as arhats, a process that has three stages: (1) stream enterer, (2) once returner, and (3) never returner. A stream enterer is one who has definitely entered the path to liberation. A once returner is a person who will attain liberation after one more rebirth, and a never returner is a person who will become an arhat in the present lifetime. Solitary realizers are Hīnayāna practitioners who attain liberation by themselves, without hearing the teachings of a buddha. According to Mahāyāna explanations, they previously listened to buddhas and followed their teachings, but in their final lives they have no teachers.[18] Seeking only personal salvation, they attain nirvana as quickly as possible and pass beyond cyclic existence. They may teach others, and often show compassion for others, but their primary goal is a personal nirvana. Tsong Khapa states that they surpass hearers through training in merit and wisdom for at least one hundred eons, but they do not amass the two collections of merit and wisdom as bodhisattvas do, and they are not motivated by a wish to benefit all sentient beings.[19] Because of this, solitary realizers (like hearers and arhats) are characterized by Mahāyānists as selfish. In the *Perfection of Wisdom in 8,000 Lines*, Buddha indicates the differences between Hīnayānists and bodhisattvas:

> Subhūti, bodhisattvas, great beings, should not train in the way that persons of the hearer vehicle and solitary realizer vehicle train.

> Subhūti, in what way do persons of the hearer vehicle and the solitary realizer vehicle train? Subhūti, they think thus, '[I] should discipline only myself; [I] should pacify only myself; [I] should pass beyond sorrow [i.e., attain nirvana] by myself.' In order to discipline only themselves and pacify themselves and pass beyond sorrow, they begin to apply themselves to establishing all the virtuous roots. Also, Subhūti, bodhisattvas, great beings, should not train in this way. On the contrary, Subhūti, bodhisattvas, great beings, should train thus, 'In order to benefit all the world, I will dwell in suchness and, establishing all sentient beings in suchness, I will lead the immeasurable realms of sentient beings to nirvana.' Bodhisattvas, great beings, should begin applying themselves in that way to establishing all virtuous roots,[20] but should not be conceited because of this . . . .
>
> Some, not speaking of the bodhisattva vehicle, say, '[I] should discipline only myself, abide in peace, and similarly just attain nirvana; [I] will remain alone and attain the fruit of a stream enterer. [I] should quickly attain the fruit of a once returner, the fruit of a never returner, and the fruit of an arhat. [I] should attain my own awakening.' Those who say, 'In this very life, having thoroughly freed the mind from contamination, without attachment, [I] will attain nirvana' are 'at the level of hearers and solitary realizers.' With respect to this, bodhisattvas, great beings, should not give rise to such thoughts. Why is this? Subhūti, bodhisattvas, great beings, abide in the great vehicle and put on the great armor; they should not give rise to thoughts of even a little elaboration.[21] Why is this? These supreme beings thoroughly lead the world and are a great benefit to the world.[22]

This passage reflects the strongly sectarian tone of many Mahāyāna discussions of their Hīnayāna rivals, which contrast the universal compassion of bodhisattvas with the supposed selfishness of hearers and solitary realizers. As Stephen Kent has noted, this tone is particularly evident in early Mahāyāna texts, probably because the emergent Mahāyāna faced strong opposition from the proponents of the path they characterized as "inferior" to their own.[23] This sectarian attitude is also found in Tibetan discussions of the differences between Hīnayāna and Mahāyāna, despite the fact that from the earliest period of Buddhism's dissemination into Tibet

Mahāyāna has been the dominant tradition. Although there is little evidence of proselytizing by Hīnayānists in Tibet, Buddhists in the Land of Snows adopted the tone of their Indian teachers in their discussions of Hīnayāna.

Why Mahāyāna is Superior

According to the Dalai Lama, Mahāyāna is superior to Hīnayāna in three ways: (1) motivation, (2) goal, and (3) level of understanding.[24] Mahāyāna surpasses Hīnayāna in terms of motivation in that bodhisattvas are inspired by great compassion, which encompasses all sentient beings, while Hīnayānists only seek liberation for themselves. The bodhisattva's goal of buddhahood is superior to the arhat's intention to attain a personal nirvana, since it takes much longer to reach and requires perfection of compassion and wisdom, along with innumerable good qualities, whereas the arhat only needs to eliminate the coarser levels of the afflictions and develop complete dispassion toward cyclic existence, along with a direct perception of emptiness. Although the Dalai Lama states that arhats do understand emptiness (since without this they would be unable to pass beyond cyclic existence), he contends that a buddha's understanding of emptiness is infinitely more profound.

In addition to these criticisms, Mahāyānists also contend that their vehicle is superior to that of their opponents because it is able to encompass more people and bring them to awakening. They characterize Hīnayāna as a narrow, limited path suitable only for monks, but Mahāyāna is portrayed as a comprehensive tradition with room for everyone. It has teachings and practices for lay people as well as monks, and Mahāyāna texts stress the importance of the ability to adapt the doctrine to the individual needs and proclivities of one's audience.

The "Hīnayāna" Response

Tibetan exegetes contend that Hīnayāna doctrines are inferior to Mahāyāna teachings, but that the Buddha taught them for the benefit of beings of lower spiritual faculties, people who are mainly concerned with their own welfare and lack the courage to devote themselves to working for all sentient beings. This assessment was not, of course, shared by those characterized as "Hīnayānists," who generally viewed themselves as

Table 4. Differences between Arhats and Bodhisattvas

Differences Between Arhats and Bodhisattvas according to Mahāyāna

	Arhats	Bodhisattvas
Motivation	Liberation for themselves	Compassion for all beings
Goal	Personal nirvana	Liberation of all sentient beings
Level of understanding	1. Direct perception of emptiness	1. Omniscience
	2. Supernatural abilities such as clairvoyance, knowledge of past lives	2. Full comprehension of emptiness
Qualities attained	1. Eliminates coarse levels of afflictions	1. Six (or ten) perfections (generosity, ethics, patience, effort, concentration, wisdom)
	2. Dispassion toward cyclic existence	2. Great compassion
	3. Ability to levitate up to the level of 7 śāla trees	3. Skill in means
		4. Full comprehension of emptiness in all its aspects at all times
		5. Supernatural abilities such as transcendence of time and laws of physics
Length of training period	Minimum of one human lifetime (after previous lives as stream enterer and once returner)	Minimum of three countless eons from manifestation of mind of awakening

upholders of a pure form of Buddhism and as heirs to the authentic teachings of Śākyamuni.

The only "Hīnayāna" school that survives today is Theravāda, which is the dominant tradition in southeast Asia. Theravāda is found in Thailand, Burma, Laos, Cambodia, Sri Lanka, and Vietnam, while Mahāyāna schools have had their greatest appeal in other parts of Asia, including China, Japan, Korea, Vietnam, the Himalayan region, Mongolia, and Tibet. Because of the geographical distance between Theravāda strongholds and Tibet, Tibetan Buddhists historically have had little contact with

Theravāda and thus lack first-hand knowledge of its practices. It is also important to note that although Tibetan Buddhists categorize Theravāda among the Hīnayāna schools, they also believe that it is a valid Buddhist path, and many Mahāyāna texts contain warnings that bodhisattvas should not denigrate Hīnayāna.

Because "Hīnayāna" is clearly a pejorative term, some contemporary scholars have proposed alternatives. Some, for instance, substitute "Theravāda" for "Hīnayāna," but this is an unsatisfactory alternative, since the term "Hīnayāna" traditionally encompasses eighteen schools.[25] Theravāda is the only one that exists today, but when Mahāyāna texts refer to Hīnayāna they do not single out any one tradition. Other proposed alternatives are equally unsatisfactory. Throughout this book I employ the term "Hīnayāna," since it is used by Tibetan exegetes, but it should be understood that it is a term that is not accepted by those to whom it is applied.

Theravādins generally reject the Mahāyāna claim that Mahāyāna sūtras are the authentic word of Śākyamuni, and contend that they are in fact later forgeries. Theravāda scholars assert that Śākyamuni's life is a paradigmatic example of the heroic struggle of an individual seeker of truth, who saw through the illusions that bind most people and who won awakening through his own efforts. He taught others and demonstrated compassion for suffering sentient beings, but Theravādins point to numerous passages in their canon in which he told his followers to pursue their own salvations. The most famous of these passages was spoken shortly before his death, when he told his followers, ". . . live with yourselves as islands, with yourselves as refuges, with no one else as refuge."[26] Such admonitions, according to Theravāda exegetes, indicate that Śākyamuni taught a path of individual liberation.

Theravāda tradition does, however, recognize the ideal of the bodhisattva as a legitimate one, but restricts it to a few exceptional individuals, such as Śākyamuni. The Pāli equivalent *bodhisatta* is used to refer to Śākyamuni in his previous lives, during which he cultivated the good qualities of a buddha, such as morality, patience, wisdom, compassion, and so on. There are numerous stories of his previous births that describe how he demonstrated Buddhist virtues in difficult circumstances. These are popular among Buddhists everywhere because they provide models for emulation.

Theravāda texts, however, indicate that very few individuals possess the fortitude to complete the training of a buddha and state that most people should be content with attaining a personal nirvana as an arhat or solitary realizer. The path to buddhahood is long and arduous, requiring a period of at least three "countless eons" to complete, according to both Hīnayāna and Mahāyāna sources. A countless eon is an unimaginably long period of time, measured in terms of cycles of creation and destruction of the universe, and the path to buddhahood contains innumerable pitfalls. Given these factors, the arhat's nirvana is a sensible alternative.

The Mahāyāna Rejoinder: All Sentient Beings Have Equal Capacities

Hīnayāna texts assert that most people lack the ability to attain buddhahood, but Mahāyānists contend that there is no fundamental difference between Śākyamuni and other sentient beings. All possess the same capacity for awakening, and Mahāyāna treatises state that all can and should aspire to buddhahood for the benefit of others. Anything less is characterized as ignoble and inferior. In the *Perfection of Wisdom in 25,000 Lines,* for example, Buddha discusses this idea with his hearer disciple Śāriputra.

> Buddha: Śāriputra, do you think that any hearers or solitary realizers think, 'After we have become completely, unsurpassably awakened, we should lead all beings to nirvana without remainder, to final nirvana?'
>
> Śāriputra: No indeed, Bhagavan . . . .
>
> Buddha: But this is the way that bodhisattvas, great beings, think. A glow-worm, or some other luminous animal, does not think that its light could illuminate the continent of Jambudvīpa or shine over it.[27] In the same way, hearers and solitary realizers do not think that they should, after attaining complete, unsurpassed awakening, lead all beings to nirvana. But the sun, when it has risen, radiates its light over the whole of Jambudvīpa. In the same way, bodhisattvas, great beings, after having completed the practices that lead to the complete, unsurpassed awakening of buddhahood, lead countless beings to nirvana.[28]

As this passage indicates, bodhisattvas are portrayed as heroic figures in Mahāyāna discourses. They are said to possess a deep sense of compassion for all suffering beings and limitless energy to work for their benefit. They eagerly sacrifice themselves to do whatever is necessary to benefit others, and they make no distinctions between friends and enemies. All sentient beings are equally dear to them, and all are equally deserving of their compassion. The ideal attitude of bodhisattvas is summed up eloquently in a famous passage by Śāntideva:

> May those who falsely accuse me, who do me harm,
> and who ridicule me all share in awakening.
> May I be a protector for those without protection,
> a guide for travelers,
> And a boat, a bridge, and passageway for those who long
> to reach the other shore.
> May I be a light for those in need of light. May I be a bed
> for those in need of rest.
> May I be a servant for those who need a servant,
> for all living beings.
> For all living beings may I be a wish-fulfilling gem, a pot
> of plenty, an efficacious spell (*mantra*),
> A universal remedy, a wish-fulfilling tree, and a wish-granting
> cow.[29]
> Just as earth and other elements are useful in many ways for
> innumerable beings dwelling throughout space,
> So may I in various ways be a source of life for beings dwelling
> throughout space until they have attained liberation.[30]

The Bodhisattva Path

The career of a bodhisattva begins with the first dawning of the "mind of awakening" (*byang chub kyi sems, bodhicitta*), which represents a fundamental alteration in one's attitudes. Ordinary beings—even those who are kind and compassionate—are primarily motivated by self-interest and work mainly for their own benefit. All of their activities and thoughts are tinged by self-serving motivations and attitudes. Even when they perform acts of kindness, they generally do so expecting praise or personal satisfaction, and not because of pure altruism.

Bodhisattvas, however, are motivated by universal compassion, and they seek the ultimate goal of buddhahood in order to be of service to others. They embark on this path with the generation of the mind of awakening, which Geshe Rabten states is "the wish for Supreme Awakening for the sake of others. The sign of true Bodhicitta is the constant readiness to undergo any sacrifice for the happiness of all beings."[31] Unlike ordinary beings, who think of their own advantage, bodhisattvas consider how best to benefit others.

> They become endowed with that kind of wise insight that enables them to see all beings as on the way to their slaughter. Great compassion thereby takes hold of them. With the divine eye they perceive countless beings, and what they see brings great agitation. So many carry the burden of a karma that will soon be punished in the hells, others have earned bad rebirths that keep them away from the Buddha and his teachings, others are doomed soon to be killed, or they are enmeshed in the net of wrong views, or fail to find the path, while others who had gained a rebirth conducive to liberation have lost it again. And they radiate great friendliness and compassion over all those beings and pay attention to them, thinking: 'I will become a savior to all those beings, I will release them from all their sufferings.'[32]

Bodhisattvas are deeply moved by the torments of sentient beings, and they consider how they can best help them. At the beginning of the bodhisattva path, they realize that at present their powers are limited and that they are unable even to prevent their own sufferings. In order to improve their ability to aid sentient beings in distress, bodhisattvas resolve to become buddhas, since buddhas have the greatest possible capacity to help others. Buddhas possess unlimited wisdom and compassion, and they have perfected the ability to adapt their instructions to suit the needs of individuals. At this point, according to Kensur Lekden,

> having come to believe that there is a great purpose in attaining Buddhahood, they generate the wish to attain the state of a Buddha—one who has abandoned all faults and has attained all realizations. They have examined their condition and seen that now, never mind helping others, they cannot free even themselves from misery . . . . Through careful study of emptiness, they see that the mind is not naturally defiled with desire, hatred, and ignorance, that these are peripheral factors, whereas the nature of the mind is intrinsically pure. They thereby ascertain with valid cognition the capacity to

> attain Buddhahood. Such persons have taken upon themselves the burden of the welfare of all sentient beings and have seen that they must and can attain Buddhahood.[33]

The Six Perfections

After generating the mind of awakening, a bodhisattva begins a training program intended to culminate in the attainment of buddhahood. Along the way, he or she will develop innumerable good qualities, the most important of which are the six "perfections" (*pha rol tu phyin pa, pāramitā*): (1) generosity, (2) ethics, (3) patience, (4) effort, (5) concentration, and (6) wisdom. These constitute the core of the awakened personality of a buddha. This list is often supplemented with an additional list of four perfections: (7) skill in means, (8) aspiration, (9) power, and (10) exalted wisdom. These ten are correlated in some Mahāyāna texts with the ten bodhisattva levels (which are discussed below).[34]

1. *The Perfection of Generosity.* The perfection of generosity involves overcoming selfishness and attachment to material things and a corresponding attitude of willingness to give everything one has to others. Those who have perfected this quality are willing even to donate parts of their bodies to those in need. On a more mundane level, bodhisattvas develop a disposition toward freely giving away all of their possessions, without feeling any sense of loss and without expecting any recompense or praise.

Mahāyāna texts stress that this faculty is not a perfection of the *ability* to give, but rather a perfection of an *attitude* that compassionately wishes to give whatever one has to those in need. This qualification is an important one, since Mahāyāna literature asserts that innumerable buddhas have perfected this quality, and if it were a perfection of the ability to give, the continued existence of poverty in the world would be inexplicable. This issue is raised in the *Sūtra Explaining the Thought*, in which Avalokiteśvara asks the Buddha, "Bhagavan, if bodhisattvas' resources are inexhaustible and they have compassion, why are there poor people in the world?" Buddha answers,

> Avalokiteśvara, that is the fault of the individual actions of sentient beings. If it were not so, if perchance individual sentient beings were not affected by the obstacles created by their own faults, then they

> would constantly engage in actions and would have inexhaustible resources, in which case how could any suffering be seen in the world? Avalokiteśvara, it is like this: For example, that a hungry ghost—whose body is pained by thirst—sees the water of the ocean as dry is a fault that is the result of the personal actions of that hungry ghost; it is not the fault of the ocean. Similarly, the oceanlike generosity of bodhisattvas is faultless, but the absence of [good] results is the fault of the faulty individual actions committed by sentient beings who are like hungry ghosts.[35]

This passage presents a fundamental problem: the continuing existence of evil and suffering despite the omnipresent goodness of buddhas and bodhisattvas. According to Mahāyāna doctrine, buddhas and bodhisattvas have great compassion that extends to all sentient beings, coupled with vast powers. Given these factors, one might wonder how there could be any suffering or poverty. Buddha's answer indicates that all dissatisfaction is the result of the negative actions of the beings who are afflicted by it. They have created the causes of their own problems, despite the best efforts of buddhas and bodhisattvas to help them.

The example of hungry ghosts illustrates how negative karma prevents beings from finding happiness. Hungry ghosts are beings that are born with large stomachs and tiny necks. They are constantly pained by hunger and thirst, but whenever they receive food or water it appears to them as putrid substances such as pus and blood. The sūtra passage indicates that they also are sometimes unable see water that is right in front of them. They are born into this state because they were greedy and self-centered in past lives, but their problems are of their own making. The nourishment they receive is neither foul nor pure, but when interpreted through the lens of their afflicted thoughts it causes revulsion and distress. In the same way, all sentient beings create the causes of their own unhappiness, despite the ongoing efforts of buddhas and bodhisattvas, who are always trying to get them to see the error of their ways. Afflicted thoughts tend to perpetuate themselves, however, and so most beings continue to pursue courses of action that will result in suffering. Thus Śāntideva concludes,

> If the perfection of generosity frees the world from poverty,
> Then how could it be that the protectors of the past attained it,
> If there is still poverty in the world today?

> The perfection of generosity is said to result from the mental attitude
> Of giving up everything one owns to all people, together with the fruits of such actions.
> Thus the perfection [of generosity] is just a mental attitude.[36]

Bodhisattvas sometimes give away material objects, and they also help others by sharing Buddhist teachings. The latter is by far the more valuable gift, since beings caught up in cyclic existence only benefit temporarily when given money or possessions. Such things inevitably are lost, the relief that they bring is only temporary, and acquiring them may have the negative side-effect of deepening attachment. Teaching sentient beings about the Buddhist path is more worthwhile, because through following it they will eventually transcend all suffering.

2. *The Perfection of Ethics.* The perfection of ethics is a basic prerequisite for the Mahāyāna path. In cultivating this quality, bodhisattvas first discipline themselves to avoid physical expressions of afflicted thoughts, the negative actions that result in future suffering. Next they must work at eliminating even the predispositions toward such actions. This process has a number of important results, including better rebirths and mental equanimity. A person who avoids negative actions and engages in ethical behavior will enjoy concordant benefits in the future, but the development of mental calm is equally essential. The minds of ordinary beings are agitated by afflicted thoughts, which lead to negative actions, which in turn result in suffering and a tendency to engage in similar actions in the future. Thus Śāntideva warns,

> One who wishes to safeguard the practice must scrupulously guard the mind.
> The practice cannot be safeguarded unless one guards the wavering mind.
> Rutting elephants roaming wild do not cause as much devastation in this world
> As that roaming elephant, the mind unleashed, causes in Avīci and the other hells.
> But if this roaming elephant, the mind, is bound in all places by the rope of mindfulness,
> Then every danger fades, and complete success results.[37]

Bodhisattvas strive to attain a state of mental balance and equanimity. This is impossible as long as the mind is troubled by passions and the desire to engage in harmful activities. Training in ethics serves to calm the mind, to diminish the force of afflictive emotions, and thus provides an important precondition to advanced meditative training, which requires mental stability.

3. *The Perfection of Patience.* The perfection of patience involves developing an attitude of unshakable equanimity. According to Śāntideva, this is important because anger can destroy the good qualities one has cultivated and eliminate hard-won equanimity.

> Anger destroys all the good conduct—such as generosity and worship of the *sugatas* [buddhas]—
> That one has gained in thousands of eons.
> There is no evil equal to hatred, and no spiritual practice equal to patience.
> Therefore, you should diligently cultivate patience by various means with great effort . . . .
> Therefore I will destroy the food of that enemy, because it has no other purpose than to harm me.
> Even if I encounter extreme adversity, I must not disrupt my happiness.
> When one is in a state of dejection, nothing seems agreeable, and one forsakes virtue.[38]

The bodhisattva learns to view all things as dependent arisings and realizes that every occurrence is the result of causes and conditions. Beings who bring harm to others are part of this causal network, and are neither evil nor good in themselves. They are reacting to external and internal stimuli and are guided by their own past actions and present attitudes. Thus the bodhisattva realizes that it makes no more sense to hate a person who harms one than it would to hold a branch personally responsible for falling on one's head.

4. *The Perfection of Effort.* The perfection of effort is necessary in order to maintain continued enthusiasm for the path. Since the training may

require an unimaginably long period of time to complete, it is necessary to cultivate an attitude of sustained fervor.

> One who has thus become patient should cultivate effort,
> Because awakening depends on effort.
> There is no merit without effort, just as there is no movement without wind.
> What is effort? It is enthusiasm for virtue.
> What is its antithesis called? It is laziness, clinging to what is reprehensible, apathy, and self-contempt.
> Laziness comes from indolence, indulging in pleasures, sleep, and wishing to lean on others,
> And from apathy regarding the miseries of cyclic existence.
> Having mounted the chariot of the mind of awakening, which takes away all weariness and toil,
> What sensible person would despair in progressing in this way from happiness to happiness?
> The powers of aspiration, steadfastness, delight, and letting go all lead to fulfillment of the needs of living beings.
> Due to fear of suffering, and while contemplating its blessings,
> One should generate that aspiration [for awakening].
> Uprooting its opposite in that way, one should strive to increase one's effort
> Through the powers of aspiration, self-confidence, delight, renunciation, and determination.[39]

One's determination is strengthened by compassion for others. One wishes to be able to help them alleviate their sufferings, and since buddhas are best able to accomplish this, one works tirelessly toward this goal.

5. The Perfection of Concentration. After developing an attitude of altruism and nonattachment toward material things, cultivating a calm mind that is spontaneously ethical and patient, and generating an unflagging determination to work toward awakening for the benefit of others, the bodhisattva is prepared for the perfection of concentration. This involves cultivating the ability to focus one-pointedly on an object of observation, without being disturbed by mental wavering.

One first leaves worldly concerns and activities behind and seeks solitude. Śāntideva states that bodhisattvas should think,

> Having developed effort in that way, one should stabilize
> the mind in meditative concentration,
> Because a person whose mind is distracted stands between
> the fangs of mental afflictions.
> Distraction does not arise if body and mind are kept secluded.
> Therefore, one should renounce the world and ignore distracting
> thoughts . . . .
> Therefore, I will always pursue the solitary life, which is
> delightful and free from strife,
> Which leads to favorable outcomes and calming of all
> distractions.
> Free from all other concerns and with a one-pointed mind,
> I will apply myself
> To taming and increasing the meditative concentration
> of my mind.[40]

6. *The Perfection of Wisdom.* The perfection of wisdom is said by Śāntideva to be the culmination of all the others: "The Sage [Buddha] taught this entire system of training for the sake of wisdom; therefore, wishing to put an end to suffering, one should develop wisdom."[41] The perfection of wisdom refers to the ability to see things as they really are, freed from false conceptuality. A person who perfects wisdom understands that all phenomena are empty of inherent existence, created by causes and conditions external to themselves, and that they are collections of parts lacking any essence.

This realization is essential because sentient beings transmigrate powerlessly due to misperceiving the nature of phenomena. They view things as naturally possessing the qualities imputed to them by conceptual thought, as truly desirable or detestable. The result of such thinking is desire, hatred, and other afflictive emotions, which are only overcome by one who recognizes that all phenomena utterly lack inherent existence and are mere collections of constantly changing parts, which are moved along by causes and conditions. This realization is so powerful, according to Kensur Lekden, that a mere suspicion that things do not exist as they appear can overturn past predispositions toward afflicted actions.

> Even if understanding of emptiness does not form and one only generates the suspicion that persons and other phenomena might be empty of inherent existence, the predispositions that cause rebirth in cyclic existence are torn to shreds.[42]

The recognition of all phenomena as empty does not, however, diminish the bodhisattva's compassion. Sentient beings are recognized as impermanent collections of changing parts, and the bodhisattva understands that their present sufferings are the results of past misdeeds. Perceiving them as psychophysical continuums whose future will be influenced by present actions and attitudes, the bodhisattva works to help them to change in ways that are conducive to future happiness.

The Ten Bodhisattva Levels

The bodhisattva's path to awakening progresses through ten hierarchically arranged stages, referred to as the "bodhisattva levels" (*byang chub sems dpa'i sa, bodhisattva-bhūmi*). The Tibetan term *sa* (Sanskrit: *bhūmi*) literally means "ground" or "foundation," since each stage represents a level of attainment and serves as a basis for the next one. Each level marks a definite advancement in one's training that is accompanied by progressively greater power and wisdom.

1. *The First Level, the "Very Joyous."* The first level, called the "Very Joyous," is attained with the first direct perception of emptiness and is simultaneous with entry into the third of the five paths to awakening, the path of seeing.[43] It is called "very joyous" because the bodhisattva is elated due to having attained the level of a "superior" (*'phags pa, ārya*) and is eager to progress to the higher stages.[44] At this stage the bodhisattva works at the perfection of generosity and develops the ability to give away everything without regret and with no thought of praise or reward. All phenomena are viewed as empty and as subject to decay, suffering, and death, and so bodhisattvas lose all attachment to them. According to Tsong Khapa, first level bodhisattvas directly understand that persons do not exist by way of their own nature. Due to this, they overcome the false idea that the five aggregates constitute a truly existent person. They also eliminate predispositions toward corrupted ethics so completely that they will not arise again.[45]

Despite having directly perceived emptiness, however, bodhisattvas on the first level are primarily motivated by faith, rather than understanding. They train in ethics in order to cleanse their minds of negativities, and so they prepare themselves for the cultivation of mundane meditative absorptions that comes on the second level.

2. *The Second Level, the "Stainless."* Bodhisattvas on the second level, the "Stainless," perfect ethics and overcome all tendencies toward engagement in negative actions. Their control becomes so complete that even in dreams they have no immoral thoughts. According to Tsong Khapa, for such a bodhisattva,

> on all occasions of waking and dreaming his movements or activities of body, speech, and mind are pure of even subtle infractions . . . he fulfills the three paths of virtuous actions—abandoning killing, stealing, and sexual misconduct—with his body; the middle four—abandoning lying, divisive talk, harsh speech, and senseless chatter—with his speech; and the last three—abandoning covetousness, harmful intent, and wrong views—with his mind. Not only does he refrain from what is prohibited but also he fulfills all the positive achievements related to proper ethics.[46]

Because of this, the bodhisattva's mind becomes purified and equanimous, which is a prerequisite for training in the meditative states called the four concentrations and the four formless absorptions (discussed in the previous chapter).

3. *The Third Level, the "Luminous."* Tsong Khapa states that the third level is called the "Luminous" because when it is attained "the fire of wisdom burning all the fuel of objects of knowledge arises along with a light which by nature is able to extinguish all elaborations of duality during meditative equipoise."[47] Bodhisattvas on this level cultivate the perfection of patience. Their equanimity becomes so profound that

> even if someone . . . cuts from the body of this bodhisattva not just flesh but also bone, not in large sections but bit by bit, not continually but pausing in between, and not finishing in a short time but

> cutting over a long period, the bodhisattva would not get angry at the mutilator.[48]

The bodhisattva realizes that his tormenter is motivated by afflicted thoughts and is sowing seeds of his own future suffering. As a result, the bodhisattva feels not anger, but a deep sadness and compassion for this cruel person, who is unaware of the operations of karma. Trainees on the third level overcome all tendencies toward anger, and never react with hatred (or even annoyance) to any harmful acts or words. Rather, their equanimity remains constant, and all sentient beings are viewed with love and compassion.

All anger and resentment rebound on the person who generates them, and they do nothing to eliminate harms that one has already experienced. They are counterproductive in that they destroy one's peace of mind and lead to unfavorable future situations. There is nothing to be gained through anger and resentment, revenge does nothing to change the past, and so the bodhisattva avoids them. Moreover, one's present suffering is only a result of one's own past misdeeds; so one's enemy is only an agent of the inevitable fruition of karma.

Bodhisattvas on this level also train in the four concentrations (the first, second, third, and fourth concentrations); the four formless absorptions (limitless space, limitless consciousness, nothingness, and the peak of cyclic existence); the four immeasurables (love, compassion, joy, and equanimity); and the five clairvoyances (magical creations, the divine ear, knowing others' minds, remembering former lives, and the divine eye).

4. The Fourth Level, the "Radiant." On the fourth level, the "Radiant," bodhisattvas cultivate the perfection of effort and eliminate afflictions. According to Wonch'uk, this level is so named because fourth level bodhisattvas "constantly emit the radiance of exalted wisdom." He also cites the *Ornament for the Mahāyāna Sūtras*, which explains that bodhisattvas on this level burn up the afflictive obstructions and the obstructions to omniscience with the radiance of their wisdom.[49] They enter into progressively deeper meditative absorptions and attain a powerful mental pliancy as a result. This eliminates laziness and increases their ability to practice meditation for extended periods of time. They destroy deeply rooted afflictions and cultivate the thirty-seven "harmonies with awakening," which are divided into seven groups:

I. The Four Mindful Establishments

1. mindful establishment on the body
2. mindful establishment on feelings
3. mindful establishment on mind
4. mindful establishment on phenomena[50]

II. Four Thorough Abandonings

5. generating virtuous qualities not yet generated
6. increasing virtuous qualities already generated
7. not generating nonvirtuous qualities not yet generated
8. abandoning nonvirtuous qualities already generated[51]

III. Four Bases of Magical Emanations

9. aspiration
10. effort
11. mental attention
12. analytical meditative stabilization[52]

IV. Five Faculties

13. faith
14. effort
15. mindfulness
16. meditative stabilization
17. wisdom[53]

V. Five Powers

18. faith
19. effort
20. mindfulness
21. meditative stabilization
22. wisdom[54]

VI. Seven Branches of Awakening

23. correct mindfulness
24. correct discrimination of phenomena
25. correct effort
26. correct joy
27. correct pliancy
28. correct meditative stabilization
29. correct equanimity[55]

VI. Eightfold Noble Path
30. correct view
31. correct intention
32. correct speech
33. correct action
34. correct livelihood
35. correct effort
36. correct mindfulness
37. correct meditative stabilization[56]

Through training in these thirty-seven practices, bodhisattvas develop great skill in meditative absorptions and cultivate wisdom, while weakening the artificial and innate conceptions of true existence.

5. *The Fifth Level, the "Difficult to Cultivate."* The fifth level is called the "Difficult to Cultivate" because it involves practices that are arduous and require a great deal of effort to perfect. It is also called the "Difficult to Overcome" because when one has completed the training of this level one has profound wisdom and insight that are difficult to surpass or undermine. According to Nāgārjuna,

> The fifth is called the Extremely Difficult to Overcome
> Since all evil ones find it extremely hard to conquer him;
> He becomes skilled in knowing the subtle
> Meanings of the noble truths and so forth.[57]

Bodhisattvas on this level cultivate the perfection of concentration. They develop strong powers of meditative stabilization and overcome tendencies toward distraction. They achieve mental one-pointedness and they perfect calm abiding. They also fully penetrate the meanings of the four noble truths and the two truths (conventional truths and ultimate truths) and perceive all phenomena as empty, transient, and prone to suffering.

6. *The Sixth Level, the "Manifest."* The sixth level is called the "Manifest" because the bodhisattva clearly perceives the workings of dependent arising and directly understands "signlessness" (*mtshan ma med pa, animitta*). Signlessness refers to the fact that phenomena seem to possess their apparent qualities by way of their own nature, but when one examines this

appearance one realizes that all qualities are merely mentally imputed, and not a part of the nature of the objects they appear to characterize.

As a result of these understandings, bodhisattvas manifest meditative wisdom and avoid attachment to either cyclic existence or nirvana.[58] Having overcome all attachments, bodhisattvas on this level can attain nirvana, but because of the force of the mind of awakening they decide to remain in the world in order to benefit others. They cultivate the perfection of wisdom, through which they perceive all phenomena as lacking inherent existence, as being like dreams, illusions, reflections, or magically created objects. All notions of "I" and "other" are transcended, along with conceptions of "existence" and "nonexistence." These sixth-level bodhisattvas abide in contemplation of suchness, with minds that are undisturbed by false ideas.

7. *The Seventh Level, the "Gone Afar."* Bodhisattvas on the seventh level develop the ability to contemplate signlessness uninterruptedly and enter into advanced meditative absorptions for extended periods of time, thus passing beyond both the mundane and supramundane paths of hearers and solitary realizers. For this reason, this level is called the "Gone Afar."[59] According to Nāgārjuna,

> The seventh is the Gone Afar because
> The number [of his qualities] has increased,
> Moment by moment he can enter
> The equipoise of cessation.[60]

On this level bodhisattvas perfect their "skill in means" (*thabs la mkhas pa, upāya-kauśalya*), which is their ability to cleverly adapt their teaching tactics to the individual proclivities and needs of their audiences. They also develop the ability to know the thoughts of others, and in every moment are able to practice all the perfections. All thoughts and actions are free from afflictions, and they constantly act spontaneously and effectively for the benefit of others.

8. *The Eighth Level, the "Immovable."* The eighth level is called the "Immovable" because bodhisattvas overcome all afflictions regarding signs and their minds are always completely absorbed in the dharma. According to Nāgārjuna,

> The eighth is the Immovable, the youthful stage,
> Through nonconceptuality he is immovable
> And the spheres of his body, speech, and mind's
> Activities are inconceivable.[61]

Because they are fully acquainted with signlessness, their minds are not moved by ideas of signs. Eighth level bodhisattvas are said to be "irreversible," because there is no longer any possibility that they might waver on the path or backslide. They are destined for full buddhahood, and there are no longer any inclinations to seek a personal nirvana. They cultivate the "perfection of aspiration," which means that they undertake to fulfill various vows, due to which they accumulate the causes of further virtues.[62] Although they resolve to work for the benefit of others and they pervade the universe with feelings of friendliness toward all sentient beings, these bodhisattvas have transcended any tendency to imagine that there are truly existent beings.

Their understanding of suchness is so complete that it overturns afflicted views, and reality appears in a completely new light. They enter into meditation on emptiness with little effort. Bodhisattvas on this level are compared to people who have awakened from dreams, and all their perceptions are influenced by this new awareness. They attain the meditative state called "forbearance regarding nonarisen phenomena," due to which they no longer think in terms of cause or causelessness. They also develop the ability to manifest in various forms in order to instruct others. Compassion and skill in means are automatic and spontaneous. There is no need to plan or contemplate how best to benefit others, since these bodhisattvas skillfully adapt themselves to every situation.

9. The Ninth Level, the "Good Intelligence." From this point on, bodhisattvas move quickly toward awakening. Before this stage, progress was comparatively slow, like that of a boat being towed through a harbor. On the eighth through tenth levels, however, bodhisattvas make huge strides toward buddhahood, like a ship that reaches the ocean and unfurls its sails. On the ninth level, they fully understand the three vehicles—of hearers, solitary realizers, and bodhisattvas—and perfect the ability to teach the doctrine. According to the *Sūtra Explaining the Thought*,

> Because of attaining faultlessness and very extensive intelligence in terms of mastery of teaching the doctrine in all aspects, the ninth level is called the 'Good Intelligence.'[63]

Ninth level bodhisattvas also acquire the "four analytical knowledges"—of doctrines, meanings, grammar, and exposition. Due to this, they develop wondrous eloquence and skill in presenting doctrinal teachings. Their intelligence surpasses that of all humans and gods, and they comprehend all names, words, meanings, and languages. They can understand any question from any being. They also have the ability to answer them all with a single sound, which is understood by each being according to its capacities. On this level they also cultivate the perfection of power, which means that because of the strength of their mastery of the four analytical knowledges and their meditation they are able to develop the six perfections energetically and to practice them continually without becoming fatigued.[64]

10. *The Tenth Level, the "Cloud of Doctrine."* On the tenth level, bodhisattvas overcome the subtlest traces of the afflictions. Like a cloud that pours rain on the earth, these bodhisattvas spread the doctrine in all directions, and each sentient being absorbs what it needs in order to grow spiritually. Thus Nāgārjuna states that

> The tenth is the Cloud of Doctrine because
> The rain of excellent doctrine falls,
> The Bodhisattva is consecrated
> With light by the Buddhas.[65]

At this stage bodhisattvas enter into progressively deeper meditative absorptions and develop limitless powers with respect to magical formulas. They cultivate the perfection of exalted wisdom, which, according to Asaṅga, enables them to increase their exalted wisdom. This in turn strengthens the other perfections. As a result they become established in the joy of the doctrine.[66]

They acquire perfect bodies, and their minds are cleansed of the subtlest traces of the afflictions. They manifest in limitless forms for the benefit of others and transcend the ordinary laws of time and space. They are able to place entire world systems in a single pore, without diminishing them or increasing the size of the pore. When they do this, the beings inhabiting the worlds feel no discomfort, and only those who are advanced bodhisattvas even notice.

Bodhisattvas on this level receive a form of empowerment from innumerable buddhas. This is called "great rays of light," because the radiance of these bodhisattvas shines in all directions. This empowerment helps them in removing the remaining obstructions to omniscience and gives them added confidence and strength. At the final moment of this stage they enter into a meditative state called the "vajralike meditative stabilization," in which the subtlest remaining obstacles to buddhahood are overcome. They arise from this concentration as buddhas.

11. *The "Buddha Level."* The culmination of the path occurs on the final level, called the "Buddha Level." According to the *Sūtra Explaining the Thought*,

> Because of becoming manifestly, completely awakened with respect to all aspects of objects of knowledge and abandoning, without attachment or obstruction, the very subtle [afflictive obstructions and] obstructions to omniscience, the eleventh level is called the 'Buddha Level.'[67]

Nagarjuna asserts that it is impossible to describe the transcendent state of a buddha with words; ordinary beings cannot even begin to imagine it.

> The stage of Buddhahood is different,
> Being in all ways inconceivable . . .
> The limitlessness of a Buddha's
> [Qualities] is said to be like
> That of space, earth, water, fire
> And wind in all directions.
> If the causes are [reduced] to a mere
> [Measure] and not seen to be limitless,
> One will not believe the limitlessness
> [Of the qualities] of the Buddhas.[68]

At this point, all afflictions have been overcome, and the natural luminosity of the mind shines forth. There is no longer even a desire to work for the benefit of others, but due to cultivating compassion in limitless ways for an unimaginable period of time, the buddha continues spontaneously to manifest compassion. The buddha's mind has attained a level of total omniscience, unhindered by any obstructions or limitations. This omniscience fully comprehends all realms, things, aspects, and times.

In addition, the buddha manifests three bodies: (1) the truth body (*chos kyi sku, dharma-kāya*); (2) the complete enjoyment body (*longs spyod pa'i sku, saṃbhoga-kāya*); and (3) emanation bodies (*sprul sku, nirmāṇa-kāya*). The first is divided into two aspects: the wisdom truth body (*ye shes chos sku, jñāna-dharma-kāya*) and the nature truth body (*ngo bo nyid chos sku, svabhāvika-dharma-kāya*). The first refers to a buddha's omniscient consciousness, and the second is the emptiness of that consciousness. The complete enjoyment body is a pure form (said in Tibetan Buddhism to be produced from subtle energies called "winds" in conjunction with consciousness), which resides in a pure land. Emanation bodies are physical manifestations that buddhas create in order to benefit sentient beings.

Notes

1. The origins of Mahāyāna still remain obscure, and a great deal of work remains to be done in this area. A good example of such research is Lewis Lancaster's "The Oldest Mahāyāna Sūtra: Its Significance for the Study of Buddhist Development," which points out some changes in the dated Chinese versions of the *Sūtra on the Perfection of Wisdom in 8,000 Lines* (*The Eastern Buddhist*, 8.1, 1975, pp. 30–41).
2. This statement is found in the *Uttaravipatti-sutta* (*Aṅguttara-nikāya* IV.163). This passage and its implications for Buddhist exegesis are discussed by George Bond in *The Word of the Buddha*, p. 30ff. He notes that this idea is not confined to this single instance but is also found in one of Aśoka's edicts (see Bond's note 37, which refers to P.H.L. Eggermont and J. Hoftizer, eds., *The Moral Edicts of King Asoka* [Leiden: E.J. Brill, 1962], p. 38). As Étienne Lamotte points out, however (*History of Indian Buddhism*; Louvain & Paris: Peeters Press, 1988, p. 53), Aśoka's statement should read, "everything that was spoken by the Blessed One is well spoken," which is praise for Śākyamuni rather than an inclusive statement about doctrinal sources.

   See also the *Adhyāśayasaṃcodana-sūtra*, in which Buddha states, "Maitreya, whatever is well spoken is the word of the Buddha" (*yat kiṃ cin maitreya subhāṣitaṃ tad buddhavacanaṃ*); *Śikṣā-samuccaya* (tr. Cecil Bendall; Delhi: Motilal Banarsidass, 1971), p. 17; and Lamotte, *History of Indian Buddhism*, p. 53 n. 117 and p. 164.
3. Overviews of some discussions of this topic can be found in Nakamura, *Indian Buddhism: A Survey with Bibliographical Notes*, pp. 149–66, and Paul Williams, *Mahāyāna Buddhism: The Doctrinal Foundations* (London: Routledge, 1989), pp. 16–33.

4. There are a number of plausible explanations for the origins of Mahāyāna. One popular view holds that it was a movement of lay Buddhists who resented the exalted status and spiritual perquisites of the monks and who developed a more inclusive form of Buddhism that could include the aspirations of laypeople. This is the thesis argued by Étienne Lamotte (see for instance, his article, "Mahāyāna Buddhism," in Heinz Bechert and Richard Gombrich, ed., *The World of Buddhism*; London: Thames & Hudson, 1984, pp. 90–93) and Akira Hirakawa ("The Rise of Mahāyāna Buddhism and Its Relationship to the Worship of Stūpas," *Memoirs of the Research Department of the Toyo Bunko*, 1963). This view is widely held among Japanese scholars, who tend to emphasize the role of the laity in Mahāyāna. Other scholars see the origins of Mahāyāna in devotional cults centered on the veneration of *stūpas*. Another view is advanced by Gregory Schopen ("The Phrase *'sa pṛthivīpradeśaś caityabhūto bhavet'* in the *Vajracchedikā*: Notes on the Cult of the Book in Mahāyāna," *Indo-Iranian Journal* 17, 1975, pp. 147–81; and "Two Problems in the History of Indian Buddhism: The Layman/Monk Distinction and the Doctrines of the Transference of Merit," *Studien zur Indologie und Iranistik* 10, 1985, pp. 9–47), who contends that the earliest traceable Mahāyāna groups were centered on veneration and propagation of particular texts. I find Schopen's arguments to be very persuasive, but there is still a great deal of uncertainty about the early phases of Mahāyāna.
5. As Graeme MacQueen notes, however, these sūtras are so different in form and content from those found in the Pāli canon that they cannot possibly be attempts to forge new sutras. Rather, their authors are clearly aware that their writings represent a decisive break with established tradition and that they are at the forefront of a new and revolutionary movement. See his "Inspired Speech in Early Mahāyāna Buddhism II," *Religion* 12, 1982, p. 51.
6. It was also noted by their opponents. A good discussion of criticisms of Mahāyāna texts can be found in Graeme MacQueen, "Inspired Speech in Early Mahāyāna Buddhism I," *Religion* 11, 1981, pp. 303–305.
7. This explanation is found in the Tibetan historian Tāranātha's *History of Buddhism in India*, tr. Lama Chimpa and Alaka Chattopadhyaya (Simla: Indian Institute of Advanced Study, 1970), p. 98.
8. See, for instance, A.K. Warder, *Indian Buddhism*, p. 13.
9. Graeme MacQueen, "Inspired Speech in Early Mahāyāna Buddhism I," p. 303.
10. In "The Oldest Mahāyāna Sūtra," Lancaster notes the absence of the doctrine of the three bodies of the Buddha in the earliest version of the text, as well as the absence of several other terms that are important in later Mahāyāna.
11. Graeme MacQueen, "Inspired Speech in Early Mahāyāna Buddhism II," p. 61.
12. For a discussion of the significance of this formula, see Jonathan Silk, "A Note on the Opening Formula of Buddhist *Sūtras*," *Journal of the International Association of Buddhist Studies*, 12.1, 1989, pp. 158–63; "Thus Spoke the Blessed One . . ." by Yuichi Kajiyama, in Lewis Lancaster, ed., *Prajñāpāramitā and Related Systems* (Berkeley, 1977), pp. 93–99; and "Thus Have I Heard . . ." by John Brough, *Bulletin of the School of Oriental and African Studies, University of London*, vol. XIII, 1950, part 2.
13. An overview of this literature may be found in Edward Conze, *The Prajñāpāramitā Literature* (The Hague: Mouton, 1960). See also Nakamura, *Indian Buddhism*, pp. 159–66, and Nakamura, "Historical studies of the coming into existence of Mahāyāna Sūtras," *Proceedings of the Okurayama Oriental Research Institute* II, 1956, pp. 2ff.

14. The Perfection of Wisdom texts are often grouped according to length, and the longer ones may be elaborations of earlier versions. There also seems to have been a corresponding move toward brevity, and some later texts appear to be condensations of earlier versions.
15. See the note provided by Étienne Lamotte in *The Teaching of Vimalakīrti* (London: Pāli Text Society, 1976), pp. 54–55, which gives a brief biography of Subhūti that is drawn from a number of sources and indicates several places where he is said to be the greatest of Buddha's disciples in realization of emptiness.
16. *Vajracchedikāprajñāpāramitāsūtra*, ed. Edward Conze (Rome: IsMEO, 1974), pp. 29–32.
17. Tsong Khapa, *Tantra in Tibet*, tr. Jeffrey Hopkins (London: George Allen & Unwin, 1977), p. 92.
18. For discussions of this concept, see K.R. Norman, "The Pratyeka-Buddha in Buddhism and Jainism," in Philip Denwood and Alexander Piatigorsky, ed., *Buddhist Studies Ancient and Modern* (London: Curzon Press, 1983, pp. 92–106) and Ria Kloppenborg, *The Paccekabuddha* (Leiden: E.J. Brill, 1974).
19. In *Compassion in Tibetan Buddhism* (London: Rider, 1980), p. 104.
20. Virtuous roots are the results of cultivating good qualities. When a person engages in meritorious conduct and cultivates corresponding attitudes, this creates positive tendencies that predispose that person to continue doing so in the future.
21. "Elaboration" (*spros pa, prapañca*) refers to proliferation of conceptual thought.
22. *Aṣṭasāhasrikāprajñāpāramitāsūtra* (*'Phags pa shes rab kyi pha rol tu phyin pa brgyad stong pa'i mdo*; Dharamsala, India: Tibetan Cultural Printing Press, 1985), pp. 11.471.4–475.3.
23. Steven A. Kent, "A Sectarian Interpretation of the Rise of Mahāyāna," *Religion* 12, 1982, pp. 311–32.
24. H.H. the Dalai Lama, in *Tantra in Tibet*, pp. 91–104.
25. For an overview of these schools and their doctrines, see Lamotte, *History of Indian Buddhism*, pp. 517–548. As Lamotte shows, although the traditional number is eighteen, there were in fact many more schools and subdivisions.
26. *Dīgha-nikāya*, ed. T.W. Rhys Davids, p. 100.
27. Jambudvīpa is the name for one of the four main continents in traditional Buddhist cosmology. It is the one that contains the subcontinent of India. Its name literally means "Island of Jambu"; it is said to be named after the *jambu* tree, which grows there.
28. *Pañcaviṃśatisāhasrikāprajñāpāramitāsūtra*, ed. Nalinaksha Dutt (London: Luzac & Co., 1934), p. 3.40–41.
29. These images are all drawn from Indian mythology. A wish-granting gem is a jewel that gives its owner whatever he or she desires. A pot of plenty never runs dry. Spells (*mantra*) are often used as magical incantations in order to bring about desired results. A universal remedy is able to cure all illnesses, and wish-fulfilling trees and cows of plenty bring riches to those who own them.
30. Śāntideva, *Entering the Bodhisattva Deeds* (*Bodhicaryāvatāra*), ed. Swami Dwarika Das Shastri (Varanasi: Bauddha Bharati, 1988), chapter III.16–20, pp. 56–57.
31. Geshe Rabten, *The Preliminary Practices of Tibetan Buddhism* (Dharamsala: Library of Tibetan Works and Archives, 1982), p. 45.
32. *Aṣṭasāhasrikāprajñāpāramitāsūtra*, p. 22.880.4.
33. In *Compassion in Tibetan Buddhism*, pp. 47–48.
34. The last four perfections will be discussed in connection with the seventh through tenth bodhisattva levels.

35. *Sūtra Explaining the Thought*, Stog Palace edition, p. 134.5.
36. *Entry into the Bodhisattva Deeds*, chapter V. 9–10, pp. 74–75.
37. *Entry into the Bodhisattva Deeds*, V.1–3, p. 73.
38. Ibid., VI.1–2, 8-9, pp. 120–121.
39. Ibid., VII.1–3, 30–32, pp. 174–175, 186–187.
40. Ibid., VIII.1–2, 38–39, pp. 206, 220–221.
41. Ibid., IX.1, p. 262.
42. In *Compassion in Tibetan Buddhism*, p. 51. His statement is based on a common Mahāyāna aphorism, which may be found in Āryadeva's *Catuḥśataka*, v. 180.
43. The five paths were discussed in the previous chapter.
44. This explanation is given by the Korean scholar Wonch'uk in his *Commentary on the Sūtra Explaining the Thought* (*Ārya-gambhīra-saṃdhinirmocana-sūtra-ṭīkā; 'Phags pa dgongs pa zab mo nges par 'grel pa'i mdo'i rgya cher 'grel pa*; Delhi: Delhi Karmapae Choedhey, Gyalwae Sungrab Partun Khang, 1985, *mdo 'grel*, vol. *thi* [119], p. 523.3). See also Nāgārjuna's *Precious Garland* (*Ratnāvalī*; tr. Jeffrey Hopkins: *The Precious Garland and the Song of the Four Mindfulnesses*; London: George Allen & Unwin, 1973), verse 441.
45. See *Compassion in Tibetan Buddhism*, pp. 140–142.
46. Ibid., pp. 193–194.
47. Ibid., p. 204
48. Ibid., p. 206.
49. Wonch'uk, vol. *thi* [119], p. 527.5.
50. See chapter 3, "Meditation" note 22 for further readings on these.
51. See chapter 3, note 23.
52. See chapter 3, note 24.
53. The five faculties are attained on the levels of heat and peak of the path of preparation (see chapter 3). They are described in *Samyutta-nikāya* V, p. 193; *Abhidharmasamuccaya* I.4 and *Abhidharmakośa* ch. 2 (pp. 111, 116, 119, 156) and ch. 4, pp. 219 and 223. Faith is confidence in the awakening of the Buddha. Effort involves working at religious practice, abandoning negative principles, and adopting good ones. Mindfulness involves remembering the teachings well and being aware of one's actions and thoughts. Concentration refers to the ability to overcome distractions and focus one's attention on a meditative object. Wisdom comes from understanding dependent arising and the four noble truths.
54. The powers are attained on the levels of patience and supreme mundane qualities of the path of preparation. They have the same names as the five faculties, and are said to be more advanced levels of the same qualities. When a faculty becomes unassailable, it is called a "power." See *Abhidharma-kośa*, ch. 6, p. 283 and pp. 286–87, which describes the difference between the powers and the forces. They are described in *Saṃyutta-nikāya* V, p. 249, *Aṅguttara-nikāya* I, pp. 39, 42ff., and III, p. 9ff.
55. For descriptions of these, see: *Dīgha-nikāya* II, p. 79, III, p. 251ff. and p. 282; *Saṃyutta-nikāya* V, p. 63ff.; *Madhyānta-vibhāga* (ed. Susumu Yamaguchi; Nagoya, 1934), p. 93.5; *Mahāyānasūtrālaṃkāra* XVIII.58; *Abhidharma-samuccaya* I.IV; and *Abhidharma-kośa*, ch. 2, p. 158; ch. 4, p. 68; and ch. 6, p. 281. These are attained on the path of seeing.
56. See chapter 2, "Some Important Buddhist Doctrines."
57. *The Precious Garland*, p. 85.
58. This explanation is given by Wonch'uk (vol. *thi* [119], p. 531.1), whose source is the *Sūtra on the Ten Levels*.

59. This explanation is given by Wonch'uk (vol. *thi* [119], p. 532.6), on the basis of a commentary on the *Sūtra on the Ten Levels*, but he does not provide the exact title.
60. *The Precious Garland*, p. 86.
61. Ibid., p. 86.
62. This explanation is found in the *Compendium of Mahāyāna* (Étienne Lamotte, tr., *La Somme du Grand Véhicule d'Asaṅga*; Louvain-la-neuve: Université de Louvain, 1973), p. 208.
63. *Sūtra Explaining the Thought*, p. 116.3.
64. See *La Somme du Grand Véhicule d'Asaṅga*, p. 208.
65. *The Precious Garland*, p. 87.
66. *La Somme du Grand Véhicule d'Asaṅga*, pp. 208–209.
67. *Sūtra Explaining the Thought*, p. 116.6.
68. *The Precious Garland*, p. 87.

Part Two

Tibetan History and Culture

5. Tibetan Religious History

Tibet: Geography and Environment

Tibet is referred to by its inhabitants as "Pö" (*bod*). The origin of this name is uncertain, but may have originally meant "native land" or "original place."[1] According to the *Blue Annals*, it is a shortened form of the earlier name "Bugyel" (*spu rgyal*), but the *White Annals* contends that it is derived from the pre-Buddhist religion of Bön (*bon*). The name "Tibet," by which it is known to the outside world, is probably derived from the Mongolian word *Thubet*.[2] It is often called "Kangchen" (*Gangs can*) by its inhabitants, meaning "Land of Snows."

A distinction should be made between the Tibetan cultural area and political Tibet. The latter includes the territories that were more or less directly controlled by the Tibetan government in Lhasa prior to the Chinese invasion of 1949–50. The Tibetan cultural area encompasses regions that are strongly influenced by Tibetan culture and religion—countries on the south side of the Himalayan divide such as Bhutan and Sikkim, as well as Mongolia, parts of Chinese Turkestan, central Asian countries bordering on political Tibet, and areas of present-day Russia.

Political Tibet encompassed three districts, traditionally referred to as the "Three Provinces," or Chölkasum (*chol kha gsum*): (1) the central provinces of Ü and Tsang, which extend from Ngari Gorsum in the west to Sokla Gyao; (2) Do Dö, which comprises the region from Sokla Gyao to the upper bend of the Machu river and includes the area of Kham; and (3) Do Mé, encompassing a region stretching from the Machu river to a monument called the White Chöden, which marked the traditional border with China. This includes the area of Amdo.[3]

The domain of political Tibet was mostly a huge plateau bordered on three sides by mountain ranges. The Kunlun and Tang-la ranges form the northern border; the western border is the Karakoram and Ladakh ranges; and the southern border is the Himalayan range, which extends for 1,500 miles. Only in the east is there a break in the mountains, but this area mostly consists of vast empty ranges, which also serve as a barrier. The area encompassed by Tibet's border mountains is about 500,000 square miles, about 75 percent of which are vast stretches of open plains interspersed with large mountain ranges. Much of this area lies at altitudes of 16,000 feet and above, making it inhospitable to humans and able to support only sparse vegetation. It is largely uninhabited, except for the hardy Tibetan nomads (*'brog pa*; pronounced "drokpa"), whose main sustenance comes from their herds of yak, sheep, and goats. Most of the population lives in the southern valleys, which are found at altitudes ranging from 9,000 feet to 15,000 feet. The lower reaches are capable of producing a wide range of agricultural products, including barley, wheat, black peas, beans, mustard, hemp, potatoes, cabbage, cauliflower, onions, garlic, celery, and tomatoes. The staple of the Tibetan diet is a flour called *tsampa* (*rtsam pa*), which is made from high-altitude barley that is roasted on heated sand and then ground. It is often mixed with Tibetan buttered tea and made into a paste.

Because of its size and its huge differences in elevation, Tibet has a wide range of climatic conditions. The northern regions, with vast open plains and an average altitude of 16,000 feet, have the harshest climate, with consistently low temperatures all year long and biting winds. In summer, temperatures range from 65 to 85°F, and in winter they sometimes drop to -30°F. Yearly rainfall averages between six and eight inches. The rocky soil is generally incapable of supporting agriculture, and the nomads who feed their herds on the sparse vegetation have to move regularly in order to avoid overgrazing.

Throughout all of Tibet, the air is thin and the sun is strong. The high altitude is often debilitating for people from lower elevations, many of whom suffer altitude sickness and shortness of breath. The central valleys enjoy a much more temperate climate than the northern plateaus, and areas below 12,000 feet are able to sustain settled agriculture. In the region of Lhasa, the capital city (which lies at the same latitude as Houston, Texas), the temperature generally ranges from 85°F in the summer to -3°F degrees Fahrenheit in the winter. The yearly rainfall is between fifteen and eighteen inches.

The Tibetan plateau is sparsely populated, and it has few large towns. Lhasa, the largest city, is the center of Tibet, both politically and culturally. Before the Chinese takeover it had a population of between 25,000–30,000. If one includes the populations of the large monasteries in the immediate area, the figure would be between 45,000–50,000. It is difficult to give an accurate estimate of the present population because the Chinese government is currently involved in a massive population transfer into Tibet, the obvious aim of which is to overwhelm the indigenous population. Reliable reports indicate that ethnic Tibetans are currently outnumbered by several million Chinese. These new settlers are mainly concentrated in the cities, where they greatly outnumber ethnic Tibetans. The Chinese government, however, denies that such a transfer is taking place and currently places the Chinese population of Tibet at 60,000, a figure that underestimates the actual number by at least several million. The recently completed Qinghai-Tibet Railway—the highest in the world—will undoubtedly bring even more Chinese to the region.

The second largest city is Shigatsé, with a pre-invasion population of about 12,000. Gyantsé, the third-largest city, had about 8,000. Both of these today have considerably more people because of the population transfer, but accurate figures are impossible to obtain. Prior to the invasion, the total population of Tibet probably ranged from five to six million, but since a true census was never taken, these figures are only estimates.

The Early History of Tibet

Scholars seeking to write about Tibetan history face many difficulties. As Giuseppe Tucci has noted, in Tibetan historical sources "true historical facts are reduced to a minimum"; he concludes that "we must discover them, almost guess them, here and there, hidden in a wilderness of pious tales."[4] Because Buddhism came to influence all aspects of Tibetan life—and because the history of their country is closely connected with Buddhism in the minds of Tibetans—traditional sources tend to overlay historical events with Buddhist significance and attribute important aspects of their narratives to the interventions of Buddhist deities. This process is so pervasive in historical works that even the pre-Buddhist history of Tibet has been cast as a story of the preparation of the country for the dissemination of Buddhism.

Because of these difficulties, there seems to be little hope of following Tucci's advice. Tibetan historical records were composed by people who saw their country's history as a record of the gradual triumph of Buddhist dharma over the indigenous forces opposing it. Their accounts presuppose a mythic structure in which forces of darkness and ignorance are defeated by proponents of dharma, and so a modern scholar who attempts to find "historical truth" in these accounts is destined to meet with a great deal of frustration, as Tucci indicates.

Fortunately for our present purposes, there are different sorts of "truths," and despite their deficiencies as history, Tibetan historical records reveal a great deal about how Tibetans have traditionally viewed themselves, their religion, and their country. The goal of the present section is to summarize the important events of the story of Buddhism's dissemination in Tibet and what the story reveals about Tibetan attitudes and beliefs. Parts of the story undoubtedly reflect historical events, but our main concern will be with what Tibetans *believe* about their history and how these beliefs reflect and influence their world view.

Tibetan Origins

As recounted in traditional Tibetan sources, the story begins in the distant past, when the land of Tibet had recently risen above the water. This aspect of the story corresponds to current scientific information on the area's geographical history. In the distant past, much of what is now the Tibetan plateau was in fact under water, but approximately forty million years ago the Indian land mass collided with Asia. It began to slide underneath the Asian land mass, eventually lifting up land that had been seabed. One result was the formation of the Himalayas, the world's highest mountains, and a huge high-altitude plateau that came to be known as Tibet.[5]

When the land was newly formed, according to traditional accounts, its only inhabitants were a monkey, who was an incarnation of Avalokiteśvara (*Phyan ras gzigs*, pronounced "Chenrézi"), and an ogress. The monkey was peaceful and contemplative, living alone in a cave and practicing meditation. The ogress, however, was a creature of wild emotion and lust. She is described as strong-willed, stubborn, and driven by sexual desire. Thinking that she was alone, she wailed piteously for a mate, and when the monkey heard her cries he was filled with compassion. He traveled to her, and their union produced six offspring, who were born without tails and walked upright. Tibetans today see themselves as descendants of these two progenitors, and believe that they have divided natures that result from the personalities of the monkey and the ogress. Their gentleness and compassion are traced back to the monkey, but their willfulness, avarice, and other negative personality traits derive from the ogress.[6]

After planting the seeds of the Tibetan race, Avalokiteśvara continued to take an interest in the spiritual development of the country. Because the early Tibetans were too primitive to be able to understand or adopt Buddhism, however, he decided to work behind the scenes to help them reach a level of maturity that would allow them eventually to embrace the dharma.

The Beginnings of Tibetan Society

A popular origin myth of early Tibet contends that its first king came from India. According to one account, he was born with unusual physical attributes, including long blue eyebrows and webbed fingers. Cast out by his people, he wandered north, eventually coming to Tibet.[7] In another version, he was a refugee from the fighting in India between the Kurus and Pāṇḍavas, which is recounted in the epic tale *Mahābhārata.* According to the *Red Annals*, he was a king of the Kurus who feared reprisals after their defeat.[8] Disguising himself as a woman, he crossed the Himalayas and encountered some people living in caves on the high plateau on the other side. The first people he saw asked him whence he came. Not understanding their question, he pointed to the sky. Those who saw this decided that he had descended from the heavens and proposed to make him king, since at the time they had no ruler. They placed him on their shoulders and carried him to their village, and so he came to be called Nyatri Tsenpo, meaning "Neck-Enthroned King." According to legend, he built Tibet's first house and began introducing Indian civilization. He is considered to be the first of the kings of the earliest ruling dynasty of Tibet, which had its capital near the Tsangpo river in the Yarlung Valley, about fifty-five miles southeast of Lhasa.[9]

Traditional histories trace the beginnings of the Yarlung dynasty to Nyatri Tsenpo. They report that when he died he ascended to heaven by means of a "sky-rope." For the next six generations his successors followed his example, but the rope was cut during the lifetime of the eighth king, Drigum Tsenpo. He was buried in a tomb in Kongpo in the Yarlung Valley in central Tibet, and this structure is the first concrete evidence of early Tibetan history. From this point on, the kings were buried in vaults, many of which are still found an area named Chong Gyé in the Yarlung Valley.[10]

The early kings are described as adherents of Bön, which at that time was not an organized religion, but rather a vaguely defined collection of shamanistic and animistic practices. The kings were believed to have descended from heaven, and their divine origin may have played a role in their eventual rise to supremacy among the many small kingdoms of Tibet. It is still unclear, however, how this lineage of petty local rulers eventually rose to preeminence. This question has been explored by a number of scholars, but available records provide no conclusive evidence.[11]

Dynastic histories indicate that many of the early kings died young and met violent deaths. Some records report that when a king's son reached the time of investiture at the age of thirteen (or, according to some sources, "when he was able to ride a horse"), the king underwent a ceremony of ritual death, after which the son was linked with the father as designated heir.[12] Dynastic records also indicate that when a king died and was buried in a specially constructed tomb, his closest associates were burned alive and buried with him, along with his belongings. As David Snellgrove notes, this practice may have originated as a pragmatic way of ensuring the loyalty of ministers and retainers, who had a personal stake in the king's survival.[13]

Beginnings of Empire

By the early sixth century, the Yarlung dynasty had brought most of the warring tribes of Tibet under its control and began to build the country into a military power.[14] As the emergent empire of Tibet expanded outward, it discovered that it was surrounded on all sides by Buddhist civilizations. Buddhism had been established in the Gangetic valley by the emperor Aśoka in the third century B.C.E., and in intervening centuries a number of major monastic universities had been built in northern India. Buddhism had also spread to Kashmir, Gilgit, and Baltistan, and had moved into Central Asia and beyond, following ancient trade routes. Buddhist missionaries traveled across the Pamir mountains, bringing the dharma to China through the caravan routes that skirted the Taklamakan Desert to the north and south. The southern route passed through the kingdoms of Shanshan and Khotan, both of which were Buddhist countries, and the northern route went through the cities of Karashahr, Kucha, and Kashgar, all of which were under Chinese control. To the south of Tibet was the kingdom of Nepal, which at that time encompassed little more than the Kathmandu Valley. It was strongly influenced by Indian culture and had a number of Buddhist monasteries and temples.[15]

In light of its later conversion to Buddhism, it is interesting that Tibet first came into contact with the religion as an invading force that ransacked Buddhist institutions in Central Asia and put many monks to death during its military incursions. Surviving records from Tibet's Central Asian neighbors speak of the Tibetan soldiers as the dreaded "Red Faces," who painted their faces with red ochre and savagely attacked Buddhist institutions, destroying all in their path. Despite this initial persecution of Buddhism, in the course of several centuries the Tibetans were converted and eventually became ardent supporters of the dharma.

In the early part of the sixth century the Tibetan army conquered and annexed large territories of Central Asia that lay between Tibet and China and were inhabited by nomadic and semi-nomadic tribes of Turkic and Tibetan stock. In 635 Tibet attacked China itself, and in successive campaigns managed to wrest control of large areas that had been under Chinese control. These included the four main Chinese strongholds in Chinese Turkestan. As a result, China lost its lines of communication with the west.

The Tibetan empire eventually conquered all of Gansu and most of Szechwan and northern Yunnan. The Chinese emperor was required to pay a yearly tribute to the Yarlung kings, and when the payment was not made in 763, the Tibetans responded by attacking, capturing, and sacking the Chinese capital of Changan. The Tang emperor was forced to flee, and the Tibetans set up a puppet emperor in the capital. It is clear from both Chinese and Tibetan dynastic records of this period that both countries were major powers in Asia that were on equal footing diplomatically, although Tibet enjoyed a military advantage.[16] In 648 the Tibetans sent an expedition into India, and in 670 they wiped out the Duyu hun people, who lived in the Kokonor area.[17] They later came to dominate Nepal and areas along the southern side of the Himalayas, sending military expeditions as far as Upper Burma. Near the end of the eighth century the Arab caliph Harun al-Rashid became concerned that the Tibetans, having reached as far as the Oxus river, were advancing toward his empire. In order to counteract the threat, he formed an alliance with the Chinese emperor.

As Luciano Petech has remarked, the fact that the two most powerful empires of the middle ages had to join forces in order to curb Tibetan expansion indicates the success of Tibetan military endeavors.[18]

The Period of the Religious Kings

The Introduction of Buddhism

The first official appearance of Buddhism is said to have occurred during the reign of the twenty-third monarch of the Yarlung dynasty, Totori Nyentsen (born c. 173 C.E.). According to Tibetan legends, one day a Buddhist text and relics consecrated to Avalokiteśvara fell from the sky to the roof of the king's palace. The scriptures were written in Sanskrit, and no one at the court understood the significance of the relics; thus it remained an isolated event. Tsepon Shakabpa cites a Tibetan account that indicates that these articles actually were brought from India, but Totori Nyentsen hid their origin after having a dream indicating that in four generations a king would be able to read and understand the books. The arrival of this text is considered to be the first introduction of Buddhism to Tibet, and is believed to have been planned by Avalokiteśvara. Its importance for Tibetans is reflected in the fact that their currency before the Chinese takeover was dated in terms of years since that event, which Tibetan historians claimed occurred in 233 C.E.[19]

According to traditional histories, the definitive establishment of Buddhism in Tibet occurred during the reign of Songtsen Gampo (c. 618–650), who later was portrayed as the first of the three *Chögyel* (*chos rgyal*), or "Religious Kings" (the others were Tri Songdétsen and Relbachen). He is considered to have been an incarnation of Avalokiteśvara, who took rebirth as a king in order to further the dissemination of the dharma. Under his military guidance, Tibet became a major power in Central Asia, and when it spread beyond its original borders it encountered Buddhism, which was widespread in Central Asia and China. During his reign Tibet conquered the kingdom of Shangshung in what is today western Tibet, and he moved his capital from Yarlung to Lhasa. At the time it was known as Rasa, meaning "enclosure," suggesting that the area was originally a hunting preserve with a royal residence on top of the Marpori Hill. A palace was built on the hill, which is now the site of the Potala, residence of the Dalai Lamas prior to the Chinese takeover in 1959.

Seeking to make political alliances, Songtsen Gampo sent emissaries to Aṃśuvarman, the king of Nepal, to request a marriage with his daughter Bhṛkutī. The king agreed, and when the princess, reportedly a devout Buddhist, traveled to Tibet, she brought with her an image of Akṣobhya Buddha. This was housed in a temple she had built in the center of a lake, which was called Ramoché. She is generally referred to by Tibetans as Belsa, meaning "Nepalese wife," or Tritsun, "Royal Lady."

The king's next attempt at a political marriage ran into some difficulties. He sent emissaries to the Chinese emperor Taizong (627–650), founder of the Tang dynasty, requesting a marriage to a royal princess. Because the emperor considered the Tibetans to be uncouth barbarians, Taizong refused, and he further angered Songtsen Gampo by promising one of his daughters to the ruler of the Duyu hun. Songtsen Gampo responded by attacking and defeating tribes affiliated with the Tang, after which he marched on the Chinese city of Songzhou. After threatening further violence against the Chinese, he sent the emperor a suit of armor inlaid with gold, along with a request that he reconsider his earlier decision. Having little choice, Taizong agreed, and the princess Wencheng was sent to Tibet in 640. She is referred to by Tibetans as "Gyasa," meaning "Chinese wife."[20] She brought with her an image of Śākyamuni Buddha as a young prince. This was installed in a temple named Trülnang, which later came to be known as the Jokhang.[21] Today the temple is Tibet's holiest shrine, and the statue, named Jowo Rinpoché, is the most sacred image in Tibet.

Little is known about Songtsen Gampo's Nepalese wife, and some scholars believe that she may have been a later invention, created as a counterpart to Wencheng. No contemporaneous records of her life or activities exist, but in later histories she is portrayed as an emanation of the buddha Tārā, as is Wencheng.

Wencheng is also a nebulous figure in records of the time, but in later Chinese histories is recast as a cultural ambassador who traveled to Tibet not as a war bride, but as the central actor in an imperial plan to convert the bellicose Tibetans to Chinese ways and thus civilize them. The Tang dynasty annals report that "[since] Princess Wencheng went and civilized this country, many of their customs have been changed."[22] She is credited with convincing the king to wear Chinese brocades, to ban the practice of painting faces red, to adopt imperial customs, and to disseminate Chinese manners, learning, and technology among the backward Tibetans. This was part of a long-term strategy to lift the Tibetans up to the Chinese standard, so that they could be assimilated into the empire. According to the Tang annals, he "praised the costume of the great empire, and the perfection of their manners, and was ashamed of the barbarism of his own people."[23]

In Tibetan histories, however, there is little mention of interest in Chinese culture, and the king's interactions with the Tang court and marriage to Wencheng are conceived as strategies to further the dissemination of Buddhism. The Tang ruler is presented as an emanation of the buddha Mañjuśrī, who colluded with Avalokiteśvara's manifestation to spread the dharma. Tibetan dynastic records present a picture of an ambitious military commander seeking to expand his empire.

Traditional Tibetan histories portray Wencheng as a physical emanation of Tārā, who worked with Bhṛkutī and Songtsen Gampo to spread Buddhism among the populace. Their coordinated activities were the culmination of centuries of behind-the-scenes maneuvering by Avalokiteśvara and other Buddhist figures to prepare Tibetans for the dharma. She is credited with sponsoring the building of several temples, and these later histories recount her prodigious efforts to establish Buddhist culture throughout the region.

Records of the time, however, fail to reflect the influence later tradition attributes to Wencheng. At the conclusion of a study of available evidence from the imperial period, Hugh Richardson concludes that she is an ambiguous figure who appears to have exerted little influence and that there is no evidence that she was even a Buddhist.[24] It should also be noted that at the time she arrived in Tibet, she was only about twelve years old, did not speak the language, and would have been a complete outsider. Her husband died several years afterwards, and there are no records that they had any children. According to traditional norms, she would have been the second wife behind Bhṛkutī, and one of five royal consorts. Records from the imperial period provide no evidence that she exerted any significant influence either before or after her husband's death.

Similarly, details of Songtsen Gampo's life and activities present a portrait of a military commander and politician who was mainly concerned with conquering new territory, making strategic alliances, and establishing himself as a monarch of high status. His marriage to Wencheng appears to be a calculated move to forge relationships with a rival neighboring kingdom, and he is also said to have married three Tibetan women from prominent aristocratic families to shore up his local power base. There is no significant evidence that he sponsored Buddhist activities, aided missionary efforts, or participated in Buddhist practices. When he died, he was interred according to the pre-Buddhist rites of Bön, and no Buddhists appear to have been involved. Further evidence of his religious orientation is a record promising that one hundred horses would be slaughtered at the tomb of a loyal vassal.[25] Had Songtsen Gampo really been an incarnate buddha (or even a devout Buddhist), wanton slaughter of animals would presumably have been abhorrent to him, and he could have devised another way to commemorate his vassal's service.

Literary Contacts with India

The period of Songtsen Gampo's tenure was characterized by a growing perception on the part of the ruling class that Tibet lagged behind many of its neighbors culturally, and some perceived Buddhism as an integral part of these advanced foreign cultures.

One of the most obvious gaps in Tibetan culture was the absence of a literary script or a common grammar. Recognizing this lack, Songtsen Gampo sent the scholar Tönmi Sambhota and some students to India to develop a script and codify the language. There may have been scholars who were involved in such projects prior to Tönmi Sambhota, but he is generally credited with actually developing what came to be recognized as a standard Tibetan script and grammar.

Since Kashmir was widely recognized as a center of learning, Tönmi Sambhota journeyed there in order to work with Sanskrit scholars. He remained in India for a number of years, studying language and literature. He adapted a northern form of the Indian Gupta script to the sounds of the oral Tibetan language, and he also modified the rules of Sanskrit in order to apply them to the much less complex grammar of the indigenous Tibetan language. Upon his return to Tibet, the king used his authority to declare that the system developed by Tönmi Sambhota would henceforth be the standard throughout the area ruled by the central government.

Tri Songdétsen

The next great religious king was Tri Songdétsen (c. 740–798), who is considered by Tibetans to have been an incarnation of Mañjuśrī. By all accounts he was a devout Buddhist who took a personal interest in propagating the dharma. In order to accomplish this, he sent a message to the Indian scholar Śāntarakṣita asking him to travel to Tibet. The abbot of Vikramaśīla, one of the greatest seats of Buddhist learning in India, Śāntarakṣita became known in Tibet as the "Bodhisattva Abbot."

When he arrived, however, he was confronted by opposition from some of the king's ministers, who are characterized in traditional accounts as adherents of Bön. Unfortunately for his mission, a series of natural disasters occurred at this time, and the ministers contended that they were caused by Bön deities, who opposed the arrival of the Buddhist scholar. Their opposition was effective enough that Śāntarakṣita was forced to leave Tibet, and it was several years before he was able to return. Before departing, he advised the king to invite the tantric adept Padmasambhava, who could defeat the gods of Bön.

According to traditional histories, Padmasambhava knew in advance that the king would invite him to Tibet, and so when the messenger arrived he was already prepared to leave. When he entered the outer reaches of Tibet, demonic forces sought to bar his progress by sending a huge snowstorm. He retreated to a cave and entered into a deep meditative absorption, and through this was able to defeat them. As he traveled toward central Tibet, the demons and deities of the country massed against him, but his power was so great that he single-handedly defeated them all. The people were amazed that a single man could challenge their powerful demons to personal combat and triumph.

As a result of this victory, Padmasambhava was also able to overcome human opposition, after which he advised the king to invite Śāntarakṣita to return. In 775, Tri Songdétsen, Padmasambhava, and Śāntarakṣita celebrated the successful establishment of Buddhism in Tibet by founding its first monastery, which was called Samyé (*bsam yas*). The monastery's buildings were arranged in a mandala pattern, with a temple in the center and its four sides oriented with the cardinal directions. It is said to have been modeled after the Indian monastery Odantapurī in Bihar.[26] It was built in three stories, each in a different architectural style—one Indian, one Chinese, and one Tibetan—and it was surmounted by a small lantern-roofed chapel. According to Erik Haarh, the monastery was completed in 766 and consecrated in 767.[27] When the monastery was finished, seven Tibetans received monastic vows. They became known as the "seven probationers," and their ordination is considered to be the inauguration of monastic Buddhism in Tibet.

After this the king turned his attention to the translation of Buddhist texts, realizing that Buddhism would never flourish in Tibet as long as its scriptures remained in a foreign language. He began inviting translators from India, Kashmir, and China, and he also sent young Tibetans to India for training.

The Debate Between Kamalaśīla and Hashang Mahāyāna

Background of the Controversy. In the early period of Buddhism's dissemination into Tibet, it faced widespread opposition from Tibetans who were adherents of indigenous religious traditions. Among Buddhists, there were also competing groups that advocated differing doctrines and practices. Two of the most prominent of these were factions that propounded traditional Indian Mahāyāna models of the Buddhist path and others that favored the approach of the Chinese Chan school. The main exponent of the Chinese position was a meditation master (*Hva shang;* pronounced "Hashang") named Mahāyāna (Chinese: *Heshang Moheyan*), who is reported to have taught that awakening is attained suddenly and is not a result of gradual training. It dawns in a sudden flash of insight, after which all mental afflictions are eliminated.

His opponents, who followed the Indic model of the five paths and ten levels,[28] contended that the process of awakening gradually removes mental afflictions. Because these are deeply rooted and are the result of countless lifetimes of familiarization with negative thoughts and deeds, they cannot be extirpated all at once. It is no more possible for an ordinary being to become a buddha in one moment of awakening than for a mountain climber to scale a high peak in one jump.

It is clear from Tibetan and Chinese records that both sides had popular support, and to settle the dispute the king arranged for a debate between representatives of the Indian school and Heshang Moheyan and his followers.[29] The Indian side was headed by Kamalaśīla, a student of Śāntarakṣita's. According to Pudön, Śāntarakṣita had foreseen the conflict before his death and had told the king that when it occurred Kamalaśīla should be invited to Tibet to argue for the Indian position.[30] Tibetan and Chinese records report that the two sides met in Lhasa around the year 792 for a debate that was intended to settle the question once and for all.[31] The system of the winner would become the standard in Tibet, and the losing side would be forbidden to spread its doctrines.

The Council of Lhasa: An Apocryphal Story? In a study of this story in *Minor Buddhist Texts II*, Giuseppe Tucci argues against the idea that the debate could have been held in Lhasa. He contends that at the time Lhasa was a small and isolated town, and during the season in which the debate is purported to have occurred, travel there would have been difficult. He believes that the debate probably took place at Samyé, the nexus of Tibetan Buddhism at that time. Paul Demiéville, whose groundbreaking study *La Concile de Lhasa* followed the traditional story of a single debate in Lhasa, later emended his position and stated that there was probably a series of exchanges between proponents of sudden and gradual awakening that took place over a period of many years, with the Indian gradualist faction eventually triumphing. Other scholars—Yoshiro Imaeda, for instance—doubt that a debate even occurred, and Luis Gómez contends that while there were probably disputes between the two factions, they were not settled in a single, definitive council, but rather took the form of "a haphazard series of indirect confrontations."[32] Gómez bases this conclusion on discrepancies in documents that purport to give an account of the debate.

Whether or not the debate took the form reported in traditional sources (and even if it never occurred at all), the story is an important one for Tibetan Buddhists, who believe that the council resulted in a clear victory for Indian gradualist Buddhism and the defeat of Chinese teachings of sudden awakening. At the very least, the prevalence of the story indicates that during the eighth century there was a conflict between Indian Buddhist models of gradual awakening and Chinese teachings of sudden awakening and that the Indian model eventually won out. If there was a single council, it seems probable that it did not end the conflict and that the relative merits of the two approaches were the subject of later disputes. All available sources agree that the Chinese suddenist teachings were popular in Tibet, but they subsequently declined. The widespread disapproval of such doctrines even among contemporary Tibetan scholars may be seen in the fact that schools which speak of sudden awakening often feel compelled to argue that their teachings are significantly different from those of Heshang Moheyan.[33]

Pudön's Account. The most influential Tibetan account of the debate is found in Pudön's *History of Buddhism*, which states that Chan doctrines and practices had gained many adherents in Tibet, to the dismay of people who followed Indian models.[34] In order to counteract the perceived heresies of the Chinese, their opponents convened a council in which they would be required to defend their positions. The greatest concern of the Indian faction was the purported antinomianism of Heshang Moheyan. Pudön reports that the Heshang and his followers eschewed the practice of moral cultivation, saying that it is irrelevant to the goal of buddhahood. Awakening, he claimed, is only found by those who attain a state of complete inactivity in which thought ceases. According to Pudön, the Heshang wrote treatises that denounced traditional dharma practice and claimed that awakening is gained by those who remain in a sleeplike state.[35] In Pudön's account, Heshang Moheyan began the debate by summarizing his position:

> He who has no thoughts and inclinations at all can be fully delivered from Phenomenal Life. The absence of any thought, search, or investigation brings about the nonperception of the reality of separate entities. In such a manner one can attain (Buddhahood) at once, like (a Bodhisattva) who has attained the tenth Stage.

> Kamalaśīla replied:

> If one has no thought concerning any of the elements of existence and does not direct the mind upon them, this does not mean that one can cease to remember all that one has experienced and to think of it. . . . If the mere absence of (consciousness and) recollection is regarded as sufficient, it follows that in a swoon or at the time of intoxication one comes to the state where there is no constructive thought. . . . Without correct analysis there is no means of attaining liberation from constructive thought.[36]

The Indian scholar Jñānendra pressed the point by asking the Chinese faction, "If you can attain buddhahood at any time, what are you doing now?" In other words, if they had the potential to become buddhas at any moment, why were they wasting their time discussing it, rather than doing it? He then stated the Indian Mahāyāna view that awakening is the result of gradual perfection of compassion and wisdom, a process that begins with moral cultivation and meditation practice. These remove mental defilements and lead to progressively deeper understanding of reality, culminating in omniscience. Jñānendra contended that if one were to follow the Chan path it would be impossible to attain the state of buddhahood, since one would simply sleep and do nothing.

According to Pudön's account, the Chinese were unable to answer these charges and remained silent. The king declared that the position of the Indian gradualists was victorious and decreed that henceforth the teachings of Heshang Moheyan should be banned. The members of the Chinese faction acknowledged their defeat and returned home to China. Pudön adds that Heshang Moheyan was so upset by this loss of face that he committed suicide with a number of his followers. Kamalaśīla, however, was not able to savor his victory for long, because some surviving disciples of the Heshang hired Chinese assassins to kill him. Pudön states that they murdered Kamalaśīla by squeezing his kidneys.

The Chinese record composed by Wangxi contradicts Pudön's statement that the Indian faction won. Wangxi reports that Heshang Moheyan and his teachings were declared the winners of the debate, but he adds that the Heshang was so upset by the degeneration of dharma in Tibet that he committed suicide along with some of his followers.[37] This seems rather suspicious, since if he had been victorious he would presumably have felt vindicated, and not suicidal.

The story of the defeat of Heshang Moheyan is well known among Tibetan Buddhists, who view it as clear evidence of the superiority of Indian gradualist Mahāyāna. Chinese Buddhism is widely regarded as a system that diverges from the tradition founded by Śākyamuni, but the original motivation for this belief may have been as much political as doctrinal. While the Chinese, Tibetan, and Indian sources give evidence of marked differences in outlook and practice, the aversion that developed toward Chinese forms of Buddhism may have been at least partially motivated by political considerations.[38] Tibetan relations with India were generally amicable, but Tibet and China had a long and bitter history of conflict.[39] Both were major powers in Central Asia, and both were involved in armed competition for supremacy in the region. Given their history, it is unlikely that the king would have ruled in favor of the Chinese faction. Moreover, even if he were as devout as traditional sources claim, his duties as ruler of a large empire probably prevented him from studying Buddhist philosophy in depth, and so in all likelihood he lacked the background knowledge to be able to understand the subtleties of the competing positions.

Relbachen, the Third Religious King

Tri Songdétsen's support of Buddhism caused the religion to spread widely, particularly among the educated classes. The tradition of royal support was vigorously continued by the king Sénalek (reigned 799-815) and reached its apogee with Relbachen (reigned 815-836), who is said to have been an emanation of the buddha Vajrapāṇi. By all accounts he was deeply committed to Buddhism, and his fervor led him to concentrate on religious matters, to the neglect of affairs of state. He spent lavish amounts of money on the construction of temples and monasteries and supported visits by Indian Buddhist teachers, as well as trips to India by Tibetan scholars. He is reported to have been so devoted to the dharma that in official state ceremonies he would tie ribbons to his long braids, and Buddhist monks would sit on top of the braids, symbolizing his submission to the *saṃgha*.[40] This angered traditional ministers, who viewed this practice as an affront to the dignity of the throne. Another source of discontent was his policy of allotting a group of seven households for the support of each monk, which meant that even people who had little or no interest in Buddhism were required to finance its propagation. Although traditional sources portray the growing opposition to his reign as underhanded plotting by adherents of Bön, his political ineptitude and financial irresponsibility were probably the root causes of his eventual downfall.

One of the major contributions of his reign was his sponsorship of a project to standardize translation equivalents for Buddhist texts. The project, headed by Beltsek, created a glossary for Sanskrit and Tibetan terms and revised the written language in order that Tibetan translations could more accurately reflect the grammar and syntax of Sanskrit. By this time there were a number of highly trained Tibetan translators (*lo tsā ba;* pronounced "lotsawa"), such as Yéshédé, and many Indian scholars-in-residence. Most texts were translated by committees made up of Indian and Tibetan scholars; the Indians were mainly responsible for checking the doctrinal accuracy of the translations, while the Tibetans made sure that they were grammatically correct. Because both the Tibetans and Indians were generally well versed in Buddhist thought and practice, there was also considerable overlap in translation duties. The translations produced during this period continue to be favored by the Nyingma school, which considers them to be more faithful to the original spirit of the texts than the later translations prepared during the period of the "second dissemination" of Buddhism.[41]

Lang Darma's Persecution of Buddhism

The reaction against Relbachen's mishandling of the government eventually became so intense that he was assassinated by two of his ministers, who crept up behind him and twisted his neck while he was relaxing in his palace. He was succeeded as king by Lang Darma (reigned 838–842), who is reported to have vigorously persecuted Buddhism. The persecution brought to a close the period of the "first dissemination" (*snga dar*) of Buddhism, which was initiated by the religious kings in the seventh century.[42]

Traditional sources portray Lang Darma as a devout adherent of Bön who was possessed by a demon.[43] Prompted by these influences, he ordered temples and monasteries closed; monks and nuns were forced to return to lay life. Some refused and were executed. He halted cultural contacts with India, and he is also said to have ordered the destruction of Buddhist texts and images. Despite his efforts to eradicate Buddhism, however, it had become so widespread among the Tibetan people that during his reign it went underground. Since the power of the throne was mainly concentrated in central Tibet, other areas were largely unaffected, and many religious leaders in the central provinces simply moved beyond the king's sphere of influence, waiting for a reversal of official policy.

Although there was widespread dissatisfaction with Relbachen, Buddhism had gained a large following, and so Lang Darma's policy of persecution prompted a backlash among people faithful to the dharma. This led to his own assassination by a Buddhist monk named Belgyi Dorjé, who killed him during a theatrical performance. Pretending to enact a traditional story, he danced in front of the king, holding a bow and arrow. Placing the arrow in the bowstring, Belgyi Dorjé aimed it at the king, still pretending to be acting, and shot Lang Darma dead. Traditional sources characterize this euphemistically as a "liberation" rather than a killing, because Belgyi Dorjé is said to have been motivated by compassion for the king, and not anger. Belgyi Dorjé was concerned that Lang Darma, possessed by a demon, was creating vast amounts of negative karma for himself due to his persecution of Buddhism, and so he decided to "liberate" the king from committing future misdeeds, thus saving him from himself.

As the king lay dying, Belgyi Dorjé, who had arrived on a black horse and wearing a white robe, turned the robe inside out. The reverse side was black, and when he rode from the murder scene his horse waded through a river, which washed off the black paint covering it. Through this ruse, soldiers hunting for an assassin on a black horse wearing a white robe passed by Belgyi Dorjé, who was riding on a white horse and wearing a black robe.

Lang Darma's death led to the collapse of the Yarlung dynasty and brought on a period of political chaos in Tibet.[44] It also marked the beginning of the end of the Tibetan empire in Central Asia. With no strong authority in Tibet to hold the empire together, China was able to regain control over the areas it had lost, while the Tibetans retreated behind their border mountains. The Tang dynasty only outlived the Yarlung dynasty for a short while, however, and in 905 it collapsed, leaving no central authority capable of holding onto the provinces of Central Asia, which were left as a no-man's-land between China and Tibet until the emergent Mongol empire began to annex them. For the next three centuries after the fall of the Tang dynasty, there was little contact between Tibet and China.

With the demise of their empire and the subsequent collapse of their main rival, the Tibetans were content to remain within the natural borders set by the Kunlun, Karakoram, and Himalayan mountains, and never again engaged in military adventures beyond these limits. It was not until 1247 that another strong central authority was established in Tibet, when Sakya Pandita was appointed overlord of Tibet by the Mongol chieftain Ködan, a grandson of Chinggis (or Genghis) Khan.

The Second Dissemination of Buddhism

With the passing of the royal house, central Tibet entered a period of political upheaval. The main source of funding for Buddhism also disappeared. In western Tibet, however, interest in Buddhism remained strong. Near the end of the tenth century, according to traditional accounts, Tsenpo Khoré, the king of the western kingdom of Gugé, renounced the throne and became a Buddhist monk, taking the ordination name Yéshé Ö. Apparently intending to revive the dharma in Tibet, he sent twenty-one promising Tibetan monks to India and Kashmir to study, and he allocated money to support Buddhist scholarship in Tibet. All but two of the monks died in India, but the two who returned became prominent scholars and translators. They were Rinchen Sangpo and Lekbé Shérap, who returned to Tibet in 978, along with some Indian scholars. In Tibetan histories, this event marks the inauguration of the "second dissemination" (*phyi dar;*

pronounced "chidar") of Buddhism to Tibet, but other factors also played important roles. The greatest Tibetan figure of this period was Rinchen Sangpo, who oversaw the translation of many Sanskrit sūtras and tantras, along with their voluminous commentaries. He made three visits to India, where he spent a total of seventeen years, traveling from teacher to teacher, receiving initiations and oral instructions, and acquiring copies of Buddhist texts. He brought these back with him to Tibet, and his literary activity played a significant role in the Buddhist renaissance.[45]

Another influential source of the reinvigoration of Buddhism was the efforts of monks who traveled to institutions in Amdo where monastic discipline and scholarship had survived, and who brought these traditions back to the central regions of Ü and Tsang. The Mūlasarvāstivāda system of vinaya, which had been declared the standard by King Relbachen, was preserved by the Amdo monks, along with the monastic curriculum that had become institutionalized during the early period of Buddhism's dissemination. Much of this had been lost in central Tibet, but these monks re-imported it and built a number of monasteries during the tenth and eleventh centuries, which attracted increasing numbers of new monks. Ronald Davidson has argued convincingly that this was the most important factor in the successful reintroduction of Buddhism during the renaissance period.[46] This was a gradual process that hardly registers in traditional Tibetan histories of the second dissemination, but it provided the institutional foundation that made it possible. Most Tibetan historians portray the mission of the Indian scholar Atiśa (also known as Dīpaṃkara Śrījñāna, 982–1054) to Tibet as the decisive event of this process, but records of the time depict him as a minor player with little real influence, despite his prestige as a renowned master from India.

Atiśa

According to Tibetan tradition, Atiśa was born into a noble family in Bengal. He entered the religious life at an early age after experiencing a vision of Tārā. During his early years he traveled around the Buddhist world to receive teachings. His first guru was a tantric yogi who initiated him into the Hevajra cycle, and he was mainly involved with nonmonastic tantric practices until in a dream Śākyamuni advised him to become a monk. He took ordination vows at the age of twenty-nine in a monastery at Bodhgayā, the site of the Buddha's awakening. Atiśa then immersed himself in the monastic curriculum current at the time, studying monastic discipline, the Perfection of Wisdom literature, and tantric texts.

Due to his great learning and realization, he rose to prominence in the monastic university of Nālandā, where he was one of the four directors. He also taught at the Buddhist universities of Vikramaśīla and Bodhgayā, and was probably the most famous and revered Buddhist teacher of his day. When he was advanced in years, a messenger sent by Yéshé Ö visited him, offered him a substantial sum of gold, and asked him to journey to Tibet in order to reintroduce the dharma, which had been damaged by the persecutions of Lang Darma. Atiśa initially rejected the request on the grounds that his teaching skills were required in India.

Fearing that the gold he had sent was insufficient, Yéshé Ö set about raising a much larger amount, in hopes that it would induce Atiśa to accept the invitation. While trying to obtain funds from a neighboring king, he was captured and imprisoned. The king demanded a ransom equal to Yéshé Ö's weight in gold, but Yéshé Ö advised his great-nephew, Jangchup Ö, not to pay it, and instead to send the gold to Atiśa. Jangchup Ö reluctantly did so, with the result that Yéshé Ö died in prison. This act of self-sacrifice is said to have been a factor in Atiśa's eventual decision to travel to Tibet.[47]

Shortly after receiving the royal request, Atiśa had a vision of Tārā, his patron deity, who told him that if he traveled to Tibet his life would be shortened. Atiśa was relieved by the news, assuming that it meant that he should not accept the invitation. He was advanced in years, and the journey to Tibet was long, difficult, and dangerous. For these reasons, Atiśa preferred to remain where he was. Tārā then added that if he did go to Tibet his visit would benefit many sentient beings and would cause the dharma to flourish there. As a devout Mahāyānist, Atiśa realized that he should choose the benefit of others over his own welfare, and so he accepted the invitation. Before he left he made a vow to the abbot of his monastery that he would return in three years. He is reported to have arrived in Gugé in 1042 at the age of sixty.

His reputation in India gave him personal authority in Tibet, and he was invited to lecture in various Buddhist establishments. Tibetan histories written after the fifteenth century cast him as the single most influential actor in the second dissemination, but records of the time indicate that his mission had little real influence until centuries later. One difficulty he faced was his ordination lineage: he adhered to the Mahāsāṃghika vinaya, but the Mūlasarvāstivāda monastic code had been normative in Tibet at least since the time of Relbachen, and he was not allowed to ordain Tibetan monks. Moreover, while he was regarded as an eminent scholar and teacher, the monks who had earlier traveled to northeast Tibet and re-imported the vinaya and scholastic curriculum already had well-established curricula in their institutions, and so they felt no need to make major changes. Despite these factors, he traveled widely and composed works that would later become influential—particularly in the Gélukpa order, which considers itself to be the successor of the Kadampa, founded by Atiśa's disciples. After the Gélukpa came to power in the fifteenth century, Tibetan historians tended to inflate his role in the second dissemination, and this has largely been echoed in studies by contemporary Western scholars.

He composed several works on Buddhism for the benefit of Tibetans, most notably his *Lamp for the Path to Awakening*, which is a summary of the Buddhist path. He reportedly wrote this work at the request of Jangchub Ö while he was staying at Toling. In this treatise, he brought together the two streams of scholastic Mahāyāna and tantra, both of which are today viewed by Tibetan scholars as complementary aspects of the Buddhist path.

Atiśa began his analysis with a distinction of three grades of human beings: (1) nonreligious people, who only focus on the present life; (2) people of middling capacity, who engage in practice for their own benefit (Hīnayānists); and (3) practitioners of great capacity, who work for the benefit of others. He then indicated that the best religious life is that of a celibate Mahāyāna monk who diligently adheres to the vinaya rules and follows the gradual path to awakening for the good of other living beings. His text integrates tantric techniques into the Mahāyāna path, and Atiśa did not seem to think that there was any discrepancy between tantra and other Mahāyāna practices. His vision of the path provided a model for the development of monastic orders in lineages that traced themselves back to noncelibate tantric yogis, particularly the Gélukpa.

Despite Atiśa's intention to keep his promise and return to India, political factors prevented this, and he died in Tibet in 1054. During his years in Tibet, Atiśa trained a number of disciples, several of whom became important figures in the development of Tibetan Buddhism. His instructions and influence led to the founding of the Kadampa order, the first school of Buddhism in Tibet, although the establishment of a clearly defined school was due primarily to the efforts of his disciple Dromdön

(1008–1064).[48] In 1057 Dromdön founded Réting Monastery, which became the main seat of the order, and later became a Gélukpa institution.

Mongol Influence and Sakya Supremacy

During the centuries after Atiśa's death, Buddhism continued to flourish in Tibet. As Tibetans became more confident in their grasp of the tradition, indigenous orders began to develop, the first of which was the Sakya sect, which takes its name from the monastery of Sakya, founded by Gönchok Gyelpo (1034–1102) of the Khön family in 1073.[49] His son and successor Günga Nyingpo (1092–1158) systematized the teachings of the lineage, which is traced to Drokmi, who traveled to India and brought back tantric and scholastic teachings. Günga Nyingpo became known as the "Great Sakyapa" (*sa chen*) because of his extensive learning.

Early in the twelfth century, the Mongols emerged as the new power in Central Asia under the rule of Chinggis Khan. In 1207, as Chinggis was moving to attack the Tangut state of Xixia, the leading religious and secular leaders of Tibet, fearing that their land might be his next target, sent an emissary to him with an offer of submission. The formal acknowledgment of his overlordship served its intended purpose of keeping Chinggis at bay. In 1240, however, the Mongol chieftain Köden invaded Tibet, raiding and looting almost as far as Lhasa. There was no attempt at this time to place Tibet under direct Mongol rule, but in 1249 Köden summoned Sakya Pandita (Günga Gyeltsen Bel Sangpo, 1182–1251), an eminent religious leader, to surrender his country to Mongol control.

When Sakya Pandita met the khan, however, the Mongol ruler was so impressed with him that Köden became converted to Buddhism. Instead of invading Tibet, he offered a special relationship: Köden would protect the country against foreign threats, and the Sakya lamas would become spiritual preceptors of the Mongol khans. In this relationship, according to Wylie, "the patron (*yon* or *yon bdag*) provides the military power to enforce the temporal prerogatives of the lama, who in turn devotes himself to the religious needs (*mchod* or *mchod gnas*) of the patron."[50] This became known as the "priest-patron" (*mchod yon*) relationship. It was based on a recognition of shared religious ideals, and although the Mongols technically controlled Tibet, they left the actual administration of the country to Tibetans.[51]

This at least is how the concord between the Sakyapa hierarchs and the

Mongol khans is presented both in traditional Tibetan histories and in contemporary accounts written by Tibetan exiles. The latter are particularly concerned with countering claims by the Chinese government that Tibet submitted to China (although the Mongols had not yet actually conquered China)[52] and that it remained a part of its empire from that time up to the present day. By putting a religious gloss on the arrangement and portraying the Mongol khans as Buddhist converts devoted to their religious preceptors, they intend to exclude China from the arrangement, which they claim lapsed after Mongol power waned in the fourteenth century, following which both Tibet and China, they claim, regained their separate independences.

Hugh Richardson rejects Chinese assertions that submission to the Mongols was tantamount to accepting Chinese sovereignty over Tibet.

> [T]here is no substance to the claim of some Chinese writers that Tibet was in unbroken subordination to China from the time of the Yuan [Mongol] dynasty. The link between Peking and Tibet came into being only through the conquest of China by a foreign power which had already been accepted by the Tibetans as their overlord. Even before their expulsion from China the later Mongol emperors enjoyed no more than a purely formal and personal relationship with Tibet; and although the Chinese recovered their own territory from the erstwhile foreign conqueror they did not take possession of that of the Mongols, nor did they exercise or attempt to exercise any authority in Tibet. China and Tibet had each recovered its independence of the Mongols in its own way and at different times.[53]

As Richardson notes, Tibetan submission was to the Mongol khans, and not the emperor of China. When China was annexed to the Mongol empire, it was one part of a vast territory that covered much of Asia and later parts of eastern Europe. After the demise of Mongol power, many regions regained their independence, including both China and Tibet, but no Tibetans participated in China's liberation, nor did Chinese play any role in Tibet's return to indigenous rule.

The real motivations of the khans in creating a special administrative system in Tibet are difficult to determine, and there is considerable evidence that the special arrangement they made with the Sakyapas was intended to provide for stable and loyal administration of a distant territory. One of the ways they secured this loyalty was by demanding that Sakya Pandita's nephew Pakpa (who had accompanied him on his journey to the Mongol court) be left behind as a virtual hostage. The khans also left clear threats of bloody retaliation against Tibet in the event of any rebellion.

Sakya Pandita's Successors

In 1251, both Sakya Pandita and Köden died, and the "priest-patron" arrangement was continued by Qubilai Khan. In 1253 Pakpa (1235–1280) became the religious preceptor of Qubilai. After giving tantric initiations to the khan, he was designated as ruler (*dishi*) of all of Tibet, from the far west to the Kokonor. When Qubilai became supreme leader of all the Mongols in 1260, Pakpa's influence made him one of the most powerful members of the royal court. When he died in 1274, another Sakya lama took his place as dishi, and this pattern continued for several generations of lamas and khans.

Despite being appointed as viceroy of Tibet, Pakpa's actual influence was limited by the fact that he was required to remain in residence in the Mongol capital, and so much of the actual administration was carried out by his lieutenants. His rapid ascent to power as a result of Mongol patronage caused some resentment among leaders of other Buddhist orders, many of whom began cultivating relationships with other Mongol chieftains. Because the Mongols were highly factionalized, with warring tribes competing for supremacy, the Tibetan religious leaders inevitably became embroiled in this factionalism, which was reflected in Tibetan politics. Among the leading competitors were the lamas of the Karmapa, Tselpa, and Driküngpa sects. This was an age of political intrigues, intense infighting, and intermittent armed conflict. Many of the large monasteries had their own armies of warrior monks, and the schools with Mongol patrons sometimes used the threat of Mongol intervention. As long as the Mongol chieftains supporting the Sakyapas remained in the ascendancy, the supremacy of that lineage was assured. When Qubilai died in 1265, he was succeeded by Timur, who continued the relationship with the Sakyapas, but with his passing in 1307 the Mongols began to exhibit diminished interest in Tibet and its internecine conflicts.

Compilation of the Tibetan Buddhist Canon

Although this was a period of conflict, it also produced a number of influential Buddhist teachers. One of the great religious events of the period was the compilation of the Tibetan Buddhist canon in two sections, the *Translations of Teachings* (*bka' 'gyur;* pronounced "gangyür") and the *Translations of Treatises* (*bstan 'gyur;* pronounced "dengyür"). The first section contains teachings attributed to the Buddha, and the second comprises the voluminous commentarial literature that had come to Tibet from India, as well as some indigenous Tibetan works. The great scholar Pudön is primarily associated with this project, although no doubt much of the preparatory work had been done before he undertook the task of finalizing the collections. He meticulously checked divergent versions of the texts, eventually producing a definitive canon.[54]

When it was completed, wood blocks were carved for the entire canon, a process that required a vast amount of effort, both in the carving and in proofreading. In this traditional Tibetan printing technique, a mirror image of the page is carefully carved in relief. The block is then inked and the paper pressed against the inked surface. The initial carving requires a great deal of time, but when it is completed numerous copies can be produced, and the texts disseminated widely. The first manuscript copies were kept at the monastery of Nartang.

End of Mongol Rule

The period of Mongol rule had created widespread resentment among Tibetans, and following the fading of a strong central authority Tibet eventually regained its independence. With the passing of the Mongol threat, the Tibetan Buddhist schools which had long chafed under Sakya hegemony were able to dislodge the Sakya hierarchs from their position of power. The next faction to gain control over the country was the Pakmodrupa. Their name derived from an area administered by Sakya which was named after Dorjé Gyelpo (1110–1170), a monk from Kham who was known as Pakmodru. He built a small hermitage in 1158, in which he practiced solitary meditation until his death. From this humble beginning, the monastery of Densatil developed, and eventually it became one of the most powerful institutions in the country when his successors gained hegemony over Tibet.

A key figure in the eventual demise of Sakya power was Jangchub Gyeltsen (1302–1364), who belonged to the Lang family. At an early age he became a monk at Sakya Monastery, and in 1332 he was made administrator of a large district. After becoming involved in political intrigue, he was imprisoned and tortured, but he was eventually released. Gradually gathering support and recruiting allies, in 1354 he attacked and conquered Sakya itself. He adopted a nationalist program and attempted to eradicate all traces of Mongol influence, while at the same time hearkening back to the glories of the dynasty of the religious kings. He discarded the Mongol titles of leadership and proclaimed himself *desi* (*sde srid*), "ruler." He restored old celebrations, such as the New Year festival, in accordance with earlier customs, and he forbade officials to wear the garments and ornaments of the former royal court. He based the legal code on the ancient laws promulgated by Songtsen Gampo, and established a system of guardposts on the frontiers, particularly those bordering on China.

His successors continued his policies, but they lacked his political abilities, and within one hundred and thirty years of his death Pakmodru rule came to an end. They were replaced as rulers by the princes of Rinbung, who had been ministers of the Pakmodru. The Rinbung were in turn superseded by the governors of Tsang, who by 1565 had consolidated their power. For a short time they were rulers of a unified Tibet.

The Gélukpa Ascent to Power

During the fifteenth century, when Jangchub Gyeltsen's successors governed Tibet, Tsong Khapa (1357–1419), one of its greatest religious figures, founded a new school, which came to be known as Gélukpa, or "System of Virtue." Tsong Khapa himself had little interest in politics, and his early successors followed his example.[55] As time went on, however, their influence grew, with the result that they eventually came out on top of the power hierarchy.

At first the new order won the respect of the older schools, mostly because of its strict observance of monastic discipline, its strong emphasis on study and meditation, and its disinterest in political involvements. However, during the lifetime of Gendün Gyatso (who was considered to be the reincarnation of Tsong Khapa's disciple Gendün Druba), this began to change. The new movement, with its high standards of discipline and scholarship, began to attract the active resentment of some of the older orders, which often suffered in comparison. Gendün Gyatso's growing prestige and the high regard in which his school was held caused the Karmapa hierarchs and their lay patrons to move against him, with the result that for most of his life he was not able to live in the Gélukpa monasteries around Lhasa. Because of this, he traveled widely throughout the country, and his personal sanctity and good reputation won many converts. He was an effective missionary and spokesman for Tsong Khapa's lineage, and his charisma—coupled with the enviable reputation of his lineage for adherence to monastic discipline, scholarship, and meditative attainments—helped him to gain large numbers of disciples and admirers.

Contacts with the Mongols

Gendün Gyatso was succeeded by Sönam Gyatso (1543–1588), who was born into a prominent family with ties to the Sakyapas and the Pakmodrupas. He continued the missionary work of his predecessors, and was even able to convert some monasteries of the older orders to the Gélukpa.

In 1578 he accepted an invitation to visit Altan Khan, chief of the Tumed Mongols. This event was to have wide-ranging repercussions, and it marked a transition of Géluk from an order that avoided politics to a ruling theocracy. Although they no longer controlled China, the Mongols were still a powerful military force, despite their continual tribal conflicts. There had been no supreme leader to match the power of Chinggis or Qubilai, but Altan was the most influential of the Mongol chieftains of his day. When the lama and the khan met, the latter conferred the title of *Ta le*, or "Ocean," on Sönam Gyatso, implying that he was an "Ocean of Wisdom." Thus he and his successors (and, retrospectively, his predecessors Gendün Druba and Gendün Gyatso) came to be known as the "Dalai Lamas." Sönam Gyatso in turn gave Altan the title "King of Dharma, Divine Purity" (*chos kyi rgyal po lha'i tshang pa*). Both apparently considered themselves to be re-establishing the "priest-patron" bond that had existed between Sakya Pandita and Qubilai Khan. There was a great difference in the two relationships, however: Altan lacked the power to confer any temporal jurisdiction on his spiritual preceptor, although he did send lavish gifts to Gélukpa monasteries and monks.

Sönam Gyatso had great success in converting the Mongols to Buddhism. He influenced Altan to ban blood sacrifices and the worship of ancestral images. Because of his missionary activity, many Mongols became adherents of the Gélukpa order. The relationship between the Gélukpas and the Mongols was further strengthened after his death in 1588, when his reincarnation was discovered in the person of a great-grandson of Altan Khan, who received the ordination name Yönden Gyatso (1589–1617). This solidified the ties between the powerful khans and the Gélukpa lamas.

The Mongols believed that his birth fulfilled a promise made by Sönam Gyatso that he would return to them in a future life. Because of political considerations connected with his being born outside of Tibet, the new Dalai Lama was not brought to Lhasa until 1601, when he was twelve years old. The procession that accompanied him included prominent Mongol leaders as well as Tibetan religious and political figures. He was taken to Ganden Monastery and to the Jokhang Temple, and everywhere he went there were celebrations indicating that he was regarded as a major religious figure. The attention and ceremony that he was shown began to arouse the animosity of other powerful religious leaders, particularly lamas belonging to the Karmapa order. Relations between the Gélukpas and the Karmapas became further strained when the Gyelwa Karmapa sent letters to the Dalai Lama that were interpreted as being insulting. The Gélukpas replied in kind, which led to open antagonism between the two groups.

The conflict simmered until 1610, when the Pakmodru carried out a raid in the Lhasa valley, which angered the king of Tsang. He retaliated by attacking and annexing Ü, giving him effective control over most of Tibet. Although the Gélukpas were partly connected with the initial raid, he made them his official representatives in Lhasa. He later requested tantric empowerments from Gélukpa lamas, but was refused. This was seen as an affront to the royal dignity, and the king responded by attacking the monasteries of Drébung and Séra. The Dalai Lama was forced to flee, and Gélukpa leaders appealed to their Mongol supporters for aid. There was no immediate Mongol intervention, but the stage had been set for further conflict. Yönden Gyatso died in 1617, and it was widely rumored that he was poisoned.

The "Great Fifth" Dalai Lama

The fourth Dalai Lama's successor was found in 1617 at Chong Gyé, the burial place of the old Tibetan kings. This is an interesting coincidence, because he was destined to become the first of a succession of religious rulers of Tibet. The fifth Dalai Lama, Ngawang Losang Gyatso (1617–1682), popularly referred to as "The Great Fifth," was the most dynamic and influential of the early Dalai Lamas. He was a great teacher, an accomplished tantric yogi, and a prodigious writer. His literary output surpasses the combined total of all the other Dalai Lamas. In addition to his scholastic achievements, he proved to be an able statesman, and he united the three provinces of Tibet (the Central, South, and West) for the first time since the assassination of King Lang Darma in the mid-ninth century.

He was born into a Nyingmapa family that had connections with the Pakmodru. From the time that he was recognized as the fifth Dalai Lama, he forged strong connections with Mongol chieftains, with the result that the king of Tsang became concerned about the threat of foreign intervention in Tibetan affairs. This fear proved to be well-founded, since in 1642, with the help of his Mongol benefactors, Ngawang Losang Gyatso consolidated power and became the first Dalai Lama to rule Tibet.

Conflict between the king of Tsang and the Mongols began early on, and it reached a crisis point in 1621 when a large Mongol army entered Tibet with the stated intention of protecting the Gélukpas. A battle was avoided through the intervention of the Panchen Lama and some other prominent religious figures, but the seeds of conflict had been sown. A series of battles followed, and by 1640 the Gélukpas, with the help of the Mongols, proved victorious. The king of Tsang was unable to withstand the foreign force, largely due to weakness among his main allies.

Further destabilizing events, the king of Ladakh invaded central Tibet, and the combined threats brought down the king of Tsang. His army was defeated by the forces of the Mongol chieftain Gushri Khan, and he was later executed. According to Tibetan historical accounts, the monks of Tashihlünpo were the ones who successfully agitated for his death. The fighting did not end with the king's demise, however, and members of the Karmapa school continued to battle the Gélukpas and their Mongol patrons. The Gélukpas emerged victorious, and the Gyelwa Karmapa was forced to flee. He disguised himself as a simple monk and lived in hiding for many years, until he was eventually reconciled with the fifth Dalai Lama.

The rulership of the fifth Dalai Lama was conceived after the model of the "priest-patron" relationship that had been established between the Mongol princes and Pakpa, but the fifth Dalai Lama in actuality wielded far greater power than Pakpa had. The Dalai Lama lived in the center of Tibetan power in Lhasa, whereas Pakpa spent most of his life at the Mongol court. The Dalai Lama also enjoyed the support of his powerful Mongol patron, and this ally had a large army to back up his wishes.

Despite the power of his benefactors, it took some time for the Dalai Lama to extend his rule over all of Tibet, but by the time of Gushri's death in 1656 he controlled an area that extended from the region of Mount Kailash in the west to Kham in the east. He began a process of determining the number of monks and monasteries throughout the country, and in several cases he forced members of some orders to convert to his own sect. The most notable of these were the monks of the Jonangpa school, whose doctrines had been judged to be heterodox by Gélukpa scholars. The Dalai Lama forced the Jonangpa monks to become Gélukpas, and the seat of the order, Jonang Monastery, was officially declared a Gélukpa monastery and renamed Ganden Püntsokling. The monks of Jonang were forbidden to teach the tenets of their school and had to adopt the Gélukpa curriculum and philosophical views. The fifth Dalai Lama also punished several Karmapa monasteries that had opposed him, but he later allowed them to rebuild.

Although he was rather heavy-handed with the Jonangpas and the Karmapas, his treatment of other orders was often generous. He was particularly supportive of Nyingma, and he himself was an ardent practitioner of several Nyingma tantric lineages. Snellgrove and Richardson contend that on the whole his actions proved to be beneficial and stabilizing, despite the obvious hard feelings they engendered among his opponents:

> The older orders may preserve some bitter memories of the fifth Dalai Lama, for no one likes a diminution of wealth and power, but there is no doubt that without his moderating and controlling hand, their lot might have been very much worse. It must also be said that at that time, despite their new political interests and responsibilities, the *dGe-lugs-pas* remained the freshest and most zealous of the Tibetan religious orders.[56]

Recognizing the power of the Dalai Lama, the Chinese Qing emperor invited him to visit Beijing, which he did in 1652. The newly unified Tibet was a rising power in Central Asia, and it is clear that this was a meeting between equals, despite later Chinese interpretations of the event. The Chinese emperor even wished to travel to the border to greet the Dalai Lama, despite standard imperial protocol, which does not admit even the possibility of China having equal diplomatic status with any other country.

The power of the Mongols diminished rapidly after Gushri's death, and they fell into the internecine rivalries that had divided them in the past. This eliminated a potential foreign threat to Tibet, and it left the Dalai Lama in control of the country. The Dalai Lama even began to minimize the role that the Mongols had played in his ascension to power and attempted to associate his rule with the past glories of the Religious Kings of Tibet.

During his reign, the connection between the Dalai Lamas and Avalokiteśvara was stressed, and this was reflected in the construction of the Potala, which was their main residence and the seat of the Tibetan government until the Chinese invasion in the 1950s. The name that was chosen for the palace was taken from a mountain in southern India that is associated with Śiva in his incarnation as Lokeśvara, or "Lord of the World," who is considered by Tibetans to be an emanation of Avalokiteśvara. This association helped to establish the Dalai Lamas as incarnations of a buddha, and they are regarded as such by Tibetan Buddhists, who have traditionally looked on the Potala as the residence of Avalokiteśvara in human form. As Snellgrove and Richardson observe, "it was clear to all Tibetans that here was a true religious king enthroned in his mountain palace in their midst."[57] The fifth Dalai Lama died in 1682 during a planned three-year retreat.

The Manchus

At this time China was still militarily weak, which allowed it to be conquered by a new power, the Manchus. They initially defeated the warring Mongol factions, and in 1633 officially took over the Chinese throne. In 1664 they overthrew the last Ming ruler and established the Qing dynasty, which was to last until 1911. There had been little contact between Tibet and China since the fall of the Yuan dynasty, and the Manchus were initially content to leave Tibet alone. During the conflicts that led to Gélukpa preeminence, the competing factions had sent envoys to the Manchus (who were not then rulers of China), but nothing came of this.

Despite current Chinese claims of long-standing sovereignty over Tibet, the fifth Dalai Lama wielded absolute power until his death, although he skillfully delegated authority to competent ministers. One of these ministers, Sangyé Gyatso, assumed power after his death, but he concealed his master's decease for several years, fearing that the news might halt construction of the Potala. When his duplicity was discovered, he was removed from office, and was later executed by the Mongol chieftain Hlasang.

The Seventeenth and Eighteenth Centuries

During the seventeenth and eighteenth centuries, Tibet became increasingly isolated from its neighbors. When it first adopted Buddhism, it was surrounded by Buddhist civilizations, but by this time it was the only country in the region in which Buddhism was predominant. Despite a growing conviction that Tibet was the only land in which the true dharma flourished, outside influences were still generally welcomed. There were communities of Muslims in Tibet, whose members often performed tasks like butchering animals that were repugnant to Tibetan Buddhist sensibilities. Many Newaris from Nepal, whose religion was a mix of Hindu and Buddhist elements, were valued craftsmen, famous for their superb religious artwork.

In the seventeenth century, Tibet was also visited by Christian missionaries. The first to arrive was the Jesuit Antonio d'Andrade, who traveled to Tsaparang in western Tibet in 1624. He was followed by two more Jesuits, Father Cacella and Father Cabral, in 1627, and by Capuchin clerics in 1707. At first some of the missionaries believed that they had stumbled on an ancient Christian community whose practice had degenerated. The missions were remarkably unsuccessful, however, because most of the visitors never bothered to learn the Tibetan language well enough to communicate effectively. Instead, they tended to preach dogmatically and denounce Buddhism, with the result that they were perceived as rude and uncouth.

An exception was the Jesuit Ippolito Desideri, who stayed in Lhasa from 1716 to 1721. Unlike other Christian missionaries, he managed to learn Tibetan well, and he impressed the Tibetans he met with his erudition and demeanor.[58] Neither he nor his fellow missionaries, however, managed to convince more than a handful of Tibetans to convert.

Mongol Intervention

With the death of the fifth Dalai Lama, the inherent problems of a political system headed by reincarnating lamas became evident. The Great Fifth had consolidated power in his own hands as a result of skillful diplomacy and his religious authority, but with his passing an interregnum period set in, during which his successor had to learn the intricacies of politics as well as the duties of the religious leader of the country. Unfortunately, the sixth Dalai Lama, Tsangyang Gyatso, proved temperamentally unsuited for the position, and was not inclined to either statecraft or religion. Instead, his interests tended toward women and poetry. He was enthroned as the sixth Dalai Lama in 1697, but he showed little proclivity toward religious affairs. When Tsangyang Gyatso reached the age of twenty, he renounced his monastic vows and moved out of the Potala to a small apartment in Lhasa.

His abdication left a vacuum in Tibetan politics. Even after the long interregnum period following the death of his successor, Tibet was still without an effective leader. The problem was compounded by the fact that he governed not just by right of royal succession, as is the case with most human dynasties; his position as Dalai Lama provided him with a divine right to rule, despite his own ambivalence toward his position. The roots of the problem lay in the application of the system of governance by reincarnating lamas—which had originally developed in relatively stable monastic institutions—to the political realm, in which strong and continuous leadership is essential.[59]

Since the time of Gushri Khan, Mongol interest in Tibetan affairs had diminished, but this changed when Hlasang, leader of the Dzungar Oriats, achieved supremacy among the Mongol commanders in 1697. He objected to Tsangyang Gyatso's open flaunting of what he considered proper behavior for a Dalai Lama, especially his renunciation of his monastic vows. Despite his unusual behavior, however, the Tibetan people still considered him to be a true incarnation, whose actions were viewed as very subtle "skill in means."

Apparently unaware of the widespread popular support for the young Dalai Lama, in 1706 Hlasang, with the approval of the Manchu emperor Kangxi (1661–1722), sent a small armed force into Tibet. The Mongols executed the Regent Sangyé Gyatso for his duplicity in concealing the death of the fifth Dalai Lama and captured Tsangyang Gyatso, declaring him a false incarnation. Kangxi then sent an imperial decree recognizing Hlasang as governor of Tibet. Hlasang agreed to an offer to become a vassal of China, but the imposition of foreign rule was widely resented by Tibetans, who neither recognized the new Mongol viceroy nor the authority of the Manchu emperor, who at any rate had no legal claim to overlordship of Tibet.[60] His Mongol predecessors had sporadically exercised control over

Tibet, but formal ties had languished after the fall of the Yuan dynasty, and there was little official contact during the Ming dynasty. Relations between Tibet and the Manchus had been of a diplomatic nature, and the Chinese rulers had exercised no effective authority in Tibet.

In a move that underestimated the depth of popular Tibetan resentment toward his rule and of devotion to the Dalai Lama, Hlasang tried to persuade the leading lamas to support his move to usurp Tsangyang Gyatso, but his overtures were refused. Despite this, Hlasang decided to remove the Dalai Lama from office. Tsangyang Gyatso was arrested and transported to China, but he died on the way, and it was widely rumored that he was murdered by the Mongols. Hlasang attempted to replace him with another young lama named Ngawang Yéshé Gyatso, declaring that he was the true incarnation. This announcement was rejected by the Tibetans, who still considered Tsangyang Gyatso to be the Dalai Lama. When news of his death reached Tibet, the search for his successor began, despite the fact that Hlasang's protégé was still installed as Dalai Lama.

The sixth Dalai Lama is best known for his romantic poetry, in which he celebrates his affairs with women. He adopted the dress and lifestyle of a layman and playboy, wearing his hair in long braids and adorning himself with jewelry. His erotic verse celebrated the ecstasy and pain of romantic love, and his songs to his lovers are still sung today. For obvious reasons, his behavior was widely considered by people of his time to be improper for a Dalai Lama, but it would probably have been tolerated if political conditions had been different. Unfortunately for Tsangyang Gyatso, he became Dalai Lama during unstable times, and his open rejection of the duties of his position and the outward appearances that were expected of him earned him powerful enemies.

The Seventh Dalai Lama

Following Tsangyang Gyatso's death, the search for his successor began. One of his poems was interpreted as foretelling that he would be reborn in Litang in eastern Tibet, and this became the area on which the search was focused.

> White crane, lend me your wings;
> I go no further than Litang
> And from there, return again.

Kelsang Gyatso, born in Litang in 1708, was judged to be the fulfillment of this prophecy, but due to ongoing political problems with the Mongols he could not be officially recognized. Kelsang Gyatso was not enthroned until 1720, after the Dzungar Mongols were expelled from Lhasa. This was effected with the help of the Manchus, which led to future political problems. The ramifications are still felt in modern times, since Chinese leaders used it as a part of their claim to Tibet during and after the invasion in the 1950s.

Kelsang Gyatso proved to be different from his predecessor and is renowned as an exemplary monk who lived a simple life in accordance with the rules of monastic discipline. He also wrote important works on several tantric sets, including *Heruka Cakrasaṃvara, Vajrabhairava, Kālacakra, and Guhyasamāja.* He is perhaps best known for his spiritual poetry and his hymns and prayers. He died in 1757 at the age of fifty.

Manchu Interest Wanes

Kangxi died in 1722, and his son Yongzheng became emperor. Soon after his ascension to power, he removed the Chinese garrison that his father had established in Lhasa in the aftermath of the conflicts associated with the death of the sixth Dalai Lama. One effect of this move was a resurgence of internecine rivalries in Tibet, which led to the murder of the minister Kangchen and the eventual victory of a Tibetan lay official named Pohla. For the next twenty years Pohla ruled Tibet, and his reign is generally seen as a time of good government under a competent leader.

The events leading up to this period established a pattern for Sino-Tibetan relations. During times when Tibet was stable, the Chinese rulers showed little interest in Tibetan affairs; imperial meddling and the Chinese military presence dwindled. When internal troubles arose, the emperor would personally intervene to restore order. During Pohla's reign, contacts with China were reduced to mere formalities, and although he allowed the continuing fiction of Chinese supremacy, the emperor's representatives (*amban*) had the status of observers who occasionally made suggestions to Tibetan leaders, but who exercised little influence in the country's affairs.

Return to Religious Rule

The brief period of lay rule by Pohla came to an end with his death in 1747. His son succeeded him, but proved to be poorly suited to the position. He was murdered by two Chinese *ambans*, who were concerned that he was intriguing with the Dzungar Mongols. In retaliation, a Tibetan mob killed the *ambans*, but the Dalai Lama was soon able to restore order. The Chinese emperor had prepared to send an armed force to Tibet, but was dissuaded from this by the Dalai Lama, who assured him that the situation was under control. A small unit of soldiers arrived, but there was no fighting between Chinese and Tibetans. After their arrival, a public execution was staged, and the Tibetan government was reorganized. In the new system, the Dalai Lama was restored to power, and a council of four ministers was created. The seventh Dalai Lama ruled until his death in 1757, after which Tibet began a period of 130 years during which none of the Dalai Lamas assumed effective control. During this time, the country was ruled by a succession of regents, all of whom were Gélukpa monks. The eighth Dalai Lama, Jambel Gyatso, was uninterested in worldly affairs, and so although he lived to the age of forty-seven, the administration of the country was handled by regents. The next four Dalai Lamas died young. By and large, the regents managed to maintain stability, and as a result Chinese interest in Tibet diminished. The *ambans* generally played no role in Tibetan politics, and the post was apparently viewed as a punishment by Chinese officials.[61]

Trouble from the South

Tibet's next major crisis was precipitated by an ambitious ruler of the Gurkha region of Nepal.[62] In the period from 1768–69, he managed to extend his rule over the entire Nepal Valley, and eventually annexed an area roughly equal to the present-day state of Nepal. Flush with success, he set his sights on Tibet, and in 1792 Nepalese troops entered the country and sacked the Panchen Lama's monastery of Tashihlünpo. This prompted the Chinese emperor Qianlong to send a military force to counteract the Gurkha invasion. The Gurkhas were expelled, and the Tibetan administration was reorganized. The *ambans* were given greater authority to intervene in Tibetan affairs, but this new influence was short-lived. When Tibet was calm again, Chinese interest in its affairs waned, and the emperor's authority diminished. An example of how little effect the emperor's wishes had in Tibet occurred in 1807, when two candidates emerged as favorites in the search for the ninth Dalai Lama. Qianlong had sent a golden urn to Tibet in 1793 with instructions that it should be used to select Dalai Lamas in a lottery system. The names of the leading candidates were to be placed in the urn, and the winner chosen by a random drawing. Despite this clear attempt to influence Tibetan affairs, the selection process followed the traditional method, and the emperor's urn was ignored.

After Qianlong's death in 1799 China was plunged into a period of social chaos. Rebellions broke out all over the country, and although the Manchu dynasty survived until 1911, it was greatly weakened. This meant that the Manchu emperors had little interest in Tibetan affairs. *Ambans* were still sent to Tibet, but they played no real role in its governance.[63] With the withdrawal of Chinese interest, Tibet became even more closed off from the outside, an attitude that was strengthened by the Gurkha invasion, which soured relations with its southern neighbor.

By the end of the century, the Chinese presence in Tibet had been reduced to two *ambans* and their garrison of one hundred soldiers. These troops were mostly sons of Chinese soldiers and Tibetan mothers. They were born in Tibet, but because of their mixed heritage were generally shunned by both Chinese and Tibetans. Most spoke Tibetan and had never even visited China, and they were poorly trained and equipped. The Manchus were beset by troubles at home and were unable to spare any imperial troops for Tibet. The emperor continued to send missives to the Tibetan ministerial council and the Dalai Lamas, but neither he nor his representatives exerted any real influence in Tibetan politics. The actual situation was summed up by Claude White, the British Political Officer in Sikkim, who was quoted by Colonel Francis Younghusband as stating that China had "no authority whatever" in Tibet and that "China was suzerain over Tibet only in name."[64]

NOTES

1. See David Snellgrove and Hugh Richardson, *A Cultural History of Tibet* (New York: Frederick A. Praeger, 1968), p. 23.
2. It is also referred to in early Arab histories as Tüpüt and Tubbat. See W. Barthold, *Encyclopedia of Islam*, vol. 4 (Leiden, 1913–36), p. 742.
3. For a discussion of the term *chol kha gsum*, see Luciano Petech, "The Mongol Census in Tibet," *Tibetan Studies in Honour of Hugh Richardson* (Warminster: Aris & Phillips, 1980), p. 234. Petech contends that the three provinces were Ü, Tsang, and Ngari, but according to Tibetan records, the area of the "three districts" also included Kham and Amdo.
4. Giuseppe Tucci, *Tibetan Painted Scrolls* (Rome: IsMEO, 1949), p. 155.
5. This process is described in Peter Molner and Paul Tapponier, "The Collision Between India and Eurasia," *Scientific American*, April 1977, pp. 30–41.
6. See Geshe Wangyal, *The Door of Liberation* (New York: Maurice Girodias, 1973), p. 59.
7. This story is found in the historical text *rDzogs ldan gzhon nu'i dga' ston* by the fifth Dalai Lama, Ngawang Losang Gyatso. For an overview of the legends surrounding the first king, see Per K. Sørensen, "Dynastic Origins and Regal Succession," *Studies in Central and East Asian Religions* 4, 1991, pp. 67–68.
8. See Giuseppe Tucci, *Deb ther dmar po gsar ma* (Rome: IsMEO, 1971), p. 141.
9. The best study to date on this dynasty is Erik Haarh's *The Yarlung Dynasty* (Copenhagen: G.E.C. Gad's Forlag, 1969). Matthew Kapstein's *The Tibetan Assimilation of Buddhism: Conversion, Contestation, and Memory* (Oxford: Oxford University Press, 2000) has several excellent articles on the Tibetan appropriation of Buddhism.
10. An early study of this area was conducted by Giuseppe Tucci, who reported his findings in *The Tombs of the Early Tibetan Kings* (Rome: IsMEO, 1950). Some of Tucci's conclusions were later disputed by Hugh Richardson in his article "Early Burial Grounds in Tibet and Tibetan Decorative Art of the VIIth and IXth Centuries," *Central Asiatic Journal*, 1972, pp. 30–39.
11. See David Snellgrove, *Buddhist Himalaya* (Oxford: Bruno Cassirer, 1957), pp. 128ff. and Erik Haarh, *The Yarlung Dynasty*, pp. 136–137.
12. See Giuseppe Tucci, "The Sacral Character of the Kings of Ancient Tibet," *East and West* 6.3, 1955, pp. 197–205.
13. David Snellgrove, *Indo-Tibetan Buddhism* (Boston: Shambhala, 1987), vol. 2, p. 382.
14. For more information on this period, see Christopher Beckwith, *The Tibetan Empire in Central Asia* (Princeton: Princeton University Press, 1987) and Géza Uray, "The Old Tibetan Sources of the History of Central Asia up to 751 A.D.: A Survey," in J. Harmatta, ed., *Prolegomena to the Sources on the History of Pre-Islamic Central Asia* (Budapest, 1979), pp. 275–304.
15. See Snellgrove and Richardson, *A Cultural History of Tibet*, pp. 26–27.
16. Despite the historical evidence, recent Chinese historians have claimed that Tibet paid tribute to China during the Tang dynasty, but the Tang records indicate that this claim is baseless.
17. Snellgrove (*Indo-Tibetan Buddhism*, p. 387) speculates that the Duyu hun correspond to the Asha ('A zha) people mentioned in early Tibetan records.
18. Luciano Petech, *A Study of the Chronicles of Ladakh* (Calcutta, 1939), pp. 73–74.
19. Shakabpa, *A Political History of Tibet*, pp. 24–25.

20. She is also known as Kongchu, or Kongjo. The highly divergent accounts of this period are discussed at length in my book, *History as Propaganda: Tibetan Exiles Versus the People's Republic of China* (New York: Oxford University Press, 2004), chapter 1.
21. This temple and its history are discussed by Hugh Richardson in his article, "The Jokhang, 'Cathedral' of Lhasa," in Ariane Macdonald and Yoshiro Imaeda, eds., *Essais sur l'art du Tibet* (Paris, 1977), pp. 157–88. He discusses the vicissitudes of the image in "The Growth of a Legend," *Asia Minor* 16, 1971, pp. 174–75.
22. F.W. Bushell, "The Early History of Tibet from Chinese Sources," *Journal of the Royal Asiatic Society*, n.s., 12, 1880, p. 457. For an example of the mythology of Wencheng from the "treasure text" *Maṇi bka' 'bum*, see Jacques Bacot, "Le marriage chinois du roi tibétain Sron bcan sgan po," *Mélanges chinois et bouddiques*, #3, 1935, pp. 1–60. Wang Furen and Suo Wenqing exemplify the contemporary Chinese party line on Wencheng's life and influence: "She was a pioneer adherent to unity and friendship between Hans and Tibetans and an enthusiastic disseminator of Tang culture": *Highlights of Tibetan History* (Beijing: New World Press, 1984), p. 14.
23. Bushell, p. 445. In some early histories written in China and Khotan, Tibetans are referred to as "Red Faces," indicating that this practice was widespread. See Paul Pelliot, *Histoire ancienne du Tibet* (Paris, 1961), pp. 130–31.
24. He states that she was she was "a dim figure . . . who made no mark on either Tibetan or Chinese history in the remaining thirty years of her life [following Songtsen Gampo's death] and whose religious affiliation is uncertain." Hugh Richardson, *High Peaks, Pure Earth: Collected Writings on Tibetan History and Culture* (London: Serindia Publications, 1998), p. 212.
25. See Ariane Macdonald, *Une Lecture des Pelliot Tibétain 1286, 1287, 1036, 1047, et 1290; Essai sur la formation et l'emploi des mythes politiques dans la religion royale de Sroṅ-bcan Sgam-po: Études Tibetaines* (Paris: Adrien Maisonneuve, 1971), p. 256. Macdonald concludes that his religion was based on indigenous beliefs, and not Buddhism. See also Turrell Wylie, "Some Political Factors in the Early History of Tibetan Buddhism," A. K. Narain, ed., *Studies in History of Buddhism* (Delhi: B. R. Publishing Co., 1980), p. 366, where he concludes that Songtsen Gampo was probably an illiterate king who adhered to the imperial cult of Bön.
26. See Giuseppe Tucci, "The Symbolism of the Temples of Bsam-yas," *East and West* 6.4, 1956, pp. 279–281.
27. Erik Haarh, "The Identity of Tsu-chih-chien, the Tibetan 'King' who died in 804 AD," *Acta Orientalia* 25.1–2, 1963, pp. 121–170.
28. These are discussed in chapters 3, "Meditation," and 4, "Mahāyāna."
29. This debate has received a great deal of attention from contemporary scholars. Some important studies are: Paul Demiéville, *La Concile de Lhasa* (Paris, 1952); Giuseppe Tucci, *Minor Buddhist Texts II* (Rome, 1958); Daishun Ueyama, "The Study of Tibetan Ch'an Manuscripts Recovered from Tun-huang: A Review of the Field and Its Prospects," Whalen Lai and Lewis Lancaster, eds., *Early Ch'an in China and Tibet* (Berkeley, 1983), pp. 327–350; Jeffrey Broughton, "Early Ch'an Schools in Tibet," in Robert Gimello and Peter Gregory, eds., *Studies in Ch'an and Hua-yen* (Honolulu, 1983), pp. 1-68; G.W. Houston, "The System of Ha Śang Mahāyāna," *Central Asiatic Journal*, 21.2, 1971, pp. 106–110; Imaeda Yoshiro, "Documents Tibétains de Touen-houang Concernant le Concile du Tibet," *Journal Asiatique*, 1975, pp. 125–145. An overview of sources may be found in G.W. Houston, *Sources for a History of the Bsam yas Debate* (Sankt Augustin: VGH-Wissenschaftsverlag, 1980).

30. See Obermiller's translation (*History of Buddhism*; Heidelberg, 1931), vol. II, pp. 188ff. and the *Blue Annals*, tr. George Roerich (Delhi: Motilal Banarsidass, 1976), pp. 41ff.
31. There are differing opinions about the date of the council (and, as we shall see, some scholars doubt that it occurred at all). Tsepon Shakabpa, following traditional sources, states that it was held over a two-year period, from 792–794 (see *A Political History of Tibet*, p. 37).
32. Luis O. Gómez, "Indian Materials on the Doctrine of Sudden Awakening," in Lai and Lancaster, eds., *Early Ch'an in China and Tibet*, p. 396.
33. Two examples are Dudjom Rinpoche's *The Nyingma School of Tibetan Buddhism* (Boston: Wisdom, 1991), pp. 887ff., and Takpo Tashi Namgyal, *Mahāmudrā: The Quintessence of Mind and Meditation*, pp. 105ff. See also Per Kværne, "'The Great Perfection' in the Tradition of the Bonpos," in *Early Ch'an in China and Tibet*, p. 368.
34. See Obermiller's translation, pp. 191–192.
35. Ibid., p. 191.
36. Ibid., p. 193.
37. See Demiéville, *La Concile de Lhasa*, p. 442. A Tibetan text associated with the dzogchen tradition entitled *Bka' thang sde lnga* also reports that the Chinese suddenists were victorious (see Tucci, *Minor Buddhist Texts II*, p. 80).
38. The political ramifications are discussed by Shakabpa, *A Political History of Tibet*, pp. 39–41.
39. This is reflected in both Tibetan and Chinese sources. An example is a Chinese historical record entitled *Jiu Tang Shu*, which has been translated by Don Y. Lee (Bloomington, IN: Eastern Press, 1981).
40. See A.H. Franke, *Antiquities of Indian Tibet* (Calcutta, 1914 and 1926), pp. 33–34.
41. See chapter 12, "Nyingma."
42. As Snellgrove and Richardson note, this scenario conceives of Buddhism's diffusion in Tibet primarily in terms of royal patronage, but even during the period of persecution Buddhism continued to spread throughout the country. While the construction of temples and monasteries may have been halted, Buddhist teachers apparently continued to circulate the dharma, and followers of Bön were incorporating Buddhist ideas and practices into their own tradition, with the result that it eventually became for all intents and purposes a divergent school of Buddhism.
43. The extent of his subsequent demonization may be seen in Tsepon Shakabpa's statement that after his death rumors circulated that he had horns on his head and a black tongue. Shakabpa asserts that the Tibetan custom of greeting people by scratching one's head and sticking out one's tongue originated as a way of indicating that—unlike Lang Darma—they lacked horns and black tongues (*A Political History of Tibet*, p. 53).
44. For a discussion of the political upheavals brought on by Lang Darma's assassination and the disputed succession to the throne, see H.E. Richardson, "The Succession to Glang Darma," *Orientalia Iosephi Tucci Memoriæ Dicata* (Rome: IsMEO, 1988), pp. 1221-29.
45. A study of his life and literary accomplishments may be found in Giuseppe Tucci, *Rin-chen-bzaṅ-po and the Renaissance of Buddhism in Tibet Around the Millennium* (New Delhi: Aditya Prakashan, 1988).
46. The details of their efforts and the overall history of the period are still very obscure, and records from the time are sketchy at best. Davidson's study is the best to date, and it examines a number of sources that have not previously been studied by contemporary scholars: Ronald Davidson, *Tibetan Renaissance: Tantric Buddhism in the Rebirth*

of Tibetan Culture (New York: Columbia University Press, 2004), particularly pp. 84–116.

47. Although the story of Yéshé Ö's act of self-sacrifice is repeated by Tibetans as an inspiring tale of religious devotion, Rinchen Sangpo's biography indicates that it may in fact be apocryphal, because in it Yéshé Ö is said to have died of a severe illness at his own palace at Toling. Rinchen Sangpo is reported to have performed the funeral ceremonies (see Snellgrove and Richardson, *The Cultural Heritage of Ladakh* [Boulder: Prajna Press, 1977, vol. 2], p. 92).
48. Snellgrove and Richardson, *A Cultural History of Tibet*, p.129.
49. Although the Nyingmapas claim greater antiquity than the later orders, during this period it can hardly be considered a separate "order," since the teachers of this time who are claimed by later Nyingmapas were a disparate group of people with no real affiliation to anything resembling a distinguishable sect.
50. T.V. Wylie, "The First Mongol Conquest of Tibet Reinterpreted," *Harvard Journal of Asiatic Studies* 37, 1977, p. 119.
51. See János Szerb, "Glosses on the Œuvre of Bla-ma 'Phags-pa: III. The 'Patron-Patronized' Relationship," in Barbara Aziz and Matthew Kapstein, eds., *Soundings in Tibetan Civilization* (Delhi: Manohar, 1985), pp. 165–73.
52. For a discussion of both Chinese and Tibetan histories of the Mongol period, see *History As Propaganda*, chapter 2.
53. Hugh Richardson, *Tibet and Its History*, p. 36. See also his article, "Regurgitating an Imperial Political Myth," *Tibetan Review* XVII.9, 1982, pp. 13–14, and Shakabpa, *Tibet: A Political History*, p. 73.
54. For an account of his life, see David S. Ruegg, *The Life of Bu-ston Rin-po-che* (Rome: IsMEO, 1966).
55. See chapter 15, "Géluk."
56. *A Cultural History of Tibet*, p. 197.
57. Ibid., p. 200.
58. His letters provide an interesting glimpse into Tibetan life during this period: *An Account of Tibet; The Travels of Ippolito Desideri of Pistoria, S.J., 1712–1727* (London, 1937).
59. See Snellgrove and Richardson, *A Cultural History of Tibet*, p. 204.
60. These events are described in Luciano Petech, *China and Tibet in the Early 18th Century* (Westport, CT: Hyperion Press, 1973), pp. 8–21.
61. See Snellgrove and Richardson, *A Cultural History of Tibet*, p. 225.
62. The background of the conflict centered on disputes over adulterated Nepalese currency and the capture of the Red Hat lama. These events are described by Shakabpa in *Tibet: A Political History*, pp. 156–158.
63. The fact of Tibetan control over internal affairs and the lack of Manchu influence are even admitted by Melvyn Goldstein, who is one of the most pro-Chinese of contemporary Western scholars working in Tibetan studies. See his *A History of Modern Tibet, 1913-1951* (Berkeley: University of California Press, 1989), p. 44. This is a well-researched study of the modern period of Tibet's history, but its pro-Chinese bias is most clearly seen in Goldstein's decision to cut his study short at the beginning of the Chinese invasion, thus allowing him to overlook the human rights abuses perpetrated in its wake. He deals with the invasion and early period of occupation in a sequel, *The Snow Lion and the Dragon: China, Tibet, and the Dalai Lama* (Berkeley: University of California Press, 1997), but tends to gloss over or justify Chinese atrocities. The four-

teenth Dalai Lama is presented as a liar and an incompetent leader. In *A History of Modern Tibet*, Goldstein presents the takeover of Tibet as an inevitable outcome of growing Chinese confidence and Tibetan incompetence and venality.

64. Cited by Shakabpa, p. 204.

6: The Twentieth Century

Foreign Conflicts

In 1875, Trinlé Gyatso, the twelfth Dalai Lama, died after a short reign of two years. His successor, Tupden Gyatso (1876–1933), proved to be much longer-lived, and he became one of the greatest rulers in Tibetan history. After the death of Trinlé Gyatso, search parties began looking for his reincarnation in southeastern Tibet, as this location had been revealed in a vision at Hlamö Latso, a lake located about ninety miles southeast of Lhasa.

The thirteenth Dalai Lama was born in 1876 in Takpo Langdün in southeast Tibet and recognized in 1878 as the reincarnation of Trinlé Gyatso. Tupden Gyatso was born into a peasant family, and he was enthroned as Dalai Lama during a time of increasing tension for Tibet. He ascended to full power in 1895 and began a program to modernize the country. Some of his public statements indicate that he recognized Tibet's friendlessness in the international community and the danger posed by the winds of change brewing in China, which would eventually engulf his country. Nor was China the only external danger, as was made clear in 1903, when a British expedition led by Colonel Francis Younghusband entered Tibet and demanded that the government open trade relations with British India.

Younghusband's troops marched into the western part of central Tibet, where they met ineffectual resistance from local militias. The British forces captured Gyantsé Fort, and later marched to Lhasa, but the Dalai Lama had fled. Younghusband then forced government officials to agree to a trade compact (generally referred to as the Anglo-Tibetan Convention of

1904) that was highly favorable to Britain, following which he withdrew to India.

Events in Eastern Tibet

It is now clear in hindsight that the British had no interest in adding Tibet to their substantial empire in South Asia, but they believed their strategic interests required that they prevent China or Russia from gaining a toehold there. Some of the provisions of the compact signed by Younghusband and the Tibetan government bordered on establishing a protectorate in Tibet, but the British government repudiated these in the following year. While the British were content to remain at arm's length, however, China grew increasingly concerned that foreign powers coveted a large piece of real estate that it was unable to rule or administer, but over which it still wished to retain sovereignty.

The situation in eastern Tibet had been fluid for centuries. The weak Tibetan central government lacked the ability to administer outlying regions effectively, and in practice they were often effectively autonomous. This situation suited the traditionally independent residents of the eastern provinces, who preferred to stay clear of the intrigues of central Tibetan politics and Chinese influences. During the imperial period, Kham had been under the administrative control of the Yarlung government, but following its collapse it regained its autonomy, and in subsequent centuries it effectively faded from the sphere of interest of central Tibet. As a result, historical records for Kham (as well as Amdo and other areas in the eastern part of the Tibetan plateau) tend to be fragmentary, and it is difficult to find reliable evidence for the history of this region.

During the period of Sakya administration of Tibet beginning in the thirteenth century, the Sakya hierarchs established some large estates in the western part of Kham, but their leaders seem to have become autonomous after Sakya hegemony faded, and they had contacts with China's Ming dynasty after that. During the reign of the fifth Dalai Lama, much of Kham came under the control of the central Tibetan government, and several major Gélukpa monasteries were built there.

Following the crisis sparked by the Dzungar invasion of Tibet and the capture of the sixth Dalai Lama, a formal boundary was established between Kham and the lands controlled by the Lhasa government. It was marked by a boundary pillar at Bumla—a pass in the southwest of Ba, and extending along the west of the Dri River (the upper portion of the Yangtse). In 1918 the boundary was formalized in an agreement which certified that the area to the west of the boundary belonged to the Dalai Lama, while the other side was under the control of the Manchu emperor of China.[1] The rulers of these regions and important tribal chieftains were given seals of authority by the emperor and ruled as semi-independent feudatories.

The Manchus continued to claim sovereignty over central Tibet and characterized the Lhasa government as a vassal state but, as we have seen, they lacked the power to enforce their claims, and their representatives, the *ambans*, had no real authority. Following the expulsion of the Gurkhas by Manchu forces, China's influence in central Tibetan affairs increased for a short period, but it soon returned to its previous nominal status.

It is difficult to gauge the level of control China exerted over its purported subordinates in eastern Tibet. The few accounts from the eighteenth and nineteenth centuries that exist indicate that it was probably nonexistent, except for areas near China.[2] Much of Kham was under the control of local chieftains, hereditary kings who ruled estates of varying sizes, and reincarnate lamas whose monasteries controlled surrounding lands. Amdo, to the north of Kham, appears to have enjoyed even greater autonomy. Mainly populated by semi-nomadic pastoralists, Amdo had few large population centers, although there were two major Gélukpa monasteries at Kumbum and Labrang, which maintained ties with the Dalai Lama's government.[3]

The Nyarong Troubles

As the Manchus' problems worsened, they lost the will and ability to interfere in the affairs of this remote region, and so when a local chieftain named Gompo Namgyel (who ruled a region near Nyarong in eastern Kham) gained control over a large part of Kham, the Manchus were unable to do anything about it. An army dispatched from central Tibet overthrew and killed him in 1865, but the Qing rulers merely watched from a distance and then conferred empty certificates on the victors. After this the Lhasa government set up an administrative office in Nyarong, and the rulers of the five Hor states and Dergé were restored to power under its ultimate authority. The top administrator in Nyarong was the Nyarong Chikyab, and after 1913 this office was superseded by the Domé Chikyab, a provincial governor. Although he had ultimate authority, in practice areas like Dergé continued to be ruled by traditional kings (*rgyal po*).

Chinese Military Adventures in Eastern Tibet

The Chinese government continued to claim all of Tibet as part of its territory, and the Lhasa government apparently saw no reason to anger China by pointing out that it had no administrators in Tibet, or that all aspects of Tibetan government and administration were solely in Tibetan hands, with no oversight, funding, or administrative control from Beijing. This changed following the Younghusband expedition and the signing of the Anglo-Tibetan Convention. The Manchu rulers decided to establish a network of sectors under Chinese control in eastern Tibet. In 1909 Chinese troops led by Ma Weiqi and later Zhao Erfeng invaded the area, destroyed several major monasteries, and killed thousands of monks and lay Tibetans. Tibetan administrators were removed from office and replaced by Chinese.

In 1907 Zhao sent a military expedition into Kham, which seized thousands of loads of grain from the local inhabitants without making any repayment. The Throne Holder of Ganden and the Kashag sent a letter of protest to the *amban,* Lianyu, but he refused to forward it to Beijing. Although this was interpreted by Tibetans as a sign that the *ambans* were in collaboration with Zhao, it was probably a reflection of the emperor's weakness. As the Manchu dynasty was breaking up, some of its generals acted independently of the central government and pursued their own programs of conquest and pillage.

In 1910, Zhao's forces reached Lhasa, but the Dalai Lama had fled to India along with his ministers, and so there was no one with whom to negotiate surrender. Zhao's advance to Lhasa had been accompanied by widespread brutality, and a number of monasteries had been sacked. Many Tibetans had been tortured or killed. The general thus came to be known among Tibetans as "Zhao the Butcher."[4]

Zhao's forces attempted to usurp control of Tibet, but were met with widespread resistance by the Tibetan people, who refused to cooperate with the invaders. In order to consolidate his power, he publicly announced that the Dalai Lama, who was still in India, was being removed from office. This proclamation, however, was widely ignored by the Tibetans, who continued to pray for his return. In 1911 Zhao's attempts to gain control unraveled after Sun Yat-sen and the Nationalists overthrew the Manchu dynasty. When the news reached Lhasa, some of the Chinese troops mutinied, and Zhao retreated to his capital in Szechuan. He was executed in 1912 by the Nationalist leader Yin Qangheng. The dispirited Chinese troops left behind in Tibet eventually surrendered. When Tibetan control was restored, the Kashag, realizing that there was no longer any purpose in continuing the fictions of Chinese overlordship or the remnants of the "priest-patron" relationship, expelled all Chinese officials and soldiers.

Chinese forces were expelled from central Tibet, but military hegemons continued to rule areas of Kham. A militia under the control of the Tibetan general Champa Tendar was dispatched to Kham, where it successfully battled Chinese commanders, resulting in a peace agreement in 1918 that gave control over much of Kham to the Lhasa government. China was given hegemony over the territories to the east of a border along the Dri River (including the Hor states and Nyarong), but Dergé and Péyul were under the control of the Tibetan government.

This situation continued until 1930–1933, when armed conflicts broke out between Gélukpa monasteries and institutions belonging to other orders. Chinese and Tibetan troops clashed in eastern Tibet, and the end result was that the Tibetan forces lost, and territories of Kham to the east of the Dri River came under the control of Chinese warlords. Records of the time indicate, however, that actual Chinese authority was largely restricted to areas near military garrisons and that the local inhabitants were largely autonomous.

The Nationalists Claim Tibet

Soon after gaining control over China, the Nationalists began to set their sights on Tibet, which they recognized as having strategic importance due to its location at the top of Central Asia, with borders on India, Nepal, Mongolia, and Russia. Another consideration was a Chinese belief that Tibet contained vast stores of natural resources, which was reflected in the Chinese term for the region—Xizang, meaning "Western Treasure House." Perhaps the most important factor was the government's nationalist agenda, which included promises to make China strong again. This involved, among other things, reconquering areas that had belonged to the Qing dynasty but that had become independent either as a result of colonialism or indigenous liberation movements. Tibet was singled out as the most important of these territories, and it was characterized as the "back door to the apartments" of China. As long as it remained independent or under the influence of foreign powers, the Nationalists proclaimed that China would be weakened and vulnerable.

The new government soon began asserting a hereditary right to Tibet, claiming that it had been a Chinese vassal since the twelfth century. The Tibetan leadership quickly realized the threat posed by a resurgent China and moved to sever all relations. There was no longer any possibility of renewing the "priest-patron" relationship, since the Nationalists were resolutely secular. The old system had continued as a shared fiction with the Manchus, but with China now threatening to annex Tibet and assume effective control, Tibet formally declared its independence.

Despite its inability to influence Tibet's internal affairs, the Nationalist government continued to proclaim its sovereignty over the country, and other nations, unwilling to anger China and uninterested in a remote region with few known natural resources, acquiesced by their silence. For the next several decades China was in a state of internal turmoil, which eventually ended with the defeat of the Nationalists by the Communists led by Mao Zedong.[5] The interregnum period allowed Tibet a brief respite, but this proved to be merely a calm before a growing storm.

The Dalai Lama's Attempts at Modernization

After his return to Lhasa, the Dalai Lama, recognizing Tibet's tenuous position in relation to its neighbors, initiated several measures designed to protect the country and bring it into the international community. He began by creating Tibet's first standing army, which was financed by a tax on all estates in Tibet. This led to conflict with the Panchen Lama, whose monastery of Tashihlünpo was the most powerful landowning institution in the country. The Panchen Lama lost the confrontation and was forced to flee to China in 1923.[6]

In order to foster understanding of the outside world, the Dalai Lama sent a number of young Tibetans to England for schooling, and he also attempted to create a Western-style system of education in Tibet. This move was strongly resisted by monastic leaders, who saw it as a threat to their long-standing hegemony over education and who feared that foreign ideas might undermine the position of Buddhism in the country. The monasteries had become deeply conservative and resistant to change, and their leaders were opposed to any innovations in society or religion. Despite the nominal supremacy of the Dalai Lama, their power was so great that their conservatism eventually defeated his attempts at modernizing the educational system.

The Death of the Thirteenth Dalai Lama

With the death of the thirteenth Dalai Lama in 1933, Tibet again entered an interregnum period. This occurred at an inopportune time, because a combination of Chinese manipulation of foreign powers and Tibetan insularity had isolated the country from the outside world. In his attempts to enlist foreign allies, the thirteenth Dalai Lama discovered that Tibet had no friends in the international community and lacked the military resources to repel a determined foreign invasion. On its borders a new power was growing, one that would eventually engulf Tibet, and all of the Dalai Lama's efforts to forestall catastrophe ultimately came to nothing. In a famous statement shortly before his death, he warned his people of imminent danger from foreign invasion and predicted that unless Tibet adopted his modernization policies the country would be overrun, its people killed or enslaved, and its religion destroyed.[7] Despite his personal authority, however, after his death the reforms were mostly scuttled, and Tibet returned to its policy of deeply conservative isolationism.

The Fourteenth Dalai Lama

Réting Rinpoché Ascends to Power

In January of 1934, Réting Rinpoché Jambel Yéshé was selected to be regent during the interregnum period. The monastic leaders in Lhasa insisted that the regent be a *tülku*, an incarnate lama (*sprul sku;* pronounced "tülku"). When the leading candidates withdrew their names from consideration, the choice fell to Réting Rinpoché, who at the time was only twenty-four years old. Although he was a widely respected tülku, he had little experience in a role of political leadership.

Unfortunately for the stability of the country, he proved to be corrupt and heavy-handed in his rule. At the beginning of his reign his authority was limited, but within a few years he gained supreme power in Tibetan politics. After consolidating his position, Réting Rinpoché began to openly flout the conventions of monastic behavior, and his personal letters indicate that despite being a monk he engaged in affairs with women. There was also speculation that he had sexual relations with men.[8] In addition, he is reported to have spent money lavishly and recklessly, and his monastery made huge profits as a result of the special trading advantages he granted it. These factors, along with widespread reports of his corruption, fueled popular resentment toward his regime.

How Tülkus are Selected

Perhaps Réting Rinpoché's greatest positive contribution was his leadership in the search for the fourteenth Dalai Lama, who was discovered in Taktsé and who proved to be an excellent choice to lead Tibet in its coming time of crisis. As we have seen, from the time of the Great Fifth, the Dalai Lamas who reached maturity exercised temporal and spiritual leadership in Tibet, and so their testing was taken very seriously by those involved in the selection process.

The tülku system is an extension of the logic of the Buddhist understanding of karma and rebirth and the Mahāyāna system of spiritual development. According to Buddhist doctrine, every sentient being is reborn over and over again in a beginningless cycle, and so from this point of view every creature is a reincarnation. Most, however, are unaware of this, and few people remember their past lives. The reason for this can be found in the process of death, in which the coarser levels of consciousness drop away, resulting in the eradication of the personality of one's past life. Sometimes, however, the process is incomplete, particularly if one's past life contained particularly powerful events that left deep imprints.[9]

According to Tibetan Buddhism, however, through meditative training it is possible to gain access to deeply buried memories of past lives and become consciously aware of them. This ability is considered to be common among advanced meditators, people who have learned to access subtle levels of mind. Such people are said to be able to perceive the events of their past lives. At higher levels of realization, it is thought that people can even develop the ability consciously to choose a rebirth, rather than simply being helplessly drawn into it. Advanced bodhisattvas have the ability to determine the life situations that best enable them to work for the benefit of others, and they consciously will themselves into these situations.

The logic of the tülku system is based on these ideas: all sentient beings are constantly reincarnating, and some exceptional beings are pursuing the path to awakening, motivated by compassion and working for the benefit of others. Since it is possible in principle to determine one's past births, it stands to reason that some beings will continually reincarnate themselves in a distinguishable lineage in a particular place for a particular group of people. Among Tibetans, such people are called tülkus, and they are greatly revered because Tibetans believe that their rebirths are motivated by compassion. Tibetan Buddhism has developed elaborate systems for detecting and testing candidates in order to ensure that the person recognized as a tülku is actually the reincarnation of a previous teacher. The most rigorous of these tests are those used to find a new Dalai Lama. Since he is regarded as the greatest of all Tibetan incarnate lamas and is the temporal and spiritual leader of Tibet, it is extremely important that the right person be found, and a number of fail-safe devices have been developed in order to ensure this.

The Testing Procedure

There are many degrees of tülkus, from the great incarnations like the Dalai Lamas, the Panchen Lamas, and the Gyelwa Karmapas, to minor figures who are associated with a particular area or with a monastery. The degree of care given to the testing procedure varies accordingly. For minor incarnations, the choice is sometimes made after a perfunctory search and often motivated by political considerations. For major tülkus, however, a great deal of care is taken to ensure the accuracy of the process.

Some lamas make the process of finding a successor relatively easy: the Gyelwa Karmapas, for instance, traditionally write instructions to their followers concerning where they will be reborn, often including such information as family name, details of one or more parents, and time of birth. Their disciples open the letter at a prearranged time after the Karmapa's death, follow the master's instructions, and according to tradition the predictions are always accurate.[10]

Most lamas, however, do not make it so easy for their disciples. In the case of the Dalai Lamas, when one is about to die, he will commonly make general predictions about his rebirth, but these must be supplemented by further tests in order to insure that the correct incarnation is located. When the thirteenth Dalai Lama foresaw his death, for example, he predicted that he would take rebirth in the eastern part of Tibet. After he passed away in 1933, this prediction was corroborated by a number of unusual signs, all pointing toward the east. One of the most striking of these occurred when an attendant looked into the sealed chamber that held the remains of the thirteenth Dalai Lama and found that the head of the corpse was turned toward the east, rather than south, the position in which it had originally been placed. After it was returned to the original position, it again was found facing toward the east after a few days. The state oracles gave signs that the incarnation was to be found in the east, and a large fungus began to grow on the eastern part of a pillar of the Potala. Another sign was the appearance of rainbows and auspiciously shaped cloud formations in the sky, all of them pointing toward the east.

The Search for the Fourteenth Dalai Lama

The beginning of the search was marked by a trip by Réting Rinpoché to the lake Hlamö Latso. This lake is well known as a source of visions, and Hlamö Latso had earlier provided a vision that aided in the discovery of the thirteenth Dalai Lama. Réting Rinpoché and other high-ranking lamas journeyed there in hopes of a similar vision. As Réting Rinpoché approached the lake, he saw on its surface the Tibetan letters *a*, *ka*, and *ma*. Then a three-tiered monastery appeared, followed by the sight of a road leading from the monastery toward the east and passing by a house near a small hill. The house had turquoise-colored tiles around the roof, and a brown and white dog was in the yard. Réting Rinpoché also saw a young boy standing in the yard.

After Réting Rinpoché returned to Lhasa, search parties were sent toward eastern Tibet, since it seemed clear that this was the area where the Dalai Lama's reincarnation was to be found. One party traveled to the province of Amdo, to the area of Kumbum, where they saw a monastery that closely resembled the vision in the lake. The members of the party began to inquire about children who had been born recently in the area and examined some likely candidates. After testing several young boys, it was determined that none was the new Dalai Lama, but the search party then decided to test a boy in Taktsé and two other candidates recommended by the seventh Panchen Lama. Kutsang Rinpoché, a member of the search party, went to examine the boy from Taktsé with a government official named Losang Tséwang and two attendants. They were concerned that the presence of a high-ranking lama and government dignitaries might cause people to try to sell them on a particular candidate, and so they hid their true intentions and disguised themselves as merchants on business. Kutsang Rinpoché dressed as a servant, and Losang Tséwang pretended to be the leader of the party.

As they approached the village of Taktsé, they passed several famous temples, the most important of which was the Shartsong Temple in which Tsong Khapa had taken his novice vows after deciding to become a monk. This was viewed as highly significant, and their hopes continued to rise when they saw a small dwelling that matched the description of the house in Réting Rinpoché's vision. As they approached the entrance, a brown and white dog began to bark at them, and the woman of the house came out to see what had caused the commotion. Losang Tséwang asked her if he could use her facilities to make some tea, and she showed him into the house. As Kutsang Rinpoché walked into the courtyard, he noticed that the roof had turquoise tiles like the ones that Réting Rinpoché had seen in his vision and that the house matched his description in other aspects.

Kutsang Rinpoché entered the kitchen and began making tea. As he was waiting for water to boil, a two-year-old boy walked up to him, sat in his lap, and began to play with the prayer beads around the disguised lama's neck. These beads had belonged to the thirteenth Dalai Lama. The young boy, named Hlamo Döndrup, then told Kutsang Rinpoché that the beads were his, and Kutsang Rinpoché offered to give them to the child if he could guess the lama's true identity. The boy said, "You are a lama of Séra," which was true. The boy then correctly identified Losang Tséwang. This was remarkable, since he had never been outside of his small village, and the two were dressed as merchants. Hlamo Döndrup then announced that the other two attendants were from Séra Monastery, which was also correct.

The members of the delegation still did not tell the parents the true purpose of their visit, and after spending the night in the house they left. As they were preparing to go, the boy came to see them and asked that they take him with them. He was so insistent that they finally had to console him by telling him that they would return later.

Testing the Candidate

The members of the search party fulfilled their promise shortly thereafter, and when they returned they asked the boy's parents for permission to speak to their son alone. This was a precautionary measure, because it is considered a great honor to have an incarnate lama appear in a family, and the search party wanted to ensure that the parents did not coach or influence their son.

The key test involved placing a number of articles in front of the boy and asking him to choose from among them. Some were personal articles belonging to the thirteenth Dalai Lama, and others were duplicates. Some were exact duplicates, and others were better-made and more aesthetically appealing. Among the objects were the former Dalai Lama's eyeglasses, a bowl, a silver pencil, his prayer beads, a small hand drum, and his walking stick. Hlamo Döndrup came into the room and began the test. He was first presented with a choice of prayer beads, and he chose the beads belonging to the thirteenth Dalai Lama without hesitation. Kutsang Rinpoché then presented him with two walking sticks, and the boy at first reached for the wrong one, and then corrected himself and chose the right one. This apparent mistake was actually seen as being significant, since the first stick had briefly belonged to the thirteenth Dalai Lama before he gave it to a friend. Hlamo Döndrup correctly chose from among the remaining items. The final choice was between the hand drum of the thirteenth Dalai Lama, which was rather worn out, and a beautifully crafted drum that was much better made than the other one. Hlamo Döndrup unhesitatingly chose the thirteenth Dalai Lama's drum, and then began twirling it in the correct manner.

This test was significant, but not definitive. Tradition holds that Dalai Lamas are marked with specific physical signs, and the boy was examined for these. Some of the signs are: large ears, long eyes, streaks on the legs like a tiger's stripes, and a conch-shell shaped imprint on one hand. All of these were found on the boy, and this finally convinced the members of the search party that the correct incarnation had been located.

The testing did not end there, however. Given the importance of the Dalai Lama, it is necessary to be absolutely certain, and so after the authorities in Lhasa were notified of the search party's findings, the state oracles were consulted, and they confirmed that Hlamo Döndrup was indeed the reincarnation of the thirteenth Dalai Lama.

The members of the search party also recognized that the area in which Hlamo Döndrup was born matched Réting Rinpoché's vision of the Tibetan letters *a*, *ka*, and *ma* in Hlamö Latso. *A* is the first letter of Amdo, the province in which the village of Taktsé is located, and *ka* is the first letter in Kumbum, the most important monastery of the area. In addition, *ka* and *ma* are a part of the name of a monastery in Taktsé named Karma Shartsong. Since the thirteenth Dalai Lama had spent time there in a retreat in 1909, this was seen as being particularly significant. He had left a pair of his boots there as a blessing, which led the villagers to believe that a great lama would be born there in the future. He had also passed the house in which Hlamo Döndrup was born and remarked that it was a beautiful place. These were recognized as confirmations of the search party's decision.

Auspicious Events Surrounding the Dalai Lama's Birth

The members of the search party wanted to bring the child to Lhasa, where he could begin his formal training. Even though Dalai Lamas are considered to be manifestations of the buddha Avalokiteśvara and retain memories of past lives, with each incarnation they must begin their education anew.[11]

The birth of the fourteenth Dalai Lama was also accompanied by a number of auspicious signs. Oddly enough, the villagers of Taktsé had expected that a high lama would be born among them because their crops had been unusually poor for several years. A popular Tibetan belief holds that good crops are preceded by bad ones, and the unusual run of bad luck was interpreted as an auspicious sign that something particularly good was about to happen to the village. The family of Hlamo Döndrup had also undergone some hard times: they had lost a number of heads of livestock for no apparent reason, and his father had been afflicted by a mysterious illness shortly before the birth of Hlamo Döndrup. The boy was born at dawn on July 6, 1935, and when he emerged from his mother's womb, his eyes were wide open, which she thought was very unusual. As soon as Hlamo Döndrup, the family's fifth child, was born, his father recovered from his illness.

As he grew, his parents realized that he was unusually bright, but they had no idea that he was the fourteenth Dalai Lama. There were other auspicious signs that his parents later recognized as being significant, such as the fact that shortly after the boy's birth two crows (who are associated with the buddha Mahākāla) sat on the roof of the house for awhile. It was recalled that a similar event had occurred with the births of the first, seventh, eighth, and twelfth Dalai Lamas. The first Dalai Lama was saved by a crow as an infant when bandits raided the tent of his nomad parents. When the parents found him, the bandits had left, and he was being guarded by a large black crow.

Hlamo Döndrup's parents also reported that from an early age the child's favorite game was to sit on the windowsill of the house and pretend that he was traveling to Lhasa. He often played at packing his bags for a journey to Lhasa and would announce to his parents that he was leaving.

The New Dalai Lama Travels to Lhasa

Although the search party was eager to bring the young Dalai Lama to Lhasa, their departure was prevented by the intervention of a local Chinese Muslim warlord named Ma Bufeng, whose troops controlled the area. He suspected that the presence of search parties in his area indicated that the Tibetans believed that their new Dalai Lama had been born there, and when the members of the search party asked him for permission to bring young Hlamo Döndrup to Lhasa, Ma Bufeng decided that the young boy was probably the successful candidate. Recognizing the value of the Dalai Lama to Tibetans, he asked for an outrageous sum of money. He initially asked for about $92,000, and when the Tibetans produced the money, he then raised the price by an additional $300,000 and asked for other valuable gifts, including the robes of the past Dalai Lama and an edition of the Buddhist canon. Realizing that they had no real choice, the Tibetan government with great difficulty raised the money and sent the required gifts to the warlord.

After the ransom had been paid, the party set out for Lhasa in August of 1939 with the blessings of the boy's parents. Although he had not been officially recognized as the Dalai Lama, he was treated as such, and people along the route to Lhasa came out in droves to see the young incarnation. At first the boy seemed distressed by the journey, but as he approached Lhasa he became very happy.

At a place that was still ten days from Lhasa, he was greeted by a delegation of the highest-ranking lamas and government officials. The whole party traveled in state to the holy city. He first caught sight of Lhasa on the morning of October 6, 1939. A huge tent encampment had been constructed on a plain about two miles from the city, in accordance with traditional protocol for the greeting of newly recognized Dalai Lamas. Prominent religious leaders and government officials gathered there, along with huge crowds of onlookers, and traditional ceremonies were performed. On October 8, the Dalai Lama was escorted into the city, while a Tibetan band played "God Save the King," which had been learned from British emissaries. Huge crowds turned out for the procession, and ambassadors arrived from China, India, Nepal, and Bhutan. The Néchung oracle also attended, taking possession of the body of his human host and performing a dance in honor of the Dalai Lama. Approaching the boy, the oracle bowed down and presented him with a ceremonial scarf, called a *kata*. The young Dalai Lama placed it over the oracle's neck in blessing.

The procession traveled to the Norbulingka, summer residence of the Dalai Lamas, and as Hlamo Döndrup passed a small box in his quarters, he said, "My teeth are in that box." When it was opened, a set of dentures belonging to the thirteenth Dalai Lama was discovered inside.

After several weeks, Hlamo Döndrup was ordained as a Buddhist monk and given the ordination name of Jétsun Jambel Ngawang Losang Yéshé Tenzin Gyatso—Most Venerable, Elegant Glory, Eloquent, Intelligent, Upholder of the Teaching, Ocean of Wisdom. On February 22, 1940, shortly before his fifth birthday, Tenzin Gyatso was enthroned as the fourteenth Dalai Lama in a grand ceremony in the Potala. His official enthronement in 1940 was attended by representatives from the British government in India, the King of Nepal, the Maharajas of Sikkim and Bhutan, and a Chinese representative named Wu Zhongxin.

The Interregnum Period

In a surprising move, in December of 1940 Réting Rinpoché offered his resignation to the Kashag. He explained that he had received portents in dreams that his life would be threatened if he did not resign. Considering the regent's fascination with the exercise of power and his indulgence in the perquisites of office, this explanation was probably a smokescreen, but his actual reasons for resigning are still a matter of debate. Goldstein speculates that Réting may have been reluctant to supervise the monastic ordination of the young Dalai Lama because he had broken his own vows.[12] His numerous affairs had rendered him unfit to bestow ordination, and if he had given monastic vows to the Dalai Lama they would have been void because of Réting's transgressions. Although he was clearly willing to violate his own vows, he may have been unwilling to risk the crisis that could have resulted from an improperly ordained Dalai Lama.

During this period, the rest of the world was in the throes of World War II, but Tibet remained virtually untouched by the international conflict. An attempt to involve Tibet occurred in 1942, when the Chinese and British governments requested permission to build a supply route through Tibet because the route between India and China through Burma had been cut off by the Japanese. Unwilling to allow Chinese troops or supplies into its territory, Tibet refused the request. The Chinese government threatened to attack Tibet unless the government changed its position, but when Tibetan troops were sent to the border the Chinese relented and withdrew the surveyors who had been sent to plan the road. After the British government requested that Tibet reconsider its position, the Kashag relented and allowed Britain to transport goods through Tibet, provided that they were not of a military nature.

The People's Republic of China

After the conclusion of World War II, the Chinese Communists made a bid for power, which eventually led to the flight of Chiang Kai-shek to Taiwan and the triumph of the Communists. Soon after assuming full power the Communist government made it clear that it intended to annex Tibet and make it a part of China. Deeply concerned about the threat posed by the Communists, in July 1949 the Tibetan government expelled all Chinese officials from the country.

On October 1, 1949, a new government that referred to itself as "The People's Republic of China" was inaugurated in Beijing. Now that China was united under a strong central government, it possessed much more power than the weak Nationalists. The Communist government soon announced that it intended to unite all of China and "reintegrate" Tibet into the "motherland." Apparently believing that Tibet had always been a part of China, the Communist leaders suspected that the expulsion of Chinese officials and severance of relations had been due to interference by "Western imperialists" and "counterrevolutionaries."

The People's Liberation Army Invades Kham

On January 1, 1950, the New Year's broadcast from Beijing announced that in the coming year the People's Liberation Army would liberate Tibet from foreign imperialists and reintegrate it with the motherland. In August of the same year, a massive earthquake shook Tibet, and its tremors were felt all over the country. As far away as Calcutta, people ran from theaters when the shockwaves hit. Mountains were toppled, and the course of the Brahmaputra river was altered. The sky over southeastern Tibet burned with an ominous red glow, and people remembered that several years earlier the Néchung Oracle had faced eastward while in a trance and predicted in great agitation that Tibet was threatened with grave danger. This was followed by the appearance in 1949 of a bright comet in the sky, which was interpreted as a further harbinger of war. In addition, the top of an ancient column at the base of the Potala was found shattered one morning. This had been built in 763 in commemoration of Tibet's victory over China.

Following these events, reports came into Lhasa from the east indicating that Chinese troops were massing at the border. The Tibetans prepared to meet them with small, poorly-armed, undisciplined local militias. The Chinese army was spearheaded by an advance force of twenty thousand combat-hardened troops armed with modern weapons.

When Chinese troops began pouring into Kham, the Tibetan militias were easily overcome. Kham was given up after only token resistance. With a foothold established in eastern Tibet, the People's Liberation Army set its sights on Lhasa.

The Fourteenth Dalai Lama Assumes Power

Tenzin Gyatso's early years were mainly taken up with the intensive program of study expected of Dalai Lamas, and during this time Tibet continued to be ruled by regents. With the Chinese incursions in eastern Tibet, the central government convened a special session with the two main state oracles, Néchung and Gadong. The Dalai Lama was in attendance, along with leading government officials and abbots from the major monasteries. Both oracles indicated that he should assume power immediately, although he had not yet reached the normal age at which Dalai Lamas take on their temporal duties. Taktra Rinpoché, who had succeeded Réting Rinpoché as regent, resigned soon after, and the Dalai Lama assumed full temporal and religious control on November 17, 1950, at the age of sixteen.

The full extent of Tibet's friendlessness in the international community was brought home when it appealed to the United Nations for help soon after the Dalai Lama's ascension to power. The members of the U.N., unwilling to provoke a conflict with China over a small and isolated country, rebuffed the Tibetans, stating that Tibet was not a member nation, and so its appeal would not be considered.

During the Dalai Lama's early tenure as ruler, China made increasingly bold forays into eastern Tibet, meeting little effective resistance. The Dalai Lama attempted to come to terms with the Chinese government and to find a way to reach a peaceful agreement, but the Chinese leadership was bent on conquest.

After establishing a power base in eastern Tibet, the People's Liberation Army began moving toward Lhasa. Along the way it met with sporadic but ineffectual Tibetan resistance, and on September 9, 1951, three thousand troops of the Eighteenth Route Army marched into Lhasa, waving portraits of Mao Zedong and Zhou Enlai above their heads, holding aloft a Chinese flag with four small circles around a blazing yellow sun. The orbs symbolized the small states that China considered to be a part of its territory, and the sun was the Han-controlled central areas of China. One of the orbs was Tibet, which was now under direct Chinese control for the first time in its history.

Within months additional Chinese troops flooded into Lhasa. They were met by angry Tibetans, who shouted insults and spat at them. This had no effect on the Chinese, and within a short time there were twenty thousand troops in Lhasa. Initially the Chinese conducted themselves with restraint and did not react to the Tibetans' antagonism. Proclaiming that their invasion was a "liberation" that would bring prosperity to Tibet, the Chinese promised schools, hospitals, roads, and other modern improvements. The new overlords of Tibet soon constructed a movie theater, bank, and hospital, but ironically they were reserved for Chinese officials and Tibetan collaborators, while the "masses" were not permitted to sample these symbols of modernization.

It soon became clear that the foreign invaders and their ideology were incompatible with Tibetan culture. While the communists firmly believed that Marxism was the cure for all the world's problems and that communization would create a perfect society, the Tibetans looked for rewards beyond the present life, since as Buddhists they believed that any sort of mundane existence is unsatisfactory. It seems clear that the Chinese initially expected that the Tibetans would join them in throwing off the "yoke of oppression" represented by Tibetan institutions and leaders. David Patt contends that in the early stages of the invasion

> they must have believed their own propaganda, that the Tibetan serfs would rise up to join their Chinese brothers and sisters to throw off the chains of feudalism. But events proved that the vast chasm that separated Communist China from Buddhist Tibet—in terms of religion, culture, language, history and political ethos—was so vast, so utterly unbridgeable, that in the end the Chinese must have come to the conclusion that the only way they could liberate Tibet was to destroy it.[13]

The Dalai Lama's Attempts at Mediation

In spite of these differences, the Dalai Lama took on the task of negotiating with the Chinese. In July of 1954 he accepted an invitation to meet with Mao in Beijing, hoping to forestall further Chinese aggression. Although he reported that his talks with the Chinese leader were cordial, when he returned to Tibet he saw that the invaders were in the process of transforming his homeland. By 1955 the process of collectivization was underway, with Kham and Amdo bearing the brunt of the changes at first. Chinese troops began confiscating arms, property, livestock, and possessions, and then they created communes. The people who were being forced into the new system resisted these moves. The Chinese answer was to use violence to force Tibetans into the golden age that awaited them. Local leaders, wealthy landowners, and religious figures were rounded up and subjected to public *thamzing* ("struggle sessions"), in which they were berated for their "crimes against the people" and forced to confess. Confession was generally preceded by beating and often followed by execution. Local people who refused to participate were accused of being "collaborators" or "reactionaries" and themselves subjected to *thamzing*. As John Avedon notes, a *thamzing* session was

> a carefully orchestrated undertaking, much like a collective Passion play. Thamzing proper took place with the people seated on the ground before a tribunal of Chinese officials ensconced behind a table. An opening speech was made by the ranking Chinese. In it the people were informed that thamzing was not a matter of one or two meetings, but would continue until a full confession, followed by repentance, had been obtained—until the accused himself, 'with the help of his revolutionary brothers,' had cleansed his mind of reac-

> tionary thoughts. Furthermore, it was designed to teach the 'serfs' to stand up, unafraid of their masters, and expose past injustices. On this dramatic note—with the official gesturing angrily and yelling, 'Bring that bad person in!'—the prisoner would be led to the head of the crowd, and made to bend over from the waist, hands on knees, eyes to the ground. A list of crimes was then read from the charge sheets, the official saying at the conclusion: 'These are the crimes committed by this person. It is now for the people to help him admit his evil ways and decide the punishment he should receive.' At this signal the first accuser, invariably an 'activist' in Chinese employ, would spring up, race forward, and denounce the 'exploiter,' by yelling such epithets as 'Kill the stinking dog! Skin him alive! Your mother's corpse! Your father's heart! Confess your crimes!' After recounting the supposed suffering he had been subjected to, the witness would beat the victim, rebels often being thrashed by their guards with the butt end of a rifle. In these cases, it would frequently be the task of those at the meeting to execute the victim.[14]

These struggle sessions were accompanied by carefully orchestrated attempts to undermine the people's attachment to their culture and diminish their respect for religious leaders and institutions. Chinese soldiers commonly tortured monks and nuns in front of crowds of horrified Tibetans. Monks and nuns were forced to copulate in public. If they refused to do so, others would be tortured until they complied. In order to break down resistance, thousands of people were executed as "counterrevolutionaries," and their families were then forced to pay for the bullets that had been used to kill them. These measures naturally led to rebellion, particularly in Kham and Amdo, where bands of guerrillas formed. Some of their attacks on Chinese garrisons were successful, but their final defeat was inevitable. The Tibetans were mostly armed with hand weapons and some old rifles, while their enemies possessed modern weapons and vastly superior numbers.[15]

The Flight of the Dalai Lama

By 1959 the situation in Tibet was grim. The country suffered under the yoke of a foreign army that was wreaking destruction throughout the countryside while proclaiming that it was "liberating" the people. As tensions increased, a message was delivered to the Dalai Lama by the Chinese general Dan Guansan, who was in command of the Chinese forces, to join him at a theatrical performance. The message stipulated that the Dalai Lama was to come alone, with no attendants or bodyguards.

Fearing that the invitation was part of a thinly disguised plot to kidnap Tibet's spiritual leader, the Dalai Lama and his advisers began planning his escape. When Radio Beijing announced that he would attend the performance, the people of Lhasa, also suspecting a plan to kidnap him, took to the streets *en masse* to protest. At dawn on March 10, 1959, a huge crowd of Tibetans gathered outside the Dalai Lama's summer palace, the Norbulingka, to prevent his capture by the Chinese. By nine o'clock there were over thirty thousand people massed outside the gates, shouting anti-Chinese slogans. During the next several days tensions continued to mount, and it became clear that the Chinese leaders intended to take drastic action. At four o'clock on March 17, the Chinese began lobbing mortar shells in the area around the Norbulingka, with the stated purpose of "freeing" the Dalai Lama from the "reactionary clique" surrounding his residence. Realizing that there was no point in continued negotiations with the Chinese, the Dalai Lama and his advisors made plans to leave that night. He and his family disguised themselves in order to pass by the Chinese patrols that roamed the countryside. The Dalai Lama himself dressed as a soldier and took off his glasses in order to make recognition more difficult in case they were stopped.[16]

Later that night he and his party slipped out of the Norbulingka undetected and began the long journey to exile in India. Along the way they were aided by bands of commandos, mainly Khampas and Goloks, who watched out for Chinese patrols and delivered supplies.

On March 24, the Dalai Lama was informed that two days after his escape the Chinese, apparently still thinking that he was in the Norbulingka, had shelled it repeatedly. On March 28, Zhou Enlai announced in a radio broadcast that the Tibetan government had been dissolved and China had taken direct control. After hearing the news, the Dalai Lama crossed the border into India to begin a new life in exile.

China Consolidates Its Control

In the aftermath of the Dalai Lama's flight, the Chinese army went on an orgy of destruction. As scores of corpses lay outside the Norbulingka,

Chinese troops attacked Lhasa, shelling the Potala, destroying the medical college on Chokpori Hill, and bombing Ganden Monastery into rubble. Prior to the Chinese invasion, Ganden had been one of the largest monasteries in the country and one of the greatest achievements of Tibetan architecture. Today it consists of piles of stones and some buildings that have been rebuilt by Tibetans. Continuing their destruction, Chinese soldiers set fire to the Ramoché temple, Tibet's second holiest shrine, and then began shelling the Tsuklakhang, the most sacred building in the country. At the time, thousands of people were inside, vainly hoping that the Chinese would not attack the sacred precincts. As the shells began to fall, machine gunners opened fire, killing scores of people. Within days the conquest of Tibet was complete, thousands of people lay dead, many ancient and holy buildings lay ruined, and Chinese flags flew over Lhasa. The Chinese authorities announced to the world that Tibet had been "liberated" and that the "darkest feudal serfdom in the world" had been eliminated.

Tibetan Refugees in India and Nepal

Although the Chinese continued to assure Tibetans of their benevolent intentions, their actions clearly revealed the true nature of the occupation. As a result, tens of thousands of Tibetans fled their country to join the Dalai Lama in exile, hoping for a better life in India or Nepal. They faced an uncertain future, however, arriving with little or nothing and confronting strange cultures, customs, languages, and environments. Many died during the difficult journey, either as a result of natural dangers or Chinese patrols, which executed any people caught fleeing. When they arrived in the warmer climates of India and Nepal many died of illnesses that were unknown in the high plateau of Tibet.

After reaching India, most of the refugees were placed in camps created by the Indian government, which also provided employment for many. The most common source of work was road crews in the Himalayan region. This was difficult and low-paying labor, but most of the refugees arrived with limited resources, and so this was one of the few options available. Fortunately, the Indian government and international relief agencies began sending food, medical supplies, and money to help them, and the Dalai Lama and his advisors soon started planning refugee settlements.

Recognizing that Tibetan culture—and the Tibetan race itself—were in danger of extermination, Tibetan leaders began to plan for an indefinite future in exile. The new Tibetan refugee society began with a donation of land by the Indian government, which offered a small hill-station named Dharamsala that had been built by the British. Located in the foothills of the Himalayas in the northern state of Himachal Pradesh, it had the Dhauladar range as a picturesque backdrop, its snow-covered peaks reminiscent of the home the refugees had left behind. It soon became the administrative center of the Tibetan exile community. The main residence of the Dalai Lama (referred to as the *Podrang*) is now located there, along with the offices of a democratically elected government-in-exile. It is also a center for Tibetan culture, with a large library containing rare texts smuggled out of Tibet by fleeing scholars, Namgyal Monastery (the personal monastery of the Dalai Lama, formerly located in the Potala), Néchung monastery (home of the state oracle), and several schools, including the first Tibetan Children's Village.

Settlements in South India

Although Dharamsala has become the center of the Tibetan exile community, the majority of Tibetan refugees live in other parts of India. Dharamsala, perched on the steep sides of a mountain, has limited room and few areas suitable for agriculture. In order to create self-sustaining Tibetan communities, the Indian government offered to lease uninhabited land in the southern state of Karnataka, which today houses the bulk of the refugee population. When the Tibetans first arrived, much of the land was jungle. Disease and wild beasts were constant threats, and the Tibetans were unused to the warm and humid climate. Despite the obstacles, the refugees persevered. The settlement of Byllakuppe, for instance, began as a small group of tents in a jungle clearing, but today is a prosperous farming community of almost 10,000 people. Other settlements were soon started in other areas, most of which are now self-sustaining. About 35,000 Tibetan refugees now live in communities in Karnataka State. In all, the Tibetan refugee population today numbers more than 150,000 in India, about 13,000 in Nepal, 1,500 in Bhutan, and about 10,000 more in small groups in Western countries.[17]

Perhaps because of their shared suffering, the exiles realized that cooperative action was necessary for survival. As a result, they shared resources and equipment, allowing the communities to maximize their ability to produce goods and render services. They also discovered the power of collective purchasing and marketing. In addition, the Tibetan penchant for trade proved to be an asset, and many Tibetans today make substantial profits from selling a wide range of goods, particularly sweaters and other wool products.

The Tibetans wisely recognize that their continued success requires good relations with their neighbors, and so they often rent out farm machinery at low rates and employ Indian workers in farming and other industries. As a result, their neighbors generally accept them as welcome guests.[18] Some grumble about the astounding success of the refugee communities, which were founded by penniless displaced people in a foreign country. In general, however, the refugees have managed to live peacefully with their neighbors. Despite the continual strain on their resources caused by an ongoing influx of new Tibetans fleeing Chinese oppression, most of the communities are financially solvent, and those in need of help are aided by others who are more affluent.[19]

Rebuilding Monastic Culture in Exile

In spite of the innumerable difficulties the refugees encountered after arriving in India, after founding new communities they began devoting considerable resources to preserving their culture in exile. Although most of Tibet's monasteries were destroyed or shut down, many of their inhabitants managed to escape the Chinese invaders and make their way to India. Once there, they soon began the task of recreating their religious institutions. Today most of the major monasteries have been rebuilt, though with greatly reduced numbers of monks. In 1959 Tibet had an estimated two hundred thousand monks, out of a population of six million, but the exile community lacked the resources to support such a large monastic population. In spite of the financial difficulties facing the monasteries in exile, many young Tibetans have chosen to enter the monastic life, ensuring the continuation of the tradition.

In southern India, the great monasteries of Drébung, Séra, and Ganden have been recreated on a smaller scale, and thousands of young monks are currently pursuing the standard monastic curriculum of study and oral debate. Yearly examinations are held for advanced degrees, and a significant number of young Tibetans have earned the *géshé* degree, the highest level of the traditional Gélukpa educational system. Female monasticism has also undergone a resurgence, and many young women have chosen to pursue the celibate monastic life. In Tibet, nuns were involved mainly in conducting religious ceremonies and prayers, but a new trend has developed at the Gaden Chöling convent in Dharamsala, in which young nuns have begun learning the oral debate style practiced in the monasteries, with the result that some are becoming proficient in philosophical dialectics. This perhaps signals a changing orientation and an increase in options for women considering the monastic life.[20]

It is important to note that Tibetans in exile have not simply sought to preserve their traditions; they are also formulating new ones and planning for the return to their homeland that they fervently desire. Most Tibetans firmly believe that they will be able to return someday to a free Tibet, and their leaders are anticipating this with plans to revamp the society. An important step in this direction was the drafting in 1963 of a constitution for a free Tibet, which instituted democratic elections and abolished many of the archaic institutions of the old order. It promises universal suffrage, equal rights to all citizens, contains guarantees concerning life, liberty, property, and ensures freedom of religion, speech, and assembly.

One of its most striking elements of Tibet's new constitution is a diminution of the power of the Dalai Lama, at his own request. He has publicly stated that upon his return to Tibet he will no longer exercise temporal leadership and will be a purely religious figure. He will not hold any public office or set government policy (although he will no doubt retain a great deal of personal authority due to the great reverence Tibetans have for him). In the new Tibet, the Dalai Lama may even be impeached by a two-thirds vote of the National Assembly. This idea was proposed by the Dalai Lama himself—who recognized that in a democracy no individual should be above the law—but was vigorously opposed by Tibetans, who were uncomfortable with treating an incarnation of Avalokiteśvara as an ordinary human.

The Chinese Occupation of Tibet

Soon after dissolving the Tibetan government, the Chinese authorities declared martial law. Any attempts at resistance were met with massive retaliation, the intent of which was to terrorize the populace into submission. Thousands were killed, and thousands more imprisoned and tortured. This reflected the general attitude of the Chinese toward the indigenous inhabitants, whom they regarded as culturally backward and genetically inferior. Han Chinese generally consider themselves to be superior to minority groups in China, and Chinese scientists have even published articles "demonstrating" this racial superiority. One such theory, which Tibetan children learn in science textbooks, holds that Tibetans are intellectually inferior to Han Chinese because the high altitude of the country has deprived their brains of oxygen.

Chinese scholars have also published numerous articles and books stating that despite reports by human rights organizations, news reporters, and travelers in Tibet, the "liberation" of Tibet was a peaceful one and was welcomed by the people of the country. An example is *Highlights of Tibetan History*, written by two researchers at Beijing's Central Institute of Nationalities, which states that Tibetans viewed the soldiers of the People's Liberation Army as saviors when they

> launched an epic march on Tibet for its peaceful liberation . . . . Whenever they were billeted they helped the local population do all kinds of jobs, took care of their needs and interests and the army medics attended to their sick free of charge. Such good deeds won the hearts of the Tibetans.[21]

In reality, the invading troops began systematically looting the country, ransacking monasteries and removing images, which were either sold at antique markets or melted down for their precious metals. An estimated one half of Tibet's voluminous religious literature was destroyed, until Chinese authorities belatedly realized that they might be able to make a profit by selling it. As a result, they began shipping loads of books to Beijing, and some of these have been copied and offered for sale.

In order to further divide the populace, the country was partitioned into three areas, with the central provinces forming a new entity called the "Tibet Autonomous Region," while most of Kham and all of Amdo were affixed to other Chinese provinces. This allowed the Chinese to claim that there are only 1.8 million ethnic Tibetans, a figure that ignores more than four million Tibetan-speaking people in the other newly-created provinces of China.

"The Socialist Paradise on the Roof of the World"

In order to handle the huge numbers of people arrested, Chinese authorities began building forced labor camps.[22] Among the most infamous were

Nachen Tang near Lhasa, Golmo, north of the Tsaidam Basin; Tsala Garpo, in the northern plains of the Changtang; and Kongpo, in the southeastern part of the country. Kongpo was built to harvest Tibet's huge timber forests and ship the logs to China. Prisoners in this camp clearcut huge areas of timber, a shortsighted practice that led to erosion problems and flooding in lowland areas. Golmo and Tsala Garpo were built as death camps, and the unfortunate people who came to them were subjected to physical torture and fed at a starvation level. In addition, the prisoners were poorly clothed and were forced to work at least twelve hours per day at harsh physical labor, with the result that many died due to the extreme weather conditions in these camps. During this period approximately one tenth of the Tibetan population spent some time in a Chinese prison, and most of the prisoners were subjected to physical torture of some kind. At the same time, the *People's Daily* carried headlines about the "new socialist paradise on the Roof of the World."

In 1959 Tibet experienced its first famine, ironically during a time of record crop production. China was in the midst of a major food shortage, and so the authorities confiscated the Tibetan harvest and shipped it to China, while allocating the Tibetans starvation rations. This led to tens of thousands of deaths. The Tibetan government-in-exile estimates that during the first decade of the Chinese invasion an estimated 1.2 million people died, either as a result of starvation, under torture, or due to being killed outright by Chinese soldiers. In addition, of the 6,254 monasteries and temples in Tibet prior to the invasion, only thirteen remained after this period.[23] In a move reminiscent of the Nazi occupation of Poland, several of the most beautiful monasteries were preserved as monuments to the culture that was being systematically destroyed. They were converted into propaganda museums in which exhibits were built by the Chinese that depicted pre-invasion Tibet as a "feudal system" and praised the "socialist paradise" that had been created.

Much of this destruction occurred during the Cultural Revolution, a program instituted by Mao as a means to shorten the time needed for full communization. He believed that by destroying all symbols of the old culture—monasteries, temples, ancient monuments, religious leaders, authority figures, books, and so on—a cultural vacuum would be created, and Marxism would move in to fill the void with a new order. Instead of collectivization by stages, the people would be quickly moved into the new millennium. This program was carried out by young zealots called Red

Guards, who swept through China destroying everything in their path. But the destruction was far worse in Tibet than in China, mainly due to the contempt the Chinese felt toward the "backward" Tibetans.

The Red Guards in Tibet

In 1966 Red Guard troops began pouring into Tibet to eradicate the "Four Olds": old ideology, culture, habits, and customs; and to institute the reverse of these evils, the "Four News." The devastation they caused was particularly severe in minority areas like Tibet, which differed from China in language, culture, and attitudes. The Red Guards perceived these as indications that minority people were dangerously "reactionary" and required strong measures to bring them to true socialism. *Thamzing* (struggle sessions) were held all over Tibet, with large numbers of people standing accused of being "enemies of the people" and harboring "counterrevolutionary attitudes."

Lacking even the limited restraint exercised by the soldiers of the People's Liberation Army, the Red Guards held mass executions, engaged in torture on an unprecedented scale, and rampaged throughout the countryside destroying monasteries, forcing monks to urinate on sacred texts, placing religious images in latrines, scrawling graffiti on the walls of temples and monasteries, and subjecting religious and political leaders (even those who collaborated with the Chinese authorities) to thamzing. The Red Guards also struck fear into the populace with marauding bands of young soldiers who staged mass gang rapes randomly throughout the countryside. International human rights organizations estimate that thousands of women of all ages were raped, often in public, with their parents, children, and neighbors being forced to watch.

The reign of terror lasted for almost a decade until Mao's death in 1976. By the end of the Cultural Revolution, tens of thousands of Tibetans had been murdered, and millions more had suffered extreme physical and mental abuse. It also brought economic devastation on such a scale that when Mao was succeeded by Deng Xiaoping the new supreme leader had to acknowledge that "mistakes were made." A more accurate assessment was offered by Alexander Solzehnitsyn, who stated that China's rule in Tibet is "more brutal and inhumane than any other communist regime in the world."[24]

When Deng assumed power, he announced a new attitude on the part of the Chinese government and promised a "more open China." Vowing to reverse the excesses of the past, Deng's policies were aimed at creating a market economy in China, although this would not be accompanied by any loosening of military control. China would have open markets, but a closed political system. Dissent would not be allowed, and the massacre of pro-democracy demonstrators in Tiananmen Square in Beijing in 1989 indicated the level of repression the new government was prepared to mete out to dissidents. Several months before this, a series of protests were staged throughout Tibet by people who called for China to respect international standards of human rights. They were met by the same type of brutal force, and scores were killed; hundreds more were arrested without being charged; most were tortured, and many were executed. Contrary to the expectations of the authorities, this did not stop the unrest, which continues today. Every year thousands of Tibetans escape into exile, most claiming that they fled persecution and human rights abuses. From time to time reports of small-scale demonstrations reach the outside world, but even the most trivial act of rebellion commonly results in lengthy prison terms and torture.

Amnesty International states that torture is "endemic" in Tibet,[25] and an estimated eight out of every nine prisoners are tortured. A study of the human rights situation by Asia Watch contends that

> all . . .manifestations of dissatisfaction with Chinese rule—whether peacefully conducted or otherwise—are viewed by the authorities as constituting 'illegal separatist activity,' and those who have led or participated in them have been punished with escalating force and severity.[26]

"Merciless Repression"

Qiao Shi, who was China's security chief in charge of controlling dissidence in Tibet until 1998, described the official policy as "merciless repression," which meant that any attempts to demonstrate against Chinese rule—or even expression of pro-independence sentiments—would be met with extreme force and brutal punishment. In 1989 Qiao contended that the previous policy toward rebels was "too lenient" and that they must be punished without mercy in order that they would come to love their "Han big brothers" who were in Tibet to bring them the benefits of communism and Chinese civilization.

The Chinese authorities today proclaim to the world that repression has been eased and that Tibetans are now free to speak their own language and practice their religion. The reality is that all important positions are held by Chinese, and in order to find a good job one must be fluent in Chinese. When I visited Tibet in 2001 every employed person I encountered in Lhasa and Shigatsé was Chinese. Throngs of beggars importuned foreigners at popular tourist spots, and a few Tibetans hawked handicrafts laid out on cloths by the edges of roads.

No position of any power is currently held by a Tibetan, and no Tibetan has ever been appointed to a position of real authority. Most of the monasteries that have been rebuilt are mainly used as tourist stops. The monks who live in them are not allowed to pursue the intensive studies that were required in pre-invasion Tibet, which means that they have little knowledge of the religion and are not able to explain it to others. The external symbols of Tibetan Buddhism are allowed—prostrations, prayer flags, images, and so on—but without the background knowledge that was possessed by Tibet's scholar-monks before the invasion, they remain symbols without substance, a sad memorial to the gutting of Tibetan culture that has been carried out by the Chinese. In a report on religious freedom in contemporary Tibet, Asia Watch concludes that "the limited leeway that religious expression has been given in Tibet in no sense permits the independent propagation of Buddhism or the unfettered management of religious institutions by Buddhist believers themselves."[27]

Despite the repression, according to all reports the overwhelming majority of the population remains committed to Buddhism and deeply devoted to the exiled Dalai Lama. An example of his continuing influence that both surprised and embarrassed the Chinese authorities was his statement to Tibetans during a Kālacakra initiation in India in 2006 denouncing the practice of wearing animal furs. He urged Tibetans to cease purchasing skins of endangered species, and when Tibetans who had traveled to India returned to their homes reported his words, within days reports surfaced from all over the Tibetan cultural area of public bonfires of animal skins. The purveyors of pelts in Lhasa saw their business plummet overnight. Although the Chinese government is officially committed to preservation of endangered species, the fact that this movement was initiated by the Dalai Lama led them to criminalize fur burning. There have been reports of several arrests, but they appear to have had little effect on Tibetans.[28]

Despite such evidence of continuing loyalty to the Dalai Lama, Chinese authorities regularly denounce him publicly and work to undermine Tibetans' attachment to their culture and religion. The most successful aspect of this plan is the ongoing population transfer of Han Chinese to Tibet, which has rendered the Tibetans a minority in their own land. In a speech commemorating the thirty-fourth anniversary of the Tibetan uprising in 1959, the Dalai Lama discussed current Chinese actions and policies, and he concluded that

> the situation in Tibet continues to remain bleak. Merciless repression of the slightest political dissent is the order. The demographic aggression of Tibet through a policy of population transfer continues unabated, escalating the marginalization of the Tibetan people and the assimilation of the Tibetan way of life into the Chinese mainstream. Cultural genocide is being committed, intentionally or unintentionally. Tibet, an ancient country on the roof of the world, is fast becoming a Chinese colony . . . Throughout human history, dictators and totalitarian governments have learned that there is nothing more powerful than a people's yearning for freedom and dignity. While bodies may be enslaved or imprisoned, the human spirit can never be subjugated or defeated. As long as we uphold this human spirit and determination, our aspirations and beliefs have the power to ultimately prevail. The sweeping global changes in recent years reaffirm my beliefs and I am more optimistic than ever before that freedom and peace for the Tibetan people is now within our reach.[29]

Despite the Dalai Lama's optimistic conclusions, today Han settlers outnumber Tibetans by several million, and in the cities Tibetans have become a minority. The Chinese authorities deny that the population transfer is taking place and accuse news organizations that report on the influx of Chinese in Tibet of attempting to "split the motherland" with false accusations. International human rights groups that document the transfer are denounced as "liars" and tools of Western "imperialists."

Tibetans observing this transfer fear that the flood of immigrants will eventually overwhelm the indigenous population in the same way that other "minorities" have been engulfed by Han settlers. In Manchuria, for example, native Manchurians now number two million, while the Han population is estimated at seventy-five million. Ethnic Mongolians are outnumbered five to one in their own country, and in Eastern Turkestan (Sinkiang) there are fifteen million Han Chinese, as compared to 7.5 million Eastern Turkestanis. This is part of a process through which, according to China's Central Institute of Nationalities, "minorities will amalgamate and disappear." Since the authorities consider Han Chinese to be racially superior to the minorities and believe that Han culture is also more advanced than those of the minority peoples, this is viewed by them as a positive development.

The Dalai Lama's Attempts at Reconciliation

In spite of the reports of ongoing human rights abuses, the Dalai Lama continues to seek a peaceful compromise with the Chinese government. In 1987 he proposed a "five-point plan" for a negotiated settlement, in which he offered to accept Chinese ownership of Tibet, while asking for a cessation of human rights abuses and a return to Tibetan control over internal affairs. His efforts won him international praise and led to his receiving the Nobel Peace Prize in 1989, but the plan was flatly rejected by the Chinese government, which accuses him of attempting to "split the motherland." Chinese officials also attacked the Nobel Commission for attempting to undermine "the unity of the nation" through what they characterized as a "gross interference in China's internal affairs."

The Dalai Lama continues to press for negotiations and puts pressure on China by bringing Tibet's cause to international forums. In discussing the Chinese occupation of his country, he remains apparently free of animosity, and resolutely declares that he bears no ill will toward the Chinese people, or even toward their leaders. Rather, he contends that in his opinion they are acting in ignorance, and through this are sowing the causes of their own future suffering.[30]

Tibetan Buddhism's Influence Today

Ironically, as Tibetan Buddhism is being destroyed in its native land, it is having an unprecedented impact in other countries. The Tibetan diaspora has forced thousands of eminent lamas to leave their country, with the result that many have met and influenced people in other cultures. Their knowledge of the philosophy and meditative practices of Buddhism—as well as their personalities, which often demonstrate the positive effects of years of training in wisdom and compassion—have attracted large numbers of followers.[31]

Tibetan Buddhism has had its greatest influence in Europe and North America, which today have hundreds of Tibetan Buddhist centers and tens of thousands of people who profess to follow its teachings. A number of Tibetan lamas have successfully translated the ideas and practices of their tradition to Western audiences, and a few Westerners have taken vows as monks and nuns. Many Tibetans view the success of their religion in America as fulfillment of a prophecy attributed to Padmasambhava in the late eighth century:

> When the iron bird flies and horses run on wheels, the Tibetan people will be scattered like ants across the face of the earth, and the dharma will come to the land of the red men.

As a result of the diaspora, Western scholars now have access to Tibetan literature to an extent that never would have been possible had Tibet remained closed. More importantly, the Chinese invasion has driven most of Tibet's great scholars and religious practitioners into exile, and now people interested in studying or practicing Buddhism are able to meet with them and receive oral explanations. Because of this, Tibetan culture has become diffused throughout the world, and eminent lamas—most notably the Dalai Lama—have been able to travel widely and spread the dharma. A veritable flood of books on Tibetan Buddhism is being published in Western languages. Tibetan lamas have appeared in television specials and movies, and the Dalai Lama has become one of the most visible religious leaders in the world. Since receiving the Nobel Peace Prize in 1989, he has been in great demand as a public speaker, and he is widely recognized as a leading figure in international efforts to promote human rights. Thus the national catastrophe of Tibet has had at least some positive results, although this fact in no way diminishes the tragedy of the Chinese invasion, nor does it lessen the shared suffering of the Tibetan people.

The Dalai Lama in Global Perspective

Westerners who study the system of reincarnating lamas are often understandably skeptical about it, but it seems clear that somehow the Tibetans who choose the Dalai Lamas have managed to find a remarkable succession of unusually gifted people. Even given the profound devotion that Tibetans feel for their Dalai Lamas, it would be difficult to disguise an incarnation who was stupid, arrogant, greedy, or belligerent. Those Dalai Lamas who attained maturity, however, have consistently distinguished themselves in their teaching, writing, and personal examples. The present Dalai Lama is a testament to the success of the system through which Dalai Lamas are found, and it is improbable that his remarkable accomplishments are merely due to good training. Many monks follow the same basic training as the Dalai Lamas, but somehow the Dalai Lamas tend to rise above others of their generation in terms of scholarship, personal meditative attainments, and teaching abilities. It is true that they receive the best training, and they also have the finest teachers, but these facts alone fail to account for their accomplishments. In Western countries, many students enroll in the finest colleges, study with the best teachers, and still fail to rise above mediocrity because they are lacking in intellectual gifts.

When one considers the origins of the present Dalai Lama, his successes are remarkable. Born in a remote village in eastern Tibet, driven from his country by an invading army and forced to start over in exile, he is today a Nobel Prize laureate and one of the world's most revered religious leaders. When one considers the odds against randomly choosing a young child from a remote Tibetan village, educating him in a traditional Tibetan monastic curriculum, and his later winning the Nobel Peace Prize, his accomplishments might give skeptics pause.[32] As Glenn Mullin remarks of the fourteenth Dalai Lama,

> the depth of his learning, wisdom and profound insight into the nature of human existence has won him hundreds of thousands of friends around the world. His humor, warmth and compassionate energy stand as living evidence of the strength and efficacy of Tibetan Buddhism, and of its value to human society.[33]

There are obviously problems with the system, particularly the lapses of leadership while newly recognized Dalai Lamas reach maturity. The system worked well enough in the past when Tibet was not beset by hostile neighbors, but it is difficult to imagine any country in the present age being able to endure periods of eighteen years or more without a true leader. It is not surprising, therefore, that the present Dalai Lama has expressed doubts about the continuing viability of the institution of the

Dalai Lamas and has indicated that he may not choose to reincarnate. He has also proposed that the office of Dalai Lama become an elected position, with the Tibetan people voting for their spiritual leader. The Dalai Lama appears to recognize the flaws in the present system and apparently hopes that the institution will be adapted to changing times. If Tibetans regain control of their country and if the lineage of incarnations continues, it seems clear that it will need to change, but this should come as no surprise to Tibetans, who recognize that everything is impermanent—even Dalai Lamas.

Notes

1. The situation in this region is described by Eric Teichman, who was involved in brokering the agreement: *Travels of a Consular Officer in North-West China* (Cambridge: Cambridge University Press, 1922), p. 2ff.
2. A detailed account of the situation in eastern Tibet exceeds the parameters of this book, but there are a number of good sources, including accounts by travelers in the region. Geoffrey Samuel provides a useful overview in *Civilized Shamans: Buddhism in Tibetan Societies* (Washington, D.C.: Smithsonian Institution Press, 1993), pp. 64–98. He cites a number of accounts that describe various perspectives on the politics and society of eastern Tibet.
3. See Paul Nietupski, "Sino-Tibetan Relations in Eighteenth-Century Labrang," Katia Buffertrille and Hildegard Diemberger, eds., *Territory and Identity in Tibet and the Himalayas* (Leiden: E.J. Brill, 2002), pp. 121–133 and Toni Huber, "Introduction: A mdo and Its Modern Transition," Toni Huber, ed., *Amdo Tibetans in Transition: Society and Culture in the Post-Mao Era* (Leiden: E.J. Brill, 2002), pp. xi–xxiii.
4. Zhao's depredations are described by Shakabpa in *Tibet: A Political History*, pp. 225–226.
5. See John Avedon, *In Exile from the Land of Snows* (New York: Vintage, 1986), p. 3.
6. The Panchen Lama's sojourn in China and the influence he had on Chinese attitudes toward Tibet are described by Gray Tuttle in *Tibetan Buddhists in the Making of Modern China* (New York: Columbia University Press, 2005).
7. This is translated in Melvyn Goldstein, *A History of Modern Tibet*, pp. 204–205.
8. See Melvyn Goldstein, *A History of Modern Tibet*, p. 333.
9. Some interesting work in this area was done by Dr. Ian Stevenson, who interviewed a number of children who reported strikingly detailed information of past lives. See, for example, *Twenty Cases Suggestive of Reincarnation* (Charlottesville: University Press of Virginia, 1980), and *Children Who Remember Previous Lives* (Charlottesville: University Press of Virginia, 1987).
10. This is not always the case, however, as the ongoing dispute over the successor to the sixteenth Gyelwa Kamapa indicates. After his death, there was no clear indication of his future plans, but one of his regents, Tai Situ Rinpoché, later produced a

locket he claimed had been given him by the Karmapa that contained a note purportedly indicating the place and situation of his reincarnation. The authenticity of the note has been disputed by Shamar Rinpoché, another regent, who has backed another candidate. The dispute has led to violent clashes between members of the two factions, and there are presently several lawsuits making their way through the Indian courts.

11. For a discussion of the development of the association of the Dalai Lamas with Avalokiteśvara, see Yumiko Ishihama, "On the Dissemination of the Belief in the Dalai Lama as a Manifestation of the Bodhisattva Avalokiteśvara," *Acta Asiatica* 64, 1993, pp. 38–56.
12. *A History of Modern Tibet*, pp. 357–360.
13. David Patt, *A Strange Liberation* (Ithaca: Snow Lion, 1992), p. 28. The Chinese and Tibetan perspectives on the invasion and occupation are discussed in *History as Propaganda*, chapter 4.
14. John Avedon, *In Exile from the Land of Snows*, pp. 229–30.
15. Some of the rebels' weapons were supplied by the American Central Intelligence Agency, although recently released records indicate that CIA officials thought that the Tibetans' eventual defeat was inevitable. Some Tibetan guerillas were even trained at secret CIA bases in Colorado and then clandestinely flown back into the Mustang region of Nepal, from where they moved back into Tibet. The CIA's involvement is detailed in Kenneth Conboy and James Morrison, *The CIA's Secret War in Tibet* (Lawrence, KS: University of Kansas Press, 2002). The story of one of the Tibetan resistance fighters can be found in Jamyang Norbu, *Warriors of Tibet: The Story of Aten and the Khampas' Fight for the Freedom of Their Country* (London: Wisdom Publications, 1979).
16. The best account to date of these events is Tsering Shakya's *The Dragon in the Land of Snows: A History of Modern Tibet Since 1947* (New York: Columbia University Press, 1999), which also discusses the events leading up to the rebellion.
17. Margaret Nowak's book *Tibetan Refugees: Youth and the New Generation of Meaning* (New Brunswick, NJ: Rutgers University Press, 1984) discusses the early period of refugee settlement in India and the vicissitudes they faced. There have been a number of studies of aspects of the refugee experience of Tibetans, including P. Christiaan Klieger, *Accomplishing Tibetan Identity: the Constitution of a National Consciousness* (Ph.D. dissertation, University of Hawai'i, 1989); and *Tibetan Nationalism: The Role of Patronage in the Accomplishment of a National Identity* (Meerut, India: Archana Publications, 1992); Dorsh Marie Devoe, "Keeping Refugee Status: A Tibetan Perspective," Scott Morgan and Elizabeth Colson, eds. *People in Upheaval* (New York: Center for Migration Studies, 1987), pp. 54–65; and Claes Corlin, *The Nation in Your Mind: Continuity and Change among Tibetan Refugees in Nepal* (Ph.D. dissertation, University of Göteborg, 1975). Toni Huber has written several excellent articles, including "Shangri-la in Exile: Representations of Tibetan Identity and Transnational Culture," Thierry Dodin and Heinz Räther, eds., *Imagining Tibet: Perceptions, Projections, and Fantasies* (Boston: Wisdom Publications, 2001), pp. 357–371.
18. This is more the case in the south than in Dharamsala, where there have been violent clashes between Tibetans and local inhabitants, many of whom complain about what they consider condescending Tibetan attitudes and mistreatment of Indians.
19. Currently about three thousand Tibetans on average flee into exile every year despite the dangers and difficulties. Given the rigors of the journey and the small

population of Tibet, these numbers are a clear sign of continuing repression by China. The largest number make their escape during the winter months, when there are fewer Chinese patrols, and have to cross some of the world's highest passes—often traveling for several weeks before reaching freedom—and then have to get past Nepali border guards who may send them back, rob them, or extort money to let them continue. After that they are examined by a refugee tribunal, and may then proceed to India or another country if their claims for refugee status are accepted. Even if they succeed, their status is still uncertain, and new arrivals are often greeted with suspicion by established refugees because they have lived under Chinese control.

20. For a study of the history and current status of Tibetan nuns, see Hanna Havnevik, *Tibetan Buddhist Nuns: History, Cultural Norms and Social Reality* (Oslo: Norwegian University Press, 1989). Another important study of women's roles in Tibetan Buddhism is Janet Gyatso and Hanna Havnevik, eds., *Women in Tibet* (New York: Columbia University Press, 2005).
21. Wang Furen and Suo Wenqing, *Highlights of Tibetan History*, tr. Xu Jian (Beijing: New World Press, 1984), p. 178.
22. Some recent publications have argued that prisons in China are built more for profit than for punishment or rehabilitation. Recent estimates place China's prison population at between sixteen and twenty million people. Prisoners commonly work long hours in dangerous conditions, and although they are paid for their work, it is barely enough to buy their food, clothes, and so on (which must be purchased from their captors). Because of this large force of what amounts to slave labor, China is able to export goods at prices which are much lower than those charged by companies with paid employees (see Steven Mosher, "Chinese Prison Labor," *Society* 29, 1991, pp. 49–59).
23. See Christoph von Fürer-Haimendorf, *The Renaissance of Tibetan Civilization* (Oracle, AZ: Synergetic Press, 1990), pp. 31–34. These figures are vigorously contested by the PRC, which at one point admitted that three hundred thousand people died during the invasion and Cultural Revolution, but now claims that only a few "reactionaries" perished.
24. Quoted in Anne Klein, "Contemporary Tibet: Cultural Genocide in Progress," *White Lotus* (Ithaca: Snow Lion, 1990), p. 45.
25. As reported by Reuters, April 16, 1993, Amnesty International contends that "the practice of torture has become endemic in Chinese detention centres in ten years and that prisoners now suffer much more severe abuses."
26. Asia Watch, *Merciless Repression: Human Rights in Tibet* (New York: Human Rights Watch, 1990), p. 3.
27. Ibid., p. 70. See also *Contemporary Tibet: Politics, Development, and Society in A Disputed Region*, ed. Barry Sautman and June Dreyer (Armonk: M.E. Sharpe, 2006), which contains articles that examine the contemporary situation from a variety of perspectives by Tibetan, Chinese, and Western authors.
28. Radio Free Asia aired a report on this phenomenon on February 22, 2006, and since then several other international media organizations have done reports on the continuing movement to burn furs and stop the sale of new ones, along with Chinese efforts to halt this embarrassing example of the Dalai Lama's continuing influence among Tibetans.
29. H.H. the Dalai Lama, March 10, 1993.

30. H.H. the Dalai Lama, "Human Rights and Universal Responsibility" (speech delivered to nongovernmental organizations, the United Nations World Conference on Human Rights), Vienna, Austria, June 16, 1993.
31. *The Renaissance of Tibetan Civilization*, p. 14.
32. This was pointed out to me by William Magee during a lecture at Grinnell College in November 1992.
33. *Selected Works of the Dalai Lama II*, tr. Glenn Mullin (Ithaca: Snow Lion, 1982), p. 220.

7. Religious Festivals and Holy Days

Mönlam

Buddhism has a pervasive influence on the Tibetan cultural area, and so it is not surprising that the year is punctuated by a multitude of religious festivals and holy days. These vary from minor observances that are only celebrated in small localities to elaborate ceremonies—like the yearly holiday called "Great Aspiration" (*sMon lam chen mo;* pronounced "Mönlam Chenmo")—which were major events in Tibet and the surrounding areas in which Tibetan Buddhists live. The great festivals drew people from far and wide, and for many they were high points of the year. During Mönlam, for example, people congregated in Lhasa from all over Tibet, Mongolia, Nepal, Bhutan, Sikkim, and even as far away as Siberia.

These pilgrims often traveled vast distances on foot or horseback in order to visit the sacred precincts for this auspicious time, during which great lamas performed powerful ceremonies for the wellbeing of sentient beings everywhere. Some people even made the journey in a series of prostrations, stretching themselves full-length on the ground and then beginning again from the place marked by the tips of the fingers. Pilgrims who traveled in this way sometimes took months to reach their destinations, but they chose to do so believing that such acts of devotion bring great merit to those who perform them. It was also thought that people who were present in the holy city of Lhasa, being in the nexus of the ceremony, received extra merit. Moreover, according to a widely held Tibetan belief, religious activities performed on important holy days yield greater results than those done at other times.[1]

In addition to their religious benefits, major festivals also provided opportunities for economic and social exchanges. The influx of pilgrims brought in money and goods from outside, as well as opportunities to meet people from other places. Products from outside the area—as well as news brought by visitors—flooded into the cities during these times, and the visitors for their part often purchased mementos and brought them home.

Many of the most popular festivals of Tibet were traditionally held in Lhasa, the religious and political capital of the country. Today they are celebrated by Tibetans in their exile communities. Many, including the Great Aspiration Festival, have been banned by the Chinese, but in recent years some of the restrictions have been relaxed. Recent reports indicate that participation in festivals and pilgrimages is growing, but the relative tolerance of religious activity could change at any time.

One of the most important of the major holy times was the Mönlam celebration, which was instituted by Tsong Khapa, founder of the Gélukpa order, in 1409. The festival commemorates the two weeks during which Śākyamuni Buddha manifested miraculous powers. According to legend, he was challenged to a contest of magic by a group of heretics, and he responded by multiplying himself into a row of manifestations stretching into infinity, each one issuing flames from its head and feet. The heretics were unable to match this and were defeated. This is referred to as the "Great Miracle." The heretics were enemies of the Buddha (and, by extension, of the dharma), and so it is not surprising that their defeat is connected with New Year rituals designed to drive out evil forces and ensure the protection of Buddhism in Tibet.

Mönlam is held during the first two weeks of the first month of the Tibetan lunar calendar and is connected with the celebration of the Tibetan New Year (*Lo gsar;* pronounced "Losar"). During this time, monks from the great monasteries of Drébung and Séra—along with other monks from all over the Tibetan cultural area—gather together to recite prayers and perform rituals for the benefit of all sentient beings. These are attended by throngs of laypeople, and as Tucci notes,

> the monks are actors, the laity spectators . . . the laymen are always beneficiaries of these religious performances, since the ceremonies generate merit which spreads out over everyone. Through the transference of the result of a good action it brings profit to all. The believers are thereby encouraged to contribute to the fruitful performance

of the sacred ceremony through donations and other services, since it is to their own moral advantage.[2]

This time is also the occasion of the yearly examinations of candidates for the *géshé* degree (the highest degree in the Gélukpa monastic system). The candidates are subjected to a rigorous set of examinations, which stress oral debate and a comprehensive knowledge of Buddhist philosophy. Each candidate's testing typically lasts for an entire day, during which he must be able to field questions from monks from both his own and other schools. Laypeople are also allowed to join in and ask questions of the monks, but even those who are unable to follow the subtleties of the exchanges come to the examinations. Huge crowds gather for these public debates, and the procedure is viewed as great entertainment by laypeople and monks alike.

Although Mönlam is primarily a religious festival, it also embraces many nonreligious activities, some of which are probably remnants of pre-Buddhist celebrations. There is evidence that New Year festivals were celebrated in Tibet prior to the establishment of Buddhism, and these included martial activities, reflecting a pre-Buddhist emphasis on warfare and conquest. Such practices continue today, despite the religious overtones of Mönlam. During the festival, people parade through the streets wearing antique armor and traditional ceremonial clothing, hearkening back to the days of Tibetan military might. There are also horse races, archery contests, wrestling matches, and other secular activities. For most, however, it remains a thoroughly religious festival, a time for contemplation and devotion. Large numbers of people perform prostrations in front of holy structures and personages, and they light butter lamps, make offerings to the monastic community, and renew their commitment to the dharma through increased devotion and religious observances. Through these practices, according to Tucci,

> the karmic content of the festival does not remain isolated; it benefits all, and provides the ethical counterpart of an efficacious defence against evil, the result of a symbiosis between old and new, between the original religiosity of Tibet and the moral doctrine of Buddhism.[3]

The Mönlam festival, through driving out evil forces and creating positive karma, has an underlying purpose of ameliorating the effects of the present degenerate age in which we live. Tsong Khapa was concerned that humanity was currently in an age in which the dharma was declining, and that this process of degeneration would continue until the birth of Maitreya, the buddha of the future. Until that time, however, Buddhists can still practice effectively if they are vigilant and take proper precautions. Major religious celebrations help people to accomplish their religious aspirations by undermining the power of the evil forces of this period of religious degeneration.

Mönlam is the most important of the major festivals, which are referred to by Tibetans as "great times" (*dus chen*). The others are also connected with the life of the Buddha. These festivals commemorate his birth on the seventh day of the fourth month; his awakening on the fifteenth day of the same month (during which his entry into final nirvana is also celebrated); his first sermon on the fourth day of the sixth month, and his descent from Tuṣita heaven during the ninth month. Tradition holds that he was born, died, attained awakening, and turned the wheel of dharma on the same date, but some of these events are celebrated on separate dates. All are also commemorated on the fifteenth day of the fourth month, referred to as "Śākya Month" (*Sa ga zla ba;* pronounced "Saga Dawa"). This is a reference to the Buddha's epithet *Śākyamuni*, "Sage of the Śākyas."

The Butter-Sculpture Festival of Kumbum

Although Lhasa remains the spiritual center of Tibet, other areas also have festivals of national importance. One of the most notable of these is the annual Butter-Sculpture Festival held at Kumbum during the first lunar month. Since its focus is a public display of butter sculptures on the fifteenth day, it is commonly known as "The Offering of the Fifteenth."[4]

Kumbum is located in eastern Tibet and is closely associated with the life of Tsong Khapa. The main monastery of the town is believed to have been built on the site where he was born. Its name derives from a popular story which reports that after his birth some drops of blood fell to the ground when the umbilical cord was cut. From these a white sandalwood tree sprang up bearing one hundred thousand (*'bum*) leaves, each of which had an image (*sku*) of Tsong Khapa on it. Thus the spot came to be known as Kumbum (*sku 'bum*), meaning "one hundred thousand images."

From early times Kumbum has been an important commercial center, since it is located at the crossroads of major trade routes. Before the Chinese invasion, caravans passed through Kumbum from all over Central Asia, transporting goods from one area to another, and bringing visitors from many places to this remote region of eastern Tibet. Although Kumbum was a small town with about three thousand permanent residents, it absorbed cultural influences from other places, since it regularly had visitors from Mongolia, other parts of Tibet, Chinese travelers and merchants, Uigurs from Central Asia, and even visitors from Russia and neighboring areas.

The Butter Sculpture Festival is held at the monastery of Kumbum, and some of its teaching faculties compete with each other in making the figures. Prior to the invasion, Kumbum had five colleges: a college of medicine, a tantric college, a college of Kālacakra studies, a college of philosophical dialectics, and a college of religious dance. Within the college of philosophical dialectics, there were thirteen separate classes on Perfection of Wisdom philosophy, each of which had its own emphases and texts. Two of these—one of which follows the textbooks of Jétsünpa Chögi Gyeltsen and another that follows the textbooks of Jamyang Shéba—were mainly responsible for constructing the butter sculptures.

These figures were often elaborate artistic masterpieces, using large quantities of hardened butter, sometimes with clever internal frames containing joints and springs that allowed them to move. The process of accumulating the necessary funds began with the completion of one festival; funding the next one often required months of work by the monks in charge, who traveled far and wide to solicit donations. The monks involved in making the sculptures sometimes spent several months on their creations, and the work was generally very detailed and carefully executed. The largest and most elaborate figures were often started in the ninth month of the previous year. As Robert Ekvall indicates, this festival became

> a noteworthy exhibition of current Tibetan art. The butter images—displayed only once and then destroyed before dawn of the very next day—are planned and executed with great care by carefully trained artists, each with his own particular skill and renown. Months of planning and lavish expenditure go into their creation; and the element of competition that has become a part of the display has helped produce, or maintain, an excellence of execution and beauty of line and coloration. The various organizations within the monastery—the colleges and the establishments of the emanation-body lamas

> [tülku]—assume responsibility for different units of the exhibition, and there is intense rivalry among them to put on the best show.[5]

Traditionally, after all the figures were completed, they were displayed on the fifteenth day of the first month in an enclosed area about twenty feet high and forty feet wide, filled with an array of colorful and intricately fashioned images. Each year a different theme was emphasized. The members of the classes responsible for creating the images would decide on what this was to be, and it would be kept secret until the sculptures were made available for public display. Popular themes included events from the stories of Śākyamuni's previous births, his twelve great deeds,[6] Tibetan folk tales (overlaid with Buddhist symbolism and imagery), or important events in Tibetan religious history. Some of the displays would consist of as many as twenty large butter figures, elaborately sculpted and carefully painted in vibrant colors. The coloring was made from natural dyes, often mixed with ash. In addition, the most important sculptures were sometimes decorated with pigments made from powdered gold and silver, as well as other precious substances. The images commonly had boards for backing, but others were freestanding sculptures with internal supports. In some cases frames from the previous year were used, but most had to be newly constructed.

The Images

While making the sculptures, the artists kept two buckets at hand, one containing hot water, and the other containing cold water. Since the butter had to be kept cold to prevent melting, warm hands could damage the artists' work. Moreover, sculptors' hands had to be kept clean, since dirty hands could stick to the figures or smudge them. While working on the images, the monks would first put their hands into the hot water to wash them, and then dip them in dry flour and rub their fingers together to remove dirt. The hands were then rinsed in hot water, and then dipped in cold water in order to cool the skin. This enabled the artists to avoid melting or discoloring the images while shaping the butter, which was first molded by hand, and later smoothed and colored.

In addition to religious scenes, the monks would sculpt images depicting life in the monasteries, often including figures of the head monks. Many of these were caricatures, as this was a time in which it was acceptable to gently poke fun at the senior officials of the monastery. If the head lama was old, for example, his figure might have a head with a spring at the neck, which would cause the head to bob up and down, symbolizing senility and feebleness. Other prominent physical features would be exaggerated, although there were commonly recognized boundaries of good taste, and the monks were expected to remain within them. In the displays of monastic life, the various figures would often be movable. Monks manipulated their movements from behind the scenes by means of ropes and pulleys, and internal spring mechanisms gave them added mobility.

When all the preparations were complete, the sculptures were displayed in a specially constructed enclosure lit by butter lamps. The monks of the Perfection of Wisdom classes greeted people at the entrance and gave their guests cups of tea; many laypeople responded by making offerings of food or money to the monks. The images were only displayed at night for a few hours. The monks and laypeople filed through the area, admiring these exquisitely sculpted images, knowing as they viewed them that all would be destroyed before dawn. This provided the audience with a graphic reminder of the Buddhist concept of impermanence, which teaches that all mundane human activities pass away, leaving nothing behind. Those who recognize the implications of this principle should understand the ultimate futility of worldly pursuits and devote themselves to religious activities, which bring lasting benefits.

After the display, the buddhas and bodhisattvas who had earlier been invited to enter the figures were asked to leave (because it would be disrespectful to destroy the images if they were inhabited), and the monks quickly dismantled the sculptures. The frames were saved, but the sculptures were stacked up, their coloring was scraped off, and they were then melted down. The end of the festival was marked by a ritual in which people tossed constructs called *sur* (*zur*) into a pit.

Sur are structures made of sticks in a pyramidal shape, connected with strong paper and decorated with images of fire, clouds, jewels, and other symbols, all made from butter. On top of the *sur* was a skull with flames coming from its mouth. Ribbons and strings were tied to the top of the tripod. These were used to steady it while it was being moved. Inside the legs of the tripod was a *torma*, which is a painted sculpture made of flour and butter. The *sur* was built as a part of a ceremony to exorcise evil forces, which were lured into it by special rituals. On the afternoon of the nineteenth day, the *sur* was carried in a procession, followed by the monastery's abbot, who held a vajra and bell in his hands. Behind him was a crowd of seventy-five to one hundred monks, who banged drums, clashed cymbals, and blew horns. A crowd of spectators was in the rear of the procession.

After rituals were conducted to bring all the evil of the area into the *sur*, the structure was taken outside the grounds of the monastery and burned, thus making a clean slate for the New Year. On the way to the burning ground, the crowd was joined by the Néchung oracle, who was in trance. His power was invoked to aid in driving out evil and making the New Year safe and prosperous. When the procession reached the designated spot, the *sur* and *torma* were thrown into a pit filled with straw and wood. A fire was lit and the structure burned, signifying that evil had been overcome and dharma had prevailed. The *sur* symbolized not only external evil forces, but also internal mental afflictions such as ignorance, desire, and hatred. The fire represented the light of wisdom that immolated them, leaving behind the clear light nature of mind. Thus the ritual had several levels of significance and could be interpreted by untutored laypeople as a straightforward exorcism ceremony, while tantric practitioners viewed it as a symbolic enactment of the meditational process, the aim of which was to purify the mind of defilements and bring about the actualization of the fully awakened mind of a buddha.

In addition to its religious aspects, the festival also had important secular elements, and it was a period of relaxed rules for laypeople. There was a great deal of drinking and celebration, and many social contacts were made. It was also a good time for young people to meet members of the opposite sex. Due to the relaxed rules it was a time of increased promiscuity.[7] There were also secular entertainments such as musical performances and horse races, and it was a period of vigorous commercial activity. A bazaar was set on the western edge of the monastery, and there were restaurants and displays all over town. The area was full of merchants from different areas, as well as seers and fortunetellers, who for a small price would prognosticate the future.

Sacred Dance

During the New Year celebrations, it is common for monks to perform ritual dances, called *cham* (*'cham*), in which they don elaborate costumes and enact performances with Buddhist themes. Traditionally held on the fourteenth day of the first lunar month, this colorful dance,

> which is ritual and drama combined, is a spectacle presented to the gods, but it is also of benefit to men. Through it, the old year, with its sins and disasters, is pushed into the background; and the new year is purged . . . and safeguarded for all who watch and worship.[8]

During the dances, monks wear brightly colored costumes and masks, which represent Buddhist themes and depict religious figures as well as demons and mythical creatures. There are also comic elements, such as a figure representing the Chinese teacher Heshang Moheyan, who according to Tibetan histories was defeated by the Indian scholar Kamalaśīla in a debate held in Lhasa.[9]

Before the dances begin, the participants prepare themselves by visualizing a maṇḍala. This provides the paradigm for the entire performance. The monastery's courtyard becomes the base of the maṇḍala, and the participants are the deities and other figures within it.

The action begins when a group of dancers in skeleton costumes enters the courtyard. They are the helpers of Yama, the Lord of Death. Holding short sticks, they carry a tray with a triangular iron box in it. This holds a human figure made out of *tsampa* (barley flour) dough, colored black, resting on its back with its knees up and hands folded at the heart. The tray is placed in the center of the courtyard, after which another group of dancers enters. These are helpers of the maṇḍala's main deity. They are followed by another contingent of heroes, whose male figures wear turbans and have mustaches, while the female figures have green faces and large eyes.

Next come three more helpers of the Lord of Death dressed as deer, holding skull cups and curved knives. Their performance is followed by dances by lions and crocodiles. A comic skit comes next, executed by monks dressed as Heshang Moheyan and his six Chinese disciples. The Heshang is portrayed as a portly monk with a flat, smiling face. He stumbles around the courtyard, and his disciples keep him from hurting himself, help him up when he falls, and fan him, but they make fun of him when he falls asleep. This is often performed as slapstick farce, and it indicates the current state of the Chinese master's reputation in Tibet.

The next character to enter is either Yama or Hayagrīva. Yama is a demonic figure with the head of a horned bull and blue skin. He carries a skull cup and staff and wears a crown of skulls. Hayagrīva has a wrathful red face, surmounted by three horse heads, and he also holds a skull cup and wears a crown of skulls. He holds a double-edged sword, symbolic of his wrathful nature. The main figure is accompanied by other fierce deities, all in bright costumes and wearing skull crowns, carrying skull cups, and wielding swords.

If the main figure is Yama, his skeleton helpers bring the triangular box to him, and the figure in it is invested with all the evil of the old year. Dancers representing Indian masters then remove the lid and Yama drives a dagger through the figure's heart and cuts off its head, arms, and legs, symbolizing the exorcizing of the evil of the old year and a fresh start in the new one. One of the deer helpers then removes the head of the figure, and others carry away the other parts and dispose of them, thus completing the exorcism.

Other Religious Festivals

An exhaustive listing and description of Tibetan holy days and festivals would require a separate book. In this section I have only mentioned some of the more prominent ones, the major celebrations that draw people from all over the Tibetan cultural area. Other important religious events include the celebration held on the fifteenth day of the third month commemorating the preaching of the *Kālacakra Tantra*, which tradition holds was first revealed at Śrī Dhānyakaṭaka in India. Each of the four orders of Tibetan Buddhism also celebrates the traditional date of the revelation of its main tantric text.

The Nyingma school has a number of festivals that celebrate events in the life of Padmasambhava, the "Precious Guru" (*Guru Rinpoché*). The tenth day of the first month is the occasion for commemorating his renunciation of the world, his taking of vows, and his meditation in cemeteries. On the tenth day of the second month, Nyingmapas celebrate his taking of vows and the occasion of his being given the name "Lion of the Śākya" (*Sakya Sengé*). The tenth day of the third month is designated as a time to remember the story of his being thrown into a fire by the king of Sahor. Padmasambhava turned the flames into a pond of clear water, after which he sat in the middle of the pond on top of a huge lotus with his consort Mandāravā. Throughout the year Nyingmapas celebrate numerous other dates of particular significance to the tradition.

Sakyapas also have a number of important holy days, including the "Summer Offering," which is held on the seventh to fifteenth days of the fourth month. The focus of this ceremony is a set of rituals connected with the Hevajra tantric cycle. A festival on the fourth day of the sixth month memorializes the sixteen (or eighteen) arhats whose legends were inherited from India. This celebration is referred to as the "Great Thousand Offering" because during the festival one thousand lamps are lit.

Another Sakya observance is an exorcism called Tordok, during which a large *torma* (along with numerous smaller ones) is constructed and carried to the bank of the Tangchu River. The main image is associated with the wrathful deity Mahākāla (an aspect of Avalokiteśvara). Amid chanting and the firing of guns, a symbol called a *liṅga* (*ling ga*) is offered to the image. The ceremony, celebrated from the twenty-second to twenty-ninth days of the ninth month, is believed to propitiate local spirits and demons, making the area safe for its human inhabitants.

Common Elements in Tibetan Religious Ceremonies

Although Tibetan ceremonies exhibit a wide range of variations, several features are commonly found: the area to be used in a ceremony is first purified by rituals and the chanting of mantras; inimical forces are subdued; and the help of buddhas, bodhisattvas, ḍākinīs, and protectors is invoked. Rituals almost invariably begin with a recitation of the refuge prayer, in which the participants declare their resolution to rely on the Buddha, dharma, and saṃgha (and in tantric ceremonies the lama and ḍākinīs are often invoked). This is followed by a recitation of the bodhisattva vows, in which the celebrants pledge to strive for awakening in order to bring all sentient beings happiness and the causes of happiness. Other common features of Tibetan rituals include acts of homage, making offerings, confession of transgressions, praising the good deeds performed by sentient beings and buddhas, asking buddhas to teach the dharma, petitioning bodhisattvas to forgo their own nirvana in order to work for others, and dedicating the merit of the ritual to all sentient beings. Most religious gatherings also involve a great deal of chanting and often include playing of drums, horns, cymbals, and other instruments.

Many modern Buddhist festivals have their origins in pre-Buddhist celebrations, but have become overlaid with Buddhist symbols. Although they retain some of their original characteristics, they have become so infused with Buddhist imagery and significance that most are thoroughly

Buddhist in character, despite the fact that some external aspects hearken back to pre-Buddhist practices. As Tucci states, Tibetan Buddhism,

> far from forbidding the festivals in honour of the various *dei loci* (*yul lha, sa bdag, klu*), has rather impressed its own imprint on the traditional rituals and festivals, which have been allowed to continue and to preserve essential features of their ancient forms. There is scarcely any place in Tibet where these old indigenous forms were not preserved from destruction by admitting them into the festal calendar.[10]

These festivals are of a primarily religious nature and are distinguished from more secular festivals, such as the ceremonies celebrating the harvest. The religious celebrations are occasions for Tibetan Buddhists to gather together in the company of religious leaders and participate in rituals that drive out evil, purify the negative karmas of the country and its people, and serve as opportunities for practitioners to confess past misdeeds and rededicate themselves to their religion. Although these gatherings are primarily religious in nature, they are by no means overly solemn. Tibetans generally appreciate a good time, and their festivals serve as occasions to meet, talk, drink, and celebrate. During these times the Tibetans' love of celebration is evident, and while the religious aspects of the festivals are important, there is also a great deal of laughter, merrymaking, and socializing. Tibetan festivals have a multifaceted character and exhibit a curious blend of the religious and the mundane, of serious Buddhist rituals and humorous skits, sacred music and secular entertainments, all mixed together. These communal gatherings are important elements in the development of a sense of shared values and traditions: people gather together from a wide area to celebrate their religion and culture, to meet new people and old friends, and to drive out negative influences and ensure a brighter future.

NOTES

1. See, for instance, Thubten Legshay Gyatsho, *Gateway to the Temple* (Kathmandu: Ratna Pustak Bhandar, 1979), p. 81.
2. Giuseppe Tucci, *The Religions of Tibet*, pp. 146–147.
3. Ibid., p. 151.

4. A description of this event may be found in Thubten Norbu, *Tibet is My Country* (London: Rupert Hart-Davis, 1960), pp. 136–139.
5. Robert Ekvall, *Religious Observances of Tibet* (Chicago: University of Chicago Press, 1964), p. 175.
6. See chapter 1, "Buddhism in India."
7. Ekvall, *Religious Observances of Tibet*, pp. 175–176.
8. Ibid., p. 174. See also René de Nebesky-Wojkowitz, *Tibetan Religious Dances* (The Hague: Mouton, 1976); P.H. Pott, "Some Remarks on the 'Terrific Deities' in Tibetan 'Devil Dances,'" in *Tibetan Studies Presented at the Seminar of Young Tibetologists, Zürich, June 26-July 1, 1977*, ed. Martin Brauen and Per Kværne (Zürich, 1978), pp. 199–208; and Nanci A. Hoetzlein, "Sacred Ritual Dance: The *Gu Tor* Tradition at Namgyel Monastery," in *Chö Yang: The Voice of Tibetan Religion and Culture*, Year of Tibet Edition (1991), pp. 314–320.
9. See chapter 5, "Tibetan Religious History."
10. *The Religions of Tibet*, p. 149.

8: Geography and Architecture

The Religious Environment

THE LANDSCAPE of Tibet is intimately connected with the theory and practice of religious architecture. Its inhabitants view the country as a special place, a sacred realm that is literally alive with spirits and demons of all types. Some of these are benevolent, while others are potentially dangerous unless held in check by rituals and mantras, or by the construction of Buddhist structures. Tibetans have traditionally viewed their country as a living being, a wild demonness *(srin mo;* pronounced "sinmo") who was initially opposed to the propagation of Buddhism. In order to subdue her and aid the dissemination of the dharma, Songtsen Gampo reportedly sponsored the construction of twelve temples at key parts of the country. Referred to as "limb-binding temples," their intention was to subdue the country and prevent its spirits and demons from creating obstacles for Buddhist teachers.

These were built in three sets of four: (1) four for the central regions, referred to as the "four horns" *(ru bzhi)*; (2) four to subdue the border regions *(mtha' 'dul)* and (3) four for the outer regions *(yang 'dul)*. After these were completed, the Jokhang temple was built over the heart of the *sinmo*, which completed the process of subjugating her.[1] From the earliest times, the spread of Tibetan Buddhism has been linked with the building of temples and monasteries, as is indicated by the fact that the founding of Samyé (the first monastery in Tibet) is believed to have marked the official establishment of the dharma in Tibet.

The building of religious structures is also connected to Tibet's geography. The Tibetan plateau is like no other place on earth; it is a land apart, a place of vast open spaces, deep blue skies, and towering snow-capped mountains. The grandeur of the land has inspired spiritual seekers for millennia. There is perhaps no better place on earth to experience emptiness; space imposes itself on the consciousness everywhere one looks, the land seems to stretch off into infinity, and the sweeping ranges of mountains naturally draw the gaze upward toward the open sky.

It is also a harsh environment, with extremes of temperature and climate, huge tracts of arid high-altitude desert, thin air, and many regions that are barely habitable. As a result, for centuries Tibetans, like the indigenous inhabitants of North America, lived in harmony with their environment and carefully shepherded its resources. Such attitudes and practices were evoked by the natural beauty of the country and were also a pragmatic response to its dangers. In addition, their Buddhist beliefs led Tibetans to develop an aversion toward killing wild animals, and they avoided angering the spirits of the land by causing it harm. According to Lobsang Lhalungpa,

> All Tibet was once a land of pristine purity due to sparse population and the people's inbred sense of respect for nature and an ecological balance . . . . The physical world was considered not only the heavenly abode of the cosmic deities but also the sacred habitat of all living beings. All mountains, lakes, rivers, trees, and even the elements were sacred dwellings of the spiritual forces indeed, the entire country was deemed a 'sacred realm.'[2]

This perception of their country as a sacred realm was reflected in the fervor that Tibetans had for their religion. Before the Chinese invasion, the people of Tibet were devoted to religious practice on a scale unparalleled in other countries. Approximately one tenth of the adult male population was monks, and Tibet had over six thousand monasteries. Many of its inhabitants believe that widespread devotion to Buddhism is at least partially attributable to the country itself, that its geography is conducive to religious practice and mystical contemplation. Such attitudes have also been expressed by foreign travelers, such as Ardito Desio, who climbed the mountain peak in the Karakoram range known as K2. In his account of the climb, he writes:

> When I find myself alone, and only then, I am wont to meditate, and from my meditations I derive immense delight and great comfort. I meditate above all on the essential nature of human life, and in the process I find myself becoming even more serene and self-assured.[3]

Mircea Eliade echoes this sentiment in a discussion of the power of mountains to inspire human consciousness:

> Mountains are the nearest thing to the sky, and are thence endowed with twofold holiness: on the one hand they share in the spatial symbolism of transcendence—they are 'high,' 'vertical,' 'supreme,' and so on—and on the other, they are the especial domain of all hierophanies of atmosphere, and therefore, the dwelling of the gods . . . The symbolic and religious significance of mountains is endless. Mountains are often looked on as the place where sky and earth meet, a 'central point' therefore, the point through which the *Axis Mundi* goes, a region impregnated with the sacred, a spot where one can pass from one cosmic zone to another.[4]

Tibetan Architecture and Tibetan Landscape

Tibetan architecture has recognized the power and symbolism of mountains, as reflected in the way they are used to enhance the visual power of religious structures. The construction of religious buildings is connected with Buddhist principles and goals, and Tibetan Buddhist buildings reflect the natural conditions of the areas in which they are built. Religious structures play an important role in establishing a sense of Buddhist identity for the people of Tibet, and as one travels in the Tibetan cultural area one is regularly confronted by impressive buildings, many perched on steep hills, often appearing to float in the air in a region midway between the ground and the sky. These serve to draw the gaze upward and provide a shared symbol of their religion for the people who pass by. Visitors to the area remark on the powerful effect of monasteries and temples perched on steep cliffs, often with a striking backdrop of snow-covered mountains.[5] As Thubten Legshay Gyatsho indicates, this effect is intentional.

> One should seek out a place for building a temple in places that have the following: a tall mountain behind and many hills in front, two

> rivers converging in front from the right and left, a central valley of rocks and meadows resembling heaps of grain, and a lower part which is like two hands crossed at the wrists.[6]

Texts on architecture recommend such places as ideal locations for building monasteries and temples. They also list negative landscape features that should be avoided, such as a pointed curved shape in back of the site of the proposed temple, which is said to signify the jaws of the Lord of Death. This is an inauspicious omen, as is the presence of a spring above the site, which is symbolic of tears of sorrow.[7] Such negative features may be countered, however, and Tibetan architectural theory recognizes that no place is completely perfect. With the proper rituals and other counteragents, unfavorable landscape characteristics are prevented from undermining the success of the building process or harming the future inhabitants.

Construction of Religious Structures

When constructing a monastery or temple it is first necessary to determine an auspicious time to begin. Astrological divinations are conducted, and the lama in charge decides how they should be interpreted. After this, the builders must make offerings of incense to local deities, because without these they might become offended and interfere with the construction. The next stage involves taking possession of the land. In order for a religious site to be successful, it must be free of any negative associations, and so the builders must make sure that they have rightfully acquired it from any human owners. After this they make offerings to the spirits in the area as a way of paying them for the property. Most importantly, they propitiate the earth goddess, who ultimately owns the land.

> A plot of land possessing good signs and characteristics is the foundation from which all happiness is produced. Whoever wishes to build a monastic temple on such a spot should first take possession of the land. One should take possession from physically-apparent land owners, such as from the king or his ministers, either by verbal agreement or by payment of wealth. Then, one must make offerings to the invisible earth goddess, and one should perform the ritual in which one receives her acknowledgment of the sincerity of one's

> endeavors . . . . If one does not vigorously apply oneself to the examination, testing, appropriation and taming of the land, no matter how one proceeds there will be the danger of obstacles and obscurations. Hence, bearing in mind the many histories of temples built in the past, it is right to devote great attention to the ways by which shrines come into being.[8]

In choosing the site, one should also be aware of such pragmatic considerations as availability of water and food, the character of the local inhabitants, and the climate. Since one is constructing a dwelling, there must be sufficient drinking water nearby, and one should look for a place that is free from conflict and in which the inhabitants have good dispositions. One should not build in regions plagued by insects, or areas with many brambles, steep precipices, avalanches, or other natural disasters. The climate should be moderate, and locales with frequent droughts or shortages of food should be avoided.

When monastic residences are constructed, they are conceived as self-contained communities, and so the plan for the monastery provides for all the needs of the monks. The complex has a separate kitchen, a heated room in which residents may warm themselves in winter, storehouses (for stockpiling grain for both monks and the local populace to ensure that they have enough to eat, even when natural disasters harm crops), meditation areas, a place for bathing, medical facilities, and so on. Those monastic orders that stress oral debate will construct a courtyard in which the monks congregate for this purpose. Monasteries also have a central prayer room in which the monks gather for ceremonies. This contains a central image of a buddha which serves as a focal point for the community.

Before beginning the actual construction, the builders should make sure that they have all the required materials. Most monasteries have thick walls of stone, packed earth, mud brick, or a mixture of earth and gravel, depending on what materials are available. Each area has its own techniques and preferred materials. Buildings in eastern Tibet, for example, generally have walls of packed earth for which retaining structures are built, and then successive layers are packed down with wooden posts or rocks that workers lift and drop repeatedly. One feature common to all Tibetan architecture is the sloping shape of the walls, which have thick bases and gradually taper toward the top. The construction is all done by manual labor. Local people generally volunteer their help in the process, which often takes on a festive atmosphere. Those who participate in building religious structures gain great merit, and volunteers offer their services gladly.

A striking example of this can be seen in the current effort to rebuild Ganden Monastery (outside of Lhasa), which was bombed into rubble by Chinese troops. As soon as the authorities lifted the ban on reconstructing it, Tibetans—many of them young people born and raised under communist rule—began to move stones up the hillside on which Ganden was built. The local people have rebuilt and painted some of the damaged buildings, though most of the complex remains in ruins. The Chinese authorities were reportedly astounded by this display of devotion to the old culture of Tibet, which they have relentlessly vilified as "oppressive" and "feudal." Although the Chinese view the rebuilding of Ganden as a "reactionary" activity, for those involved it is an attempt to recapture a symbol of their religious tradition, which is still treasured by Tibetans despite decades of antireligious Chinese propaganda.

Framing and Decoration

Throughout the Tibetan plateau, the roofs of buildings are generally flat and are built with joists between supporting beams. Smaller boards are placed across them and covered with earth and small stones, to which is added another layer of stones on top. This mixture is moistened with water and packed down. The resulting roof is very hard and strong, as well as waterproof.

Tibetan religious structures are generally built with internal supports of large columns and beam structures. Windows and doors have wooden frames, often decorated with intricate carvings and painted in vibrant colors. The main entrance is often a vestibule with an open side, whose walls are covered with murals depicting Buddhist motifs and deities. Others may depict monastic scenes or examples of the clothing and conduct expected of the residents.

> There is a widespread tradition of painting, on the walls inside the door of the assembly hall, examples of the proper measures and designs of the robes and requisite articles for the livelihood of the assembly of fully-ordained monks as set forth in the *Vinaya.* Also common are paintings illustrating meditation experiences where one

material element predominates, depictions of yogis practicing the meditation of calming and setting the mind, and paintings illustrating other topics.[9]

Another common motif is the "Wheel of Life," symbolizing the workings of cyclic existence. This is frequently found at the doorway to the main assembly hall and serves to remind the inhabitants of the dangers of mundane existence. This striking image has a large central circle divided into two halves. The top half has three sections, representing the three "happy transmigrations"—humans, demi-gods, and gods. The lower half also has three sections, indicative of the three bad transmigrations—animals, hungry ghosts, and hell beings. A pigeon symbolizes the mental affliction of desire, a snake represents hatred, and a pig—symbol of ignorance—holds the tails of the first two in its mouth. These three afflictions are the primary factors that bind people to cyclic existence, causing them to transmigrate helplessly from birth to birth. The theme of cause and effect is further illustrated by twelve sections around the rim of the wheel, symbolizing the twelve links of dependent arising (a summary of the process of transmigration).[10] The whole wheel is held in the jaws of the Lord of Death, indicating that death is inevitable for those who are caught up in this cycle. Outside of the wheel are buddhas and bodhisattvas, often shown teaching the dharma, which provides an avenue of escape for those who are perceptive enough to recognize this and follow their instructions.

The paintings of a given monastery reflect its primary emphasis as well as its lineage. Tantric monasteries emphasize tantric themes, while those devoted mainly to study and debate will have pictures of great scholars from India as well as luminaries of the school.

Structures built by wealthy orders or patrons often have gilded roofs, surmounted by two deer on either side of a wheel, symbolizing the Deer Park in Sarnath, where Śākyamuni Buddha first "turned the wheel of dharma." These features reflect the tantric emphasis on symbolism: both the exteriors and interiors of Tibetan religious structures are commonly replete with religious images and symbols, the intention of which is subtly to influence the minds of those who see them. The inhabitants are constantly confronted by pictorial representations of key Buddhist concepts, which are meant to evoke corresponding responses in their thoughts and attitudes. The tantric influence on Tibetan architecture is noted by Thubten Legshay Gyatsho: "Tibet's own pure tradition of temple architecture is a system that incorporates the good and harmonious from among various architectural features of the celestial palaces described in the tantric divisions of scripture."[11]

Even the internal structure of religious buildings often reflects Buddhist ideas, as is illustrated by the common practice of building prayer halls with four columns and eight beams, symbolizing the four noble truths and the eightfold noble path. The outsides of the buildings are generally painted white, which is an auspicious color symbolic of purity, and the areas around them are invariably festooned with prayer flags, which are inscribed with Buddhist mantras and prayers to deities. Every time the breeze moves a flag it sends out a prayer for the benefit of all sentient beings. A similar sentiment is found in the construction of the rows of prayer wheels which often surround the outside walls of monastic establishments. It is a common sight to see monks or local laypeople circumambulating the sacred precincts, turning each wheel in turn, with the intention of benefiting others. Many monasteries also have prayer wheels that are turned by water, constantly sending out blessings that fill the universe and ease the suffering of sentient beings in all realms.

As Tucci notes, the images and symbols adorning Tibetan religious structures are intended "to prepare the right mood, and converge the spirit towards supreme visions, so as to complete with the help of art the apostolate work undertaken."[12] These symbols operate on multiple levels: for ordinary people, they are straightforward representations of buddhas, bodhisattvas, and other beings to whom they may pray for blessings, protection, prosperity, and so forth, while for those who are initiated into their deeper significance they are viewed as representations of states of consciousness that practitioners should seek to actualize in their own minds through meditative cultivation. Because of the differences in their respective training and worldviews, monks and uneducated laypeople looking at the same symbols perceive them in very different ways. A monk who has been initiated into the relevant tantric practices should view them as symbols whose esoteric meanings, revealed by his guru, represent the goals and techniques of his religious training. Most laypeople will likely perceive them as forces and beings to whom they pray and make propitiatory offerings for mundane and pragmatic ends. As Tucci notes, these are two parts of a continuum of attitudes, ranging from the simple faith of uninitiated laypeople to the developed perceptions of tantric adepts,

> but there is no opposition between the two ways of approaching the divine; they rather correspond to two different moments in the spiritual ascension that every religion proposes as [the] ultimate goal to the faithful, and that consists . . . in a progressive purification. The first way to approach the divine is to have glimmers of grace about it, which create ardours and renunciations, enkindle the desire of feeling its contact in an ever more intimate way through those visible forms that inspire dedication and élan of faith and tear us away from the tyranny of daily contingencies. In this way the cult of images is helpful in a first moment; because, later, the merit so acquired will bear fruits and the individual will be inclined to understand less material and sensory forms of the divine and could ascend to those experiences that, progressively refining themselves, will make him worthy, one day, to approach the doors of the greatest mystery.[13]

Buddhism recognizes that there are different levels of understanding, and its teachings respond to this by providing a wide range of symbols and techniques which can accommodate various types of practitioners. In the same way, the symbols of Tibetan religious structures are intended to be understood differently by different individuals, who interpret them in accordance with their particular predilections and perceptions.

Rituals and Consecrations

Rituals and consecrations accompany every stage of the construction of Tibetan religious structures. These ensure the pacification of negative forces and alleviate any faults that may have occurred during the building process. In addition, the power of these rituals ensures the future protection of the structure. Most monasteries and temples also have a special chapel for the protector deities of the order, who are expected to safeguard the buildings and their inhabitants. The importance of these protectors was noted by Tucci, who states that Tibetan temples

> are the architectural and plastic projection of a mystical process or of a liturgy; the presence of the dharmapāla [protectors of the dharma] or the dvārapāla [door guardians] . . . leads us back to an essential moment of every act of worship . . . . No ritual ceremony can have the desired result, if first the evil forces . . . have not been sent away,

> since these are the impediments to the formation of that sacred aura in which the compliance with the rite can only take place . . . . And consequently, in the temple, which is consecrated soil and the place in which the atmosphere of purity and sanctity must always be preserved, near the doors almost unfailingly the images of these dharmapāla are arranged or depicted, the supreme mercifulness of whom becomes active and pugnacious to reject all that which is from outside.[14]

Tibetan texts on architecture indicate that one must also take steps to ensure that human workers have positive attitudes about their labor. Before construction begins, the masons and carpenters are given offerings of beer, rice, tea, and *tsampa* (barley flour). The workers are presented with *katas*—silk scarves given by Tibetans to mark important occasions. Similar offerings are given after the completion of each floor of the building.[15] It is also common to have rest days during which no one works, and all the people involved in the construction gather together to admire their handiwork and enjoy each other's company. No work is done on important holy days, and since most of the volunteers are unpaid, many must take time off to attend to their own business. In addition, the requisite rituals and consecrations are often very time-consuming, and by Western standards Tibetan construction generally proceeds at a very slow pace.

Stūpas

Stūpas (*mchod rten*) are found throughout the Tibetan cultural area. They proliferate in all regions where Buddhism has had a significant impact on the local culture. Sometimes they are built in groups, and sometimes they stand alone. Stūpas are even constructed in very remote or uninhabited areas, often by people who regularly travel in such places, since stūpas are believed to subdue and propitiate local spirits and make an area safe for people to pass through.

The stūpa motif originated in India around the third century C.E. These monuments were reportedly first used as receptacles for the cremated remains of religious figures or for sacred objects, but in Tibet they exhibit a wide range of motifs and purposes. As Tucci notes, Tibetan stūpas only rarely serve a funerary function.[16] The Sanskrit term *stūpa* literally means "heap" or "mound," reflecting the simple designs of Indian versions of this architectural form.[17] Lokesh Chandra contends that in India stūpas were originally used to mark the domains of kings, but the design was later adopted by Buddhists for religious purposes.[18] Initially constructed by Buddhists primarily to house the remains of great teachers, their symbolism gradually was expanded, although they retained their pre-Buddhist function of designating territory. The building of a stūpa is a concrete manifestation of the establishment of the dharma in an area, marking it as a place whose inhabitants have embraced Buddhism.

The Tibetan translation of the Sanskrit term stūpa—*chöden*—is an interpretive one, meaning "receptacle for offerings." This reflects the fact that in Tibet they often contain religious objects, texts, images, and the like, and are invested with spiritual energy by being consecrated in special ceremonies. As a result, pilgrimages to stūpas are thought to earn merit, as are prostrations and circumambulations. Their construction and veneration are strongly associated with the practice of accumulating merit through virtuous activities. They are often built to commemorate an auspicious event, or for the spiritual wellbeing of the inhabitants of an area. Those who construct them receive a great deal of merit, since stūpas also bring benefit to others who venerate them.

The rewards for builders of stūpas are sometimes described as a sort of spiritual pyramid scheme, in which the original builder continues to gain merit due to the ongoing utilization of the stūpa for religious purposes. A stupa's function of bringing merit to those who build or venerate it has wide-ranging benefits. People who engage in devotional activities with virtuous intentions purify their thoughts, which helps them to cultivate morality and positive feelings toward others. The merit they acquire brings them good fortune in this and future lives; even more importantly, it helps them to purify their mental continuums of afflictions, which is a necessary part of the path to awakening.

In Tibet stūpas often serve as repositories for sacred articles that have outlived their usefulness, such as texts, paintings, images, and so on. When these become old, worn, or damaged, they are not discarded like common garbage, but are generally deposited in stūpas. Even sacred articles that are damaged still retain their sacral character, and so it would be an act of desecration simply to discard them. Since religious texts or images represent the dharma itself, they cannot be tossed onto a garbage heap; such an act would be an insult to the Buddha and his teaching. Such negative actions inevitably rebound on those who commit them, bringing suffering and pain, and so Tibetans use stūpas—which are themselves sacred spaces—as repositories for religious articles that have served their purpose but are no longer useful.

Types of Tibetan Stūpas

The size and shape of Tibetan stūpas vary greatly. Some stūpas are only a few inches in height, while others are towering structures with many levels. Most towns have several stūpas along roads at their outskirts, and in rural Nepal it is common to see stūpas built over the roads entering a town. People coming into the town pass through an opening at the bottom of the stūpa; this act brings a blessing to all who enter the town, and the stūpa is thought to protect the inhabitants from outside evils. Often the approach to the town will be marked by several stūpas, generally joined together by long walls of stones inscribed with the mantra *oṃ maṇi padme hūṃ*. These "maṇi walls" are sometimes over one mile long and consist of tens of thousands of stones, each one of which has the mantra either carved or written on it.

According to Tibetan architectural theory, stūpa designs are based on eight paradigmatic Indian models, each of which commemorated a particular aspect of the Buddha's career:

1. A stūpa at the Lumbinī grove in Kapilavastu (where Siddhārtha was born), reportedly built by Śuddhodana;
2. A stūpa in Magadha, credited to Ajātaśatru, commemorating the Buddha's awakening;
3. A stūpa in Vārāṇasī, built by Brahmadatta, that represents his teaching activities;
4. A stūpa in Śrāvastī, built by Prasenajit, that portrays a miraculous display he created in order to defeat a group of heretics;
5. A stūpa in Kānyakubja, on the site from which he ascended to Tuṣita heaven and then returned again;
6. A stūpa at Rājagṛha, where the Buddha mediated an argument between groups of monks; this was reportedly built by Bimbisāra;
7. A stūpa in Vaiśālī, where he contemplated how long he would live; this was constructed by a prince of the Licchavis;
8. A stūpa in Kuśinagara, attributed to Malla, where the Buddha attained final nirvana.[19]

Buddhist Symbolism

The design of stūpas reflects Buddhist motifs. They employ the basic design of the maṇḍala, and their form symbolizes the structure of the universe according to traditional Buddhist cosmology and the path to liberation. A common design for stūpas utilizes a square base, representing the earth element.[20] The base is oriented toward the four cardinal directions and is surmounted by a dome, which corresponds to the earth element and the system of universal genesis. It is symbolic of our world, in which beings are born and die, transmigrating endlessly under the dome of the sky until they comprehend the path to release. This path is indicated by a series of rings above the dome, often ten in number, designating the ten bodhisattva levels and the fire element.[21] Stūpas are often capped by a parasol, symbolic of the awakening of buddhas, who have transcended the mundane world but still retain a connection to it through compassionate activity. On top of the parasol are a half-moon and a sun disk, which signify space. The hierarchical structure of the stūpa denotes the stages of ascension of a Buddhist practitioner, who begins at the level of an ordinary being helplessly transmigrating in cyclic existence, but who heroically attains liberation through accumulating merit, practicing morality and developing virtuous mental qualities, working for the benefit of others, and cultivating direct perception of the true nature of reality. There is a separation between the states of ordinary sentient beings and buddhas, but the former constitute the raw material for the latter, and so are the basis for the attainment of awakening. This is reflected in the clear distinction between the shapes of the base, body, and spires of stūpas, each of which represents a particular aspect of the path, but all of which are connected as integral parts of the structure.

Stūpas play an important role in the religious life of Tibetan Buddhist communities. They are a concrete manifestation of the establishment of the dharma in the physical environment, and they also serve as a focus for devotional activities. It is common to see people circumambulating them in a clockwise direction (except for followers of Bön, who walk in the opposite direction), often softly intoning mantras or performing prostrations. It is believed that such activities work on the mind of the practitioner, eliminating mental afflictions and promoting the development of virtuous mental states. Because of the role they play in the process of accumulating merit, stūpas serve as focal points for the religious life of the community.

Notes

1. See Keith Dowman, *The Power-Places of Central Tibet* (London: Routledge & Kegan Paul, 1988), p. 285, and Michael Aris, *Bhutan. The Early History of a Himalayan Kingdom* (Warminster: Aris & Phillips, 1979), pp. 8–23.
2. Lobsang Lhalungpa, "Tibetan History," *White Lotus*, p. 32.
3. Ardito Desio, *Ascent of K2* (London, 1955), p. 12.
4. Mircea Eliade, *Patterns of Comparative Religion* (Cleveland, 1963), pp. 99–100.
5. Early temples and monasteries were generally built on flat plains, as is evident in surviving examples of old Tibetan architecture. In this section, however, I am mainly concerned with modern structures and contemporary architectural theories. But as Helmut Hoffman notes, (*Tibet: A Handbook;* Bloomington, IN: Research Center for the Language Sciences, 1975, pp. 225–226), while there have been some changes in construction techniques and preferred locations, Tibetan architecture has by and large been a conservative art, and modern buildings share many features in common with older ones.
6. Thubten Legshay Gyatsho, *Gateway to the Temple* (Kathmandu: Ratna Pustak Bhandar, 1979), p. 29.
7. A lengthy list of positive and negative features is provided by Thubten Legshay Gyatsho, pp. 29–30.
8. Ibid., pp. 30–33.
9. Ibid., p. 46.
10. See chapter 2, "Some Important Buddhist Doctrines."
11. *Gateway to the Temple*, p. 35.
12. Giuseppe Tucci, *The Temples of Western Tibet and their Artistic Symbolism* (New Delhi: Aditya Prakashan, 1988), p. 160.
13. Ibid, p. 161.
14. Ibid., pp. 107–108.
15. *Gateway to the Temple*, p. 43.
16. Giuseppe Tucci, *Stupa: Art, Architectonics and Symbolism* (New Delhi: Aditya Prakashan, 1988), p. 26.
17. Lokesh Chandra provides a good discussion of Sanskrit sources that mention this term in his introduction to Tucci's *Stupa* (pp. xi–xiv).
18. Ibid., p. xxiii.
19. This list is found in Tucci, *Stupa*, pp. 21–24. He notes that there are several extant lists of the eight stūpas, which differ in some details.
20. Earth is one of the primary elements that constitute the universe according to Buddhist cosmological theory. The other elements are fire, water, air, and space.
21. As Tucci (*Stupa*, pp. 41–45) notes, there are often thirteen rings, and there are also different systems of interpretation of the ten-ring and thirteen-ring designs.

Part Three

Tibetan Buddhist Doctrines and Practices

9: Tantra

The Place of the Tantras in Buddhist Literature

The term *tantra* (*rgyud;* pronounced "gyü") refers to systems of practice and meditation derived from esoteric texts emphasizing cognitive transformation through visualization, symbols, and ritual. These in turn gave rise to a vast commentarial literature, as well as oral traditions, and tantric practices, ideas, and images today permeate all aspects of Tibetan Buddhism. The root texts of this system are generally called "tantras"; most of these highlight a particular buddha who is the focus of ritual and meditative practices (in the *Hevajra Tantra,* for example, the buddha Hevajra is the central figure).

Although many of the fundamental treatises of this tradition are called tantras, there are some that do not contain the term "tantra" in the title, and there are some non-tantric works that do. As David Snellgrove notes,

> some of the works that were subsequently catalogued by the Tibetans as tantras are referred to in their titles as sūtras. Thus there is a slight overlapping between these two classes of Buddhist literature, although clear distinctions of content can be drawn between them.[1]

Each order of Tibetan Buddhism has its distinctive tantric practices, and individual lineages are often based on particular tantras or on groups of tantras that are considered to be related.

Tantric Buddhism is often referred to by its adherents as the Vajra Vehicle (*rDo rje'i theg pa, Vajrayāna*). The *vajra* (*rdo rje*; pronounced "dorjé") is an important symbol in the tantras: it is described as the hardest substance, something that is pure and unbreakable, like the omniscient wisdom of a buddha. Iconographically, the vajra is a five-pointed scepter that represents the method aspect of a buddha's realization. In tantric images, it is commonly held in the right hand by a buddha or bodhisattva, and a bell is held in the left hand. The bell denotes the wisdom aspect, and the two arms are often crossed, symbolizing the inseparable union of method and wisdom in the mind of a buddha. According to the *Vajra Crown Tantra* (*Vajraśekhara-tantra*), a vajra is "adamantine, hard, nonempty, with a nature that is imperturbable and indivisible; because it cannot be burned and is indestructible and empty, it is called 'vajra'." [2]

> It is symbolic of the awakened mind of a buddha—which combines compassion for all sentient beings with full understanding of reality—and the activities of a buddha, which are characterized by compassionate manifestations with direct perception of emptiness. Thus the vajra represents the final aspiration of Mahāyāna practitioners.

Tantric Buddhism is also referred to as the "Method Vehicle," because it contains numerous special techniques for rapid attainment of buddhahood, and the "Effect Vehicle," because it takes the final result of Buddhist practice—buddhahood—as the path and trains directly in the attributes of awakening. Vajrayāna is considered by its adherents to be a separate vehicle, along with Hīnayāna and Mahāyāna, and they believe it to be the supreme Buddhist system. It follows the general outlines of Indian Mahāyāna (which tantric exegetes often refer to as the "Sūtra Vehicle," because it is based on the Mahāyāna sūtras, or the "Perfection Vehicle," because it enjoins the gradual cultivation of the perfections as the path to buddhahood) and also valorizes the bodhisattva as its ideal, but Vajrayāna claims to have special and more effective methods of practice that can greatly shorten the path to buddhahood. As in the standard Mahāyāna, tantric bodhisattvas cultivate the six perfections, follow the five paths and ten levels, and their training also culminates in the awakening of a buddha, but highest yoga tantra texts maintain that practitioners can complete the path in one human lifetime instead of the three countless eons required for bodhisattvas of the Perfection Vehicle.

Origins of Vajrayāna

Most tantras claim to have been spoken by Śākyamuni Buddha, or sometimes by other buddhas. This assertion is accepted by most Tibetan Buddhists, but is generally rejected by contemporary historically-oriented scholars, because no reliable evidence supports the appearance of tantras for at least a millennium after the death of Śākyamuni.[3] The discrepancy between the time of the Buddha and the period of Vajrayāna's flourishing in India has also been noted by Tibetan historians, and Tāranātha (1575–1635) attempts to explain it away by stating that Śākyamuni taught the tantras during his lifetime, but some were passed on in secret from master to disciple, while others were hidden in the Heaven of the Thirty-Three or Tuṣita until humans were ready to receive them.[4] The origins of tantra are extremely obscure, and there are numerous theories concerning when, where, and by whom various texts were composed.

Tāranatha reports that the tantric teachings were first given to the Indian king Indrabhūti of Zahor. The Buddha created an emanation body, and then appeared in his enjoyment body form in the center of a vast maṇḍala. The king was sitting in his palace surveying his domain. Seeing what appeared to be a flock of red birds flying in the distance, he asked his advisors what they were, and was informed that it was the Buddha and his arhat disciples. He ordered that the Buddha be invited to the palace.

When the Buddha and his retinue arrived at the royal court, he gave the king Hīnayāna teachings, but Indrabhūti was dissatisfied with what he had heard and requested something deeper. The Buddha responded by making the Hīnayānists in his entourage disappear, and then created a huge maṇḍala and delivered tantric instructions. At this point, Vajrayāna entered the world of humans and was transmitted in secret to the few advanced practitioners who could comprehend and effectively practice it. Indrabhūti, however, was initially unable to understand the new dispensation, but the sage Kukura was given a special empowerment by the buddha Vajrasattva, following which he was able to explain it to the king.

There are no historical records of an Indian king Indrabhūti receiving or transmitting tantric teachings, nor is the story of the creation and dissemination of Vajrayāna likely to be as straightforward as those found in traditional accounts. Sources relating to the origins of tantra are notably scarce, and often contradictory, and so much of the early history must be inferred (or guessed) from fragments of the past.

There are no records from the Buddha's time that suggest he gave teachings resembling developed Vajrayāna. The tantras only began to appear in India toward the end of the seventh century—over a millennium after the Buddha's passing—and new ones continued to be composed until the twelfth century, and possibly later. It is clear from Tibetan records that when Buddhism was first disseminated in Tibet during the ninth and tenth centuries tantric texts and practices were well established in India and that many of the monastic universities that were centers for the transmission of the dharma were also centers of Vajrayāna study and practice.

When the Chinese pilgrim Xuanzang (596-664) visited India between the years 629 and 645 C.E., he made no mention of tantric texts or practices in his writings.[5] This is significant because he traveled all over Buddhist India and through Central Asia, and his reporting is notable for its scrupulousness. He recorded in great detail the places he visited, the pilgrimage spots and shrines he saw, the numbers of monks he found in particular areas, and the types of practices in which they were engaged. He reported the existence of many people belonging to Hīnayāna or Mahāyāna sects, but there is no record of his ever encountering any type of Buddhism that resembles Vajrayāna. When another Chinese pilgrim named Wuxing traveled to India sometime around 680, he reported that Vajrayāna had entered the monastic mainstream in the north Indian monastic centers, and he also indicated that this was a recent phenomenon. Tibetans did not begin translating tantric texts until the eighth century, and Chinese Buddhists began to import and translate them around the same time, and so it appears that the first tantras were probably composed somewhere around the end of the seventh century and that their appearance and acceptance in India probably happened rather quickly, over the period of several decades.

Tantric lineages commonly claim Indian luminaries like Nāgārjuna (ca. 150–250 C.E.) and Asaṅga (ca. fourth century C.E.), but this was done retrospectively; there is no evidence to indicate that they were involved in tantric practices. Vajrayāna was not a completely new system, however, and it incorporated elements of earlier Buddhist traditions, including doctrines and practices. For example, tantric texts presuppose the doctrine of emptiness, which is central to the Madhyamaka and Yogācāra schools, and places a high value on skill in means, which is a core theme in a number of Mahāyāna sūtras. The symbol of the vajra predates Buddhism, as does the use of mantras, symbolic diagrams, and fire rituals (*sbyin sreg, homa*), all of which are central to Vajrayāna. Before the late seventh or early eighth centuries, however, there is no evidence of anything resembling the elaborate systems of doctrine and practice that characterized the developed Vajrayāna, nor are there records of adherents proclaiming it as a separate "vehicle."

Whatever their origins, it is clear that the production of the new tantric texts in India—and the claim that these had been taught during the time of Śākyamuni—generated both great interest and strong opposition. These reactions are also found in the writings of contemporary Western scholars. Some view tantra as a development that accords with the ideals and doctrines of Mahāyāna, while others consider it to be a new phenomenon that marks a major paradigm shift. Some early Western researchers—apparently shocked by the presence of sexual imagery and practices, as well as a plethora of demonic figures—characterized tantra as the final degeneration of Indian Buddhism, a corruption of the ideals and practices of the dharma of Śākyamuni.

These thoughts are not, however, shared by Tibetan scholars, who generally view tantra as the supreme of all Buddhist teachings and who consider tantric practices to be the shortest and most effective path to buddhahood. Tantric texts and practices are considered by Tibetans to be a part of Mahāyāna, since they emphasize both the path of the bodhisattva, which leads to the supreme goal of buddhahood, and the central importance of compassion, which is the primary motivating factor in the bodhisattva's pursuit of awakening. As David Snellgrove has noted, however, tantric texts were not accepted wholesale in Tibet, and in order for a work to be acknowledged as authoritative Tibetan scholars generally required validation in the form of a Sanskrit original. Thus Tibetan Buddhists

> followed their Indian masters in treating the tantras . . . as authoritative Buddhist works, canonically valid as Buddha Word just as much as were the Mahāyāna sūtras. When they finalized the contents of their own canon in the thirteenth century, they strictly excluded from the Tantra section certain tantras for the existence of which no direct Indian authority in the form of a Sanskrit original or other acceptable Indian original could be proved.[6]

Moreover, there was some opposition to the tantras during the early part of the first dissemination, and both Trisong Détsen and Relbachen forbade their translation into Tibetan. Later in the eleventh century, the *Official Edict* catalogue of Yéshé Ö characterized such tantric practices as sexual union (*sbyor ba*) and "deliverance" (*sgrol ba*; "liberating" beings from cyclic existence by killing them) as heretical and rejected tantras that contained descriptions of them. The famed translator Rinchen Sangpo (958–1055) made similar claims in his *Refutation of Errors Regarding Secret Mantra*.[7] Such controversies continue today, and Tibetan exegetes tend to construe the more outrageous passages in tantric texts symbolically.

The Socio-Political Environment of Early Indian Vajrayāna

The dynasties of the Guptas and Vākāṭas (ca. 320–550) were a time of relatively stable centralized government in India. After they fell, a feudal period ensued during which much of the subcontinent was divided into smaller states. The larger ones commonly had smaller allies and vassals that made alliances of convenience. As power relations shifted, however, so did the associations, and armed conflict between these kingdoms was common. A powerful state might suffer losses as a result of its military campaigns and be reduced to a vassal of an emergent rival, or be subsumed altogether. Records of the time speak of devastation resulting from warfare and the corresponding breakdown of social order, large population shifts, and negative effects on trade and the sort of royal sponsorship that had been essential for the founding and maintenance of large monastic institutions. In this new environment, Buddhists borrowed from rival groups like the Pāśupatas and Kāpālikas, who had practices and doctrines that resembled those of the developed Vajrayāna. Ronald Davidson persuasively argues that the emergence of Buddhist Vajrayāna was part of an attempt to adapt to changing social conditions and develop new paradigms to suit the times.[8]

The origins of Indian Vajrayāna lie in this feudal period of medieval India, and so it is not surprising that the emerging system appropriated elements of the surrounding society. Much of the symbolism and organization of Vajrayāna ritual reflects post-Gupta India; an example is the maṇḍala, which often depicts an Indian royal residence or a central deity with a surrounding retinue of subordinates, like an Indian monarch or a powerful state surrounded by vassals. And as in medieval India, the center can shift in changing circumstances, and one of the peripheral elements can become central. In visualization practice, one generates a mental image of the maṇḍala and populates it with various deities, each with its own subsidiary entourages, and at the conclusion of the rite dissolves them into one's own mind. As a result, one acquires the attributes of the deities, and meditators are supposed to experience the "divine pride" of a lordly buddha who exerts dominion over his or her domain, a pride that is free from afflictions such as desire, anger, or obscuration.

Tantric consecration ceremonies also incorporate a number of elements that reflect the paraphernalia of Indian kingship, and the stated goal of tantric initiation—becoming a supreme lord with dominion over a particular area—is derived from royal consecration rituals. Moreover, during their training bodhisattvas accrue vast stores of merit that allow them to create buddha realms with conditions that are suitable to particular types of beings, and after attaining buddhahood they become lords of these domains. An example is Sukhāvatī, the realm of Amitābha, which is the focus of popular cults throughout the Mahāyāna world. The buddha who creates a realm is also its overlord, and this notion is extended in Vajrayāna: tantric adepts are said to become "supreme overlords," and they also possess the charisma of kings, extensive magical powers, and the ability to conquer sorcerers and gods.

Even today tantric consecrations employ the accoutrements of royal consecrations from the Indian feudal period following the demise of the Guptas, and initiates commonly wear crowns and carry vajras, which in some texts are related to the king's staff of office (*'khar, daṇḍa*), the symbol of regal power in medieval India. Moreover, the language and symbolism of these rituals contain elements of the imperial paraphernalia of the time. Initiates are instructed to view themselves as monarchs who acquire power through their meditation and performance of rituals, and who exercise dominion in the manner of a universal monarch (*'khor los bsgyur ba'i rgyal po, cakravartin*). During the ceremony, they also learn mantras that purportedly have the power to defeat rival armies, ensure good crops, control the weather, counter black magic by enemies, and so on, all of which were part of the lore of medieval Indian kingship.

Along with the appropriation of symbols of royalty and medieval Indian social structures, Vajrayāna texts also contain significant antinomian elements, and some of the most influential practitioners of early tantra were the "adepts" (*grub thob, siddha*) who lived at the margins of society and frequented cemeteries, charnel grounds, and wildernesses while engaging in practices that were abhorrent to orthodox Brahmanism.

These included tantric "feasts" (*tshogs 'khor, gaṇacakra*) in which siddhas with long matted hair, wearing ornaments of human bones, dressed in animal skins, and sometimes smeared with ashes from cremation fires, fornicated with their consorts and consumed forbidden substances like alcohol and dishes made from the flesh of humans.

The most influential grouping of Buddhist *siddhas* (adepts) is found in Abhayadatta's (ca. twelfth-century) hagiography *Lives of the Eighty-Four Adepts*, which includes such luminaries as Virūpa, Kāṇha, Tilopa, and his student Nāropa. Many of the siddhas are also known through their works of prose and poetry, particularly inspired verse compositions *(dohā).*

The siddhas constitute a strange collection of tribal people, outcastes, beggars, criminals, and some upper caste members. They reportedly defeat demons, fly through the air, pass through solid objects, and travel to the land of the *ḍākinīs* (female buddhas who are guardians of tantric lore), where they receive esoteric instruction. The goal of siddha practice is the acquisition of supernatural powers (*dngos grub, siddhi*), which are said to be aids on the path to buddhahood. Their pantheon incorporated various fearsome tribal and local deities that were associated with lowcaste groups, as well as demons and other unsavory characters. Their antinomian practices are portrayed as skillful means to help adepts transcend ordinary conceptuality and are connected with the doctrine of emptiness; all phenomena are devoid of any inherent nature, and so by extension anything can be appropriated in the path to liberation.

The tantras commonly employ the opening formula of sūtras, "Thus have I heard at one time . . . ," and are sometimes situated in Indian locations found in the Hīnayāna and Mahāyāna discourses, but in others the Buddha is said to reside in transcendental realms, and often engages in activities that he proscribed in his discourses and the *vinaya.* The *Hevajra Tantra* (II.3,29), for example, begins by asserting that the Buddha "dwelt in the vagina of the Vajrayoginī who is the body, speech, and mind of all buddhas." He tells the assembled bodhisattvas: "You should kill living beings, speak lying words, take things that are not given, and have sex with many women." They are so scandalized to see the Buddha *in flagrante delicto* and uttering such apparently scandalous words that they collectively faint. He magically revives them and informs them that the new teachings are more advanced versions of what they had previously learned. He then explains that these teachings are to be understood symbolically: "killing living beings" involves cultivating "singleness of thought"; "speaking lying words" refers to the vow to save all sentient beings; "what is not given" is a woman's bliss (presumably in sexual yoga); and "frequenting others' wives" is meditation focused on Nairātmyā, Hevajra's consort.

The Buddha explains that in the final analysis there is no difference between cyclic existence and nirvana (*'khor 'das dbyer med, saṃsāra-nirvāṇa-abheda*) and that the goal of tantric practice is to become indifferent to all notions of good and bad, pure and impure, permitted and proscribed: "There is nothing that one may not do, and nothing that one may not eat. There is nothing that one may not think or say, nothing that is either pleasant or unpleasant." (I.7,24)

Tantra As a Branch of Mahāyāna

Sūtra and Tantra

Tantras differ from other Mahāyāna texts primarily in the area of method: they contain practices, symbols, and teachings that are not found in other Mahāyāna works, and these are held by their adherents to be more potent and effective than those of the Perfection Vehicle. Through tantric practice, according to Lama Thubten Yeshe, one is able to overcome afflictions and deluded thoughts, progress rapidly through the Buddhist paths, and attain the state of buddhahood in order to benefit others.

> Speaking generally we can say that all the many practices of tantra involve the principle of transformation . . . . Through the practice of tantra *all* our energies, including the subtle yet very powerful energies we are not ordinarily aware of, are harnessed to accomplish the greatest of all transformations. This is our evolution from an ordinary, limited and deluded person trapped within the shell of a petty ego into a fully evolved, totally conscious being of unlimited compassion and insight.[9]

Vajrayāna focuses on ritual, visualization, and symbols in order to effect rapid transformation to the state of buddhahood. Many tantrists even claim that it is *only* possible to become a buddha through practice of highest yoga tantra. The Dalai Lama, for instance, asserts that "one must finally engage in Mantra [another name for tantric practice] in order to become a Buddha."[10] As we saw in earlier sections, this claim runs counter to the popular biographies of Śākyamuni, which make no mention of tantra. This discrepancy is explained away by stating that although Śākyamuni *appeared* to take rebirth in India and attain awakening, in reality he had become awakened in the distant past. His birth, life in the palace, pursuit of awakening, and so on, were really only a display put on for the benefit of people of limited intellect. Like all buddhas, he attained buddhahood through the special practices of highest yoga tantra.

In the *Compendium of the Truth of All Tathāgatas*, it is related that as Siddhārtha Gautama sat under the Tree of Awakening he was roused from his meditation by the buddhas of the ten directions, who informed him that it is impossible to attain buddhahood without engaging in the sexual yogas of highest yoga tantra. Realizing that this was the case, he left his physical body under the tree and traveled to a transcendent tantric realm, where he received consecrations and engaged in sexual yogas with a consort named Tilottamā. He then returned to Bodh Gaya and resumed his display.[11]

Motivation

Although in Tibet tantra is generally considered to be the culmination of Buddhist teachings, it is not suitable for everyone. Tantric practice is a powerful and effective means of bringing about spiritual transformation, but for this very reason it is also thought to be dangerous. Thus Tibetan teachers contend that it is only appropriate for certain exceptional individuals, while others should follow the slower but less dangerous path of the Mahāyāna sūtra system or of Hīnayāna.

What sort of people are suitable receptacles for tantric teachings? According to the Dalai Lama, only those with unusually strong compassion and an overpowering urge to attain buddhahood in order to benefit others should undertake the training of Vajrayāna:

> A person who has practised the stages of sūtra and wishes to attain quickly the state of a blessed Buddha *should* enter into the Secret Mantra Vehicle that can easily bestow realisation of Buddhahood. However, you cannot seek Buddhahood for yourself, engaging in Mantra in order to become unusual . . . . You must develop great compassion from the very orb of your heart for all sentient beings traveling in cyclic existence . . . . You need to have a very strong mind wishing to free all sentient beings from suffering and its causes.[12]

Practitioners of tantra must have greater compassion—and greater intelligence—than those who follow the sūtra path. The special methods and powerful techniques of Vajrayāna are intended for those whose compassion is so acute that they cannot bear to wait for a long time in order to benefit others.

> Although the goal is the same (as in Mahāyāna sūtras),
> (in tantra) there is no ignorance,
> There are many skillful means and less hardship.
> It is for people of sharp intellect.
> Hence, the tantrayāna is superior.[13]

The Faults of Cyclic Existence

In addition to the motivation of compassion, tantric practitioners must be perceptive enough to recognize the faults of cyclic existence. Ordinary, ignorant beings are caught up in fleeting and transitory pleasures and fail to recognize the pervasiveness of suffering and the inevitability of death. Intelligent people who meditate on the nature of things, however, recognize the unsatisfactoriness of cyclic existence and generate a strong desire to escape it.

In common with the exoteric sūtra path, tantric texts teach that transmigratory existence is a vicious cycle that is driven by afflicted desires and mistaken thoughts. The minds of ordinary beings run after fleeting stimuli and are easily distracted by things that appear to promise satisfaction but which in the end turn out to be disappointing. Human beings, for example, have a tendency to believe that material possessions can lead to happiness, and so they expend great amounts of energy in an effort to acquire them. Others seek fulfillment in worldly fame or power, sexual activity, adventures and dangerous pursuits, but none of these are able to provide more than momentary gratification. Wealth, power, and fame are easily lost, and those who have them are as prone to discontent and suffering as anyone else. The stimulation of sexual activity and the excitement of adventure quickly fade, leaving feelings of emptiness and disappointment.

While most exoteric Buddhist texts advise practitioners to reduce desire in order to attain liberation, tantric treatises propose to incorporate the energy of desire into the path. The problem lies not in desire *per se*, but rather in a misdirection of the energy of desire toward objects that lead to suffering and bondage.

> Instead of viewing pleasure and desire as something to be avoided at all costs, tantra recognizes the powerful energy aroused by our desires to be an indispensable resource for the spiritual path. Because the goal is nothing less than the realization of our highest human potential, tantra seeks to transform *every* experience—no matter how 'unreligious' it may appear—into the path of fulfillment. It is precisely because our present life is so inseparably linked with desire that we must make use of desire's tremendous energy if we wish to transform our life into something transcendental.[14]

Tantric Buddhism accepts the idea found in many Buddhist texts that buddhas have overcome desire, but holds that the path to extinction of desire does not necessitate its suppression. In fact, since desire is a very powerful force in human beings, suppressing it requires the expenditure of a great deal of energy and diligent practice over an extended period of time. The skillful means of Vajrayāna, however, provide methods to redirect this energy by utilizing it in the spiritual path, so that desire itself becomes a means to overcome desire. This process is compared to the way that two sticks can be rubbed together to create a fire that consumes them.

This does not mean, however, that tantra involves unrestrained wallowing in pleasure. Rather, desire and bliss are carefully channeled through meditative practices, and they are used in very specific ways. The path of tantra involves great discipline and requires keen intelligence, and it is based on a strong wish to help others. It has nothing to do with sensual indulgence.

Desire and Skillful Means

Human beings want happiness and seek to avoid suffering. These are accepted as legitimate goals by Vajrayāna, but the methods commonly used to achieve them are rejected. Most people seek pleasure for themselves alone, and look for it in material objects, the approval of others, interpersonal relationships, and so on. None of these things are able to provide lasting contentment, since they are all impermanent and thus subject to change and death.

The problem lies in looking for fulfillment in external things, since tru happiness is found in the mind. Tantric texts claim that the human mind contains the seeds of both suffering and of lasting joy, and that one's state of mind determines which one will experience. Unlike ascetic traditions that seek to find satisfaction through difficult or painful meditative practices, Vajrayāna practice cultivates blissful mental states. In tantra, one actualizes progressively deeper understanding of the nature of reality through experiencing pleasurable cognitions, gaining control over physical and mental energies, and conjoining blissful consciousnesses with realization of the nature of reality. The goal of tantra is

> to transform all pleasures into the transcendental experience of deep penetrative awareness. Instead of advocating separation from worldly pleasures the way many other traditions do, tantra emphasizes that it is much more effective for human beings to enjoy themselves and channel the energy of their enjoyments into a quick and powerful path to fulfillment and awakening. This is the most skilful way of using our precious human potential.[15]

Through the skillful methods of Vajrayāna, meditators are able to cultivate enjoyment in a way that aids in spiritual progress. Afflicted grasping and desires based on mistaken ideas are the problem, not happiness and pleasure. If the pursuit of contentment can be separated from afflictive emotions, then it can be incorporated into the path and will even become a powerful aid to the attainment of awakening. The *Hevajra Tantra*, for example, states,

> That by which the world is bound,
> By the same things it is released from bondage.
> But the world is deluded and does not understand this truth,
> And one who does not possess this truth cannot attain perfection.[16]

Tantra, however, is not concerned merely with cultivation of pleasure, nor is its purview restricted to actions and practices that are traditionally associated with "religion." Tantra proposes to incorporate all actions, all thoughts, all emotions into the path. Nothing in itself is pure or impure, good or bad, mundane or transcendent; things only appear to us in these ways because of preconceived ideas. In the Vajrayāna systems, any action

—even walking, eating, defecating, or sleeping—can be elements of the spiritual path. Tantric practitioners seek to overcome the pervasive sense of ordinariness that colors our perceptions of daily life. Sleep, for example, should be viewed by a tantrist as a time to recharge one's strength in order that one may wake up and engage in meditation with renewed vigor. Eating is a chance to replenish one's energy in order to be able to continue to work for the benefit of others.

A particularly vivid example of the tantric attitude can be found in the story of a tantric lama who escaped Tibet when the Chinese invaded and who made his way to northern India, where he dressed as a layman and worked on a road construction crew for several years. One day a former student happened by and recognized him. Surprised to find an important lama performing lowly manual labor, the student asked why he had remained an anonymous road worker when he could have told his fellow Tibetans who he was and been returned to his monastery. Had he done this, he could have lived in ease, surrounded by devoted students. The lama replied that for him there was no difference between working on roads and living in a monastery. He explained that when he shoveled dirt he visualized it as pure offerings to buddhas. Moving heavy boulders symbolized his struggle to eliminate recalcitrant mental afflictions. And his fellow workers were fully awakened beings whose actions were performed for his benefit. Through his visualization practice, the world he inhabited had become a pure land, uncontaminated by the negativities that most people see as a result of their mental afflictions.

Tantric Symbols

Maṇḍalas

The Sanskrit term *maṇḍala* (*dkyil 'khor*) literally means "circle," both in the sense of a circular diagram and a surrounding retinue. In Buddhist usage the term encompasses both senses, because it refers to circular diagrams that often incorporate depictions of deities and their surroundings. The maṇḍala represents a sacred realm—often the celestial palace of a buddha—and it contains symbols and images that illustrate aspects of the awakened psychophysical personality of the buddha and that indicate Buddhist themes and concepts. The Dalai Lama explains that the image of the maṇḍala "is said to be extremely profound because meditation on it serves as an antidote, quickly eradicating the obstructions to liberation and the obstructions to omniscience as well as their latent predispositions."[17] The obstructions to liberation and the obstructions to omniscience are the two main types of mental afflictions that inhibit one's attainment of buddhahood. The maṇḍala serves as a representation of an awakened mind that is free of all such obstacles, and in the context of tantric practice it is a powerful symbol of the state that meditators are trying to attain.

Maṇḍalas often consist of a series of concentric circles enclosed by a square, which in turn has a circular boundary. The square contains a gateway in the middle of each side, the main one facing east, with three other openings at each of the other cardinal directions. They represent entrances to the central palace of the main deity and are based on the design of the classical Indian four-sided temple. Such maṇḍalas are elaborate floor plans of the palace, viewed from the top. The portals, however, are often laid down flat, as are outer walls. These portals are lavishly decorated with tantric symbols. The architecture of the maṇḍala represents both the nature of reality and the order of an awakened mind. The two dimensional blueprint is then used as a template for visualization. The image, emanated from the empty nature of mind through the power of creative visualization, is intended to evoke attitudes and understandings that correspond to its internal symbolic structure.

The middle of the maṇḍala represents the inner sanctum of the main deity and is the sacred center of the whole image. There are innumerable variations on the primary theme, some of which are very simple, with a single deity dominating the center, while others are complex and may contain hundreds of attendants, buddhas, mythical creatures, symbols, and landscapes. All are intended to represent the state of awakening iconographically, and the palace is a creation of the awakened mind of the main buddha.

Maṇḍalas depict the realms of particular buddhas, and the images used in a given maṇḍala will be chosen in light of how they represent the mythology and special attributes of the main deity. The maṇḍala of Bhaiṣajyaguru, for example, contains images of therapeutic herbs and medicines, since this particular buddha is associated with healing. As another example, Mañjuśrī is said in Mahāyāna literature to be the embodiment of wisdom, and so his maṇḍalas generally emphasize images associated with learning and insight, such as Perfection of Wisdom sūtras and his flaming sword of gnosis that cuts through ignorance. Practitioners are regularly reminded, however, that the figures in the maṇḍala have no real ontological status; they are representations of the mental qualities toward which tantric adepts aspire and are intended to provide templates for mental transformation, but they are empty of inherent existence. This is also true of demons and wrathful deities, which represent factors of human consciousness that are transmuted through meditation into virtuous qualities.

Other maṇḍalas depict a particular buddha in several different emanations, and many also contain images of fierce guardian figures, great teachers, and bodhisattvas. In tantric practice the maṇḍala provides a blueprint for one's own mental transformation. The central deity represents the state of awakening toward which one is striving, and the various parts of the palace indicate key aspects of the awakened personality. The wrathful deities signify one's own negative emotions—such as anger, hatred, desire, and ignorance—transformed into the awakened consciousness of a buddha. The Buddhist symbols that fill the diagram indicate important doctrines, myths, deities, and so forth that are meant to be incorporated into the idealized worldview of a tantric practitioner, in which cyclic existence and nirvana are known to be undifferentiable, and in which all sense of dualistic thinking is overcome.

> Thus the maṇḍala represents the self-identification of the microcosm (the human person) with the macrocosm, which has the nature of saṃsāra for the unenlightened mind; conversely, it reveals itself as the perfect expression of buddhahood when all misleading distinctions disappear in the enlightened state of nonduality.[18]

In tantric literature, there are descriptions of various types of maṇḍalas, some of which exist in concrete form as painted canvas maṇḍalas or sand maṇḍalas that are used as aids in meditation or as the focal points of initiation ceremonies. In some texts, the external maṇḍalas are said to be representations of natural maṇḍalas, which are nonphysical and represent the awakened qualities of buddhahood. Other maṇḍalas are internal: meditational maṇḍalas are visualized by the mind of a practitioner as three-dimensional figures. In tantric theory, the body itself is also considered to be a maṇḍala, and is the crucible of training designed to transform it into the body of a buddha.

Once constructed and consecrated, maṇḍalas are believed to be imbued with the presence of the relevant buddha(s), and thus become focal points for devotion and visualized offerings. They are also thought to have magical power, and can prolong life, bring wealth, protect against evil, and are often worn as amulets.

Mantras

Mantras are invocations to buddhas, magical spells, prayers, or a combination of these. Tantric practitioners repeat them in order to forge karmic connections between themselves and meditational deities and to effect cognitive restructuring through internalizing the divine attributes that the mantra represents. A person who wishes to develop greater compassion, for instance, might recite the mantra of Avalokiteśvara, who embodies this quality: *oṃ maṇi padme hūṃ*. As we saw in the opening section, the mantra is well known to Tibetans. It represents for them the perfect compassion of Avalokiteśvara, who they believe has taken a special interest in the spiritual welfare of the Tibetan people. He epitomizes universal compassion that is unsullied by any trace of negative emotions or mental afflictions.

Among ordinary beings there are, of course, many acts of compassion, but these are generally tinged by self-interest, pride, or desire for recognition. Avalokiteśvara's compassion, by contrast, is completely free from all afflictions and is so vast that it encompasses all sentient beings without exception and without distinction. People who wish to develop such a perspective recite Avalokiteśvara's mantra over and over, meditating on its significance, and in so doing they try to restructure their minds in accordance with the cultivation of his exalted qualities. According to the Dalai Lama,

> *maṇi* . . . symbolizes the factors of method—the altruistic intention to become enlightened, compassion, and love. Just as a jewel is capable of removing poverty, so the altruistic mind of enlightenment is capable of removing the poverty, or difficulties, of cyclic existence and of solitary peace . . . . The two syllables, *padme* . . . symbolize wisdom. Just as a lotus grows forth from mud but is not sullied by the faults of mud, so wisdom is capable of putting you in a situation of non-contradiction whereas there would be contradiction if you did not have wisdom . . . . Purity must be achieved by an indivisible unity of method and wisdom, symbolized by the final syllable *hūṃ*, which indicates indivisibility . . . . Thus the six syllables, *oṃ maṇi padme*

> *hūm,* mean that in dependence on a path which is an indivisible union of method and wisdom, you can transform your impure body, speech, and mind into the pure exalted body, speech, and mind of a Buddha.[19]

The Dalai Lama's comments are, of course, an interpretive overlay, and other Tibetan exegetes have proposed alternative associations for the syllables of the mantra. As David Snellgrove notes,

> even when the words themselves are normally intelligible, such a mantra can have no essential meaning outside the prescribed ritual. Thus normal intelligibility is of secondary concern. What is primary is the spontaneous significance of a particular mantra to those who have been initiated into its proper use.[20]

Tantric practitioners should recognize that the conventional meanings of words are not fixed, and the significance of anything lies in the mind of the beholder. Mantras mean what they need to mean in the context of a particular practice, and so conventional usage is often irrelevant. Thus Kalu Rinpoche states that

> in the Vajrayāna context, we recite and meditate on mantra, which is awakened sound, the speech of the deity, the Union of Sound and Emptiness . . . . It has no intrinsic reality, but is simply the manifestation of pure sound, experienced simultaneously with its Emptiness. Through mantra, we no longer cling to the reality of the speech and sound encountered in life, but experience it as essentially empty. Then confusion of the speech aspect of our being is transformed into enlightened awareness.[21]

The use of mantras is central to Vajrayāna practice, and so the system is often referred to by its adherents as the "Mantra Vehicle" or the "Secret Mantra Vehicle." Mantra repetition is not simply an external activity in which one vocalizes sounds; it is primarily an act intended to awaken the cognitive potential of the meditator. According to Lama Zopa Rinpoche,

> Mantras are effective because they help keep your mind quiet and peaceful, automatically integrating it into one-pointedness. They

> make your mind receptive to very subtle vibrations and thereby heighten your perception. Their recitation eradicates gross negativities and the true nature of things can then be reflected in your mind's resulting clarity. By practising a transcendental mantra, you can in fact purify all the defiled energy of your body, speech, and mind.[22]

The external vocalization of the sounds of the mantra serves as a focus for mental development. By concentrating on the significance of the mantra as explained by their gurus and opening themselves to their transforming power, meditators actualize their own latent potential for awakening. Through this the sounds of their bodies come to be perceived as divine sounds, and their speech becomes the speech of a buddha.

In some Hindu systems, mantras are said to be primordial sounds that possess power in and of themselves. In Tibetan Buddhist tantra, mantras have no such inherent power. Unless they are recited by a person with a focused mind, they are only sounds. For people with the proper attitude, however, they can be powerful tools that aid in the process of transformation.

Entering Tantric Practice

Initiation

Vajrayāna is presented as a secret system by its texts and practitioners, and so it is not surprising that special initiations (*dbang, abhiṣeka*) are required in order to enter the tantra path. The bestowal of initiation is a necessary precondition for tantric practice, since this forges a special bond between the student, the guru (*bla ma;* pronounced "lama"), and the meditational deity (*yi dam, iṣṭa-devatā*). Nor is initiation open to everyone: only those who are judged by the teacher to possess the necessary intelligence and spiritual aptitude are considered fit for initiation. For people who lack the necessary qualifications, tantra is dangerous, and the texts repeatedly warn that such people can greatly harm themselves if they enter into Vajrayāna practice. Thus the Dalai Lama cautions that tantra

> is not appropriate for the minds of many persons . . . . If one's mental continuum has not been ripened by the practices common to both Sūtra and Tantra Mahāyāna—realisation of suffering, impermanence, refuge, love, compassion, altruistic mind generation, and emptiness

> of inherent existence—practice of the Mantra Vehicle can be ruinous through one's assuming an advanced practice inappropriate to one's capacity. Therefore, its open dissemination is prohibited; practitioners must maintain secrecy from those who are not vessels of this path.[23]

Although tantra is said by its adherents to be an effective and rapid means of gaining awakening, it should not be taught to everyone, only to those who demonstrate the necessary prerequisites. This is hardly a surprising attitude, and analogies may be found in other areas. For example, jet airplanes are effective means of getting from one place to another very quickly, but it is extremely dangerous to pilot them without the necessary initiation of extensive flight training under a qualified instructor. In addition, admission to such training is generally restricted to people with the preconditions for successful piloting, such as good eyesight, coordination, mental stability, and so forth. Operation of jet airplanes by people without proper training or who are physically or mentally impaired could be disastrous, and so potential pilots are screened thoroughly and regularly tested to ensure that their skills have not deteriorated.

Tantric initiation is intended to accomplish many of the same goals. Lamas should test those who desire initiation, making sure that their commitment is genuine and is motivated by an altruistic determination to attain buddhahood and not by desire to impress others through acquiring magical powers or by other negative goals. If one wrongly enters the tantric path, one can bring great harm to oneself and others, and so lamas are warned to screen candidates carefully.

Aspirants who are judged to be suitable receptacles for tantric initiations are sworn to secrecy. Initiates are required to take a series of vows (*dam tshig, samaya*), one of which is not to reveal tantric teachings openly. The promised retributions for breaking the vows include painful suffering in "vajra hells" reserved for those who transgress their tantric promises.

Despite the solemnity of the vows and the fearsomeness of the threatened punishments for transgression, initiation is generally viewed with joyful anticipation, because the aspirant is being established on the fastest and most effective path to awakening. Initiation empowers the initiate and awakens the hidden potential for buddhahood that lies dormant in everyone.

All beings possess the "buddha nature," meaning that they have the capacity to perfect themselves and become buddhas. It is the source of all intelligence and good qualities, and is the ground of every being's personality. The basic nature of mind, as we have seen, is clear light, pure luminosity untainted by any mental constructions. During initiation, the lama introduces students to the nature of their own minds. The ideal student-teacher relationship is not, however, that of a master and a slave, but a true meeting of two minds. The teacher is a person who has successfully cultivated the esoteric teachings of tantra and thus actualized the latent potential of the buddha nature, and students possess the same potential and rely on their instructions in order to attain the same level of realization themselves.

Initiation introduces students to a new vision of reality, one that is not bound by ordinary conceptuality. Nothing is conceived as substantially existent or permanent, and everything is known to be the interplay of luminosity and emptiness. This reality is open and expansive; there are no limits, and so it is also frightening at first. It is as though the firm ground under one's feet has been removed and one is set adrift in a realm of infinite possibilities, but no rules, no boundaries, and no certainties.

Tantric initiation is often a complex ritual involving detailed visualizations, prayers and supplications, offerings, special ritual implements and substances. The purpose is to establish the initiate in the proper frame of mind, forge a karmic bond with the lama and meditational deity, purify defilements, grant permission to practice a particular tantra, and to give instruction concerning how this should be done.

Successful initiation requires active participation from initiates and an openness to the new teachings and practices. They must be in a receptive state of mind and should be thoroughly coached in their role in the ceremony and its importance. In addition, the master must set the proper tone and establish an atmosphere that will impress the initiate with the gravity of the situation and the tremendous opportunity being conferred. In order to accomplish this, the teacher must have progressed spiritually to the point where he or she can perceive the needs and predilections of individual students and adapt teachings and symbols accordingly. Teachers should impress upon their students the importance of an attitude of renunciation, developing the mind of awakening, and the proper view of emptiness.

For serious practitioners of Vajrayāna, initiation is not something that is received only once. Tantric texts speak of the great power of the process, and initiates are urged to participate in initiation again and again, since each experience of these rites has the potential to confer profound blessings on trainees and inspire them to pursue their practice with renewed vigor.

Types of Initiations

There are many different types of initiation in tantra. Four of the most important are: (1) vase initiation; (2) secret initiation; (3) knowledge initiation; and (4) word initiation. The first involves giving initiation using water in a vase and is found in all four tantra sets.[24] The other three are only used in highest yoga tantra. In the vase initiation, according to Khetsun Sangpo,

> The vase symbolizes the bodies of all Buddhas, and receiving this initiation causes you to attain the rank of an Emanation Body. This is the stage of generating yourself as a deity and your surroundings as his habitat. Through such imagination you will be able so to cleanse the channels in your body that you become capable of physical manifestation at will.[25]

The vase initiation is a ritual that uses a maṇḍala. This may be a cloth painting, a maṇḍala made from colored sand, a body maṇḍala, or a meditation maṇḍala. Body maṇḍalas require the meditator to visualize the guru's body as a maṇḍala, with its various aspects constituting parts of a celestial palace and its inhabitants. Concentration maṇḍalas involve a maṇḍala visualized simultaneously by both guru and student. These are only possible for advanced practitioners with highly developed powers of visualization.

The secret, knowledge, and word initiations have various permutations. Sometimes they include practice with a consort and ingestion of substances that are commonly viewed as impure (in order to overcome attachment to reifying views).[26] The consorts and substances may be either imagined or real. Initiations that make use of actual consorts and so forth are reserved for very advanced practitioners.

The secret initiation uses a mixture of the fluids produced by male and female deities in sexual union, which together constitute a maṇḍala referred to as the "conventional mind of awakening." The wisdom initiation uses a "vagina maṇḍala." This practice, according to Khédrup Jé,

involves sexual union with a consort.[27] A guru's instructions co
the union of pure body and pure mind generated in highest yoga
constitutes the "ultimate mind of awakening maṇḍala" used in the w
initiation.

When initiation is conferred, some people develop profound experiences, but others only have a small stirring. Still other initiates feel nothing, and must imagine that something has been experienced.

The lowest level involves imagining that bliss arises with the bestowal of initiation. Those on the next level experience a little bliss when they are touched by water or one of the initiation implements. The third level is reached by those who develop a similitude of meditation on emptiness with a blissful consciousness. The highest level occurs when one fully experiences profound bliss when initiation is given and uses this blissful consciousness to meditate on emptiness.

Deity Yoga

According to Tsong Khapa, deity yoga is the central practice of tantra and is the feature that most clearly differentiates it from the sūtra path.[28] As an indication of how important it is, the Dalai Lama states that "without deity yoga the Mantra path is impossible; deity yoga is the essence of Mantra."[29] He adds that all the distinctive practices of the tantra path are based on this technique, which is the supreme path to awakening.

Deity yoga involves creative visualization of oneself as a fully awakened buddha in order to achieve the state of buddhahood more quickly than is possible using sūtra practices alone.[30] The meditational deity one uses in this practice represents one's own potential for awakening; it is an archetype for the state one is trying to achieve. One generates a mental image of a buddha who is endowed with perfectly developed wisdom and compassion, as well as the other attributes of buddhas, such as ethics, patience, generosity, use of skillful means, and so forth. According to Khenpo Könchog Gyaltsen, in this practice one receives empowerment from tantric deities, which heightens one's sense of potential buddhahood, and so

> through the empowerment of the yidam deities we identify and become one with the yidam itself so that the ordinary vision of the mind is purified. The yidam is the individual's special deity or guide, inseparable from himself, and taking him to Enlightenment. So

> when we visualize certain Enlightenment deities, we are not simply imagining them or indulging in wishful thinking; rather we are realizing what already exists within. This is the method for fully awakening the mind and achieving complete Buddhahood.[31]

Underlying the theory of this system is the idea that the more one familiarizes oneself with something the more likely one is to manifest it. Thus, if one engages in lying, lying becomes progressively more natural and spontaneous. If, however, one becomes familiar with visualizing oneself as having the body, speech, and mind of a buddha—and as performing the activities of a buddha—one will gradually come to approximate the state of buddhahood. The tantric adept recognizes that his present perceptions are powerfully influenced by the predispositions created by former actions and attitudes and that in order to attain the freedom of buddhahood it is necessary to establish control over this process. This is accomplished by making idealized substitutions for present situations and appearances. The meditator envisions everything that appears as a manifestation of the luminous and empty nature of mind. Everything becomes part of the environment of a deity, and through this process the meditator's actual surroundings progressively come to approximate this ideal vision.

When, for example, meditators visualize themselves as Avalokiteśvara, the embodiment of compassion, they are attempting to develop their own latent capacity for compassion. There is no fundamental or truly existent difference between ordinary beings and fully awakened buddhas; the only difference is that the minds of ordinary beings are plagued by deluded thoughts which result from mental afflictions, but these are adventitious and not a part of the nature of the mind. When ordinary beings remove the afflictions and perfect wisdom and compassion, they become buddhas.

Deity yoga is a technique for becoming progressively more familiar with the thoughts and deeds of a buddha, until the state of buddhahood is actualized through repeated practice. As one develops an increasing ability to identify with the meditational deity, one approximates the awakened attributes of that deity, and in so doing one simulates in oneself the qualities that the deity represents. Through this practice, according to tantric teachings, the mind of the meditator becomes indistinguishable from the mind of the deity, and his or her experiences are transformed into the blissful cognitions of a buddha.

Because in Vajrayāna one trains in the effect that one is trying to achieve—the state of buddhahood—it is often referred to as the "Effect Vehicle." In tantric training one engages in practices that develop the various awakened qualities of a buddha, particularly those of body, speech, and mind. One also creates a symbolic world in which one lives in the exalted environment of a buddha. According to Tsong Khapa,

> the word 'Effect' refers to the four thorough purities—abode, body, resources, and deeds—which are a Buddha's palace, body, fortune and activities. In accordance with them one meditates on oneself as one presently having an inconceivable mansion, divine companions, sacred articles and deeds such as purification of environments and beings. Thus, it is called the 'Effect Vehicle' because one is progressing through meditation in accordance with the aspects of the effect [i.e., buddhahood].[32]

The Dalai Lama explains this practice has two features: developing pride in oneself as a deity and a clear appearance of the deity.[33] Divine pride is essential because it overcomes the sense of oneself as ordinary. Since one's goal is to become a fully awakened buddha, one attempts to view oneself in this way. Divine pride is different from ordinary, afflicted pride because it is motivated by compassion for others and is based on an understanding of emptiness. The deity and oneself are both known to be empty, all appearances are viewed as manifestations of the luminous and empty nature of mind, and so the divine pride of deity yoga does not lead to attachment, greed, and other afflictions. The tendency toward developing afflicted pride is counteracted by meditation on emptiness because in deity yoga,

> induced by ascertaining the emptiness of one's own inherent existence, this consciousness itself appears in the form of the face, arms, and so forth of a deity. The wisdom consciousness vividly appears as a divine body and at the same time ascertains its non-inherent existence.[34]

One who develops this divine pride has the ability to view appearances as the sport of a buddha, and one thinks of oneself as performing the activities of an awakened being for the benefit of others. In this way, tendencies toward afflicted attitudes are overcome by proper motivation and the correct view of emptiness.

Deity Yoga as a Union of Method and Wisdom

Deity yoga is said by its adherents to be superior to sūtra practice because it utilizes a "union of method and wisdom." Wisdom refers to a consciousness that realizes emptiness, the lack of inherent existence of all phenomena. Method refers to one's motivation and the activities that one performs for the benefit of others in order to establish them in awakening. Both are essential aspects of the awakened mind of a buddha. According to tantric texts, practitioners of sūtra train in these two characteristics separately, which means that each is cultivated independently. Because of this, the sūtra path requires a very long time to complete. Tantra, however, has methods in which one develops both at the same time, and so they quickly become manifested in the continuum of one's consciousness. This is accomplished by the practice of deity yoga, in which the subtle consciousness that meditates on emptiness is actualized in a physical form embodying compassion. This unites wisdom and compassion within the continuum of a single mind, allowing one to amass the collections of merit and wisdom simultaneously.[35] Those who successfully train in this way make far more rapid progress than is possible through sūtra practices alone. The Dalai Lama explains that in the sūtra system

> 'inseparable method and wisdom' refers to method conjoined with wisdom and wisdom conjoined with method. When the altruistic mind of enlightenment is manifest, the mind actually cognising emptiness is not present, and when an actual cognition of emptiness is manifest, an altruistic mind of enlightenment is not present . . . . In Mantra . . . the inseparability of method and wisdom does not mean that wisdom and method are different realities conjoined; rather, method and wisdom are included in one entity. In Mantra these two are complete in the different aspects of one consciousness.[36]

In sūtra one separately develops the collections of merit and of wisdom, but in tantra they are perfected simultaneously. This is important because the collection of merit leads to actualization of the form bodies of a buddha, while the collection of wisdom leads to actualization of the truth body.[37] These are developed quickly through deity yoga, because one familiarizes oneself with the idea that one is already a fully awakened buddha possessing the body, speech, and mind of a buddha; one also performs the activities of a buddha. Thus one actually trains in the result one is trying to achieve and is not simply cultivating qualities that are concordant with it, as in sūtra practice.

As an analogy, if one wishes to learn to play the flute it might be helpful to study flute music, listen to great performances, read the biographies of accomplished musicians, study the dynamics of how the flute produces sounds, and so forth; but if one only does these things one may know a great deal about the flute but will never master the technique of actually playing it. It would be far more beneficial to actually begin playing the flute under the guidance of a qualified teacher. Through engaging in training, and through diligent practice, one may eventually become skilled in flute playing. From the point of view of tantra, sūtra practitioners are like people wishing to play the flute who only train in related activities. They have greater understanding than those who never begin instruction at all, but their progress is very slow because they fail to familiarize themselves with the effect they are trying to achieve. In the context of tantric practice, this goal is buddhahood, and although engagement in such concordant qualities as the six perfections, skill in means, and so on is very beneficial, it will not bring about the state of a fully awakened buddha without the special techniques of tantra, in which one actually cultivates the bodies of a buddha.

The perfections and other bodhisattva practices are effective means of spiritual development, but they bear no resemblance to the form body of a buddha, and thus they cannot become a form body. A form body is a manifestation of the wisdom consciousness of a buddha in a form embodying compassion, and this can only be developed by an awakened consciousness in which direct perception of emptiness and the mind of awakening are conjoined. Proponents of Vajrayāna assert that this is only accomplished by means of the practice of deity yoga.[38] In deity yoga, the consciousness perceiving emptiness is manifested as a buddha. The buddha's wisdom consciousness, motivated by compassion, is a projection of one's own mind and serves as a template for one's development. The appearance of the deity develops into a buddha's form body, while one's mind develops into a truth body, and thus both bodies are complete in one consciousness.

How a Buddha's Bodies Are Manifested

Form bodies are of two types: emanation bodies and complete enjoyment bodies. Emanation bodies are creations of buddhas that are designed to benefit sentient beings. The complete enjoyment body is a pure form that resides in a pure land and can only be perceived by advanced practitioners. It is a very subtle entity that according to the Dalai Lama is "the sport of mere wind and mind."[39] This means that it is created by the pure mind of a buddha from subtle energies called "winds" (which will be discussed below in the section on highest yoga tantra). Both types of bodies are the result of perfecting the collection of merit.

Truth bodies are also of two types: the wisdom truth body and the nature truth body. The wisdom truth body is the buddha's omniscient consciousness, which continually resides in a nondual meditative equipoise on emptiness. The nature truth body is the emptiness of that consciousness—its lack of inherent existence—which is the nature of the mind and of all other phenomena. Truth bodies are the result of perfecting the collection of wisdom.

Tantric texts stress that neither form bodies nor truth bodies can be achieved separately, since the attainment of either one requires the conjoined cause of the collections of merit and wisdom. Tsong Khapa contends that form bodies are

> achieved through the appearance of the wisdom apprehending [emptiness] as a divine maṇḍala circle, and a Truth Body is achieved through the cognition of its nature—emptiness. One should know that joining such method and wisdom non-dualistically is the chief meaning of the method and wisdom and of the yogas set forth in the Mantra Vehicle.[40]

For those who wish to attain buddhahood it is not sufficient to cultivate method by itself or wisdom by itself; the two must be conjoined in a single consciousness at the same time. Because sūtra cultivates both separately, its followers must enter the path of tantra in order to fully actualize buddhahood.

Central to this system is the use of meditational rituals called "means of achievement" (*sgrub thabs, sādhana*), in which one combines prayers, visualizations, hand gestures, and bodily movements that represent the awakened aspects of the mind of a particular buddha. These practices are based on meditational manuals that outline ritual practices for particular deities. Sādhanas describe the qualities of the deity and its retinue, contain recitations of mantras and prayers, and they are connected with visualization of the deity's maṇḍala. By repeatedly performing the prescribed activities of the means of achievement, meditators enhance their powers of visualization, until eventually the entire diagram appears clearly.

During the process of emanating a maṇḍala, the meditator praises the deity, asks for blessings, and envisions the deity's maṇḍala, but is not simply a devout supplicant. The meditation process requires that meditators view themselves as inseparable from the deity and as possessing all the attributes of a fully awakened buddha. Thus, they are not simply praising someone else's good qualities, but are using the meditation to develop the same attributes themselves. Through repeated familiarization with the rituals of the means of achievement, meditators begin to approximate the state of awakening.

Means of achievement range from simple rites that can be done in a relatively short time to elaborate combinations of prayers, offerings, and visualizations of vast numbers of deities in various patterns. They generally begin with recitation of the refuge prayer and an indication of one's intention to manifest the mind of awakening. This is followed by visualization of the central deity, generally accompanied by other buddhas and various attendants.

The next phase involves paying homage to the deity and repetition of his/her mantra, and one may imagine that all sentient beings are also participating in the practice and deriving merit from it. The deity is viewed as responding positively to one's prayers and bestowing blessings. In the next phase one visualizes the deity being dissolved into emptiness, and one abides in nonconceptual contemplation of suchness. The concluding part of the ritual involves dedication of the merit generated by it to all sentient beings and hoping that they benefit from one's practice.

More elaborate *sādhana*s may incorporate initial purificatory practices for oneself and the surrounding environment, complex visualizations, extended verses of homage and dedication of merit, and detailed sequences of imagery that are built up progressively and then comprehensively dissolved into emptiness. The dissolution is crucial because ideally the visualization itself is generated from the wisdom consciousness realizing emptiness, which enables one to understand that there is no real difference between oneself and the deity. This fundamental nondifference makes possible the transformation of an ordinary being into a fully-actualized buddha, and comprehending that oneself, the deity, and the environment are empty serves as a counteragent to false pride and afflicted perceptions.

This practice enables meditators to reconstruct the world in accordance with the meditation. Those who become adepts know that they are no longer bound by the fetters of ordinariness; their surroundings become the environment of a buddha. Their companions are viewed as a buddha's retinue, and their actions are the compassionate activities of a buddha.

> Those who have attained slight mastery with respect to wisdom are able to visualize clearly and firmly the entire maṇḍala, even the subtle deities at the sense organs of the larger deities, at one time. They have by this stage become so familiar with the images visualized that those images can appear with the slightest effort; thus, it is said that it is no longer necessary to distinguish meditative sessions from non-sessions, since one can do deity yoga at all times, maintaining the sense that one is a deity while carrying out all manner of daily activities.[41]

Advanced meditators develop the ability to create environments of their own choosing, and they are able to transcend the sufferings that seem so real to ordinary beings who are bound by mundane conceptions. According to Tsong Khapa, for one who attains advanced levels of meditation painful cognitions no longer occur, no matter what external experiences one encounters. All of one's cognitions are a union of bliss and emptiness. One recognizes that nothing is inherently what it appears to be. Whatever occurs is perceived by one's unshakably blissful consciousness as the sport of luminosity and emptiness, and so

> for a Bodhisattva who has attained the meditative stabilisation of bliss pervading all phenomena, only a feeling of pleasure arises with respect to all objects; pain and neutrality do not occur, even though [pieces from his body] the size of a small coin (*kārṣhāpaṇa*) are cut or even though his body is crushed by elephants, only a discrimination of bliss is maintained.[42]

Tantric texts stress that such bodhisattvas are not creating a delusional system in order to hide from the harsher aspects of reality. Rather, they are transforming reality, making it conform to an ideal archetype. Since all phenomena are empty of inherent existence, they have no fixed nature. No one ever apprehends an object as it is in its true nature, because there is no such nature. Even if phenomena had fixed natures, we would still never be able to perceive them, since all we ever experience are our cognitions of objects, which are overlaid with conceptions about them. All our perceptions are *ideas about* things, and not real things. These ideas are also empty, arising from nothingness and immediately dissolving again into nothingness, leaving nothing behind. Tantric adepts develop the ability to reconstitute "reality," which is completely malleable for those who train in yogas involving blissful consciousnesses realizing emptiness. The sense of bliss pervades all their cognitions, and their understanding of emptiness allows them to generate minds that are manifestations of bliss and emptiness.

The Four Classes of Tantra

Action Tantra

Tibetan exegetes have developed numerous classification systems for tantric texts, the most common of which is a fourfold division into: (1) action tantras; (2) performance tantras; (3) yoga tantras, and (4) highest yoga tantras. This method of differentiating tantras was developed in the thirteenth and fourteenth centuries and used to classify these texts in the definitive version of the Tibetan Buddhist canon by the scholar Pudön. The system is based on the types of practices emphasized in a particular tantra and the relative importance of external rituals or internal yogas.[43]

Action tantras are primarily taught for meditators who require external activities. The special trainees of action tantras are people who lack the capacity for profound meditation on emptiness but are able to engage enthusiastically in external rituals and activities.[44] The practice of action tantra

> emphasizes external development leading towards purification through the observance of ritual actions of body and speech. The divine power (*lha*)—the supreme essence of Buddhahood—is the

> embodiment of pristine awareness (*ye-shes*) and confers temporal and lasting benefits like a donor to his beneficiaries. In more psychological terms, an individual identifies himself as a servant to the divine power with the conviction that such patterning of behavior will eventually lead one to realize the origin of that power.[45]

Action tantra trainees engage in activities in which symbolic representations of aspects of the path are created or acted out. For example, one may make or buy a painting of a deity, place it in a special spot and make offerings to it, imagining that the deity is actually present there. Other activities include ritual bathing in which one envisions the external activity of washing as purifying mental afflictions. The activities of action tantra are designed for those who are not adept at internal visualization and who can benefit from having physical symbols as focal points for their meditation.

Practitioners of action tantra understand that in reality all phenomena are an undifferentiable union of appearance and emptiness, but on the conventional level of practice they perceive themselves and the meditational deity as separate entities. They view the deity as a master or lord and themselves as servants, performing acts of devotion in stylized ritual dramas involving activities of body and speech. According to Jikmé Lingpa,

> generally the practitioner visualizes before himself the deity, and invites it to be present as a servant would a lord by making offerings and singing praises. He then concentrates on visualizing the deity's body, speech and mind, the celestial palaces, the spreading and contracting of rays of light from the deity and thereby receives the blessings of the deity through supplication, recitation and meditative stability.[46]

Through successful engagement in action tantra, practitioners can greatly shorten the path to awakening and can attain the state of the tantric deity Vajradhara in as little as sixteen human lifetimes.

Performance Tantra

Performance tantras, according to the Dalai Lama, equally emphasize external activities and internal yoga.[47] The training of performance tantra

> places equal emphasis on external ritual purity and internal meditative development. The basis of realization is the view of oneself as of equal status with the divine power, like a friend or brother. In these practices, meditative activity involves the creative visualization of the embodiment of pristine awareness so that beliefs in the distinction between the enlightened patterns of action and those of oneself dissolve.[48]

The main practices of performance tantra involve mentally creating an image of oneself as an awakened being and also generating the form of a deity in front of oneself as a template. One views oneself and the deity as companions or friends, strives to emulate the deity, chants the mantra of the deity, and endeavors to perfect one's ability to visualize it without mental fluctuation. There are two aspects to this meditation: a yoga with signs and a signless yoga. The first type involves stabilizing the mind by developing one-pointed concentration on the deity, the letters of its mantra (visualized at the heart), its hand-gestures (*phyag rgya, mudrā*), and its form. Signless yoga focuses on the deity's final nature—emptiness—and not on external characteristics. Those who train in performance tantra can attain the state of Vajradhara in as little as seven human lifetimes.

Yoga Tantra

In *yoga tantra* one visualizes oneself as an actual buddha, and not merely as a devotee or companion of a buddha. Yoga tantra consists of two parts: outer yoga tantra and highest yoga tantra. The difference between them is that

> With the Outer Yoga-tantra, ritual purity and other observances found in the former Tantras are only aids to the realization of the path. The primary concern of these teachings is inward contemplation and introspection to directly perceive, in the atmosphere of meditative settledness, the functioning of the mind. Here, realization is attained through the contemplation of non-duality which comes about by the fusion of the individual committed to the service of the divine power with the power itself, as an embodiment of primordial awareness.[49]

Yoga tantras emphasize internal yoga. One visualizes oneself and the archetypal deity as separate beings, and then one causes the deity to enter oneself. In highest yoga tantra one develops a profound awareness of one's body as being composed of subtle energies called "winds" (*rlung, prāṇa*) and "drops" (*thig le, bindu*) which move through a network of seventy-two thousand "channels" (*rtsa, nāḍī*). One then generates oneself as a fully awakened buddha composed entirely of these subtle energies and possessing a buddha's wisdom consciousness.

Practitioners of yoga tantra view all phenomena as being naturally free from the signs of mental projection and as manifestations of luminosity and emptiness. On the conventional level, meditators train in perceiving all appearances as maṇḍalas of deities. Although trainees of yoga tantra engage in some external activities, ritual is viewed as being symbolic of the primary practice of internal yoga.

There are two aspects of yoga tantra: a yoga with signs and a yoga without signs. The former type involves visualizing oneself as a deity in terms of five qualities of awakening: (1) a perfect moon disk, representing the pure nature of reality; (2) perfect seed syllables of deities, which are their primary mantras (these represent the speech of buddhas); (3) perfect ritual implements held by the deities, representing the pure minds of buddhas; (4) the perfect form of a deity, representing the deity's complete maṇḍala; and (5) the perfection of wisdom, visualized within the heart of the deity, which represents the essence of a buddha's awakened consciousness. In yoga tantra one first generates a vivid appearance of the deity, together with its retinue, contemplating both its wondrous form and exalted attributes, and then one absorbs the deity into oneself, imagining that one becomes merged with it.

In the yoga without signs, one dispenses with external symbols and meditates directly on suchness (*de kho na nyid, tathatā*). One views nondual suchness as inseparable from the appearances of deities, which are themselves representations of perfect awakening. Practitioners of yoga tantra are able to attain buddhahood in a minimum of three human lifetimes.

Highest Yoga Tantra

Highest yoga tantra is divided into two stages: the stage of generation and the stage of completion. Both are factors in the transformation of one's mind and body into the mind and body of a buddha. In the stage of generation, one creates a vivid image of a deity, and in the stage of completion one transforms oneself into an actual deity possessing the exalted form and awakened mind of a buddha.

There are three primary prerequisites for entering the stage of generation: (1) previous practice of paths common to both sūtra and tantra; (2) initiation into a highest yoga tantra; and (3) taking on tantric pledges and vows. The first prerequisite entails correct motivation: the mind of awakening. The practice of the common paths serves to establish the proper orientation and attitudes. This is important, because in order to endure the rigors of highest yoga tantra one should have a clear idea of why one is traveling the path to awakening and what one's goals are. With this as a basis, one trains in the six perfections and in the activities of bodhisattvas. Proponents of tantra claim that all the practices of sūtra are included in tantra, although tantra transcends sūtra because of its profundity and effectiveness. Thus, in tantra one cultivates the qualities characteristic of bodhisattvas—generosity, ethics, patience, effort, concentration, wisdom, and so on—but one develops them much more quickly through engaging in deity yoga. The techniques of tantra supplement the bodhisattva's training, but they do not contradict or supersede the wish to attain awakening for the benefit of others. Rather, they are practical enhancements that allow meditators to progress more quickly by giving them access to subtle levels of consciousness in order to bring about profound transformations.

To enter into the training program of the stage of generation, one must first receive the vase initiation. Practice of the stage of completion requires the vase initiation, plus the secret initiation, the knowledge initiation, and the word initiation.

These two stages are intimately connected in that the generation stage is a necessary precondition for the completion stage. The generation stage prepares the mind for the completion stage by gradually enhancing the clarity of one's visualizations until they are made manifest in the completion stage.

The conferral of initiation serves as an empowerment, which creates a karmic connection between the student, the deities of the maṇḍalas, and the lama. There are also special tantric pledges that initiates are required to take. These hold students to a strict code of conduct and provide an ethical basis that is essential to successful tantric practice. This is important, because many of the techniques of highest yoga tantra are dangerous, and the vows serve as a counterbalance to tendencies toward possible negative attitudes and behaviors.

The Stage of Generation

In the stage of generation one trains the mind with imaginative visualizations. One creates a vivid image of a deity that possesses all the physical marks of a buddha, as well as its mental qualities. The purpose of this stage is to develop one's imaginative powers to such a degree that one's mental creations become real. In the stage of completion, one finalizes the process by transforming oneself in accordance with the visualizations of the stage of generation.

This system conceives trainees in terms of a mystical physiology. The body contains seventy-two thousand energy channels, through which winds circulate. The most important ones are a central channel, which is roughly contiguous with the spine, and a left and right channel that wrap around the central channel at certain points and constrict the movements of winds in the channels. These constriction points are called *cakras* (*rtsa 'khor*, which literally means "wheel").

In tantric physiology, consciousnesses are said to travel throughout the body "mounted" on the winds, which serve as their support. Consciousnesses cannot function without the support of the winds, but the winds lack direction without consciousnesses. Because of this, consciousnesses by themselves are said to be like people without legs, while winds by themselves are like blind people. Each needs the other, and they function in tandem, with winds providing movement and consciousnesses providing direction. Because of this intimate connection, whatever affects one also affects the other, and so meditators wishing to gain control over consciousness must also learn to influence the movements of winds.

In tantric meditation, one learns to manipulate the winds in order to bring about particular types of consciousness. In the system of highest yoga tantra, one acquires the ability to control them with great precision in order to gain access to very subtle levels of mind. In the stage of generation, yogis cause the winds to move into the central channel, remain there, and then dissolve. The dissolution of the winds results in profound bliss and the manifestation of subtle consciousnesses, which can be used to bring about specific realizations, such as direct cognition of emptiness.

Through learning to influence the movements of winds, meditators simulate the process of death, in which progressively subtler levels of mind manifest as the winds dissolve in stages.[50] With the dissolution of winds, a succession of consciousnesses appears, each more subtle than the last, until the arising of the "mind of clear light," which is the most subtle and basic of all minds. In ordinary death, the stages of this process occur involuntarily, but through the special techniques of highest yoga tantra yogis can cause the subtle minds to manifest under their conscious control.

Developing proficiency in the visualizations used in the stage of generation requires a great deal of practice for most meditators. According to Roger Jackson, a person who has perfected the stage of generation in the Kālacakra system "can visualize the entire *maṇḍala* in a drop the size of a mustard seed at the tip of one's nose, with such clarity that one can see the whites of the eyes of all 722 deities—and can maintain the visualization with uninterrupted one-pointed concentration for four hours."[51]

The Stage of Completion

In the stage of completion, the meditator is actually transformed into the buddha that was visualized in the stage of generation. In the stage of generation, one learns to visualize oneself as a deity with intense clarity and vividness, one's environment is perceived as the environment of a fully actualized deity, and one develops the nonafflicted pride of a deity. In the stage of completion, one acquires the ability to cause winds to enter the central channel and dissolve in the "indestructible drop" in the center of the heart. This drop was created at birth from the fluids of one's father and mother, and it remains in the heart until death. As one causes winds to enter into it and dissolve, one experiences a profound bliss, and concomitantly one actualizes progressively subtler levels of mind. When all the winds have been dissolved in the indestructible drop, the mind of clear light manifests, and this can be used to cognize emptiness directly. According to the Dalai Lama, in tantra

> the main technique is for one consciousness to contain the two factors of observing a maṇḍala circle of deities and of simultaneously realizing their emptiness of inherent existence. In this way, the vast—the appearance of deities—and the profound—the realization of suchness—are complete in one consciousness.[52]

At this point, one is no longer bound by the physical and cognitive restraints of ordinary beings, and one attains a subtle body in the form of a deity possessing all the physical marks of a buddha. This body is made of subtle winds which manifest in the ideal form of the deity.

In the stage of generation, one visualizes a maṇḍala, complete with mansions and deities, in a tiny drop, which is either at the upper or lower opening of the central channel. According to the *Guhyasamāja Tantra*, during the stage of completion

> everything from the crown of the head to the feet dissolves into the heart; you engage in the perfect yoga (meditation on emptiness). . . . All sentient beings and all other phenomena dissolve into clear light and then dissolve into you; then you yourself, as the deity, dissolve into your heart . . . . Just as mist on a mirror fades toward the center and disappears, so does everything—the net of illusory manifestation—dissolve into the clear light of emptiness. Just as fish are easily seen in clear water, so does everything—the net of illusory manifestation—emerge from the clear light of emptiness.[53]

Six Levels of the Stage of Completion

There are six levels of the stage of completion: (1) physical isolation; (2) verbal isolation; (3) mental isolation; (4) illusory body, (5) actual clear light; and (6) learner's union. In preparation for the stage of *physical isolation*, one causes winds to enter, remain, and dissolve into the drop in the heart *cakra*. This leads to the manifestation of a subtle consciousness. One result is that the yogi transcends the conception of herself as ordinary, and her body appears in the aspect of a deity. Because of this, her physical form is "isolated" from ordinary appearances, and so this stage is called "physical isolation."

In the stage of *verbal isolation*, yogis cause winds to enter, remain, and dissolve in the central channel. The practice of verbal isolation is connected with breathing exercises, and meditators come to realize that the natural whisper of the breath sounds like the syllables *oṃ*, *ah*, and *hūṃ*. In this way, breathing is isolated from ordinariness.

The stage of *mental isolation* begins with dissolution of winds into the indestructible drop at the center of the heart. It is referred to as "mental isolation" because one's mind becomes isolated from conceptuality through appearing as a union of undifferentiable bliss and emptiness. This is a prerequisite for the next stage, the development of an illusory body (*sgyu lus, mayā-deha*).

The *illusory body* is a creation of one's imaginative visualization. It is made from subtle winds that are manifested in the form of a deity. In this meditation, one uses an "action seal" (*las kyi phyag rgya, karma-mudrā;* i.e., a tantric consort) in connection with a practice that causes all the winds to dissolve into the indestructible drop. At this point the illusory body arises in the appearance of a buddha. This is called an "impure illusory body" because one still has not overcome all afflictions. The second Dalai Lama advises that

> the way to hold the visualization is to see the visualized mystic drop and one's own mind as entering into a unity. When this is done well, the visualized drop and the visualizing mind no longer appear as separate entities. By means of blending the two and causing them to become inseparable, one gains especially subtle tantric pride.[54]

The stage of *clear light* refers to the manifestation of the mind of clear light, the most fundamental level of consciousness. Compared to this, all other minds are merely adventitious. For most people, this mind is only experienced involuntarily and not as a result of one's conscious choice. Ordinary beings have flashes of the mind of clear light at the time of death, just before going to sleep, at the moment of fainting, and so on, but since these experiences are not under one's control, one is not able to do anything with them. Tantric adepts, however, develop the ability to cause the mind of clear light to become manifest as a result of meditative practice, and this mind can be used to cognize emptiness directly and nondualistically. This is the mode of cognition of buddhas, who always remain in the state of clear light. For them, all the appearances of phenomena are perceived as a union of luminosity and emptiness. The arising of the mind of clear light occurs when all the winds are completely dissolved in the indestructible drop, which leads to a profound and subtle bliss and the manifestation of the mind of clear light. The second Dalai Lama connects this with dissolution of the substances that constitute the subtle drops:

> When the substance melts, descends, and arrives at the channel below the navel, it touches the sensory power inside the channel and gives

> rise to a special sensation. This sensory power is a principal condition that, when combined with control of the drop, gives rise to a special sensory consciousness of bliss. This in turn acts as a simultaneous condition that arises in the nature of great bliss as a mental consciousness. By combining this with a recollection of the view of emptiness one can generate great bliss in the nature of insight into the emptiness nature of mind. It is this that is to be cultivated and maintained.[55]

After this, the winds begin to move again, and the meditator arises in an illusory body. The level of *learner's union* is attained when one is able to manifest an illusory body after having overcome all of the obstructions to liberation from cyclic existence. This illusory body is called the "pure illusory body" because it is not afflicted by these obstructions. It is created from an extremely subtle wind, and one becomes progressively more familiar with the mind of clear light. According to the second Dalai Lama,

> this means that one should arise in the actual form of a deity. This is to be done not by mere imagination but by manifesting the most subtle aspects of energy and mind and then arising in a tantric form from these.[56]

The beginning of the stage of learner's union is also marked by the attainment of the second bodhisattva level and entrance onto the path of meditation. As one deepens one's practice, one overcomes the obstructions to omniscience, and through this progresses to the final level, a non-learner's union. This is the stage of buddhahood, in which one attains the form bodies and truth body of a fully awakened being. At this point, one has eliminated even the subtlest traces of the afflictions, and the actual clear light is fully manifest.

In the Gélukpa tantric system, the ability to generate an illusory body is considered to be essential for the attainment of buddhahood. Geshe Kelsang Gyatso attributes this sentiment to Nāgārjuna:

> Nāgārjuna stated that if one does not realize the illusory body then there is no purpose in studying or practising either sūtra or secret mantra. He said this because buddhahood—the ultimate goal of all study and practice—cannot possibly be attained unless you achieve the illusory body. To become a buddha you must attain a buddha's

> form body and the illusory body is its primary or substantial cause. . . . no matter how much you might study and meditate upon the teachings of sūtra and secret mantra, if you do not attain the illusory body it will be impossible to reach buddhahood. However, once you do actually attain the illusory body it is definite that you shall reach perfect buddhahood within that very lifetime.[57]

Tantric Seals

At advanced levels of the stage of completion, yogis also utilize special sexual techniques that involve a "seal," or partner. In these practices, one visualizes oneself and one's partner as specific deities, and one's sexual union is used as a way of generating very subtle minds. According to tantric theory, in orgasm coarser levels of mind drop away, but most people do not see the potential meditative benefits of the experience. In the practices using seals, the occurrence of orgasm is conjoined with yogas that draw the winds into the central channel. The result is an indescribable sensation of bliss and direct perception of emptiness. The partner is referred to as a "seal" because the practice seals the realization that all phenomena are a union of bliss and emptiness. According to the second Dalai Lama, one relies on a seal

> as an external condition and the experience of the compression process as the inner condition. This causes one's illusory body, which is as clear and vibrant as a rainbow, to melt like a cloud into space. When this occurs, the dualistic appearance of the illusory body and the clear light subsides. The actual clear light which directly perceives emptiness then brings realization of the Yoga of Pure Wisdom. This pulls out the seed of grasping at true existence, destroying it once and forever at its root.[58]

The bliss of union—which is combined with the wisdom consciousness realizing emptiness—approximates the mental state of buddhas, who perceive all appearances as manifestations of luminosity and emptiness and who are untroubled by the vicissitudes of phenomenal reality. Sexual yogas often involve retention of semen by male practitioners. In such contexts, the semen is referred to as "mind of awakening" (*bodhicitta*), and the movement of subtle energies through the central channel is equated with generation of the aspiration to become a buddha.

Tantric texts stress that practice with consorts is not a form of sexual indulgence, but rather a technique of controlled visualization that uses the special bliss of sexual union. It is restricted to very advanced practitioners, yogis who have gained control over the emanation of a subtle body and have awakened the mystical heat energy, or *dumo (gtum mo, caṇḍālī)*. Those who have not progressed to this level are not qualified to practice with an actual consort; people without the necessary prerequisites who mimic tantric sexual practices thinking that they are practicing Vajrayāna are simply deluded, and may do themselves great harm. Sexual union is only appropriate to the highest levels of the stage of completion, and so those who have not developed sufficient realization and control over subtle energies are unable to generate the blissful wisdom consciousness realizing emptiness that is the basis for this practice. They may succeed in fooling others—or even themselves—but they will be utterly unable to use sexual energy in accordance with the practices of highest yoga tantra.

According to the Dalai Lama, only a person who views all the phenomena of cyclic existence with complete impartiality is qualified to engage in tantric sexual practices:

> Truthfully, you can only do such practice if there is no sexual desire whatsoever. The kind of realization that is required is like this: If someone gives you a goblet of wine and a glass of urine, or a plate of wonderful food and a piece of excrement, you must be in such a state that you can eat and drink from all four and it makes no difference to you what they are. Then maybe you can do this practice.[59]

When asked to name any lamas who he thought were at this level, he admitted that he could not. He mentioned that there are well-known stories of great teachers like Tilopa who had transcended all attachment to conventional thinking and so were able to engage in sexual practices without harming themselves or their students, but he added that such exceptional individuals are very rare.[60]

Types of Seals

There are various types of seals, some real and some imagined. Tsong Khapa asserts that it is possible to access subtle levels of mind by working with seals that are merely visualized, but he contends that in order to attain buddhahood in one lifetime it is necessary to use an "action seal," because the great power of practice with an actual consort allows one to generate an illusory body that arises as a deity. According to Geshe Kelsang Gyatso, a tantric yogi who does this

> will enter into the meditative equipoise in which the very last obscurations preventing omniscience are removed. At that point he has achieved the path of no more learning, full omniscience and the resultant mahamudra union having the seven features: perfect buddhahood.[61]

The only other way to accomplish this is to transform the clear light of death into a deity, but this can only be done when actual death occurs. According to Gélukpa tradition, this was the choice that Tsong Khapa made. He was concerned that some of his followers might go astray if he were to practice with an actual consort, and so he postponed the generation of an illusory body until his death. When the clear light of death manifested, he effected the transformation of a subtle body and arose as a fully awakened buddha.

> The use of an Action Seal is one of two ways to proceed to the level of illusory body. The only other way to rise in an illusory body is to use one's actual death as the means of withdrawing all the winds, practicing vajra repetition as one is dying. (If one is capable of performing it, this practice would result in the attainment of awakening without again being reborn into a coarse body.) Shākyamuni Buddha, in his last lifetime prior to awakening, used an Action Seal, but it is said that although [Tsong Khapa] became a Buddha, he did not use an Action Seal, becoming awakened in the intermediate state instead . . . because he feared his followers would imitate him without being properly prepared, thus hampering instead of enhancing their practices.[62]

As Geshe Kelsang Gyatso's describes this process,

> The method of embracing the action seal can be explained as follows by taking the example of a man whose personal deity is Heruka. He visualizes himself as Heruka embracing his consort Vajravarahi and

> through the force of this embrace all his winds enter, abide and dissolve within the indestructible drop at his heart. With this dissolution the eight signs appear and are experienced in conjunction with emptiness. With arisal of the all empty clear light his mind will mingle indistinguishably with emptiness, like water being poured into water. At this stage the experienced yogi can remain in the state of the all empty clear light for as long as he wishes. Until perfect buddhahood is attained this practice must be performed frequently.[63]

The culmination of the stage of completion occurs when one actually transforms oneself in accordance with the deities one had previously imagined. One is no longer an ordinary being, but has transcended all vestiges of ordinariness. One perceives all phenomena as a union of bliss and emptiness. Nothing is coarse, painful, or contemptible; everything is regarded as the play of the luminosity and emptiness of mind. All appearances are the creative visualization of a tantric deity, and one understands that one has been transformed into this deity. One has transcended all egoistic attachments, all desire, and even the subtlest traces of mental afflictions. Because of this, one's mind is characterized by profound compassion and direct perception of emptiness, and thus one is able to manifest in limitless forms for the benefit of others. According to the *Hevajra Tantra*,

> Therefore, a buddha is neither an existent thing nor a non-existent thing;
> He has a form with arms and faces, yet in supreme bliss is formless;
> Therefore, the whole world is the innate, because the innate is said to be its essential nature.
> Due to purification of the mind, nirvana is also its essential nature.[64]

In the final stages of this process, the manifestation of the mind of clear light becomes the antidote to the remaining traces of the afflictions. One enters into the "vajralike meditative stabilization," which is one's final mind as an ordinary being. In this concentration, one removes the subtlest traces of afflictions, and

> at dawn you become a fully awakened buddha. At that time your mind of clear light realizing emptiness becomes indestructible and

> constant . . . . From that time onwards you experience th
> clear light realizing emptiness without a single break in c
> With the total annihilation at dawn of the obscurations p
> omniscience, your mind of meaning clear light will bec
> resultant truth body of a buddha and your pure illusory b
> become the resultant form body . . . all objects of knowledge will be simultaneously realized within a single mind in a single moment because even the most subtle dualistic appearance has been totally eliminated. Your clear light mind will simultaneously perceive all objects of knowledge as clearly as ordinary beings see their reflections in a mirror.[65]

Levels of Desire

As mentioned previously, one of the special features of Vajrayāna is its use of desire in the path to awakening. According to Gélukpa exegetes, the four types of tantras are distinguished by the respective levels of sexual desire that their followers are able to use in the path. The four levels are: looking, laughing, holding hands, and union of the male and female organs. These correspond to the four levels of satisfaction found among inhabitants of the Desire Realm. According to Lama Yeshe,

> Each class is designed for a particular type of practitioner and what differentiates one class from another is the intensity of desirous energy the practitioner is skilful enough to direct into the spiritual path. Traditionally, these differing levels of blissful energy are illustrated by examples of increasing sexual intimacy. Thus it is said that the practitioner of the lowest level of tantra is one who is able to use and transform the blissful energy that arises merely from looking at an attractive partner. On the second level, it is the energy of exchanging smiles or laughter with this partner that is transformed. On the third level, the energy used is that of holding hands while the qualified practitioner of highest yoga tantra has the skill to direct into the spiritual path the desirous energy of sexual union itself. This very powerful imagery gives us an idea of the steadily increasing range of energy that can be channeled and transformed through the practice of tantra.[66]

Practitioners of action tantra are able to visualize themselves as either male or female deities who generate desire while looking longingly at deities of the opposite sex. (Since tantric texts assert that ordinary ideas of gender are based on false conceptuality and lack inherent existence, women may visualize themselves as either women or men, and men may visualize themselves as either men or women.) Performance tantra practitioners train in utilizing the desire generated by laughing with a partner. Yoga tantra trainees are able to use the stronger desire that arises from physical contact, and highest yoga tantra adepts employ the energies of sexual union. Through this training, one becomes familiar with applying the energy of desire in meditative stabilizations. Repeated familiarization with these techniques allows meditators to transform desire into blissful wisdom consciousnesses, and in this way desire is overcome. This is often compared to the manner in which some insects are born in wood but consume the wood as they grow, leaving nothing behind. Thus Vīryavajra's *Commentary on the Sampuṭa Tantra* contends that

> within the sound of laughter non-conceptual bliss is generated; or it is generated from looking at the body, the touch of holding hands and the embrace of the two; or from the touch [of union] . . . . just as an insect is generated from the wood and then eats the wood itself, so meditative stabilisation is generated from bliss [in dependence on desire] and is cultivated as emptiness [whereupon desire is consumed].[67]

The Preliminary Practices

According to Tibetan Buddhism, ordinary beings are born into life situations in which they are destined to suffer and die. This is the result of former contaminated actions and afflictions, which have been accumulated since beginningless time. Because of this process, physical and mental afflictions are deeply rooted in sentient beings, and so it is generally considered necessary to prepare oneself for tantric practice by engaging in the "preliminary practices," or *ngöndro* (*sngon 'gro, pūrvagama*) in order to begin to reverse one's negative conditioning. Jikmé Lingpa states that preliminary practices are crucial elements in mental preparation because

> when the mind is prepared through the preliminary practices, just as food is made edible by being cooked, the mind will be capable of

> entering the actual path of meditation. There will be no likelihood of disturbances such as laziness and fluctuation in the practice, and the meditations will be accomplished.[68]

These practices combine physical movements with visualization in order to transform the mind from one that is fixated on mundane concerns and desires into one that is primarily oriented toward religious practice for the benefit of others. Some teachers consider these preparatory trainings to be so essential to successful tantric practice that they will not give advanced tantric initiations to those who have not completed them, and even teachers who are willing to waive them generally stress their importance. The preliminary practices are: (1) taking refuge; (2) prostration; (3) Vajrasattva meditation; (4) maṇḍala offering; and (5) guru yoga.

Taking Refuge

Before entering into the practice of tantra, it is necessary to "take refuge," a practice that is common to all schools of Buddhism. The theory behind it is based on the idea that people who are unhappy with their present circumstances should consider the causes of the dissatisfaction and evaluate possible solutions. According to Buddhism, the root cause of all the sufferings of cyclic existence is ignorance, which causes us mistakenly to imagine that transitory things like money, sex, power, possessions, or relationships will bring enduring joy and fulfillment. If we consider this widespread assumption, however, we find that many people who have such things in abundance are profoundly unhappy, and so it is clear that they offer no guarantee of satisfaction. The problem with seeking contentment in such things, according to Buddhist thinkers, is that they are transitory, impermanent, and subject to change, and so they cannot be a source of lasting happiness.

Another potential source of happiness lies in religious practice, and there are many religions that offer a path to salvation for their followers. Some, like Christianity and Islam, promise a blissful existence in a heaven for those who follow certain rules and who worship particular divinities. Others, like Jainism, hold that asceticism and self-denial are the keys to enduring contentment; in this system, people who undergo prolonged physical austerities eventually transcend all suffering and experience bliss. Buddhism, however, rejects these two options and contends that the route to lasting happiness lies in meditation that eliminates suffering through destroying the bases of suffering—ignorance and the afflictive emotions it engenders.

Many Buddhist texts caution, however, that most people cannot accomplish this on their own, because the afflictive emotions are so deeply ingrained that they color all our thoughts and distort our perceptions. In order to transcend them successfully, it is necessary to find a qualified spiritual guide and follow a path that, according to our best evidence, is able to bring trainees to a state of happiness. Buddhists, not surprisingly, contend that when one examines the available paths, one will conclude that Buddhism holds out the strongest possibility of true salvation. According to the Dalai Lama, a true source of refuge

> must have completely overcome all defects forever; it must be free of all faults. It must also have all the attributes of altruism—those attainments which are necessary for achieving others' welfare. For it is doubtful that anyone lacking these two prerequisites can bestow refuge; it would be like falling into a ditch and asking another who is in it to help you out. You need to ask someone who is standing outside the ditch for help; it is senseless to ask another who is in the same predicament. A refuge capable of protecting from the frights of manifold sufferings cannot also be bound in this suffering but must be free and unflawed. Furthermore, the complete attainments are necessary, for if you have fallen into a ditch, it is useless to seek help from someone standing outside it who does not wish to help or who wishes to help but has no means to do so. Only a Buddha has extinguished all faults and gained all attainments. Therefore, one should mentally go for refuge to a Buddha, praise him with speech, and respect him physically. One should enter the teaching of such a being.[69]

Those people who reach this conclusion should commit themselves to Buddhist practice. This is accomplished by taking refuge vows, in which one formally declares that one has decided to rely on the "three jewels" of Buddhism—the Buddha, the Dharma, and the Saṃgha (the community of Buddhist monks and nuns). Kalu Rinpoche contends that ordinary people, beset by mistaken ideas and afflicted mental states,

> need some help; we need to look somewhere outside of our own limited situation for something that can provide that source of refuge.

> This is the reason, first and foremost, for taking refuge in the Buddha. The attainment of Buddhahood implies the removal of all levels of obscuration and confusion in the mind, and the unfolding of all the incredible potential which is the nature of mind itself . . . . Therefore, the Buddha, as one who attained omniscience, provides us with a source of refuge and with the guidance for our own spiritual practice. Taking refuge in the Dharma, the teachings which were presented by the Buddha to enlighten other beings, provides us with a source of guidance and refuge . . . . Taking refuge in the Saṃgha, those beings who attain to high states of realization . . . and who transmit the dharma, provides us with an additional source of guidance and refuge . . . . Through our own efforts in seeking refuge and through the blessings which are inherent in the sources of refuge, the connection is made whereby we can make effective progress along the path to awakening.[70]

Buddhism recognizes that there are many possible motivations for taking refuge. Some people are looking for comfort, for meaning, or for escape, while others decide to follow the Buddhist path in order to benefit others. Ngorchen Konchog Lhundrup contends that the various reasons can be reduced to three basic motivations: fear, faith, and compassion:

> Seeking refuge through fear means that, being alarmed by the miseries of worldly existence experienced by others or oneself, one seeks refuge from them . . . . Seeking refuge through faith means that in seeking refuge one is motivated by any of the three kinds of faith. Faith of clear appreciation signifies that one discerns clearly the value of refuge, which has the ability to shield one from those fears of suffering; faith of aspiration signifies that one wishes to attain the stage of the refuge itself; and faith of confidence means that one trusts in the profound teaching of interdependent origination. Seeking refuge through compassion refers to a person who has awakened into the Mahāyāna race. Being moved by unbearable compassion for others who are afflicted by sufferings, which one infers from one's own sufferings, one seeks refuge in order to shelter them entirely.[71]

Any of these constitutes a valid reason for taking refuge. Many people initially develop interest in Buddhist practice because it holds out the promise of a peaceful state in which all suffering is overcome. This is not, of course, a particularly noble motivation, but is recognized as a valid basis for commitment to the dharma. For those who wish to follow the Mahāyāna path, genuine compassion is also necessary, since the goal of Mahāyāna is attainment of awakening for the benefit of others.

When one takes refuge, one declares that one believes, on the basis of the available evidence, that the three jewels are reliable guides and that the Buddhist path offers the best chance for salvation. The actual ceremony of taking refuge is a simple affair: generally the initiate, in the presence of a lama, declares three times, "I take refuge in the Buddha; I take refuge in the Dharma; I take refuge in the Saṃgha." Those who make this declaration with conviction are Buddhists. Because one's main teacher plays a central role in tantric practice, tantric initiates commonly take refuge first in the guru, and then in the three jewels. Initiates of highest yoga tantra also often take refuge in wisdom beings called *ḍākinīs*, who play a central role in the practice and dissemination of tantras of the highest yoga tantra class.

Whatever Buddhist path one follows, taking refuge is viewed as a necessary precondition, since it focuses the mind on the goal of Buddhist awakening, clearly identifies the guides one will follow, and forges a connection with the sources of refuge. Before entering into advanced tantric practice, it is customary to recite the refuge prayer at least one hundred thousand times.

Faith as a Prerequisite

Tantric texts all stress the importance of faith. It is commonly asserted that without faith in the three jewels, in the guru, and in one's chosen practice there is no chance of attaining buddhahood. Thus the *Sūtra on Ten Dharmas* states,

> Just as a green sprout never springs from seeds
> That have been scorched by fire, so no virtues
> will arise in people who have no faith.

Ngorchen Konchog Lhundrup comments that this means that

> If one lacks faith, then the very foundation of virtue does not exist and, as a result, one will not seek the path to liberation. For such a

one, the good qualities of the Noble Ones will not be gained, nor will one obtain the blessing of the Preceptor and the Three Jewels.[72]

This is not a blind faith that holds to tantric tenets and practice in spite of empirical evidence or common sense, but a reasoned conviction—based on one's own observation and reasoning—that the tantric path holds out the best promise of salvation. Without such an attitude, it is unlikely that one will be fully committed to Vajrayāna. Tantric texts stress the idea that awakening is only attained by those who dedicate themselves wholeheartedly. This dedication requires reasoned belief that will sustain one's practice in times of difficulty.

Prostration

Prostration (*phyag 'tshal;* pronounced "chaktsel") is a crucial preparatory activity in which one prostrates oneself on the floor, generally in front of an image, altar, painting, or some other religious symbol. Because it involves vigorous physical activity, it is considered to be particularly effective in overcoming negative physical karma. It requires a complete physical abasement of the individual before symbols of deities—who are viewed as completely surpassing the meditator in good qualities—and so it is a counteragent to false pride. In bowing down, the meditator recognizes the superior wisdom and compassion of buddhas and bodhisattvas and requests their aid in attaining their exalted state.

Prostration begins in a standing position. The practitioner's hands are in the "gem holding position," in which the base of the palm and the tips of the fingers are touching, with a space between the middle of the palms. The thumbs are tucked in. The folded hands are raised above the head, and with them the practitioner touches either three or four points on the body. In the first method, one touches the crown of the head, throat and heart, and in the second, the crown, forehead, throat, and heart are touched. Touching the crown symbolizes one's wish to attain the body of a buddha; touching the throat symbolizes one's goal of attaining the speech of a buddha; touching the heart symbolizes the aim of actualizing the mind of a buddha.

There are two types of prostrations that are commonly used: a full prostration and a partial prostration. In the partial prostration, one touches the knees, forehead, and palms on the ground, while in the full prostration the whole body contacts the ground and the arms are outstretched. The practice of prostration is very popular among all sections of Tibetan society, both laity and monastics, and in Tibetan cultural areas one often sees crowds of people prostrating in front of religious sites, such as temples or monasteries, or in front of important religious figures, such as incarnate lamas. One particularly striking Tibetan custom involves circumambulating a religious site making a series of full prostrations. In this practice, people will make a complete circuit around an area—such as the Potala, former residence of the Dalai Lamas—by making a full prostration and then beginning a new one at the place where the tips of the fingers reached. In the popular pilgrimage around Mt. Kailash, it is a common sight to see pilgrims in the process of making the whole circuit by means of full prostrations, which may take weeks to complete.

While performing prostrations it is important to have the proper mental orientation. The whole process is connected with tantric visualizations, and practitioners should imagine that standing in front of them are innumerable buddhas and bodhisattvas, as well as the lineage gurus, with the root guru at the front. One should strive to retain awareness of the religious significance of the practice, of the ultimate goal of buddhahood and the immediate goal of purifying afflictions, and of the guru and meditational deities. Without the proper mental orientation, prostrations are just empty movements that have as little spiritual significance as calisthenics. Jikmé Lingpa states that while making prostrations meditators

> should visualize the assembly of the Refuge Objects [buddhas, bodhisattvas, ḍākinīs, gurus, etc.] in the sky above us, and with reverence perform full bodily prostrations while reciting the relevant verses. This should be done with strong devotion and faith towards the objects of prostration, never allowing our mind to wander towards any other object . . . . We should rise immediately, and think that our defilements are purified and that we have received the blessings of the Body, Speech, Mind, Qualities and Activity of the Buddhas. We should meditate in this way while performing prostrations with a strong faith and belief.[73]

During prostration practitioners commonly chant a prayer of confession and mentally recite their faults and transgressions to the buddhas and gurus. They also vow to avoid committing negative acts and thinking negative thoughts in the future. Because prostration combines physical movements with verbal recitation and mental visualizations, it simultaneously purifies the "three doors" of body, speech, and mind and provides a powerful counteragent to afflictions. When used as a preparatory practice for tantra, it is customary to perform one hundred thousand prostrations, but Tibetans commonly do many more. There is no outer limit to the amount of merit one may acquire, and so practitioners are encouraged to do as many as possible, since prostration serves to undermine the power of afflictive emotions. It is important to note that prostrations—as well as the other preliminary practices—are not performed only prior to entry into tantric practice. Because they serve to diminish the force of afflictions, they are said to be effective at all levels of the path, and it is common for even advanced meditators to begin retreats with prostrations and other practices in order to purify their minds and set the proper tone for religious practice. It is also common for committed tantrists to make them a part of their daily practices.

Vajrasattva Meditation

Vajrasattva (*Rdo rje sems dpa'*; pronounced "Dorjé Semba") is a buddha associated with mental purification. The preliminary practice of Vajrasattva meditation involves picturing this deity at the crown of one's head and mentally associating the image with all the physical, mental, and spiritual perfections characteristic of fully awakened buddhas. One thinks of Vajrasattva as being identical with one's own root lama, who manifests in a form of purity as a sign of blessing. According to Kalu Rinpoche, this is the most effective practice for mental purification found in Buddhist meditation texts.[74] The aim of this meditation

> is to purify us of the different levels of obscuration and confusion in the mind and the negativity and negative karmic patterns that develop as a result of that confusion and obscuration.[75]

There are many variations in this practice, and individual lineages have their own distinctive teachings. The description that follows is a short version that contains the most common aspects of the visualization process. At the beginning of a session of Vajrasattva meditation, one should find a quiet place free from distractions and assume a position in which the spine is straight, the eyes slightly open, and the jaw parallel with the floor. The back of the right hand should be resting in the left palm, with thumbs lightly touching. The meditator may sit on a cushion in order to facilitate a posture in which the spine is comfortably straight.

The practice generally begins with a confession, in which the meditator reflects on past transgressions and vows not to commit them again. Khetsun Sangpo states that in this practice one must recognize that non-virtuous actions result in rebirths in the lower realms and that they harm oneself and others, but "confession will bless your continuum and free you from the fault of hiding misdeeds."[76] This must be combined with a faculty of mindfulness and a strong desire not to repeat one's misdeeds.

> In order to carry out your intention to refrain from non-virtue in the future, you need mindfulness and introspection that are able to catch even slight tendencies towards non-virtue. Coupled with watchfulness there must be a very strong and urgent resolution not to repeat the mistake even if it should cost your life. Without a strong sense of restraint it is not possible to purify sins.[77]

After generating contrition and resolving to avoid future wrongdoing, one then offers homage to all the buddhas and bodhisattvas and dedicates the merit gained through one's religious practice toward the welfare of all other sentient beings. Ideally the practice of Vajrasattva meditation should be combined with the mind of awakening, since one's ultimate goal should be attainment of buddhahood for the benefit of others.

With this mental preparation one is ready to begin the visualization practice. One first generates a mental image of a throne shaped like a lotus flower, with a cushion in the middle, and in the center of the disk is the syllable *hūṃ*. The *hūṃ* transforms into Vajrasattva, whose body is colored a luminous white. He is seated in the half-lotus posture, and the toe of his right foot rests on the head of the meditator. He has one face and two arms.[78] This mental image is often connected with guru yoga, and the meditator is instructed to imagine that Vajrasattva is his or her guru manifesting in a pure form.[79]

Vajrasattva's right hand is at his heart and holds a golden vajra, while his left hand, at his waist, holds a bell with the hollow part facing upwards. These symbolize the key qualities toward which tantric meditators aspire: compassion and wisdom. The vajra is the symbol of wisdom united with skillful means, and the bell is the symbol of emptiness. He is wearing ornaments of precious jewels that adorn complete enjoyment bodies, and the *hūṃ* syllable is at his heart. The hundred-syllable mantra of Vajrasattva surrounds him in a counterclockwise direction, and the *hūṃ* radiates light in all directions. This light pervades all of space and benefits all sentient beings by removing their mental obstructions. It is crucial that the meditator also cultivate the understanding that the image is empty of inherent existence, completely insubstantial like a rainbow, a union of empty form and pure appearance. This is necessary because one should avoid reifying the image and becoming attached to it. The visualized Vajrasattva, like oneself, is a creation of mind and lacks true substantial existence.

Beginning meditators will be unable to get beyond the idea that this is a mental creation, but in advanced states of realization one understands that the image is one's own mind manifesting as Vajrasattva, who represents one's potential for awakening. It is neither more nor less real than the phenomena of ordinary experience, which are also manifestations of mind. Kalu Rinpoche states that the idea that the visualized Vajrasattva is a mere creation of mind may be overcome:

> . . . for the beginner, the particular aspect of the divinity that we call forth, visualized above the crown of our heads, is what is termed Samayasattva . . . . This is the bonded or consecrated aspect, and is our own mental creation, our own visualized concept of the divinity. At this point, we meditate that from the HUNG [*hūṃ*] syllable in the heart of the Samayasattva, light shines throughout the universe and invokes the awareness aspect, Jnanasattva . . . . The awareness aspect of the divinity, that is, the actual divinity, is called to imbue the bonded aspect with the awareness aspect. We visualize this by meditating the Buddhas and Bodhisattvas from all directions manifesting in myriad forms of Dorje Sempa [Vajrasattva]: they are absorbed into the aspect meditated above the crown of our heads. We can rest assured that the awareness aspect has blended with the consecrated aspect, and the divinity is actually present above the crown of our heads.[80]

One now visualizes a stream of ambrosia (symbolizing the wisdom and compassion of Vajrasattva) issuing from the central syllables of the mantra, entering through a hole at the top of one's head, and flowing downward through the body. As it descends, it displaces all of one's negative emotions, bad karmas, and mental afflictions, which are visualized as a dark, viscous substance that is expelled through the lower extremities, the pores of the skin, the palms of the hands, and the soles of the feet. In this way, all of one's negativities are replaced by the healing ambrosia, which permeates one's whole body and suffuses it with a sense of wellbeing.

After this initial purification, the meditator cultivates the feeling that her body has been transformed into that of Vajrasattva. The more convinced one is of this transformation, the more effective the meditation will be. One should dispel all sense of ordinariness and cultivate the idea that one has become Vajrasattva. One perceives oneself as having the body, speech, and mind of Vajrasattva, and one engages in the awakened activities of a buddha, acting spontaneously and effortlessly to benefit all sentient beings throughout space. In order to sustain this idea, one repeats Vajrasattva's hundred syllable mantra:

> *oṃ vajrasattva samayam anupālaya / vajrasattva tvenopatiṣṭha / dṛḍho me bhava / sutoṣyo me bhava / supośyo me bhava / anurakto me bhava/ sarva siddhi me prayaccha / sarva karmasuccha me / cittaṃ śrīyaṃ kuru / hūṃ ha ha ha ha hoḥ / bhagavan-sarva-tathāgata vajra ma me muñca vajra bhava / mahāsamaya-sattva āḥ hūṃ /*
>
> *Oṃ* Vajrasattva, protect the pledge. Vajrasattva, may I be supported by you. Remain firmly with me; be pleased with me; be happy with me. Be affectionate toward me. Bestow all attainments on me. Purify my karma. Make my mind virtuous. *Hūṃ ha ha ha ha hoḥ* all the blessed Tathāgatas, may I be liberated in the vajra, O great pledge being of the nature of the vajra, *āḥ hūṃ.*

In *ngöndro* practice, one repeats this mantra one hundred thousand times. It is often recommended that one also repeat the short Vajrasattva mantra, *oṃ vajrasattva hūṃ.* This should be done as often as possible, ideally six hundred thousand times. The purpose of this is to focus the mind on Vajrasattva and contemplate his function of mental purification. Through this one becomes increasingly familiar with the concept of purification, and this in turn contributes to its actualization within the psychophysical continuum. This is based on a key notion in Buddhist meditation, that the more one focuses the mind on a particular object of observation, the more the mind itself is transformed in accordance with the object. In the case of Vajrasattva, one gradually purifies the mind through familiarizing it with a being who embodies mental purification.

The meditator then recalls all past faults and transgressions of religious vows. He confesses them to Vajrasattva, asks for his blessings, and resolves not to commit such offenses in the future. Vajrasattva then dissolves into the meditator, and the meditator contemplates the fact that this image, like his own psychophysical continuum, is empty of inherent existence. He realizes that his own faults and negativities are similarly empty, void of substantial existence, and so they may be purified through appropriate practices.

Despite the fact that mental afflictions are empty, they are not easily eradicated. The process requires a great deal of effort, and it is often compared to washing a very dirty shirt. The first washing eliminates most of the stain, but in order to get rid of the more subtle traces one must wash it again and again. With every laundering the stain diminishes a bit, but only repeated application will bring the shirt to a point where the stain is no longer visible. Even then, there are undoubtedly subtle traces of the stain in the fabric.

In the same way, the discipline of meditation initially serves to counteract the grossest levels of affliction, but subtler aspects remain. Only repeated training diminishes their force, and the subtlest remnants of affliction are only removed through prodigious amounts of meditation.

At the end of every session of practice one offers any benefits that derive from it for the benefit of all sentient beings. This is an essential element of closure, since it assures that one's motivation is not a selfish one, but that one is pursuing this practice due to altruistic intentions. In order to assure that one does not become attached to the form of the image, one then visualizes Vajrasattva being absorbed into light, and then he is absorbed into oneself. One thinks of one's own body, speech, and mind as being transformed into those of Vajrasattva, and one realizes that one has internalized the awakened qualities of the deity.

This is a powerful practice, because one cultivates the actual state of the deity, rather than merely working at qualities that are concordant with it. Tantric meditation puts one into the situation of a buddha, and one cultivates the understanding that one is in fact a fully awakened being, endowed with the exalted qualities of Vajrasattva, and one further visualizes oneself as engaging in his awakened activities, with the result that one becomes progressively more familiar with the state of buddhahood. Through such practice one moves very quickly toward the final goal of buddhahood, because it is not a distant goal, but rather an integral part of one's present practice and an unfolding of one's basic nature.

Maṇḍala Offering

As with the practice of prostration, maṇḍala offering involves physical activities conjoined with visualization. Practitioners making maṇḍala offerings imagine themselves giving valuable substances such as gold, jewels, and so on to buddhas and bodhisattvas, as well as the guru. According to Geshe Rabten,

> maṇḍala means to take the essence. Although this is a simple practice it is an effective means of accumulating merit. It is offered to the Object of Refuge which is free from all impurity and attachment, therefore the practice is for one's own benefit.[81]

Generally the ritual requires a base, which is a round plate about six inches in diameter. Ideally it should be made of gold, silver, or another precious metal, but in practice any surface may be used, even one made of stone or wood. No matter what the material is, the plate should be visualized as pure gold. This symbolizes the pure innate buddha nature of each person.

People of limited means often make offerings of grains or rice, and sometimes common stones, but those who can afford it may use precious gems. Other offerings may be added, such as coins, jewelry, and the like. When grains are used, the practitioner begins by holding some in the left hand while holding the base at the level of the heart. With the right hand, she drops some grains into the center of the base while reciting the refuge prayer and attempting to generate the mind of awakening. With the right forearm, she wipes the grain off the base in a clockwise direction. This symbolizes the removal of the three afflictions of desire, hatred, and ignorance, which obscure the innate buddha nature. The right arm is used because an energy channel associated with wisdom runs along it.

Next the practitioner drops some grains on the base and wipes it three times in a counterclockwise direction. This is symbolic of the wish to develop the exalted qualities of the body, speech, and mind of a buddha.

The succeeding stage involves pouring grain in the hand and then into the center of the base. One then makes a fence around the perimeter by pouring more grain in a clockwise direction. After this, a hill of grain is formed in the middle, symbolizing Mount Meru, the center of the universe in traditional Buddhist cosmology. Around it are piles of grain representing the four primary continents described in traditional Buddhist literature, one at each of the cardinal points. One then makes two more piles on either side of the central one, which correspond to the sun and moon. For those who make this offering with the proper motivation, according to Geshe Lobsang Tharchin,

> contained in every grain of this offering there is a fertile seed for the attainment of Perfect Enlightenment. This is because of the sincere aspiration for Perfect Enlightenment, which has motivated you to perform the offering. One strives for Enlightenment in order to become able to benefit all sentient beings in the universe. Thus, as the number of living beings in the universe is infinite, the virtue which is derived from this act is also without limit.[82]

While creating this maṇḍala, the practitioner should be creatively visualizing it as containing the entire universe and all its desirable things. The universe in the form of the maṇḍala is then given to the buddhas while one recites a prayer of offering:

> By virtue of offering to this assemblage of Buddhas visualised before me this maṇḍala built on a base, resplendent with flowers, incense, saffron water, and adorned with Mount Meru, the four continents, the sun and the moon, may all sentient beings share in its good effects.[83]

After the prayer has been recited and one has imagined oneself giving everything in the universe to the buddhas, one tilts the maṇḍala toward oneself and pours the grains into one's lap, imagining that the buddhas reciprocate by bestowing blessings. This practice is said to be an effective way of generating merit and of overcoming attachment to material things. By symbolically proffering everything imaginable to the buddhas for the benefit of all sentient beings, one diminishes one's desire for wealth and possessions. As with the practice of prostrations, it is customary for practitioners to perform this at least one hundred thousand times.

Three Levels of Maṇḍala Offering

The process described above, using grains and plates, is referred to as the "outer maṇḍala offering." It is considered to be a powerful method of cultivating merit and proper attitudes, but it is still only a beginning technique because it uses external props. The deeper levels of maṇḍala offering are the "inner maṇḍala offering" and the "secret maṇḍala offering," which do not use physical movements, external gestures, or material objects. The practice takes place in the mind, and one's own body becomes the offering.

In the inner maṇḍala offering, one visualizes one's body as a maṇḍala, which represents the entire universe. At the beginning of the meditation, one imagines that the outer parts of the body, the skin and so forth, are of the nature of pure gold. They take the place of the base used in the outer maṇḍala offering. After this one mentally pictures the flesh and blood of the body, imagining the blood as a celestial ambrosia that covers the base and eliminates all impurities. One's flesh is conceived as celestial flowers with fresh blooms and vibrant colors. The trunk of the body is Mount Meru, which is viewed as being composed of precious materials, such as rubies, sapphires, gold, and silver. One's arms and legs are the four continents, and the toes and feet are smaller land masses. One's head is the mansion of the Lord of Deities, which is located at the top of Mount Meru, and one's eyes are the sun and moon. The heart becomes the most valuable jewel in the universe, and the other internal organs are repositories of vast wealth.

In this way, the body itself is transformed into a maṇḍala, and through this one diminishes the sense of ordinariness. This practice also undermines fixed views and negative attitudes toward the body. Once the mental image is complete, one transforms the body-maṇḍala into a pure land and offers it to the guru and the three jewels while reciting a prayer of offering. One then imagines that this gift has greatly pleased the objects of refuge and that oneself and all sentient beings receive the blessings of the guru, buddhas, and bodhisattvas.

The secret maṇḍala offering requires a thorough familiarity with the mystical physiology of highest yoga tantra, and because much of the practice involves great skill in subtle manipulation of vital energies, it will only be possible to provide a brief sketch of the process. The secret maṇḍala offering is said to be more profound—and also more difficult—than the previous two, because there is no external basis for visualization. Instead, one's own mind becomes the maṇḍala. The goal of the practice is transformation of one's mind into the consciousness of a fully awakened buddha through imagining that aspects of one's cognition are transmuted into the bodies of a buddha. As noted before, according to Mahāyāna buddhology, buddhas develop three primary bodies: (1) the truth body, which is the result of a fully developed wisdom consciousness realizing emptiness; (2) a complete enjoyment body, a perfect body created out of subtle energy; and (3) form bodies, which are compassionately emanated for the benefit of others and result from perfecting the cultivation of the mind of awakening. Form bodies are the fulfillment of the collection of merit. The truth body is the outcome of cultivating the collection of wisdom; it is actualized through perfecting understanding of emptiness.

These two types of consciousness—the mind of awakening and the mind directly perceiving emptiness—are the basis of the secret maṇḍala offering. The mind of awakening consists of the mental awareness accompanied by two aspirations: the aspiration to benefit all sentient beings through establishing them in the state of buddhahood; and the wish personally to attain complete awakening in order to be able to accomplish the first aspiration. The wisdom consciousness realizing emptiness penetrates beyond false appearances and correctly perceives things as they are, that is, as utterly lacking inherent existence, as composite, produced, and impermanent.

In the secret maṇḍala offering, one offers the mind of awakening and the wisdom consciousness realizing emptiness to the objects of refuge. One adorns the maṇḍala with the activities of these minds—which are suffused with wisdom and compassion—and gives them to the guru, the buddha, and other awakened beings. The merit gained from successfully completing this practice is said to be immeasurable, but the mental training is more important. The mind is extremely subtle, an entity of luminosity and emptiness, and those who are able effectively to manipulate mental energies in this way overcome deeply rooted afflictions and purify their mental continuums.

Guru Yoga

All schools of Tibetan Buddhism emphasize the necessity of finding a qualified teacher. Such a teacher is one who has successfully traversed the path and attained the highest levels of realization. Because of this, the guru can guide students around the pitfalls they will encounter, warn them of dangers, correct their errors, and skillfully help them to actualize their potential buddhahood. It is stated throughout Tibetan meditation literature that one cannot successfully follow the path of tantra without a guru, and Tilopa contends that

> the ignorant may know that sesame oil—the essence—exists in the sesame seed, but because they do not know how, they cannot extract the oil. So also does the innate fundamental wisdom abide in the heart of all migrators; but unless it is pointed out by the guru, it cannot be realized. By pounding the seeds and clearing away the husks, one can extract the essence—the sesame oil. Similarly, when it is shown by the lama, the meaning of suchness is so illuminated that one can enter into it.[84]

Guru yoga purifies one's awareness through practices that involve visualizing the teacher as an embodiment of the pure, exalted wisdom of buddhahood. Unlike a deity mentally generated in front of one, arising from emptiness and again dissolved into emptiness at the end of the session, the guru remains with one as a symbol of the goal of awakening. Kalu Rinpoche states that from the point of view of individual meditators, the guru is even kinder than buddhas and bodhisattvas, because the guru is the one who actually reveals the teachings to them.[85] Most of us never have the good fortune to meet a buddha in person, but if we are able to visualize the guru as an awakened being, the result is the same as if we had. The guru transmits Buddhist teachings, instructs us on their proper application, and provides an example of a person who puts them into practice; thus the relation of a tantric practitioner with the guru is much more intimate than relationships with buddhas.

Imagining one's guru as a buddha provides a concrete example of the awakened state one is trying to achieve. Lama Yeshe states that through guru yoga meditators "are able progressively to cut through our superficial ways of relating to the world and make contact with the innate wisdom at the heart of our being."[86] Successful Vajrayāna practice requires the ability to see the guru as a buddha, and to understand that any apparent faults the guru might have are only reflections of one's own inadequacies. The guru is a reflection of one's own mind, and a meditator who perceives the guru as having faults develops corresponding flaws. One who views the guru as a buddha actualizes the innate potential for buddhahood in each sentient being. Jikmé Lingpa contends that this is

> the finest method for realizing the innate wisdom within oneself. It is accomplished through one's own faith and by the grace or blessing of the Spiritual Guide. All Fully Awakened Beings abide inseparably in the expanse of Primordial Awareness, and all are in essence one. The Spiritual Master is the embodiment unifying all wisdom, compassion and power of an Awakened Being. Understanding this with strong devotion and belief will lead to a direct experience of the essence of the path. By these means the emotional defilements are purified and the accumulation of merit and wisdom is perfected.[87]

Lineage

In addition to providing meditators with living examples of realized beings, gurus also belong to lineages of teachings and practices that are traced back to the beginnings of Buddhism. The lineage is a guarantee of the authenticity of the teachings. Tibetan Buddhism is a traditional system, and its leaders are revered not for their innovations but for how closely they approximate its ideals. Great teachers and adepts are presented in Tibetan literature as archetypal models, and their biographies tend to stress the ways in which they embody the shared values of the tradition.

In keeping with these attitudes, gurus are important because they belong to established lineages, and students who receive initiation from a guru are told of the succession of awakened teachers who have passed on that particular teaching. This is partly due to a respect for precedent and a backward-looking orientation found in all traditional systems, but it is also a recognition that Vajrayāna is not transmitted primarily through texts and scriptures, but from mind to mind, from teacher to student. Gurus do not simply learn the texts and practice the relevant meditations: they also receive a rich oral heritage from their own teachers, and each successive generation augments this legacy, while striving to retain a perceived connection with the past.

> Each tantric deity has its own unbroken lineage of practitioners. To be authentic and reliable this lineage must have had its source in the fully enlightened experience of a true master. Furthermore, this experience must have been passed down to us through an unbroken succession of adepts, each of whom attained realizations by accomplishing the practices of this deity. The strength of tantra—which has the literal meaning of 'continuous' or 'continuity'—lies in its preservation and transmission of the enlightened experience through a continuous, unbroken lineage of practitioners.[88]

This oral transmission is essential for newly initiated students to enter into the system at all, since many tantric texts are deliberately cryptic. Tantric teachings are secret, and the texts assume that their words will be explained by a qualified master who has studied and internalized Vajrayāna lore from his or her own teachers and whose meditation has led to advanced states of spiritual development. The ideal guru is a person who is firmly rooted in the tradition, who has studied the texts and commentaries extensively, who has deeply internalized oral instructions from awakened masters, and who has put the teachings into practice in meditation. Tantric texts also emphasize that the guru should be a person whose meditations have borne fruit, since only those who have purified their own mental continuums are able to perceive the spiritual defects and needs of others and adapt their teachings to them. Such a person provides students with a model to emulate, a once-ordinary being like themselves who through meditative practice has become extraordinary. Role models of awakened behavior are essential in order for beginners to be able to imagine themselves as awakened masters embodying wisdom and compassion, working ceaselessly for the benefit of others.

The Problem of Faulty Gurus

Although ideally the guru should be an advanced meditator who embodies the highest ideals of the system, if one's guru is not such a person, one should still view him or her as such in meditation. Kalu Rinpoche states that

> once the formal bond of empowerment and teaching has been established and we have accepted a particular teacher as a guru, then . . . it is extremely important for us to have nothing but pure views toward the teacher. Even in the case of discovering qualities in the teacher that we find repulsive, the bond has been established, and purely from the personal point of view of making spiritual progress, the only attitude which is beneficial is to view that teacher as an emanation of Buddha. To view the teacher as an ordinary person and become critical does not help us and in fact can be a serious obstacle.[89]

As Kalu Rinpoche explains this, the proper attitude of reverence toward the guru is based on pragmatic considerations. Even if the guru is utterly lacking in good qualities, the student should still strive to imagine him or her as a buddha. Those who succeed in perceiving the guru in this way develop corresponding qualities themselves—whatever the spiritual condition of the guru—and there are numerous stories in tantric literature of students attaining complete awakening through pure devotion to the guru, even though he or she is a less than ideal model.[90] There are also stories of people who denigrated their gurus and were born in terrible "vajra hells" which are specially reserved for tantric practitioners who transgress their vows (one of which is a promise to venerate the guru).

In Vajrayāna, one works at transcending ordinariness through creative visualization, and those who critically focus on the guru's faults remain trapped by the ordinary, mired in the false appearances of cyclic existence. Meditators who learn to view the guru and themselves as fully awakened deities alter their own reality in accordance with the visualization and develop the qualities of a deity. Throughout this practice, one should be aware that the mind of the guru is by nature empty, as is one's own mind. Both are indistinguishable in nature from the mind of a buddha. By conjoining a perception of one's guru as being a buddha with the thought that the guru's mind and one's own are indistinguishable in that both have the pure buddha nature, one quickly purifies adventitious mental afflictions and progressively comes to approximate the state of buddhahood.

Visualizing the Guru as a Deity

When one has received initiation into the practice of a particular deity, one works at generating a mental image of this deity, its retinue, and its maṇḍala. The visualization process is also conjoined with guru yoga, and tantric practitioners develop the ability to perceive the guru as indistinguishable from the buddha. A typical practice of this sort involves creating a projection of the meditational deity in front of oneself, surrounded by the succession of gurus belonging to the lineage in an unbroken stream, including one's own guru. One then asks the gurus and deities to bestow blessings and aid one's progress. It is important that the meditator believes that this actually occurs.

At this point in the ritual, the deities and gurus merge into one another, then they enter into one's body through the aperture at the crown of the head and descend into the central channel. They dissolve into the energy center (*cakra*) at the heart. At this point, all conventional dualistic appearances dissolve into emptiness. Through this practice, one should develop a feeling of close connection with the guru, who is perceived as identical with the meditational deity and with one's own consciousness. One should regularly reflect on the great wisdom of the guru and on the guru's kindness in teaching the path to awakening. The guru embodies the goal of the path—fully developed compassion and wisdom—and should be viewed as a buddha. But this abstract consideration is only the first step; one must also recognize that the exalted qualities of buddhas are present in one's own mind. Thus one trains in the understanding that the guru, meditational deity, and oneself are one. In this meditation, it is necessary to have unwavering faith in the guru because

> if, when you are practicing it, there is a limitation in your devotion, it will not work. To practice true guru yoga, you must think—from the very depths of your heart—of the kindness of the root and lineage gurus and of their good qualities of body, speech, and mind. So intense is this devotion that the hairs on your body will rise, tears will well into your eyes, and your voice will break. You have only the lama in your mind; your mind is attracted to the lama; you then wish to pray day and night to the lama. Until such blazing experiences of true guru yoga arise, you must make effort.[91]

Faith in the guru is an essential precondition for awakening, and Tibetan meditation literature has many stories of meditators who made progress due to faith, as well as cautionary tales of people with great potential whose training stagnated due to questioning the lama. Of course, a system like this, which emphasizes absolute, unquestioning devotion to the lama, is ripe for abuse, and there are notable examples of lamas who exploit their positions and take advantage of the faith of their disciples. For this reason, spiritual seekers are advised to choose carefully, because a person who follows a charlatan is apt to be brought down by him.

It is important to note, however, that the purpose of exalting the guru is not to give praise to one's teacher. An awakened being has no need for praise, and is unaffected by censure. Gurus are extolled and visualized as deities in order to enhance one's own spiritual practice. Learning to perceive an apparently ordinary being as a deity helps people to overcome their attachments to feelings of ordinariness, to transform the mundane through creative visualization. Through this practice, one learns to overcome one's own limitations and to recast the world in accordance with the symbols and practices of tantra.

The Fourteen Root Downfalls

When receiving initiations, tantric practitioners commonly take a series of vows (*dam tshig, samaya*) in which they promise to perform certain actions and avoid particular harmful deeds and attitudes. Upholding these vows is considered to be essential to successful tantric practice, and those who transgress them cause themselves great harm. Tantric practitioners are required to uphold the bodhisattva vows (which include eighteen root vows and forty-six subsidiary vows). Practitioners of yoga tantra and highest yoga tantra also have to fulfill fourteen root tantric vows and ten additional vows. Moreover, initiation into a particular tantric practice often includes more vows.[92]

Failure to uphold the fourteen root tantric vows leads to the "fourteen root downfalls." They are generally enumerated in descending order of severity, with the first being the most serious, the second less serious, and so forth.

The first root downfall is contradicting the guru, which weakens the close bond required for successful tantric practice. Before one has received initiation, it is considered appropriate to examine potential gurus thoroughly in order to determine whether or not they are genuine teachers who practice what they preach. It is also important to determine whether or not a particular guru is a person for whom one feels respect and closeness; but after initiation has been bestowed the only appropriate attitude is one of unquestioning reverence and confidence. Whether or not the teacher is actually awakened, students should view him or her as a buddha. People who develop antipathy toward their teachers, who speak ill of them or displease them—or who even recognize negative qualities that their teachers actually possess—violate their tantric vows and commit the most serious of the root downfalls.

The second root downfall involves contradicting or denigrating the teachings of the buddhas or those of one's guru. It is essential that Vajrayānists take the teachings to heart and put them into practice diligently. They should avoid looking for faults either in the teachings themselves or in those who present them.

Because Vajrayāna is designed for people with exceptional compassion and intelligence who seek to become buddhas due to altruistic motivations, it would be unseemly to quarrel with others on the same path. It would not only diminish the practitioners of tantra in the eyes of others, but would lead to schisms among them and to negative mental qualities. The third root downfall, therefore, is fighting with other tantrists, and initiates vow to cultivate positive feelings toward them and to develop relationships with them that are mutually beneficial and harmonious. Thus Kalu Rinpoche cautions that

> quarreling, spite, competitiveness, malevolent attitudes toward each other, bickering, and discord between ourselves and these people are completely out of the question from the point of view of samaya [vows]. We must respect the very important bond that we have with these people through our commitment to Vajrayāna. The bond exists and we must attempt to promote harmony and mutual accord, mutual help and benefit, as much as possible among the vajra saṃgha.[93]

When one receives tantric initiation, one becomes part of a community and is expected to regard fellow tantrikas as one's "vajra brothers and sisters." One's immediate community includes those who belong to one's particular lineage, who have received empowerments from the same lama, and who regularly perform the same *sādhanas*. Feelings of belonging may vary considerably among groups, and some who receive initiations may view them as a form of blessing and not undertake tantric practice commitments. Most serious practitioners, however, consider themselves to be bound by their connections to others who have received the same empowerments from the same lama, and many groups gather regularly for communal practice. For many tantrikas, members of their community constitute a support group for religious practice.

Tantric practitioners should be deeply committed to the bodhisattva vow to work for the benefit of all sentient beings without exception. Those who deviate from this principle are guilty of committing the fourth root downfall. This is a particularly difficult vow to keep, because it is violated not only by harmful acts, but even by negative thoughts or intentions. Bodhisattvas should seek to help others in all circumstances and avoid doing them any harm, which requires constant mindfulness and unwavering compassion.

The fifth root downfall is connected with the mystical physiology of tantra, which postulates the existence of subtle drops residing in the cakras. The two most important of these are a red drop and a white drop that each person inherits from the mother and father respectively. Those who harm these drops are guilty of the fifth root downfall. This occurs in several ways, and especially as a result of sexual indulgence. Because of this, illicit sexual activity should be avoided by tantric practitioners, who seek to channel the energy of sexual desire as an aid on the path.

In keeping with the nonsectarian nature of Vajrayāna, practitioners vow not to denigrate the teachings and paths of other systems. Those who do commit the sixth root downfall.

Tantra is a secret system that should only be revealed to those who demonstrate that they are fit to receive the teachings, and then only by a fully qualified Vajrayāna master. Those who reveal the secrets to noninitiates—people who are not ready to receive them or who will be harmed by them—are guilty of the seventh root downfall.

Although ordinary beings have physical, impermanent bodies that are subject to degeneration, sickness, old age, and death, they are still bodies in which they are able to practice Vajrayāna and become buddhas. Thus the eighth root downfall involves viewing the five aggregates that make up the psychophysical personality as impure and defiled. Tantric practitioners should train in viewing themselves as fully awakened buddhas, with the perfect body, speech, and mind of a buddha. Thinking of the body as defiled would be an impediment to the visualization process, and so it should be avoided. It is a great fault

> because Vajrayāna sees everything as sacred. All appearance is a form of divinity, all sound is the sound of mantra, and all thought and awareness is the divine play of transcending awareness . . . . The potential for that sacredness exists within our present framework . . . of the five skandhas [aggregates]. Acknowledging psycho-physical aggregates of an individual as the potential of the Buddhas . . . is to recognize that, in tantra, the potential for that transformation exists within our present situation. To disparage that potential as something useless or impure or unwholesome is a root downfall, a basic contradiction, from the point of view of tantric practice.[94]

Because tantra requires total commitment and sustained effort, initiates promise to maintain unwavering faith. Those who develop doubts about their decision to enter Vajrayāna are guilty of the ninth root downfall.

Sometimes advanced bodhisattvas must make difficult choices for the benefit of others. There are stories in Buddhist literature of advanced bodhisattvas who are able to know the minds of others and who realize that certain people will inevitably commit acts of great evil that will result in suffering for themselves and others. Such bodhisattvas sometimes elect to save the evil beings from themselves by killing them in order to prevent them from carrying out their plans. This is referred to euphemistically as a "liberation" because the person who is killed is liberated from the negativities of his or her present life situation. If the liberation is carried out in a spirit of true compassion and love, it will result in a better future life for the being who is liberated. This should only be done by those who have reached a high enough level of awareness that they can directly perceive the mental continuums of others and accurately predict their futures. When such beings recognize a potentially disastrous situation and fail to act to prevent it, they are guilty of the tenth root downfall.

Buddhist literature cautions against holding extreme views, since they cause biases and lead to negative thoughts. The most important of these are the view of permanence and the view of nihilism. The former naively believes that everything one experiences is real, while the other misunderstands the concept of emptiness by thinking it means that nothing exists. The latter view is more dangerous, since it may lead one to believe that one's actions have no effects, to deny the possibility of liberation, and thus to renounce the path and engage in harmful activities. Those who hold either of these extreme views commit the eleventh root downfall.

The twelfth root downfall is committed by tantrists who refuse to teach others who seek instruction from them and who are qualified recipients. When someone with sincere faith and the proper motivation requests instruction, it is the duty of tantric adepts to teach them. Failure to do so constitutes the twelfth root downfall.

Tantric initiates train in the understanding that nothing is inherently foul or pure and that all our ideas about such things are merely based on false conceptuality. In order to weaken our attachment to such ideas, tantric ceremonies sometimes involve consumption of small amounts of substances that are commonly considered to be impure. Those who refuse to partake of these things remain enmeshed in a limited view of reality because they

> have failed to appreciate the view of tantra which attempts to transcend purity and impurity, attempts to transcend dualistic thinking . . . . To indulge in this kind of superficial, dualistic clinging to appearances during the course of a tantric ritual, is to commit this thirteenth root downfall and to go against the spirit of our tantric practice.[95]

In tantric literature, women are associated with wisdom, and so practitioners of tantra are cautioned against denigrating any woman, either verbally or mentally. Those who do so are guilty of the fourteenth root downfall.

Notes

1. David Snellgrove, *Indo-Tibetan Buddhism*, vol. I, p. 148.
2. *Vajraśekhara-tantra*, To. 480.149a7-b1. Quoted in David Snellgrove, "The Notion of Divine Kingship in Tantric Buddhism," *La Regalitá Sacra—Contributi al Tema dell' VIII Congresso Internazionale di Storia delle Religioni* (Leiden: E.J. Brill, 1959), vol. 2, pp. 104–105. In some contexts, the vajra is also a thunderbolt that is used to defeat enemies or a diamond, and in texts of the highest yoga tantra class, the vajra is often equated with the penis.
3. For an overview of discussions of the place of the tantras in Buddhist literature, see Nakamura, *Indian Buddhism*, pp. 311–343.
4. *Tāranātha's History of Buddhism*, ed. A. Schiefner (Simla, 1970), p. 82.
5. This text contains a wealth of historical information concerning the state of Indian

Buddhism during the seventh century. For a translation, see Samuel Beal, *Si-yu-ki, Buddhist Records of the Western World* (Delhi, 1969).

6. Snellgrove, *Indo-Tibetan Buddhism*, vol. I, p. 118.
7. For more information on controversies regarding authentic tantric practices, see David Seyfort Ruegg, "Problems in the Transmission of Vajrayāna Buddhism in the Western Himalaya about the Year 1000," *Acta Indologica* VI, 1984, pp. 369–381. Samten Karmay discusses and translates Yéshé Ö's *Official Edict* in "The Ordinance of Lha Bla-ma Ye-shes-'od," Michael Aris and Aung San Ssu Kyi, eds., *Tibetan Studies in Honour of Hugh Richardson* (Warminster: Aris & Philips, 1980), pp. 150–162.
8. Ronald Davidson, *Indian Esoteric Buddhism: A Social History of the Tantric Movement* (New York: Columbia University Press, 2002), pp. 26–168.
9. Lama Thubten Yeshe, *Introduction to Tantra* (Boston: Wisdom Publications, 1987), pp. 16–17.
10. H.H. the Dalai Lama, in *Tantra in Tibet*, tr. Jeffrey Hopkins (London: George Allen & Unwin, 1977), p. 69.
11. The passage is translated in Snellgrove, *Indo-Tibetan Buddhism*, vol. I, p. 120. In another version, he practiced highest yoga tantra with Tilottamā during the life before the one in which he manifested as a buddha. As a result of this practice, he was already fully awakened before taking birth in India, and his whole life was a manifestation for the benefit of others. See also Mkhas-grub-rje's *Fundamentals of the Buddhist Tantras*, ed. Lessing and Wayman (The Hague/Paris: Mouton & Co., 1968), pp. 28–37.
12. *Tantra in Tibet*, p. 18.
13. Tulku Thondup Rinpoche, *Buddha Mind* (Ithaca: Snow Lion, 1989), p. 5.
14. Lama Thubten Yeshe, *Introduction to Tantra*, p. 21.
15. Ibid., p. 29.
16. *The Hevajra Tantra*, ed. David Snellgrove (London: Oxford University Press, 1959), I.9,19, vol. 2, pp. 34–35.
17. *Tantra in Tibet*, p. 77.
18. Snellgrove, *Indo-Tibetan Buddhism*, vol. I, p. 200.
19. *Kindness, Clarity, and Insight*, pp. 116–117.
20. *Indo-Tibetan Buddhism*, vol. I, p. 122.
21. Kalu Rinpoche, *The Dharma*, p. 52.
22. Lama Zopa Rinpoche, *Wisdom Energy* (London: Wisdom, 1976), p. 23.
23. H.H. the Dalai Lama, in *Tantra in Tibet*, p. 47.
24. The four tantra sets are: action tantra, performance tantra, yoga tantra, and highest yoga tantra. This classification scheme is based on differences in the types of yogas involved, and is discussed below. For a translation of a ritual text describing the vase initiation, see *Indo-Tibetan Buddhism*, vol. I, pp. 223–227.
25. Khetsun Sangpo Rinbochay, *Tantric Practice in Nying-ma* (Ithaca: Snow Lion, 1982), p. 176.
26. These include the five meats: bull meat, dog meat, elephant meat, horse meat, and human meat; and the five nectars: excrement, brains, semen, blood, and urine.
27. See Mkhas grub rje's *Fundamentals of the Buddhist Tantras*, pp. 321–323.
28. See John Powers, "Stealth Polemics: Tsong Khapa on the Differences between Sūtra and Tantra," Damien Keown, ed., *From Ancient India to Modern America: Buddhist Studies in Honor of Charles Prebish* (London: Routledge/Curzon, 2005), pp. 128–145.
29. *Tantra in Tibet*, p. 68. Other Tibetan scholars dispute this idea. Ngorchen Günga Sangpo (1389–1456), for example, pointed out that some tantras make no mention of

deity yoga. As we will see in chapters 12 and 13, however, the Nyingma and Kagyu orders have methods that involve formless meditations that they consider to be superior to deity yoga. Because these yogas they do not employ visualizations, they are considered to be non-tantric, but they are based on the physiology and theory of highest yoga tantra.

30. "Sūtra practices" are the trainings of bodhisattvas outlined in chapter 4, "Mahāyāna." These include training in the mind of awakening, the six perfections, and so forth. Such practices are also integral aspects of the tantra path, but they are cultivated in different ways.
31. Khenpo Könchog Gyaltsen, *In Search of the Stainless Ambrosia* (Ithaca: Snow Lion, 1988), p. 93.
32. *Tantra in Tibet*, p. 106.
33. Ibid., p. 47.
34. Ibid., p. 63.
35. The two collections are discussed in chapter 3, "Meditation."
36. *Tantra in Tibet*, pp. 50–51.
37. As we saw previously, the truth body is equated with reality itself. It is beyond all physicality and all form. It is the mind-essence of all buddhas, and it is characterized by perfect clarity. The bodies of buddhas are discussed in chapter 4, "Mahāyāna."
38. See, for example, *Tantra in Tibet*, p. 134.
39. Ibid., p. 26.
40. Ibid., pp. 127–128.
41. Daniel Cozort, *Highest Yoga Tantra* (Ithaca: Snow Lion, 1986), p. 53.
42. Tsong Khapa, *Tantra in Tibet*, p. 143.
43. Ronald Davidson argues that this classification scheme probably reflects the chronology of their respective compositions, with the first two sets appearing first, followed by yoga tantras, and finally highest yoga tantras. This is a plausible scenario, but it is based on the fact that each successive set tends to have more developed doctrines and practices than the previous ones; but aside from this internal evidence, there is no historical data to conclusively prove or disprove the hypothesis. As we have seen, adherents of tantra assume that all were spoken by the Buddha and that each tantra set is designed for a particular type of practitioner. See *Indian Esoteric Buddhism*, pp. 113–167.
44. See, for example, Tsong Khapa, *Tantra in Tibet*, pp. 163–164.
45. *Lineage of Diamond Light: Crystal Mirror V* (Berkeley: Dharma Publishing, 1991), p. 170.
46. Jig-me Ling-pa, *The Dzogchen Innermost Essence Preliminary Practice* (Dharamsala: Library of Tibetan Works and Archives, 1982), p. 88.
47. *Tantra in Tibet*, p. 75.
48. *Lineage of Diamond Light*, p. 170.
49. Ibid., p. 171.
50. See chapter 10, "Death and Dying in Tibetan Buddhism," for a detailed description of this process.
51. Roger Jackson, "The Kalachakra in Context," in *The Wheel of Time: The Kalachakra in Context*, ed. Geshe Lhundub Sopa, Roger Jackson, and John Newman (Madison, WI: Deer Park Books, 1985), p. 32.
52. *Kindness, Clarity, and Insight*, p. 199.
53. This passage is quoted by Khenpo Könchog Gyaltsen in *The Garland of Mahamudra Practices*, pp. 56–57.

54. *Selected Works of the Dalai Lama II*, p. 115. Illusory body practices are stressed in the *Guhyasamāja Tantra* and other highest yoga tantras of the "father tantra" class. They are called father tantras because the generation of a subtle body is associated with the practice of method, which is characterized as male in the tantra system. Tantras like the *Cakrasaṃvara* are categorized as "mother tantras" because they emphasize the generation of clear light, which is associated with cultivation of wisdom and categorized as female.
55. Ibid., p. 121.
56. Ibid., p. 127.
57. Geshe Kelsang Gyatso, *Clear Light of Bliss: Mahamudra in Vajrayana Buddhism* (London: Wisdom, 1982), pp. 188–189.
58. *Selected Works of the Dalai Lama II*, p. 89.
59. "Advice from the Dalai Lama," in *Inquiring Mind*, vol. 10, no.1 (Fall 1993), p. 16.
60. Ibid., p. 17.
61. *Clear Light of Bliss*, p. 218.
62. *Highest Yoga Tantra*, p. 92.
63. *Clear Light of Bliss*, pp. 219–220.
64. Snellgrove, *The Hevajra Tantra*, II.2.43–44, vol. 2, p. 51. My translation differs slightly from Snellgrove's in vol. 1, p. 92.
65. *Clear Light of Bliss*, p. 221.
66. *Introduction to Tantra*, p. 32.
67. Quoted in *Tantra in Tibet*, p. 161.
68. Jig-me Ling-pa, *The Dzogchen Innermost Essence Preliminary Practice*, p. 31. In the Nyingma, Kagyu, and Sakya orders, completion of the preliminary practices is required before any tantric initiations are conferred. Some Gélukpa teachers, however, will sometimes give initiation to students who have not completed them. The reasoning behind this is that their interest in tantra must have been linked to previous practice, and so they probably performed the preliminaries in a previous life. Trainees are generally expected to integrate these practices into their subsequent training, however, and higher-level initiations will not be conferred until they have been completed.
69. *Tantra in Tibet*, pp. 29–30.
70. Kalu Rinpoche, *The Gem Ornament of Manifold Oral Instructions* (Ithaca: Snow Lion, 1986), p. 40.
71. Ngorchen Konchog Lhundrup, *The Beautiful Ornament of the Three Visions* (Ithaca: Snow Lion, 1991), pp. 9–10.
72. Ibid., p. 4.
73. Jig-me Ling-pa, *The Dzogchen Innermost Essence Preliminary Practice*, p. 63.
74. Kalu Rinpoche, *The Gem Ornament*, p. 51.
75. Ibid., p. 49.
76. Khetsun Sangpo, *Tantric Practice in Nying-ma*, p. 142.
77. Ibid., p. 143.
78. This may seem obvious to people unfamiliar with the iconography of tantric deities, but many of them have multiple faces and arms.
79. See, for example, Kalu Rinpoche, *The Gem Ornament*, p. 51.
80. Ibid., p. 52.
81. Geshe Rabten, *The Preliminary Practices of Tibetan Buddhism* (Dharamsala: Library of Tibetan Works and Archives, 1976), p. 85.

82. Geshe Lobsang Tharchin, *A Commentary on Guru Yoga and Offering of the Maṇḍala* (Ithaca: Snow Lion, 1980), p. 75.
83. Geshe Rabten, *The Preliminary Practices of Tibetan Buddhism*, p. 87.
84. Quoted in Khenpo Könchog Gyaltsen, *The Garland of Mahamudra Practices*, p. 58.
85. Kalu Rinpoche, *The Gem Ornament*, p. 73.
86. *Introduction to Tantra*, p. 97.
87. *The Dzogchen Innermost Essence Preliminary Practice*, p. 64.
88. *Introduction to Tantra*, p. 101.
89. *The Gem Ornament*, p. 69.
90. An example is the story of the Indian teacher Śāntipa, who had extensive knowledge of Buddhist literature, but failed to put the teachings into practice. One of his students received his instructions and then went into solitary meditative retreat for three years, during which he became awakened through practices that included visualizing Śāntipa, his root guru, as a fully awakened buddha. Even though this was not the case, the student himself became awakened through his practice, and then he returned to visit Śantipa. Śāntipa, however, did not even remember the student, but when he realized that the student had become awakened through practicing his teachings, Śāntipa regretted his failure to practice what he preached and asked that the student allow him to become his disciple. Śāntipa eventually became awakened also.
91. Khenpo Könchog Gyaltsen, *The Garland of Mahamudra Practices*, pp. 37–38.
92. See, for example, Daniel Cozort, *Highest Yoga Tantra*, pp. 36–37, for a list of behaviors prohibited by the vows of the *Kālacakra Tantra*.
93. *The Gem Ornament*, p. 123.
94. Ibid., pp. 124–125.
95. Ibid., p. 126.

10: Death and Dying in Tibetan Buddhism

Introduction

According to traditional stories of his life, the Buddha first decided to leave his home and seek awakening after encountering the "four sights": (1) a sick person; (2) an old person; (3) a corpse; and (4) a world renouncer. The first three epitomize the sufferings to which ordinary beings are subject, and the last indicates that one can transcend them through meditation and religious practice. The greatest problem of all is death, the final cessation of all our hopes and dreams, our successes and failures, our loves, hates, worries, and plans.

From its inception, Buddhism has stressed the importance of death, since awareness of death is what prompted the Buddha to perceive the ultimate futility of worldly concerns and pleasures. Realizing that death is inevitable for a person who is caught up in worldly pleasures and attitudes, the Buddha resolved to renounce the world and devote himself to finding a solution to this most basic of existential dilemmas. After years of diligent and difficult practice he became awakened, and through this he transcended death. His life story provides his followers with a model to emulate, and even today Buddhist teachers strongly advise their students to meditate on death and impermanence, since they are powerful counteragents to shortsighted concern with mundane matters and one's own transitory happiness. Buddhist teachers also point out that according to tradition Buddha began his teaching career discussing death and impermanence in his first sermon on the four noble truths, and he also ended his career with teachings on death and impermanence, which indicates how important they are in Buddhist doctrine and practice.

Tibetan Buddhism places a particularly strong emphasis on instructions concerning death, and Tibetan literature is full of admonitions to be aware of the inevitability of death, the preciousness of the opportunities that a human birth presents, and the great value of mindfulness of death. A person who correctly grasps the inevitability of death becomes more focused on religious practice, since he or she realizes that death is inevitable, the time of death is uncertain, and that every moment counts.

An example of this attitude can be found in the biography of Milarépa, who began his meditative practice after having killed a number of people through black magic. The realization of his impending death and the sufferings he would experience in his next lifetime prompted him to find a lama who could show him a way to avert his fate. His concern with death was so great that when he was meditating in a cave his tattered clothes fell apart, but he decided not to mend them, saying, "If I were to die this evening, it would be wiser to meditate than to do this useless sewing."[1]

This attitude epitomizes the ideal for a Buddhist practitioner, according to many teachers. Atiśa is said to have told his students that for a person who is unaware of death, meditation has little power, but a person who is mindful of death and impermanence progresses steadily and makes the most of every precious moment. A famous saying of the school he founded, the Kadampa, holds that if one does not meditate on death in the morning, the whole morning is wasted; if one does not meditate on death at noon, the afternoon is wasted; and if one does not meditate on death at night, the evening is wasted.

In stark contrast to this attitude, most people frantically run after transitory pleasures and material objects, foolishly believing that wealth, power, friends, and family will bring lasting fulfillment. This is particularly prevalent in Western cultures, which emphasize superficial images of happiness, material and sensual pleasures, and technological innovation as avenues to contentment. We are taught to crave such things, but inevitably find that the wealthy and powerful die just as surely as the poor and powerless. We try to cover up the signs of aging through cosmetics and surgery, and we attempt to hide the reality of death by putting makeup on corpses to make them appear "lifelike." We are even taught to avoid discussion of death, since this is seen as inappropriate in polite company and overly morbid. Instead, people tend to focus on things that turn their attention from death and surround themselves with images of superficial happiness. As Dr. Richard Kalish states,

> death is blasphemous and pornographic. We react to it and its symbols in the same way that we react to pornography. We avoid it. We deny it exists. We avert our eyes from its presence. We protect little children from observing it and dodge their questions about it. We speak of it only in whispers. We consider it horrible, ugly and grotesque.[2]

From its inception, Buddhism has taken a far different course. Anyone who has studied with a Tibetan lama has been regularly reminded of the importance of mindfulness of death. Discussions of death and impermanence are found in every facet of Tibetan Buddhist teaching, and any student who tries to overlook them is soon reminded that dharma practice requires a poignant awareness of death. Buddhist doctrines emphasize the idea that although one's destiny is always influenced by past karma, every person has the ability to exercise free will and influence the course of both life and death. We all shape our own destinies, and in every moment there are opportunities for spiritual advancement. According to many Buddhist texts, death presents us with a range of important possibilities for progress.

Meditation on Death

Buddhist meditation texts point out that we have ample evidence of death all around us, since everything is changing from moment to moment. A person wishing to ponder death need not go to a cemetery or a funeral home: death is occurring everywhere and at all times. Even the cells of our bodies are constantly being born and dying. All of us are inexorably moving toward physical death in every moment. Since every created thing is impermanent, everything we see, hear, touch, taste, love, despise, or desire is in the process of dying. There is nothing to hold onto, nothing that remains unchanged from moment to moment, and so anyone who tries to find happiness among transient, created things is doomed to disappointment.

This transience is the reason why we are prone to discontent and suffering, since everything we desire eventually breaks down, and we often have to put up with things that we find unpleasant. Impermanence is also essential for liberation, since the constantly changing nature of cyclic existence makes progress possible. Every moment presents an opportunity to train the mind in the direction of awakening, and since there is no fixed element to personality, every person is always engaged in the process of becoming something else. We do, of course, tend to fall into patterns of behavior, and it is all too easy to become caught up in negative patterns, but since every moment is a rebirth, there is always an opportunity to initiate change. A wise person, according to Chagdud Tulku Rinpoche, understands the imminence of death and plans ahead.

> Warned of a hurricane, we don't wait until the storm pounds the shore before we start to prepare. Similarly, knowing death is looming offshore, we shouldn't wait until it overpowers us before developing the meditation skills necessary to achieve the great potential of the mind at the moment of death.[3]

Each moment is said to give us a glimpse of the *bardo* (*bar do, antarā-bhāva*), the intermediate state between death and rebirth, since every moment of mind passes away and is replaced by a successive moment. Reflection on one's own mental processes graphically indicates the fleeting nature of consciousness: thoughts flow along in unending succession, each one giving way to its successor. Cognitions and emotions change in response to our experiences and perceptions, and even our most cherished ideas and aspirations are subject to change. Thus, for a person who has awareness of death, every moment becomes a lesson in death and impermanence.

Our dreams also provide an opportunity for mindfulness of death. In Tibetan Buddhist death literature it is said that at the moment of falling asleep one experiences an instant of clear light like the one that arises at the time of death. Moreover, the dream state is like the bardo, since in dreams one often conceives of oneself in a body and undergoes vivid experiences that are creations of mind, just as beings in the bardo do. Waking from a dream is similar to rebirth, since the illusory dream body passes away and we awaken to a new "reality." Because of these similarities, dream yoga is an important method for gaining control over the production of mental images, a skill that is extremely useful in the bardo.[4]

How to Develop Mindfulness of Death

A person wishing to develop mindfulness of death should first cultivate awareness of its inevitability. Everyone who has ever lived has died, and there is no reason to suppose that anyone presently alive will be able to escape the same fate. Even the buddhas, bodhisattvas, and Buddhist saints of the past have all died, and so it should be clear to a person who thinks on this that death awaits us all.

This understanding should not result in passivity, resignation, or morbidity; rather, it should spur us to greater diligence in religious practice. Every moment should be viewed as infinitely precious, and we should make the utmost effort to use our time to the best advantage.

After making this decision, the meditator considers the uncertainty of the time of death and decides that it might occur at any moment, which should lead to a resolve to begin practicing dharma immediately. Practice should not be put off until the future, but should begin right now. A person who thinks, "I'll wait until the children are grown," "After I finish this semester I'll start meditating," or "I just don't have enough time right now" will probably never get around to meditation, and even if he does, practice will most likely be half-hearted. A person who wishes to make real progress must feel a strong sense of urgency, like someone caught in a burning house looking for a way out.

The next stage in this process is coming to understand that at the time of death only spiritual accomplishments will be of any worth. Material possessions, friends and relatives, worldly acclaim and power all vanish when life ends, leaving nothing behind. None of these can be carried over into the next existence. Moreover, one's future birth will be determined by one's actions in this life, and so one should resolve to practice meditation and other religious activities diligently.

It is also important not to think that in one's next lifetime one will not necessarily be born as a human. According to Buddhist teachings on rebirth, a human life is very rare, and it is much more likely that one will be born in some other situation, and if this happens one's chances for becoming aware of the problems of cyclic existence and seeking a solution are greatly diminished. Humans are uniquely situated in cyclic existence: we are intelligent enough to recognize its problems and sufferings (unlike lower types of beings such as animals), and we are not so overwhelmed by either suffering or happiness that we are blinded to its realities. A person who understands this situation should become keenly aware of death and resolve to "extract the essence" of the present life.

Death Meditation: Exoteric and Esoteric Traditions

Types and Causes of Death

According to treatises on death, there are two kinds of death: untimely death, which is the result of violence or accidents; and death that is the result of the natural end of one's lifespan. The latter occurs when the karmic predisposition that provided the impetus for the present life is exhausted. One can also die prematurely, through violence, accident, or through lack of the necessities of life, such as food and water.

Untimely death may be averted through long-life meditations or religious practices, but the second type is the inevitable result of one's own karma, and so cannot be prevented. A person whose lifespan is exhausted is like a car that has run out of gas: it simply stops running, but in this case there is no possibility of refueling it, since its ability to sustain life is gone.

According to the first Dalai Lama, the three causes of death are: (1) the end of one's lifespan has been reached; (2) all positive, life-sustaining energy has been used up; or (3) all the karmic supports of life have been exhausted.[5] There are various techniques for counteracting each of these, but when all three are present, there is no way to overcome all of them, and a person in this situation should prepare for death.[6] Moreover, even if one does engage in practices to prolong life, this is at best a temporary measure, since everyone inevitably dies anyway. In order that one will not be unprepared when the time of death arrives, Buddhist teachers strongly emphasize the importance of immediately beginning to meditate on death.

Using the Death Process to Advantage

In both exoteric and esoteric traditions of Buddhism there are many techniques for developing awareness of death. A common exoteric practice involves visualizing corpses or skeletons and recognizing that these represent the final fate of one's own body. Meditators sometimes even go to cemeteries or cremation grounds in order to be confronted with the inevitability of death.

Another powerful technique for developing awareness of death involves visualizing oneself lying on one's deathbed, with life slowly ebbing away. All one's friends and relatives are gathered around, weeping and lamenting, and one's body progressively degenerates. The glow of life fades from the face, and the pallor of death replaces it. Breathing becomes shallow. The lips dry up, slime forms on the lips, and the body becomes like a lump of flesh, unable to move freely. Bodily temperature drops, eyesight, hearing, and other senses lose clarity, and one becomes aware of past negative deeds.

These transgressions weigh heavily on a dying person, since they will negatively affect one's future birth. One should think of how one will look around for help, but none will be possible. One is responsible for one's own actions, and no outside force can intervene. Through cultivating this meditation one should develop a sense of urgency regarding religious practice and a poignant awareness of death.

The esoteric tantric systems also have techniques for death meditation. In these practices, death is portrayed as an opportunity for spiritual progress and not simply as a limiting condition that represents the termination of life. One applies generation stage yogas to the death process, using the procedure of "taking the three bodies as the path." This involves perceiving the clear light of death as the truth body, the bardo as the complete enjoyment body, and the rebirth process as the emanation body.[7]

In the first method, one realizes that the truth body is of the nature of one's own mind, which is a union of clear light and emptiness. A person who successfully cultivates this understanding transforms the clear light nature of the mind into the truth body, thus quickly actualizing the state of buddhahood.

Perceiving the bardo state as the complete enjoyment body involves taking control of the bardo process. In this yoga one directs the manifestations and contents of the visions of the bardo, rather than being helplessly moved along through the process. One learns that all perceptions are creations of mind, and a person who becomes skilled in this practice develops the conscious ability to direct the production of mental images. Most beings in the bardo are assaulted by strange and unnerving sights, sounds, and smells, but the experienced meditator understands that they are creations of mind. After realizing this and learning to exercise control over the process of emanation, the meditator works at developing the level of skill necessary to visualize herself as a complete enjoyment body.

Perceiving the rebirth process as the emanation body is founded on the same principles as the previous two practices. In this technique the meditator develops awareness that a buddha's ability to produce emanation bodies is an extension of the sort of control that advanced meditators gain in creating mental images that appear to be real but are produced from emptiness. The process of rebirth can be influenced by a person who attains the mental discipline required for advanced visualization. Thus, one need not be thrown helplessly toward the next birth, and a yogi who becomes skilled in taking control over the rebirth process can develop the ability to determine the sort of life situation into which she will be born.

The esoteric process of death meditation focuses on the "twenty-five coarse substances," which are the constituents of an ordinary being. These include the five aggregates (form, feelings, discriminations, consciousness, and compositional factors), which form the nucleus of the psychophysical personality, the four basic elements (earth, wind, fire, and water), the "twelve entrances" (objects of sight, hearing, touch, taste, and thought, together with the sense powers that enable us to perceive them), and the "five basic wisdoms" (basic mirrorlike wisdom, basic wisdom of equality, basic wisdom of accomplishment, basic wisdom of discrimination, and the basic wisdom of the sphere of reality; these are wisdoms that belong to a person who has not yet attained buddhahood).

The basic mirrorlike wisdom is an ordinary consciousness that has many objects appearing to it simultaneously, in the way that objects appear in a mirror. The basic wisdom of equality is an ordinary consciousness that is aware of pleasure, pain, and neutral feeling as being of one nature. When one experiences this consciousness, one is no longer cognizant of the pleasure, pain, or neutral feelings that previously accompanied sensations which gave rise to these feelings. The basic wisdom of analysis is an ordinary consciousness that recognizes the names of people who are dear to one. During the process of death this fades and vanishes, signaling one's imminent detachment from things that had previously been viewed as important. The basic wisdom of accomplishment is a consciousness that is aware of ordinary activities and goals. As one's life fades, this diminishes and disappears, signaling that one is losing interest in worldly activities. The basic wisdom of the sphere of reality is the subtlest of these, and its passing indicates that attachments to one's previous life have been cut off.

When a person dies naturally (that is, when death is not a result of a violent act or sudden accident), the various constituents of the psychophysical continuum begin to disintegrate. Initially the form aggregate and the basic mirrorlike wisdom begin to degenerate simultaneously, along with the earth element and the eye sense power.[8] Physically, the earth element dissolves into the water element. The external signs of this process include a noticeable decrease in vitality and a weakening of the body, which feels very heavy. The dying person's eyes begin to blur, and it becomes increasingly difficult to move the limbs. These changes are apparent both to the dying person and to others. At the same time, the dying person perceives an inner sign, which is a miragelike appearance that seems to fill all of space. This is similar to the appearance of water in a desert mirage in the summer. As the Dalai Lama describes this process,

> The first stage is represented by the dissolution of the aggregate of forms. In rough terms, when the aggregate of forms begins to disintegrate, this means that the earth constituent is losing its force in the sense of becoming less capable of serving as a basis of consciousness. Simultaneously with this, the capacity of the water constituent in your body to serve as a basis for consciousness becomes more manifest; this process is called "dissolution of the earth constituent into the water constituent."[9]

The second phase of the death process involves the degeneration of the feeling aggregate simultaneously with the basic wisdom of equality, together with the water element and the ear sense power. Physically the water element dissolves into the fire element, and then the fire element begins to weaken. The outer signs of this process are a loss of the ability to discriminate between pleasant and unpleasant sensations, a drying of the lips, a stopping of perspiration, and coagulation of blood and semen. One loses the ability to hear external sounds, and as an inner sign one perceives a smokelike appearance that seems to fill all of space. This appears like billowing smoke coming from a chimney.

In the third stage, the discrimination aggregate dissolves simultaneously with the basic wisdom of discrimination, together with the fire element and the nose sense power. The wind element begins to dissipate. One loses the ability to understand what is being said, forgets even the names of parents, close friends, and relatives, and body temperature drops. One is unable to digest food, and exhalation is strong while inhalation is weak, indicating that the vital force is leaving the body. The ability to distinguish smells fades, and as an inner sign the dying person perceives a subtle flame-like appearance that seems to fill all of space.

The fourth stage involves the dissolution of the compositional factors aggregate, simultaneously with the basic wisdom of accomplishment, together with the wind element and the tongue sense power. The outer signs are a complete failure of all physical abilities, loss of a sense of purpose, a dissolution of the greater and lesser bodily energies into the heart, a change of the color of the tongue from pink to bluish-gray, and a loss of the ability to taste. The inner sign is a flickering light, like the light given off by an oil lamp.

This is the point at which Western medicine considers a person to be dead, but according to Tibetan physiology and meditation theory, actual death has not yet occurred. Consciousness still inhabits the body, and until it departs one is not considered to be truly dead, although to all outward appearances this is the case.

Signs of Death as Premonitions

Just prior to death, there are certain physical signs that indicate the dying person's most probable rebirth situation. If wind and mucus move in the left nostril at the time of death and physical warmth first withdraws from the area of the left eye, the dying person will probably be born as a human, unless something is done to reverse this tendency while in the bardo. If the dying person's hands shake and he babbles incoherently, and if physical warmth first withdraws from the area of the right armpit, the dying person will likely be reborn as a demi-god. Those who make animal sounds with their mouths and whose body heat withdraws at night will generally be reborn as animals. If a dying person's skin turns yellow and its glow fades, and if he feels hungry and emits semen, this is an indication of probable rebirth as a hungry ghost. Finally, when a dying person's right leg shakes uncontrollably, his body heat exits from the sole of the right foot, and he simultaneously emits saliva, urine, and excrement, this indicates that rebirth in a hell realm is likely.

The Dalai Lama states that the dying person's previous actions and attitudes are the most important determining factor in rebirth, and the result of these actions can be seen in how one dies:

> For those strongly involved in nonvirtuous actions, the warmth of the body withdraws first from the upper part of the body and then from other parts; whereas, for those strongly involved in virtuous actions, the warmth first withdraws from the feet. In both cases, the warmth finally gathers at the heart, from which the consciousness exits. Those particles of matter, of the combined semen and blood, into which the consciousness initially entered in the mother's womb at the beginning of the life, become the centre of the heart; and from that very same point the consciousness ultimately departs at death.[10]

For a person who dies in a state of afflicted pride, consciousness exits through the opening of the ear and heat begins to leave in that area. This indicates that the dying person will probably become a malevolent spirit. If, however, one is able to die in a state of equanimity or positive feeling, this is a predictor of a pleasant rebirth. If just before death the illness appears to recede—and if the dying person can bring to mind clear thoughts of her guru and other religious teachers—this will positively influence the rebirth process. If the dying person successfully performs the appropriate meditations for the time of death, a sign of success is the disappearance of the yellow fluid from the fontanel opening at the crown of the head, and consciousness departs from the body through that opening. One who accomplishes this will either go to a high rebirth or attain full awakening.

In order to prepare for death and take full advantage of the opportunities it offers, previous training is important. Whatever attitudes a person cultivates during life will most likely manifest themselves during the process of death. The Dalai Lama contends that when one is dying

> attitudes of long familiarity usually take precedence and direct the rebirth. For this same reason, strong attachment is generated for the self, since one fears that one's self is becoming nonexistent. This attachment serves as the connecting link to the intermediate state between lives; the liking of a body, in turn, acts as a cause establishing the body of the intermediate being.[11]

The whole process of death and rebirth in ordinary beings is driven by past habits, attitudes, and actions. In order to avoid falling into the traps one finds along the way in the death process, prior preparation and training are crucial. They help the dying person to recognize what is happening and to cultivate attitudes that will result in either a good rebirth or awakening.

The Internal Process of Death According to Tantric Theory

The bardo state has many pitfalls that trap the unwary and lead to future pain and suffering. Fortunately, there are ways to prepare for the dangers and increase one's chances of being able to take advantage of the opportunities afforded by the bardo. Among the most effective of these are yogic practices that simulate the process of death. A person who becomes familiar with these is not shocked or terrified by what he experiences in the bardo, but rather recognizes everything as images created by the mind. A meditator who has developed proficiency in the yogic practices of the bardo is also less likely to become terrified by the process of physical and mental degeneration that precedes death. Understanding the stages of death and the physiological reasons that underlie them enhances one's ability to remain calm during the process, and this can also help one to recognize the events of the bardo for what they are.

The yogas of bardo preparation are based on simulating death. They are founded on the mystical physiology of Vajrayāna that describes the human body in terms of winds—subtle energies that are the bases of various levels of consciousness—and channels through which the winds travel. According to this system, death is the result of the progressive collapse of the ability of the winds to act as supports for consciousness. When they are no longer able to perform this function, death occurs.

According to tantric medical literature, there are five types of winds: (1) life-bearing wind, which resides in the heart area and which is responsible for inhalation and exhalation, burping, and spitting; (2) upward-moving wind, located in the chest, which operates in the throat and mouth and is responsible for speech, swallowing food and saliva, and also operates in the joints; (3) pervasive wind, residing at the crown of the head, which is responsible for pliancy, extending and contracting the limbs, and closing the mouth and eyes; (4) fire-dwelling wind, whose abode is the stomach, which moves throughout the internal organs and the channels in the limbs, and is responsible for digestion; and (5) downward-moving wind, which resides in the lower abdomen and moves throughout the womb or seminal vesicle, the urinary bladder, and the thighs, and which initiates and stops urination, defecation, and menstruation.

Certain meditative techniques of highest yoga tantra manipulate the movements of these winds and cause them to dissolve into the subtle life-bearing wind at the heart. This parallels a part of the death process and gives the yogi a measure of control over the winds and energy channels.

There are seventy-two thousand channels, of which three are the most important for tantric yoga: (1) the central channel (*rtsa dbu ma, avadhūti*) in the center of the body; (2) the channel to the left of the central channel (*rtsa brkyang ma, lalanā*); and (3) a channel to the right of the central channel (*rtsa ro ma, rasanā*). The left and right channels wrap around the central one at the cakras, the most important of which are located at the top of the head, forehead, throat, heart, solar plexus, base of the spine, and sexual organ. They constrict the central channel and inhibit the movements of winds. When a person dies, the winds that are the bases of consciousness dissolve into the right and left channels. These then dissolve into the wind in the central channel, causing a loosening of the pressure exerted on the central channel by the right and left channels at the cakras. This allows a freer movement of wind in the central channel, which leads to the manifestation of subtle minds.

These minds are always present, but are normally submerged beneath the coarser levels of consciousness; these coarser minds are what ordinary beings experience most of the time. When the restrictions are loosened, however, the more subtle minds manifest, which presents a valuable opportunity to work with them in a meditative context. Unfortunately, most people do not realize this opportunity for what it is, and instead people generally react with fear, since they feel that they are being annihilated. Practitioners of highest yoga tantra should recognize these subtle minds and understand that there is in fact no "I" that can be threatened with annihilation. Adepts can take advantage of the arising of the subtle minds and manipulate them in accordance with the goals of tantric practice.

At each of the cakras are red and white "drops" (*thig le, bindu*), which are the bases for mental health. The white drops are more numerous at the top of the head, while the red drops are more common at the solar plexus. The origins of these drops are the white and red substances one inherits from one's father and mother, respectively. At the time of conception, white matter from the father's sperm and red matter from the mother form the nucleus of the zygote, and the matter one receives from them at conception resides at the heart in what is called the "indestructible drop," which is the size of a small pea. It is white at the top and red at the bottom, and it is called "indestructible" because it remains until death. The subtle life-sustaining winds reside in it, and when one dies all winds dissolve into it. After it has absorbed all winds, the clear light of death becomes manifest.

According to tantric theory, the residence of the mind is not the brain, but the heart. The mind abides in the indestructible drop at the heart cakra. There are two types of indestructible drop, one coarse and one subtle. The coarse drop is a coalescence of cells from the semen of the father and the ovum of the mother, and the subtle drop is a coalescence of subtle levels of consciousness and subtle physical energies. The coarse drop is "indestructible" because it endures throughout one's life from the moment of conception until the final moment of physical death. The subtle drop is "indestructible" because it endures throughout all of one's lives, from beginningless time into the future until the time of awakening, at which point one's body is transformed into the perfect body of a buddha.

When the vital energies that sustain life break down, the dying person experiences a reversal of the process of conception that initiated his life. According to Tibetan medical theory, during one's life the cells that came from one's father and the cells that came from one's mother (both of which joined at conception) separate and subsequently reside in different parts of the body. The cells of the original sperm from one's father are located at the cakra at the top of the head during one's life, and the cells from the mother's ovum are at the navel cakra. Throughout one's life, these are kept separate by the vital energies in the body, particularly those in the central channel. As one's energy fades, however, the vital energies are no longer sufficient to separate these two sets of cells, and they begin to move from the cakras where they were stored.

The white cells of the father's sperm move downward from the crown cakra through the central channel until they come to the heart. While they are moving, one experiences a vision of snowlike whiteness as they travel through the cakras. Then the cells of the mother's ovum move upward toward the heart where the two types of cells meet. At this point the dying person has a vision of darkness similar to a sky that is completely covered with dark clouds.

People who have not meditated in advance of this faint when the vision appears, but skilled meditators recognize what is happening and remain conscious. This is a particularly potent opportunity for meditative progress, since the grosser levels of mind are dropping away, making access to subtle consciousnesses easier.

Physically, the body continues to degenerate, and eventually the heart gives a slight tremble, which signifies that consciousness has left the body. One experiences a vision of clear light that is like dawn breaking in a cloudless sky. This is termed the "clear light of death," and according to Tibetan medical literature this is the actual point of death.

Ordinary people undergoing these changes are terrified. Tantric yogis, however, prepare for them during their lifetimes and simulate the process of death in meditation, and so they are untroubled by these experiences. A person who has practiced preparatory yogas and used them to gain control over the mind can use the death process to great advantage, since it presents a tremendous opportunity for spiritual progress.

The most important trainings involve gaining control over the vital energies and recognizing the subtler levels of consciousness. A meditator who becomes skilled in the practices of highest yoga tantra learns to influence the movements of subtle energies and gains access to the subtler levels of consciousness, and so when the coarse energies dissolve into the subtler ones and grosser levels of mind dissolve into the subtler ones, she is not surprised. One who has simulated this process during life is well prepared for death, and when the images and sensations of the bardo appear, she will recognize them as products of the mind, which can be influenced and manipulated in accordance with a yogi's wishes in order to produce particular soteriological results.

Influencing the Death Process

A skilled tantric practitioner who takes control over the process of death is able to transform the subtle energies and consciousnesses into the bodies of a buddha. Consciousness is transmuted into the truth body, wisdom and energy into the complete enjoyment body, the clear light of death arises as the truth body, and the visions of the bardo are transformed into emanation bodies.

An important part of this process is the recognition of subtle levels of mind. As the physical supports of life dissolve and the energies that sustained consciousness break down, the grosser levels of consciousness drop away and are replaced by more subtle ones. Each of these subtle minds is characterized by a particular type of light that distinguishes it.

The process of the dissolution of consciousness begins when the winds of the left and right channels above the heart enter the central channel at the top of the head. At this point one has a perception of light similar to that given off by a butter lamp. Now the mind begins to dissolve, and coarser levels of consciousness are sublated while progressively subtler ones become manifest. The winds in the right and left channels below the heart enter the central channel at the base of the spine. According to Yangjen Gaway Lodrö,

> at the time of death all the winds in the seventy-two thousand channels gather in the right and left channels. Then the winds in these two dissolve into the central channel. The winds in the upper and lower parts of the central channel finally dissolve into the indestructible life-bearing wind at the heart.[12]

Conceptuality also dissolves and the "mind of white appearance" becomes manifest. The sign of this is an experience of a clear void filled with white light. At this point the mind is free from coarse conceptuality but retains some elements of dualistic thought. The Dalai Lama states that

> when the eighty conceptual thoughts together with the winds or energies that serve as their mounts dissolve, the internal sign is that a white appearance dawns; this is the mind of radiant white appearance. It is compared to a clear autumn sky filled with just moonlight.[13]

The mind of white appearance in turn dissolves into a subtler mind, the "mind of red increase." This occurs when the upper and lower winds come together at the heart and the winds enter the drop at the heart. According to the Dalai Lama, this is "compared to a clear autumn sky filled with just reddish or orange sunlight."[14] A yogi who abides in this state and recognizes the red light as a manifestation of mind can transmute it into the form of a complete enjoyment body buddha; if this does not occur, he moves on to the next phase.

The mind of red increase now dissolves into the "mind of black near-attainment," in which all one perceives is a void pervaded by blackness. The sign of this mind is a void filled with dense darkness, followed by a feeling of faintness. This occurs when all winds dissolve into the very subtle life-sustaining wind in the indestructible drop at the heart. One then experiences a clear void that is free from the previous white, red, and black appearances and is referred to as "the mind of clear light." The Dalai Lama states that the mind of clear light

> is called the fundamental mind because it is the root of all minds; in relation to it, all other minds are just adventitious. It is this mind that exists beginninglessly and continuously in each individual through each lifetime and into Buddhahood.[15]

When the mind of clear light manifests, one experiences it as a completely nondualistic voidness. It is the subtlest and most fundamental level of consciousness. A person who is proficient in generation-stage yogas can take advantage of this extremely subtle level of mind and transmute the light into the truth body.[16] Yogis who successfully merge the clear light into the truth body instantaneously attain buddhahood and pass through the bardo.

The Bardo Process

In tantric physiology, the sign of actual death is not the cessation of inhalation or circulation of blood, but the appearance of the mind of clear light. People remain in this state of lucidity for three days, but most are so frightened by the strangeness of the experience that they lapse into unconsciousness and pass through the period of the arising of the mind of clear light unaware of what is happening. At the end of this stage, external signs of death appear, such as pus or blood emerging from the nose and sexual organ. This indicates that consciousness has departed from the body, and only at this point should the corpse be disposed of. Before this time, consciousness is still in the body, and if it is handled violently, buried, or cremated, this could negatively influence the consciousness of the dying person, possibly resulting in a lower rebirth.

Since the body and mind are no longer able to sustain life, this is the end of one's life and the beginning of an interim existence in the bardo. After the clear light ceases, the previous process of manifestation of progressively subtler minds is reversed, and one is born into the bardo.

At this point one acquires a subtle body that accords with one's future rebirth. If one is to be reborn as a human, one will have a bardo body that is human in appearance; if one is to be reborn as an animal, one's bardo body will resemble the type of animal one will become, and so forth. The bardo body is unhampered by physical restrictions and can travel wherever one wills and can pass through walls and other physical objects. This state can last from a moment up to seven days. If one either averts rebirth through yogic practice or is unable to locate a suitable rebirth situation, one undergoes a "small death" in which one experiences the death sequence outlined earlier, but this time it happens very quickly. Then the rebirth process is repeated and one takes a second rebirth in the bardo, with a new bardo body. This can happen as many as seven times, making a total of forty-nine days in which one may be in the bardo. After this one must find a place of rebirth.

According to highest yoga tantra meditation theory, the small death that occurs between bardos or immediately before taking rebirth is similar to the process of sleep, and so there are a variety of yogic practices that involve exerting control over the dream process, practices which are said to prepare one for the bardo. There are other states that living people experience which are similar to those of the death process and bardo, and these also are bases for tantric practices that help yogis to become familiar with and manipulate subtle minds and energies in preparation for death. In particular, the states of increasing subtlety of the death process and increasing coarseness during rebirth are similar to what one undergoes during and after sleep, fainting, and orgasm, but these are only adumbrations of the full range of experiences of the bardo. Still, a person who learns to properly manifest and manipulate the subtle consciousnesses present in orgasm or dreams can gain valuable expertise in techniques that will be useful in the bardo state. When one experiences orgasm or sleep, coarser levels of consciousness drop away and are replaced by more subtle ones. Most people, of course, do not exercise any conscious control in these states, but tantric yogis learn to recognize the manifestation of subtle minds and to use them as a basis for diminishing the power of conceptual thought and accessing the clear light nature of mind. The Dalai Lama advises practitioners that

> it is very important to identify your own basic mind, the mind of clear light. To realize the subtlest mind, the first step is realization of the nature of mind on the conventional level. With realization of the nature of mind you can concentrate on mind itself, gradually increasing the power of realization of the entity of consciousness. Through

> that method, the mind can be controlled. The strength of control, in turn, helps to stop coarse minds, and once those are stopped, subtler minds will automatically manifest. If, before death, you can realize the subtle mind, this subtle mind can be transformed into wisdom—the strongest weapon to destroy ignorance and the suffering it induces.[17]

There are various methods for accomplishing this. Trainees of the highest capacity who are prepared for the bardo and have developed proficiency in generation stage yogas can manifest the clear light of death as a tantric deity in accordance with a tantric system (Guhyasamāja or Cakrasaṃvara, for example). A person who accomplishes this bypasses the bardo altogether and arises in the form of a tantric deity, endowed with all the outer and inner signs of perfection. This is a result of previous successful simulation of the process of death and training in such practices as dream yoga and illusory body yogas.[18] A person who becomes adept in these practices realizes that all appearances are creations of mind and that mind itself is a union of clear luminosity and emptiness. The yogas of the bardo begin with this insight, and the meditator transforms the clear light nature of the mind into the fully awakened mind of a buddha and the vital energies into a buddha's subtle body.

Those who are not advanced enough to accomplish this but who have gained a measure of control over the vital energies have other options. If one is able to recognize the stages of the process of dissolution of vital energies, when the twenty-five coarse elements dissolve and the clear light of death manifests, one can generate the clear light of death into the "clear light of the path," thus making the nature of the mind indistinguishable from the path. This is called "merging the mother and son clear light."

Bardo Experiences

Advanced tantric meditators recognize the dawning of the clear light of death for what it is and strive to take advantage of the opportunities it affords. Most people, however, are disoriented by the experience and fall into unconsciousness. Beings who fail to manipulate the clear light in accordance with generation stage yogas are drawn into the bardo, where a new set of opportunities and dangers awaits.

Beings in the bardo are bombarded by strange and powerful sensations, and these have a profoundly disorienting effect on the mind. Bardo beings hear loud sounds caused by the four elements—earth, water, fire, and wind. In the bardo all of one's senses are functioning, and one hears a sound like a huge avalanche continually falling behind one, the sound of a massive blazing fire like a volcano, and the sound of a powerful storm. There are also bright and unnerving colors, smells, and tastes, all of which are products of one's own mind, but which are no less real than ordinary perceptions; in fact, they have greater power and are more compelling than anything one experienced while alive. The combined effect of all these strange perceptions is a sense of disorientation, confusion, and desperation for beings who are unprepared for them. This in turn tends to lead to negative emotional responses, which then bring about a connection to one's next birth.

In addition to the powerful and confusing sights and sounds of the bardo, however, tantric deities also manifest as beings in the intermediate state. These deities, like the other perceptions, are products of mind, but also have tremendous power and can become bases for awakening for a person who recognizes them and responds appropriately. [19]

When the five elements dissolve and the coarser levels of consciousness progressively dissipate into more subtle ones, eventually all that remains is the fundamental innate mind of clear light. This manifests at the final stage of dissolution, called "spontaneous presence dissolving into primordial purity." After this a pantheon of tantric deities appears, many of which are specific to the bardo. These deities can arise in vast numbers, even seeming to fill all of space. They are seen by everyone in the bardo, because everyone has the buddha nature, and everyone's mind is of the nature of clear light, just like the mind of a buddha. Thus the deities of the bardo are merely manifestations of aspects of one's own consciousness. Chökyi Nyima Rinpoche contends that

> all sentient beings are buddhas, but this fact is veiled by our temporary obscurations. When these veils are removed, we are actual buddhas. When a gap occurs in our dualistic fixation during the process of death, then all these different manifestations of our buddha nature are experienced unveiled.[20]

Some of these manifest in peaceful forms, while others assume wrathful aspects. A person who recognizes the peaceful deities and successfully generates himself as one either manifests as a fully actualized complete enjoyment body buddha or takes rebirth in the deity's pure land, a place where conditions are optimal for meditative training. This is also true of one who sees the wrathful deities for what they are, and either practices generation stage yogas or responds to them with feelings of faith and devotion. This can lead to attainment of buddhahood or rebirth in a pure land, but a person who reacts negatively to the bardo deities creates harmful emotions that impel him toward rebirth.

In addition to the images of deities, bardo beings are also confronted with five lights: white, blue, yellow, red, and green. For a person who is to be reborn in the lower realms, they appear to be malignant and unpleasant, but a person who will have a good rebirth sees them as the "five wisdom lights of awakening." One who successfully merges the mind with one of these lights manifests as a buddha or is reborn in a particular buddha land. A yogi who remains in the white light either experiences the "mirrorlike primordial wisdom" and emerges as Akṣobhya, or is reborn in the central buddha land. One who remains in the blue light either generates the "primordial wisdom of the sphere of reality" and emerges as Vairocana, or goes to the eastern buddha land. One who remains in the yellow light either transmutes the mind into the "primordial wisdom of equality" and generates herself as Ratnasambhava, or goes to the southern buddha land. Remaining in the red light either leads to actualization of the "primordial wisdom of discrimination" and attainment of the state of Amitābha, or to rebirth in the western buddha land. A meditator who remains in the green light either attains the "primordial wisdom of accomplishment" and the state of Amoghasiddhi, or goes to the northern buddha land. Longchenpa describes this as

> the attainment of full enlightenment at the primordial ground. This is the (method of) instant liberation by unifying (the primordial wisdom) with the clarity of the intermediate state by recognizing the spontaneously present and unsearched for primordial wisdom of bliss, clarity, and no-thought, which has naturally arisen and has been naturally recognized when one gained experience in this crucial point of instant self-liberation in the past.[21]

This description of the intermediate state process indicates some of the potential advantages to be gained by those who prepare for it, recognize the experiences of the bardo as manifestations of mind, and successfully transmute the clear light nature of the mind into the clear light of buddhahood.

Westerners confronted by the descriptions of the bardo often wonder whether these perceptions are universal and are found across different cultures, or if they are specific to Tibetan Buddhists. It is reasonable that Buddhists who are confronted by strange sights and sounds while in the process of death would conceive them in terms of previously learned images and concepts, but what of non-Buddhists? Does everyone see Buddhist deities and symbols? According to a number of Tibetan teachers, the manifestations of the bardo are the same for everyone, but a person who has no familiarity with Buddhism will most likely not see Buddhist deities, and instead will only perceive the images of the bardo as random and confusing lights, forms, and sounds. According to Chökyi Nyima Rinpoche,

> we cannot really say what non-practitioners experience at this point, but they certainly experience very colorful and intense forms that can be as big as Mount Sumeru, the enormous mythical mountain, or as minute as a sesame seed. Images are extremely brilliant and colors are overwhelmingly clear. Incredibly loud noises resound like one hundred thousand simultaneous thunderclaps. The light can be so bright that we feel like we are being completely perforated by light rays. If someone has practiced there is a great chance of success, but someone who has absolutely no experience of Dharma practice might faint from sheer fright.[22]

Although non-Buddhists will probably not recognize the images of the intermediate state in the same way that a Buddhist will, the rules are still the same for both, and since a Buddhist is more likely to be familiar with the manifestations of the bardo and more likely to feel comfortable with both the peaceful and wrathful deities, he or she has a greater chance of taking advantage of the opportunities afforded by this state. The process is the same for everyone, whether or not one actually knows what the rules are.

Taking Rebirth

According to Tibetan tradition, everyone who dies enters the intermediate state, but the amount of time a person spends in the bardo varies: some move through it very quickly, while others take as long as forty-nine days.

The most common time for people who die natural deaths is seven days. After this period the dead person moves toward a life situation that is concordant with the karma of the past life. If a suitable life situation is not found—or if the deceased is able to forestall rebirth—then a "small death" occurs, and one is born again in the bardo. This may happen for as many as seven cycles, but most people exit the bardo before this.

At the end of the bardo process, one is drawn toward a rebirth appropriate to one's future life situation. If one is to be reborn as a human, one will be attracted to human parents, if an animal to animal parents, and so forth. While still in a bardo body, one will become captivated by a particular set of parents of the appropriate type who are in the act of copulating. Seeing one's future parents lying together, the bardo being is filled with desire. If it is to be reborn as a male, it feels strong attraction toward its future mother and hatred for its future father; if it is to be reborn as a female, it will feel desire for its future father and hatred toward its future mother. Experiencing an overwhelming sense of desire, it rushes toward the copulating partners, but its lust is so strong that it only sees the sexual organ of the person toward whom it is drawn. The bardo being also wishes to displace the other person: if it is to be reborn as a male, it wants to displace the father and copulate with the mother, and if it is to be a female, it wants to displace the mother and copulate with the father. Since a bardo body is unable to accomplish this, it feels a strong sense of anger and rage, which brings about the end of the bardo state and causes it to be reborn.

The bardo being now enters the mother's womb and begins a new life. When the father's semen mingles with the mother's ovum, consciousness enters the zygote that is produced. The Dalai Lama states that

> one is desirously attracted to one's future birthplace, even if it is to be a hell. For instance, a butcher might see sheep in the distance as in a dream; upon his rushing there to kill them, the appearance would fade, causing him to become angry, whereupon the intermediate state would cease and his new life in a hell begin . . . . in the end, one rushes to the place of rebirth and, when one's wish is not achieved, one gets angry, whereupon the intermediate state ceases and the new life begins.[23]

Ordinary beings rush heedlessly toward their own suffering, not realizing the pitfalls their attitudes create for them. Feelings of desire, anger, resentment, and the like create the connection between lives and are responsible for making the final move from the bardo state to a new life. As long as one has such mental afflictions, one will continue to be reborn helplessly, pushed along by past actions and dispositions. Until one breaks this vicious cycle, one is like a prisoner: there is some possibility for movement in many cases, but one is still trapped by one's previous karma.

Tibetan Rituals of Death and Dying

In Tibetan Buddhist literature there are a variety of practices concerned with "caring for the dead" (*rje 'dzin*). These provide guidelines for how to prepare a person for death so that the death process will result either in a good rebirth or in liberation from cyclic existence. The state of mind of a dying person is vitally important in determining what sort of rebirth that person will have. If a person has strongly negative thoughts at the time of death—thoughts of anger, resentment, hatred, and so on—this can erase the effects of a lifetime of virtuous conduct and lead to a rebirth characterized by suffering. By contrast, a person who generates positive thoughts at the time of death can reverse a lifetime's negativities and bring about a better rebirth. Of course, it is best to engage in religious practice throughout one's life, since this sort of training is more likely to be effective at the time of death, but if one has failed to take advantage of life's opportunities, death presents a new range of possibilities.

In addition to potential advantages, death also holds many pitfalls which must be carefully avoided. It is important to guard one's thoughts at the time of death, since these have a strong effect on future rebirth. Even apparently innocuous thoughts and desires can have very negative consequences: for instance, a person who loses bodily warmth while dying might have a strong wish for heat, which can generate predispositions for rebirth in a hot hell. These feelings can make a very hot place seem attractive, and so the dying person may inadvertently end up in a place of extreme heat and suffer as a result. Similarly, a dying person might yearn for coolness or a drink of cool water, which could lead to rebirth in a cold hell. Any sort of desirous thought can have negative consequences, and a dying person should strive to avoid them and to focus the mind on religious images, concepts, and motivations.

Dying persons should be helped to relax, since tension and discomfort can easily lead to negative emotions. In addition, surrounding the dying person with religious images and chanting mantras and prayers into her ear can help turn the mind toward positive thoughts. Religious images are said to have a calming effect on the mind, and they prompt positive associations for devout Buddhists.

Mantras of buddhas (such as *oṃ maṇi padme hūṃ*, the mantra of Avalokiteśvara) are particularly effective, since they help either to create or strengthen a karmic link between the buddha invoked by the mantra and the dying person. They are even more powerful if the person to whom they are recited is a Buddhist with strong faith, since hearing them can spark feelings of devotion in the dying person's mind, thus leading to more positive thoughts. If a person is a religious practitioner who has a root lama, reciting the name mantra of the lama is particularly effective, since it should induce feelings of love and devotion toward the lama. A religious practitioner should see the lama as being inseparable from the buddha, and so hearing the name of the lama at the time of death should awaken strongly positive associations.

After a person has died, there are still further opportunities to influence the course of her future rebirth. Giving a dead person's possessions to the poor and needy leads to good karma, and any prayers that are said on behalf of the deceased can positively influence the bardo process. If her lama performs ceremonies on her behalf, this will be particularly powerful because of the strong karmic connection that exists between a lama and a disciple. In addition, parents, siblings, friends, and relatives should offer prayers, since they also have strong links to the deceased.

Tibetan Burial Practices

In Tibetan communities, three methods of disposal of corpses are practiced: (1) "sky burial"; (2) cremation; and (3) ground burial. The last is rarely performed, and the second is generally reserved for incarnate lamas or religious leaders who become recognized as spiritually advanced. The most common method of disposal of the dead is sky burial, which is a ritual that seems particularly strange to many Westerners. In this practice, the body of the deceased is cut up and offered to vultures as a final act of charity.

There are cases in which people who die are buried, but this generally only happens when a person dies of a virulent disease (such as leprosy or smallpox), because the corpse is considered unfit for sky burial. Corpses of people killed by weapons are often thrown into rivers. There are very good pragmatic reasons why Tibetans avoid burying people in the ground, apart from the Buddhist motivations of generosity involved in the sky burial: the soil of Tibet is very rocky in many areas, making the digging of graves difficult, and the long winters of Tibet make burial impossible for much of the year in many places. Cremation is also not practical in much of Tibet due to the scarcity of wood, and so sky burial is a pragmatic solution that also accords with Buddhist ideas of charity.

The process of sky burial is handled by specialists called *rogyapa*s ("body cutters"). An astrologer is generally consulted in order to determine the most auspicious time for disposal of the corpse. The deceased's birth date and time of death are the primary determining factors. The astrologer also decides whether or not any special rituals are required before burial can safely take place. These are for the benefit of the deceased and his or her family, since a close relative's death can threaten relatives.

After all the rituals and ceremonies to help the deceased through the intermediate state have been performed, the rogyapas take the corpse to a place reserved for sky burial. Monks are hired to wash it and chant prayers for the benefit of the deceased. Washing the body is said to make it more attractive to vultures, and it is a bad omen if they refuse to eat its flesh. In order to make it more palatable, the corpse is washed in a tub made of iron, wood, or copper, filled with warm water scented with saffron, camphor, or other perfumes. Soap is generally not used, and after bathing the body is dried with a clean towel.

The corpse is generally wrapped in a robe, except for the head, which is uncovered. It is carried on a palanquin (or sometimes a wooden table) borne by close friends and relatives. At dawn of the day determined by the astrologer, the body is carried to the burial ground. The sky burial usually takes place within a few days after the deceased is considered dead according to tantric medical theory. The corpse often has an initiation collar and a crown signifying the five meditation buddhas,[24] and each of the bearers and other helpers places a ceremonial silk scarf on the body. Incense is burned in the house where the deceased passed away as a way of purifying it.

The burial process begins when a tantric master marks a maṇḍala on the chest and stomach of the corpse, after which rogyapas cut across the chest with large knives in accordance with the master's instructions. They then remove the internal organs and slice flesh from bone. Next the bones are beaten with stone hammers and mixed with barley flour (*tsampa*) in order to make them more palatable to the vultures, which by this time have generally gathered in anticipation.

The feeding of the birds usually takes place in an area of flat rock called a *maṇḍala*. The rogyapas wait until a sufficient amount of flesh and bones has been prepared to feed all the vultures that appear (in order that they not begin fighting among themselves and thus cause each other injury). The corpse is tied down in order to prevent the vultures from carrying it off before this. Then the rogyapas begin tossing pieces of flesh into the maṇḍala, where the vultures eagerly consume them. One rogyapa generally has the task of keeping the hungry vultures at bay with a long rope, which he swings around in order to prevent them from entering the maṇḍala until the proper time.

When the flesh and bone have been disposed of, the tantric master takes the skull of the deceased and inserts a long needle into the "Brahmā opening" at the top, allowing the consciousness to escape (if it has not already done so). Then the skull is smashed and the brains and skull are fed to the vultures. After the disposal of the corpse is complete, the house of the deceased is cleaned and the bricks on which the corpse rested are thrown into a river or taken far away. The house is then fumigated with incense, and often monks are brought in to chant the text of the *Perfection of Wisdom in 8,000 Lines*. After this there are traditional ceremonies offered at regular intervals for the benefit of the deceased.

The somewhat gruesome ceremony of sky burial is full of significance for Tibetan Buddhists, since it graphically illustrates the impermanence of human life and the certainty of death. Burials performed out in the open serve as a reminder to everyone that this is the final fate of all ordinary beings. This sort of funeral is more difficult to deny or avoid than those found in Western societies, and it is meant to wake people up to the imminence of death. In addition, it illustrates the cyclic nature of life, since the return of one's body to the environment—something that Western mortuary practices try to hide—is enacted for all to see. A Buddhist watching this process should be moved toward thoughts of impermanence, uplifted by the final act of generosity of the deceased, and impelled to stronger effort in pursuit of awakening, since the burial process shows what inevitably comes to those who remain in cyclic existence.

Notes

1. See *The Life of Milarepa*, tr. Lobsang Lhalungpa (New York: Arkana, 1984), p. 119.
2. Dr. Richard Kalish, "Some Varieties of Death Attitudes," in *Death and Identity*, ed. Robert Fulton (New York: Wiley, 1965). Quoted in Glenn Mullin, *Death and Dying: The Tibetan Tradition* (Boston: Arkana, 1986), p. 4.
3. Chagdud Tulku Rinpoche, *Life in Relation to Death* (Cottage Grove, OR: Padma Publishing, 1987), p. 8.
4. For a description of dream yoga, see the "Six Yogas of Nāropa" portion of chapter 13, "Kagyu."
5. *Death and Dying: The Tibetan Tradition*, p. 128.
6. A description of some of the techniques for prolonging life can be found in *Death and Dying: The Tibetan Tradition*, pp. 149–172. For a Tibetan Buddhist perspective on the use of extraordinary medical means to prolong life, see John Powers, "Withdrawal of Care from Terminally Ill Patients: A Tibetan Buddhist Perspective," *Medical Journal of Australia*, 183(10), 2005, pp. 616–621.
7. Chapter 4, "Mahāyāna," discusses the "three bodies."
8. This is the faculty that allows the eye to perceive objects. Each of the other senses has a similar faculty, which enables it to perform its function.
9. *Kindness, Clarity, and Insight*, p. 173.
10. Lati Rinbochay and Jeffrey Hopkins, *Death, Intermediate State, and Rebirth in Tibetan Buddhism* (Ithaca: Snow Lion, 1979), pp. 10–11.
11. Ibid., p. 9.
12. Ibid., p. 31.
13. *Kindness, Clarity, and Insight*, p. 176.
14. Ibid., p. 176.
15. Ibid., p. 177.
16. See Khenpo Könchog Gyaltsen, *In Search of the Stainless Ambrosia*, p. 106.
17. *Kindness, Clarity, and Insight*, p. 179.
18. These are described in the "Kagyu" chapter in the section on the six yogas of Nāropa.
19. These are described in detail in the classic work on the subject, *Liberation Through Hearing in the Intermediate State (Bar do thos grol)*, attributed to Padmasambhava and discovered by the famed "discoverer of secret treasures" *(gter ston)* Karma Lingpa (ca. fourteenth century). See the translation by W.Y. Evans-Wentz (*The Tibetan Book of the Dead* [London: Oxford University Press, 1957]), pp. 101–152, and the translation by Francesca Fremantle and Chögyam Trungpa of the same title (Berkeley and London: Shambhala, 1975), pp. 41–71.
20. Chökyi Nyima Rinpoche, *The Bardo Guidebook* (Hong Kong: Rangjung Yeshe, 1991), p. 120.
21. Tulku Thondup Rinpoche, tr., *Buddha Mind: An Anthology of Longchen Rabjam's Writings on Dzogpa Chenpo* (Ithaca: Snow Lion, 1989), p. 368.
22. *The Bardo Guidebook*, p. 119.
23. *Death, Intermediate State, and Rebirth*, pp. 10–11.
24. These are Akṣobhya, Vairocana, Ratnasambhava, Amitābha, and Amoghasiddhi.

PART FOUR

THE ORDERS OF TIBETAN BUDDHISM

11: The Four Orders

ADHERENTS of the four main orders of Tibetan Buddhism —Nyingma, Kagyu, Sakya, and Géluk—tend to emphasize the differences that distinguish them, but much more striking is how much they share in common. The following chapters contain short overviews of important events in the history of each order, synopses of the religious biographies of some major figures, their philosophical systems, and their distinctive meditative practices.

Readers will see a number of themes recurring in these sections, such as the importance of overcoming attachment to the phenomena of cyclic existence and the idea that it is necessary for trainees to develop an attitude of sincere renunciation. Another important point of agreement lies in rules of monastic discipline: all orders of Tibetan Buddhism follow the vinaya of the Mūla-Sarvāstivāda school, which has been the standard in Tibetan monasteries since the founding of the first monastic institution at Samyé. In addition, they also share the same corpus of philosophical and liturgical texts imported from India, and all four orders present a path to awakening that incorporates practices of sūtra and tantra systems.

They also share some common assumptions about the doctrines and practices they inherited from India. It is generally agreed that the Buddha provided divergent dispensations for various types of trainees, and these have been codified by Tibetan doxographers, who categorize Buddha's teachings in terms of three distinct vehicles—the Lesser Vehicle (Hīnayāna), the Great Vehicle (Mahāyāna), and the Vajra Vehicle (Vajrayāna)—each of which was intended to appeal to the spiritual capacities of particular groups. Hīnayāna was presented to people intent on personal salvation in which one transcends suffering and is liberated from cyclic existence. The audience of Mahāyāna teachings included trainees with the capacity to feel compassion for the sufferings of others who wished to seek awakening in order to help sentient beings overcome their sufferings. Vajrayāna practitioners had a strong interest in the welfare of others, coupled with determination to attain awakening as quickly as possible, and the spiritual capacity to pursue the difficult practices of tantra.

Indian Buddhism is also commonly divided by Tibetan exegetes of the four orders into four main schools of tenets—Great Exposition School, Sūtra School, Mind Only School, and Middle Way School. Each of these is associated with particular teaching lineages, texts, doctrines, and practices, and all are thought to have value for particular people and in particular contexts.[1] Moreover, although the classification scheme is a hierarchical one, none of the practices and doctrines is disparaged, since all are thought to have been taught by Buddha and to be conducive to spiritual progress. As a result, all four orders of Tibetan Buddhism incorporate elements of the three vehicles and the four tenet systems in their philosophical systems and meditative practices. Their curriculums reflect this eclectic approach, and students in Tibetan monastic schools generally study a wide range of Buddhist texts and learn the tenets of the four Indian philosophical schools, along with the practices and teachings of the three vehicles.

All four Tibetan orders agree on the basic outline of the path to be followed to escape from cyclic existence and the sorts of practices that one should adopt. All share a Mahāyāna orientation, and so they agree that the path begins with the generation of the mind of awakening and progresses through the bodhisattva levels, during which one cultivates the six (or ten) perfections. It is assumed by members of the four orders that Vajrayāna is the supreme of all Buddhist paths, although there are differences between them regarding which tantras they favor and which lineages they follow. The Nyingma order, for instance, emphasizes the "great perfection" (*rdzogs chen;* pronounced "dzogchen"), and its tantric practices are mainly based on the so-called "Old Tantras" (such as the *Secret Basic Essence Tantra*) and on instructions found in "hidden treasures" (*gter ma;* pronounced "terma"). The Kagyupas emphasize the *mahāmudrā* system inherited from the Indian master Tilopa, and its tantric practices are mainly derived from the *Guhyasamāja Tantra* and the *Cakrasaṃvara Tantra.* The Gélukpa system of tantric theory and practice is based on the *Guhyasamāja Tantra*, the

Cakrasaṃvara Tantra, and the *Kālacakra Tantra*. The Sakyapas favor the *Hevajra Tantra*, which is the basis of their "path and fruit" (*lam 'bras;* pronounced "lamdré") system.[2]

Each order traces its lineage to particular Indian masters. There are distinctive differences in their actual tantric practices, but despite these differences there are many points of commonality. This has been noted by the Dalai Lama, who states that the philosophical view of all orders is that of the Middle Way School of Nāgārjuna, and in terms of practice all follow the program of Mahāyāna (which he refers to as the "bodhisattva vehicle"). In addition, their paths and tenets incorporate the systems of the sūtras and tantras in their entirety, and so he concludes that all of them are equally effective programs for bringing sentient beings to liberation.

> In Tibet, due to differences in the time of translation of texts from India and the development of lineages formed by particular teachers, eight distinct schools of Buddhism arose. Nowadays, four are widely known, Nyingma, Sakya, Kagyu, and Gelugpa. From the point of view of their tenets, they are all Mādhyamika. From the point of view of their vehicle, they are all of the Bodhisattvayāna. In addition, these four schools are all complete systems of unified Sūtra and Tantra practice, each having the techniques and quintessential instructions necessary for a person to achieve Buddhahood within one lifetime. Yet each has its own distinguishing features of instruction.[3]

If one compares the four orders of Tibetan Buddhism to Theravāda Buddhism, or to Chinese, Japanese, or Korean schools, the disparities are more pronounced. This is a result of important differences in their respective histories of transmission of Buddhism, and the style of practice and teaching in each country is reflective of this history, as well as cultural and linguistic factors and subsequent political and religious developments.

Tibetan Buddhists share a common heritage that came to them from the great scholastic institutions of northern India during the period of the dissemination of Buddhism to Tibet and the *siddha* lineages that mainly centered in Bihar and Bengal, combined with cultural factors that influenced later developments. At the time of the early transmission of Buddhism to Tibet, the philosophical views of Nāgārjuna and the Madhyamaka school were dominant, and one finds that all four orders of Tibetan Buddhism hold this to be the supreme of all philosophical views. In terms of practice, many of the influential masters who came to Tibet viewed Vajrayāna as the supreme of all Buddhist teachings and practices, and so it is not surprising that Tibetan Buddhism also regards it in this way.

This is not the case in other Buddhist traditions. In Theravāda countries, for example, tantric practices and techniques were introduced and enjoyed brief popularity in some areas, but were eventually eclipsed. In China Vajrayāna was influential during the seventh and eighth centuries, but was later absorbed into other traditions. During this time Japanese monks (most famously Kūkai and Saichō) traveled to China and brought back tantric lineages, but the Shingon school founded by Kūkai is today one of the smallest orders in Japan, and the Tendai school incorporates tantric practices as part of an eclectic range of influences. In Japan, tantric schools tend to emphasize rituals and ceremonies, and not the distinctive yogas of highest yoga tantra, which are the central Vajrayāna practices in Tibetan Buddhism.

In Tibet, the dominant form of religious practice is the tantric Buddhism inherited from India, and there is also a high degree of compatibility in the philosophical views of the four orders. Particularly important is their agreement on the nature of the mind, since mental training is the focus of the Buddhist path as practiced in Tibet. All four orders agree that the mind is of the nature of clear light. All posit various levels of consciousness that are differentiated in terms of relative coarseness or subtlety, and all agree that the most subtle and basic level of mind is of the nature of pure luminosity and emptiness. They have different terms for it and different ways of realizing it, but, as the Dalai Lama states,

> this innate fundamental mind of clear light is emphasized equally in the Highest Yoga Tantra systems of the New Translation Schools[4] and in the Nying-ma system of the Great Perfection and is the proper place of comparison of the old and new schools.[5]

Teachers of the four orders also agree on the role of the mind in perpetuating cyclic existence and in the attainment of liberation. All teach that the ordinary mind acts under the influence of afflictive emotions and misconceptions. These cause people to engage in negative deeds, which then rebound on those who commit them. The process is maintained by the nature of the mind itself, which tends to repeat patterns of behavior with which it is familiar. So if one regularly falls into anger, for example, one becomes progressively more habituated to this emotion, and it becomes easier to generate angry thoughts. By contrast, if one trains in compassion and love, one will become progressively habituated to them and manifest them spontaneously.

In the practices of highest yoga tantra that are found in the New Translation orders, one cultivates the awareness that the mind is of a nature of luminosity and bliss and that all mental defilements are adventitious and not a part of the nature of mind. The same is true of the *dzogchen* system (the supreme teaching in the Nyingma order), which takes this insight as the key element of its program of meditative training. In both systems, one learns to view phenomena as the creative sport of mind, and thoughts are perceived as arising from emptiness and again merging into emptiness. The Dalai Lama contends that all four orders train in this insight, and that

> if one can cause all these phenomena to appear as the sport of the basic mind within not deviating from the sphere of that mind, one does not come under the influence of conventional conceptions. When we identify our own basic entity ourselves and directly ascertain its meaning continuously and forever in meditative equipoise, then even though acting in the world, we are Buddhas.[6]

As the brief overviews presented in the following chapters will indicate, this sums up the core meditative practices of all four orders of Tibetan Buddhism. Each has its own distinctive ways of leading trainees toward buddhahood, and each has developed characteristic styles and terminology, but all of them share fundamental assumptions about the path and about Buddhist doctrine. More importantly, as the Dalai Lama argues, all can demonstrate that their methods have succeeded in producing outstanding meditators who embody the highest ideals of Tibetan Buddhism and whose lives and teachings stand as testaments to the effectiveness of the systems of each of the four orders.

The Nonsectarian Movement

In spite of the many similarities in view and practice among the traditions of Tibetan Buddhism, sectarian controversy has been a recurring feature in Tibet since earliest times. Every order has produced scathing attacks on its perceived rivals, and the history of Tibetan Buddhism is marked by oral debates between competing groups as well as persecutions and factional wars. In the late nineteenth century, several prominent lamas in eastern Tibet began a countermovement, commonly referred to as "Nonsectarian" (*Ris med*; pronounced "Rimé"). It was a direct challenge to the scholastic approach of the Gélukpa order, whose educational system mainly relies on textbooks (*yig cha*) that summarize key philosophical and doctrinal points. The definitions (*mtshan nyid*) they contain are derived from Indian "root texts"; these are memorized by students and form the basis of their curriculum and examinations.

The Nonsectarian lamas, by contrast, required their students to study Indian *sūtras* and philosophical texts, and much of the Nonsectarian literature consists of original commentaries on them. The philosophical basis of most Nonsectarian lamas is the "other-emptiness" (*gzhan stong*) view, which posits a self-existent ultimate reality that can only be understood by direct meditative perception. Another important aspect of Rimé is the vision of the great perfection developed by the "treasure discoverer" (*gter ston*) Jikmé Lingpa (1730–1798). His revelation of the *Heart Essence of Longchenpa* cycle of practice is one of the foundational sources of the movement.

His reincarnation Jamyang Khyentsé Ongbo (1820–1892) became one of the leading figures in the Nonsectarian movement. Like other Nonsectarian lamas, he advocated a universalist approach to Buddhist teachings, according to which all were said to have value for particular practitioners. Students were encouraged to study extensively in various traditions, and as Gene Smith has pointed out, one of the key features of the movement was an encyclopedic orientation.[7] Nonsectarian lamas produced a number of compendia of Buddhist learning, most notably Jamgön Kongtrül's (1813–1899) *Compendium of All Knowledge.* Unlike some scholars of his time, who focused on certain works they regarded as normative and rejected others, Kongtrül and his students traveled throughout Tibet searching for texts, initiations, and oral lineages—both those that were widely popular and others that were obscure and local—and brought them together in huge collections. Contrary to those who claimed that one approach was superior to all others, they sought to make available as many teachings and practices as possible so that students could choose those that were most effective. Their sources were not limited to religious or philosophical texts, and they incorporated folk traditions and popular literature, including such classics as the *Epic of Gésar of Ling.*[8]

By contrast, the Gélukpa scholars of the time tended to reiterate the paradigms that had been handed down to them and to engage in rote and unoriginal scholarship. There were some notable and original scholars among the Gélukpas, but the main monasteries of the order were generally bastions of dogmatic conservatism, and authors of the time mainly composed textbooks that elaborated on definitions and debates found in earlier texts. Many of these laid out possible debates and counterarguments in great detail, and these were memorized by students. They provided set refutations against potential opponents, and so students learned to simply identify a mistaken view and apply the appropriate label rather than examining philosophical positions on their own merits. The Rimé masters, however, urged their students to look at the Indic root texts and to take in the oral instructions of a variety of teachers in order to become acquainted with a range of perspectives. The emphasis was on direct understanding rather than repetition of established "correct" positions.

The Gélukpa tradition following Tsong Khapa sought to sift through texts, doctrines, practices, and opinions and discern the most philosophically cogent or normative ones. These were encoded in set definitions and debates, which were memorized by students. The Nonsectarian lamas took an eclectic approach that valued the multitude of tantric practices and lineages as suited to the proclivities of certain practitioners. Thus Jamyang Khyentsé Ongbo—a Sakya lama who also practiced the Nyingma great perfection—and Jamgön Kongtrül, a Kagyupa, gathered tantric lineages from Nyingma, Sakya, Kagyyu, Kadam, Jonang, and other sources. Kongtrül and his students compiled them in large collections. When the texts, empowerments, and oral instructions from various sources had been incorporated in one individual, he or she could then pass on the whole range of what they had received to students.[9]

The Nonsectarian masters took a similarly open approach to religious practice. Many of the main figures of the tradition were nonmonastics, and some of the treatises associated with the movement disparage monks as plodding dogmatists of limited intelligence. Some Nonsectarian lamas moved between the state of ordination and that of lay tantrics (*sngags pa*), but others maintained monastic vows throughout their lives. The general attitude of Rimé practitioners was one that recognized the potential value of different modes of practice and lifestyles and that refused to categorically regard one as superior to another in all circumstances.

In keeping with its nondogmatic approach, the Nonsectarian movement was not a distinct school with fixed doctrines, nor did it create a distinctive monastic order with its own institutions. Instead, its proponents maintained allegiance to their own lineages, but adopted elements from the various Buddhist traditions available to them. No one approach to Buddhist doctrine and practice was dogmatically asserted, and the essence of the movement was an openness to different approaches.

Like Jikmé Lingpa, many of the great Rimé masters came from nonaristocratic backgrounds, and generally shunned institutional Buddhism. Because of the emphasis on lineage, there is generally a particularly close bond between lamas and students. Retreats are a core element of the tradition, and students are often guided by their teachers for extended periods of practice in solitude. The literature of Rimé emphasizes the beneficial results of long retreats and the importance of regular engagement in solitary meditation. Not surprisingly given this emphasis, biographies of the luminaries of the tradition emphasize visions, trances, revelations, and oral instructions. Many of the prominent Nonsectarian lamas were also treasure-discoverers, and disclosures of new "hidden treasures" are an important aspect of its history.

Most contemporary lamas of the non-Gélukpa traditions are directly influenced by this important movement, and many of its practices have also found their way into the Gélukpa order. One key difference between Nonsectarian traditions and the Gélukpas is the doctrine of other-emptiness, which is a cornerstone of most Rimé practice, but is staunchly rejected by the Gélukpas. (Not all Rimé masters hold to this view, however; Mipam is a prominent example of a Rimé lama who adhered to the self-emptiness view.)

Other-Emptiness

As we have seen, the doctrine of emptiness figures prominently in Indian and Tibetan Buddhist thought. Questions regarding how emptiness should be interpreted have been a major source of debate between the various orders of Tibetan Buddhism, and they continue to generate controversy today.

The two most influential factions advocate respectively the doctrines of "other-emptiness" (*gzhan stong*; pronounced "shendong") and "self-emptiness" (*rang stong*; pronounced "rangdong"). The latter position is held by the Gélukpa order, which follows the interpretation of Madhyamaka developed by Tsong Khapa. He contended that emptiness is a "nonaffirming negative," meaning that it is simply a radical denial of inherent existence (*rang bzhin, svabhāva*), a quality falsely attributed to phenomena by ordinary beings. From the perspective of an ignorant consciousness, phenomena appear to exist by themselves and are not viewed as composites of smaller parts created by causes and conditions and subject to decay, and persons appear to possess enduring selves that are independent of the vicissitudes of birth, death, and change. The Gélukpas deny that there is any enduring substance and hold that all phenomena are collections of parts that are constantly changing due to the influence of causes and conditions.

According to the other-emptiness interpretation, emptiness is the ultimate truth and is conceived as a self-existent, unchanging reality that pervades all phenomena. It is empty of what is other than itself—that is, the mistaken perceptions attributed to it by deluded beings.[10] But it is not void of itself, since it is the final nature of all phenomena. The emptiness of the Gélukpas is said to be "dead emptiness" (*bem stong*) because it would be a state devoid of any qualities. Proponents of other-emptiness claim that it is in fact the repository of all the qualities of buddhahood and is inherent in all beings. It cannot be known by logic or conceptuality, and is only realized by advanced yogis through direct, nonconceptual insight. The Gélukpas denounce this position as an attempt to reify the Absolute and smuggle Indian substantialist notions into Buddhism.

One of the key debates between the Gélukpas and their opponents who advocate the "other-emptiness" position concerns how the doctrine of the "womb of the *tathāgata*" (*de bzhin gzhegs pa'i snying po, tathāgata-garbha*) should be understood. This notion, found in some Indian Buddhist texts, holds that all sentient beings have the potential to become buddhas. Advocates of other-emptiness conceive of this potential as a positive, self-existent essence that pervades all existence and is made manifest through meditative training, but is not created by it.

Buddhahood is the basic nature of mind, and it is subtle, ineffable, and beyond the grasp of conceptual thought. It cannot be described in words, and can only be understood through direct experience. According to this position, all phenomena are of the nature of mind, which is a union of luminosity and emptiness. They have no substantial existence, and merely exist within the continuum of mind. Initiations by Rimé masters—particularly those who belong to the Nyingma and Kagyu orders, which emphasize the formless meditations of the great completion (*dzogchen*) and great seal (*mahāmudrā*) respectively—commonly feature oral instructions in which lamas "point out the nature of mind" to students, who are then instructed to cultivate a direct apprehension of this reality themselves. Those who succeed in grasping the nature of mind and perceiving all phenomena as emanations of luminosity and emptiness are able to attain buddhahood in a single instant of awakening.

The Gélukpas follow the Indian gradualist tradition, which holds that the path to buddhahood consists in progressively perfecting the matrix of good qualities that characterize awakened beings. This is accomplished during many lifetimes of arduous training, during which meditators follow a step-by-step approach and progressively rid themselves of negative propensities while simultaneously acquiring deeper insight and qualities like generosity, ethics, and patience, which they did not have when they began the path. According to this interpretation, *tathāgata-garbha* should be understood as being equivalent to emptiness, conceived as a nonaffirming negative. It is another way of expressing the idea that beings lack any enduring essence, and so they have the ability to effect changes in their psychophysical continuums. If they choose to follow the Buddhist path, they can move toward buddhahood because there is no self, soul, or essence that endures from moment to moment.

NOTES

1. These classifications are the focus of an extensive literature in Tibetan, and a discussion of the details exceeds the limits of this study. For further information, see Katsumi Mimaki, *Blo gsal grub mtha'* (Kyoto: Université de Kyoto, 1982), Geshe Lhundup Sopa and Jeffrey Hopkins, *Cutting Through Appearances* (Ithaca: Snow Lion, 1989), Jeffrey Hopkins, *Meditation on Emptiness* (London: Wisdom, 1983), pp. 305–697, and Dudjom Rinpoche, *The Nyingma Order of Tibetan Buddhism,* pp. 151–237.
2. Each order also has particular deities that are featured in its tantric practices. Nyingma, for example, favors practices associated with Avalokiteśvara, Mañjuśrī, Vajrapāṇi, Green Tārā, Red Tārā, White Tārā, Vajrasattva, and Padmasambhava. Kagyu emphasizes practices associated with Avalokiteśvara, Mañjuśrī, Vajrapāṇi, Green Tārā, Bhaiṣajyaguru, Vajrayoginī, and Heruka Cakrasaṃvara. Sakya focuses on practices associated with Avalokiteśvara, Mañjuśrī, Vajrapāṇi, Green and White Tārā, and Hevajra. Géluk favors practices associated with Avalokiteśvara, Mañjuśrī, Vajrapāṇi, Green and White Tārā, Bhaiṣajyaguru, Guhyasamāja, Yamāntaka, Heruka Cakrasaṃvara, Vajrayoginī, and Kālacakra. The different Tārās are considered to be individual emanations of the same buddha, each of which is manifested with a particular skin color.

3. H.H. the Dalai Lama, Tenzin Gyatso, "Talk of His Holiness the Dalai Lama at the Nyingma Institute," *Gesar* 6.3, 1980, p. 4.
4. The New Translation orders are the Kagyu, Sakya, and Géluk, who base their philosophical systems and practices on the translations that were prepared according to the rules and standards developed during the period of the second dissemination of Buddhism into Tibet (see chapter 5). The "old translations" are those prepared during the first dissemination, which began with the arrival of Padmasambhava and Śāntarakṣita in Tibet. These are favored by the Nyingma order.
5. *Kindness, Clarity, and Insight*, p. 208.
6. Ibid., p. 213.
7. E. Gene Smith, *Among Tibetan Texts: History and Literature of the Himalayan Plateau* (Boston: Wisdom Publications, 2001), pp. 227–272. The term *Rimé* is sometimes rendered as "eclectic" by contemporary scholars, but the products and teachings of this tradition indicate that this is inappropriate. David Seyfort Ruegg points out that *Rimé* is more encyclopedic or universalistic than eclectic. *Ris med* is the antonym of *ris su chad pa*, and so it has connotations of being unbounded, all-embracing, and impartial ("A Tibetan's Odyssey: A Review Article," *Journal of the Royal Asiatic Society*, 1989, 2, p. 310.
8. The Gésar epic was particularly important for Mipam, who wrote several works based on the legends of the mythical hero, including a number of rituals focusing on him as a deity associated with longevity
9. See Geoffrey Samuel, *Civilized Shamans*, pp. 533–543.
10. This doctrine was initially propounded in Tibet by the Jonangpa thinker Dolpopa Shérap Gyeltsen (1292–1361). A good overview of his life and thought, along with his responses to critics, can be found in Cyrus Stearns, *The Buddha from Dolpo: A Study of the Life and Thought of The Tibetan Master Dolpopa Sherab Gyaltsen* (Albany: State University of New York Press, 1999). See also David S. Ruegg, *Buddha-Nature, Mind, and the Problem of Gradualism in a Comparative Perspective* (London: School of Oriental and African Studies, 1989) and S.K. Hookham, *The Buddha Within* (Albany: State University of New York Press, 1991).

12: Nyingma

History and Doctrines

The Nyingma order has the longest established history of transmission of all of the four major traditions of Tibetan Buddhism. This is reflected in the name *Nyingma* (*rNying ma*), which literally means "Old Order." The other three main schools of Tibetan Buddhism—Sakya, Kagyu, and Géluk—are collectively referred to as *Sarma* (*gSar ma*), or "New Orders," because they rely on the Tibetan translations of Indian Buddhist texts that were prepared under the system established during the period of the second dissemination of Buddhism into Tibet.

Nyingma primarily relies on the old translations, particularly of tantric texts, and its Tibetan origins are traced to Buddhist pioneers of the time of King Tri Songdétsen. Because of this, it is also called the "Old Translation Order" (*sNga 'gyur*). This school's preference for the early translations is due to the feeling of many Nyingma teachers that although the newer translations are often more technically polished, the early translations were prepared by realized masters whose own spiritual attainments guided their work. Thus, these editions are thought to more closely capture the spirit of the Indian texts than the later ones, which are not as reliable because their authors were more concerned with technical accuracy than with transmitting the spirit of the awakened experience of the Indian masters who revealed or composed the texts.

According to Nyingma lineage histories, the original teacher of the doctrines that came to be associated with the Old Order was Samantabhadra (Güntu Sangpo), who is the "primordial buddha" (*dang po'i sang rgyas, ādibuddha*) and who embodies the truth body of all buddhas. In discussing the place of Samantabhadra in the Nyingma tradition, Dudjom Rinpoche indicates that this buddha is

> the teacher in whom both saṃsāra and nirvāṇa are indivisible, the antecedent of all, who holds sway over existence and quiescence in their entirety, and who is the expanse of reality and the nucleus of the sugata [buddha]. Thus buddhahood is attained in the naturally present pristine cognition, without thoughts of the three times, beginning, middle, and end, or of all else that can be known.[1]

Nyingma also identifies Vajradhara (an emanation of Samantabhadra)[2] and the buddhas of the five buddha families as the original promulgators of many of its teachings and practices.[3] These are complete enjoyment bodies, whose teachings are primarily adapted to the cognitive capacities of very advanced practitioners.

In addition to these exalted figures, this lineage also has a succession of distinguished human teachers, the most important of whom is Padmasambhava, the north Indian tantric yogi who according to traditional histories was instrumental in the introduction of Buddhism into Tibet. Because of their strong links to Padmasambhava—as well as other eminent first dissemination teachers like Vimalamitra, Vairocana and Śāntarakṣita—the Nyingmapas feel that their lineage represents the most authentic and complete teachings of the early masters who brought Buddhism to the Land of Snows.

Lineages of Translations and Texts

Nyingmapas trace the beginning of their translation lineage to Samyé, the first monastic center in Tibet. According to traditional histories, over one hundred scholars and translators congregated there in order to translate the sūtras and tantras. The tantric master Buddhaguhya is said to have trained two of the most important of these, Bé Jambel and Drenka Mukti, at his hermitage on Mt. Kailash. Buddhaguhya had been invited to Tibet during the time of King Tri Détsuktsen (r. 710–755), but instead opted to instruct disciples who then returned to Tibet with his teachings, which they used to guide their translations.

Nyingma tradition contains a complex array of intersecting lineages, including lineages of transmission of vinaya teachings and practices, sūtras, tantras, "hidden treasures" (*terma*), and so on. Of crucial importance for Nyingma masters is the "teaching" (*bka' ma*) tradition, which begins with Samantabhadra and consists of doctrines, texts, practices, rituals, and realizations that have been passed on from master to disciple in an unbroken chain. It is divided into three main groups: (1) apparitional (*sgyu*), which consists of the eighteen tantric cycles of great yoga (*rnal 'byor chen po, mahāyoga*), and for which the primary text is the *Secret Basic Essence Tantra;* (2) sūtra (*mdo*), which includes the subsequent yoga (*rjes su rnal 'byor, anuyoga*) practices and realizations, and for which the primary text is the *Collection Sūtra;* and (3) mind (*sems*), which includes the teachings of the great perfection.

All of these systems originate with Samantabhadra. As the primordial buddha, Samantabhadra embodies the essence of the awakened mind of all buddhas. He skillfully and spontaneously emanates teachings throughout all of space in ways that are appropriate to the spiritual capacities of sentient beings. He radiates a fivefold light that emanates from the sphere of reality (*chos nyid, dharmatā*) that represents a maṇḍala that is found throughout all aspects of space and time. He effortlessly disseminates teachings, which are entrusted to "knowledge bearers" (*rigs 'dzin, vidyādhara*), who pass on those that are appropriate to particular disciples. Initially they are imparted to Dorjé Chörap, the knowledge bearer of the complete enjoyment body realm. He gives them to the ḍākinī Légi Wangmoché and to Vajrasattva. These beings in turn instruct human adepts.

Transmission of the Teaching Tradition

Vajrasattva is credited with transmitting the teaching tradition to Garap Dorjé (b. 55 C.E.), the first human teacher in this tradition.[4] Garap Dorjé is an emanation body, and according to tradition he had three visions of Vajrasattva in which he received teachings. He perfectly penetrated their meaning, and then passed them on to Jambel Shé Nyen in the area of Trashi Trigo in China. Jambel Shé Nyen taught them to his student Śrī Siṃha (b. 289 C.E.), who in turn gave them to Vimalamitra in the cremation ground of Śītavana and to Jñānasūtra in Trashi Trigo. According to tradition, after they had completed their transmission of the teachings, Garap Dorjé, Jambel Shé Nyen, Śrī Siṃha, and Jñānasūtra transformed into bodies of light and disappeared without leaving a trace behind.

Vimalamitra continued the process of diffusion. Born in western India, he received a comprehensive education in Hīnayāna and Mahāyāna doctrines and studied with a number of teachers. After completing studies of sūtra, vinaya, and abhidharma, he began his education in tantra with Buddhaguhya. He later traveled to China to learn from Śrī Siṃha, with whom he studied for nine years. He received teaching in the inner, outer, and secret cycles of dzogchen. He later traveled widely, eventually coming to Oḍḍiyāna, where he taught King Indrabodhi. While in residence in Oḍḍiyāna, a delegation sent by King Tri Songdétsen of Tibet arrived to invite him to spread the dharma in the Land of Snows. The delegation consisted of Gawa Beltsek, Chokro Lügyeltsen, Ma Rinchen Chok, and other notable figures. They presented him with golden statues and gold dust, and he agreed to their request, despite King Indrabodhi's objections. According to traditional accounts, that night people across India dreamed that the sun, moon, trees, and crops were leaning toward Tibet, signifying that Vimalamitra's departure was a great loss for India.

When he arrived in Samyé, he was greeted by Tri Songdétsen, but the inauspicious signs accompanying his departure proved prophetic. Some of the king's ministers, jealous of Vimalamitra's stature, spread rumors that he was merely a black magician, which began to undermine the king's confidence in him. Vimalamitra silenced his critics with an act that demonstrated his yogic powers: sitting in meditation in the central courtyard of Samyé, he uttered a powerful mantra that shattered a statue of Vairocana. The ministers thought that this confirmed their misgivings about him, but then he restored the fragments into a more beautiful image of Vairocana. Radiant beams of light issued from the statue, filling the entire monastery, which allayed all doubts concerning Vimalamitra's character.

Tri Songdétsen recognized that Vimalamitra was a tantric master of a high level of spiritual attainment, and under the king's patronage he soon became involved in translating Sanskrit texts into Tibetan. Working with Tibetan scholars, he helped to translate and explain numerous sūtras, tantras, and commentaries. According to Nyingma tradition, Vimalamitra and his Tibetan collaborators were not ordinary people, but incarnate bodhisattvas who had taken rebirth in order to aid the transmission of dharma into Tibet. Vimalamitra remained in the country for thirteen years, during which he was active in teaching and translation. Many of his students in turn became important figures in the early history of Buddhism in Tibet and are revered by Nyingma tradition as key members of the lineage. Traditional accounts of his life state that he spent his later years in a mountain retreat in China called Riwo Tsé Nga ("Mountain with Five Peaks"), where he lived to well beyond the age of two hundred. Before his death, he predicted that he would reincarnate in every century for as long as the dharma remained in Tibet. The purpose of these incarnations would be to breathe new life into Tibetan Buddhism, and several of the recognized incarnations have played important roles in revitalizing the dharma. Among these are Longchen Rapjampa in the fourteenth century and Jikmé Lingpa in the eighteenth. The incarnational lineage continues, and tradition holds that it will do so until Buddhism is no longer practiced in Tibet.

Longchen Rapjampa is considered by Nyingma teachers to be one of the greatest figures in the tradition. A master of all aspects of Buddhist teachings and practices, he was both one of Tibet's great scholars and among its most renowned meditators. He transmitted the teachings he had received from his teachers and revitalized them through his writings and oral instructions. Some of the most renowned Nyingma lamas trace their lineages back to him. Among the great teachers who are spiritually descended from him are Orgyen Terdak Lingpa (1646–1714), Jikmé Lingpa (1730–1798), Patrul Rinpoché (b. 1808), Mipam (1848–1912), and the second Jamyang Khyentsé Ongbo (b. 1896). The Nyingma order continues to produce influential masters today, including the late Dudjom Rinpoche, Khetsun Sangpo Rinpoche, and Pema Norbu Rinpoche, who is currently the head of the Nyingma lineage.

Padmasambhava

By far the most influential of Nyingma teachers is Padmasambhava—known to Tibetans as "Guru Rinpoché"—who probably lived during the eighth century C.E. He received the teaching transmission from Jambel Shé Nyen and Garap Dorjé, and traditional histories report that his missionary work spread the lineage into Tibet. He is regarded by Nyingmapas as an emanation of the buddha Amitābha whose particular goal was to facilitate the dissemination of Buddhism in the crucial early period.

According to the biography written by his disciple Yéshé Tsogyel, many aspects of his early life closely paralleled similar events in the life of Śākyamuni Buddha. Like Śākyamuni, he had a miraculous birth in a small north Indian kingdom. Popular legends hold that he was born in the country of Oḍḍiyāna from the bud of a large, multicolored lotus that sprang up in the middle of a lake. On the lotus was a golden vajra marked with the syllable *hrīḥ* that had emanated from the heart of Amitābha. At the time of his birth, he already had the physical development of a child of eight years and had all the major and minor marks of a "great man." When the lotus opened, Padmasambhava was standing in the middle, holding in his hands a vajra and lotus. The name Padmasambhava means "born from a lotus."

Indrabodhi, the king of Oḍḍiyāna, had no son, and so he decided to adopt Padmasambhava. Like Śākyamuni, Padmasambhava grew up in a palace and learned the arts and sciences appropriate to princes. His adoptive father wanted him to follow in his footsteps and rule the kingdom, but Padmasambhava realized that such a life would be of little use to others, particularly in comparison to the great benefit he could accomplish through spreading the dharma.

He asked his father for permission to leave the palace and pursue a religious life, but the king refused. In order to convince Indrabodhi to let him leave, Padmasambhava performed a dance during which he pretended to fumble with a trident, which killed the son of a minister. This is referred to as a "liberation" rather than a killing, since Padmasambhava was able to effect the release of the minister's son through his yogic power. This was not recognized by the king or ministers, however, and as Padmasambhava had intended, he was exiled from the kingdom and ordered to live in cremation grounds.

Although this might seem like a harsh and oppressive punishment for an apparent accident, it suited Padmasambhava's purposes, because cremation grounds are favorite meditation spots for tantric adepts. During his exile he spent time in the cremation grounds of Śītavana, Nandanavana, and Sosadvīpa, and in each of these places he developed his tantric insight and powers, and he received teachings and initiations from ḍākinīs.

He then traveled to the island of Dhanakośa and the forest of Paruṣakavana, where he continued to meet ḍākinīs and enhance his insight and power. He next went to Vajrāsana (the place of Buddha's awakening) and then to the country of Sahor, where he encountered the teacher Prabhāhasti, from whom he received ordination. He studied the whole range of Buddhist literature and sciences, mastered the texts of exoteric and esoteric traditions, and became widely recognized for his spiritual prowess. He was given the teachings of the "eight classes of attainment" by the eight great knowledge bearers, the *Magical Net* teachings by Buddhaguhya, and instructions on the great perfection by Śrī Siṃha. At this point in his development he was able instantly to understand and memorize any teachings and texts, even after hearing them only once. He could perceive any deities without even propitiating them.

For several months he performed advanced tantric rites with his consort Mandāravā in a cave called Māratika. He cultivated longevity techniques and received empowerment directly from Amitāyus, the buddha of long life. Through this practice he attained the level of a knowledge bearer and gained complete control over the duration of his own life. Since through these practices his physical form was able to transcend birth and death, he became effectively immortal, and nothing could harm him without his allowing it. This proved to be a valuable attainment, because when he traveled to the kingdom of Sahor the king and his ministers attempted to immolate him. Through his tantric power he transformed the pyre into a lake of sesame oil, and he remained unharmed in the center of it, sitting on a lotus. The king and ministers were so impressed that they asked him to teach them the dharma.

He next traveled to Oḍḍiyana in the guise of a beggar, but the inhabitants recognized him as the banished prince, and the minister whose son he had slain tried to have him and his consort burned on a pyre of sandalwood. He transformed the pyre and appeared to the bystanders with his consort on a lotus in the middle of a lake, completely unharmed by the fire. He wore a necklace of skulls, a symbol of his status as a tantric master who liberates sentient beings from cyclic existence. This display so impressed the king that he asked Padmasambhava to become his guru.

He served in this capacity for thirteen years, during which he converted the entire kingdom to Buddhism. He also disseminated the dharma to neighboring countries, and he is said to have emanated the monk Indrasena, who converted King Aśoka. In addition, he inspired people to build physical monuments to the dharma (such as *stūpas*), which both spread the fame of the teachings and marked their advance. Traditional histories of his life recount numerous mighty deeds that he performed in order to vanquish opposition and convert his enemies to the truth. In every case, minds full of hate and rancor were transmuted into minds uplifted by faith in the Buddha and his teachings.[5]

Padmasambhava's Conversion of Tibet

He began to widen the scope of his missionary activity, visiting China, Shangshung and Turkestan, and eventually he decided that the time was ripe to introduce the doctrine to Tibet. Traditional histories portray his journey to Tibet as a triumphant victory over demonic forces bent on keeping Buddhism out of the country. They report that Śāntarakṣita, the first great missionary to Tibet, encountered demonic opposition, which turned the minds of the king's ministers against him. The demons of Tibet—which were partial to the pre-Buddhist tradition of Bön—threw bolts of lightning at Marpori Hill (the present site of the Potala palace) and destroyed the harvest. Śāntarakṣita advised the king to invite Padmasambhava to Tibet to subdue the demons, and in the interim he went to Nepal.

The king followed Śāntarakṣita's instructions and sent a delegation to Padmasambhava, but the great tantric yogi already knew of the situation. He traveled to the Tibetan border, but his advance was blocked by a fierce snowstorm created by the country's demons. The snow made the passes into Tibet inaccessible, but Padmasambhava overcame the demons by retiring to a cave and entering a meditative contemplation that enabled him to subdue them and bind them to his will. After this, he traveled the length and breadth of Tibet on foot, meditating in caves all over the country, challenging the demons he encountered to personal combat and converting them to Buddhism. None were able to withstand his power, and many became protectors of the new religion. They took solemn and lasting vows never to work against the dharma and to do their utmost to ensure its propagation.

The king, his ministers, and the common people were all amazed that a single man had challenged all the supernatural forces of their country to mortal combat and that none had the power to stop him. The king announced that from this point onward Buddhism would be the religion of Tibet, and he asked Padmasambhava what needed to be done in order to facilitate the dissemination of the dharma. Padmasambhava advised him to invite Śāntarakṣita to return, which he did, and after this the first Buddhist monastery was built at Samyé. The king realized that in order for Buddhism to be successfully transplanted to Tibet the scriptures would have to be translated, and so he funded translation teams, which began the long process of rendering the texts of Indian Buddhism into Tibetan. In addition, he began sending Tibetans to study in India and inviting renowned Indian masters to Tibet.

Traditional histories disagree on how long Padmasambhava remained in Tibet to ensure the successful spread of dharma. According to some accounts, he only remained for six or eighteen months, while others contend that he stayed for three, six, or twelve years. Some state that he lived in Tibet for over fifty years. According to the *Statement of Ba*, the discrepancy can be explained: Padmasambhava appeared to leave Tibet after a short time, but in reality the Padmasambhava that left was only an emanation created by the master, who remained in meditative solitude in caves. In the final analysis, it probably matters little from the point of view of the tradition, since it ascribes to Padmasambhava a multitude of wondrous deeds. If these were accomplished in a short period of time, this is a testament to his power, and if they were effected over a longer period, it indicates his great compassion and skill in overseeing the transmission of dharma.

He eventually left Tibet to continue his missionary work in neighboring regions, subduing demons and forces antithetical to Buddhism. Immediately after leaving the country he traveled to Küngtang Mountain, where he subdued Totreng, king of the ogres. During their struggle, Padmasambhava "liberated" Totreng, after which he entered the ogre's body. He then created a palace that became the seat of his power among his subjects.

Padmasambhava continues to live in this world and to engage in missionary activity for the benefit of all sentient beings. He is the regent of Vajradhara, whose presence assures that the true essence of the dharma will always remain in the world.

This account of Padmasambhava's life follows the outlines of traditional Tibetan histories, but in the ancient records he is a minor figure. The earliest mention of him in the *Statement of Ba* only briefly alludes to him as an itinerant Indian water-diviner, and does not accord him any role in the propagation of Buddhism.

The Nine Vehicles

The Nyingma order has a distinctive classification of Buddhist teachings into nine vehicles (*theg pa, yāna*). The first three are the commonly recognized trio of (1) hearer vehicle, (2) solitary realizer vehicle, and (3) bodhisattva vehicle. The next three are connected with the outer tantras: action tantra, performance tantra, and yoga tantra. The final three vehicles are the inner tantras: great yoga, subsequent yoga, and great perfection (*rdzogs chen*).[6]

The outer tantra instructions were primarily transmitted to Tibet through disciples of Buddhaguhya, whose own lineage descends from Indrabhūti and Līlavajra. Buddhaguhya is counted among the great knowledge bearers of yoga tantra, along with Ānandagarbha and Śākyamitra. Each of the outer tantras is traced back to a complete enjoyment body buddha: Vajrasattva gave human beings action tantra, Mañjuśrī disseminated performance tantra, and Avalokiteśvara taught yoga tantra.

During the period of the early transmission of Buddhism in Tibet, Buddhaguhya and his disciples were mainly associated with the propagation of action and performance tantras. Tantras included in these groups by Nyingmapas are *The Tantra Called 'Questions of the Superior Subāhu,' The Secret Tantra of the General Precept of All Maṇḍalas, The Stages of Final Meditations*, and their commentaries.

The eighteen major works of inner tantra recognized by Nyingma were brought to central Tibet by Padmasambhava and Vimalamitra and later translated by them.[7] Samantabhadra, the essence of the wisdom of the truth body, is the origin of the inner tantras. The most important of the inner tantras is *The Secret Basic Essence Tantra*, the authenticity of which was questioned by teachers of other orders for centuries, since there was no extant Sanskrit manuscript. In the thirteenth century, however, a Sanskrit text of this work was found in a column of Samyé, with handwritten notations by Padmasambhava. It was authenticated by Jomden Rikpé Sangyé and Sakya Pandita, and when it was translated into Tibetan by Tarpa Lotsawa it was an almost exact match with the extant Tibetan translation. This has continued to be a fundamentally important text for Nyingmapas, and a number of commentaries on it have been written. Other principal tantras for Nyingmapas include the *Hevajra, Cakrasaṃvara, Guhyasamāja*, and *Kālacakra*.

Nyingma Tantric Lineages

The Nyingma order recognizes three primary lineages, corresponding to the three groupings of teachings, all of which converged in the stream that later became known as Nyingma. After these teachings had been brought into Tibet, they were preserved by the disciples of the great Indian masters, such as Vairocana, Ma Rinchen Chok, Nyak Jñānakumāra, and Nup Sangyé Yéshé. The disciples primarily responsible for preserving and transmitting the great yoga lineages were So Yéshé Wangchuk, Surpoché, Surchung, Drobukpa, and their successors.

Nup Sangyé Yéshé is credited with introducing Tibet to subsequent yoga. He received the teachings from such luminaries as Hūṃkāra, Dharmabodhi, and Vasudhara. Nup Sangyé Yéshé in turn passed on the lore of this lineage to Yönden Gyatso and other students.

The great perfection teachings are traced back to Surativajra (Garap Dorjé), a form body emanation of Vajrasattva. He initiated human masters like Jambel Shé Nyen (Mañjuśrīmitra), Śrī Siṃha, and Jñānasūtra. Śrī Siṃha imparted "supreme yoga" (*rdzogs chen, atiyoga*) instructions to Padmasambhava, Vimalamitra, and Vairocana. Vairocana was the primary transmitter of the teachings of "mind class" (*sems sde*) and "spatial class" (*klong sde*) supreme yoga teachings, and the lineages of "secret instruction class" (*man ngag sde*) supreme yoga were conferred by Padmasambhava and Vimalamitra.

Tulku Urgyen states that

> There is the outer Mind Section, which is like the body. There is the inner Space Section, which is like the heart, and the secret Instruction Section, which is like the veins within the heart. Finally there is the innermost Unexcelled Section, which is like the life-energy inside the heart, the pure essence of the life-force. What is the difference between these four sections, since all four are Dzogchen? The outer Mind Section of Dzogchen emphasizes the cognizant quality of mind, while the inner Space Section emphasizes its empty quality, and the secret Instruction Section emphasizes the unity of the two. The innermost Unexcelled Section teaches everything—ground, path and fruition . . . . [8]

Basis, Path, and Fruit

The path of the nine vehicles is divided into four categories: (1) basis continuum (*gzhi rgyud*); (2) path continuum (*lam rgyud*); (3) result continuum (*'bras bu rgyud*); and (4) method continuum (*thabs rgyud*).

The first, *basis continuum*, refers to Samantabhadra, the primordially awakened truth body that is beginningless and endless and perfectly free from all defects. The basis is also the correct view (*lta ba*), which has three aspects: (1) entity (*ngo bo*); (2) nature (*rang bzhin*); and (3) compassion (*thugs rje*).

Path continuum comprises practices that eliminate the afflictions through accumulation of merit and wisdom. These serve as antidotes to the tendencies toward the afflictive obstructions and the obstructions to omniscience. The term "path continuum" also embraces all Mahāyāna teachings and practices, which together constitute innumerable paths to awakening.

Result continuum refers to the eleventh "level," the attainment of awakening after training as a bodhisattva.[9] *Method continuum* corresponds to the awakened being's ability to work constantly and effectively for the benefit of sentient beings. The buddha's awakened mind is able skillfully to perceive the backgrounds and problems of trainees and is not disturbed by preconceived notions or biases. This enables a buddha to determine the most effective teachings for each sentient being and to instruct every trainee in ways ideally suited to his or her needs.

The tantric doctrines and practices of Nyingma are passed on through two main types of transmission lineages: (1) teachings (*bka' ma*) and (2) hidden treasures (*gter ma*). The first of these is the unbroken tradition of instructions from the Buddha to his disciples, which continues to the present day. These instructions are passed on from master to disciple. The "teaching" lineage is divided into (1) sūtra, (2) tantra, and (3) mind transmission. These correspond to the categories of subsequent yoga, great yoga, and supreme yoga (great perfection) respectively.

Most of the teaching instructions have been preserved in the Nyingma tantric canon (*rnying ma'i rgyud 'bum*), which was compiled by Ratna Lingpa in the fifteenth century, mostly from texts in Sur Ukpalung Monastery. Several other collections have been produced by Nyingma scholars, such as Jikmé Lingpa, Katok Rikdzin Tséwang Norbu, and most recently by Tarthang Tulku in the United States.

Hidden treasures are texts, instructions, images, and the like, which were concealed by past masters who anticipated a particular future need for a certain teaching. These will be discussed in the following section.

Terma: Hidden Treasures

The fortunes and developments of the New Orders are often closely connected with political and social factors, and all of them to a greater or lesser extent became involved in Tibetan politics. The Nyingma order, by contrast, has remained remarkably aloof from political intrigues. One result of this orientation, however, was that the tradition at times became insular and detached from current events. Nyingma histories report that the early teachers of the lineage had foreseen this problem, and they created the institution of hiding texts and artifacts that would be discovered at a later date and would breathe new life into the tradition. These "hidden treasures" are said to be secreted throughout the land of Tibet, and they are safeguarded by spells that prevent them from being found before the appropriate time.[10] When conditions are ripe for their dissemination, the *terma* are discovered by *tertön* (*gter ston*), or "treasure discoverers." These people are prophesied by the masters who hid the treasures, and there are strict controls and tests regarding the finding and propagation of *terma.*[10] According to Tarthang Tulku, *terma* can be

> anything that is precious or worthy of preservation. In addition to texts or fragments of manuscripts, *gter* can take the form of religious figurines, reliquaries, or ritual objects, denoting anything that stands for spiritual value. *gTer* may also manifest as natural objects, such as trees, rocks, and signs in the earth; *gter* can also be gifts of silver, gold, or precious jewels which may be exchanged for materials needed to build a temple or other religious monument . . . . Furthermore, *gTer-ma* may serve as a catalyst to aid in deciphering a text or fragment concealed by Padmasambhava or one of his disciples.[11]

According to Dudjom Rinpoche, each hidden treasure manuscript outlines the path to awakening in a way that is particularly appropriate to the time in which it will be discovered because

> the all-seeing master Padmasambhava composed . . . each requisite for the path in its entirety, including means for attainment, ritual collections and esoteric instructions, for he knew the manner in which those requiring training would appear in the future. He arranged them in yellow scrolls as verbal tantras and entrusted them to their respective non-human treasure lords . . . . He then concealed them to be invisible along with their seals of entrustment which were in the form of prayerful aspirations that they be discovered in the future by the worthy and fortunate individuals who were empowered to do so. At a later date, the power of those prayerful aspirations would awaken in the individuals endowed with suitable fortune. The indications of the appropriate times and the prophetic declarations

> would come together, whereupon the great master would actually reveal his visage, confer empowerment, and inspire [the treasure-finders] with the seals of entrustment and prophetic declarations.[12]

Historically the most influential terma have been the "eight Heruka *sādhanas*" (liturgical cycles) and the *Innermost Essence of the Great Expanse*, which were hidden by Padmasambhava. Anticipating a time in which they would be needed, he concealed them, predicting the occasion of their discovery and the people who would find them. Other texts were secreted by his consort Yéshé Tsogyel, who memorized his teachings and then hid them with the help of Padmasambhava. Although later Nyingma tradition tends to emphasize Padmasambhava and his disciples as the sole proprietors of hidden treasures, the earliest ones were attributed to the dharma kings Songtsen Gambo and Tri Songdétsen.

According to the tradition, treasure discoverers are bodhisattvas who possess special qualities that enable them to find terma. When the time comes for a terma to be discovered, the discoverer finds a secret "hint" or "key" (*kha byung* or *lde mig*) that indicates the place of concealment. The great tertöns are emanations of Padmasambhava whose primary purpose is to locate the appropriate treasure at the appropriate time. In addition, each tertön is specially qualified to explain and transmit the terma he or she finds. This system is necessary because

> the essence of the teachings can become confused, misinterpreted, or lose its potency. The *gTer-ma* masters have thus appeared at various times throughout history in order to clarify, reinterpret, or re-energize the meaning of the original teachings.[13]

This system has proven remarkably effective in regularly breathing new life into the Nyingma order while maintaining a perceived link with its origins. Each age finds the terma appropriate to its spiritual needs, and each new terma becomes a part of the tradition. A number of Nyingma monasteries were founded to preserve and transmit these religious treasures, which facilitated their institutionalization. This, in turn, helped the recipients of this lore to develop the sort of structures that could guarantee its continued survival through the vicissitudes of Tibetan history.

The hidden treasures are often written in a code called "ḍākinī language" that can only be deciphered by people who have been taught how to read it. Ḍākinīs commonly aid in the process of discovery and in interpreting the terma. There are numerous safeguards that prevent terma being discovered before the appropriate time, including a "time-lock formula" (*gtsug las khan*). This ensures that only the ordained discoverer can locate the treasure at the appropriate time.

Transmission Lineages

At the present time, there are two recognized methods of transmission for Nyingma teachings: (1) the distant lineage of the teachings and (2) the close lineage of terma. The first group is concerned with the instructions of great yoga, subsequent yoga, and supreme yoga, collectively transmitted as "the trio of sūtra, magical net, and mind class." The second collection comprises "the trio of guru, great perfection, and the great compassionate one" (*bla rdzogs thugs gsum*). These are instructions attributed to the guru (*bla ma*) Padmasambhava, the great perfection (*rdzogs chen*), and Avalokiteśvara, the embodiment of compassion (*thugs rje*).

There are a number of hidden treasure lineages, including the "royal thought," which is a transmission by the truth body of the awakened wisdom of the buddhas. This is imparted directly by the truth body to qualified recipients without any need of words. Another tradition, the "symbols of knowledge bearers," emanates from complete enjoyment body buddhas who impart their wisdom by means of nonverbal symbols. This is a symbolic (*brda*) lineage, and it is not communicated through ordinary language. It includes the great perfection, which is the supreme teaching among humans and advanced bodhisattvas.

The "personal instruction" lineage refers to the oral traditions passed on from master to disciple through use of words. These were first imparted to King Indrabodhi by five buddhas.

The "directed ḍākinī" teachings are given by knowledge ḍākinīs to terma masters. They point the way for tertöns to find the appropriate terma. The "yellow parchment" lineage comprises instructions written in code on yellow paper, which are conferred by ḍākinīs to treasure discoverers. The "pure vision" lineage consists of secret lore imparted directly to tertöns by knowledge bearers.

The basic texts of terma are the eight Heruka sādhanas, which were brought to Tibet by Padmasambhava. These are based on the tantras of the teaching class and contain instructions on how to practice the techniques of the inner tantras. Each sādhana is connected with a particular text, maṇḍala, mantra, deity, and family of buddhas. They constitute a complex and interrelated system of visualization and practice aimed at developing the awareness of trainees by dividing tantric practice into discrete but connected sādhanas. The first five are related to the "meditation buddhas" (Akṣobhya, Vairocana, Ratnasambhava, Amitābha, and Amoghasiddhi) and have sādhanas that enact and cultivate the existence, teachings, mind, virtues, and activities of the buddhas. The last three are referred to as "world class."

The Treasure Discoverers

Most of the influential terma were purportedly secreted by Padmasambhava or his immediate disciples, and specific instructions were also laid down for each terma at the time of its concealment. The theory behind this system is that certain teachings would be especially effective at particular points in the future, and so they were hidden in a "time release" system which assured that at the appropriate time a tertön would locate the teaching and disseminate it. When Padmasambhava hid these treasures, he prophesied the circumstances for the discovery of each terma and the tertön who would find it. He predicted that there would be three "grand" tertöns, eight "great" ones, twenty-one "powerful" ones, one hundred eight "intermediate," and one thousand "subsidiary" tertöns. Most of these were to be recognized as emanations of Padmasambhava or his chief disciples.

The first tertöns were Sangyé Lama and Drapa Ngönshé in the eleventh century. They were followed by Nyang Rel Nyima Öser (1124–1192) and Chögi Wangchuk (1212–1270), who are referred to as the "sun and moon" of tertöns. The terma they found are called the "upper and lower treasures." They are two of the three "grand" tertöns, along with Rikdsin Gödem (1337–1409). They are held to be emanations of the mind, speech, and body of Padmasambhava.

The fourteenth and fifteenth century saw a great deal of activity among tertöns, including Orgyen Lingpa (1323–1360), Sangyé Lingpa (1340–1396), Péma Lingpa (1346–1405), Karma Lingpa (ca. fourteenth century), and Ratna Lingpa (1403–1479). The tertön tradition continued in the following centuries, which produced such important figures as Terdak Lingpa (1634 or 1646–1714), Jikmé Lingpa (1729–1798), Péma Ösel Mongak

Lingpa (1820–1892), and Chogyur Déchen Lingpa (also known as Shikpo Lingpa, 1829–1870).

Many hidden treasures still remain undiscovered, awaiting the proper time for their dissemination. They continue to reinvigorate the Nyingma tradition, and a number have been incorporated into other lineages. The institution of terma serves as a link with the past of the tradition, a link that periodically revitalizes the present and points the way to the future. The system reflects the Mahāyāna ideal of skill in means, the ability to adapt teachings to changing circumstances.

Many of the lineages of Nyingma are based on particular terma. For instance, Mindroling Monastery in central Tibet is strongly associated with the transmission and propagation of the "upper and lower treasures" discovered by Nyang Rel Nyima Öser and Chögi Wangchuk. Dorjé Drak Monastery in central Tibet (founded by Rikdzin Ngagi Ongpo in 1659) is particularly associated with the terma teachings known as the "northern treasures." Katok Monastery in Kham (founded by Dampa Déshek Shérap Sengge in 1159) is an important training center for the inner tantras. Dzogchen Monastery, the largest Nyingma institution, was founded by Dzogchen Péma Lingpa in 1685. It maintains the lore of the inner tantras of the teaching tradition and the terma of Nyima Drakpa.

Distinctive Practices: Dzogchen

According to lineage histories of the great perfection (*rdzogs chen*), the system originated with Samantabhadra, who passed it on to Vajrasattva. It then entered the world of human beings and continues today in an unbroken chain of transmission. Its adherents assert that dzogchen is not a school or system of philosophy, but rather a view of reality that is based on a profound understanding of the nature of mind. It is primarily imparted through direct oral instructions of a master to a disciple, but there is also a large corpus of texts belonging to the teaching tradition and hidden treasures.

Nyingma tradition maintains that great perfection teachings first appeared in the world in the area of Dhanakośa Lake in Oḍḍiyāna. The basic text of the tradition is the *Fourfold Innermost Essence*, and the proponents of dzogchen hold that the philosophical basis of the system is the Madhyamaka view of Nāgārjuna. The lore of dzogchen was first imparted to Garap Dorjé by Vajrasattva, and then Garap Dorjé passed it on to Jambel Shé Nyen in a golden box. The teachings in the box consisted of six million four hundred thousand verses summarizing the quintessence of dzogchen. Jambel Shé Nyen divided them into the three categories of mind class, spatial class, and secret instruction class.

Of the three inner tantras (great yoga, subsequent yoga, and supreme yoga), supreme yoga (dzogchen) is considered to be the highest path. The three represent a hierarchy of progressive profundity and subtlety, beginning with visualizations, progressing through a comprehensive view of the nature of reality, and culminating in a union of appearance and emptiness. Great yoga is primarily oriented toward visionary experiences, while subsequent yoga is concerned with the cognitive implications of such experience. In great yoga, one realizes that all phenomena are emanations of mind, which is an indissoluble union of appearances and emptiness (*snang stong*). In subsequent yoga, all thoughts and forms are perceived as being of the nature of emptiness, and emptiness is identified with Samantabhadrī, the female counterpart of Samantabhadra, embodiment of the truth body. Appearance is identified with Samantabhadra, and subsequent yoga adepts cultivate the insight that all appearances are of the nature of the truth body. Meditators seek to comprehend the union of appearance and emptiness and to understand that all phenomena arise from this conjunction, but not in the manner of cause and effect.

Great perfection is the culmination of this awareness, and the view of this system is based on the realization that appearance and emptiness interpenetrate and are inseparable. In this practice, the goal becomes the path, and one seeks to examine the fundamental nature of mind directly, without the need for images or visualizations. The *Tantra of the Great Natural Arising of Awareness* states that meditative systems which utilize images and visualizations are inferior to dzogchen, which works on the mind itself.

> Because you yourself are the divine maṇḍala,
> naturally manifest to yourself,
> Do not offer worship to the deity,
> for if you worship you will be fettered by it . . . .
> Do not renounce saṃsāra, for if you renounce it
> you will not attain buddhahood.
> Because the Buddha is not elsewhere,
> he is naught but awareness itself.
> Saṃsāra is not elsewhere;
> all is gathered within your own mind.

Do not practise conditioned fundamental virtues,
for if you do you will be fettered by them.
Renounce conditioned fundamental virtues,
such as [building] stūpas and temples.
There is no end to contrived doctrines,
but by leaving them they will end.
Not renouncing the yoga of abandoning deeds,
should you renounce deeds, you will become a tathāgata [buddha].
So it is that you must know the path
of the authentic buddhas in everything.[14]

Great perfection is considered by its adherents to be a practice transcending highest yoga tantra, since in the view of dzogchen even tantric visualization is only a preliminary technique of artificially creating mental images that are concordant with liberation. Dzogchen, by contrast, works with the fundamental nature of the mind itself. It dispenses with mental imagery and manipulation of subtle winds and drops; instead, it aims at direct experience of the nature of mind. Great perfection also surpasses practices that aim at cultivating ethics in order to acquire good karma, since if one trains in actualizing the clear light nature of mind such actions are unnecessary. This is because in dzogchen

> a philosophy of freedom from deeds with respect to the disposition of reality, when the ultimate, definitive meaning of pristine cognition, which does not rest in the sphere of causal conditioning, is indicated directly; it is explained that there is no need to orient oneself to contrived doctrines that require efforts associated with the causes and effects of good and evil.[15]

People who become attached to "virtue" and to acquiring good karma fail to understand that the basis of transformation is the mind itself, which is of the nature of clear light. This light cannot be enhanced by the practice of virtue nor diminished by nonvirtue, and so the great perfection adept recognizes that both "virtue" and "nonvirtue" are simply conceptual constructs that ultimately constitute obstacles to spiritual realization.

Virtue is not to be practised,
nor sin to be renounced;

> Awareness free from both virtue and sin
> is the buddha-body of reality.
> Virtue is not to be practised,
> if practised there is no buddhahood.
> Neither is sin to be renounced
> if renounced, buddhahood is not achieved.[16]

Great perfection practice involves cultivating a union of essential purity (*ka dag*) and spontaneity (*lhun grub*). Essential purity refers to the mode of being (*gnas lugs*), which is emptiness. According to the view of this system, all positive qualities are spontaneously established in the sense that all are contained in the "basis-of-all" (*kun gzhi, ālaya*), the psychophysical continuum of existence. When sentient beings realize the natural purity of the basis-of-all, they attain buddhahood; when they fail to do so, they wander in cyclic existence.

Dzogchen Practice

The key practice of the great perfection is referred to as "cutting through" (*khregs chod*), in which yogis see through appearances to perceive the primordially pure mind. Meditators eliminate discursive thought, allowing primordial awareness to shine through mental obscurations. Through this, they perceive reality from the perspective of the nondual awareness of awakened beings. The "direct approach" (*thod rgal*) involves recognizing spontaneity. In cutting through, one dissects the ego and directly trains in the primordial innate awareness without relying on appearances or signs. This is described as an effortless path, while the yoga of direct approach requires work. According to Jikmé Lingpa, the direct approach involves

> relying on appearances (or visions), the spontaneous accomplishment of purifying the gross aspects into the clarity [luminous absorption] and dissolving the (phenomena into the) ultimate nature of appearances.[17]

The visions used in this practice are of four kinds: (1) direct perception of reality, (2) development of experiences, (3) perfection of pure awareness, and (4) dissolution into the nature of reality. Through this technique meditators acquire two kinds of power: control of birth and control over arising (*skye 'jug*). Control over birth allows one to dissolve the elements of the body into light in order to benefit sentient beings. Through this, one is liberated through actualizing the innate primordial purity of mind. Control over arising involves transcending physicality (or even the appearance of physicality). The adept dissolves the body into light, which in turn merges into the sphere of reality. In this state, one is co-extensive with all of reality, and thus able to work for the benefit of all beings in all places and times.

Longchen Rapjampa summarizes the practices of cutting through and direct path as follows:

> The appearances of clarity are the primordial wisdom of direct path, and
> The self-present peace (free) from projections and withdrawal
> Is the spontaneously accomplished emptiness of cutting through.
> The aspect of cessation of mind is cutting through.
> The spontaneously accomplished self-clarity is direct path.
> The union of (both), which is the self-arisen intrinsic wisdom,
> Is the secret path of innermost essence.
> When all the elaborations are completely pacified,
> At that time the self-awareness intrinsic wisdom will naturally arise.[18]

Tulku Urgyen explains that cutting through is the emptiness aspect of the training and direct approach relates to use of skill in means, which allows one to master all aspects of the awakened consciousness. Cutting through eliminates ego and its permutations, while direct approach examines the manifestations that remain.[19] Both techniques are described as effortless and formless, and both are linked in this system. Mastery of cutting through enables the yogi to abide in understanding of emptiness free from all concepts. The yogi perceives the innate purity of all phenomena, and they are regarded as empty of any conceptual limitations or impurity. This banishes delusion and ignorance and reveals the true nature of reality.

Direct approach yogas enable one to comprehend that everything is innately pure. It works directly with the clear light nature of mind; the yogi views everything as naturally and spontaneously present to awareness. It is immediate realization, with no coloring by concepts or thought. It enables one to actualize all aspects of awakening in one lifetime.

Mental Training

The basic nature of mind is clear light, which from beginningless time has been free from all defilements. All of our experience is merely a series of ripples on the surface of the primordially pure mind, which is unproduced and unchanging. The self-existent, uncontaminated nature of mind becomes the basis for practice, and the meditator seeks to manifest this in meditation. Great perfection texts draw a distinction between the ordinary mind (*sems*), which is enmeshed in discursive and dualistic thought, and the "mind itself" (*sems nyid*), or basic nature of consciousness, which is equated with the "buddha nature," a fundamental level of awareness that is untouched and unsullied by any afflicted cognitions. The basic quality of the mind is "pure awareness" (*rig pa*). The "mind itself" is the buddha mind, the innate capacity for buddhahood that is present in all sentient beings, and it is the basis upon which ordinary consciousness rests, although only spiritual adepts are even aware of it.

Because the mind is of the nature of clear light, all defilements and afflictions are adventitious. For this reason, great perfection texts claim that with the proper training the basic nature of mind can be revealed and that this need not be the result of a long process of training. Rather, awakening can be a sudden flash of insight. The contemporary dzogchen master Khetsun Sangpo Rinpoche distinguishes two modes of practice,

> the sudden and the gradual. The sudden mode is for someone who over many lifetimes has accumulated the proper actions and predispositions, so that when he receives initiations and the lama's identification of reality, he attains high realization. The gradual mode . . . . is not that of the sūtra systems in which one achieves awakening only after countless eons of practice, but that of someone on the Mantra path who completes the auspicious qualities, finishing the grounds [levels] and paths gradually even in one lifetime. However, when he identifies reality, he is unable to progress along these paths simultaneously, but has to proceed in stages.[20]

Although this is the most rapid of all paths to awakening, few have the necessary cognitive capacities to practice it successfully. Great perfection texts often contain stories of people who failed in this path because they thought that it required no effort, since it dispenses with rituals, visualizations, and other externally observable activities. Such an attitude is mistaken; dzogchen is only suitable for a small number of advanced practitioners with the unusual capacity to quickly grasp its profound and simple truths. Most people, however, are so blinded by accumulated delusions that they require a long process of gradually removing the veils that obscure the truth before they can grasp it in its simplicity and immediacy.

> If through such quintessential instructions one can identify the basis of the mind, then in that instant one has become a Buddha without engaging in the difficulties of the gradual path. Among a hundred thousand trainees there are only one or two such persons and thus although they do occur, they are very rare.[21]

Only those who have prepared their minds through successful meditative training are able to understand great perfection teachings, and so, although this is a sudden path, it requires preparatory training prior to sudden realization.

Another important prerequisite for successful dzogchen training is an awakened teacher. In order to be able to point out the nature of a student's mind, the lama must have personally realized the nature of his or her own mind. When the awakened master speaks to a properly prepared trainee, the student is shown the nature of mind, and if this is successfully apprehended, he or she becomes a "superior" (*'phags pa, ārya*). Since the only difference between a superior and an ordinary being is that the former recognizes the nature of mind while the latter does not, the moment of understanding transforms an ordinary being into a superior. Most people are unable to accomplish this sudden transformation, however, and so the sudden path is only for a small elite.

One great difficulty lies in the fact that "pure awareness" is so omnipresent and so fundamental that it is difficult to perceive. It is even more subtle than air and space, which are also all around us, although we are seldom consciously aware of them. Pure awareness is not something that exists on a rarefied plane of mystical awareness; rather, it is the most basic element of all experience. It is closer than one's own heart, closer than the breath, more fundamental than any feelings, emotions, or perceptions. It is the basis of consciousness and of every moment of awareness. It is the space in which all conscious life takes place, and like the physical environment, we only begin to recognize it when our attention is drawn toward it for some reason. Most of the time, however, we simply move and act within this space without generating any conscious awareness of it. In an oral commentary on Mipam's *Three Cycles of Fundamental Mind*, Khetsun Sangpo Rinpoche stated,

> Because it is beyond causes and conditions, it is self-arisen. Because it is not something that did not exist before and adventitiously arose, it is the pristine wisdom that is of the nature of primordially abiding basic knowledge. It is the basis from which all of the [phenomena] of cyclic existence and nirvana appear. That basis is expressed as being a buddha that is naturally, spontaneously established.[22]

Observing the Mind Itself

The primary meditative technique of great perfection is remaining in the state of pure awareness. This is accomplished by calming the mind and then abiding in comprehension of its basic clear light nature. Unlike other forms of meditation in which the eyes are partly or mostly closed, dzogchen masters often urge their students to meditate on the nature of mind with their eyes wide open. The meditative practice involves being cognizant of the arising and passing away of feelings, emotions, sensations, and so on, but understanding them within the context of pure awareness. The more one does this, the more one realizes that all phenomena arise from mind and re-merge into it. They are of the nature of pure awareness and are a projection of luminosity and emptiness. Through cultivating this understanding, mental phenomena of their own accord begin to subside, allowing the clear light nature of mind to become manifest. They appear as reflections on the surface of a mirror and are perceived as illusory, ephemeral, and nonsubstantial.

The meditator should consider how minds arise and pass away. The first examination involves searching for the place from which a mind arises. After considering the various parts of the body, one realizes that none are suitable to be the basis of this arising and that the mind does not abide in external phenomena. Rather, it appears to reside now in one area, and later in another, but there is no constant foundation for the arising of mind. The meditator then considers where mind goes after it passes away. The mind of last year does not exist today, and today's mind will be gone tomorrow, but where do they go? How does a mind arise, abide, and pass away? After considering these questions in the light of meditative introspection, the yogi recognizes that mind arises from nowhere, abides nowhere, and goes nowhere. This leads to the realization that the mind is emptiness and that the images of cognition arise from this emptiness and again merge into it without leaving a trace behind, in the same way that waves arise from the ocean and then flow back into it, leaving no trace of their passing. A series of verses by the first Karma Chakmé captures this realization.

> Mind has no form, color, or concrete substance.
> It is not to be found anywhere outside or within your body, nor in between.
> It is not found to be a concrete thing.
> Even if you were to search throughout the ten directions,
> It does not arise from anywhere, nor does it abide and disappear at any place.
>
> Yet, it is not non-existent, since your mind is vividly awake.
> It is not a singularity, because it manifests in manifold ways.
> Nor is it a plurality, because all these are of one essence.
> There is no one who can describe its nature.
> But, when expressing its resemblance, there is no end to what can be said . . . .
> It is the very basis of all of saṃsāra and nirvāṇa.[23]

Results of Dzogchen Training

There are three stages in great perfection training: basis, path, and result. In the basis phase, the meditator cultivates the understanding that cyclic existence and nirvana are the same and overcomes the tendency to distinguish cause and effect. The path phase is concerned with transcending the propensity to engage in discursive thoughts and to accept some aspects of reality while rejecting others. The result phase is characterized by an attitude of confidence that overcomes thoughts of hope and fear concerning the goal of meditative practice. The final level of this stage is reached when the meditator perceives all phenomena as being emanations of mind, which itself is a union of luminosity and emptiness.

One result of this process is that compassion and wisdom become spontaneous. Since these are expressions of the basic nature of mind, when this is allowed to manifest, positive mental qualities are actualized of their own accord and are uncontrived. At this point, cyclic existence disappears, and nirvana also disappears, since it is only the counterpoint of saṃsāra. In the realm of pure awareness, all such dichotomies are transcended. One perceives the nature of mind as being like space: it is omnipresent, clear, transparent, unobstructed, undefiled, pure, unmoving, limitless, eternally the same in all times and places.

Since the nature of mind is always a union of luminosity and emptiness, great perfection practice makes no distinction between meditation and nonmeditation. All activities, if performed with mindfulness of the nature of mind, can become occasions for awareness of its essential nature. This is manifest in all activities and at all times, and a person who is directly aware of this becomes awakened. Due to the ever-present possibility of awakening, dzogchen is considered by its adherents to be the most powerful and rapid of all paths to buddhahood.

Those who succeed in this practice attain a state of radical freedom: there are no boundaries, no presuppositions, and no habits on which to rely. One perceives things as they are in their naked reality. Ordinary beings view phenomena through a lens clouded by concepts and preconceptions, and most of the world is overlooked or ignored. The mind of the great perfection adept, however, is unbounded, and everything is possible. For many beginners, this prospect is profoundly disquieting, because since beginningless time we have been constricted by rules, laws, assumptions, and previous actions. One who is awakened, however, transcends all such limitations; there is no ground on which to stand, no limits, nothing that must be done, and no prohibitions. This awareness is bottomless, unfathomable, immeasurable, permeated by joy, unboundedness, and exhilaration. One is utterly free, and one's state of mind is as expansive as space. Those who attain this level of awareness also transcend physicality and manifest the "rainbow body" (*'ja lus*), a form comprised of pure light that cannot decay, which has no physical aspects, and which is coterminous with the nature of mind. Tulku Urgyen describes it as

> [t]he dissolution of the physical body at death into a state of rainbow light. Such practitioners leave behind only their hair and fingernails . . . . Among the three kayas [bodies of a buddha], sambhogakaya [the complete enjoyment body] manifests visually in the form of

> rainbow light. So, attaining a rainbow body in this lifetime means to be directly awakened in the state of enlightenment of sambhogakaya . . . There has been an unceasing occurrence of practitioners departing from this world in the rainbow body up until the present day . . . So this is not just an old tale from the past, but something that has continued to the present day.[24]

The Three Classes of Great Perfection Tantras

In contrast to the standard Mahāyāna hierarchy of ten "levels" (*sa, bhūmi*), the Nyingma tradition recognizes sixteen levels. The first ten are the same as those found in the perfection vehicle,[25] but the remaining five are distinctively tantric. The eleventh level is called "path continuum" (*lam rgyud*) and is the result of successful completion of highest yoga tantra practices that lead to direct awakening. The twelfth level is the outcome of successful practice of great yoga. The thirteenth is the result of successful subsequent yoga practice, and the fourteenth through sixteenth are the results of successful practice of the mind class, spatial class, and secret instruction class divisions of supreme yoga (dzogchen).

The mind class consists of teachings that are concerned with the fundamental nature of mind, and the spatial class comprises yogas of "freedom from activity" (*bya bral*). These techniques emphasize the effortlessness of realization, which consists of simply becoming aware of the nature of mind.

According to traditional classifications, mind class tantras are those which teach that all elements of cyclic existence and nirvana arise from the emanational power of mind. According to Gyurmé Tséwang Chogdup, the view of this system

> transcends all the various levels of *yānas* [paths], two truths, six perfections and two stages, all the composed and contaminated aspects of the 'truth of the path' which are bound with the rigid concept of apprehending. (These are transcended by) the great ultimate sphere which is the nature of innate awakened mind, the primordial wisdom of the great equalness purity, the ultimate sphere free from elaborations, the nature of absolute truth. It is the total liberation from causes and results, virtues and unvirtues and acceptances and rejec-

> tions. In brief, it is the transcendence of all the phenomena of dual perceptions of apprehended and apprehender.[26]

Spatial class tantras are those which teach that self-arisen pure awareness and phenomena are emanations of the nature of reality (*chos nyid*) and are primordially liberated. They are characterized by the view that all appearances of reality are free from activity and also transcend the extreme of antidotes, since they are all contained within Samantabhadrī, who is co-extensive with the sphere of reality. According to Longchen Rapjampa, these tantras teach that

> phenomenal existents are present as various self-appearing modes, but they do not exist since they are originally liberated and are naturally pure result. So even the aspect of mind and the play, the appearances of mind, do not exist . . . . Whatever imputations one makes (about the appearances), whether as pure or impure, at the very point of their appearance, their self-essence transcends (the extremes of) existing or non-existing. All are the great original liberation and infinite expanse.[27]

Secret instruction tantras point to the spontaneously present and primordially pure nature, which is free from all terms, expressions, conceptualizations, and discriminations. These tantras are characterized by the view that all the aspects of truth transcend the extremes of renunciation and antidote because they abide in accordance with the mode of subsistence of being (*yin lugs*). Jikmé Lingpa states that in these tantras

> the glow of originally pure essence, the great freedom from concepts and expressions, arises naturally through the doors of spontaneously accomplished self-appearances, there are no deviations and obscurations in the appearances of power (*rtsal snang*); and the appearances of phenomena are perfected in the ultimate nature of phenomena, free from elaborations.[28]

Secret instruction class teachings are considered by Nyingmapas to be the most profound in all of Buddhism. They are divided into two sections: (1) hearing lineage (*snyan brgyud*) and (2) explanatory lineage (*bshad brgyud*). The secret instruction class was uncovered at Vajrāsana by Śrī

Siṃha, a disciple of Jambel Shé Nyen. Śrī Siṃha divided these teachings into four sections: (1) exoteric cycle (*phyi skor*), (2) esoteric cycle (*nang skor*), (3) secret cycle (*gsang skor*), and (4) unsurpassably secret cycle (*gsang ba bla na med pa skor*).

In a summary of the distinctive characteristics of the three types of supreme yoga tantras, Dudjom Rinpoche states:

> The Mental Class, by referring positively to the mind, has mostly achieved the area of profundity rather than radiance, and yet, by not realising the expressive power of radiance to be reality, it almost clings to mental scrutiny. The Spatial Class, though equally achieving profundity and radiance, rather than the mental scrutiny which apprehends reality, almost lapses into a deviation point within the range of emptiness. The Esoteric Secret Instruction Class, on the other hand, is actually superior because it gathers within the expanse of reality that is free from conceptual elaboration, all apparitions of reality which appear through the self-manifesting, spontaneously present and natural, expressive power. As such [these apparitions] are the tone of the primordially pure, inexpressible essence, the supreme transcendence of intellect.[29]

The perspective of the third class transcends all positions, all views, and all conceptuality. It takes the fundamental reality of mind as its object and cultivates the awareness that this reality is primordially free from bondage and liberation, cyclic existence or nirvana, or any other limiting categories. It points directly to emptiness, the emptiness that is the fundamental nature of mind and phenomena. In this practice, no activities are of any use, there are no rituals, no visualizations, and no need for ethical training; one simply cultivates direct awareness of reality as it is.

Notes

1. Dudjom Rinpoche, *The Nyingma School of Tibetan Buddhism: Its Fundamentals and History*, vol. I (Boston: Wisdom Publications, 1991), p. 116.
2. See *The Nyingma School*, p. 120.
3. For an overview of the attributes and practices associated with the five buddha families, see David Snellgrove, *Indo-Tibetan Buddhism*, vol. I, pp. 189–198.

4. A traditional biography of Garap Dorjé is summarized in Tarthang Tulku et al., *Crystal Mirror V* (Berkeley: Dharma Publishing, 1977), pp. 183–186.
5. Some of these are recounted in *The Nyingma School*, pp. 471–474.
6. It should be noted that *dzogchen* (*rdzogs chen*) is an unlikely Tibetan equivalent of the Sanskrit term *atiyoga*, but it is often given in Tibetan lexicons. *Mahāsampanna* is another Sanskrit term that is often given as the equivalent of *dzogchen*, but I know of no Sanskrit text that confirms this.
7. A list of these can be found in *Crystal Mirror V*, pp. 198–199.
8. Tulku Urgyen Rinpoche, *Rainbow Painting* (Hong Kong: Rangjung Yeshe, 1995), p. 34.
9. See the section on the "bodhisattva levels" in chapter 4, "Mahāyāna."
10. The terma have an ambiguous status in Tibetan Buddhism. They are generally associated with the Nyingma and Kagyu orders, but there have also been Géluk and Sakya treasure discoverers, and some of these texts are part of the paracanonical literature of all four orders. There has been considerable debate, however, regarding the authenticity of certain terma, and many are rejected by the other orders. Early terma claimed to have been hidden by figures from the early dynastic period, and later most terma were attributed to Padmasambhava or his disciples. Many contain "prophecies" that purport to predict future events, but the texts appear to have been "discovered" well after the predicted events occurred, which has fuelled suspicions regarding their provenance. Some opponents view the tradition of hidden treasures as a device to put a veneer of antiquity on new doctrines and practices, but the Nyingmapas staunchly defend the validity of their main terma.
11. *Crystal Mirror V*, pp. 261–262. See also Tulku Thondup Rinpoche, *Hidden Teachings of Tibet* (London: Wisdom, 1986), pp. 61–62.
12. *The Nyingma School*, vol. I, pp. 927–928.
13. *Crystal Mirror V*, p. 265.
14. Quoted in *The Nyingma School*, vol. I, p. 900.
15. Ibid., p. 896.
16. *Tantra of the Great Natural Arising of Awareness* (quoted in *The Nyingma School*, vol. I, p. 901).
17. Tulku Thondup Rinpoche, *Buddha Mind*, p. 73.
18. Ibid., p. 403. I have substituted English equivalents for the key terms, which were untranslated in the original text.
19. *Rainbow Painting*, p. 159.
20. Khetsun Sangpo, *Tantric Practice in Nying-ma*, p. 187. Critics of dzogchen often charge that this system is linked with the teachings and practices of Heshang Moheyan, the Chinese Chan master who is portrayed in traditional histories as the opponent of Kamalaśīla in the debate at Lhasa. The traditional histories agree that at that council the Indian faction, which advocated the position that awakening is only attained in stages, defeated the Chinese faction, which propounded a doctrine of sudden awakening. Since dzogchen masters contend that awakening may be attained very quickly through their practices, and because dzogchen, like Chan, dispenses with images, visualizations, ceremonies, and so on and focuses on the mind itself, Tibetan opponents have often dismissed dzogchen as merely a disguised form of Chan. This charge is vigorously denied by dzogchen masters. See, for instance, *The Nyingma School*, vol. I, p. 896, and *Buddha Mind*, pp. 89ff.
21. *Tantric Practice in Nying-ma*, p. 189.

22. This passage is from a series of lectures given by Khetsun Sangpo Rinpoche in Charlottesville, Virginia, during the summer of 1986 and translated by Jeffrey Hopkins. I have revised Hopkins' translation somewhat. Khetsun Sangpo is commenting on p. 10b of Mipam's *Three Cycles of Fundamental Mind* (*gnyug sems skor gsum*).
23. These verses are from a root text by the First Karma Chakmé that is the basis for an oral commentary by Chökyi Nyima Rinpoche in *The Union of Mahamudra and Dzogchen,* tr. Erik Pema Kunsang (Hong Kong: Rangjung Yeshe Publications, 1989), pp. 143–144.
24. *Rainbow Painting,* p. 31.
25. See the section on the "bodhisattva levels" in chapter 4, "Mahāyāna."
26. *Buddha Mind,* p. 49.
27. Ibid., pp. 49–50.
28. Ibid., pp. 51–52.
29. *The Nyingma School,* p. 329.

13. Kagyu

History and Doctrines

The Kagyu (*bka' brgyud*) order traces its lineage back to the Indian tantric sage Tilopa (988–1069), who is said to have received instructions directly from Vajradhara (*Dorjé Chang*). Vajradhara's teachings are considered to be superior to those of Śākyamuni (the historical Buddha) in that he is a "complete enjoyment body," while Śākyamuni is only an "emanation body." In order to receive teachings from a complete enjoyment body buddha, one must have reached a high level of mystical awareness, and so the instructions of such buddhas are vastly superior to those of emanation bodies, since the latter must adapt their message to the limited capacities of their audiences.

In addition to Tilopa, the Kagyu order also counts such important Indian figures as Nāgārjuna, Saraha, Śavari, and Maitripa as members of its lineage. The name Kagyu literally means "teaching lineage," and its adherents claim that its doctrines and practices are passed down through a succession of awakened teachers, each of whom directly understands the true nature of reality through spontaneous, nonconceptual awareness and then transmits the essence of his or her teaching to the next generation of meditators.[1] Tilopa, for example, transmitted the teachings to his student Nāropa (1016–1100), who first underwent a series of trials that tested his determination and purified his mind.

According to his religious biography, Nāropa was renowned as a scholar and was widely recognized as a person who had conceptually mastered the teachings of the sūtras, tantras, and vinaya. He eventually rose to the position of abbot of Nālandā Monastery, the greatest seat of learning in the

Buddhist world at the time, which indicates that he was one of the foremost scholars of his day. His philosophical acumen and debating prowess were so great that no one could exceed him in knowledge of Buddhist scriptures, and he decisively vanquished all who dared debate him. Despite his learning and prestige, however, he had not penetrated the meaning of the teachings, and one day this was pointed out to him by a hideously ugly old woman who appeared before him and challenged him to explain the essence of the dharma.

He confessed his inability to do so, and the old woman (who was an apparition sent to him by Tilopa) advised him to seek out a guru who could help him to find the truth. The ugly physical characteristics of the apparitional woman were revealed to be reflections of his own mind, and he realized that his learning and scholarship had made him proud and arrogant. He only understood Buddhist teachings conceptually, but the apparition informed him that such an approach is inadequate. He was told that Tilopa could help him to penetrate the true meaning of the teachings.

After a series of trials, he met Tilopa, who became his teacher.[2] Because of his attachment to conceptuality, however, Nāropa was not yet ready to receive his instructions, and so Tilopa subjected him to a series of tasks, most of which resulted in pain or frustration. In one case, Tilopa climbed up to the roof of a high building and said to Nāropa, "If I had a true disciple, he would willingly jump to the ground from the top of this building." In response, Nāropa unhesitatingly did so, with predictable results: the fall caused him serious injuries, and as he lay broken on the ground Tilopa pointed out that his problems arose from his still-powerful attachment to conceptual thought. Tilopa then healed him through his magical powers, and Nāropa continued to follow his orders until he had been released from the most debilitating of his false conceptions and mentally purified through his intense and unwavering faith in his teacher. His trials lasted for twelve years, during which he never lost confidence in Tilopa. At the completion of his trials, Tilopa was able to give him the teachings of the great seal (*phyag rgya chen po, mahāmudrā*), which the Kagyu order considers to be the quintessence of all Buddhist doctrines. After receiving them and meditating on them, Nāropa attained supreme awakening.[3]

Tilopa's discourses were not lengthy discussions of doctrine or detailed instructions on practice: he pointed to the empty sky and said to Nāropa, "Kyeho! Here is the primordial wisdom of self-awareness which transcends words and mental objects. I, Tilo, have nothing to show. Just understand by looking at self-awareness." Hearing these words, the veils of delusion were lifted from Nāropa's eyes and he was able to understand the primordially pure nature of mind. With this he attained the state of the buddha Vajradhara, which completely transcends all conceptuality.

The main disciple of Nāropa was Chögi Lodrö of Mar, generally referred to as Marpa (1012–1097).[4] He is the first Tibetan member of the lineage, and he began his career as a translator of Buddhist texts. He made three visits to India in search of the dharma, and while in India met Nāropa and became his disciple. On each of his journeys, Nāropa gave him more of the teachings and initiations into tantric practices, particularly the practice of Cakrasaṃvara, the main tutelary deity of the Kagyu order. During Marpa's third trip Nāropa gave him his final instructions, including the quintessence of the great seal.

It is significant that the Kagyu tradition considers Marpa to have attained a level of awakening equivalent to that of Vajradhara, because he was a householder with a wife and family. The lineage also holds, however, that he was not like ordinary householders, because he was completely unattached to worldly things, and his perception was like that of a buddha who can live and act in the world while still perceiving the nondifference of nirvana and cyclic existence. In other words, Marpa was in the world but not of it, since his perception was developed to a point where he could view the world as a completely purified buddha land and all beings as awakened deities.

Marpa's main disciple was Milarépa (1040–1123), who is renowned throughout the Tibetan cultural area as one of the greatest figures of Tibetan Buddhism. According to his biography, his family was cheated of its property by his unscrupulous uncle and aunt, which led to Milarépa's studying black magic. After he had mastered several destructive spells, he cast one on the uncle and aunt, with the result that a number of people were killed. Reflecting on his actions, Milarépa understood that his deeds had created a great debt of negative karma, and so he sought a lama who could help him to avoid the consequences of his act of revenge.

His search led him to Marpa, who recognized that Milarépa had the potential to become awakened. Marpa assigned his new student a series of difficult and dispiriting tasks (most notably building several towers by hand), which were designed to purify Milarépa's karma. After these were completed, Marpa gave him the teachings of his lineage, after which Milarépa decided to devote himself to meditation in solitude. After meditating in a cave for a number of years, Milarépa attained a high level of realization and began teaching students.[5] He had a number of famous disciples, including Réchung Dorjé Drakpa (1088–1158) and Gampopa (1079–1153). The transmission of this lineage continues today, and its vibrancy is attested by the number of widely acclaimed lamas it has produced, including the Gyelwa Karmapas and the late Kalu Rinpoche, who was a major figure in the dissemination of this lineage to the West.[6]

The Kagyu order is traditionally divided into "the four great and the eight lesser schools." The former derive from Gampopa and his nephew Takpo Gomtsül (1116–1169). They are: (1) Karma Kagyu or Karma Kamtsang, founded by Tüsum Khyenpa (1110–1193), who was later recognized as the first of the Karmapa lamas; (2) Tselpa Kagyu, which was founded by Shang Tselpa and derives its name from the district of Tsel; (3) Baram Kagyu, founded by Darma Wangchuk; and (4) Pakmo Kagyu, founded by Pakmodrupa Dorjé Gyelpo (1110–1170), a disciple of Gampopa.

The eight lesser schools are: (1) Drikung, (2) Taklung, (3) Tropu, (4) Drukpa, (5) Mar, (6) Yerpa, (7) Shuksep, and (8) Yamsang. Today only the Drukpa, Drikung, and Taklung survive, and the newer lineages of Shangpa Kagyu and Ugyen Nyendrup should be added to the list of Kagyu schools.

The first great monastery of the Kagyu order was Densatil, founded by Pakmodrupa. This monastery began as a simple hut in which he lived, but as he attracted students numerous buildings were constructed, and due to the patronage of the aristocratic Lang family, it was eventually transformed into a large and powerful monastic complex. Today the Kagyu lineage is spreading in the West, due to the efforts of a number of lamas who have set up teaching centers overseas. Although most of the great Kagyu monastic complexes in Tibet were destroyed by the Chinese, many have reopened in India, Nepal, Sikkim, and Bhutan. An example is Rumtek in Sikkim (the seat of the Karmapa in exile).

Gampopa and the Development of a Monastic Tradition

Someone visiting the great Kagyu monasteries of present-day India and Nepal might wonder how a lineage that began with ascetic, iconoclastic hermits developed into one of the major orders of Tibetan Buddhism, with large monasteries and centers all over the world. The period of transition begins with Gampopa, who received the teachings of Milarépa and incorporated them into a system of cenobitic monasticism. Gampopa combined the yogic practices and meditational techniques of the early Kagyu teachers with the monastic structures of the Kadampas (the lineage founded by Atiśa's disciple Dromdön), and the result was a new order that could transmit the yogic teachings of Milarépa and his predecessors and preserve them within a monastic framework.

Gampopa became a monk in his early twenties after his wife and children died. These events brought home to him the transient nature of human existence, and he took the vows of a monk of the Kadampa order. From an early period he displayed an eclectic approach to Buddhist teachings and practice, and he received instructions and empowerments from a number of teachers. According to the *Blue Annals*, he heard of an accomplished yogi named Milarépa and decided to visit him, despite the objections of his teachers, who asked him, "Are our teachings not sufficient?" He persisted in his request, and they gave him permission to leave, but told him, "Go, but do not abandon our ways."[7]

When Gampopa neared the place where Milarépa was meditating, he met a monk who informed him that his coming had been prophesied. When he heard that Milarépa had been expecting him, he was filled with pride, and in order to counteract this Milarépa refused to receive him for two weeks. When Milarépa finally consented to meet, Gampopa offered him a piece of gold and some tea. Milarépa informed Gampopa that he had no interest in such things and handed him a skull cup full of *chang* (an alcoholic brew made from barley).

Gampopa at first was reluctant to drink it, since doing so would conflict with his monastic vows, which expressly forbade him to drink liquor. Milarépa, reading his mind, ordered him to drink it, which he did. This act began a process of weaning him from attachment to religious conventions, which, although they are designed to help people to escape from cyclic existence, may prove to be a hindrance if one fails to realize that even Buddhist teachings can become an object of negative attachments.

Milarépa then asked him what initiations he had received, to which Gampopa replied,

> From the Sage of Mar-yul I have received many initiations including the 'Sixfold Jewel Ornament' and the *Saṃvara Tantra*. Also I have studied the teachings relating to the Kadampa scriptures in north Uru, and I have experienced for thirteen days a state of trance devoid of all sensations.[8]

In reply, Milarépa laughed and told Gampopa that such practices are "useless for achieving buddhahood, even if one is free from sensations for a whole eon." He told Gampopa, "Although the initiations that you have received previously are not altogether unsatisfactory, you should now practice according to my system," after which he gave Gampopa tantric initiations.[9]

Gampopa diligently practiced in accordance with Milarépa's instructions, and the *Blue Annals* report that he made rapid progress. He learned to harness the energy of breath and live on breath alone. After he had attained a high level of meditative control, Milarépa advised him to return to central Tibet and to abandon the world. He further urged him to apply himself diligently to meditation, avoid evil people who might distract him, frequent solitary places, and remain apart from society.

The tension between monastic life and the tantric practices of his teacher is evident in this story, and it continued throughout Gampopa's life. After leaving Milarépa, he went to Nyal and stayed at the Kadampa monastery of Séwalung, where he participated in religious ceremonies. This led to a sense of conflict, however, because he felt that such external rituals were incompatible with his tantric practice. After this he devoted himself to meditation for three years, with the result that he fully comprehended the luminous nature of mind and directly perceived the true nature of all phenomena.

After leaving the monastery, he continued to obey Milarépa's advice to remain in solitary places, coming eventually to Gampo (which is why he later became known as Gampopa, "Man of Gampo"). He was visited by some lamas from Uru, who asked him to work for the benefit of sentient beings. He replied, "I have no doubt about the good of living beings, as I have no more than three years to live." One of his previous teachers gave him a mantra that would prolong his life, and by reciting it he was able to live beyond the time he had expected. After this he attracted a circle of disciples, and he is reported to have given each the instructions that would be most beneficial. To some he presented the Mahāyāna teachings of the six perfections and the bodhisattva path, and to others he taught basic tantric practices, while to the most advanced he gave the final great seal instructions. In this way he paved the way for the development of a Kagyu order that could attract a large number of students.

Previous masters had reserved their instructions for a small number of specially qualified initiates, but Gampopa expanded the range of Kagyu. By combining the tantric teachings of Marpa and Milarépa with the established monastic practices of the Kadampas, he made it possible to develop training centers, monastic universities, and curricula that could meet the needs of spiritual seekers of different levels of spiritual attainment and with different interests and proclivities. This development is somewhat surprising in light of the aversion that both Milarépa and Marpa felt toward established monasticism. Milarépa was a hermit who spoke eloquently about the dangers of society, family life, and monasticism, and Marpa was a householder who saw the monastic life as appropriate only for people of limited capacities. For both, the eremitic life of the unattached tantric yogi, free from the artificial constraints of society and religion, was thought to be best suited to attaining awakening.

Gampopa, however, was able to combine both elements, and this is the probable reason that the Kagyu lineage continues to be one of the most dynamic orders of Tibetan Buddhism. It has successfully blended the esoteric tantric teachings of Marpa and Milarépa with a monastic structure that is well suited to preservation of the words of previous masters. In addition, this order strongly emphasizes the necessity of meditative training, and Kagyu practitioners are expected to spend long periods of time in solitary retreats. Anyone who wishes to become a teacher must have completed a three-year meditative retreat, a practice that severely tests the fortitude of even the most strong-willed person. This combination of monasticism and solitary retreats has served the Kagyu order well, allowing it to transmit its teachings and practices to successive generations of students while maintaining a spiritual continuity with the tantric yogis who were its founders.

Meditation Practices

The Six Yogas of Nāropa

Among the most important practices of the Kagyupas are the "six yogas of Nāropa" (*nā ro chos drug*), which are named after the Indian master, although according to some traditions he did not develop them himself. The six yogas are: (1) heat (*gtum mo*); (2) illusory body (*sgyu lus*); (3) dream (*rmi lam*); (4) clear light (*'od gsal*); (5) intermediate state (*bar do*); and (6) transference of consciousness (*'pho ba*).

Heat Yoga. The first of these yogas involves developing the ability to increase and channel inner heat through visualizing fire and the sun in various places of the body. Through training, the meditator is able to imagine her entire body being surrounded by flames, and Western medical researchers have reported significant increases in body temperature among yogis who are proficient in this practice.[10]

The technique requires the yogi to become aware, through introspective meditation, of the body's subtle energy channels and the winds that course through them. The winds are "mounts" (*rta*, literally "horses") for consciousnesses. The channels are too subtle to be perceived through dissection of the body, as are the winds. The physiology used here is a mystical one, and the movements of the winds, their function as mounts, and the operation of the channels are only understood by advanced yogis whose experience has awakened them to such things.

Through meditation adepts learn to harness the energy current called "mind of awakening" (*byang chub sems, bodhicitta*) and cause it to move from the left and right channels into the central channel. The yogi then causes it to rise through the cakras.[11] This causes a sensation of increasing heat and light, which often alters bodily temperature at the extremities. It is important to be aware, however, that this is not simply a substitute for warm clothing or central heating: the process is not primarily designed to produce heat, but rather to help the yogi to experience directly the luminous nature of consciousness, which is being manifested in the form of heat and light. This yoga represents mind's luminosity in visual and tactile terms, but the primary goal is to experience directly the fluid, clear nature of mind, which in this meditation is represented by experiences of heat and light.

In one technique, the yogi sits in meditation and concentrates on the presence of four "fires" below the navel, one in each of the four cardinal directions. Then she draws in air from the two nostrils and another subtle wind from below, mingling the two. This causes the fires to blaze brightly and become bright red, which in turn raises body temperature. This is accompanied by a feeling of bliss. One remains in this state, holding the breath for as long as possible, and then exhales slowly through the nostrils.

In the next stage one visualizes the central channel and the channels on the left and right, each about the width of a wheat straw. One mentally pictures a sun disk at the point where they meet. This has a blazing red letter *ram* on it. As in the previous stage, one draws the outer and inner breaths, and this causes fires to burst forth from the letter *ram*, after which one makes the fire rise through the central energy channel. This gives rise to a feeling of blissful heat.

As one works at these practices, the energy channels open and allow energy to flow more freely. This yoga is then combined with meditation on the nature of mind. One visualizes the subtle drop that rises through the central channel as being of the same nature as one's own mind, and through deepening this perception the drop and the mind come to be viewed as undifferentiable. Meditators who are adept at this technique also experience the subtle "pride" or dignity of being a fully awakened deity. This experience is different from ordinary pride, because it is free from false conceptuality and afflicted mental states.

A person who works at this yoga gains control over the energy channels and subtle drops, which is a necessary precondition for the other five yogas, all of which require familiarity with, and proficiency in, this mystic yoga of psychophysical control and manipulation of energies.[12]

The latter five yogas are based on heat yoga. When practicing them, one generally spends one-third to one-half of each session training in heat yoga, and the rest with the specific techniques of each yoga.

Illusory Body. The technique of illusory body begins with the insight that the phenomena of cyclic existence are mental creations. This yoga involves visualizing a subtle body that is different from the physical body, which is composed of the five aggregates.[13] One imagines an illusory body imbued with the six perfections that is being transformed into the "vajra body" (*rdo rje'i sku, vajra-kāya*), symbolizing supreme buddhahood.

This practice is compared to the way that magicians in India were said to be able to create illusory images that appeared as concrete and real to the audiences which came to see them.[14] In the context of the yoga of illusory body, the reason for visualizing an unreal image and imbuing it with apparent reality is to analyze whether or not it is different in essence from the phenomena of ordinary experience. Diligent analysis and meditation reveal that all phenomena are empty of inherent existence. They emerge from mind and return to it, like waves rising from water. The yogi realizes that there is no inherently real difference between his mind and the mind of a buddha, and this technique is said to be a powerful tool for quickly transforming one's ordinary consciousness into that of an awakened being.

Having gained a measure of control over the vital winds and channels, the meditator now uses subtle energies and mind to produce an illusory body in the form of a tantric deity which appears to be real, although it lacks substantial existence. It is compared to a mirror image, which seems like the thing of which it is a reflection, but is completely devoid of substantial reality. Unlike the mirror image, however, the illusory body is created from subtle aspects of energy and mind that are generated as the form of the deity. The energies and mind used in this exercise should be visualized as residing at the heart as an indestructible drop. These should be thought of as the most subtle basis for the imputation of "self."

One causes the vital energies to enter the central channel, remain there for a while, and then dissolve into clear light. The clear light is then generated as a tantric deity, which means that the meditator is visualizing his vital nature and mind as a fully awakened deity. The form of the deity enters into the clear light, and so one's vital energy and mind become the deity. This experience is a counteragent to feelings of desire and aversion, and it quickly leads to actualization of the state of Vajradhara. In addition, gaining proficiency in generating and manipulating the illusory body is essential for related exercises in the next stage, dream yoga, which utilizes similar techniques.

Through gaining familiarity with the practice of generating an apparently real illusory body from one's vital energies and mind, one comes to realize that one is of the same nature as this image and that all sentient beings share the same ontological status. One perceives them as being of the nature of light and develops compassion for those creatures who foolishly grasp at other illusory forms, which have as much substantial reality as images in dreams. All appearances of cyclic existence are seen to lack inherent existence, and one visualizes all sentient beings as being liberated and as residing in pure buddha lands. Even negative mental states, disease, and evil spirits are illusions, and one mentally transmutes them into pure forms, which then become aids on the path to awakening. The meditator understands that "reality" is pliable and malleable, not fixed and determinate. This perception is a precondition for the practice of dream yoga.

Dream Yoga. The yoga of dreams involves taking control of one's dreams, determining their contents, and using this practice to influence the activity of mind. Ordinary people are helpless in their dreams: they are buffeted by images and emotions that are beyond their control. The tantric yogi, by contrast, learns to control dreams by manipulating the vital energies that operate during sleep. Waking perceptions are understood to have no more (and no less) veracity than images in dreams, and this yoga helps to weaken one's rigid attachment to conventional "reality."

There are two primary aspects of this yoga: (1) manipulating the contents of dreams so that they no longer reflect negative mental states, but are transformed in accordance with tantric symbolism; and (2) gaining awareness of the fact that one is dreaming while one is in the dream state. In the first practice, one mentally generates tantric deities, bringing to mind the symbolism associated with them, and using these visualizations to replace the random, afflicted images of dreams with Buddhist images and positive mental states that counteract mental afflictions. For example, a yogi who in the waking state has visualized the identification of Vajradhara and Prajñā (Wisdom) will in the dream state visualize a red and white triangle below her own navel. This is symbolic of the visualization of the union of the two deities in the waking state, and with this practice even dreams become occasions for tantric practice. In this way, one brings meditational images into one's dreams, with the result that the dreams become imbued with tantric symbolism.

The second aspect is closely connected, because it allows one to become aware of the dream process as it unfolds and to exercise control over it, and so

> by becoming aware of the infinite modes to counter one thing by another, as in the case of diseases by medicines, not to become confused as to the proper means and in recognizing the mystery of the inseparableness of the opposites to clarify the state of bewilderment-errancy and to attain a state of non-bewilderment.[15]

The training begins with developing the ability to focus on the energy center (*cakra*) at the throat and visualizing a soft, glowing light there. One then cultivates this image until it becomes clearer and more radiant. This exercise is important in that it marks a measure of control over one's dreams while one is in the dream state. The next phase involves becoming aware of the unfolding of dream images and watching their arising and cessation within recognizing their illusory nature. This in turn helps meditators to determine the contents of dreams, and those who become skilled in this yoga are able to populate their dreams with buddhas, ḍākinīs, and so on, thus subtly transforming their consciousnesses in accordance with these images. In this way, the yogi

> transforms the unfolding drama into pure Buddha-realms and the like, and creates various enhancing situations. In some cases he will purify his former Karma . . . in others he will enter, stay in, and emerge from a great variety of meditative absorptions; or he will listen to the Dharma under the Buddhas of many and various realms. By practising this dream-state the bewilderment of holding as true what appears as an outer object in the waking life will be annihilated and internally the rigid interconnexions of the pathways will be resolved.[16]

The Second Dalai Lama's Presentation of Niguma's System

The second Dalai Lama, in accordance with the system of Niguma,[17] divides the training of dream yoga into six categories: (1) awareness of dreams, (2) purifying dreams, (3) increasing the objects of dreams, (4) emanating within the dream, (5) awareness of objects of perception, and (6) meditating on their suchness.

The training in dream recognition begins with guru yoga and reciting an aspirational prayer. During the day the meditator should cultivate a sense that all objects perceived in the waking state are like the images of dreams, and she views the waking state as a form of dream. Through this training, the apparent solidity of things begins to diminish, and she becomes aware that the objects of waking consciousness are no more real than those experienced in sleep. This enables the meditator to recognize dream objects for what they are while asleep.

Before going to sleep, the meditator imagines herself as a tantric deity and also visualizes the three energy channels. At the base of the central channel is the syllable *ah*, and at the highest cakra is the syllable *ham*. A white drop comes from the *ham*, and a red drop comes from the *ah*, and both are shining brightly. The meditator mingles them together and visualizes them moving to the heart and then encircling it. While doing so, she affirms a commitment to be aware of dreaming while in the dream state. The drop is then brought to the throat cakra, where it remains while one goes to sleep.

While dreaming, one engages in visualizations concordant with one's practice. One mentally pictures oneself as a tantric deity, and this deity can be either peaceful or wrathful. In this way, one controls the dream and learns to manipulate the subtle drops while in the dream state. The skill that one has gained in the previous two yogas is essential to successful practice in dream yoga, which involves working with the vital energies and illusory images.

In the next stage, the meditator learns to purify the dream. She performs various tantric meditations in which deities are visualized out of emptiness, radiate lights that purify the psychophysical continuum, and are then re-merged into emptiness. Throughout this process, it is necessary for the meditator to remain aware that she is in the dream state.

Increasing the objects of dreams requires the ability to control the production of images. One first creates a second dream body, and then doubles these two. This enables the meditator to populate the dream with objects concordant with the goal of meditation, and advanced practitioners of this yoga can create as many of these bodies as they wish.

Emanating within the dream represents a further development of mastery. In this stage the meditator creates tantric images concordant with current meditative goals. For instance, a person who wants to overcome death will emanate in the form of the deity Yamāntaka (Destroyer of Death).

A yogi who successfully completes these practices gains progressively greater control over dreams, and at the same time also gains greater awareness of the dream process. A person at the level of "awareness of objects of perception" has a heightened understanding of how mental images arise and pass away, and this in turn leads to greater awareness of how both dreams and waking reality operate.

The previous practices are required for the sixth, "meditating on their suchness," which refers to comprehension of the nature of dream objects. These are viewed as being of the nature of mind, which is clear light. The images of dreams are seen as arising from this clear light and again being re-absorbed into it without any change in ontological status taking place. One realizes that the same is true of the waking state, and this understanding serves to weaken one's attachment to, and unquestioning acceptance of, waking "reality."

Clear Light. In the yoga of clear light, the practitioner becomes aware of the nature of mind. Its luminosity is visualized as radiating out everywhere in all directions, like a lamp that illuminates both itself and other objects.

The mind of clear light is seen as both an unwavering radiance that is untouched by the apparent negativities of mental afflictions and a pure, vibratory sound that encompasses all other sounds. Its luminosity is unrestricted, and its purview is universal. It is also perceived as radiant emptiness, an emptiness from which images and concepts arise, but one realizes that these are not different from mind. They are simply manifestations of the creative power of consciousness, and so one understands that they have no power in themselves.

In Niguma's system, this practice is connected with the completion stage of highest yoga tantra. There are two primary techniques: (1) generating the pure light consciousness through reliance on the lama, and (2) generating it through the syllable *hūṃ*. One first imagines oneself as the deity Heruka and his consort, and the central channel is filled with substances that are distillations of the mind of awakening and look like newly fallen snow. At the heart one visualizes a cakra representing the wheel of doctrine, and one's lama, in the form of a tiny drop, sitting on it. The drop is mostly white, with some red color, and at its center is a white letter *hūṃ* the size of a mustard seed. This radiates silver lights that are of the nature of primordial bliss.

The meditator concentrates on this letter, which emanates light that fills the entire world and dissolves its inhabitants into light. These lights then are dissolved into the meditator, who is still manifesting as Heruka and consort. The meditator in turn dissolves into light from the head downward and from the feet upward simultaneously. This light is then merged into the drop at the heart, which itself disperses into the letter *hūṃ*. This dissolves into itself and becomes a flame, which finally resolves into emptiness. One remains in this state, contemplating emptiness, and this causes the vital energies to enter the central channel, remain awhile, and then dissolve. This gives rise to the wisdom of clear light.

A person who successfully completes this meditation perceives all objects as empty, and the emptiness appears as pure bliss, and the bliss as a tantric deity such as Heruka. This awareness and the feeling of bliss should continue to pervade all of the yogi's perceptions after the meditative state.

Bardo. The Kagyu lineage distinguishes six bardos (intermediate states): (1) our normal waking experience, from the moment of birth until death, called "the bardo between birth and death" (*skye shi'i bar do*); (2) the bardo of the dream state, which is the time between when one falls asleep and the time of awakening, called "dream bardo" (*rmi lam bar do*); and (3) the "reality bardo" (*chos nyid bar do*), the time of unconsciousness that people experience when the mind is overwhelmed by death. This is called "reality bardo" because in this state the mind is thrown into its own nature, but ordinary beings are so confused that they tend to escape into unconsciousness rather than confront it directly.

The next stage in the process of death is called (4) "bardo of becoming" (*srid pa bar do*). In this phase a person experiences all sorts of fantastic and terrifying sights, all of which are projections of mind, but no less real to the perceiver than the contents of ordinary waking consciousness. This stage begins at the first moment of awakening from unconsciousness and lasts until one takes rebirth in one of the six realms of cyclic existence.[18] It is called "bardo of becoming" because it leads to the next phase of one's existence.

A person who successfully practices meditation gains a greater familiarity with the mind, and such a person is able to enter (5) "the bardo of meditative absorption" (*bsam gtan bar do*). This is a state of cessation in which one attains a meditative equipoise in which the senses are withdrawn from external objects and focused on a meditative object of observation. This bardo is said to last for the duration of successful meditation and ends when normal worldly consciousness resumes.

The last bardo is (6) "the bardo of birth" (*skye gnas bar do*), which begins after the bardo of becoming. At this time, consciousness is attracted to a copulating couple in accordance with its past karma. The consciousness enters the zygote at the moment of fertilization, at which point the process of gestation and birth begins. This period of bardo lasts from the point of fertilization until the moment of physical birth.

All of these bardos are common to beings caught up in cyclic existence, and in most of them one is propelled forward by the force of past karma. The bardos of death, however, are potentially liberating opportunities. A person with the proper meditative training can make great progress at this time because the coarse levels of mind that normally dominate one's awareness drop away, and one actualizes very subtle states of mind that before death are only accessible to advanced meditators. A person who takes advantage of this opportunity can more easily become aware of the fundamentally pure and luminous nature of mind than a living person in the normal waking state, and so Tibetan meditation theory stresses the importance of training prior to death. Kalu Rinpoche states that a person who correctly understands the workings of bardo realizes that the appearances of peaceful and wrathful deities, of colors and sounds and the like, are all projections of mind, and so is not frightened by them. Through deepening this realization,

> liberation arises at the moment in the after-death state when consciousness can realize its experiences to be nothing other than mind itself . . . . The possibility of awakening in the after-death state rests upon three things. The first is the fundamentally enlightened nature of mind, the seed of Buddhahood, without which nothing would be possible. The second is the blessing inherent in the pure forms of the deities. The third is the connection we have established with those deities through empowerment, and the understanding we have, both intellectually and intuitively, of what is actually taking place. When all these three elements come together, the possibility exists of achieving liberation during the instant of confronting the maṇḍalas of the deities.[19]

If, however, one does not take advantage of this opportunity, one continues on through the later stages and again undergoes rebirth in accordance with past karma.

Transference of Consciousness. The practice of transference of consciousness has a number of levels, some of which are geared toward nonadepts, and others that are only attained by people who are very advanced on the path. For beginners, it is said that just receiving empowerments for this practice from a qualified lama can result in transference to a pure buddha land if one brings the teachings to mind at the time of death. After receiving the empowerment, a practitioner should develop a strong yearning for a pure buddha land and should continue to cultivate this throughout his life. If successful, at the moment of death the consciousness escapes through the "Brahmā aperture" (the fontanel, which is the place at the crown of the head where the bones of the skull meet). A person who is about to die should also repeat the mantra *hik* over and over, as this is said to aid in the process of transference.

According to the second Dalai Lama, it is best to begin this practice while one is healthy, because "once severe illness has set in one will not be able to master the trainings, no matter how strong one's wish may be."[20]

If one is doing this while still healthy in order to practice for the time of actual death, pronouncing the mantra *hik* sends the consciousness out, and the mantra *ka* causes it to return. The process is repeated three times, and one sign of success is the appearance of a small hole (or sometimes a pustule) at the fontanel, out of which a small amount of blood or lymph flows.

This practice may also be used at the time of death to transfer one's consciousness into a suitable, newly deceased body. As an example, Marpa's son, Darma Dodé, died prematurely as a result of his father's disobeying Nāropa's command to pass the teaching of "transference of consciousness" to Milarépa. Marpa instead only gave this teaching to Darma Dodé, and the karmic consequence of his disobedience was his son's death. Since Darma Dodé knew how to effect the transfer of consciousness, at the moment of death he took over the body of a dove that had just died (which happened to be the only body available). Marpa then advised him to fly to India, which he did. There he found the body of a recently deceased brahman boy that was being carried in a funeral procession. Darma Dodé entered and awakened the body, but one result was that this particular practice of transference was lost in Tibet.

Other types of transference, however, are still practiced by Tibetan lamas, and the ordinary empowerments are widely bestowed on people who wish to have an "insurance policy" when they die. By receiving the empowerments, they hope to gain rebirth in a Buddhist pure land, where the conditions are optimal for attainment of buddhahood.

Gampopa also identifies three levels of transference for tantric practitioners: (1) in the lowest, one manifests one's consciousness in the generation stage, and one is able to visualize oneself as a deity, such as Vajradhara or Vajravārāhī; (2) in the next highest, one shifts oneself into an illusory body; and (3) the supreme level involves transferring consciousness into the realm of clear light, which is identified with the basic nature of mind and with the "rainbow body" of supreme buddhahood.

All of these yogas serve to undermine fixed attachment to the phenomena of ordinary experience as being fixed and immutable. They give the successful meditator a measure of control over the unfolding of experience and allow him to manipulate it in ways that are thought to be impossible by people still bound by the conceptual limitations of ordinary beings. Even death is no longer the inevitable cessation of existence, but rather a doorway of opportunity for spiritual progress.

Mahāmudrā, the Great Seal

There are three primary features of Kagyu tantric practice: (1) visualizing oneself as a deity and practice of sādhanas; (2) practice of inner yogas, which work with the subtle body; and (3) formless meditations, in which one rests in the nature of mind. All Kagyu schools emphasize the primacy of the great seal, which Kagyupas consider the essence of all Buddhist teachings. This essence lies not in the texts or doctrines of Buddhism, but rather in direct, personal realization of truth, which is epitomized in mahāmudrā practice. As Khenpo Könchog Gyaltsen describes it,

> mahāmudrā . . . is the Buddha nature, the basic mind within all sentient beings. To know it is to know the true nature of all phenomena, and to actualize it is to become a Buddha, to be one with all the Buddha qualities.[21]

Lobsang Lhalungpa states that the term mahāmudrā

> stands for the ultimate nature of mind and reality. Just as a royal seal wields unchallengeable authority, so the all-encompassing voidness of the ultimate reality prevails upon the cosmic phenomena. It also stands for the path of self-realization, which integrates authentic vision, contemplation, and action into one perfect insight.[22]

Like the practice of great perfection (*dzogchen*) in Nyingma, the path of great seal involves directly realizing the luminous nature of mind, which leads to instantaneous self-realization.[23] Kagyu tradition regards this as the most rapid of all paths to awakening. A meditator of sharp faculties who diligently pursues this path can reach awakening at any moment through directly experiencing the clear, luminous nature of mind, which in its essence is the same in buddhas and ordinary beings.

In order to penetrate the mysteries of mahāmudrā, it is necessary to find an awakened teacher, a person who has successfully traversed the path and thus acquired the ability to look directly into the minds of students and skillfully guide them past the pitfalls they will encounter in their training. The student must have a strong desire to transcend the sufferings of cyclic existence, well-developed compassion for other sentient beings, a high level of intelligence, and, most importantly, an intense and unwavering faith in the lama.

Initially the student is expected to undergo the training of the preliminary practices, which help to purify past karma and focus one's attention on the goal of awakening. This in turn brings blessings and empowerments, which serve to overcome obstacles on the path.

Great seal practice is divided into three aspects: basis, path, and result. The basis is correct understanding, which is founded on comprehending the nature of mind. The meditator quiets the mind through meditation that stabilizes it and thus begins a process of disengagement from the habitual tendencies of random, deluded thoughts. This is expanded by means of the practices of the path, which involve meditation on the nature of mind. The result is the culmination of the process, in which one actualizes the potential for buddhahood inherent in the nature of mind.

Calm Abiding and Higher Insight

After the student completes the preliminary practices, the next stage is cultivating calm abiding and higher insight. In the Kagyu system, the former involves a state of single-minded concentration in which one rests in the mind's natural condition of blissful, clear awareness. This is a state in which one is able to focus on the object of observation for extended periods of time without being distracted by either laxity or excitement. The former is the tendency to fall away from the object due to mental dullness, and the latter causes the meditator to lose the object due to becoming overly agitated. When these are in equipoise and one is able to focus on the object without wandering, one has attained calm abiding.

Higher insight in this system involves analyzing the nature of mind within the meditative state and perceiving its pure, mirrorlike nature. Like a clear mirror, it reflects what is put in front of it, but its nature is eternally unsullied and unaffected by its contents. According to Kalu Rinpoche, higher insight

> is often called the experience of selflessness which has two aspects: the absence of a personal self, and the non-existence of all phenomena as independent entities. We begin to realize that the self and the objects we perceive as external lack any ultimate reality.[24]

The Four Faults

If mind is essentially pure and unsullied, then why do we not perceive the mind in its pure state? Why are we beguiled by appearances, drawn toward conceptuality, and motivated by mental afflictions? The answer, according to Kagyu teachers, is that ordinary beings have "four faults" that impede our realization of the omnipresent reality of mind. The first is that the mind is "too close" (*nye drags*) to us, and so we are unable to perceive it. Just as one never looks directly at one's own face, the mind is too close to be perceived in its nature by one who has not undergone meditative training.

The second fault is that the nature of mind is "too profound" (*zab drags*) because it is something completely beyond the scope of ordinary awareness. A person who correctly understands the true nature of mind is a buddha, and such understanding is unimaginable to ordinary beings.

The third fault is that mahāmudrā is "too easy" (*sla drags*), and so ordinary people fail to grasp it. For one who has successfully actualized the highest realizations of mahāmudrā, direct perception of reality is spontaneous and effortless. There is nothing easier than letting the mind remain in its natural state, and so finally there is nothing to do in the great seal—one simply lets the mind be what it is.

The fourth fault is that awakening is "too excellent" (*bzang drags*), and so ordinary, deluded beings are unable even to begin to conceive what it is like. Buddhahood is the final actualization of one's highest potential, the dawning of full realization of the primordial buddha nature that is inherent in the mind of every sentient being, but a person whose mind is bound to ordinariness, to conceptual thought and delusion, cannot even begin to imagine what it would be like to perceive reality as a buddha does.

Understanding the Nature of Mind

The path to overcoming the four faults initially involves developing positive mental qualities, which serve to counteract the negative emotions that cloud the perception of ordinary beings. One must also cultivate pure devotion to the lama; this is said to be essential to successful meditation.

Through following the lama's instructions and engaging in meditation on the nature of the phenomena of experience, one finds that they are all empty of inherent existence and are merely manifestations of mind. Mind is also found to be empty, and all of its apparent contents are illusory. Through cultivating this insight, one realizes that all mental afflictions and negative mental states are empty like space, are not a part of one's own nature, and are not different from mind. When an emotion like anger arises, one looks for its basis and decides that it is a manifestation of mind, and that mind is empty, clear, and unimpeded. Thus the emotion has no independent existence and has no real claim on one's mind.

Once one begins to perceive emotions in this way, their strength diminishes, as does their motivating force. A thought or emotion is perceived as being essentially empty, a creation of mind. Mind itself is also empty, and so the emotive force is transmuted through this realization. There is no need to repress or suppress emotions, since they are nothing in themselves. The meditator should simply experience them as they appear, while subjecting them to scrutiny to determine whether or not they have any substantial reality. Thus the arising of passions and afflictions becomes an occasion for meditative practice, and even powerful negative sensations like hatred, rage, lust, and so on are transformed into unconquerable bliss through realizing their lack of inherent existence. Wangchuk Dorjé advises meditators,

> do not wander for even an instant. Be as (attentive as) when threading a needle. Do not let your mind be turbulent, rather have it be like an ocean without any waves. Do not self-consciously try to accomplish anything, rather fix your mind like an eagle soaring. Be completely free from all expectations and worries.[25]

Meditative Therapy

The method described above is very different from a number of currently popular therapy techniques in which people are urged to express negative emotions and painful past experiences in order to encounter them directly and thus overcome them through "catharsis." These techniques think of the mind as a reservoir in which people store past memories and emotions, and the purpose of the therapy is to get them out in the open so that one can move beyond them. When the reservoir is dry, one achieves a state of psychic health. In Buddhist meditation, by contrast, the mind is empty, and so one's mental state at any given moment is the result of the sort of emotions and thoughts one is currently producing. Because they too are empty, there is no limit to the mental states that can arise. Any mental quality can be developed and cultivated limitlessly, whether this is a negative tendency such as anger or a positive quality like compassion. If one chooses to work at anger, one's capacity for anger will increase; conversely, a person who cultivates compassion can develop this quality limitlessly.

We do, of course, tend to fall into patterns of thought and behavior, but Buddhist psychology contends that if we exert control over the process the mental continuum can be transformed through applying antidotes to negative mental states. These are replaced by positive qualities concordant with the antidotes, and so the tendency to produce negative mental states progressively diminishes. As this occurs, the propensity toward positive and healthy mental attitudes becomes stronger. This is possible because the mind is empty, and, as Kalu Rinpoche states:

> If we are looking for a medicine to cure the disease of emotional imbalance, we are not going to find a better remedy than emptiness. Experiencing the emptiness of emotion is what liberates us from that need to recapture the balance, because we have not been knocked off balance by emotional upheavals in the first place. Contentment and well-being arise first and foremost from understanding the nature of mind and the nature of emotionality.[26]

Through continually examining the mind and realizing that mental states arise from emptiness and again pass into emptiness, one penetrates the true nature of mind. All thoughts and perceptions are recognized as mental creations, and mind itself is also understood to be unreal. Even such apparently obvious distinctions as subject and object, male and female, self and world are mental overlays on essentially undifferentiated experience. There is no inherently existent perceiver or perceived object, no good or evil, no cyclic existence or nirvana. A meditator who cultivates this insight enters into a state of spontaneous awareness in which all distinctions are sublated in pure, nondual awareness. One perceives all sound as a union of sound and emptiness, all form—including one's own physical form—as a union of form and emptiness, and one realizes that mind and its contents are also a union of appearance and emptiness. The mind becomes liberated from the limitations of ordinary thought and perception. One perceives that the mind is all-pervasive; like space, it has no outer limits, no boundaries, no color or form, no shape or size, no real qualities of any kind. A meditator who reaches this level of awareness should strive to remain within this realization free from distractions, directly experiencing the essential emptiness of mind without clinging to or being disturbed by thoughts and concepts.

The meditator comprehends that mind and its thoughts are neither the same nor completely different. If they were the same, then there would be no way to bring conceptual thoughts to rest, since they would be of the nature of mind itself. If mind and thoughts were different, then one could have thoughts without a mind. The great seal adept realizes that the relationship between the two transcends what can be encompassed by conceptual thought and that thoughts are the temporary play of mind. They have no more ultimate reality than the fleeting images of dreams. The nature of mind is pure and clear, primordially undisturbed by the images that appear to it. The meditator strives to remain in a state of simply observing these images within being aware that they are mind's sport.

Effects and Benefits of the Training

Mahāmudrā adepts are particularly renowned for developing supranormal powers, which are said to result from cultivating the insight that the phenomena of experience are the play of mind. The phenomenal world is viewed as empty, as a projection of mind, and those who fully realize this are able to manifest miracles and to actually transform the phenomenal world in accordance with their wishes. Kalu Rinpoche contends that

> by understanding this and coming to experience it, teachers such as Milarepa can demonstrate miracles and make things happen contrary to the normal laws that govern the universe. If the universe were something ultimately real in its own right, its laws would be inviolable, and miraculous events impossible. In fact, the laws governing conventional reality are flexible, and once we realize this we have at least some limited power to manipulate the phenomenal world.[27]

This is only possible for a person who is free from attachment to conceptual thought. As long as the mind clings to "reality" as being solid and immutable, one is limited by such conceptions. By contrast, a person who knows phenomena and mind to be of one nature of emptiness perceives them as malleable, transitory images arising from emptiness and receding again into emptiness. This state is referred to as "the union of appearance and emptiness" (*snang stong zung 'jug*).

The more one remains in this state, the greater one's equanimity becomes. Distraction diminishes, and eventually one reaches the state of "one-pointedness," in which one is able to focus on a single thing for extended periods of time without distraction. The next important level of progress is one in which the yogi is able to engage in meditation spontaneously, with little mental effort. Simply thinking of meditation on the nature of mind is enough to bring about the experience, and awareness of the wonderful simplicity of mind pervades all the yogi's activities. This stage is termed "simplicity." Gampopa describes this as "understanding the essential state of that awareness [of one-pointedness] as non-arising [emptiness], which transcends conceptual modes of reality and unreality."[28] One eliminates conceptual superimpositions, even such notions as existence and nonexistence. Phenomena are viewed in their most simple aspect, free from terms and concepts.

The stage of simplicity is followed by the level of "one taste," in which all of one's experiences—all thoughts, emotions, desires, and so on—are perceived as being of one taste with the essential emptiness of mind. Prior to this stage, one's equanimity is easily distracted, and one is only able to meditate for periods of a few minutes, but a yogi at the level of "one taste" can sustain meditative concentration for extended periods and apply it to all types of mental states. The perception of these as being of one taste of emptiness, and as being of the nature of mind, becomes so pervasive that one no longer has to exert any effort in meditation. Wangchuk Dorjé states that

> on the stages of a single taste, appearances and the mind become completely mixed. At the early stages all things of a dual nature mix into an equal taste of Voidness. At the intermediate, appearances and the mind are like water mixed with water. At the advanced you see the arisal of the five types of pristine awareness out of the same taste.[29]

According to Pakmodrupa's explanation,

> By meditating on the one flavor of all things
> The meditator will cognize the one flavor of all these things.
> The diversity of appearances and nonappearances,

Mind and emptiness, emptiness and nonemptiness,
Are all of one flavor, nondifferentiable in their intrinsic emptiness.
Understanding and lack of understanding are of one flavor,
Equipoise and postequipoise are nondifferentiable,
Meditation and absence of meditation are unified into one flavor,
Discrimination and lack of discrimination are of one flavor
In the expanse of reality.[30]

At this point, meditation becomes a spontaneous experience of the nature of mind, and one no longer even thinks of meditating. Since one is always meditating, there is no distinction between meditation and nonmeditation. As thoughts arise, they are understood to come from emptiness and return to emptiness. This level is termed "beyond meditation."

Even ordinary meditation at some point becomes a hindrance to realizing the natural, spontaneous, free flow of mind. At this point, one's meditation is effortless, and one lets go of any attachment to meditation. One cultivates the understanding that all appearances, thoughts, emotions, and forms are merged into the primordially pure truth body and that one has from beginningless time been awakened. Nothing new is added, and nothing is taken away; rather, the innate luminosity of mind asserts itself and one abides in unshakable equanimity. One is unfettered by conceptuality, remains in the state of bliss characteristic of buddhas, and one is able to act spontaneously for the benefit of others. As Jikden Sumgön describes this,

> mahāmudrā is simply this self-awareness. Sustaining this practice without distraction is cultivation of the fundamental Truth Body. That which brings about enhancement of mahāmudrā is devotion to the excellent lama. To understand every appearance whatsoever as the Truth Body is to understand mahāmudrā. To realize conceptuality as the Truth Body is to realize mahāmudrā. The happiness that arises both in cyclic existence and beyond it is the quality of mahāmudrā. The benefiting of beings by the Four Bodies is the activity of mahāmudrā.[31]

The meditator who successfully actualizes this state sees all mental phenomena as merely illusory fabrications. They become merged into the truth body, which is identified with the nature of mind. Awakening is of the nature of all thought, and a person in this state recognizes this in every moment. In this way, the meditator quickly actualizes the state of Vajradhara, which is possible because there is no real difference between the mind of Vajradhara and the minds of ordinary beings caught up in cyclic existence. A person who comprehends this instantly eliminates the mental obscurations that previously concealed this fact. The meditator thus overcomes the limitations that hinder ordinary beings, and all of reality is perceived as the spontaneous play of mind. The primordially pure nature of mind is realized as the truth body, and one actualizes one's full potential of awakening.

The final level of attainment is a state of pure spontaneity, radical freedom of thought and action without boundaries. All previous limitations are transcended, and there is nothing that one must do, no rules, and no set guidelines. Even imagining such a state is disquieting for ordinary beings, who are always constrained by notions of who and what they are, of what must be done, of gender, age, nationality, clan, expectations, and habitual patterns of behavior. The mahāmudrā adept has no foundation on which to stand, no fixed identity, and is utterly free. He or she perceives phenomena through naked awareness, without the mediation of presuppositions or concepts, as they are in reality, and this reality has no solidity, no fixed nature, and it is utterly malleable. Reality is what one makes it, and one's freedom is absolute. This is the realm of buddhas, who transcend all limitations and develop godlike powers, the ability to know whatever they wish, and insight into the minds of other beings. Their compassionate activity for the benefit of others arises spontaneously from their nature, without planning or hesitation. While understanding the concerns of ordinary beings, they are not bound by them, and their actions are the play of the luminous nature of mind.

Chö, "Cutting Off"

Chö (*gcod*) is a meditative technique developed in Tibet as a tool to help people eliminate attachment to the ego. The system is traditionally traced back to Padampa Sangyé (ca. eleventh–twelfth centuries), an Indian tantric yogi whose disciple Machik Lapdrön (1055–1143)[32] codified and refined his teachings into the developed practice of *chö*.[33] Traditional biographies report that Machik was born an Indian brahman male near Vārāṇasī. He became a Buddhist, after which he engaged in a debate with a group of heretics. He won the debate, but was told by a ḍākinī that he should flee in order to avoid their planned revenge. The ḍākinī told him to go to Tibet, and then separated his consciousness from his body and transferred it to Tibet, where it was reborn in Mé province in a female body.

At an early age, Machik was deeply interested in Buddhist practice. She was also unconcerned with her physical appearance and shunned society. She is reported to have married a tantric yogi named Töpa Bhadra, after which she gave birth to three sons and two daughters. Later in life she met Padampa Sangyé, who gave her tantric instructions. His student Gyodön Sönam Lama became her root guru. After studying with him for awhile, she built a hermitage, where she remained for the rest of her life. During her later years she attracted a number of disciples and systematized the practice of *chö*.[34] She reportedly died at the age of ninety-five at her hermitage in Sangri Khangmar, in the area of Hlokha. She is widely believed to have been an emanation either of the buddha Tārā or of a wisdom ḍākinī who took birth as Machik in order to transmit the practice of *chö* to the world of humans.

The term *chö* literally means "cutting off," indicating that through this practice one severs the tendency to cling to the body and to a sense of "I." Its purpose is to destroy attachment through cultivating visions in which the body—which is the pivotal point of intersection for ego-clinging and its resultant mental afflictions—is offered as a sacrifice. *Chö* involves meditative practices and rituals in which one visualizes one's body being cut up and devoured by demons, leaving behind nothing toward which attachment can arise.[35] *Chö* is based on the idea that the body is empty of inherent existence and unworthy of interest. In keeping with Buddhist teachings that ignorance and desire are the root causes of suffering, *chö* practitioners seek to uproot them through offering their bodies as food for demons, leaving behind a purified consciousness that no longer clings to physical things.

Through offering up one's body one undermines the tendency to reify such dichotomies as subject and object, self and others, and conventional ideas of good and evil. Thus one recognizes that one's fears are only the result of mental afflictions, which themselves are empty of inherent existence. In order to confront them directly, a *chö* practitioner enacts a complex drama consisting of visualizations, rituals, and prayers in which deities and demons are initially conjured up, but later found to be insubstantial, utterly lacking inherent existence, and products of mind. According to Jamgön Kongtrül, this practice involves

> accepting willingly what is undesirable, throwing oneself defiantly into unpleasant circumstances, realising that gods and demons are one's own mind, and ruthlessly severing self-centered arrogance through an understanding of the sameness of self and others.[36]

Practitioners of *chö* often underscore their lack of concern with physical things by neglecting their outward appearance. Well known among Tibetans for their often unconventional behavior, *chö* adepts commonly frequent cemeteries, dark forests, deserted wastes, and other frightening places which are believed to be the preferred abodes of demons and spirits. In order to prepare themselves for their encounters with powerful forces, they generally approach frightening spots with a particular gait. This is believed to help in overcoming demons.[37] In addition, they are often armed with ritual instruments symbolic of their triumph over primal fears concerning death and demonic forces, such as a trumpet made from a human femur (*rkang gling*) and a small hand drum called a *ḍāmaru.* Purposely traveling to frightening places, they seek to confront their deepest fears, which their studies and meditations on the perfection of wisdom have revealed to be only mental creations. Although the demons they meet appear to be real, substantial entities, they are products of the unconscious and cannot exist independently of the mind. Those who fully recognize this transmute their demons into the light of undifferentiated awareness, free from all afflictions.

Unlike other types of Buddhist practices, *chö* does not seek to avoid potentially harmful forces, but rather purposely seeks contact with them, because through this one may subdue them and thus overcome their power over one's thoughts. As a result of the control they gain over evil forces, *chöpa*s (practitioners of *chö*) are believed to be immune from disease, and they are often asked to cure illness and end plagues.

Despite their often unkempt appearance, *chöpa*s are required to develop strict discipline. This is essential in dealing with inimical forces, because an uncontrolled mind will succumb to the primal fears that surface in the perceptions of people faced with demons and malevolent spirits. Based on perfection of wisdom doctrines of emptiness, *chö* teaches that all demons are empty of inherent existence. They are products of the mind, and in *chö* rituals these inimical forces are used to represent one's own mental afflictions. According to Machik, through confronting and defeating apparently external demons, one "cuts off" the power of one's internal demons and eventually eliminates them.

> What we call devils are not materially existing individuals . . . . A devil means anything which hinders us in our achievement of liberation. Consequently, even kind and loving friends and companions may become devils as far as liberation is concerned. In particular, there is no greater devil than this present ego-clinging, and because of this all the devils will rear their ugly heads as long as one has not severed this clinging to ego.[38]

The central practice of *chö* involves making an offering of one's body to demons, deities, and ḍākinīs. This is said to be an expression of the "perfection of generosity," in which one cultivates an attitude of willingness to give up all one has—even one's own body—in order to benefit other sentient beings. The offerings to demons are divided into several types of "feasts," the most important of which are "red feasts" (*dmar 'gyed*) and "white feasts" (*dkar 'gyed*). In red feasts, the body is cut up into bloody parts and offered to flesh-eating demons, who consume one's flesh, leaving behind a consciousness purified of defilements. White feasts involve visualizations in which one mentally transforms the body into light-colored ambrosia, after which deities feast on it and are satisfied. In the white offering, all the parts of one's body become idealized symbols, as is indicated in the following passage, which outlines the process:

> One's mind re-emerges from the heart of Machikma in the form of a red *hrī* which becomes Dorje Phagmo [a wrathful ḍākinī]. With the hooked knife in her right hand she divides up one's own inanimate form. Briskly peeling off the skin, she spreads it out and on it piles the corpse; the skin is the golden ground, the blood and lymph are lakes of sweet-scented water, fingers and toes form the iron mountains of the perimeter, the trunk is the massive central mountain, the four limbs are the four continents and their sub-continents, the head is the residence of the gods, the eyes form the sun and the moon, the heart is the wish-fulfilling jewel, and the inner organs become the eight delights, etc. This array of all manner of excellent things, com-

> plete and entire, resembles Samantabhadra's offering clouds: their extent, like space, is unlimited . . . . Meditate that the offering produces the gathering of the accumulations and the purifying of veils for oneself and all other living beings, after which [you should] rest in a state where the three spheres are completely purified.[39]

Both red and white feasts begin with the meditator ejecting the consciousness from the body, after which the mind is visualized as being that of a fully awakened buddha or ḍākinī. The lifeless corpse is offered as a sacrifice in a ritual designed to sever all physical attachments and eliminate mental defilements. Tantric practices are an important aspect of *chö*, which incorporates tantric visualizations, as well as tantric deities and ḍākinīs. Among the more important ḍākinīs are Vajrayoginī—who commonly appears in the aspect of the fierce Vajravārāhī or Tröma—and the Tibetan saints Machik Lapdrön and Yéshé Tsogyel, who are believed to have been ḍākinīs who took human form.

The inception of the practice of *chö* is closely associated with the Kagyu lineage, but it has been adopted by the other orders of Tibetan Buddhism as well. The fifth Dalai Lama, for example, is reported to have become a practitioner of *chö* after receiving instructions from Terdak Lingpa. Machik also holds the distinction of being the only Tibetan lama whose lineage was transmitted to India. During the time she was teaching in her hermitage in Sangri Khangmar, a group of brahmans from India visited her, received her instructions, and were reportedly so impressed that they brought them back to India and taught *chö* to others, after which it became popular among Indian tantric yogis.

Notes

1. In his introduction to *The Life of the Saint of Gtsaṅ* (New Delhi, 1969), Gene Smith indicates that there are several ways of construing the term *Kagyu*; E. Gene Smith, *Among Tibetan Texts: History and Literature of the Himalayan Plateau* (Boston: Wisdom Publications, 2001), p. 40.
2. According to his biography, Nāropa underwent twelve major trials and twelve lesser trials.
3. His biography is translated by Herbert Guenther in *The Life and Teachings of Nāropa* (Oxford: Oxford University Press, 1963).
4. According to the Kagyu tradition, he was not an ordinary person, but rather a mani-

festation of Ḍombī Heruka who took the form of Marpa in order to facilitate the transmission of the Kagyu lineage to Tibet. For translations of his biography, see *The Life of Marpa the Translator*, tr. Nalanda Translation Committee (Boulder, CO: Prajna Press, 1982) and Jacques Bacot, *La vie de Marpa, le "tradacteur,"* (Paris: Paul Geuthner, 1937).

5. For further information on his life and teachings, see Lobsang Lhalungpa, *The Life of Milarepa* (Boston: Shambhala, 1977); John Powers, "Conflict and Resolution in the Biography of Milarepa," *Tibet Journal* 17.1, Spring 1992; Garma C.C. Chang, *The Hundred Thousand Songs of Milarepa* (Boulder: Shambhala, 1989); and W.Y. Evans-Wentz, *Tibet's Great Yogi Milarepa* (London: Oxford University Press, 1928).
6. The sixteenth Gyelwa Karmapa, Rangjung Rikpe Dorje, was a major figure in the dissemination of the Kagyu lineage in the West. After his death, the search for his successor was complicated by the fact that the seventeenth Karmapa was born in Tibet. He has now been recognized and was officially enthroned at Tsurpu Monastery on September 27, 1992. He later escaped from his Chinese guards and made his way to India, and presently resides in Dharamsala. His recognition has been complicated by the opposition of Shamar Rinpoche, who has proposed another boy as the true Karmapa. The fight over the succession has been marked by acrimony and even occasional violence, and several cases are making their way through the Indian courts.
7. See George Roerich, tr., *The Blue Annals* (Delhi: Motilal Banarsidass, 1976), pp. 454–456. For a traditional biography of Gampopa, see *The Life of Gampopa: The Incomparable Dharma Lord of Tibet*, tr. Jampa Mackenzie Stewart (Ithaca: Snow Lion, 1995) and *Life and Teachings of Gampopa*, tr. Thrangu Rinpoche (Auckland, NZ: Zhyisil Chokyi Ghatsal Trust, 2004).
8. *Blue Annals*, p. 455.
9. Ibid., p. 456.
10. Some interesting findings concerning the physiological effects of this practice have been reported by Dr. Herbert Benson in "Mind/Body Interactions including Tibetan Studies," in *Mind Science*, H.H. the Dalai Lama et al. (Boston: Wisdom, 1991), pp. 37–48. See also Benson et al., "Body Temperature Changes during the Practice of *gTum-mo* (Heat) Yoga," *Nature* 295 (1982), pp. 234–236, and M.S. Malhotra et al., "Three Case Reports of the Metabolic and Electroencephalographic Changes During Advanced Buddhist Meditative Techniques," *Behavioral Medicine* 16 (1990), pp. 90–95.
11. See chapter 9, "Tantra."
12. See, for example, *Selected Works of Dalai Lama II*, pp. 117–118.
13. The five aggregates (*phung po, skandha*) are the constituents of the psychophysical continuum on the basis of which we create false notions of "I" and "mine": form, feelings, discriminations, consciousness, and compositional factors. See chapter 2, "Some Important Buddhist Doctrines."
14. A good example of this analogy is found in the opening part of the first chapter of the *Sūtra Explaining the Thought*. See *The Wisdom of Buddha* (*Saṃdhinirmocana Sūtra*), tr. John Powers (Berkeley: Dharma Publishing, 1994), chapter 1.
15. Herbert Guenther, tr., *The Life and Teachings of Nāropa*, p. 188.
16. Ibid., pp. 68–69.
17. See *Selected Works of the Dalai Lama II*, pp. 134ff. Niguma (or Vimalaśrī) was a consort of Nāropa who is said to have attained awakening. Nāropa divided the teachings he had received between his disciples, and Niguma received the six yogas, which

she in turn passed on to her own disciples, most notably Kyungpo Nenjor. He brought her teachings to Tibet, where they became associated with the Kagyu order. The six yogas are also practiced by adherents of the Sakya, Géluk, and Nyingma orders.

18. These are the state of gods, demi-gods, humans, animals, hungry ghosts, and hell beings.
19. Kalu Rinpoche, *The Dharma*, p. 61.
20. *Selected Works of Dalai Lama II*, p. 143.
21. Khenpo Könchog Gyaltsen, tr. *The Garland of Mahamudra Practices*, p. 14.
22. Takpo Tashi Namgyal, *Mahāmudrā: The Quintessence of Mind and Meditation*, tr. Lobsang P. Lhalungpa (Boston: Shambhala, 1986), p. xxi. See also pp. 92–94, in which Takpo Tashi Namgyal discusses various ways of construing this term.
23. The similarities between dzogchen and mahāmudrā have been noted by Lobsang Lhalungpa in his introduction to *Mahāmudrā: The Quintessence of Mind and Meditation*, p. xxxvii, and by Chokyi Nyima Rinpoché in his translation of a text by Karma Chakmé Rinpoché I entitled *The Union of Mahamudra and Dzogchen* (Hong Kong: Rangjung Yeshe, 1989). It should be noted that although mahāmudrā is most closely associated with Kagyu, other orders of Tibetan Buddhism have their own mahāmudrā practices. The Géluk order, for instance, highly values a text entitled *The Bright Lamp of Mahāmudrā*, composed by Losang Chögi Nyima (1570–1662), the first Panchen Lama. An important work of the Sakya order is a text by Sakya Pandita (1181–1251) entitled *The Eye-Opening Tools of Mahāmudrā*.
24. Kalu Rinpoche, *The Dharma*, p. 119.
25. Wangchuk Dorjé, Karmapa IX, *The Mahamudra Eliminating the Darkness of Ignorance*, tr. Alexander Berzin (Dharamsala: Library of Tibetan Works and Archives, 1978), p. 52.
26. Kalu Rinpoche, *The Gem Ornament*, p. 151.
27. Kalu Rinpoche, *The Dharma*, p. 116.
28. Quoted in *Mahāmudrā: The Quintessence of Mind and Meditation*, p. 358.
29. *The Mahamudra Eliminating the Darkness of Ignorance*, p. 143.
30. Quoted in *Mahāmudrā: The Quintessence of Mind and Meditation*, p. 360.
31. Quoted in *The Garland of Mahamudra Practices*, p. 94.
32. These dates are taken from Sumpa Khenpo's *Re'u mig*, in *Dpag bsam ljon bzang*, part 3 (ed. Lokesh Chandra; New Delhi: International Institute of Indian Culture, 1959). According to T.G. Dhongthog Rinpoche, however, Machik was born in 1031 (*Important Events in Tibetan History*; Delhi, 1968, p. 86).
33. A good source for the life and thought of Padampa Sangyé is Barbara Aziz, ed., *The Tradition of Pha Dam-pa Saṅs-rgyas* (Thimphu: Druk Sherik Parkhang, 1979, 5 vols.); volume 5 contains a biographical sketch (pp. 324–363).
34. Janet Gyatso ("The Gcod Tradition," in Barbara Aziz and Matthew Kapstein, eds., *Soundings in Tibetan Civilization*; New Delhi: Manohar Publications, 1985, p. 332) reports that it is often stated that Machik codified teachings she received from others, and gave her new system the name "*chö*."
35. As Rinjing Dorje and Ter Ellingson note, many of these rituals use music and dance (see Rinjing Dorje and Ter Ellingson, "Explanation of the *gCod da ma ru*: An Exploration of Musical Instrument Symbolism," *Asian Music* 10.2, 1979, pp. 63–91).
36. *Cutting Through Ego-Clinging*, tr. Anila Rinchen Palmo (Landrevie, France: Dzambala, 1988), p. 11.

37. Four of the most well-known gaits are referred to as “hero tiger,” “dancing ḍākinī,” “swift black snake,” and “proud yogi.”
38. *Cutting Through Ego-Clinging*, p. 52.
39. Ibid., p. 28.

14. Sakya

Origins of the Sakya Tradition

THE SAKYA ORDER traces its origins to India, particularly to the great adept Virūpa, who is the first human to disseminate the most distinctive of its teachings, the practices of "path and result" (*lam 'bras,* pronounced "lamdré"). According to traditional histories, Virūpa was born in Bengal during the reign of King Devapāla. As a child he entered the monastic university of Somapurī, where he was given the ordination name Dharmapāla.[1] In the monastery, he pursued the standard scholastic curriculum and tantric studies. During the day he devoted himself to the three duties of a scholar-monk: debate, teaching, and writing. At night he engaged in secret tantric practices. He received the initiation and empowerment of Cakrasaṃvara and assiduously applied himself to tantric liturgical cycles (*sādhana*) and meditation, but with little result. He repeated the mantra of Cakrasaṃvara twenty million times, but after twelve years he could see no signs of progress. He began to fear that he lacked the necessary karmic connections for tantric practice.

In what appeared to be a confirmation of his fears, he had a series of dreams that contained disturbing images. In one, he saw a huge fire burning in the lower end of a valley, while a flood came from the upper end. In another, hailstorms raged, huge glaciers fell, and icicles and icebergs appeared in the sky. In an even more disturbing dream, he saw his lama, meditational deity (*yi dam, iṣṭa-devatā*), and spiritual guides hanging upside down or with their faces torn apart, noses cut off, eyes gouged out, and blood dripping. He interpreted the images as indications that his practice and realization were degenerating, and so in despair he threw his prayer beads in a urinal and resolved to devote himself only to exoteric Mahāyāna practices.

When the time came for evening prayers, he did not have his rosary, but the tantric deity Nairātmyā (consort of Hevajra) appeared to him and presented him with a beautifully carved set of beads. She told him that she was the buddha with whom he had a karmic connection and that henceforth he should treat her as his meditational deity. She then informed him that his interpretation of his dreams was incorrect and that his practice had indeed been effective. What he took to be inauspicious signs in fact were indications of spiritual accomplishment: he had attained the level of "heat" (*drod, ūṣmagata*) of the path of preparation and would soon enter the path of seeing. The vital energy of his mind was about to merge in the syllables *kṣa* and *ma* in the navel *cakra* (*lte ba'i 'khor, nābhimaṇḍala*). The rising fire and descending flood were indications of the immanent movement of vital energies and mastery of heat yoga (*dumo*). The circulation of subtle drops was symbolized by the hailstorms, icicles, and icebergs. The appearances of his lama and preceptors were signs that he was about to transcend attachment to conventional perceptions. When this was explained to him, he immediately realized that all appearances are manifestations of mind. Traditional sources indicate that Virūpa's failure to recognize the true significance of his dream visions was due to the fact that his guru had not properly prepared him for such events.[2]

The following evening, Nairātmyā again appeared in her maṇḍala of fifteen goddesses and bestowed tantric empowerments on Virūpa. As a result, he attained the first bodhisattva level and the path of seeing. After twenty-nine days he reached the sixth bodhisattva level. He later collected Nairātmyā's instructions in his most important text, the *Vajra Verses*.[3]

Virūpa returned to diligent practice, and after another twelve years arrived at the supreme realization of the great seal (*phyag rgya chen po, mahāmudrā*). At this point, he knew that he had transcended the narrow confines of monastic life, and he began to behave in ways that caused his fellow monks concern. On one occasion he asked an attendant to make him a pie with the pigeons that roosted in the eaves of the monastery, which went against the monks' vows never to take life.

An older monk noticed that the pigeons had disappeared, and when he inquired about this he was informed that Virūpa had ordered them made into a pie. The monk went to investigate this disturbing story and found Virūpa sitting down to his meal. The outraged monk had Virūpa expelled from the monastery for this flagrant violation. Virūpa removed his robes after prostrating in front of a buddha image and left with no regrets, since he realized that he had transcended the need for monastic structures and restrictions.

Before leaving, he ordered his attendants to bring the scraps of bone and wings left over from the pigeon pie, and then snapped his fingers, at which point the pigeons were all restored to life and flew away. He told the amazed spectators that the pie and dead pigeons were merely an illusion. Virūpa had become a master *siddha* (a tantric adept) and had control over life and death. He could create appearances at will, and the limitations of ordinary people no longer applied to him. Before leaving, he renounced his monastic appellation and gave himself the name Virūpa, meaning "ugly" or "ill-formed," symbolizing his nonattachment to worldly conventions.

After departing the monastery, he traveled widely, and stories of his miraculous deeds circulated wherever he went. One of the most famous of these concerns his visit to a small village, where he entered a tavern and ordered food and wine. After finishing the first flagon, he asked for more, and as he continued to drink heavily the tavern keeper became concerned about Virūpa's ability to pay. Virūpa assured him that he would pay for his food and drink shortly, and then he stuck his dagger in the table in front of him, saying, "When the sun crosses this dagger, I will pay you." Satisfied, the tavern keeper waited for the sun to move past the dagger, but with his magic power Virūpa kept the sun from moving in the sky.

For almost three days Virūpa sat in the tavern with the sun motionless overhead, drinking huge quantities of wine. The sun scorched the town, endangering the crops and causing the townspeople to complain of the heat, until finally they petitioned the king to save them. In order to get the sun to move again, the king had to pay Virūpa's bar bill, after which he allowed the sun to resume its course.

He subsequently traveled all over India, amazing people with wondrous displays of yogic power, and he used his abilities to convert sentient beings to Buddhism. He is reported to have lived for seven hundred years, during which he performed countless miraculous deeds, and finally he attained complete liberation and ascended to the heaven of the ḍākinīs.

The Sakya Order in Tibet

The Sakya tradition in Tibet begins with the establishment of a monastery in an area called Sakya, in the province of Tsang in south-central Tibet.

The name "Sakya" literally means "gray earth," because the ground in this area was of gray color, which was considered auspicious. Sakya Monastery was founded in 1073 by Gönchok Gyelpo (1034–1102), and with the later ascension to power of the Sakya lineage this became one of Tibet's great monastic centers. Gönchok Gyelpo was a disciple of the translator Drokmi (ca. 993–1077), who had traveled to Nepal and India, where he studied Sanskrit with Śāntipa, one of the great masters of his day and author of a commentary on the *Hevajra Tantra.* Drokmi brought the text to Tibet and translated it, and it later became the basic text of Sakya tantric practice.

Gönchok Gyelpo's choice of the site of Sakya Monastery was a fortuitous one, because it was at the nexus of major trading routes. It was a connecting point for the rich agricultural lands around Shigatsé, the Nepal Valley, and the lands of the Tibetan nomads, which supplied the rest of Tibet with butter and wool. The Sakyapas capitalized on the investment opportunities that their location provided them, with the result that the fortunes of the order rose quickly.

According to traditional histories, the importance of the site had been foreseen by Atiśa. On his journey to Tibet in 1040, he saw an elephant-shaped mountain named Pönpori while he rested at the bank of a river that flows by the base of the mountain. On its slopes, he saw a patch of gray earth and two black wild yaks grazing near it. He told one of his attendants that this was an auspicious place and that the two yaks symbolized that in the future two emanations of the buddha Mahākāla would manifest there.[4]

Atiśa made prostrations in the direction of the gray patch of earth, and while he did so seven shining images of the syllable *dhī* (the seed-syllable of Mañjuśrī, embodiment of wisdom) appeared on the ground, along with the syllables *hrīh* and *hūṃ*, symbolic of Avalokiteśvara (embodiment of compassion) and Vajrapāṇi (embodiment of skillful actions). Atiśa told his attendants that the appearance of the mantric syllables indicated that in the future seven incarnations of Mañjuśrī would manifest there, along with one each of Avalokiteśvara and Vajrapāṇi. Sakya lineage histories contend that this prediction was fulfilled in nine great scholars of the lineage.[5]

The Khön Lineage

Just as traditional Sakya histories indicate that the main monastery of Sakya was presaged by auspicious events, so also the Khön family (which founded and continues to direct the Sakya tradition) is said to have had auspicious beginnings.[6] In the distant past, three brothers of the heavenly race called *Hla Rik* descended from the Ābhāsvara heaven and landed on the peak of a salt-crystal mountain in Tibet. The two eldest brothers, Chiring and Yuring, then returned to the heavens, but Yusé, the youngest, stayed on earth with his family. His great-grandson, Yapang Kyé, married Yadruk Silima, who gave birth to a boy named Khön Bargyé. Khön Bargyé is said to be the founder of the Khön family.

For generations the Khön were closely associated with the Nyingma lineage, and Khön Bargyé's son Khön Nāgarakṣita was reportedly a student of Padmasambhava and one of the seven Tibetan "probationers" who were initiated at Samyé and became the first Tibetan monks.

The Sakya patronage of Nyingma ended when Khön Bargyé's descendant Shérap Tsültrim saw a public display of tantric ritual at a Nyingma center. Shérap Tsültrim was outraged that secret rites were being performed for the entertainment of the populace, and he felt that such public advertisement of tantric mysteries cheapened them and did immeasurable harm to people who were not prepared for them. He concluded that because this cavalier attitude toward esoteric rites it was no longer possible for people to gain liberation through following Nyingma practices, and he decided to separate the Khön family from Nyingma.

Eschewing the older tantras favored by the Nyingmapas, he sent his younger brother, Gönchok Gyelpo, to study the new tantric translations with Drokmi. Through his studies with Drokmi and his students, Gönchok Gyelpo gained a comprehensive understanding of Vajrayāna, as well as sūtra literature and philosophical treatises. At the age of forty, having become widely recognized as one of the great Buddhist scholars of his day, he decided to build a monastery. The place he chose was the patch of gray earth near Pönpori mountain that Atiśa had predicted would be the site of a great place of Buddhist learning.

The Development and Dissemination of Sakya Doctrines and Practices

Gönchok Gyelpo's son, the "Great Sakyapa" (*Sa chen*) Günga Nyingpo (1092–1158), played an important role in systematizing Sakya teachings.[7] An accomplished scholar with a comprehensive knowledge of Buddhist learning, he brought together sūtra and tantra practices and doctrines in a synthetic vision of the path. According to Sakyapa accounts, he was an incarnation of Mañjuśrī, and he received teachings directly from Mañjuśrī.

Among the most important of these were four injunctions given to him by Mañjuśrī when he was twelve years old that became an important basis for commentary by later Sakya masters:

> If you cling to this life, then you are not a dharma practitioner.
> If you cling to existence, then you do not have renunciation.
> If you are attached to your own interests, then you do not have the mind of awakening.
> If you hold to [a position], then you do not have the correct view.

Sachen immediately realized that these verses summarized all of the essential teachings and practices of Buddhism. They later became the basis of the cycle of Sakya teachings called "separation from the four attachments" (*zhen pa bzhi bral*). Among the Sakya masters who wrote commentaries on these teachings were Drakpa Gyeltsen, Sakya Pandita, Ngorchen Günga Sangpo, and Gorampa Sönam Senggé.

The first line indicates the initial prerequisites for following the Buddhist path. In order to practice the dharma, one must first overcome attachment to the present life and focus on religious practice. This requires that one recognize the sufferings that are inevitable for ordinary beings and develop an understanding of the valuable opportunity afforded by a human rebirth. Human beings are in an excellent position to become aware of the dissatisfactions of cyclic existence and to practice dharma. A person who realizes this should make a concerted effort to take advantage of the opportunity. One should also be aware that rebirth as a human being is very rare, and this should spur one to diligence in religious activities.

The second verse continues the theme of the first. In order successfully to travel the path to awakening, one must overcome attachment to the present life and to continued existence. One should understand that cyclic existence is painful, fraught with suffering, and pointless. A person who fully realizes this will become truly dedicated to religious practice. A sincere practitioner of dharma should seek to avoid nonvirtuous actions, cultivate virtue, and transform neutral deeds into positive ones. (Neutral deeds are those that have no particular negative or positive effects, like eating and sleeping, but if properly considered, even these can become occasions for religious consciousness.) Thus Ngorchen Gönchok Hlündrup states that

> after having first produced a mind desiring to accomplish good for all beings, one should engage in any activity related to that object, together with mindfulness and alertness.[8]

In this practice, even such prosaic activities as eating, sleeping, and walking are infused with religious significance. For example, while eating, one should think of oneself as doing this in order to gain strength to work for others and should wish that all beings also receive food. Before sleeping, one views the period of rest as necessary for further meditation practice with renewed vigor. While walking, one wishes that all beings will be motivated to follow the path to awakening. Through such thoughts, one's daily activities become overlaid with religious symbolism and one's acts are seen has having spiritual significance and as contributing to the goal of awakening.

The third verse urges people to overcome selfish clinging to personal interests and to develop the mind of awakening, which marks the beginning of the bodhisattva path and is the result of cultivating love and compassion until they become the primary motivating factors of one's actions.

The fourth verse indicates that the most important transformation effected by successful Buddhist meditation is mental. Ordinary beings are plagued by constant sufferings, but these sufferings are the result of cognitive error. The only difference between the buddhas who have transcended suffering and ordinary beings who are its victims lies in their respective views of reality. The perceptions of buddhas are in accord with reality, and so they do not suffer as a result of afflicted views, while ordinary beings are deluded by mental afflictions such as desire, hatred, and ignorance, and these lead to continued dissatisfaction.

These wrong views are overcome by meditative practice. An important breakthrough occurs when a meditator attains the level of calm abiding, which is the ability calmly to hold one's attention on an object without allowing attention to waver. The next important breakthrough is higher insight, in which one analyzes the object in order to ascertain its final nature, which is emptiness. When one attains the "union of calm abiding and higher insight," one understands that everything that appears is only mind, and mind itself is also empty of inherent existence. One examines mind to determine its basis and finds that it has none. One seeks to determine where mind arises and where it goes, and understands that it arises from emptiness and merges into emptiness, leaving no trace behind. One then recognizes that all appearances have the same level of "reality" as dreams.

From his lamas, Sachen received the entire range of Buddhist teachings: he studied abhidharma, epistemology, Madhyamaka, the "five treatises of Maitreya," medicine, sūtras, and tantras. Since he was an incarnation of Mañjuśrī, he only needed to hear or read something once in order to understand it completely and memorize it perfectly. In addition to his studies of exoteric subjects, he also received instructions on path and result from his father and from the *siddha* Chöbar. Traditional histories state that he was

> a man of immeasurable virtue who did not infringe the three vows[9] in any way and whose uncontrived bodhicitta [mind of awakening] was all-embracing . . . . He had realized all the inner signs of accomplishment, encountered the deities and possessed the gift of clairvoyance.[10]

His sons, Lobön Sönam Tsémo (1141–1182) and Jétsun Drakpa Gyeltsen (1147–1216), continued the tradition of scholarship and Vajrayāna practice. The former was one of the great systematizers of tantric doctrine and literature, and the latter wrote an influential history of the development of Buddhism in Tibet. He also authored texts on medicine. He was renowned as a great tantric yogi, and traditional accounts of his life report that he received teachings directly from Mañjuśrī.

Sakya Pandita Günga Gyeltsen

One of the greatest figures in the early Sakya lineage was Günga Gyeltsen Bel Sangpo (1182–1251), popularly known as Sakya Pandita, "The Scholar of the Sakyas." Considered by the tradition to have been an incarnation of Mañjuśrī, his birth was accompanied by auspicious signs. A great light filled the sky, and he began to speak in Sanskrit; people who were present at his birth noticed that his body had the major and minor marks of a buddha. He was so beautiful that all who saw him were unable to take their gaze from him. People around him claimed that even as an infant he would write Sanskrit characters in the dirt and then carefully avoid crawling over them. Because of his divine wisdom, as he grew older he instantly comprehended everything he heard and memorized it perfectly. His family recognized his aptitude for monastic life, and he was ordained at an early age by Kaché Śākyaśrībhadra.[11] According to the traditional histories, from the time of his ordination until he died, he never transgressed even the most minor rule.

According to hagiographies of his life, by the age of eight he had memorized Saroruhavajra's *sādhana* of Hevajra, and by his eleventh year he memorized the *Hevajra Tantra* and could explain it correctly. By the age of fourteen he mastered the *Vajra-pañjara Tantra* and the *Sampuṭa Tantra*, as well as all the important texts and rituals of his tradition. In addition to these standard subjects, he also studied medicine, astrology, calligraphy, painting, poetry, and music.

At the age of seventeen he had two dreams that he considered highly significant: In the first, he dreamed that he heard the Indian scholar Vasubandhu teaching the *Treasury of Abhidharma* at the Achi Stūpa at Sakya, and Sakya Pandita saw himself in the audience. In the second dream, he saw himself in a place called "Dignāga's cave" at Korlochen in eastern India. In the cave he was presented with many volumes of scripture, including Dignāga's *Compendium of Valid Cognition* and the seven treatises of Dharmakīrti (which are fundamental texts for Sakya studies of epistemology). His biographers view these dreams as prophecies of future accomplishment, because he later excelled in the study of abhidharma and epistemology.

In his late teens it was decided that in order to broaden his education he should travel to other centers of learning. When he was eighteen he journeyed to Trang, where he studied with Shudön Dorjé Gyap, and in the next year he went to the temple of Gyangdur to learn from Tsur Shönnu Senggé, who taught Sakya Pandita about the Epistemology school (*tshad ma, pramāṇa*) and the Middle Way Consequence school (*dbu ma thal 'gyur pa, prāsaṅgika-madhyamaka*). In 1204, after a brief return to Sakya, he again left to pursue further studies, and in Tsang Chumik he met Śākyaśrībhadra and his student Sugataśrī. From these teachers he studied a wide range of Sanskrit texts, particularly works relating to epistemology and tantra.

During his scholarly training he became a master of all fields of learning, both Buddhist and non-Buddhist, and he was recognized as one of the greatest debaters of his day. His most famous victory was over the Vedānta philosopher Harinanda, who had heard of his erudition and debating prowess and decided to challenge him. Harinanda brought a retinue of scholars with him, but Sakya Pandita bested all of them, and after his defeat Harinanda cut his hair as a sign of his submission to Sakya Pandita, and he then became a Buddhist.

Sakya Pandita's life changed dramatically in 1216 when Drakpa Gyeltsen died. Drakpa Gyeltsen had been the head of the Sakya lineage, and with his death this position fell to Sakya Pandita, who by this time was regarded as the preeminent Sakya scholar of his generation. For the next twenty-eight years he presided over the lineage, and this was the period of his major literary activity.

One of the greatest figures in Tibetan intellectual history, he wrote influential treatises in widely diverse areas of Buddhist philosophy and practice, music, grammar, poetics, and epistemology. Perhaps his most famous philosophical work is his *Treasury of the Knowledge of Valid Cognition*, which systematizes the thought of Dharmakīrti and Dignāga. Among Tibetans and Mongolians he is best known for his *Treasury of Well-Spoken Jewels*, which contains 457 verses full of pithy sayings and moral injunctions.

Another influential work is his *Differentiation of the Three Vows*, which discusses the three Buddhist vows of individual liberation, the bodhisattva vows, and the *samaya* vows of tantric practitioners. In this text he elucidates the nature and functions of Buddhist religious vows. The vows of individual liberation serve the function of eliminating tendencies toward afflictive actions of body and speech. Sakya Pandita views the next group, the bodhisattva vows, as mental factors that influence the makeup of one's consciousness. As such, they are not fully lost at death, but become a part of the mental continuum and serve to counteract mental afflictions. The tantric vows aid in overcoming dualistic thought and help one to cultivate the insight that all appearances are manifestations of primordial wisdom.

Sakya Pandita became widely renowned as one of the great intellectual figures of his generation, and traditional histories report that "his reputation paralleled that of the great Indian masters Dharmakīrti and Dignāga and the qualities of his body, speech and mind spread like a banner for all to see."[12]

Sakya Becomes a Political Force

Because of his reputation, in 1244, when Sakya Pandita was sixty-two years of age, the Mongol prince Ködan requested that Sakya Pandita visit him in order to negotiate Tibet's submission to his growing empire. Although traditional histories report this summons as a polite request from an admiring monarch, in fact it was phrased as an order, and Sakya Pandita responded to it as such. He quickly set out for Mongolia with his nephews Drogön, who was nine years old, and Pakpa, who was five. Although his business with the Mongol prince was of great importance, so great was his reputation that during his trip people wanted to meet and receive blessings from him, and so the journey took much longer than initially expected. In the latter part of 1246 he reached the Mongol capital of Liangzhou, and he had his first audience with Ködan in early 1247.

Traditional accounts claim that the summons had been predicted by his uncle Drakpa Gyeltsen shortly before his death, when he told Sakya Pandita,

> You will be summoned by the lord of the Mongols in the East, who wear hats looking like perched hawks and who wear boots looking like pig snouts, and who have houses looking like wooden nets; their lord [Ködan], who is a reincarnation of a Bodhisattva, will summon you. At that time you must go. There your religion will spread greatly.[13]

When he met Ködan, the prince was suffering from an illness, and Sakya Pandita cured him. By all accounts, Sakya Pandita's mission to Mongolia was a great success, because Ködan converted to Buddhism and became a disciple of Sakya Pandita.[14] In consideration of their special relationship, the Mongol prince decided not to invade Tibet, and Sakya Pandita became the most powerful religious figure of his day.

Traditional accounts report that some of the prince's ministers were jealous of the prestige of the foreign lama, and so they decided to test him by having a magician create an illusory temple and challenge Sakya Pandita to destroy the illusion. Instead, Sakya Pandita gave it substance, and the magician who created it was unable to dissolve it again. The temple was then named "Magical Temple of the North," and it is said to still stand today in the area of Wutai Shan in China.

Sakya Pandita spent his last years in Mongolia, where he passed away at the age of seventy while residing in the "Magical Temple." The death of this great lama was signaled by many auspicious signs. As a result of his practice, he had completed all the Buddhist paths, and in his next birth he became the buddha Vimalaśrī.

The Sakya Hierarchs and the Mongols

The strong links between the lamas of Sakya and powerful Mongol princes led to Sakya being proclaimed the ruling lineage in Tibet. Pakpa, a nephew of Sakya Pandita, developed an association with Qubilai Khan that was termed the "priest-patron" relationship. Sakya Pandita ceded temporal authority over Tibet to the Mongol khans, and they in return agreed to protect the religion and people of Tibet. In this system, the patron offered to provide the military power to back the temporal and religious power of the lama, who for his part agreed to see to the religious needs of the khan. In 1253, Pakpa gave the Hevajra maṇḍala initiation to Qubilai, his queens, and twenty-five ministers at the palace of Hutu, and as an offering of thanksgiving Qubilai gave him vice-regal status over Tibet.

Pakpa continued the missionary activity of Sakya Pandita, becoming the spiritual preceptor of the Mongol prince Sechen. Like his predecessor, Pakpa had a wide-ranging intellect, and he is credited by Mongolians with developing a script that is now named after him. In addition to his scholastic background, he was also a renowned Vajrayāna yogi. There are numerous tales of his displays of miraculous powers, such as the story that at one time he cut off his head and limbs and transformed them into the five buddha families, which radiated countless beams of light. His scholarship, tantric powers, and moral uprightness greatly impressed the Mongolians, and the khan made him the religious and secular ruler of Tibet. He was succeeded in this position by his brother, Dromgön Channa.

Because of the authority they derived from their Mongol patrons, the Sakya hierarchs were the most powerful figures in Tibet for several generations. From 1245 until 1358, they were the acknowledged rulers of the country, but just as their ascendancy was tied to the Mongols, when Mongol power diminished so did that of the Sakyapas. Their influence was greatly weakened with the death of Qubilai Khan in 1294, and Sakya hegemony ended with the collapse of Mongol control of China (1358–1360).

The Sakya Lineage from the Fifteenth Century to the Present

The Sakya lineage continued to produce notable scholars and tantric adepts, including Gorampa Sönam Senggé (1428–1489) and Shakya Chokden (1428–1507). More recently, Jamyang Khyentsé Ongpo (1811–1892) was a leading figure in the Nonsectarian (*ris med*) movement, which had a wide-ranging impact on Tibetan Buddhism, particularly among the Kagyu, Nyingma, and Sakya orders.

The Sakya order has two main subsects, the Ngorpa and the Tsarpa. The first is named for Ngor Monastery, founded by the great path and result master Ngorchen Günga Sangpo (1382–1457) in Tsang province. The Tsarpa tradition began with the founding of Nālendra Monastery by the Vajrayoginī master Tsarchen Losel Gyatso (1502–1556) in Penyül in Ü province.

Sakya lineage histories contend that the great teachers of Sakya were fulfillments of Atiśa's predictions: Günga Nyingpo's four sons and Sakya Pandita, Sangtsa Sönam Gyeltsen, and Pakpa are the seven incarnations of Mañjuśrī predicted by Atiśa. Dromgön Channa Dorjé was the incarnation of Vajrapāṇi whose birth Atiśa predicted. The wild yaks Atiśa saw represent the wrathful deities who were chosen by Sachen Günga Nyingpo to protect the Sakya lineage, and Sachen is held to be the incarnation of Avalokiteśvara whose birth Atiśa predicted.

The present head of the Sakya lineage is H.H. Sakya Tridzin Ngawang Günga, the forty-first person to hold the throne of Sakya.[15] He is considered by his followers to be an emanation of Mañjuśrī. He was born in the Dolma clan of the Khön family in 1945, and during his training he studied with such masters as Jamyang Khyentsé Chögi Lodrö, Chogé Trichen, and Ngawang Lodrö Shenpen Nyingpo. In 1959, following the Chinese invasion of Tibet, he fled to India along with many of his followers, and he re-established his headquarters in Dehradun in Uttar Pradesh.

The Sakya Monastic Order

The Ngorpa and Tsarpa subsects are named for the locations of the monasteries from which the respective lineages derive. Ngor Éwam Chöden Monastery was founded by Ngorchen Günga Sangpo, and Nālendra Monastery was founded by Tsarchen Losel Gyatso. The Ngorpa tradition has been noted for its many eminent scholars, most notably Gorampa Sönam Senggé, who was a student of Ngorchen and Muchen Gönchok Gyeltsen (1388–1469). One of the greatest scholars Tibet has produced, his collected works cover thirteen volumes and discuss a wide range of Buddhist teachings.

The Tsarpa tradition is particularly noted for its transmission of the "thirteen golden doctrines" (*gser chos bcu gsum*) and teachings on the greater and lesser Mahākāla. The thirteen golden doctrines consist of the cycles of three ḍākinīs: Naro, Metrī, and Indrā; cycles of three great red-colored deities: Kurukullā, Gaṇapati, and Kāmarāja; cycles of three lesser red-colored deities: Garbhasuvarnasūtraśrī, Hinudevī, and Vasudhara; the three deities Prāṇasādhana, Siṃhanāda, and Śabalagaruḍa; and teachings concerned with Amaravajradevī, Siṃhavaktrā, and white Amitāyus.

In keeping with the scholastic traditions of Sakya, Tsarchen was a scholar whose learning spanned all major areas of exoteric and esoteric teachings. He was also renowned for his mastery of the doctrines of other schools, and he is said to have studied the systems of Nyingma, Géluk, and Kagyu without bias. In recognition of his vast learning, he was appointed to the seat of the great scholar Pudön at Shalu Monastery.

He received the "initiate teachings" (*slob bshad*) from Ngorchen and maintained the essential lore of the Ngorpa tradition in the monastery he founded, named Drongmoché. His tradition diverged from the Ngorpa due to a feud between the house of Dar, who were his patrons, and the Dongga, the family of the wife of the Sakya hierarch Ngakchang Günga Rinchen (1517–1584). This feud led to a split between the Tsarpas and the rest of Sakya, which was heightened by the fact that Tsarchen and his disciple Nésar Jamyang Khyentsé Wangchuk (b. 1525) had an eclectic attitude toward Buddhist practice and included texts and practices in their tradition that had been rejected by earlier Sakya teachers. In particular, they practiced Vajrakīla tantric cycles that were associated with Nyingma.

The Sakya order places a great deal of emphasis on scholarship, and its monasteries were among the greatest seats of learning in Tibet. The traditional curriculum was divided into six main units: (1) perfection of wisdom (which focuses on the "five treatises of Maitreya": *Ornament for Clear Realization, Ornament for the Mahāyāna Sūtras, Differentiation of the Middle and the Extremes, Differentiation of Phenomena and the Nature of Phenomena,* and the *Sublime Continuum*, as well as Śāntideva's *Entry Into the Bodhisattva Deeds*); (2) epistemology (the primary texts are Dignāga's *Compendium of Valid Cognition*, Dharmakīrti's *Commentary on the Compendium of Valid Cognition* and *Ascertainment of Valid Cognition*, and Sakya Pandita's *Treasury of the Knowledge of Valid Cognition*); (3) vinaya (which emphasizes the *Sūtra on Individual Liberation* and the *Sūtra on Monastic Discipline);* (4) abhidharma (which concentrates on Vasubandhu's *Treasury of Abhidharma* and Asaṅga's *Compendium of Abhidharma*); (5) Madhyamaka (based on Nāgārjuna's *Root Verses on the Middle Way,*

Candrakīrti's *Entry Into the Middle Way*, and Āryadeva's *Four Hundred*); and (6) differentiation of the three vows (the major source for which is Sakya Pandita's *Differentiation of the Three Vows*).

These topics comprise the standard curriculum for monks at Sakya monasteries. A monk who successfully completes this course of study can be awarded one of several degrees, each of which signifies a particular level of accomplishment. The first hurdle is an oral examination called "the ten teachings" (*bka' bcu*), in which monks must demonstrate their proficiency in all of these subjects. Those who pass this exam are allowed to advance. A person who excels in the study of all the eighteen texts listed above can submit to testing for the degree of *géshé* (*dge bshes*).[16] In ascending order, the primary géshé degrees are: "master of the four teachings" (*bka' bzhi pa;* pronounced "gashipa"), "master of the ten teachings" (*bka' bcu pa;* pronounced "gachupa"), and "master of extensive learning" (*rab 'byams pa;* pronounced "rapjampa"). Those who attain the level of "master of extensive learning" then have the option of pursuing tantric study.

The Sakya tradition holds that a comprehensive grounding in the fundamental texts of Buddhism serves as a necessary basis for tantric training. Sakya monks study Vajrayāna all through their schooling, but intensive tantric practice is generally reserved for those who have completed the scholastic education program.

Distinctive Practices: "Path and Result"

The characteristic meditative system of Sakya is termed "path and result" (*lamdré*), which is a comprehensive vision of Buddhist practice based on the *Hevajra Tantra. Lamdré* is a shortened form of the term "path including its result," which signifies that in this system the two are held to be inseparable, and not two distinct factualities. One cannot legitimately differentiate path from result, nor can result be distinguished from path; from the point of view of awakening, all such dichotomies vanish. The result subsumes the path, since the latter leads to the former; and the path subsumes the result, since it is the means whereby the result is actualized. Just as a seed contains the potential to give rise to a sprout if the proper conditions are present, so a qualified student has the aptitude to attain the fruit of awakening if he or she meets with the necessary conditions: the essential instructions (*gdams ngag, upadeśa*), an awakened teacher, tantric empowerment (*dbang skur, abhiṣeka*), and the diligence necessary to practice successfully. The result is already present in the mental continuum of the practitioner, and the path is the technique for making it actual.

In this system, the path includes the cause, because on the path one purifies the defilements that prevent actualization of awakening. The path also includes the result, because the result can only be realized through successful practice of the path. The result includes the cause, because the result is a transformed aspect of the cause. A person who attains the result makes manifest a previously unperceived aspect of the cause and dispels the misconception that they were different. Tugen Losang Chögi Nyima (1737–1802) states that according to the lamdré view,

> because the ultimate truth is not expressible in words, it is inconceivable. Because neither the object of meditation nor a meditator exists, there is no object [on which] to meditate. Because there exists neither an object that is viewed nor a viewer, from the point of view of exalted wisdom there is no continuum of viewing.[17]

Adherents of the tradition claim that its integrity is ensured by the "four authenticities": authentic teachers, authentic direct experiences, authentic scriptures, and authentic treatises. Teachers are certified by realized masters in an unbroken chain of transmission. Their meditations, based on hearing and practice of the secret oral instructions, lead to direct perception of the truths realized by adepts of the past. The scriptures are inherited originally from buddhas and passed on to human masters, and they in turn compose treatises that explain the system for students.

There is little material on path and result in Western languages, mainly due to the fact that Sakya masters have traditionally viewed it as the most secret and profound of all Buddhist teachings and have closely guarded its transmission. According to lineage histories, it originally existed only as an oral tradition (*snyan brgyud*) which was passed on in secret by a master to a few exceptional and advanced students. Before the eleventh century, writing down the explanations and practices of path and result was not allowed, unless a disciple received special permission from his teacher.

Traditional histories report that Drokmi gave the complete path and result instructions to just three students, the most important of whom was Sékhar Chungwa (ca. 1025–1135). His student Shangdön Chöbar (ca. 1053–11350) gave them to Sachen Günga Nyingpo (1092–1158). Sachen wrote several treatises on path and result, which became some of the most important texts of the lineage. Currently there are thirty-one volumes in Tibetan containing lamdré teachings, most of which were written in Tibet.[18] The only Indian work recognized as belonging to the path and result lineage is Virūpa's *Vajra Verses*, which is considered to be the basic text of the system. Even today, however, its lore is still primarily disseminated orally by a master to a small group of disciples, and they are sworn to secrecy, with the result that this is one of the least accessible tantric lineages for modern scholars. An example of this attitude is Chöbar's admonition to his student Sachen: "Secret mantra is realized through secret [practice]; one must practice a hidden yoga in order to attain experience and realization."[19] This approach appears to have a long pedigree: path and result is unusual among tantric lineages in that it appears to have been entirely oral in India, with no written treatises. The first text committed to writing was probably the *Vajra Verses*; before that, it and other lamdré instructions were imparted by masters to a small group of students.[20]

The most esoteric instructions were often reserved for one disciple in a generation.[21] According to tradition, the *Vajra Verses* were first spoken to Kānha, who gave them to his student Damarupa. Damarupa in turn transmitted them to Avadhūti, whose student Gayadhara (d. 1103) traveled to Tibet in 1041 and taught Drokmi. Although Sakya tradition holds that the *Vajra Verses* were originally composed in Sanskrit, the Tibetan version has no Sanskrit equivalent title. This is explained by the assertion that Drokmi memorized the verses in their original Indic dialect but translated them into Tibetan to his disciples. Ronald Davidson contends that it is more probable that Gayadhara composed the text himself in response to Drokmi's request for esoteric teachings and passed it off as Virūpa's work in order to give it a pedigree dating back to the great siddha.[22]

According to Sakya tradition, Sachen received the path and result instructions from Chöbar over a period of four years beginning in 1120, but was forbidden to transmit them for eighteen years. Most of this time was spent in solitary meditation. In 1138, when he was forty-six, he received a revelation from Virūpa, following which he penetrated the deepest mysteries of the system. After the restriction against teaching ended in 1141, he taught Aseng Dorjé Denpa the essentials of path and result, and composed a commentary that is known as the *Asengma* by the tradition. This is the most important explication of the system, and is supplemented by another ten works, most of which were reportedly also given to individual students. These circulated in manuscript form for hundreds of years before they were compiled as a set by Jamyang Gyeltsen (1870–1940) and published at Dergé in the twentieth century.[23]

The "Triple Appearance" and the "Triple Continuum"

An important tenet of path and result teachings is the similarity of the three aspects of the "triple appearance" (or "triple perspective": *snang gsum, tryavabhāsa*) and the "triple continuum" (*rgyud gsum, tritantra*). The triple appearance consists of: (1) the appearance of phenomena as impure error; (2) the appearance of experience in meditation; and (3) pure appearance.[24] Lamdré texts indicate that these are fundamentally the same and that the only difference lies in how they are perceived. The triple continuum consists of basis (*gzhi, ādhāra*), path (*lam, mārga*) and result (*'bras bu, phala*). As with the parts of the triple appearance, the components of the triple continuum are fundamentally nondifferentiable. All divisions are creations of mind, and mind in lamdré is the locus of such distinctions as "basis," "path," and "result," although in itself it is luminous and empty.[25] According to the *Hevajra Tantra*,

> This exalted wisdom arises from self-awareness, which is free from notions of self and other. It is spotless and empty like the sky, the supreme essence of the actual and non-actual, a union of wisdom and method, a union of desire and absence of desire. This very [exalted wisdom] is the life of living beings, the supreme unchanging unity. It is all-pervasive and abides in all bodies. All the actual and non-actual arise from it . . . . It is the essential nature of all things and the pure basis of illusory forms.[26]

In discussions of the triple continuum, the basis is said to be the two truths (conventional truths and ultimate truths), the path consists of cultivating method and wisdom, and the pure vision is the result. These are also linked to the triple appearance, since ordinary beings perceive reality in terms of conventional truth, and thus phenomena appear to them in the impure aspect. Those who are on the path engage in meditative practice in order to cultivate method and wisdom. Method involves training in love and compassion and developing the mind of awakening. The wisdom aspect focuses on meditation on emptiness. The result is the attainment of buddhahood, which is characterized by the pure vision in which one no longer perceives the distinctions of basis, path, and result, method and wisdom, ordinary beings and buddhas.

In the *Vajra Verses*, Virūpa sums up the characteristics of each part of the triple appearance:

> For sentient beings with the afflictions is the impure appearance.
> For the meditator with transic absorption is the appearance of experience.
> For the ornamental wheel of the Sugata's [Buddha's] inexhaustible enlightened body, voice and mind is the pure appearance.[27]

The first line refers to the perceptions of sentient beings, which are conditioned by afflicted mental states. These in turn lead to suffering and continued affliction. The cycle is only broken by those who overcome attachment to mundane enjoyments and who conquer mental defilements through meditative training. Because ordinary beings constantly experience the results of past karma, the first perspective is referred to as the "karmic appearance."

The second line is concerned with people who engage in common Mahāyāna practices like cultivating compassion and love, training in the six perfections, and so on. One should reflect on the difficulty of obtaining a human rebirth, a human body with the necessary prerequisites for religious training, and the even greater obstacle of encountering the necessary leisure and resources to be able to engage in practice. After considering this, one should become fully devoted to meditation. The most important meditative trainings of the second appearance are calm abiding and higher insight. This verse is also said to refer to people at the beginning levels of Vajrayāna practice, who study, meditate, and perform tantric rituals and who have attained some benefits from them. Such trainees selflessly undertake the practice of dharma in order to benefit others.

The third line describes the mindset of buddhas, who have attained the final result of the tantra path and thus have perfected compassion and wisdom to the highest degree and who work ceaselessly for the benefit of others. Buddhas have the pure vision, which understands that all the phenomena of cyclic existence and nirvana are the display of primordially undefiled mind. From the perspective of their exalted wisdom, there is no afflicted world to be abandoned, no pure state of liberation to be gained, no sentient beings, and no buddhas. For awakened beings,

> both worldly existence and liberation are seen to be of one taste (i.e., nondual). Previously one was a sentient being, but through the power of practicing the path, one has become a Buddha; hence the mind-stream of a sentient being and that of a Buddha are one. Previously there was the practitioner on the path, but through that path dissolving into the result, both the path and the result are of one taste. Previously all conceptualizations were to be discarded, but through the power of habituation to discarding them all conceptualizations are dissolved into the ultimate truth, so the conceptualizations to be discarded and their antidotes are of one taste.[28]

In a discussion of the nondual nature of cyclic existence and nirvana, the *Hevajra Tantra* states,

> Such is cyclic existence, and such is nirvana. There is no nirvana apart from cyclic existence, we say. Cyclic existence comprises form, sound, etc., cyclic existence comprises form and the other [four aggregates], the sense faculties, anger, obscuration, and the other three [afflictions]. But all of these are really subsumed by nirvana, and they only appear as cyclic existence due to obscuration. Through purifying cyclic existence by eliminating obscuration, cyclic existence manifests as nirvana. The mind of awakening is nirvana, which encompasses the modes of conventional and ultimate [truths].[29]

Initiation

In keeping with the strict secrecy considered necessary for authentic practice and transmission of teachings, anyone wishing to train in the system of the triple continuum must receive initiation from a qualified master who has not only been initiated, but who has also received authorization to confer initiation to students. Only those who have successfully completed a three-year, three-month, and three-day solitary retreat can receive such certification. Extensive study of both esoteric and exoteric topics is also expected of anyone who is serious about path and result practice.

Prior to conferring initiation, the lama enters into a meditative state in which he assumes the form of the buddha into whose cycle of practice students are being inducted. The lama assumes the role of an awakened being and feels the pride and confidence that make true initiation possible. The students are perceived as potential buddhas, and through the power of their faith and practice they will one day become fully awakened. They receive the blessings of the luminaries of the lineage, which increases their own power and awakens the seed of buddha nature lying dormant in their minds. The blessings are compared to water that rains down on the students and nourishes the seed of buddhahood. During this time, musical instruments are sometimes played, and the lama touches a consecrated vajra on various parts of the students' bodies, particularly the heart, throat, and forehead. This serves to protect them from negative influences of body, speech, and mind, but its effectiveness also requires their devotion and confidence in the lama and his realization.

Further elements of the ritual purify the students' five aggregates; each is symbolically transformed into one of the five meditation buddhas, and the five afflictions (desire, hatred, obscuration, jealousy, and arrogance) are transmuted into the five potential wisdoms associated with the five buddhas. Each is the opposite of the afflicted mental state and is the transformation of its energy into an aspect of the awakened consciousness. During this process, the students are handed ritual objects—a vajra, bell, or crown, for example—as symbols of this change of status.

Those who are preparing for path and result training commonly receive the teachings over a six-week period. The lama generally begins with accounts from lineage histories; the biographies of the luminaries of the tradition are intended to inspire faith and to provide role models for aspirants. During the first week or so, students are also given teachings on exoteric topics such as the nature of cyclic existence, the sufferings of the lower realms (hell beings, hungry ghosts, and animals), and the preciousness of a human birth. These are general instructions that are common to Hīnayāna, Mahāyāna, and Vajrayāna, and they must be fully understood before one can move on to more advanced topics. Without a firm grounding in the common subject matter, there is no hope of grasping the more subtle and profound teachings of tantra. They are generally given at least four times to ensure that students grasp their import. Core points are repeated throughout each day, and before beginning a new set of teachings, lamas review the previous day's main themes before starting on new ones.

After the first day of instructions, students are told to be aware of their dreams, because all such experiences are particularly significant during the initiation period. The things one witnesses in dreams serve as indications of the success of the blessings one has received and are signs of future progress.

In the initiation, students are exposed to a range of teachings relating to the triple appearance, complete with analogies and stories that highlight their application to meditation practice. They learn about the causes and implications of the impure appearance, how to attain the preliminary understanding of the vision of experience, and the characteristics of the perspective of awakened beings in the pure vision.

After this has been fully covered, the lama moves on to discussions of the triple continuum and gives initiations that allow the students to begin Vajrayāna practice. During this time the bodhisattva vows are also given, followed by tantric instruction and vows. At this point the master may discuss the subsidiary topics of the "six yogas."[30] Not all students are given all of the teachings; lamas decide which are appropriate to particular individuals, and withhold those that are not considered suitable.

Initiation is referred to as "causal continuum" because it gives students the necessary preparation for tantric practice. After it is completed, aspirants are introduced to the nature of mind, the main subject matter of the triple continuum. The lama first discusses the nondifference of all apparent dichotomies, and then analogies are used to describe the nature of mind. Unlike other tantric traditions in which the nature of mind is introduced to beginners, Sakya holds that such instructions are only appropriate for those who have attained some insight and that a thorough grounding in Buddhist doctrine is a necessary prerequisite. From the earliest times, Sakya tradition has held that students must have a firm grounding in faith, cultivation of morality, renunciation, and study before such teachings are given.

Successful initiation is the causal continuum, which plants the seeds of buddhahood. It is not merely mechanical, however: a student may sit through the ceremony and intone the words, but unless there is a basis of faith in the lama and lineage figures and comprehension of the teachings, it will be like a seed planted on barren soil. The path continuum, the second stage of the process, involves transformation of the subtle physiology of winds, drops, and channels. Students are instructed to respect the body and to view it as a maṇḍala. They are taught about the subtle body according to the highest yoga tantra system and learn to visualize the channels in the shape of letters. The lama tells them how to transmute afflicted emotions into positive ones, and they are told that there is no real difference between their minds and the mind of a buddha. Through this process, the cause becomes the path, and the path becomes the result. All dualities are understood as mental projections, without substance.

The Tibetan Appropriation of the Lamdré System

The scriptural basis of path and result, the *Hevajra Tantra*, was brought to Tibet by Drokmi, who studied with the Indian master Gayadhara (d. 1103), to whom Drokmi paid a large sum of money so that he would impart his teachings.[31] Drokmi later returned to Tibet and translated the *Hevajra Tantra*, which provides the guiding vision for lamdré practice. He also is credited with translating two explanatory tantras and Virūpa's *Vajra Verses*.

The *Hevajra* was viewed by the founders of the Sakya lineage as a distillation of the teachings of both sūtra and tantra, and many of the great Sakya masters wrote commentaries on it or developed liturgical cycles based on its teachings. An exception to this was Sakya Pandita, who, despite his exalted position among Sakya scholars, contributed little to the literature of path and result. The practice of lamdré was systematized by his uncle Drakpa Gyeltsen, who formulated an integrated system based on four primary factors: correct view of emptiness, meditation, ritual, and accomplishment.[32] According to his system, exalted wisdom (*ye shes*) is innate, and he defines it as "clear and knowing" (*gsal zhing shes pa*). This innate exalted wisdom transcends all limiting and dichotomizing categories, such as self and other, subject and object, cyclic existence and nirvana, delusion and awakening. He further indicates that all phenomena are in fact reflections of it and have no substantial existence.

In the system formulated by Drakpa Gyeltsen, there are five primary stages in the process of gaining direct understanding: (1) initiation (*dbang*) and the interpretation (*lta ba*) of the experience produced by the initiation; (2) the generation stage (*bskyed rim*); (3) the completion stage (*rdzogs rim*); (4) training (*spyod pa*); and (5) a concluding practice that involves use of tantric seals (*phyag rgya*).

Initiation is crucial for all tantric practice, since it forges the necessary connections to tantric deities. Correct interpretation of this experience is also essential, since it aids in developing the proper orientation toward one's practice. The generation stage in this system is similar to the procedure outlined in the "Tantra" chapter: one visualizes a deity which embodies all the positive physical and mental qualities of an awakened being. The completion stage uses practices of "self-empowerment" (*rang byin brlab*), which involves heat yoga, and "maṇḍala practices" (*dkyil 'khor 'khor lo*), which include sexual yogas.

During the generation stage, one generates a mental similitude of the goal of buddhahood, transforming the mind's images into the body of a buddha within its maṇḍala, surrounded by a retinue of other deities. Everything is perceived as aspects of the maṇḍala, all sounds are heard as mantras, and all of one's thoughts are imagined to be the awakened understanding of a buddha. In the completion stage, one trains in increasing familiarity with the result. This is conjoined with the techniques of heat yoga and manipulation of winds and drops. The deities cause psychic energy to move upward through the channels. This leaves the body and fills the universe, bringing benefits to sentient beings and making offerings to buddhas and bodhisattvas. When one gains the level of control necessary to cause the winds to enter the central channel, dualistic thought vanishes. Until this point, one's perceptions will always be tinged with duality and conceptuality, and one will reflexively differentiate self and other, inner and outer, cyclic existence and nirvana.

Path and result initiates are generally first given preliminary teachings on the triple appearance, and then the bodhisattva vows. Next they receive Hevajra initiation, and then the full teachings of the triple appearance. Instructions on the triple continuum are reserved for students who have attained a degree of meditative accomplishment that will enable them to understand their significance.

Before initiation is conducted, the place where the ceremony will be held is first prepared. Inimical forces are pacified, and purification rituals are performed. The ritual implements are consecrated one at a time, and the outline of the maṇḍala is drawn. There are three types of maṇḍala: painted maṇḍalas, sand maṇḍalas, and body maṇḍalas (in which the lama's body is the maṇḍala).

The initiation generally requires two days. During the first, aspirants are given preliminary instructions and prepared for admission into the maṇḍala. The physical maṇḍala is constructed by specially trained disciples of the master, who are skilled in the relevant meditations and artistic lore. It is completed by the morning of the second day, when the lama consecrates it, blessing each deity and symbol. After it is ritually prepared, it is shielded from view, and the master enters into meditation involving self-generation as the principal deity. When the maṇḍala has been consecrated, the individual deities are invited to enter their respective places and to remain during the initiation. At this point the ritual paraphernalia are consecrated and placed in their appropriate positions.

The actual initiation is in four parts, resembling the outline we saw earlier in the "Tantra" chapter: (1) vase initiation; (2) secret initiation; (3) knowledge initiation; and (4) the fourth initiation. In the first, the students drink sanctified water, which purifies the five afflictions and transmutes them into the pure qualities of the five buddha families. Various points of the body are anointed, and the students imagine that the matter of their bodies is cleansed of impurities. This also serves to purify the subtle aspects of the body: the winds, drops, and channels. This plants the seed of future actualization of form bodies.

Each aspirant is given a secret name, following which the teacher rings a bell. The name is to be memorized and never repeated to anyone. During subsequent meditation sessions, each initiate will recall his or her secret name and visualize the lama, which re-creates the deep bond created by the ceremony.

A copy of the *Hevajra Tantra* is placed inside the left arm of each student, a bell is held in the left hand, a wheel is placed under the right foot and the right hand holds a conch shell. These symbolize the actions of a buddha, who teaches the scriptures, who has mastered the wisdom aspect of the teachings (symbolized by the bell), and who turns the wheel of dharma for the benefit of sentient beings.

In the secret initiation, students are given "nectar" from a skull cup, which represents conquest of ego-clinging and understanding of emptiness. The lama pours a small amount of the nectar into each student's hand, and they recite a mantra while drinking it. They are told to visualize the liquid circulating throughout the channels, moving through the cakras, and purifying the subtle constituents of the body.

The third initiation also involves drinking nectar from the skull cup, but now students imagine it as the "mind of awakening" (*byang chub kyi sems, bodhicitta*), which in highest yoga tantra is pictured as a white liquid. The lama tells the aspirants that the nectar is a condensation of the bliss of the union of male and female during the climax of sexual intercourse when the mind of clear light manifests. Students try to imagine this bliss and visualize the white substance moving through the channels. It should be viewed as a physical manifestation of the altruistic aspiration to become awakened. It purifies all the elements in the channels, and the bliss is equated with the pure enjoyment of tantric deities in sexual embrace.

This part of the initiation confers permission to visualize the deities in "father-mother" (*yab yum*) position, that is, in sexual union. Initiates imagine themselves as the male deity (whether they are male or female), embracing his consort and experiencing pure bliss.

The fourth initiation is related to supreme bliss, which is unbounded and as vast as space. It is beyond any ordinary enjoyment, and is unconnected with conceptuality or words. It is a state of pure understanding of the nature of reality free from dichotomies or notions of inherent existence. This initiation is connected with the essential wind maṇḍala and purifies the subtle energies.[33]

At the conclusion of the initiation, offerings are given to the lama, who asks the deities of the maṇḍala to depart. After this, the maṇḍala is dismantled (if it is a sand maṇḍala, the sand is swept up, beginning at the outer edges, and collected together in a vessel). The lama then asks to be forgiven for any inadvertent mistakes during the rite, and everyone participates in a ritual feast. The lama may give an oral transmission of the text, along with instructions regarding subsequent practice. At this point the lama—who has been enacting the role of Hevajra during the ceremony—enters into meditation and returns to his normal state. From this point, students are required to perform daily *sādhana*s for the rest of their lives, and any breach of their commitments will have negative consequences for their practice and wellbeing.

After the initiation, students often have eight days of instructions in the triple continuum and are introduced to the nature of mind. They learn that all appearances are produced by mind and are not caused by external phenomena. Moreover, changing the mind transforms the world one inhabits, and they are given secret instructions on how to do this.

At the next level of practice, initiates learn to view all appearances as like a magician's illusions, which fool audiences but have no real substance. Various analogies are used to drive home this point, such as the way we assent to the reality of dreams, but realize them to be false upon awakening. While in the dream state our experiences seem unquestionably veridical, but later we know them for what they are, and they generally fade into nothing. From the awakened perspective, the images of ordinary consciousness are like this. In the next level of training, one learns to discriminate positive and negative appearances and to cultivate the former. Although all are illusory, some are pleasant and beneficial, while others have negative outcomes. Just as a buddha can create and dissolve appearances at will as a form of play, so the initiate also learns to take control over the products of mind. The mind is seen to be as expansive as the sky, and thoughts are like fleeting clouds that come and go. The sky has no edges, no top or bottom, and our minds are equally expansive.

According to Lama Choedak Yuthok,

> That incomprehensible self is articulated in the form of deities, using gestures and symbolism to help us identify with this ideal self. We try to meditate in that form, rather than as the ordinary self. We assume the role of a Buddha, who can express different moods and shapes, hold different implements and express divine enlightened qualities. Therefore we do not meditate on the 'nihilistic' concept of emptiness which focuses on nonexistence. We employ a creative concept of emptiness, which makes everything possible. We create a world, a celestial mansion. The meditator himself is the Buddha. The whole process becomes an expression of the ideal self, which is no different from the universal consciousness of all enlightened beings.[34]

Advanced meditators move beyond conceiving of meditation as something one does in formal settings, such as sitting on a cushion, and all activities become aspects of practice. Eventually the entire world and all of one's perceptions are transformed as one becomes increasingly familiar with adopting the perspective of an awakened being. These are powerful techniques, and according to the tradition students who maintain their commitments and train within the proper mental attitude can attain buddhahood in one lifetime. Those who do not succeed will still plant potent seeds that will bear fruit in the future.

The Inseparability of Cyclic Existence and Nirvana

The central insight of path and result is "the inseparability of cyclic existence and nirvana" (*'khor 'das dbyer med*), which is expressed in a famous verse in the *Hevajra Tantra*:

> Then the essence is described, pure and embodying wisdom, there is not the slightest difference between cyclic existence and nirvana. In the highest bliss there is no meditation and no meditator, no body, nor form, and likewise no object or subject. There is neither flesh nor blood, neither excrement nor urine, no sickness, no delusion, and likewise no purification, no lust, no anger, no delusion, no envy, no

> malevolence, no self-pride, no visible object . . . . The innate is calm and undifferentiated.[35]

According to this system, both cyclic existence and nirvana originate in mind (*sems*), which in its basic nature is a union of luminosity and emptiness. When mind is obscured by afflictions, there is cyclic existence, and when these are removed, there is nirvana. There is, however, no substantial or real difference between the two states, and so in the *Hevajra Tantra* Buddha states that all beings

> are buddhas, but this is obscured by adventitious defilements. When this is cleared away, they are buddhas at that very [moment] . . . There is no being that is not a buddha if it knows its own true nature. Hell beings, hungry ghosts, animals, gods, humans, and demi-gods—even worms on a dung-heap and so forth—have an eternally blissful nature . . . [36]

There is no real difference between the mind of a buddha, a beginner on the path, an advanced spiritual adept, or even a worm in a lump of manure. The only distinction lies in their respective perceptions of their environment: a buddha perceives reality in a manner that is free from defilements, while the consciousnesses of other beings are tainted by varying degrees of afflictions. When afflictions are removed, the causal buddha—which was previously unrecognized due to adventitious obscuration—becomes an actualized buddha, who differs from the causal buddha in terms of perception of reality.

In this practice, one realizes that all phenomena are creations of mind, and so nothing is either good or bad in itself. A central insight of path and result is that our ordinary notions of good and evil, or cause and effect, are only conceptual constructs that do not exist as they appear to conventional awareness. Nothing inherently exists outside of mere cognitions of mind, and all such cognitions are manifestations of mind itself, although in its basic nature it is free from all activities. Even such apparently obvious distinctions as path and result are seen as conceptual constructs, and these are transcended through meditation on the nature of mind.

> Through the practice of the inseparability of the ground [basis], path, and fruit, the profound meaning of all the tantras is immediately

> revealed and one develops the capacity to transform defilements into wisdoms and obstacles into powers. With the onset of auspicious internal signs, realization of all the *Path and Its Fruit* teachings becomes a certainty. The possessor of the three vows must guard the vows and pledges as he would guard his own life. Through practising the four empowerments at each of the four periods of meditation the continuity of the stream of initiation will be preserved and the eminent nature of this teaching will be realized.[37]

Mind as a Union of Luminosity and Emptiness

In path and result texts the character (*mtshan nyid*) of mind is said to be luminosity, and its basic nature is emptiness. Luminosity does not detract from (*'dor*) emptiness, nor does emptiness undermine luminosity. Rather, the final nature of mind is an inexpressible state of union of these two factors. Mind is without beginning, middle, or end, and it transcends any attempts to limit, conceptualize, or analyze its nature. In a discussion of meditation, Ngorchen Gönchok Hlündrup advises practitioners that in order to become aware of the nature of mind, one should first relax and allow thoughts to disappear gradually and,

> when the functioning of thoughts disappears, then place the mind for a long time on the sparkling clarity of consciousness. When one's meditation upon that sparkling clarity of consciousness becomes steady, one should not look on the meditation object but strongly look at the clear appearance of the radiance of mind itself. If one experiences this in the manner of singular clarity, then relax the mind upon that experience. Do not reflect on the past, do not think about the future, do not keep an account of your present activities, but completely cut any conceptualizations, regardless of [their] being good or bad, as they arise one after another. Remain in the manner of being inwardly at ease but outwardly attentive.[38]

The basis of all ordinary thoughts and conceptions is the "fundamental mind" (*gnyug pa'i sems*), which is innate (*lhan cig*) and is a union (*zung 'jug*) of luminosity and emptiness. All that appears to exist is nothing but a projection of the luminous nature of mind. But since the nature of mind transcends all dichotomization or conceptualization, all appearances are viewed as illusions, as forms projected by mind with no substance. Mind itself is also devoid of substance, and so

> when the place of residence of the nature of consciousness is sought, it is found to reside neither inside the body, nor outside the body, nor in between the two. It has neither color nor form. No matter how one may search, one will fail to find its essence. Therefore, consciousness is stainlessly non-abiding. In the end, when one looks for where it ceases, one finds that the resultant consciousness does not cease anywhere. Therefore, consciousness is utter blissful noncessation.[39]

Path and Result

In path and result practice, the characteristic of luminosity is connected with the stage of generation, since in this practice one emanates deities from the luminous nature of mind. Mind's characteristic of emptiness is linked with the completion stage, in which the images are merged with the meditator, who understands that the nature of the deities and the nature of mind are both emptiness. The exalted wisdom that results from successful practice of these two stages is the outcome of repeated familiarization. It should be noted, however, that according to lamdré masters this wisdom is not something newly produced by meditative practice; rather, meditation makes manifest the "naturally innate exalted wisdom."

In the "result" aspect of this method of training, the techniques connected with luminosity result in the ability to produce emanation bodies, and meditation concerned with meditation on emptiness is connected with actualization of the truth body. The complete enjoyment body is the coincidence of both aspects.

"Initiate Teachings" and "General Teachings"

The lamdré system is generally divided into two subsections: "initiate teachings" (*slob bshad*) and "general teachings" (*tshogs bshad*). The latter are given to large groups of students, while the former are reserved for a small number of advanced students.[40] The origins of this division are traced back to Muchen Gönchok Gyeltsen, who presented the most esoteric teachings in private to his student Dakchen Lodrö Gyeltsen (1444–1479), while giving general teachings to groups of students in more public lectures. The initiate teachings lineage continues this tradition, and is generally reserved for only a few particularly gifted students. The initiate teachings tend to be clear and pithy instructions written in an intimate colloquial style, while the general teachings are more scholastic, are written in religious language (*chos skad*), and contain numerous quotations from sūtras and tantras.

The Nine Path Cycles and the Six Lineages

Another common division of path and result is referred to as "the nine path cycles": (1) Virūpa's *Vajra Verses*, which distill the essence of all sūtras and tantras and are based particularly on the *Hevajra Tantra;* (2) Saroruhavajra's *Nine Profound Methods of the Generation Stage* and *The Flame Point of the Completion Stage*, which are based on the Hevajra tantra called *The Fundamental Tantra of the Two Examinations;* (3) Nāgārjuna's *Treatise on the Mind of Awakening*, which is based on the *Guhyasamāja Tantra;* (4) Dombī Heruka's *Spontaneous Birth and Attainment*, based on the *Fundamental Tantra of the Two Examinations;* (5) Indrabodhi's *The Complete Path of the Great Seal*, which is based on the *Essential Drop of Wisdom Tantra;* (6) Doktséwa's *Beyond Thought*, which is based on the *Kiss Tantra;* (7) Kṛṣṇacārin's *Olapati*, which is based on the *Cakrasaṃvara Tantra;* (8) Vāgīśvarakīrti's *The Great Seal*, which is based on the *Fundamental Tantra of the Two Examinations;* and (9) Nakpo Utsita Chiwa Mépa's *Instructions on Straightening the Crooked*, which is based on all the mother tantras.

The lamdré system is traditionally divided into six primary lineages: (1) the teaching tradition of Padmavajra, (2) the teaching tradition of Durjayacandra, (3) the teaching tradition of Śāntipa, (4) the teaching tradition of Śāntabhadra, (5) the teaching tradition of the Kashmiri Kīrtibhadra, and (6) the teaching tradition of Maitripa.

Notes

1. According to *lamdré* lineage histories, he was the same Dharmapāla who was the abbot of Nālandā Monastery and a great scholar of the Yogācāra tradition. See, for instance, Musashi Tachikawa ("The Tantric Doctrine of the Sa skya pa according to the Śel gyi me loṅ," *Acta Asiatica* 29, 1975, p. 97 n. 6), who cites *The Religious Biographies of Path and Result* (*Lam 'bras rnam thar*). Tachikawa doubts that Virūpa was the Yogācāra

scholar Dharmapāla, but the identification is commonly asserted in *lamdré* sources. One of the best studies in a Western language for the path and result lineage is Cyrus Stearns, *Luminous Lives: The Story of the Early Masters of the Lam 'Bras Tradition in Tibet* (Boston: Wisdom Publications, 2001).

2. Lama Choedak Yuthok, *Origin of the Lam 'Bras Tradition in India* (B.A. thesis, Australian National University, 1990), p. 16.
3. According to lineage histories, he originally composed the *Vajra Verses* for his student Kānha, who had a proclivity for a gradual approach to the path. Kānha had been a wandering Hindu yogi before meeting Virūpa, who gave him the teachings of the *Vajra Verses* as a concise summary of the Buddhist path. As Ronald Davidson has noted in the introduction to his translation of the text, its language is extremely cryptic, and according to Sakya tradition it was intended as a mnemonic tool. It is a brief summary of the essentials of the path, but is not sufficient by itself. A student should use it as an aid for meditation, but its significance only emerges through long-term practice. See Ronald Davidson, *Tibetan Renaissance: Tantric Buddhism in the Rebirth of Tibetan Culture* (New York: Columbia University Press, 2005), pp. 477–493.
4. The name Mahākāla means "Great Black One." This tantric deity is the wrathful aspect of Avalokiteśvara.
5. These are named below.
6. Gene Smith provides an overview of the history of the Khön family in "The Early History of the 'Khon Family and the Sa skya School," E. Gene Smith, *Among Tibetan Texts* (Boston: Wisdom, 2001), pp. 99–109.
7. A short traditional account of his life is translated by Cyrus Stearns: "A Quest for 'The Path and Result'" in Donald S. Lopez, ed., *Religions of Tibet in Practice* (Princeton: Princeton University Press, 1997), pp. 188–199.
8. Ngorchen Konchog Lhundrub, *The Beautiful Ornament of the Three Visions*, tr. Lobsang Dagpa and Jay Goldberg (Ithaca: Snow Lion, 1991), p. 105.
9. The three vows are the "individual liberation" (*prātimokṣa*) vows, the bodhisattva vows, and the *samaya* vows of tantra. Jan-Ulrich Sobisch has done an extensive study of debates regarding the three vows in Tibet in his book *Three-Vow Theories in Tibetan Buddhism: A Comparative Study of Major Traditions from the Twelfth through Nineteenth Centuries* (Wiesbaden: Dr. Ludwig Richert Verlag, 2002).
10. *The History of the Sakya Tradition*, by Chogay Trichen (Bristol: Ganesha Press, 1983), p. 15.
11. Śākyaśrībhadra is often referred to as "The Kashmiri Scholar" (*kha che paṇ chen*). The term *kha che* literally means "big mouth," and is used by Tibetans to refer to Kashmiris and Muslims.
12. *The History of the Sakya Tradition*, p. 19.
13. Alfonsa Ferrari, *Mk'yen Brtse's Guide to the Holy Places of Central Tibet* (Rome: Serie Orientale Roma, 1958), p. 64.
14. This is how Sakya Pandita's mission is presented in traditional histories, but sources from the time are more ambiguous. It appears that Ködan had some interest in Buddhism, and he may well have been personally impressed by the great lama, but he and other Mongol leaders patronized various religions as a means of control over their conquered subjects. Given the importance of Buddhism to Tibetans, it would have been prudent statecraft for the khan to let them know that he respected their tradition and its leaders. There is no reason to conclude that he saw himself as exclusively Buddhist, but Sakya Pandita's negotiations with the Mongols did provide an oppor-

tunity for missionizing among them, and in later centuries most Mongol tribes converted to Buddhism.

15. Although he is now generally regarded as the head of the Sakya lineage, his ascension was disputed for a number of years, and there are still Sakyapas who do not accept his leadership.
16. This is short for *dge ba'i bshes gnyen* (Skt. *kalyāṇa-mitra*), which literally means "good friend" and implies that such a person is a qualified spiritual guide. This title is also used in the Gélukpa monastic system.
17. Thu'u bkwan Blo bzang chos kyi nyi ma, *Grub mtha' thams cad kyi khungs dang 'dod tshul ston pa legs bshad shel gyi me long* (Delhi: Ngawang Gelek Demo, 1969-1971), vol. II, p. 22a.3-5.
18. These are listed in Yuthok, *A Study on the Origin of the Lam 'Bras Tradition in India*, Appendix D, pp. 106–138.
19. Cha rgan dbang phyug rgyal mtshan, *Lam 'bras kyi bla ma bod kyi lo rgyus rgyas pa bod dang btsan pa'i byung 'dems ma* (Beijing: Library of the Cultural Palace of Nationalities); cited in Stearns, *Luminous Lives*, p. 14. My translation differs slightly from his. The traditional limit for any initiation is twenty-five, following Sachen's decision that he could not effectively confer empowerments to more than that number.
20. It was first written down by Sachen Günga Nyingpo after he began giving the path and result teachings around 1141. Lineage histories assert that it was only transmitted orally for eight generations.
21. Jamyang Khyentsé Wangchuk (1524–1568) asserts that the Indian lamdré tradition was a "single lineage" (*chig brgyud*) given only to one disciple in a generation. See Cyrus Stearns, *Luminous Lives*, p. 10.
22. Ronald Davidson, *Tibetan Renaissance*, pp. 183–195.
23. See Stearns, *Luminous Lives*, pp. 16–17. He adds that they do not seem to have circulated as a group before this; rather, particular commentaries were recommended for certain students, but few read all of them. Some of these works seem to have not been very popular, and so their reading lineage had almost disappeared before their collection as a group.
24. An account of the triple appearance from a traditional Sakya perspective can be found in *Three Visions: Fundamental Teachings of the Sakya Lineage of Tibetan Buddhism* by Ngorchen Konchog Lhundrub, tr. Lobsang Dagpa and Jay Goldberg (Ithaca: Snow Lion Publications, 2001). Deshung Rinpoche's commentary on this text has also been translated into English by Jared Rhoton: *The Three Levels of Spiritual Perception: An Oral Commentary on the Three Visions (Nang Sum) of Ngorchen Könchog Lhündrub* (Boston: Wisdom Publications, 1995).
25. The teachings of the triple continuum are discussed at length by Lama Choedak Yuthok in *The Triple Tantra* (Canberra: Gorum Publications, 1997).
26. David L. Snellgrove, *The Hevajra Tantra: A Critical Study* (London: Oxford University Press, 1959), part 2, p. 36. My translation differs slightly from Snellgrove's.
27. Cited in *The Beautiful Ornament of the Three Visions*, p. xvi.
28. *The Beautiful Ornament of the Three Visions*, p. 204.
29. *The Hevajra Tantra*, part 2, p. 67.
30. These are described in the "Kagyu" chapter. All orders of Tibetan Buddhism practice a version of these six techniques, which according to tradition were given to Nāropa by Niguma, but Sakya does not refer to them as the "six yogas of Nāropa" because they are the common property of Tibetan practitioners of highest yoga

tantra. Sakya does not link them with any particular master, but refers to them as "subsidiary practices."

31. According to traditional accounts, the amount he paid was so large that he was able to extract a promise from Gayadhara not to give the lamdré teachings to any other Tibetans.
32. His two most influential lamdré works were his *Great Jeweled Wishing Tree* (*Rin po che'i ljon shing chen mo*) and *The Precious Appearance of the Inseparability of Cyclic Existence and Nirvāṇa, The Essential View of All Tantras* (*Rgyud thams cad kyi snying po lta ba 'khor 'das dbyer med rin po che snang ba*), along with his own commentary.
33. Each initiation relates to a particular section of the thirteen-level (*sa, bhūmi*) tantric path. The first is connected with levels 1-6, the second with 7-10, the third with 11 and 12, and the fourth with the thirteenth level, which is equivalent to buddhahood. Each of the four bodies of a buddha is actualized through the respective practices of these four initiations.
34. Lama Choedak Yuthok, *Lamdre: Dawn of Enlightenment* (Canberra: Gorum Publications, 1997), p. 196.
35. *The Hevajra Tantra*, part 2, p. 39.
36. Ibid., pp. 72–73.
37. *The History of the Sakya Tradition*, p. 42.
38. *The Beautiful Ornament of the Three Visions*, p. 170.
39. Ibid., p. 194.
40. For a more detailed discussion of this division, see Ronald M. Davidson, "Preliminary Studies on Hevajra's *Abhisamaya* and the *Lam-'bras Tshogs-bshad*," in Steven D. Goodman and Ronald M. Davidson, eds., *Tibetan Buddhism: Reason and Revelation* (Albany: State University of New York Press, 1992), pp. 107–132.

15. Géluk

History of the Lineage

The Gélukpa order was founded by Tsong Khapa Losang Drakpa (1357–1419), one of the great figures of Tibetan religious history. A renowned scholar, meditator, and philosopher, his written work contains a comprehensive view of Buddhist philosophy and practice that integrates sūtra and tantra, analytical reasoning, and yogic meditation. He was also one of Tibet's great religious reformers, a devout monk who dedicated his life to revitalizing Tibetan Buddhism and recapturing the essence of Buddha's teachings as he understood them. The beginning of his order can be traced to his founding of Ganden Monastery in 1410. This monastery was intended to provide a center for his reformed order of Buddhism, an order in which monks would strictly adhere to the rules of vinaya, sharpen their intellects in philosophical debate, and engage in high-level tantric practice. The school he founded was originally referred to as *Gandenpa*, after its first monastery, and later became known as *Gélukpa*, or "System of Virtue," in accordance with its reformist orientation.

The Life of Tsong Khapa

Tsong Khapa was born in the Tsongkha Valley in the Amdo province of eastern Tibet. According to traditional biographies, his birth was the culmination of a process of spiritual development that began during a previous life, at the time of Śākyamuni Buddha. As a young boy, he offered a crystal rosary to the Buddha, who presented him with a conch shell and told his attendant Ānanda that in a future life the young boy would be born in Tibet. There he would found a great monastery and become one of the most influential figures in the spread of the dharma in the "Land of Snows." The Buddha then predicted that in his future life the young boy would be named Sumatikīrti (the Sanskrit equivalent of Losang Drakpa).

A further prophecy is attributed to Padmasambhava, who is said to have predicted the birth of a great lama named Losang Drakpa. He said that Losang Drakpa would be born in the eastern part of Tibet, near China, that he would be an emanation of a bodhisattva, and that he would attain the complete enjoyment body of a buddha.

The fulfillment of these prophecies came in 1357. The event of Tsong Khapa's birth was presaged by auspicious events. During the previous year, Tsong Khapa's future mother had dreamed that she and a multitude of other women were in a flower garden and that a young boy carrying a vessel came to them from the east. A girl holding peacock flowers approached them from the west. The boy walked up to each of the women and asked the girl holding the flowers if any of them would make a suitable mother for him. Only one—Tsong Khapa's future mother—was deemed to have the necessary prerequisites to give birth to the future religious master. The boy and girl then bathed her. She reported that she felt unusually light when she awoke.

His future father also had auspicious dreams. In one he dreamed that a young monk came to him from Wutai Shan in China. This is a mountain that is associated with Mañjuśrī (which is significant because the Gélukpa tradition considers Tsong Khapa to be an incarnation of Mañjuśrī). The young monk asked for shelter for nine months, and the father agreed, offering him his shrine room.

The auspicious dreams continued, and shortly before she was due to give birth, Tsong Khapa's mother had a dream in which a statue of Avalokiteśvara appeared before her and entered her body through the crown aperture at the top of her head. She had another dream in which she saw many monks coming to her with offerings in order to pay respect to the child she was carrying. Then the boy she had seen in a previous dream appeared and pointed toward her womb. She saw a golden statue of Avalokiteśvara there, and the combination of signs connected with Mañjuśrī and Avalokiteśvara was interpreted to mean that the child would be an emanation of both of these buddhas. The morning after the dream, Tsong Khapa was born. It is said that his mother experienced no pain as a result of the birth, and an auspicious star appeared in the sky when he emerged from her womb.

It was clear that this unusual child was destined to be a great religious figure, and he was ordained at the age of three by the fourth Karmapa, Rolbé Dorjé (1340–1383), who gave him the name Günga Nyingpo. At the age of seven he received novice vows and was named Losang Drakpa. Even at this young age, he was fully devoted to religious practice, and he excelled in the study of Buddhist philosophy and in tantric meditation. His first great teacher, Chöjé Töndrup Rinchen, told him to study Maitreya's *Ornament for Clear Realizations* and initiated him into the practices of the tantric deities Yamāntaka, Vajrapāṇi, Mañjuśrī, Amitāyus, and others.

At an early age he began to travel widely throughout Tibet in order to find lamas who could teach him the dharma. His approach was eclectic and nonsectarian; he was willing to learn from anyone of any lineage, and he soaked up the knowledge and insights of many of the greatest figures of his day. The teachings and empowerments he received were integrated into the comprehensive and synthetic view of Buddhism that characterized his mature thought. As he traveled, he discussed the tenets of Buddhism, engaged in oral debate with the foremost scholars of his day, and began to teach on his own. As a result, the reputation of his remarkable intellect and meditational accomplishments began to spread.

During his travels he met the lama whom he would later consider to be his greatest teacher, the Sakya master Rendawa (1349–1412). Rendawa quickly recognized that Tsong Khapa was a prodigy and is said to have commented that he learned as much from his student as his student did from him. Tsong Khapa initially remained with Rendawa for only a short while, however, and soon returned to his travels in search of the dharma. During this time, he studied a wide range of Buddhist teachings, exploring the ramifications of such seminal texts as Vasubandhu's *Treasury of Abhidharma*, the treatises of Dharmakīrti, Asaṅga's *Compendium of Abhidharma*, Candrakīrti's *Entry into the Middle Way*, and treatises on monastic discipline. Traditional accounts of his life report that he quickly understood everything he was taught, memorized prodigious amounts of material, and excelled in debate on all the subjects he studied. At the same time, he was also engaged in Vajrayāna practices of the highest order and was renowned both for his scholarship and his success in meditation.

Despite his growing reputation, he is reported to have lived simply and to have been free of ostentation and arrogance. He had the ability to impress people with his learning and profound wisdom, while simultaneously helping them to remain at ease in his presence. He was never rude or disrespectful to his debating opponents, and always retained his equanimity and answered all questions with equal respect.

At the age of thirty-two he began writing his most influential works. By this time he had a national reputation as an accomplished scholar of all aspects of Buddhist learning, and he began to synthesize his insights into written works that encapsulated his vision of how Buddhism ought to be practiced and conceived. One of his great early compositions is his *Golden Rosary of the Good Explanations*, a commentary on the Perfection of Wisdom literature that incorporates all twenty-one Indian commentaries on Maitreya's *Ornament for Clear Realizations*, a text that summarizes the thought of the Perfection of Wisdom sūtras.

In addition to his work with Buddhist philosophy, he concurrently dedicated himself to practicing a wide range of tantric meditations. Shortly after completing the *Golden Rosary of the Good Explanations*, he entered into a long and intensive retreat during which he trained in practices connected with the deity Heruka in accordance with the teachings of the Kagyu tradition. He became proficient in the six yogas of Nāropa and the tantric cycles of Niguma, particularly in heat yoga (*dumo*).[1] He also became interested in Kālacakra practices, and he was concerned that the living tradition of Kālacakra was in danger of disappearing from Tibet. He collected the teachings and empowerments of Kālacakra from various lamas all over the country, and his efforts ensured that the tradition would be preserved. Kālacakra practices today are particularly important in the Gélukpa tradition.

During this time he is said to have reached such a high level of attainment that he was able to meet directly with Mañjuśrī and receive teachings from him. Mañjuśrī also advised him on his practice, giving him guidance concerning what texts he should study, lamas he should visit, empowerments he should seek, when he should go into retreat, and so on.

In one of his most important periods of meditative seclusion, he led a four-year retreat with eight of his most advanced disciples. In order to prepare himself, he began by doing three and one-half million full-length prostrations and one million eight hundred thousand maṇḍala offerings. The stone floor on which he performed the prostrations has grooves worn into it and is still preserved today as a testament to the dedication of this great lama. During the retreat, a number of wondrous mental images came to the participants, including a vision of a golden Maitreya, another of Bhaiṣajyaguru, the buddha of healing, and a third apparition of Nāgeśvara, king of the nāgas. As he and his students continued to meditate, they saw more visions, and after the completion of this retreat people often saw Tsong Khapa accompanied by tantric deities, particularly Mañjuśrī.

Following this period of meditation practice, he briefly considered traveling to India, but was dissuaded by another lama, who consulted Vajrapāṇi and was told to advise Tsong Khapa against the idea. Tsong Khapa was told that it would be better to give up the idea of journeying to India, since he would be of greater benefit to sentient beings if he were to remain in Tibet and continue teaching. As a result, he decided to compose treatises on the Buddhist path, the most important of which was his masterwork, *The Great Exposition of the Stages of the Path*, which is the central work on Buddhist practice in Gélukpa monastic colleges. It is based on Atiśa's seminal work, *A Lamp for the Path to Awakening*. Tsong Khapa later composed a similar treatise on Vajrayāna entitled *The Great Exposition of Secret Mantra*, which is the basis of the Gélukpa system of tantric practice.

Tsong Khapa's Reforms

One of the main goals of his teaching, writing, and practice was the reform of Tibetan Buddhism. He was greatly concerned with what he perceived to be lapses in monastic discipline, shoddy thinking on exoteric and esoteric topics, and a decline in tantric practice. Part of his reform program was the creation of a new order which, like its founder, has traditionally stressed the importance of strict adherence to the rules of the vinaya, the importance of comprehensive study of Buddhist thought, and reformed tantric practice that accords with the vows of monks.

This was important to Tsong Khapa, who was concerned that many of his tantric contemporaries were involved in sexual practices that were incompatible with monastic vows. These were mainly practitioners of highest yoga tantra. It was commonly thought that highest yoga tantra was the supreme of all tantric sets and that it could not be practiced by monks. Tsong Khapa agreed that highest yoga tantra was the supreme Vajrayāna system, but he also thought that it could be reconciled with a monastic lifestyle.[2] Part of his reform program was concerned with how to accomplish this. His attempt to do so will be discussed below.

The Formation of a New Order

In his late thirties he had a vision of Mañjuśrī, who confirmed that Tsong Khapa had directly perceived emptiness and that there was no longer any need for him to ask for advice on this topic. Mañjuśrī then counseled Tsong Khapa to continue to teach in accordance with the systems of Nāgārjuna and Atiśa. Shortly after this, Tsong Khapa traveled in areas south of Lhasa, and he encountered his future disciple Gyeltsap Darma Rinchen (1364–1432), who at the time belonged to the Sakya order and was already regarded as a great scholar and debater in that tradition.

Their first meeting occurred when Tsong Khapa was preparing to give teachings. Gyeltsap openly challenged Tsong Khapa's authority by sitting on the throne that had been prepared for the lectures, but as Tsong Khapa began to speak, Gyeltsap realized that the master's understanding far surpassed his own. He found that Tsong Khapa answered questions that had long troubled him, and as the discourse progressed he realized that he had been presumptuous in taking Tsong Khapa's seat. Humbly offering three prostrations to the master, he took his place among the assembly. He later became one of Tsong Khapa's two greatest disciples. The other was Kédrup Gélek Belsangpo (1385–1438), who had become his follower several years earlier. After Tsong Khapa's death, these two carried on their teacher's system and institutionalized it, assuring that it would continue and flourish.

The Great Exposition of the Stages of the Path *and Other Works*

Tsong Khapa continued his travels, residing briefly at Réting, a monastery that had been founded by the Kadampa scholar Dromtönpa (1004–1064). There he completed much of *The Great Exposition of the Stages of the Path*, along with numerous smaller works. He began by asking for inspiration from Atiśa and his tutelary buddhas, which resulted in a vision of a multitude of awakened beings appearing around him in all directions. All of them dissolved into Atiśa, and Tsong Khapa was able to ask questions of the great master. At the conclusion of the teachings, Atiśa placed his hand on Tsong Khapa's head in blessing.

Following the vision and the benediction, Tsong Khapa completed the portion of the text that discusses higher insight. At first he feared that the profundity of these teachings would prevent people from being able to practice them successfully, and he briefly considered omitting this section altogether, but Mañjuśrī appeared to him and urged him to complete the work for the benefit of the few who would be able to understand and practice its instructions. Mañjuśrī also told him to write short and medium length texts on the stages of the path for those of inferior spiritual capacities. The eight great "dharma protectors" then manifested in front of him and asked him to continue his work, which they said would be beneficial to countless sentient beings. At this point Tsong Khapa was about forty years of age.

During the next few years, he continued to meditate, teach, and write, producing a prodigious amount of written material. His collected works comprise eighteen large volumes and contain analyses of a wide range of topics relating to Buddhist doctrine and practice. One of the striking aspects of his life is his incredible productivity, which is all the more impressive considering that he lived in a time in which there were no computers, interlibrary loan departments, fax machines, or telephones. In addition to his literary output, he was also in great demand as a teacher and gave lectures regularly. He even managed to find time for long periods of meditative retreat. As Robert Thurman remarks,

> on careful consideration of the list of Tsong Khapa's discourses and teachings, it would also appear that he must have spent his whole life discoursing. Yet from the point of view of his daily practice it seems that he spent his life in meditative retreat. But on reading his literary output, it would seem that he could only have read and composed texts. His Holiness the Dalai Lama feels that Je Rinpoche's greatest feat was to have done all three.[3]

In his early fifties, he wrote one of his most influential treatises, *The Essence of Good Explanations, Treatise Differentiating the Interpretable and the Definitive*, in which he discussed the strategies for scriptural interpretation of the two main schools of Indian Buddhism, the Madhyamaka and the Yogācāra. Shortly after completing this work, he conceived the idea of inaugurating a yearly religious festival that would begin at the Tibetan New Year (*Lo gsar;* pronounced "Losar"). The Great Aspiration Festival, or *Mönlam Chenmo*, is still celebrated today in Tibetan communities and is one of the major religious events of the year.[4]

The Founding of Ganden Monastery

After the first Mönlam was celebrated, several of Tsong Khapa's disciples requested that he curtail his travels. At this time he was fifty-two. They proposed to build a monastery for him, and he agreed. Tsong Khapa prayed before an image of Śākyamuni for advice concerning the site of the monastery and was told to build it near Lhasa, in the area of Drokri. When it was constructed, he named it Ganden (the Tibetan translation of the Sanskrit *Tuṣita*), which is the legendary abode of Maitreya, the next buddha.

Tsong Khapa traveled to the site of the future monastery with one of his disciples, Gendün Druba (1391–1474), who was posthumously recognized as the first Dalai Lama. Gendün Druba appointed two other students to oversee the construction, and the main buildings were completed within a year. The monastery was officially opened in 1409. Ganden later became a huge monastic complex, housing as many as four thousand monks. The founding of this institution was followed by the founding of Drébung in 1416 and Séra in 1419, both also near Lhasa. Ganden, Drébung, and Séra became the three principal centers of the Gélukpa order and were the lineage's primary seats of power in central Tibet. They were ransacked by the Chinese army in 1959, and Ganden was largely bombed into rubble. All three have been rebuilt in India, where they continue the scholastic and meditative traditions established by Tsong Khapa.

Tsong Khapa's Death

Around the time of his fifty-fifth year, Tsong Khapa began receiving signs of impending bad health. His students responded by performing rituals and saying prayers for his continued good health and long life. Despite their efforts, the omens persisted, and Tsong Khapa realized that his life was drawing to a close. At the age of sixty-two, aware that he would soon pass away, he gave a series of final instructions to his students that summed up his profound and original insights into Buddhist thought and practice. In the main hall of Ganden, he conducted a ritual, the merit of which he offered to all sentient beings. At the conclusion of the ceremony, he recited prayers requesting rebirth in Tuṣita heaven. Later he complained of back pains and illness. In response, many of his disciples gathered to perform rites to cure him and extend his life.

The next day his pain had increased, and he told his students that they should devote themselves to the cultivation of the mind of awakening. He withdrew into seclusion and engaged in tantric practices, particularly meditations connected with Heruka. At dawn of the morning of the twenty-fifth day of the tenth month, he began to meditate on emptiness, and he entered into a profound contemplation of the final nature of phenomena. Later in the morning, while sitting in a full lotus posture, he relinquished his hold on life. This event was marked by many auspicious signs, which were witnessed by his assembled disciples. Tsong Khapa's body took on the appearance of a youthful Mañjuśrī, and multicolored rays of light poured forth from it.

During the next forty-nine days numerous offerings were made at Ganden and Drébung. Oracles were consulted, and they agreed that Tsong Khapa's remains should be enshrined at Ganden in a specially constructed stūpa. This became an important pilgrimage site, but it was desecrated by the Chinese army in the 1960s during the Cultural Revolution.

The Continuation of Tsong Khapa's Tradition

Tsong Khapa's work was continued by his two greatest students, Kédrup and Gyeltsap. At the request of the other disciples, Gyeltsap ascended the throne of Ganden, indicating that he was recognized as the primary successor to Tsong Khapa's lineage. He held this position for twelve years until his death. He composed a number of important treatises, and his collected works are contained in eight volumes. Gyeltsap was succeeded as throne-holder of Ganden by Kédrup, who retained the position for seven years until his passing at the age of fifty-four. These two lamas came to be regarded as the "spiritual sons" of Tsong Khapa and are commonly depicted sitting on either side of their master in *tanka*s and other religious paintings.

During the following centuries, the fortunes of the Gélukpa order rose quickly, mainly because it continued to produce an impressive number of eminent scholars and tantric adepts. Another factor in its success was its initial reluctance to become involved in Tibetan politics. Instead, for several centuries after the death of Tsong Khapa, the Gélukpa order was mainly renowned for its strict adherence to monastic discipline, its accomplished scholars, and its intensive meditative training.[5]

This attitude of aloofness toward politics was not to last, however. As

Gélukpa leaders continued to enjoy an enviable reputation for scholarship, monastic discipline, and tantric attainments, the order attracted growing numbers of novice monks and built new monasteries, such as Tashihlünpo, which was founded in 1445 by Gendün Druba. This later became the seat of the Panchen Lamas, who are second only to the Dalai Lamas in prestige in the Gélukpa order. Gélukpa monastic institutions grew and flourished, and these began to attract students from all over the Tibetan cultural area.

The Gélukpas began to acquire significant political power in the sixteenth century as a result of the discovery of the third Dalai Lama among the Mongols. Sönam Gyatso (1543–1588)—who was recognized by the leaders of the Gélukpa order as the third Dalai Lama—was the grandson of Altan Khan, one of the most powerful Mongol chieftains. This initiated a long-standing bond between the two groups, which paid political dividends for the Gélukpas in the seventeenth century.[6]

After the defeat of the last ruler of Tsang province by Gushri Khan in 1642, the victorious khan appointed Ngawang Losang Gyatso (1617–1682), the fifth Dalai Lama, as temporal and spiritual leader of Tibet. This ensured the future supremacy of the Gélukpa order. The Mongol victory effectively ended centuries of bitter and divisive fighting. The fifth Dalai Lama proved to be an able statesman as well as an influential religious figure, and he consolidated the hegemony of the Dalai Lamas, who continued to be recognized as the rulers of Tibet until the Chinese annexation of the region in 1959. His ascension to power also ensured the political dominance of the Gélukpa order.

In addition to its successful political maneuvering, the Gélukpa order has been able to produce a succession of eminent religious leaders, people who embody the ideals of scholarship and meditative practice initiated by Tsong Khapa. Among these are the great scholar Jamyang Shéba (1648–1721), who wrote some of the most influential Gélukpa scholastic literature, and his reincarnation Gönchok Jikmé Ongpo (1728–1791), who is best known for his *Precious Garland of Tenets* and his seminal work on the bodhisattva levels and the five Buddhist paths, entitled *Presentation of the Levels and Paths, Beautiful Ornament of the Three Vehicles.*

Other important figures include Jang Gya (1717–1786), who also authored an influential "Presentation of Tenets," Ngawang Belden (b. 1797), who wrote an important commentary on Jamyang Shéba's *Great Exposition of Tenets,*[7] and Pabongka (1878–1941), a renowned scholar and debater who was known as a fierce sectarian and defender of Gélukpa tenets. Tsong Khapa's tradition of scholarship and meditative training continues today in the Gélukpa monasteries that have been rebuilt in India, as well as in centers in Europe and North America. The present Dalai Lama is perhaps the greatest living embodiment of the tradition's intersecting ideals of intellectual achievement and tantric training. He is viewed by the overwhelming majority of Tibetans as the greatest symbol of all that is best and most worth preserving in their culture, and he impresses people who meet him with his unusual blend of saintliness and humility, profound understanding of Buddhist thought, and meditative realization.

The Gélukpa Monastic System

The Gélukpa order stresses both monasticism and scholarship. Thus, it is not surprising that it has a highly structured monastic order that contains hierarchically arranged levels of academic achievement. The first division is the distinction, made in all orders of Tibetan Buddhism, between ordinary monks and incarnate lamas (*tülku*). The latter are people who have been recognized as reincarnations of deceased lamas. They are commonly ordained as monks at an early age and begin their religious training soon after. Monks can enter a monastery at any age, but it is common for them to join when they are still young, often as a result of urging by their families.

A novice monk is referred to as a *gétsül* (*dge tshul, śrāmaṇera*), and after learning the rules of conduct, he can petition to receive full ordination as a *gélong* (*dge slong, bhikṣu*). According to traditional standards, in order to become a *gétsül*, a boy must be able to chase away a crow on his own. *Gélongs* must be at least twenty years of age.

Once ordained, young monks generally pursue a standard program of study that spans a wide range of topics in Buddhist literature. As a rule, a monk must successfully complete a particular unit of study before being allowed to move on to the next. The primary units of study are: (1) monastic discipline (*'dul ba, vinaya*), the basic text of which is the *Vinaya-sūtra* by Guṇaprabha; (2) abhidharma, which focuses on Vasubandhu's *Treasury of Abhidharma* and is primarily concerned with metaphysics and cosmology; (3) epistemology (*tshad ma, pramāṇa*), which is based on Dharmakīrti's *Commentary on [Dignāga's] 'Compendium of Valid Cognition',* concentrates on logic, reasoning, the nature of mind, and learning theory; (4) the Middle Way School (Madhyamaka), in which monks mainly study Candrakīrti's *Entry Into the Middle Way* and which focuses on emptiness, the ten perfections, and reasoning; and (5) perfection of wisdom, which also focuses on the ten perfections, on the mind of awakening, and the career of the bodhisattva. Its main text is Maitreya's *Ornament for Clear Realizations.*

The Géshé Degree

A monk who successfully completes all aspects of this scholastic program may then compete for the degree of *géshé* (*dge bshes, kalyāṇamitra*), which is a recognition of superior scholarship. Very few of those who begin the training program ever earn this degree, since it may take from fifteen to twenty-five years and is extremely rigorous. The primary method of examination is oral debate, in which a monk must be able quickly to evaluate a wide range of philosophical positions, defend any of them against any other, and triumph (or at least hold his own) in a no-holds-barred intellectual contest. The debates are generally very lively, with monks enthusiastically jumping, pivoting, shouting, and sometimes even pushing their opponents. Some participants will use techniques designed to undermine the assurance of their adversaries, such as raising eyebrows in mock surprise, intending to cause opponents to question the wisdom of their positions. The stated purpose of the exercise is to develop the intellects of the monks, and it is felt that direct dialectical confrontation accomplishes this goal by training them to defend philosophical positions, to think on their feet, and to critically examine their doctrines and positions.

The Géshé Examination Process

Candidates for the géshé degree must first pass oral examinations at their own monasteries in all of the five subjects listed above.[8] They next must complete a second set of assessments in their monastic universities. Those wishing to earn the degree of *géshé hlarampa* (*dge bshes lha ram pa*)—the highest level among those who receive the géshé degree—must then pass the most difficult of all examinations in the Gélukpa order. Prior to the Chinese invasion, candidates for the géshé hlarampa degree were examined in the Potala by the top scholars of the order: the Dalai Lama, the throne-holder of Ganden, the senior tutor of the Dalai Lama, the junior tutor, seven assistant tutors, as well as the Jangtsé Chöjé and the Sharpa Chöjé, two senior abbots whose offices are described in more detail below.[9] The assistant tutors are drawn from the seven main Gélukpa monastic colleges, each of which provides one tutor. They are appointed by the respective abbots of the monasteries and are géshés who have been chosen for their scholarship and debating skills.

After successfully completing the examinations at the Potala, the candidates for the degree of géshé hlarampa are next subjected to another round of assessments. These are conducted annually during the Mönlam festival, which is held for several weeks after the Tibetan New Year. During the exam period, monks, géshés, and abbots from the three major Gélukpa monasteries used to gather in the courtyard of the Jokhang Temple in Lhasa; today the examinations are conducted at exile institutions in India. The géshé hlarampa candidates are subjected to questions from all sides and must demonstrate a comprehensive knowledge of Buddhist scriptures and exceptional skill in debate. Each year, only a few of the géshé candidates are awarded the degree of hlarampa.[10]

Qualifications and Restrictions

Although the Gélukpa tradition recognizes some people as tülkus—beings who are reincarnations of great lamas—the various levels of scholarly achievement are open to any male who is able to complete the program successfully.[11] The formal géshé degree and the ranking system that recognizes varying levels of achievement was instituted by the thirteenth Dalai Lama (1876–1934). In this system, any qualified monk who is either a novice or full ordinand may study for the géshé degree. Monks may come from any level of society and from any geographical region. There are even a number of Western monks currently working toward the géshé degree, and one who has received the degree of géshé hlarampa.[12]

The only restrictions for the final awarding of the degree are the requirement that the candidate be a fully-ordained monk who is at least twenty-five years old, and he must have received training at one of the seven major Gélukpa monastic colleges in the three main monastic universities in Ü province: Ganden, Séra, or Drébung. The seven colleges are: Ganden Jangtsé, Ganden Shardzé, Séra Jé, Séra Mé, Drébung Loseling, Drébung Gomang, and Drébung Déyang.[13]

The Senior and Junior Tutors to the Dalai Lama

After completing the géshé degree, there are a number of further advancements that one can make in the monastic hierarchy. One of these is the office of assistant tutor to the Dalai Lama, which is given to a géshé who demonstrates exceptional abilities. Above that is the office of junior tutor, which is given to a géshé hlarampa who is widely recognized for scholarship and debating skills. Among the tutors, the highest office is that of senior tutor, which passes to the junior tutor when the senior tutor dies or retires. A new junior tutor is then appointed by a committee composed of eminent lamas and two oracles—the Néchung oracle and the Gadong oracle.

During the selection process, the names of the leading candidates are written on small pieces of paper, and each is inserted into equal-sized balls of roasted barley flour. These are placed in a bowl in front of a buddha statue or a *tanka*. A special ceremony is performed to ensure that the best candidate is chosen, and the ball that first comes out of the bowl determines who will be the next junior tutor. It is believed that the oracles and buddhas decide which person is the best candidate and ensure that the ball containing his name will be chosen.

Postgraduate Study

Those who successfully attain the level of géshé commonly follow this by entering a long retreat, often lasting for three years. The logic behind this system is based on the idea that one should first gain a thorough grounding in Buddhist scriptures, philosophy, doctrines, and practice before engaging in full-time meditation. Trainees who thoroughly understand what they are meditating on will be less likely to go astray in meditation than those whose understanding is merely superficial. A person who earns the géshé degree is recognized as having gained a profound and wide-ranging knowledge of the major areas of Buddhist learning, and such people are considered by the Gélukpa tradition to be uniquely suited to meditation practice.

Following the retreat, many géshés choose to pursue tantric training at one of the Gélukpa tantric monasteries, generally the Upper Tantric College or the Lower Tantric College, which are named for their positions in the city of Lhasa.

Administration of the Tantric Colleges

The next level of the Gélukpa hierarchy is the position of assistant abbot of one of the two main tantric monasteries. This position is chosen by the Dalai Lama every three years and is held by a géshé hlarampa. After a three-year term, the assistant abbot becomes abbot, and the former abbot retires as a "precious abbot emeritus" (*mKhan zur Rin po che*, pronounced "Kensür Rinpoché") The new abbot is given the title *rinpoché,* meaning "precious jewel."[14] A person who becomes an abbot may initiate an incarnational lineage, and all of his successors will bear the title of rinpoché. The abbot emeritus may either choose to continue teaching or withdraw into meditative seclusion.

The most senior abbot emeritus of the Upper Tantric College becomes the Sharpa Chöjé when the current holder retires, dies, or is promoted. The Sharpa Chöjé may advance to the highest rank within the Gélukpa hierarchy, the position of throne-holder of Ganden (Ganden Tripa). The position of Jangtsé Chöjé of Ganden Jangtsé monastic college is held by a former abbot of the Lower Tantric College.

The throne-holder of Ganden inherits the seat of Tsong Khapa, the founder of the lineage. The throne-holder generally serves a seven-year term. The present throne-holder is Yeshe Dönden, the ninety-ninth person to hold this position. The throne-holder is chosen from among the best scholars in the Gélukpa order, and only those who have earned the degree of géshé hlarampa, served as abbot of one of the two main tantric monasteries, and have then been selected to be an assistant tutor are candidates for the top position.

Distinctive Practices: The Stages of the Path

Perhaps the greatest legacy of Tsong Khapa was his brilliant synthesis of Buddhist doctrine and practice outlined in his two seminal treatises, *The Great Exposition of the Stages of the Path* and *The Great Exposition of Secret Mantra.* Each of these voluminous texts contains a comprehensive vision of the path to awakening that is based on the classical Indian model. In this system, the beginner is conceived of as a person whose mind is afflicted by mental defilements that prevent him or her from perceiving reality correctly. The defilements prompt ordinary beings to engage in nonvirtuous activities, and these in turn result in suffering. More importantly, ordinary beings become conditioned to such negative mental states by repeatedly engaging in nonvirtuous deeds. The key to overcoming suffering lies in eliminating the basic ignorance that blinds sentient beings to the consequences of their actions. Tsong Khapa's presentation of the path begins with beings at this level and describes their condition and its causes. After this description, he outlines a graduated path by means of which they can overcome their afflictions, engage in virtuous actions, remove mental defilements and their predispositions, and finally, through diligent training, attain final awakening.

Tsong Khapa begins his presentation with the practices and doctrines that are common to both the sūtra and tantra systems. This is the subject matter of *The Great Exposition of the Stages of the Path.* He continues his analysis in *The Great Exposition of Secret Mantra,* which presents a graduated path to awakening in accordance with the Vajrayāna system.

The characteristic Gélukpa system of the path to awakening is referred to as *lamrim* (*lam rim*), "stages of the path." As this term indicates, the path is envisioned as proceeding in hierarchically arranged stages, and trainees are expected to complete each level before moving on to the next one. This is important because later trainings require successful completion of the preceding stages.

Each aspect of the path prepares the mind and alters the perceptions of trainees in ways that help them to overcome suffering and its causes. The basic problem is ignorance, and this results in a multitude of nonvirtuous actions. The only way to overcome this ignorance and the actions that result from it is gradually to wean the mind from afflicted mental states. Tsong Khapa's *Great Exposition* is a blueprint for this process.

The Three Principal Aspects of the Path

The stages of the path system is also summarized by Tsong Khapa in several shorter treatises, the most important of which is his *The Three Principal Aspects of the Path.* In this work, Tsong Khapa divides the Buddhist path into three primary features: (1) the intention definitely to leave cyclic existence, (2) generating the intention to attain awakening for the sake of all sentient beings, and (3) the correct view of emptiness. These crystallize the essence of all Buddhist teachings and practices, and they are said to be the primary goals of all Buddhist sūtras, tantras, and commentaries. Tsong Khapa also contends that they are common to both the sūtra and tantra paths. He indicates that these should not be viewed as partial or introductory, since they are the foundation of all practice and are as necessary for successful Vajrayāna training as they are for nontantric meditation. Jeffrey Hopkins notes that although tantric techniques in general are viewed as being superior to those of the sūtra path,

> all of them require these three principal paths as prerequisites and none of them at any time forsakes these three. The intention definitely to leave cyclic existence is as essential to the practice of tantra as it is to that of sūtra; in tantra the discipline is even stricter than that of the sūtra systems. The aspiration to enlightenment for the sake of all sentient beings is the assumption of the burden of freeing all sentient beings from misery and joining them with happiness and one's consequent wish for Buddhahood, the state wherein one actually has the power to effect one's promise to free all beings through teaching the path. It forms the motivation for tantra practice as well as for sutra practice. The correct view is the realization of emptiness, the realization that all phenomena do not exist inherently, are just imputations by thought, nominally existent and effective but not to be found under ultimate analysis. Emptiness itself is the life of sūtra and tantra.[15]

The Great Exposition of the Stages of the Path

Tsong Khapa's *Great Exposition of the Stages of the Path* also stresses these three components, but goes into great detail on all features of the techniques that are common to both sūtra and tantra. The *Great Exposition* is based on Atiśa's seminal work, *A Lamp for the Path to Awakening*, which became the basis of the meditative system of the Kadampa, the first order of Buddhism founded in Tibet. Tsong Khapa saw himself as following Atiśa's approach and reforming inaccuracies in its transmission, and so his order is sometimes referred to as the "New Kadampa." His *Great Exposition of the Stages of the Path* attempts to draw out the thought of Atiśa's work, using it as a basis for his vision of a graduated path to awakening.

Atiśa's paradigm conceived the path in terms of stages and levels of attainment. The most important of these are the five paths and ten bodhisattva levels.[16] Each of these phases represents a certain degree of accomplishment and is marked by a particular realization or set of realizations.

The culmination of the process is the tenth level, at the end of which one becomes a buddha. All of the paths and levels are connected with meditational practices that are summarized in the three principal aspects of the path.

According to Gélukpa scholastics, there are two primary presentations of stages of the path, one of which was transmitted by Mañjuśrī to Nāgārjuna, and a second that was taught to Asaṅga by Maitreya. Atiśa's text derives from the first lineage, and Tsong Khapa's presentation relies on this tradition, while incorporating the other into his system.

How to Develop Genuine Compassion

Tsong Khapa begins his exposition on the development of compassion by pointing out that all sentient beings are alike in that they seek to find happiness and avoid suffering. From this standpoint, there is no difference between individual sentient beings, and if one recognizes this fact one's own desire to avoid suffering is seen to be equivalent to that of all others. One should then realize that if one looks at the big picture, no one being has a greater claim to happiness than any other, and through cultivating this insight one realizes that all are equal in this regard. This is called "equating self and others."

One should then think about the consequences of the unbridled pursuit of selfish happiness. We all intuitively think that if one wishes to be happy one should pursue one's own ends, even if this leads to the suffering of others. If we observe selfish and greedy people, however, we find that they are never truly fulfilled, while conversely those who work for the benefit of others do tend to be content. One should then recognize that seeking happiness selfishly leads to suffering, while working for others produces benefits for oneself and others.

The Nature of Mind

As we have seen in previous chapters, in the Gélukpa system the mind is said to be of the nature of clear light. Although ordinary beings are plagued by discontent, which is caused by afflicted mental states, their defilements are not related to the nature of mind. They are "adventitious," meaning that they are caused by certain actions and emotions, but these never become part of the mind itself. If, for instance, one feels hatred for others and continues to indulge in this emotion, it will become progressively stronger, and one will find that it is easier to hate. No matter how strong the tendency grows, however, it never changes the basic clear light nature of mind, and one can weaken and even eliminate hatred (or any other negative emotion) through familiarizing oneself with the proper meditative antidotes. If one wishes to eradicate hatred, one should cultivate love and compassion, and if one repeatedly and diligently familiarizes oneself with these attitudes, the force of hatred diminishes and one becomes progressively less likely to experience it. As the Dalai Lama describes this training,

> Certain types of consciousness are undesirable in that when they arise they torment the individual's mind, but there are others whose arisal ushers in calmness and peace. So our task now is to discriminate skillfully between these two categories of consciousness. Generally speaking, consciousness is of a nature of clarity and knowing; it is susceptible to change and transformation. Therefore, the essential nature of consciousness is pure and clear, which suggests that the delusions that pollute the mind have not penetrated into its nature. All the mental stains, such as ignorance and the other delusions that torment us, are adventitious and hence not indivisible aspects of our minds.[17]

A person who engages in this training is not newly producing the clear light nature of mind; consciousness is primordially free from all defilements, and one's meditation simply allows the clear light to manifest.

Tsong Khapa recognizes that most people cannot eliminate deeply ingrained mental defilements quickly, and so his presentation of the "stages of the path" begins at the beginning and outlines the cognitive changes that are required for ordinary beings. The first of these is a recognition of impermanence. One must realize that all human life is transitory, that the time of death is uncertain, and that a human birth is extremely rare. Gélukpa teachers warn their students that

> one should not have the wrong notion that the practice of dharma is to be put off for the future when one can set aside a specific time for it; rather, it should be integrated into one's life right now.[18]

Buddhist literature from the earliest times in India has asserted that a human rebirth is extremely unusual. Even rarer is to have a human rebirth in which one is fortunate enough to hear someone mention the dharma. Rarer still is a life in which one encounters realized teachers and their written works. A person who finds all of these and also has the leisure time and resources necessary to engage in the practice of dharma is extraordinarily fortunate. Once one recognizes all of these things, the next prerequisite is the development of an unwavering intention to make the most of the opportunity by devoting oneself to religious practice. Since the time of one's death is uncertain and one may not find another human rebirth for a long time, one should resolve to begin immediately, and not put training off until a later and more convenient time. People who wait for such times seldom find them.

The proper response to these factors is a sense of urgency, which is summarized in the fourth Panchen Lama's commentary on *The Three Principal Aspects of the Path*, in which he advises meditators to think:

> Now I have attained the special body of a human that has leisure and fortune, is difficult to find, and, if found, is extremely meaningful. If at this time of meeting with Buddha's precious teaching I do not attain the state of completely perfect Buddhahood, the supreme liberation that eradicates all suffering, I must again undergo the suffering at least of cyclic existence in general and perhaps also of the three bad transmigrations in particular.[19]

The Faults of Cyclic Existence

One should now consider the faults of cyclic existence. Saṃsāra is beginningless and endless. Every person has been born countless times in the past, has grown old, suffered, and died, and each successive birth was determined by the actions of its predecessors. If one does not do something to escape the treadmill of cyclic existence, one will continue to be reborn in it, and there is no certainty that one's future births will even be as good as the present one. Rather, if one thinks on the fact that most of the people in the world are plagued by suffering, poverty, war, disease, natural disasters, and so on, one realizes that even if one is fortunate enough to be reborn as a human, the odds are good that one's next rebirth will be full of unpleasantness. It is more likely, however, that one will end up in one of the lower realms (of animals, hungry ghosts, and hell beings), which are characterized by constant suffering. Those born in these destinies experience hardships and pain beyond what most humans could endure or even imagine.

Given the fact that cyclic existence is beginningless and endless, one should also recognize that one has been reborn countless times and that one has been in all of the unpleasant destinies and suffered horribly. Moreover, given the transitory nature of fortunes in cyclic existence, if one remains on the treadmill, in the future one will inevitably find oneself in the lower realms. A person who truly comprehends the facts of the situation should develop a profound aversion toward cyclic existence and a powerful resolve to escape it as quickly as possible. It is said that a proper understanding of the nature of cyclic existence leads to the attitude of a prisoner toward his prison and an overwhelming desire to be free from it. Tsong Khapa indicates that without such an outlook, one will be unable to follow the path to awakening successfully:

> Imagine your mother very clearly in front of you. Consider several times how she has been your mother numberless times, not only now, but from beginningless cyclic existence. When she was your mother, she protected you from all danger and brought about your benefit and happiness. In particular, in this life she held you for a long time in her womb. Once you were born, while you still had new hair, she held you to the warmth of her flesh and rocked you on the tips of her ten fingers. She nursed you at her breast, gave you food with her mouth, cleaned your snot with her mouth, and wiped away your filth with her hand.[23] In various ways she nourished you tirelessly. When you were hungry and thirsty, she gave you drink, and when you were cold, clothes, and when poor, money. She gave you those things that were precious to her. Moreover, she did not find these easily . . . . When you suffered with a fever she would rather have died herself than have her child die; and if her child became sick, from the depths of her heart she would rather have suffered herself than have her child suffer.[24]

The love of a mother for her child and the child's gratitude and affection are the primary paradigms for cultivating an attitude of cherishing all other beings. Tsong Khapa assumes that one has a close bond with one's mother and that anyone who contemplates his or her mother's kindness will wish to repay it. The seven-point cause and effect method is based on the assumption that a mother's affection for her child is the strongest love of ordinary beings, and this becomes the model for Buddhist practitioners.

After becoming aware of the kindness of one's own mother, one then extends to all other sentient beings the feelings of warmth and gratitude that this awareness engenders. Then one considers the fact that one's present life is contingent on various causes and conditions and that one's current relationships are merely accidental: in the past, the person who is now one's worst enemy was one's mother or dearest friend, and one's friends and relatives were one's most bitter enemies. Moreover, there is no certainty even with respect to present relationships: one's foe can become a friend, and one's friends can become foes.

> From one's own viewpoint, since one has cycled beginninglessly, there are no sentient beings who have not been one's friends hundreds of times. Therefore, one should think, 'Whom should I value?' 'Whom should I hate?'[25]

According to the Dalai Lama, people who successfully cultivate this understanding are able to love even those who hate and harm them. He mentions the poignant example of the Chinese soldiers who invaded his country, slaughtered his fellow Tibetans, drove him into exile, and are working to destroy his culture and religion. He states that they are his greatest friends in meditation, since learning to love them, despite the atrocities they have committed, has been a great challenge:

> Concepts of enemy, friend, and so forth are relative and exist only at the conceptual level. They are mutually dependent, as are the concepts of long and short . . . . It is your misapprehension of friends, relatives, and enemies as inherently existent that gives rise to your fluctuating emotions towards them. Therefore, by realizing that there is no such inherently existent enemy and friend, you will be able to overcome your biased feelings toward all beings.[26]

Contemplating in this way, one comes to understand that there is no necessity for a particular person's being either cherished or despised. When one fully comprehends the kindness of one's own mother and realizes that all other sentient beings have been equally kind, one experiences a pervasive affection and respect that extends to all other living beings, even those toward whom one previously felt animosity.

The next step is to recognize that one owes each sentient being a debt of gratitude for past kindnesses and, thinking in this way, one resolves to repay each one. After considering how best to accomplish this, it becomes clear that at present one's resources are limited. Since Tsong Khapa is a Buddhist thinker, it is not surprising that he concludes that the type of person best able to help others is a buddha, and so he suggests that at this point one should decide to pursue buddhahood in order to benefit others most effectively.

Meditation on Emptiness

The third principal aspect of the path in the Gélukpa system is meditation on emptiness, which is one of the two primary characteristics of the awakened mind of a buddha. The other is compassion, which is closely related to the practices of learning to view all sentient beings as one's mothers and working for the benefit of others. In Tsong Khapa's view, training in wisdom is not dissociated from cultivation of compassion; rather, both are intimately linked, and each fortifies and enhances the other. Thus the Dalai Lama states,

> To cultivate compassion—altruism—in meditation it is necessary to have the assistance of wisdom. It is said that with the help of wisdom, compassion can become limitless. This is because afflictive emotions prevent the development of limitless compassion, and in order to destroy these afflictive emotions it is necessary to know the nature of phenomena. The reason for this is that the afflictive emotions superimpose a goodness and badness upon phenomena which exceeds the measure of what is there . . . . To counter this superimposition and hence prevent the arising of afflictive emotions it is necessary to know the final nature of phenomena correctly, without superimposition; we need to know the absence of inherent existence in all phenomena.[27]

Through familiarizing oneself with altruism, one's appreciation of emptiness deepens, and as one becomes more advanced in meditation on emptiness, one develops a progressively greater capacity for compassion, and so,

> because the ultimate nature of all phenomena is this emptiness of inherent existence, it is also necessary to cultivate wisdom. When these two aspects—compassion and wisdom—are practiced in union, wisdom grows more profound, and the sense of duality diminishes. Due to the mind's dwelling in the meaning of emptiness, dualistic appearance becomes lighter, and at the same time the mind itself becomes more subtle. As the mind grows even more subtle, reaching the subtlest level, it is eventually transformed into the most basic mind, the fundamental innate mind of clear light, which at once realizes and is of one taste with emptiness in meditative equipoise without any dualistic appearance, mixed with emptiness. Within all having this one taste, anything and everything can appear; this is known as "All in one taste, one taste in all."[28]

A person who successfully contemplates emptiness comes to recognize that "nothing is either good or bad, but thinking makes it so." We constantly superimpose interpretations on the things we perceive, and we generally are completely unaware that we do so. When we analyze phenomena in order to determine whether or not they inherently possess the qualities that we impute to them, however, we find that in their final nature they are empty, completely lacking any inherent existence, constantly changing and impermanent.

In the Gélukpa system, one initially uses reasoning in order to ascertain whether or not phenomena exist in the way that they appear. When examined in this way, we find that although things seem to exist inherently and to naturally possess the qualities that we impute to them, in reality they do not. Gélukpa texts contain numerous reasonings that help one to gain a conceptual grasp of emptiness, because emptiness is said to be a "slightly hidden phenomenon," meaning that although we are generally unaware of it, we can comprehend it through reasoning.

The initial use of reasoning enables the meditator to recognize that all phenomena are empty of inherent existence, and the fact that one is able to demonstrate this through reasoned proofs makes the conviction unshakable. Merely gaining a conceptual apprehension, however, is not enough: one must deepen the understanding of emptiness through repeated familiarization. The more one trains in emptiness, the deeper one's discernment becomes, until one transcends the need for conceptual thought, and one's awareness of emptiness reaches the level of direct perception, such that when one considers a phenomenon in meditation, one immediately apprehends its absence of inherent existence.

Meditation as Familiarization

Such progress is possible because the mind is trainable; it becomes familiarized with whatever it is used to. Ordinary beings are plagued by the afflictive emotions because they have become habituated to them through repeated practice. If one chooses to pursue the Buddhist path, the mind can also become attuned to compassion and wisdom.

> You might think, 'My mind is so full of the afflictive emotions. How could I possibly do this?' However, the mind does what it is used to. What we are not used to, we find difficult, but with familiarity, things which were once difficult become easy. Thus Śāntideva's *Engaging in the Bodhisattva Deeds* says, 'There is nothing which, with time, you cannot get used to.'[39]

In Tsong Khapa's system, the third principal aspect of the path involves familiarizing oneself with the insight that all compounded phenomena are created by causes and conditions, that they are impermanent and transitory, and that they do not exist in the way that they appear. Although they seem to be solid, naturally possessing the qualities that we impute to them, and existent from their own side, in reality they do not exist in this way. The more one trains in this insight, the more profound one's understanding becomes, until one no longer needs to recreate the reasoning process through which one initially came to know that phenomena are empty of inherent existence. The perception of emptiness operates at the level of direct cognition, and one develops the ability to recognize the emptiness of any phenomenon through directing one's attention toward it. At this point, one transcends the conceptual thought that was necessary for initial understanding.

This is not, however, the final level of attainment, since even when one directly cognizes emptiness one is not able simultaneously to perceive the appearances of phenomena and their emptiness. One initially is only able to apprehend one or the other, and one can only directly perceive emptiness while in a meditation in which one contemplates the final nature of phenomena. Only buddhas are able to view appearances and emptiness at the same time, and so further training is required until one is able to do so.

One is also unable to manifest the spontaneous and universal compassion of a buddha, and so one must continue to practice in order to deepen and expand the purview of one's compassion. As noted above, in the Gélukpa system these two aspects of training work together, and each strengthens and enhances the other. The final result of this practice is buddhahood, which is the culmination of cultivating compassion and wisdom, completing the training of the six perfections, and the attainment of omniscience.

The Géluk System of Tantra

The techniques outlined above are part of the exoteric lore that Gélukpas refer to as the "sūtra path." It is shared by the other orders of Tibetan Buddhism. All four traditions emphasize the necessity of preliminary study prior to serious meditation practice. Just as one needs to know where one is going and how to get there before deciding to journey from one place to another, so Buddhist meditators must learn the outline of the path, the sorts of practices in which they will engage and the experiences they can expect to have—along with the dangers and antidotes—and so Tibetan Buddhists who are serious about either exoteric yogas or Vajrayāna are expected to spend years learning their respective systems. Most Tibetan masters have devoted decades to scholastic training before beginning serious tantric meditation, and this approach has its antecedents in ancient India, where the monastic universities were centers both of learning and practice. Even among the *siddha* lineages, trainees generally spent many years of apprenticeship under a master's guidance before venturing into remote areas for solitary contemplation.[30]

Like the other four orders, the Gélukpas have an extensive and highly developed system of tantric practice, which includes the training of deity yoga described in the "Tantra" chapter, the six yogas of Nāropa, formless meditations of great seal and great perfection lineages held in common with Kagyu and Nyingma lineages, as well as distinctive techniques derived from their own sources. The Gélukpa system of deity yoga and visualization practice is identical in all major respects with that outlined in the "Tantra" chapter, and so readers should refer to it.

The main tantra for Géluk is the *Cakrasaṃvara*, and the *Kālacakra* is also an important source for doctrine and practice. The Gélukpa tradition, like the Sakyapa, generally contends that because of the difficulty of the path and the rigors of tantric practice, one must have a thorough education in exoteric and esoteric topics prior to engaging in Vajrayāna training. Once this has been accomplished, Géluk masters emphasize the supremacy of tantra and encourage students to apply themselves to it diligently. Unlike some other Tibetan orders, the Gélukpas do not consider formless meditations by themselves to be sufficient for attainment of buddhahood: one must also master the techniques of heat yoga, illusory body, and visualization, along with long-term engagement in daily repetition of liturgical cycles (*sādhana*). Furthermore, while some orders contend that the practice of sexual yogas with a physical consort (an "action seal") is not necessary for the attainment of buddhahood and that one may do so through visualizations alone, Gélukpa masters from the time of Tsong Khapa have contended that the subtle physiology of the winds, drops, and channels can only be transmuted into that of an awakened being through yogas involving an actual consort. On the other hand, Gélukpa tradition has tended to reserve such practices to an elite few adepts who have undergone years of rigorous training prior to receiving the instructions of sexual yoga. Most practitioners are advised to remain monks or nuns and to employ meditations in which the consort is imagined, as this is safer and more effective for the vast majority of Buddhists.

Gélukpas also emphasize the importance of frequent retreats, and like the other three orders maintain meditation centers in which trainees can engage in three-year periods of solitary contemplation after receiving a thorough grounding by their instructors. Some Western converts to other Tibetan traditions dismiss the Gélukpas as a group of scholars who neglect tantric practice, but this is a naïve and uninformed prejudice; in reality, the Gélukpas have an extensive repertoire of Vajrayāna lineages and traditions of practice going back to the origins of the system in India. Its major figures were both accomplished scholars and tantric adepts, and they are revered as much for their meditative accomplishments as their learning.

It is true that Géluk has traditionally emphasized the centrality of study as a prerequisite for successful practice, but this in no way diminishes its commitment to meditation, and there is general agreement that without extensive training none of the advanced levels of the path are attainable. The Dalai Lama (who as noted previously was trained in the Gélukpa scholastic system but is not the head of the order) is an example of the dual emphasis on study and practice. He spent his early years under the tutelage of senior scholars, mastering the lore of exoteric and esoteric Buddhist systems, and attained the highest level in his géshé examinations. He is one of the greatest debaters of his generation and has an impressive knowledge of Buddhist literature. He also spends a significant part of each day engaged in tantric meditation. He receives ongoing instruction in the Vajrayāna cycles of a range of lineages, and also has tutors for the formless meditations that are most closely associated with Kagyu and Nyingma, but which also have become part of the Géluk lineage.

This is true of many other senior Gélukpa lamas, who spend years memorizing and debating the fine points of the textbooks of their respective colleges, but then expand their horizons and delve into other areas of Buddhist learning. Most also engage in tantric practice from an early age, and this is integrated into the monastic curriculum. Following the successful completion of each level of the scholastic system, students generally go into long-term solitary retreat, where their conceptual knowledge is integrated into the visualizations of deity yoga and the techniques of their order's distinctive tantric practices. Many Gélukpas decide to leave the scholastic stream at some point and become full-time meditators, and spend most of their lives in caves or meditation huts. The system recognizes that there is a range of proclivities among practitioners, and has corresponding options for study and practice. All Géluk masters agree that the techniques of highest yoga tantra are the fastest and most effective means for attainment of buddhahood, and the order maintains a range of lineages, each with its particular approach and esoteric lore, and this allows Géluk teachers to accommodate different aptitudes and orientations.

Notes

1. See chapter 13, "Kagyu."
2. The core issues and Tsong Khapa's solutions are discussed at length in John Powers, "Stealth Polemics: Tsong Khapa on the Differences between Sūtra and Tantra," *From Ancient India to Modern America: Buddhist Studies in Honor of Charles Prebish*, ed. Damien Keown (London: Routledge/Curzon, 2005), pp. 128–145.
3. Robert A.F. Thurman, ed., *The Life and Teachings of Tsong Khapa* (Dharamsala: Library of Tibetan Works and Archives, 1982), p. 28. "Je Rinpoche" is an epithet of Tsong Khapa.
4. See chapter 7, "Festivals and Holy Days."
5. See Snellgrove and Richardson, *A Cultural History of Tibet*, p. 181.

6. See chapter 5, "Tibetan Religious History."
7. The title of this work is *Annotations for [Jamyang Shéba's] 'Great Exposition of Tenets,' Untying the Knots of the Difficult Points, Precious Jewel of Clear Thought* (*Grub mtha' chen mo'i mchan 'grel dka' gnad mdud grol blo gsal gces nor*).
8. Georges Dreyfus, the first Western student to complete the géshé degree successfully, describes the examination process in *The Sound of Two Hands Clapping: The Education of A Tibetan Buddhist Monk* (Berkeley: University of California Press, 2003), pp. 254–266. This book also provides an insider's view of the Gélukpa monastic system as practiced today in exile universities.
9. These are two of the most senior positions within the Gélukpa monastic hierarchy. The Sharpa Chöjé (*Shar pa Chos rje*), "Dharma Master of Ganden Shardzé College" (*dGa' ldan Shar rtse Grwa tsang*), is the most senior retired abbot (*mkhan zur*) from Gyüto Tantric College (*rGyud stod Grwa tsang*). The Jangtsé Chöjé (*Byang rtse chos rje*), "Dharma Master of Jangtsé College" (*Byang rtse Grwa tsang*), is the most senior retired abbot of Gyümé Tantric College (*rGyud smad Grwa tsang*). These two alternate in assuming the position of throne-holder of Ganden, the head of the Gélukpa order. This format continues today in exile institutions, but sometimes there is no central examination, and candidates must travel to different monasteries during the testing process.
10. As Dreyfus notes, however, the fact that a person has received the *lharampa* degree does not necessarily mean that he has an outstanding intellect; as with the Western Ph.D., some candidates earn it more by persistence and determination than by their superior intelligence (*Two Hands Clapping*, p. 255). What the degree does certify is that the successful candidate has memorized a prodigious amount of scholastic material and can defend a range of philosophical positions in dialectical debate.
11. Traditionally women have not been candidates for the géshé degree because a géshé must have full ordination, and a lineage of full ordination for nuns was never established in Tibet. See Hanna Havnevik, *Tibetan Buddhist Nuns*, pp. 50–51.
12. Georges Dreyfus, whose memoir is mentioned in notes 8 and 10. He was born in Switzerland, traveled to India, and studied at several Gélukpa monasteries.
13. The géshé degree is only awarded by the three main monasteries of Ganden, Séra, and Drébung, but other Gélukpa monasteries have their own degrees. Tashihlünpo Monastery, seat of the Panchen Lamas, awards the degree of "master of the teaching" in recognition of mastery of the five primary topics listed above. Shédrupling Monastery awards the degree of "master of extensive learning" to its best scholars. Recipients of these degrees are able to pursue tantric studies at the tantric colleges, but are not candidates for the position of abbot of these monasteries, nor can they be appointed abbots of the three major non-tantric monasteries.
14. This is a term by which Tibetans refer to people who are recognized as great teachers. It is given to incarnate lamas, respected scholars, important teachers, and renowned meditators, all of whom are considered by Tibetans to be great cultural resources.
15. Geshe Lhundup Sopa and Jeffrey Hopkins, *Cutting Through Appearances* (Ithaca: Snow Lion, 1989), p. 18.
16. See chapters 3 and 4.
17. H.H. the Dalai Lama, Tenzin Gyatso, *Path to Bliss* (Ithaca: Snow Lion, 1991), tr. Geshe Thubten Jinpa, p. 14.
18. Ibid., p. 15.
19. Losang Belden Denbé Nyima, *Instructions on the Three Principal Aspects of the Path*, in *Cutting Through Appearances*, p. 47. The "three bad transmigrations" are those of ani-

mals, hungry ghosts, and hell beings. These are "bad" because they involve a great deal of suffering.

20. *Cutting Through Appearances*, p. 71.
21. This passage is drawn from a version of Tsong Khapa's *Great Exposition of the Stages of the Path*, entitled *Four Interwoven Commentaries on the Great Exposition of the Stages of the Path*, which contains Tsong Khapa's root text and interlineal commentaries by Baso Chögi Gyeltsen, Dédruk Khenchen Ngawang Rapden, Jamyang Shéba, and Dradi Géshé Rinchen Töndrup (*Lam rim mchan bzhi sbrags ma*; New Delhi: Chos 'phel legs ldan, 1972), p. 559.3. Passages quoted from the *Great Exposition of the Stages of the Path* in this section will be taken from this text.
22. At this point someone could object that the logic of the practice could just as easily lead one to hate others, since they also have been murderers, torturers, and so on, and that there is just as much reason to feel enmity toward them as affection. This objection misses the point of the exercise, which is to give compelling reasons for love and to show that in the past one has loved and cared for every other sentient being, and so there is no particular reason to value some and not others, since the relationships with others whom one currently loves and cares for are merely the result of accidental circumstances. Thus, there are equally good reasons for valuing all other beings.
23. The last three things refer to common practices in pre-industrial societies where prepackaged baby food, Kleenex, and Pampers are not available. As explained in the commentaries (see note 18 above), mothers will chew a baby's food first in order to make it easier for the child to digest. They will use their tongues to wipe away mucus from a baby's face in order to avoid irritating its skin, and will even use their own hands to clean the infant's filth. The main import of the passage is to make the meditator aware of the depth of his or her mother's kindness.
24. *Four Interwoven Commentaries on the Great Exposition of the Stages of the Path*, p. 575.1.
25. Ibid., p. 572.5.
26. *Path to Bliss*, p. 164.
27. *Kindness, Clarity, and Insight*, p. 161.
28. Ibid., p. 71.
29. Ibid., p. 104.
30. One of the recurring ironies of the Western appropriation of Tibetan Buddhism is a common anti-intellectual bias on the part of many newly converted enthusiasts, particularly those who do not speak Tibetan. The Tibetan lamas these converts revere generally spent decades in intensive scholastic study, and this is a prerequisite for certification as a teacher. The anti-intellectual attitude is particularly prevalent among Westerners who study with lamas from the Kagyu and Nyingma orders (but is by no means restricted to them)—who often assert that study by itself is insufficient and that one must also engage in meditation in order to attain advanced levels of realization—although they themselves received a thorough grounding in exoteric and esoteric lore as part of their training. I know of no Tibetan lamas who did not receive such instruction and simply entered solitary retreat; the idea that one might successfully meditate without any prior knowledge of the path—of Buddhist systems of meditation, of pitfalls and antidotes—would be as ridiculous to Tibetan lamas as the idea that one might decide to drive from New York to California blindfolded, simply getting into a car without consulting a map or asking directions, gunning the gas, and hoping that one might reach one's destination.

16: Bön: A Heterodox System

Introduction

Tibetans commonly draw a distinction between three religious traditions: (1) the divine dharma (*lha chos*), or Buddhism, (2) Bön dharma (*bon chos*); and (3) the dharma of human beings (*mi chos*), or folk religion. The first category includes doctrines and practices that are thought to be distinctively Buddhist. This classification implicitly assumes that the divine dharma is separate and distinct from the other two, although Tibetan Buddhism incorporated elements of both of these traditions.

Bön is commonly considered to be the indigenous religious tradition of Tibet, a system of shamanistic and animistic practices performed by priests called *shen* (*gshen*) or *bönpo* (*bon po*). Although this is widely assumed by Buddhists, historical evidence indicates that Bön only developed as a self-conscious religious system under the influence of Buddhism.

When Buddhism entered the country, practitioners of indigenous traditions recognized that there were clear differences between their own practices and those of the foreign faith, and in time people who considered themselves adherents of the old religion of Tibet developed a separate tradition, but one that incorporated many Buddhist elements. Although later historical works state that the introduction of Buddhism was initially opposed by Bön, this term is not even used in the early dynastic records to refer to indigenous systems and practices. Instead, they are called *chö* (*chos*), the same term later used to translate the Sanskrit term *dharma*, which in Buddhist literature refers to Buddhist doctrine and practice. In inscriptions on the tomb of King Sénalek (799–815), for example, the term *bön* refers to the royal priests whose job was to conduct ceremonies for the Yarlung kings.

In early records, "bön" denotes a particular type of priest who performed rituals to propitiate local spirits and ensure the wellbeing of the dead in the afterlife. It is only much later, under the influence of Buddhism, that "Bön" comes to designate pre-Buddhist Tibetan religious practices in general. It should also be noted that the rites performed by these early priests as reported in the old records appear to differ substantially from contemporary Bön. As Per Kværne notes, for example, they were by all accounts concerned with taking care of the dead through ceremonies intended to ensure their safe journey to the afterlife and their material prosperity after arrival.[1] The rituals of the bön often involved sacrificing animals (mainly horses, yaks, and sheep), making offerings of food and drink, and burying the dead with precious jewels, the benefits of which were apparently transferred to them in the afterlife through shamanistic rituals. The most elaborate of these were the observances for the kings, each of whom was buried in a specially-constructed tomb, and apparently joined in death by servants, ministers, and retainers. The royal priests then officiated special ceremonies, which according to old records sometimes lasted for several years. These were intended to ensure the wellbeing of the kings in the afterlife and to solicit their help in mundane affairs.

Animism in Tibetan Folk Religion

The Tibetan folk religion encompasses indigenous beliefs and practices, many of which pre-date the introduction of Buddhism and which are commonly viewed as being distinct from mainstream of Buddhist practice. These are primarily concerned with propitiation of Tibet's spirits and demons, which are believed to inhabit all areas of the country. Folk religious practices rely heavily on magic and ritual and are generally intended to bring mundane benefits, such as protection from harm, good crops, healthy livestock, health, wealth, and so on. Their importance to ordinary people should not be underestimated, since in the consciousness of most Tibetans the world is inhabited by multitudes of powers and spirits, and the welfare of humans requires that they be propitiated and sometimes subdued. Every part of the natural environment is believed to be alive with various types of sentient forces, which reside in mountains, trees, rivers and lakes, rocks, fields, the sky, and the earth. Every region has its own native supernatural beings, and people living in these areas are strongly aware of their presence. In order to stay in their good graces, Tibetans give them offerings, perform rituals to appease them, and sometimes refrain from going to particular places so as to avoid the more dangerous forces.

In the often harsh environment of Tibet, such practices are believed to give people a measure of control over their unpredictable and sometimes hazardous surroundings. With the almost total triumph of Buddhism in Tibet, the folk religion became infused with Buddhist elements and practices, but still remains distinct in the minds of the people, mainly because its focus is on pragmatic mundane benefits and not on final liberation or the benefit of others. By all accounts, Tibetans have always been fascinated by magical and occult practices, and from the earliest times have viewed their country as the abode of countless supernatural forces whose actions have direct bearing on their lives. Since Buddhist teachers tend to focus on supramundane goals, Tibetans naturally seek the services of local shamans, whose function is to make contact with spirits, to predict their influences on people's lives, and to perform rituals that either overcome harmful influences or enlist their help.

When Buddhism entered Tibet, it did not attempt to suppress belief in the indigenous forces. Rather, it incorporated them into its worldview, making them protectors of the dharma who were converted by tantric adepts like Padmasambhava, and who now watch over Buddhism and fight against its enemies. An example is Tangla, a god associated with the Tangla mountains, who was convinced to become a Buddhist by Padmasambhava and now guards his area against forces inimical to the dharma. The most powerful deities are often considered to be manifestations of buddhas, bodhisattvas, ḍākinīs, and so on, but the mundane spirits are merely worldly powers, who have demonic natures that have been tempered by Buddhism. Although their conversion has ameliorated the worst of their fierceness, they are still demons who must be kept in check by shamanistic rituals and the efforts of Buddhist adepts. Nor should it be thought that Buddhist practitioners are free from the influences of the folk religion. These beliefs and practices are prevalent in all levels of Tibetan society, and it is common to see learned scholar-lamas—masters of empirically-based dialectics and thoroughly practical in daily affairs—refuse to travel at certain times in order to avoid dangerous spirits or decide their travel schedules after first performing a divination to determine the most auspicious time. Such attitudes may be dismissed as "irrational" by Westerners, but for Tibetans they are entirely pragmatic responses to a world populated by forces that are potentially harmful.

Types of Spirits

According to folk beliefs, the world has three parts: (1) sky and heavens; (2) Earth; and (3) the "lower regions." Each of these has its own distinctive spirits, many of which influence the world of humans. The *upper gods* (*steng lha*) live in the atmosphere and sky, the *middle tsen* (*bar btsan*) inhabit the earth, and the lower regions are the home of *yoklu* (*g.yog klu*), most notably snake-bodied beings called *lu* (*klu, nāga*), which live at the bottoms of lakes, rivers, and wells and which hoard vast stores of treasure. The spirits that reside in rocks and trees are called *nyen* (*gnyan*); they are often malicious, and Tibetans associate them with sickness and death. *Lu* bring leprosy, and so it is important to keep them away from human habitations. *Sadak* (*sa bdag*, "lords of the earth") are beings that live under the ground and are associated with agriculture. *Tsen* are spirits that reside in the atmosphere, and who shoot arrows at humans who disturb them. These cause illness and death. *Tsen* appear as demonic figures with red skin, wearing helmets and riding over the mountains in red horses. *Dü* (*bdud*) were apparently originally atmospheric spirits, but they came to be associated with the Buddhist demons called *māra*, which are led by their king (also named Māra), whose primary goal is to lead sentient beings into ignorance, thus perpetuating the vicious cycle of saṃsāra.

There are many other types of demons and spirits, and a comprehensive listing and discussion of them exceeds the focus of this book. Because of the great interest most Tibetans have in these entities and the widespread belief in the importance of being aware of their powers and remaining in their good graces, the folk religion is a rich and varied system, with a large pantheon, elaborate rituals and ceremonies, local shamans with special powers who can propitiate and exorcise, and divinatory practices that allow humans to predict the influences of the spirit world and take appropriate measures. All of these are now infused with Buddhist influences and ideas, but undoubtedly retain elements of the pre-Buddhist culture.

Bön Teachings and Practices

Adherents of Bön view their tradition as distinct from Buddhism, although it clearly contains many Buddhist elements. The term *bön* for Bönpos (practitioners of Bön) signifies "truth," "reality," and "the true doctrine," which provides a path to liberation. For Bönpos, *bön* has roughly the same range of meanings that the term *chö* (*chos, dharma*) has for Tibetan Buddhists: it refers to their religion as a whole—teachings, practices, and so on—which are believed to have been revealed by awakened beings who took rebirth in order to lead others to salvation. Bön today has absorbed many Buddhist elements, and many of its teachings are strikingly similar to those of Tibetan Buddhism. David Snellgrove contends that it has incorporated so many Buddhist elements that it has become

> a form of Buddhism that may fairly be regarded as heretical, in that those who follow it have persisted in claiming that their religion was taught not by Śākyamuni Buddha, but by gShen-rab [Shenrap], likewise accepted as Buddha, and that it came not from India, but from Ta-zig [Taksik] and by way of Zhang-zhung [Shangshung]. Such are the Bonpos, who have managed to hold their own down to the present day against the enormously more powerful representatives of orthodox Buddhism, while they are constantly and quite wrongly identified by other Tibetans . . . as the persistent practitioners of pre-Buddhist Tibetan religion.[2]

In Buddhist sources, the Bönpos are commonly portrayed as malicious reactionaries whose manipulations hindered the dissemination of the dharma, who caused Śāntarakṣita to be driven from the country, and who tried to prevent Padmasambhava's arrival. As Snellgrove and Richardson contend, however, such characterizations are probably unfair to Bön and are written from a rather narrow perspective.

> Like all national historians, Tibetan writers of history see everything from a Tibetan point of view, and being fervent Buddhists as well, they inevitably see everything from a rather special Tibetan Buddhist point of view. Their view of the world around them is a simple one: in so far as it furthers the interests of their religion in general and their own religious order and monastery in particular, it is good; in so far as it works against their religion, their order and their monastery it is evil. Internally the Bon-pos tend to become the scapegoat for everything that had rendered the Buddhist conversion of Tibet at all difficult, while most Tibetan Buddhists themselves remain almost innocently unaware of the great variety of pre-Buddhist beliefs and

practices that they have absorbed as an accepted part of their daily thoughts and actions.[3]

Origins of the Tradition

According to Bön sources, the tradition came to Tibet from Taksik (which appears to roughly refer to the area of Persia). Shenrap, the founder of Bön, brought the religion from Taksik to the kingdom of Shangshung (which was probably an area in western Tibet with Mount Kailash at its center).[4] From there it was disseminated into Tibet. The location of Taksik (also known as Ölmo Lungring) is unclear in early Bön texts. As Kværne notes, it may refer to the land of the Tajiks, located in Central Asia, but this identification is based mainly on the similarity of their names and the fact that Bön references to Taksik indicate that it is somewhere to the west, and so this hypothesis is at present impossible to prove or disprove with any degree of confidence.[5]

Early Bön texts are said to have been written in a language called the language of Shangshung, which appears to be an archaic Tibetan dialect. Unfortunately, it is difficult to speculate on the nature of this language, since it only exists in the titles of early Bönpo works and some mantras. Snellgrove contends that the claim that Bön came from Shangshung has a ring of authenticity to it, since Shangshung refers to a remote area in the western part of Tibet, and so tracing the tradition to it could not be a ploy to impress others. Prior to Buddhism's dissemination into Tibet, it had already been introduced to neighboring areas, probably including Shangshung, which was undoubtedly visited by caravans traveling through Central Asia. Since much of Central Asia at one time was Buddhist, it is very plausible that a form of Buddhism could have been transmitted to western Tibet prior to the arrival of Buddhist missionaries in the central provinces. Once established, it might then have absorbed elements of the local folk religion, eventually developing into a distinctive system incorporating features of Central Asian Buddhism and Tibetan folk religion. Thus, according to Snellgrove, when the adherents of this tradition later encountered Buddhism,

> remaining staunch in their own already established tradition, they would quite reasonably urge that this same religion must have reached India from Ta-zig and that Śākyamuni must be either a man-

ifestation of gShen-rab or else just another religious teacher who was passing on gShen-rab's teaching in his own name. Only a theory such as this can explain the Bonpo claim that their religion comes originally from Ta-zig via Zhang-zhung and that all Buddhist teachings, whenever they have learned of them, are already theirs by right.[6]

Shenrap, the Founder of Bön

According to Bönpos, the founder of this original tradition was Dönpa Shenrap, whose name means "Supreme Holy Man." He is considered by Bönpos to be a fully awakened buddha who took physical form in order to teach others the true path to awakening. His biography bears some similarities to that of Śākyamuni, although there are enough notable differences to indicate that it is not an attempt to copy the Buddhist story.

Like Śākyamuni Buddha, Shenrap began his teaching career after deciding to descend from a heavenly realm and take rebirth among humans in order to teach them a path to salvation. Shenrap's birth was accompanied by miraculous signs and auspicious events. His mother conceived him after a magical cuckoo perched on her head, flapped its wings three times, and beamed a white and red light from its genitals into her head, following which she became pregnant. After taking rebirth in Shangshung as a prince, Shenrap encountered opposition by demonic forces, and like Padmasambhava he subdued them and converted them to Bön, after which they became guardians of the religion. As with Śākyamuni's legends, Shenrap's career is highlighted by twelve great deeds. After manifesting the stages of awakening, Shenrap set out on a program of conversion, first successfully bringing Bön to China, and then traveling to Tibet and converting its inhabitants. His entry into final nirvana closely parallels the story of Śākyamuni's death.

Although some of the aspects of his hagiography resemble events reported in traditional accounts of Śākyamuni's life, there are also important differences, such as the fact that Shenrap is said to have spent most of his teaching career as a layman, and that his many wives, sons, daughters, and disciples are important figures in stories of the dissemination of Bön doctrines and practices. His biographies report that he traveled far and wide, and with help from others spread the teachings of Bön, built temples and stūpas, and converted multitudes of people. Later in life he became a monk and retired to a hermitage in the forest, in which he continued to teach his disciples. His missionary efforts were most effective in regions to the west of the Tibetan plateau, and Bönpos believe that their tradition entered Tibet from the west during the time of the earliest kings, centuries before the introduction of Buddhism. They also believe that Shenrap is the "primordial buddha," far superior in stature to Śākyamuni, and their tradition bases itself on his authority. He is credited with revealing their most important texts, and the fact that many of these correspond closely to Buddhist texts is taken by Bönpos as evidence of the primacy of their own tradition, which—as they point out—existed in Tibet prior to the introduction of Buddhism (although there is no historical evidence that early Bön had anything resembling the extensive literature that is today included in its canon). Thus the common charge that Bönpos appropriated Buddhist texts is turned around, and they contend that they had the teachings first, but that Bön scriptures and teachings were later adopted by Buddhists, who failed to realize that they had actually originated with Shenrap.

Although it seems clear that in fact the Bönpos borrowed liberally from Buddhism, as Kværne states, their assertion of primacy is a pragmatic response to their minority status:

> Both Buddhists and Bon-pos agree that when Buddhism succeeded in gaining royal patronage in Tibet in the eighth and ninth centuries, Bon suffered a serious setback. By the eleventh century, however, an organized religious tradition, styling itself Bon and claiming continuity with the earlier, pre-Buddhist religion, appeared in central Tibet. It is this religion of Bon that has persisted to our own times, absorbing doctrines from the dominant Buddhist religion but always adapting what it learned to its own needs and its own perspectives. This is . . . not just plagiarism, but a dynamic and flexible strategy that has ensured the survival, indeed the vitality, of a religious minority.[7]

Monastic and Scholastic Traditions

The special focus of Bön priests is the propitiation and manipulation of the indigenous spirits and deities of Tibet, but Bön has also developed a monastic system based on the Buddhist model. According to Bön histories, the first Bön monastery was Yéru Ensa, founded by Ḍruchen Yungdrung Lama near the end of the eleventh century in Tsang province, about thirty miles east of Shigatsé. The most important Bön monastery is Menri, built in 1405 in Tsang province, to the north of the Tsangpo river. Bön monastic establishments, like Buddhist ones, have both novices and fully ordained monks. The latter are called *trangsong* (*drang srong*, a term that is also used to translate the Sanskrit word *ṛṣi*, the "seers" of the Vedas). Bön monks, like their Buddhist counterparts, are bound by vows of celibacy, and they undergo an intensive training program that includes study of scripture, oral philosophical debate, and ritual practices. As Kværne notes, however, although Bön has been influenced by the monastic structures of Tibetan Buddhism, it has maintained a strong tradition of nonmonastic tantric yogis.[8]

The Bön tradition also developed an extensive canon of religious and philosophical texts, many of which are Buddhist texts with Bön titles and with key terms changed into Bön terminology. Before the introduction of Buddhism to Tibet, Bön became the state religion of the early Yarlung kings, who retained Bön priests for all sorts of rituals and ceremonies. Perhaps the most important role was that of personal protector of the king, whose duty was to safeguard the ruler's life-force, or *la* (*bla*). Every person is believed by Bönpos to possess a *la*, which is able to move independently of the body. It may reside temporarily in trees, rocks, animals, and so on, but if one's connection with it is cut off, one will inevitably die. It is often necessary to perform special rites designed to bring it back into the body, and it is important to keep it safe from harmful influences. If the *la* comes under the power of demons or spirits, it must be ransomed by animal sacrifices or other rituals.

During the early imperial period, Bönpo ministers were closely associated with the state cult and were retained to perform ceremonies to ensure the wellbeing of the country, guard against evil, protect the king, and enlist the help of spirits in Tibet's military ventures. After the introduction of Buddhism, the new religion began to gain converts, thus threatening the hegemony of the indigenous traditions, which at this time were not an organized system of beliefs and practices, but rather a diffuse mixture of various elements of folk religion and imperial cults. At first the two coexisted (although there was some friction from the beginning), but during the reign of Tri Songdétsen a decisive split is reported. The king is said to have organized a debate between Bönpos and Buddhists, with Tangnak Bönpo representing the former group, while Padmasambhava spoke for the latter. At its conclusion, the king declared that the Buddhist position was more persuasive and that Bön had been vanquished. He ordered the defeated Bönpos to go into exile. Bön rituals involving animal sacrifice were outlawed, and Bön priests were banished to remote border regions. Although their tradition continued to flourish in these areas, in the central provinces of Tibet they mainly became relegated to legend as the early opponents of the dharma. Only a few Bönpos remained in central Tibet, but others managed to create viable communities in areas of the west, north, and east, as well as Dolpo and Mustang (which today are parts of Nepal). Not surprisingly, while Buddhist sources treat the demise of Bön as a victory of truth over falsehood, Bön texts report it as a catastrophe. They contend that their religion is the true dharma and that the triumph of the foreign faith resulted from the collective evil karma of Tibetans, who in their ignorance failed to realize the truth of Bön.

Cosmology

Bönpo tradition holds that all of reality is pervaded by a transcendent principle, called "All-Good." It has a male aspect, Güntu Sangpo, and a female aspect, Güntu Sangmo, and it is described as a universal reality of dynamic potentiality. It is identified with another principle, the "bön body" (*bon sku*), which represents the final nature of all phenomena (and is roughly identical to the truth body of Buddhism). It is equated with the fundamental principle of existence, the "bön nature" (*bon nyid*), which is the source of everything. All the elements of existence (*bon*) derive from it, and intuitive understanding of it leads to liberation. This reality was experienced by Shenrap, who taught a path whereby other beings might come to know it through direct perception.

According to Bön scriptures, in the beginning there was a great god named Yangdak Gyelpo ("Absolute Ruler"), who existed before the sun and moon, and even before time. From him two lights were created, one white and the other black, and these became a white man and a black man. The black man, Nyelwa Nakpo ("Black Suffering"), brought forth the stars and the plethora of demons that today inhabit the world. He is also responsible for all the evil in the world, including drought and other natural disasters, thunder and lightning, diseases, and the discord and fighting that divide the human race. The white man, Öserden ("Radiant One"), represents good, and is the source of virtue. He created the sun and moon, and taught human beings how to build temples, make copies of religious texts, pay respect to holy teachers, and construct roads and bridges. The ongoing struggle between these two beings reflects the competing forces of good and evil that vie with each other in the heart of every human being.

The Bön cosmos also contains numerous other deities, such as nine gods and nine goddesses, who were born of the union of a being named Shangpo and Chucham, goddess of water. Nyelwa Nakpo produced numerous demons, and Öserden similarly created good deities. These interbred with the eighteen children of Shangpo and Chucham, resulting in many beings of ambiguous nature. As this process continued, the universe became populated with all sorts of creatures. Other important deities include the 360 Kékhö, who live on the holy mountain Tisé (Kailash, which is also believed to be the residence of the Hindu god Śiva) and the 360 Werma deities. Both of these groups are associated with the 360 days of the year.

Bön is closely linked to the land of Tibet, and many of its prominent geographical features have special significance for Bönpos. Mount Tisé, for example, is an important holy spot for Bön, as is a peak in the southeastern province of Gongpo that is referred to by Bönpos as "Bön Mountain." Also called Lari (*bla ri*), Tisé is believed to be a link with the heavens, connecting the sky and earth. When Shenrap came to earth, his physical emanation descended to Tisé, and from there to the world of humans. It is believed to be the central axis of the world, and according to Bön tradition is a gigantic stūpa that houses many families of gods. These were the original inhabitants of the world, and they often resent the encroachments of humans. Much of Bön literature is concerned with describing and categorizing the various forces that inhabit the earth and sky and with rituals designed both to propitiate them and to overcome their attempts to cause harm to humans who trespass on their domains or otherwise incur their displeasure.

According to Bön creation myths, in the distant past there was only emptiness, which was not absolute void, but rather pure potentiality. This produced the five elements (earth, air, fire, water, and space), which coalesced into a vast "cosmic egg." From this was produced a primordial being named Belchen Kékhö, along with 359 other Kékhö gods. In the next stage, the "White Yak of Being" was born. The yak then descended to Shangshung. After coming to the earth, he ripped its surface with his horns, which produced mountains and valleys, and flowers then began to grow in the valleys. This made the earth inhabitable and thus completed the process of creation.

Perhaps as a result of the fact that they are often characterized by Buddhists as mere magicians, many Bön teachers today make a distinction between three types of Bön: (1) the old Bön, consisting of shamanistic practices; (2) the new or reformed Bön, which developed as a result of competition with Buddhism, and in the process absorbed Buddhist elements; and (3) swastika Bön (*g.yung drung bon*), the "eternal Bön," which refers to the tradition established by Shenrap.[9]

Bön Religious Literature

Bönpos, like Tibetan Buddhists, have divided their scriptures into two main sections, *Translations of Teachings* and *Translations of Treatises.* The former includes the revelations of Shenrap, while the latter comprises philosophical and commentarial texts. Many Bön scriptures are nearly identical to texts in the Buddhist canon, but often have different titles and Bön technical terms. There are only a few Bön texts that seem to predate Buddhism, and historical evidence suggests that the tradition's literary efforts were initially linked to a perceived need to compete with Buddhism, which had a large and varied canon, a highly-developed cosmology, elaborate rituals, and sophisticated metaphysical doctrines. The Bön canon today consists of about three hundred volumes, which were carved onto wood blocks around the middle of the nineteenth century and stored in Trochu in eastern Tibet. Copies of the canon were printed until the 1950s, but the blocks were destroyed during the Cultural Revolution, although it appears that most of the texts were brought to India or hidden in Tibet.

The Bön system shares most of its key doctrines with Buddhism. Like Buddhism, Bön teaches that the world is a place of suffering, and its primary concern is to find ways to escape from it. Bönpos assert that sentient beings are reborn in accordance with their karmas, and that for ordinary beings rebirth occurs in one of the six states of existence.[10] Escape from the cycle is achieved by those who become awakened, and good rebirths are won by beings who cultivate virtue and work for the benefit of others. There are also notable similarities in external symbols: Bönpos—like their Buddhist counterparts—use prayer flags and prayer wheels in order to multiply their prayers and gain merit, and they make pilgrimages to holy spots, which they circumambulate. Unlike Buddhists, however, Bönpos circle holy places in a counterclockwise direction, and prayer wheels are also spun counterclockwise.

Bönpos separate their teachings into nine vehicles. These in turn are divided into two groups, with the first four vehicles being termed "causal" (*rgyu*), while the next five are classed as "resultant" (*'bras bu*). The main Bön scriptures are divided into the "four doors" (*sgo bzhi*) and "five treasures" (*mdzod lnga*). In the nine vehicles schema, the first vehicle encompasses the teachings of the "*shen* of good fortune." Practices of this vehicle include creating images called *do* (*gto*), which are used in divination rituals and are connected with offerings of libations, meat, *chang* (an alcoholic beverage), and so forth.

The second vehicle includes teachings revealed to the "apparent *shen*," who perform rituals for the benefit of their clients. These bring worldly prosperity and depend upon the magical powers of those who execute them. Many of their practices are involved with exorcism. The teachings of the "magic *shen*" constitute the third vehicle. These are concerned with counteracting the influences of demonic beings, protecting people from harmful forces, and rituals of exorcism. The priests who conduct these rituals wear jackets and coats of tiger skin, carry banners with pictures of tigers on them, and wear ornaments of tiger paws, teeth, and claws.

The fourth vehicle encompasses the teachings of the "life *shen*," whose purpose is to care for the living and the dead. They are able to protect the life force of living beings and bring back the spirits of the dead. These first four vehicles include indigenous folk religious practices of Tibet, many of which are probably of ancient origin.

The fifth and sixth vehicles refer to the respective practices of laypeople and monastics. The teachings of the "virtuous *shen*" contain practices for laypeople, which are designed to bring merit and cancel evil deeds. They are also concerned with separating winter and summer through ceremonies designed to create a harmonious transition. Teachings of "swastika bön" constitute the sixth vehicle. These include ascetic practices and special meditative trainings for monks. The symbol of this vehicle is the swastika. The Bön swastika differs from the symbol used by Buddhists in that it is oriented in a counterclockwise direction, while the Buddhist swastika's orientation is clockwise.

The seventh vehicle contains the teachings and practices of the "bön of the white letter *A*," and focuses on secret mantras (*gsang sngags*) and tantric meditations. The term for this vehicle refers to the emanation of a five-part maṇḍala from the translucent center of a Tibetan letter *A*. Those who undergo the trainings of this vehicle are responsible for making offerings to deities using nine vessels and nine *torma* (images made from barley flour and butter and then painted). They are responsible for maintaining the order of the world through their rituals and chants, and with special songs called *shenlu* (*gshen glu*). The practices of this vehicle correspond to those of Nyingma yoga and mahāyoga tantras.[11]

The eighth vehicle encompasses the practices and teachings of the "bön of the superior *shen*," who are said to have special knowledge of the past, present, and future. The lore of this vehicle includes sexual yogas and corresponds to those of the Nyingma anuyoga tantras.

The ninth vehicle includes Bön teachings of the great perfection (*dzogchen*), which correspond to those of the Nyingma order. Like the Nyingmapas, Bönpos consider dzogchen to be the supreme of all meditative paths.[12] According to Samten Karmay, the primary Bön great perfection texts are a collection of hidden treasures (*terma*) referred to as *The Three Cycles of Revelation*.[13] This collection contains the primary Bönpo great perfection text, entitled *The Golden Tortoise*, which was "discovered" by Ngödrup Drakpa (ca. late eleventh century). Bönpos divide their great perfection teachings into the categories of "hidden" (*gab pa*) and "revealed" (*bsgrags pa*); according to Karmay, both of these are similar to Nyingma texts of the mind class.[14]

Bönpo sources contend that many of their hidden treasures were originally concealed as a response to Buddhist persecution. From about the tenth century onward, some Bön masters hid scriptures in temples, buried them underground, or walled them up in caves so that they would be preserved until they could be openly disseminated. Later these texts were discovered by Bönpo treasure discoverers (*tertön*). Other hidden treasures were directly revealed to *tertön* by buddhas and ḍākinīs. Because of the present climate of religious persecution in Tibet, some Bönpos there are reportedly repeating history by hiding texts, hoping that eventually the Chinese oppression will end and that they will be able to take the scriptures from concealment and openly practice their religion.

The Bön canon contains numerous ritual and liturgical treatises, which are used in the cultic practices of the tradition. These are often quite similar to those practiced by their Buddhist contemporaries. The deities invoked have Bön names, although they are otherwise similar to those found in Mahāyāna Buddhism. In addition to the differences in names, Bön deities have a distinctive iconography, which differs in significant features from Buddhist iconography, and the myths associated with them reflect Bön themes, beliefs, and symbols. The mantras associated with Bön deities also differ from those of Buddhist figures.

The Nature of Mind in Bönpo: Great Perfection

In Bön great perfection texts, the world is said to be an emanation of luminous mind. All the phenomena of experience are its illusory projections, which have their being in mind itself. Mind in turn is part of the primordial basis of all reality, called "bön nature." This exists in the form of multicolored light and pervades all of reality, which is merely its manifestation. Thus Shardza Tashi Gyaltsen contends that everything exists in dependence upon mind, which is an expression of the bön nature.

> Nothing exists independently of mind. Nothing exists beyond the natural state [bön nature]. Earth is not independent of the natural state; stone is not independent of the natural state; visions are not independent visions. Everything is a vision of the natural state.
>
> The natural state is like a single point; the natural state is like where birds fly—behind there is no trace. If you understand this point you will realise that the natural state is the creator of all things—the king of creators.[15]

He explains that mind is a primordially pure entity that is co-extensive with bön nature, an all-pervasive reality that is only perceived by those who have eliminated adventitious mental afflictions and actualized the luminous potentiality of mind. Those who attain awakening transform themselves into variegated light in the form of the rainbow body, after which their physical forms dissolve, leaving nothing behind. Both cyclic existence and nirvana are mind, the only difference being that those who have attained nirvana have eliminated illusory afflictions, and so their cognitive streams are manifested as clear light, while beings caught up in cyclic existence fail to recognize the luminous nature of mind and so are plagued by its illusory creations.

Bön Today

In accordance with Marxist-Leninist-Maoist dogma—which views religion as the "opiate of the masses" and a remnant of the "feudal" past—the

Chinese overlords of present-day Tibet have actively suppressed religious activity and have vigorously sought to undermine the beliefs of the Tibetan people while placing severe restrictions on expressions of religion (while at the same time proclaiming to the rest of the world that they protect freedom of religion). This has affected both Buddhists and Bönpos in Tibet, and Bönpos have also fled into exile and built centers in which they can maintain their traditions. One such center was established at Dolanji, about fifteen miles from the town of Solan in the Indian state of Himachal Pradesh.[16] Constructed in 1969, its design was based on Tibetan models, and it contains artwork and decorations illustrating Bön themes and depicting Bön deities.

Shortly after its completion, about seventy Bönpo families relocated to the area, forming a small but devoted lay community. It houses about one hundred and twenty monks, who follow rules similar to those of their Buddhist counterparts, but which are traced back to the teachings of Shenrap, and not Śākyamuni. In the monastery there are about sixty novices, ranging in age from fifteen to thirty, most of whom were born in exile. The curriculum includes training in the proper performance of rituals, classes in Bön *abhidharma* and cosmology (*mdzod phug*), astrology, medicine, logic, grammar, monastic discipline, and philosophy. Philosophical training includes courses in the Bön equivalents of perfection of wisdom (*phar phyin, prajñā-pāramitā*), Middle Way (*dbu ma, madhyamaka*), and epistemology (*tshad ma, pramāṇa*). The students also study tantra and great perfection.

The scholastic program includes frequent oral debate, in which the students match wits in spirited contests of dialectical proficiency. These debates require a thorough knowledge of Bön scriptures, along with clear thinking and the ability to respond quickly to challenges.[17] Those who successfully complete the curriculum—which generally requires about eight years of study—may compete for the degree of géshé. The Dolanji center has been very active in publishing and disseminating texts.

In addition to Dolanji, there are other centers in the areas of Dolpo and Mustang, where Bön established itself after leaving the central provinces of Tibet due to Buddhist opposition. Bön institutions have also been established in Kathmandu (most notably Triten Norbutsé near Swayambhu, just west of Kathmandu) and the Lubra area in Nepal, and several Bön teachers have set up centers in North America and Europe, which have attracted a number of Western students. It remains a tradition that is little studied by contemporary scholars, and only a small number of books and articles on Bön have been published to date. As a result, reliable information on Bön is limited, a situation that will hopefully be remedied as more Bön texts are published and Bön teachers make themselves available for consultation.

Notes

1. Per Kværne, "Bön," in Mircea Eliade, ed., *The Encyclopedia of Religion* (New York: Macmillan, 1987), vol. 2, p. 277.
2. Snellgrove, *Indo-Tibetan Buddhism*, p. 390.
3. Snellgrove and Richardson, *A Cultural History of Tibet*, p. 175.
4. As Per Kværne notes in his introduction to Shardza Tashi Gyeltsen's *Heartdrops of Dharmakaya: Dzogchen Practice of the Bön Tradition* (Ithaca: Snow Lion, 1993, pp. 8–9), although Bön claims of Persian origin were often dismissed out of hand by scholars of Buddhism, there is growing evidence in their favor. He notes, for example, that some pre-Buddhist Bon structures exhibit Persian features, and some original Bön teachings bear some similarities to ideas found in ancient Persian religious traditions.
5. Per Kværne, "Bön," p. 278.
6. *Indo-Tibetan Buddhism*, p. 391.
7. Per Kværne, "Bön," p. 280.
8. Ibid., p. 279.
9. This distinction is found in Shardza Tashi Gyeltsen's *Heartdrops of Dharmakaya*.
10. These are gods, demi gods, humans, animals, hungry ghosts, and hell beings.
11. For a description of the practices of this vehicle, see Per Kværne, "'The Great Perfection' in the Tradition of the Bonpos," in Whalen Lai and Lewis Lancaster, eds., *Early Ch'an in China and Tibet* (Berkeley: Asian Humanities Press, 1983), pp. 372ff.
12. For a more detailed discussion, see David Snellgrove, *The Nine Ways of Bon* (London: Oxford University Press, 1967) and Samten Karmay, "A General Introduction to the History and Doctrines of Bon," *Memoirs of the Research Department of the Toyo Bunko* 33 (1975), pp. 171–218.
13. Samten Karmay, *The Great Perfection* (Leiden: E.J. Brill, 1988), p. 201.
14. Ibid., p. 202.
15. *Heartdrops of Dharmakaya*, pp. 43–44.
16. See Tadeusz Skorupski, "Tibetan g-Yung-drung Bön Monastery at Dolanji," *Kailash* 8.1–2 (1981), pp. 25–43; reprinted in *The Tibet Journal* 11.2 (1986), pp. 36–49.
17. See Krystyna Cech, "The History, Teaching, and Practice of Dialectics according to the Bön Tradition," *The Tibet Journal* 11.2 (1986), pp. 3–28.

Chronology of Indian and Tibetan Buddhism

422–399 B.C.E.	Life of Śākyamuni Buddha
405	First Buddhist Council at Rājagṛha
305	Second Buddhist Council at Vaiśālī
284	Third Buddhist Council at Pāṭaliputra
272–236	Reign of Aśoka
100	Beginnings of Mahāyāna Buddhism in India
1st century C.E.	Buddhism enters Central Asia and China
150–250	Life of Nāgārjuna
233	Buddhist text and relics fall on roof of King Totori Nyentsen
4th century	Life of Asaṅga and Vasubandhu
350–650	Gupta Dynasty in India; flourishing of Buddhist philosophy and art
400–500	Life of Buddhaghosa
5th century	Founding of Nālandā Monastic University
414	Chinese pilgrim Faxian travels to India
6th century	Tibet invades Chinese territories in Central Asia
530–600	Life of Dharmakīrti; flourishing of Epistemological tradition
618–650	Life of Songtsen Gampo, first of Tibet's "religious kings"
618–906	Chinese Tang Dynasty; apogee of Buddhism in China

629–645	Chinese pilgrim Xuanzang travels to India
640	Chinese princess Wencheng travels to Tibet to marry Songtsen Gampo
650–950	Pala Dynasty in India; sponsorship of major Buddhist centers
700	Reign of Emperor Düsong (d. 704); construction of first Buddhist temples
720–1200	Tantric Buddhism arises and develops in India
740–798	Life of Tri Songdétsen, second "religious king"
760	Śāntarakṣita and Padmasambhava travel to Tibet; beginning of "first dissemination" of Buddhism
763	Tibetan army conquers Chinese capital Changan
767	Consecration of Samyé, first monastery in Tibet
780	Tibetan forces conquer Dunhuang
792	Council of Lhasa (?) in Tibet
799–815	Reign of Sénalek
815–836	Reign of Relbachen, third "religious king"
838–842	Reign of Lang Darma; end of first dissemination
845	Persecution of Buddhism in China
950	Beginning of revival of monastic Buddhism in central Tibet
late 10th century	Tibetans travel to India to study Buddhism
958–1055	Life of great translator Rinchen Sanpo
978	Rinchen Sangpo returns from India; beginning of "second dissemination"
999–1026	Mahmud Ghori attacks northern India, sacks Buddhist monasteries
1008–1064	Life of Dromdön; establishment of Kadampa, first order of Buddhism in Tibet
1012–1097	Life of Marpa; beginnings of Kagyupa order
1016–1100	Life of Nāropa
1040–1123	Life of Milarépa

1042	Atiśa arrives in Tibet
1073	Sakyapa order founded by Gönchok Gyelpo
1079–1153	Life of Gampopa; establishment of Kagyu monastic order
1092–1158	Life of Sachen Günga Nyingpo; systematization of Sakya teachings
1110–1170	Life of Pakmodru Dorjé Gyelpo
1158	Founding of Densatil
1200	Destruction of Nālandā by Mahmud Ghori
1235	Tibetan pilgrim Dharmasvāmin visits north India; Buddhism largely dies out in India after this time
1235–1280	Life of Pakpa; establishment of priest-patron relationship with Qubilai Khan
1244	Sakya Pandita travels to Mongolia; conversion of Mongols begins
1290–1364	Life of Pudön; Tibetan canon compiled by 1334
1292–1361	Life of Dolpopa, who initiated "other-emptiness" doctrine
1354	Jangchub Gyeltsen conquers Sakya Monastery; beginning of Pakmodrupa rule
1357–1419	Life of Tsong Khapa; beginning of Gélukpa order
1409	Founding of Ganden Monastery near Lhasa; Tsong Khapa initiates first Mönlam Chenmo
1543–1588	Life of Sönam Gyatso, the third Dalai Lama; beginning of Dalai Lama lineage
1565	Governor of Tsang overthrows Rinpungs
1589–1617	Life of Yönden Gyatso, fourth Dalai Lama
1617–1682	Life of fifth Dalai Lama, Ngawang Losang Gyatso; beginning of rule of Tibet by Dalai Lamas
1624	Jesuit missionary Antonio d'Antrade arrives in Tsaparang
1644–1912	Qing Dynasty in China; patronage of Tibetan Buddhism

1697	Tsanyang Gyatso enthroned as sixth Dalai Lama
1706	Mongol chieftain Hlasang overthrows sixth Dalai Lama
1716–1721	Jesuit missionary Ippolito Desideri resides in Lhasa
1720	Kelsang Gyatso enthroned as Dalai Lama VII
1749	Mongolian Buddhist canon completed
1792	Gurkha invasion of Tibet
19th century	Beginning of academic scholarship of Buddhism by Western scholars
1813–1899	Life of Jamgön Kongtrül; beginning of Rimé movement
1865	Gompo Namgyel killed by Tibetan troops, ending Nyarong troubles
1876–1933	Life of Tupden Gyatso, Dalai Lama XIII
1903–4	Younghusband expedition reaches Lhasa, forces officials to sign Anglo-Tibetan Convention
1909–10	Chinese troops under command of Ma Weiqi and Zhao Erfeng invade eastern Tibet, sack monasteries, and march on Lhasa
1911	Nationalists overthrow last Qing emperor and gain control of China
1912	Kashag declares Tibet's independence and expels Chinese nationals
1918	Formal boundary between Tibet and China established
1934	Réting Rinpoché named regent following death of Dalai Lama XIII
1935	Birth of Tenzin Gyatso, fourteenth Dalai Lama
1950	People's Liberation Army enters Tibet
1955	Process of collectivization begins in Kham; monasteries destroyed, monks and nuns killed

1959	March 10 uprising; fourteenth Dalai Lama flees to India, establishes government-in-exile; persecution of Buddhism by Chinese
1964–1974	Cultural Revolution in China and Tibet; widespread destruction of religious monuments
1976	Death of Mao Zedong; some easing of religious repression
1987	Dalai Lama proposes Five-Point Peace Plan
1989	Dalai Lama awarded Nobel Peace Prize; Nobel Committee accused by China of "politicizing" the prize and interfering with its internal affairs; riots by scores of Tibetans suppressed by Chinese security forces
2006	Dalai Lama denounces wearing of fur during Kālacakra ceremony in India, sparking fur-burnings all over Tibetan cultural area

Lexicon of Buddhist Terms

abhidharma (*chos mngon pa, abhidharma*): the scholastic system derived from the discourses of the **Buddha** which summarizes key points and classifies teachings.

action seal (*las kyi phyag rgya, karma-mudrā*): an actual tantric consort used in the sexual practices of **highest yoga tantra.**

action tantra (*bya rgyud, kriyā-tantra*): the tantric system that emphasizes external ritual activities (the first of the four classes of tantra).

actual clear light (*don gyi 'od gsal*): the fifth of the six levels of the **stage of generation**, in which one manifests the mind of clear light.

aggregates (*phung po, skandha*): the components of the psychophysical personality, on the basis of which beings commonly impute the false notion of self. The five aggregates are: form, feelings, discriminations, consciousness, compositional factors.

arhat (*dgra bcom pa, arhat*): a person who has destroyed the mental defilements and become detached from the phenomena of cyclic existence.

bardo (*bar do, antarābhāva*): the intermediate state between death and rebirth.

bodhicitta (*byang chub kyi sems, bodhicitta*): literally "mind of awakening," the altruistic intention to become awakened in order to benefit others.

bodhisattva (*byang chub sems dpa', bodhisattva*): literally "awakening being," one who has generated **bodhicitta** and seeks awakening for the benefit of others.

bodhisattva level (*byang chub sems dpa'i sa, bodhisattva-bhūmi*): the hierarchy of stages (usually ten in number) through which bodhisattvas progress on their way to the state of buddhahood.

brahman (*bram dze, brāhmaṇa*): a member of the priestly caste of Hinduism.

Buddha (Śākyamuni): the historical **Buddha**, named Siddhārtha Gautama at birth, who is credited with establishing Buddhist doctrine in the present era.

buddha (*sangs rgyas, buddha*): one who has perfected compassion and wisdom through following the **bodhisattva** path, who has become fully omniscient and has actualized the three bodies: **complete enjoyment body**, **truth body**, and **emanation bodies**.

cakra (*rtsa 'khor, cakra*): an energy nexus in the physiological system of **highest yoga tantra**. A cakra is a place where the left and right **channels** wrap around the central channel and constrict the flow of energies.

calm abiding (*zhi gnas, śamatha*): a meditative state in which one is able to focus on an internal meditative object for as long as one wishes without becoming distracted by laxity or excitement.

channel (*rtsa, nāḍī*): according to the subtle physiology of **highest yoga tantra**, the energy pathways through which subtle energies called **winds** and **drops** move. The most important of these are the central channel and channels to the left and right of it.

chö (*gcod*): see **cutting off**.

compassion (*snying rje, karuṇā*): sensitivity to the sufferings experienced by other beings, coupled with a desire to help them to overcome suffering and its causes.

complete enjoyment body (*longs spyod pa'i sku, saṃbhoga-kāya):* one of the three bodies of buddhas (the others are the **truth body** and **emanation bodies**). It is a pure form composed of light that appears to advanced **bodhisattvas**.

compositional factors (*'du byed, saṃskāra*): volitional activities, both good and bad, which influence future mental states; one of the five **aggregates**.

consciousness (*shes pa, vijñāna*): the continuum of dualistic cognition, which encompasses the six types of ordinary consciousness (eye, ear, nose, tongue, body, and mind); one of the five **aggregates**.

cutting off (*gcod*): a meditative practice in which one mentally visualizes one's body being cut up and devoured by demons in order to reduce ego clinging.

cutting through (*khregs chod*): a method used in **dzogchen** practice that involves seeing through appearances to perceive the primordially pure mind.

cyclic existence (*'khor ba, saṃsāra*): the endless cycle of birth, death, and rebirth that is based on ignorance.

ḍākinī (*mka' 'gro ma, ḍākinī*): female wisdom beings who are particularly associated with transmission of secret teachings to tantric practitioners.

deity (*lha, deva*): a tantric **buddha**.

deity yoga (*lha'i rnal 'byor, devatā-yoga*): the practice of visualizing a buddha and mentally transforming oneself in accordance with this visualization.

dependent arising (*rten cing 'brel bar 'byung ba, pratītya-samutpāda*): the process of causation, in which phenomena are created, sustained, and pass away in dependence on causes and conditions.

dharma (*chos, dharma*): (1) the teaching and practice of Buddhism; (2) a phenomenon.

direct approach (*thod rgal*): a method used in **dzogchen** practice that involves understanding the spontaneity of the operations of mind.

discrimination (*'du shes, saṃjñā*): mental differentiations of the phenomena of experience, based on **feelings**; one of the five **aggregates**.

doctrine: see **dharma**.

drop (*thig le, bindu*): the subtle energies found in specific places in the body according to the **highest yoga tantra** system.

dzogchen (*rdzogs chen*): literally "great perfection," this is a meditative practice closely associated with the Nyingma school that is based on the idea that all appearances are creations of mind (which is said to be an entity of luminosity and emptiness).

emanation body (*sprul pa'i sku, nirmāṇa-kāya)*: a form created by a **buddha** for the benefit of sentient beings; one of the three bodies of a buddha.

emptiness (*stong pa nyid, śūnyatā*): the final nature of phenomena, their absence of inherent existence.

excitement (*rgod pa, auddhatya*): the tendency to lose attention to one's meditative object due to becoming agitated.

feeling (*tshor ba, vedanā*): sensations of things; one of the five **aggregates**.

first dissemination (*snga dar*): the period of the initial introduction of Buddhism to Tibet.

form (*gzugs, rūpa*): things that constitute the physical world, including the senses; one of the five **aggregates**.

gélong (*dge slong, bhikṣu*): a fully ordained monk.

gétsül (*dge tshul, śrāmaṇera*): a novice monk.

higher insight (*lhag mthong, vipaśyanā*): a meditative practice in which one analyzes the object of observation in order to ascertain its final nature.

highest yoga tantra (*rnal 'byor bla na med kyi rgyud, anuttara-yoga-tantra*): considered by Tibetan exegetes to be the supreme of the four classes of **tantras**, it involves visualization exercises that manipulate and transform subtle energies called **winds** and **drops**.

Hīnayāna (*theg pa dman pa, hīnayāna*): literally "Lesser Vehicle," this encompasses Buddhist teachings and practices aimed at removing mental afflictions and attaining **nirvāṇa**.

illusory body (*sgyu lus, māyā-deha*): a subtle body created by visualization (fourth of the six levels of the **stage of generation**).

initiation (*dbang, abhiṣeka*): a ceremony that allows a meditator to engage in the practices of a particular tantric cycle.

intermediate state: see **bardo**.

karma (*las, karma*): action (which is linked with its causes and effects).

kṣatriya (*rgyal rigs, kṣatriya*): the warrior and ruling caste of Hinduism.

lama (*bla ma, guru*): a spiritual preceptor.

lamdré (*lam 'bras, mārga-phala*): literally "path and fruit," a meditative practice closely associated with the Sakya school and based on the *Hevajra Tantra*, which emphasizes the inseparability of the path and its resultant effects.

laxity (*bying ba, laya*): the tendency to lose attention to one's meditative object due to mental dullness.

mahāmudrā (*rgya chen po, mahāmudrā*): literally "great seal," this is a meditative system closely associated with the Kagyu school that emphasizes direct realization of the luminous and empty nature of mind and phenomena.

Mahāyāna (*theg pa chen po, mahāyāna*): literally "Great Vehicle," this is the Buddhist system that emphasizes the path and practices of the **bodhisattva.**

maṇḍala (*dkyil 'khor, maṇḍala*): a diagram used in tantric meditation as an aid to visualization, which represents the residence and perfected attributes of a **buddha.**

mantra (*sngags, mantra*): a ritual formula used in tantric meditation.

meditational deity (*yi dam, iṣṭa-devatā*): a **buddha** which serves as the archetype for one's meditative aspirations.

mind of clear light (*'od gsal sems, prabhāsvara-citta*): the most basic and fundamental level of mind.

mind of awakening: see **bodhicitta**.

New Schools (*gsar ma*): the schools whose teachings and practices are primarily based on the translations of the period of the second dissemination (Sakya, Kagyu, and Géluk).

ngöndro (*sngon 'gro, pūrvagama*): the "preliminary practices" of **tantra.**

nirvāṇa (*mya ngan las 'das pa, nirvāṇa*): the state of liberation from the sufferings of cyclic existence.

object of observation (*dmigs pa, ālambana*): a focal point of meditation.

ordinary being (*so so'i skye bo, pṛthagjana):* one who has not yet attained the path of seeing and so is not able to perceive **emptiness** directly.

path and result: see **lamdré**.

path of accumulation (*tshogs lam, saṃbhāra-mārga*): the first of the five Buddhist paths, during which one amasses the collections of merit and wisdom.

path of meditation (*sgom lam, bhāvanā-mārga*): the fourth of the five Buddhist paths, during which one removes subtle traces of false conceptions of inherent existence.

path of no more learning (*mi slob lam, aśaikṣa-mārga*): the fifth of the five Buddhist paths, during which one eliminates the subtlest traces of the conception of inherent existence and attains awakening.

path of preparation (*sbyor lam, prayoga-mārga*): the second of the five Buddhist paths, marked by attainment of a union of **calm abiding** and **higher insight**.

path of seeing (*mthong lam, darśana-mārga*): the third of the five Buddhist paths, so called because one directly perceives **emptiness**.

perfections, six (*pha rol tu phyin pa, pāramitā*): the six qualities in which **bodhisattvas** train, which become the matrix of the awakened personality of a buddha: generosity, ethics, patience, effort, concentration, and wisdom.

performance tantra (*spyod rgyud, caryā-tantra*): **tantras** that equally emphasize external activities and internal yogas (second of the four tantra sets).

preliminary practices: see **ngöndro**.

rainbow body (*'ja lus*): a subtle body composed of pure light.

sādhana (*sgrub thabs, sādhana*): a tantric meditational ritual, generally focused on a particular **deity** or group of deities.

Śākyamuni (*śā kya thub pa, śākyamuni*): the historical **Buddha**.

saṃgha (*dge 'dun, saṃgha*): the community of Buddhist monks and nuns.

Sarma (*gsar ma*): see **New Schools**.

seal (*phyag rgya, mudrā*): a tantric consort.

second dissemination (*phyi dar*): the period of Buddhism's transmission into Tibet that followed the death of King Lang Darma.

sentient being (*sems can, sattva*): a being that possesses consciousness.

skill in means (*thabs la mkhas pa, upāya-kauśalya*): the **Mahāyāna** practice of adapting the doctrine to the capacities of one's audience.

six yogas of Nāropa (*nā ro chos drug*): tantric practices closely associated with the Kagyu school and traced back to the Indian adept Nāropa: (1) heat (*gtum mo*); (2) **illusory body** (*sgyu lus*); (3) dream (*rmi lam*); (4) clear light (*'od gsal*); (5) **intermediate state** (*bar do*); and (6) transference of consciousness (*'pho ba*).

solitary realizer (*rang sangs rgyas, pratyeka-buddha*): a Buddhist practitioner who attains **nirvāṇa** without a teacher.

stage of completion (*rdzogs rim, niṣpanna-krama*): the **highest yoga tantra** practice in which one transforms oneself into a **buddha**.

stage of generation (*bskyed rim, utpatti-krama*): the **highest yoga tantra** practice of creating a vivid image of a **deity**.

stūpa (*mchod rten, stūpa*): a structure symbolizing Buddhist motifs that is used to store sacred objects such as texts, images, and relics of deceased **lamas**.

suchness (*de bzhin nyid, tathatā*): the final nature of phenomena, which is equated with **emptiness**.

superior (*'phags pa, ārya*): one who has reached the **path of seeing** and is able to perceive **emptiness** directly.

sūtra (*mdo, sūtra*): a teaching attributed to the historical **Buddha**.

tantra (*rgyud, tantra*): Buddhist texts that outline the practices of the **vajra vehicle**.

tathāgata (*de bzhin gshegs pa, tathāgata*): literally "thus gone one," an epithet of buddhas.

terma (*gter ma*): "hidden treasures" concealed by Padmasambhava or his disciples.

tertön (*gter ston*): "treasure discoverers," generally reincarnations of Padmasambhava or his disciples, who find **terma**.

three jewels (*dkon mchog gsum, triratna*): the **Buddha**, the **dharma**, and the **saṃgha** (also referred to as the "three refuges").

vajra (*rdo rje, vajra*): a tantric symbol that represents the indestructible union of method and wisdom that is the goal of the tantric path.

vajra vehicle (*rdo rje theg pa, vajra-yāna*): the Buddhist system of practice based on texts called **tantras**, which emphasizes the practice of deity yoga (also called the "secret mantra vehicle" and "tantra vehicle").

wind (*rlung, prāṇa*): the subtle energies that course through pathways called **channels**, according to the system of **highest yoga tantra**.

yoga tantra (*rnal 'byor rgyud, yoga-tantra*): tantric practices that involve visualizing oneself as a tantric **deity** (third of the four tantric sets).

English-Tibetan-Sanskrit Glossary

Technical Terms

abandonment of nonvirtuous phenomena already generated (*sdig pa mi dge ba'i chos skyes pa rnams yongs su spang pa, utpannākuśala-dharma-prahāṇa*)

abandonments, four (*yang dag par spong ba, samyak-prahāṇa*)

abbot (*mkhan po, upādhyāya*)

abhidharma (*chos mngon pa*)

absorption (*snyoms 'jug, samāpatti*)

absorption of limitless consciousness (*rnam shes mtha' yas kyi snyoms 'jug, vijñānānantya-samāpatti*)

absorption of limitless space (*nam mkha' mtha' yas kyi snyoms 'jug, ākāśānantya-samāpatti*)

absorption of nothingness (*ci yang med kyi snyoms 'jug, ākiṃcanya-samāpatti*)

action (*'du byed kyi las, saṃskāra-karma*)

action seal (*las kyi phyag rgya, karma-mudrā*)

action tantra (*bya rgyud, kriyā-tantra*)

actual clear light (*don gyi 'od gsal*)

adept (*sgrub thob, siddha*)

adventitious (*glo bur, agantuka*)

affliction (*nyon mongs, kleśa*)

afflictive obstructions (*nyon mongs pa'i sgrib pa, kleśa-āvaraṇa*)

aging and death (*rga shi, jarāmaraṇa*)

aggregate (*phung po, skandha*)

all empty (*thams cad stong pa, sarva-śūnya*)

all-good (*kun tu bzang po, samāntabhadra*)

amban (*am ban*)

analysis (*dpyod pa, vicāra*)

analytical knowledges, four (*so sor yang dag par rig pa, pratisaṃvid*)

animals (*dud 'gro, tiryak*)

antidote (*gnyen po, pratipakṣa*)

anuyoga (*rjes su rnal 'byor*)

apparent shen (*snang gshen*)

appearance (*snang ba, pratibhāsa*)

appearance of experience in meditation (*ting 'dzin nyams kyi snang ba, samādhyanubhavābhāsa*)

appearance of phenomena as impure error (*ma dag 'khrul pa'i snang ba, aśuddhabhrāntyavabhāsa*)

arhat (*dgra bcom pa*)

aspect (*rnam pa, ākāra*)

aspiration (*smon lam, praṇidhāna*)

assistant abbot (*bla ma dbu mdzad*)

assumptions of bad states (*gnas ngan len, dauṣṭhulya*)

atiyoga (*shin tu rnal 'byor*)

attachment (*sred pa, tṛṣṇā*)

awakening (*byang chub, bodhi*)

bardo (*bar do, antarābhāva*)

bardo between birth and death (*skye shi'i bar do*)

bardo of becoming (*srid pa bar do*)

bardo of birth (*skye gnas bar do*)

bardo of meditative absorption (*bsam gtan bar do*)

bases of magical emanations, four (*rdzu 'phrul gyi rkang pa, ṛddhi-pāda*)

basic winds (*rtsa ba'i rlung, mūla prāṇa*)

basis continuum (*gzhi rgyud*)

basis of magical emanation that is an analytical meditative stabilization (*dpyod pa'i ting nge 'dzin gyi rdzu 'phrul gyi rkang pa, mīmāṃsā-samādhi-ṛddhi-pāda*)

basis of magical emanation that is aspiration (*'dun pa'i rdzu 'phrul gyi rkang pa, chanda-ṛddhi-pāda*)

basis of magical emanation that is effort (*brtson 'grus kyi rdzu 'phrul gyi rkang pa, vīrya-ṛddhi-pāda*)

basis of magical emanation that is mental attention (*sems kyi rdzu 'phrul gyi rkang pa, citta-ṛddhi-pāda*)

beginner (*las dang po pa, ādikarmika*)

Bhagavan (*bCom ldan 'das*)

birth (*skye ba, jāti*)

bliss (*bde ba, sukha*)

bodhicitta (*byang chub kyi sems*)

bodhisattva (*byang chub sems dpa'*)

bodhisattva level (*byang chub sems dpa'i sa, bodhisattva-bhūmi*)

bodhisattva vehicle (*byang chub sems dpa'i lam, bodhisattva-mārga*)

body (*lus, kāya*)

bön body (*bon sku*)

Bön dharma (*Bon chos*)

bön nature (*bon nyid*)

bön of the superior shen (*ye gshen bon*)

bön of the white letter *A* (*a dkar bon*)

bönpo (*bon po*)

brahman (*bram dze, brāhmaṇa*)

branch (*yan lag, aṅga*)

branches of awakening, seven (*byang chub kyi yan lag, bodhyaṅga*)

buddha (*sangs rgyas*)

buddhahood (*sangs rgyas nyid, buddhatva*)

buddha land (*sangs rgyas kyi zhing, buddha-kṣetra*)

buddha level (*sangs rgyas kyi sa, buddha-bhūmi*)

cakra (*rtsa 'khor*)

calm abiding (*zhi gnas, śamatha*)

cause (*rgyu, hetu*)

central channel (*rtsa dbu ma, avadhūti*)

Cham (*'Cham*) dance

channel (*rtsa, nāḍī*)

character (*mtshan nyid, lakṣaṇa*)

chö (*gcod*)

classes of attainment, eight (*sgrub sde brgyad*)

clear light (*'od gsal, prabhāsvara*)

clear light of death (*'chi ba'i 'od gsal*)

close lineage of terma (*nye brgyud gter ma*)

close setting (*nye bar 'jog pa, upasthāpana*)

cloud of doctrine (*chos kyi sprin, dharma-megha*); tenth bodhisattva level

coarse (*rags pa, audārika*)

collection (*tshogs, saṃbhāra*)

collection of merit (*bsod nams tshogs, puṇya-saṃbhāra*)

collection of wisdom (*ye shes tshogs, jñāna-saṃbhāra*)

compassion (*snying rje, karuṇā*)

complete enjoyment body (*longs spyod pa'i sku, saṃbhoga-kāya*)

compositional factors (*'du byed, saṃskāra*)

compositional suffering (*'du byed kyi sdug bsngal, saṃskāra-duḥkhatā*)

concentration, perfection of (*bsam gtan gyi pha rol tu phyin pa, dhyāna-pāramitā*)

concentrations, four (*bsam gtan, dhyāna*)

conceptuality (*rtog pa, vikalpa*)

consciousness (*shes pa, vijñāna*)

contact (*reg pa, sparśa*)

continuous setting (*rgyun du 'jog pa, saṃsthāpana*)

continuum (*rgyun, saṃtāna*)

conventional mind of awakening (*kun rdzob byang chub kyi sems, saṃvṛti-bodhicitta*)

conventional truth (*kun rdzob bden pa, samvṛti-satya*)

correct aims of actions (*yang dag pa'i las kyi mtha', samyak-karmānta*)

correct effort (*yang dag pa'i rtsol ba, samyag-vyāyāma*)

correct livelihood (*yang dag pa'i 'tsho ba, samyag-ājīva*)

correct meditative stabilization (*yang dag pa'i ting nge 'dzin, samyak-samādhi*)

correct mindfulness (*yang dag pa'i dran pa, samyak-smṛti*)

correct realization (*yang dag pa'i rtog pa, samyak-saṃkalpa*),

correct speech (*yang dag pa'i ngag, samyag-vāc*)

correct view (*yang dag pa'i lta ba, samyak-dṛṣṭi*)

countless eon (*bskal pa grangs med pa, asaṃkhyeya-kalpa*)

cutting off (*gcod*)

cutting through (*khregs chod*)

cyclic existence (*'khor ba, saṃsāra*)

ḍākinī (*mka' 'gro ma*)

ḍāmaru (*ḍa ma ru*)

dead emptiness (*bem stong*)

death (*'chi ba, maraṇa*)

deeds (*spyod pa, caryā*)

definition (*mtshan nyid, lakṣaṇa*)

deity (*lha, deva*)

deity yoga (*lha'i rnal 'byor, devatā-yoga*)

deliverance (*sgrol ba*)

demigod (*lha ma yin, asura*)

demon (*bdud, māra*)

dependent arising (*rten cing 'brel bar 'byung ba, pratītya-samutpāda*)

Dési (*sDe srid*)

desire (*'dod chags, rāga*)

development of experiences (*nyams gong 'phel*)

dharma (*chos*)

dharma of human beings (*mi chos*)

difficult to overcome (*shin tu sbyang dka' ba, sudurjayā*); fifth bodhisattva level

direct approach (*thod rgal*)

directed ḍākinī teachings (*mkha' 'gro gtad rgya*)

direct perception of reality (*chos nyid mngon sum*)

discipline (*'dul ba, vinaya*)

disciplining (*dul bar byed pa, damana*)

discrimination (*'du shes, saṃjñā*)

dissolution into the nature of reality (*chos nyid zad pa*)

distant lineage of the teachings (*ring brgyud bka' ma*)

divine dharma (*lha chos*)

divine pride (*lha'i nga rgyal, deva-māna*)

do (*gto*)

doctrine (*chos, dharma*)

doors, four (*sgo bzhi*)

downward-moving wind (*thur sel gyi rlung*)

dream (*rmi lam, svapna*)

dream bardo (*rmi lam bar do*)

dream yoga (*rmi lam rnal 'byor, svapna-yoga*)

drokpa (*'brog pa*)

drop (*thig le, bindu*)

dü (*bdud, māra*)

dzogchen (*rdzogs chen*)

Effect Vehicle (*'Bras bu'i theg pa, Phala-yāna*)

effort (*brtson 'grus, vīrya*)

eightfold noble path (*'phags pa'i lam yan lag brgyad, āryāṣṭāṅgamārga*)

elaborations (*spros pa, prapañca*)

Elders (*gNas brtan pa, Sthavira*)

emanation body (*sprul pa'i sku, nirmāṇa-kāya*)

empowerment (*dbang skur, abhiṣeka*)

emptiness (*stong pa nyid, śūnyatā*)

empty (*stong pa, śūnya*)

energy pathways (*rtsa, nāḍī*)

epistemology (*tshad ma, pramāṇa*)

equanimity (*btang snyoms, upekṣā*)

essential purity (*ka dag*)

ethics (*tshul khrims, śīla*)

exalted wisdom (*ye shes, jñāna*)

excitement (*rgod pa, auddhatya*)

exertion (*rtsol ba, vyāyāma*)

existence (*srid pa, bhava*)

explanatory lineage (*bshad brgyud*)

factor of stability (*gnas cha*)

faculties, five (*dbang po, indriya*)

faith (*dad pa, śraddhā*)

feeling, (*tshor ba, vedanā*)

final nirvana (*yongs su mya ngan las 'das, parinirvāṇa*)

fire ritual (*sbyin sreg, homa*),

fire-dwelling wind (*mnyam gnas kyi rlung*)

first dissemination (*snga dar*)

forbearance (*bzod pa, kṣānti*)

forbearance regarding nonarisen phenomena (*mi skye ba'i chos la bzod pa, anutpatti-dharma-kṣānti*)

forgetfulness (*gdams ngag brjed pa, avavāda-saṃmoṣa*)

form (*gzugs, rūpa*)

form body (*gzugs sku, rūpa-kāya*)

formless absorptions (*gzugs med kyi snyoms 'jug, ārūpya-samāpatti*)

freedom from activity (*bya bral*)

fruit (*'bras bu, phala*)

fully ordained monk (*dge slong, bhikṣu*)

fundamental mind (*gnyug pa'i sems*)

Gachupa (*bKa' bcu pa*)

Gashipa (*bKa' bzhi pa*)

gélong (*dge slong, bhikṣu*)

general teachings (*tshogs bshad*)

generation of the mind of awakening (*byang chub sems bskyed pa, bodhicittotpāda*)

generation of virtuous phenomena not yet generated (*dge ba'i chos ma skyes pa rnams bskyed pa, anutpanna-kuśala-dharma-ropaṇa*)

generation stage (*bskyed rim, utpatti-krama*)

generosity (*sbyin pa, dāna*)

géshé (*dge bshes*; short for *dge ba'i bshes gnyen, kalyāṇa-mitra*)

géshé hlarampa (*dge bshes lha ram pa*)

gétsül (*dge tshul, śrāmaṇera*)

god (*lha, deva*)

golden doctrines, thirteen (*gser chos bcu gsum*)

gone afar (*ring du song ba, dūraṃgamā*); seventh bodhisattva level

good intelligence (*legs pa'i blo gros, sādhumatī*); ninth bodhisattva level

grasping (*len pa, upādāna*)

Great Assembly (*Phal chen pa, Mahāsāṃgika*)

great compassion (*snying rje chen po, mahākaruṇā*)

great deeds, twelve (*mdzad pa bcu gnyis*)

great perfection (*rdzogs pa chen po*)

great man (*skyes bu chen po, mahāpuruṣa*)

Great Aspiration Festival (*sMon lam chen mo*)

great seal (*rgya chen, mahāmudrā*)

great times (*dus chen*)

guru (*bla ma*)

guru yoga (*bla ma'i rnal 'byor*)

happiness (*bde ba, sukha*)

harmonies with awakening, thirty-seven (*byang chub kyi phyogs, bodhi-pakṣa*)

hearer (*nyan thos, śrāvaka*)

hearing lineage (*snyan brgyud*)

heat (*gtum mo, caṇḍālī*)

heat yoga (*gtum mo, caṇḍālī*)

hell (*dmyal ba, naraka*)

hell beings (*dmyal ba, nāraka*)

hidden (*gab pa*)

hidden treasures (*gter ma*)

higher insight (*lhag mthong, vipaśyanā*)

highest yoga tantra (*rnal 'byor bla na med kyi rgyud, anuttara-yoga-tantra*)

humans (*mi, manuṣya*)

hungry ghosts (*yi dwags, preta*)

ignorance (*ma rig pa, avidyā*)

illusory body (*sgyu lus, māyā-deha*)

immovable (*mi g.yo ba, acalā*); eighth bodhisattva level

impermanence (*mi rtag pa, anitya*)

imprint (*lag rjes*)

impure illusory body (*ma dag pa'i sgyu lus*)

incarnate lama (*sprul sku, nirmāṇa-kāya*)

increase (*mched pa, vṛddhi-prāpta*)

increasing of virtuous phenomena already generated (*dge ba'i chos skyes pa rnams 'phel ba, utpanna-kuśala-dharmavṛddhi*)

indestructible drop (*mi gzhigs pa'i thig le*)

individual liberation (*so sor thar pa, prātimokṣa*)

inhalation (*dbugs rngub pa, āpāna*)

inherent existence (*rang bzhin gyis grub pa, svabhāva-siddhi*)

initiate teachings (*slob bshad*)

initiation (*dbang, abhiṣeka*)

innate (*lhan cig, sahaja*)

innate joy (*lhan skyes kyi dga', sahajānanda*)

inseparabilty of cyclic existence and nirvana (*'khor 'das dbyer med*)

isolation (*dben, viveka*)

intermediate state (*bar do, antarābhāva*)

introspection (*shes bzhin, saṃprajanya*)

Jangtsé Chöjé (*Byang rtse Chos rje*)

Jātaka (*sKyes rabs*)

jewels, three (*dkon mchog gsum, triratna*)

joy (*dga' ba, prīti*)

junior tutor to the Dalai Lama (*yongs 'dzin chung ba*)

karma (*las*)

Kashag (*bKa' shag*)

knowledge bearer (*rigs 'dzin, vidya-dhāra*)

knowledge initiation (*shes rab ye shes kyi dbang, prajñā-jñānābhiṣeka*)

knowledge woman (*rig ma, vidyā*)

kṣatriya (*rgyal rigs, kṣatriya*)

la (*bla*)

lama (*bla ma, guru*)

lamdré (*lam 'bras*)

laxity (*bying ba, laya*)

laziness (*le lo, kausīdya*)

learner (*slob pa, śiṣya*)

left channel (*brkyang ma, lalanā*)

level (*sa, bhūmi*)

liberation (*thar pa, mokṣa*)

life-bearing wind (*srog 'dzin kyi rlung*)

life force (*bla*)

life shen (*srid gshen*)

light drop (*'od thig, ābhāsa-bindhu*)

liṅga (*ling ga*)

lords of the soil (*sa bdag*)

Losar (*Lo gsar*)

lotsawa (*lo tsā ba*)

lu (*klu, nāga*)

luminous (*'od byed pa, prabhākarī*); third bodhisattva level

magic shen (*'phrul gshen*)

mahāmudrā (*rgya chen po*)

mahāyoga (*rnal 'byor chen po*)

maṇḍala (*dkyil 'khor*)

manifest (*mngon du gyur pa, abhimukhī*); sixth bodhisattva level

mantra (*sngags*)

mantra adept (*sngags ram pa*)

mantra drop (*sngags thig, mantra-bindu*)

mantra vehicle (*sngags lam, mantra-yāna*)

master of extensive learning (*rab 'byams pa*)

master of the teaching (*bka' chen*)

master of the ten teachings (*bka' bcu pa*)

meditation (*bsgom pa, bhāvanā*)

meditational deity (*yi dam, iṣṭa-devatā*)

meditational maṇḍala (*ting nge 'dzin kyi dkyil 'khor, samādhi-maṇḍala*)

meditative equanimity (*btang snyoms, upekṣā*)

meditative equipoise (*mnyam bzhag, samāhita*)

meditative stabilization (*ting nge 'dzin, samādhi*)

mental abidings, nine (*sems gnas, citta-sthiti*)

mental continuum (*sems rgyud, citta-saṃtāna*)

mental factor (*sems 'byung, caitta*)

mental image (*don spyi, artha-sāmānya*)

mental isolation (*sems dben pa, citta-viveka*)

merit (*bsod nams, puṇya*)

metaphoric clear light (*dpe'i 'od gsal*)

method (*thabs, upāya*)

method continuum (*thabs rgyud*)

Method Vehicle (*Thabs kyi theg pa, Upāya-yāna*)

middle tsen (*bar btsan*)

mind (*sems, citta*)

mind class (*sems sde*)

mind itself (*sems nyid*)

mindful establishments, four (*dran pa nye bar gzhag pa, smṛtyupasthāna*)

mindfulness (*dran pa, smṛti*)

mind of black near-attainment (*nyer thob nag lam pa'i sems*)

mind of clear light (*'od gsal sems, prabhāsvara-citta*)

mind of awakening (*byang chub gyi sems, bodhicitta*)

mind of red increase (*mched pa dmar lam pa'i sems*)

mind of white appearance (*snang ba dkar lam pa'i sems*)

mind-only (*sems tsam, citta-matra*)

mode of being (*gnas lugs*)

mode of subsistence of being (*yin lugs*)

monastery (*dgon pa, araṇya*)

monastic discipline (*'dul ba, vinaya*)

Mongol (*Hor pa*)

mount (*rta, aśva*)

nāga (*klu*)

name and form (*ming gzugs, nāma-rūpa*)

natural maṇḍala (*rang bzhin dkyil 'khor, svabhāva-maṇḍala*),

naturally innate exalted wisdom (*rang bzhin lhan cig skye pa'i ye shes, prakṛti-sahaja-jñāna*)

nature truth body (*ngo bo nyid chos sku, svabhāvika-dharma-kāya*)

near attainment (*nyer thob*)

never returner (*phyir mi 'ong, anāgamin*)

New Schools (*gSar ma*)

ngöndro (*sngon 'gro, pūrvagama*)

Ngorpa (*Ngor pa*)

nirvana (*mya ngan las 'das pa*)

no-self (*bdag med, nairātmya*)

noble truths, four (*'phags pa'i bden pa rnam bzhi, caturāryasatya*)

nonaffirming negative (*med 'gag, prasajya-pratiṣedha*)

nonconceptual (*rtog med, nirvikalpa*)

nongeneration of nonvirtuous phenomena not yet generated (*sdig pa mi dge ba'i chos ma skyes pa rnams mi skyed pa, anutpannākuśala-dharmāropaṇa*)

nonsectarian (*ris med*)

northern treasures (*byang gter*)

novice monk (*dge tshul, śrāmaṇera*)

nun (*dge slong ma, bhikṣuṇī*)

nyen (*gnyan*)

object of negation (*dgag bya, pratiṣedhya*)

object of observation (*dmigs pa, ālambana*)

obstructions to omniscience (*shes sgrib, jñeya-āvaraṇa*)

Offering of the Fifteenth (*bCo lnga mchod pa*)

Old Translation School (*sNga 'gyur*)

once returner (*phyir 'ong, āgāmin*)

one-pointedness (*rtse gcig pa, ekāgra*)

ordinary being (*so so'i skye bo, pṛthagjana*)

pacifying (*zhi bar byed pa, śamana*)

painted canvas maṇḍala (*ras bris kyi dkyil 'khor*)

parinirvāṇa (*yongs su mya ngan las 'das pa*)

path (*lam, mārga*)

path and result (*lam 'bras, mārga-phala*)

path continuum (*lam rgyud*)

path cycles, nine (*lam skor dgu*)

path including its result (*lam 'bras bu dang bcas pa*)

path of accumulation (*tshogs lam, saṃbhāra-mārga*)

path of liberation (*rnam grol lam, vimukti-mārga*)

path of meditation (*sgom lam, bhāvanā-mārga*)

path of no more learning (*mi slob lam, aśaikṣa-mārga*)

path of preparation (*sbyor lam, prayoga-mārga*)

path of seeing (*mthong lam, darśana-mārga*)

patience (*bzod pa, kṣānti*)

patron (*yon bdag*)

peak of cyclic existence (*srid rtse, bhavāgra*)

perfection (*pha rol tu phyin pa, pāramitā*)

perfection of aspiration (*smon lam gyi pha rol tu phyin pa, praṇidhāna-pāramitā*)

perfection of concentration (*bsam gtan gyi pha rol tu phyin pa, dhyāna-pāramitā*)

perfection of effort (*brtson 'grus kyi pha rol tu phyin pa, vīrya-pāramitā*)

perfection of ethics (*tshul khrims kyi pha rol tu phyin pa, śīla-pāramitā*)

perfection of exalted wisdom (*ye shes kyi pha rol tu phyin pa, jñāna-pāramitā*)

perfection of generosity (*sbyin pa'i pha rol tu phyin pa, dāna-pāramitā*)

perfection of patience (*bzod pa'i pha rol tu phyin pa, kṣānti-pāramitā*)

perfection of power (*stobs kyi pha rol tu phyin pa, bala-pāramitā*) perfection of pure awareness (*rig pa tshad phebs*)

perfection of skill in means (*thabs la mkhas pa'i pha rol tu phyin pa, upāya-kauśalya-pāramitā*)

perfection of wisdom (*shes rab kyi pha rol tu phyin pa, prajñāpāramitā*)

perfection vehicle (*phar phyin theg pa, pāramitā-yāna*)

performance tantra (*spyod rgyud, caryā-tantra*)

person (*gang zag, pudgala*)

personal instruction (*gang zag snyan*)

pervasive wind (*khyab byed kyi rlung*)

phenomenon (*chos, dharma*)

physical isolation (*lus dben, kāya-viveka*)

pledge (*dam tshig, samaya*)

pliancy (*shin tu sbyangs pa, praśrabdhi*)

power (*stobs, bala*)

precious abbot emeritus (*mkhan zur rin po che*)

predisposition (*bag chags, vāsanā*)

preliminary practices (*sngon 'gro, pūrvagama*)

presentation of tenets (*grub mtha', siddhānta*)

pride (*nga rgyal, māna*)

priest-patron (*mchod yon*)

primordial buddha (*dang po'i sangs rgyas, ādi-buddha*)

probationers, seven (*sad mi bdun*)

proctor (*dge skos*)

progressively developed (*bskyed rim pa*)

prostration (*phyag 'tshal*)

protector (*chos skyong, dharmapāla*)

pure appearance (*dag pa'i snang ba, śuddhāvabhāsa*)

pure awareness (*rig pa, vidyā*)

pure illusory body (*dag pa'i sgyu lus*)

pure land (*dag zhing, kṣetra-śud-dhi*)

pure vision (*dag snang*)

radiant (*'od 'phro ba can, arciṣmatī*); fourth bodhisattva level

rainbow body (*'ja lus*)

reality bardo (*chos nyid bar do*)

realization (*rtogs pa, prativedha*)

realizational union (*rtogs pa zung 'jug*)

realm (*khams, dhātu*)

red feast (*dmar 'gyed*)

refuge (*skyabs 'gro, śaraṇa-gamana*)

reliances, four (*rton pa bzhi, catvāri pratiśaraṇāni*)

religious kings (*chos rgyal*)

renunciation (*nges 'byung, niḥsaraṇa*)

resetting (*slan te 'jog pa, avasthāpana*)

result (*'bras bu, phala*)

result continuum (*'bras bu rgyud*)

retention (*'dzin pa, dhāraṇa*)

revealed (*bsgrags pa*)

right channel (*rtsa ro ma, rasanā*)

ritual (*bsnyen pa, sevā*)

rogyapa (*ro rgyab pa*)

root downfall (*rtsa ltung, mūlāpatti*)

royal thought (*rgyal ba dgongs*)

sadak (*sa bdag*)

sādhana (*sgrub thabs*)

saṃgha (*dge 'dun*)

saṃsāra (*'khor ba*)

sand maṇḍala (*rdul phran gyi dkyil 'khor*)

Sarma (*gSar ma*)

seal (*phyag rgya, mudrā*)

secondary wind (*yan lag gi rlung*)

second dissemination (*phyi dar*)

secret (*gsang, guhya*)

secret initiation (*gsang dbang, guhyābhiśeka*)

secret instruction class (*man ngag sde*)

secret mantra (*gsang sngags, guhya-mantra*)

secret mantra vehicle (*gsang sngags kyi theg pa, guhya-mantra-yāna*)

secret place (*gsang gnas*)

self (*bdag, ātman*)

self-empowerment (*rang byin brlab*)

self-generation (*bdag bskyed*)

self-grasping (*bdag 'dzin, ātma-grāha*)

senior tutor of the Dalai Lama (*yongs 'dzin che ba*)

sense faculty (*dbang po, indriya*)

sentient being (*sems can, sattva*)

separation from the four attachments (*zhen pa bzhi bral*)

setting in equipoise (*mnyam par 'jog pa, samādhāna*)

setting the mind (*sems 'jog pa, citta-sthāpana*)

sexual union (*sbyor ba*)

Sharpa Chöjé (*Shar pa Chos rje*)

shen (*gshen*)

shenlu (*gshen glu*)

shen of good fortune (*phya gshen*)

skill in means (*thabs la mkhas pa, upāya-kauśalya*)

siddha (*grub thob*)

singleness of thought (*sems gcig, eka-citta*)

signlessness (*mtshan ma med pa, animitta*)

similar in aspect (*rnam pa dang mthun pa, ākāra-bhāgīya*)

sinmo (*srin mo*)

six yogas of Nāropa (*Nā ro chos drug*)

skill in means (*thabs la mkhas pa, upāya-kauśalya*)

sky-goer (*mkha' 'gro ma, ḍākiṇī*)

smokelike appearance (*du ba lta bu'i snang ba*)

solitary realizer (*rang sangs rgyas, pratyeka-buddha*)

spatial class (*klong sde*)

special joy (*khyad par gyi dga' ba, viśeṣānanda*)

spontaneity (*lhun grub, anābhoga*)

stability (*gnas cha*)

staff of office (*'khar, daṇḍa*)

stage of completion (*rdzogs rim, niṣpanna-krama*)

stage of generation (*bskyed rim, utpatti-krama*)

stainless (*dri ma med pa, vimalā*); second bodhisattva level

stream enterer (*rgyun zhugs, śrotāpanna*)

stūpa (*mchod rten*)

subsequent realization (*rjes thob, pṛṣṭa-labdha*)

substance drop (*rdzas thig, dravya-bindu*)

subtle (*phra ba, sūkṣma*)

subtle mind (*phra ba'i sems, sūkṣma-citta*)

subtle wind (*phra ba'i rlung, sūkṣma-prāṇa*)

suchness (*de bzhin nyid, tathatā*)

suffering (*sdug bsngal, duḥkha*)

suffering of change (*'gyur ba'i sdug bsngal, vipariṇāma-duḥkhatā*)

suffering of misery (*sdug bsngal gyi sdug bsngal, duḥkha-duḥkhatā*)

summer offering (*dbyar mchod*)

superior (*'phags pa, ārya*)

supreme joy (*mchog dga', paramananda*)

sūtra (*mdo*)

sūtra vehicle (*mdo'i theg pa, sūtra-yāna*)

swastika bön (*g.yung drung bon*)

symbols of knowledge bearers (*rig 'dzin brda*)

tantra (*rgyud*)

tantric empowerment (*dbang skur, abhiṣeka*)

tantric feast (*tshogs 'khor, gaṇacakra*)

tathāgata (*de bzhin gshegs pa*)

teaching tradition of Durjayacandra (*Grub chen mi thub zla ba'i bshad srol*)

teaching tradition of the Kashmiri Kīrtibhadra (*Kha che sNyan grags bzang po'i bshad srol*) teaching tradition of Maitripa (*mNga' bdag Me tri pa'i bshad srol*)

teaching tradition of Padmavajra (*sLob dpon Pad ma ba dzra'i bshad srol*)

teaching tradition of Śāntabhadra (*Śān to bha dra'i bshad srol*)

teaching tradition of Śāntipa (*Śān ti pa'i bshad srol*)

teachings, four (*bka' bzhi pa*)

teachings, ten (*bka' bcu*)

temple (*lha khang*)

tenet system (*grub mtha', siddhānta*)

terma (*gter ma*)

tertön (*gter ston*)

textbook (*yig cha*)

thing (*dngos po, bhāva*)

thorough abandonings, four (*yang dag par spong ba, saṃyak-prahāṇa*)

thorough pacifying (*nye bar zhi bar byed pa, vyupaśamana*)

thought treasures (*dgongs gter*)

throne holder of Ganden (*dGa' ldan khri pa*)

Tibetan New Year (*Lo gsar*)

time (*dus, kāla*)

time-lock formula (*gtsug las khan*)

torma (*gtor ma*)

transference of consciousness (*'pho ba, saṃkrama*)

translator (*lo tsā ba*)

trangsong (*drang srong, ṛṣi*)

treasures, five (*mdzod lnga*)

trio of guru, great perfection, and the great compassionate one (*bla rdzogs thugs gsum*)

trio of sūtra, magical net, and mind class (*mdo sgyu sems gsum*)

truth (*bden pa, satya*)

truth body (*chos sku, dharmakāya*)

truth of suffering (*sdug bsngal bden pa, duḥkha-satya*)

truth of the cessation of suffering (*'gog bden pa, nirodha-satya*)

truth of the origin of suffering (*kun 'byung bden pa, samudaya-satya*)

truth of the path (*lam bden pa, mārga-satya*

ultimate (*don dam pa, paramārtha*)

ultimate mind of awakening (*don dam byang chub kyi sems, paramārtha-bodhicitta*)

ultimate truth (*don dam bden pa, paramārtha-satya*)

uncommon preliminaries (*mthun mong ma yin pa'i sngon 'gro*)

uninterrupted path (*bar chad med lam, ānantarya-mārga*)

union (*zung 'jug, yuganaddha*)

union of abandonment (*spangs pa zung 'jug*)

union of appearance and emptiness (*snang stong zung 'jug*)

union of calm abiding and higher insight (*zhi gnas dang lhag mthong gi zung 'brel, śamatha-vipaśyanā-yuganaddha*)

union of no more learning (*mi slob pa'i zung 'jug, aśaikṣa-yuganaddha*)

universal monarch (*'khor los bsgyur ba'i rgyal po, cakravartin*)

unusual attitude (*lhag pa'i bsam pa, adhyāśaya*)

upper gods (*steng lha*)

upward-moving wind (*gyen rgyu'i rlung*)

vagina (*bha ga, bhaga*)

vajra (*rdo rje*)

vajra body (*rdo rje sku, vajra-kāya*)

vajra recitation (*rdo rje bzlas pa, vajra-jāpa*)

vajra repetition (*rdo rje bzlas pa, vajra-jāpa*)

vajra vehicle (*rdo rje theg pa, vajra-yāna*)

vajra-like concentration (*rdo rje lta bu'i ting nge 'dzin, vajropama-samādhi*)

vase initiation (*bum dbang, kalaśābhiṣeka*)

vehicle (*theg pa, yāna*)

very joyous (*rab tu dga' ba, pra-muditā*); first bodhisattva level

very subtle mind (*shin tu phra ba'i sems*)

very subtle wind (*shin tu phra ba'i rlung*)

vinaya (*'dul ba*)

virtuous shen (*dge gshen*)

vitalizing wind (*srog 'dzin kyi rlung*)

vow (*sdom pa, saṃvara*)

wheel of doctrine (*chos kyi 'khor lo, dharma-cakra*)

white feast (*dkar 'gyed*)

wind (*rlung, prāṇa*)

wind yoga (*srog rtsol, prāṇāyāma*)

wisdom (*shes rab, prajñā*)

wisdom being (*ye shes sems pa, jñāna-sattva*)

wisdom initiation (*shes rab ye shes kyi dbang, prajñā-jñānābhiṣeka*)

wisdom seal (*ye shes kyi phyag rgya, jñāna-mudrā*)

wisdom truth body (*ye shes chos sku, jñāna-dharmakāya*)

withdrawal (*sor 'dus, pratyāhāra*)

womb of the *tathāgata* (*de bzhin gzhegs pa'i snying po, tathāgata-garbha*)

word initiation (*tshig dbang*)

world class (*'jig rten, loka*)

wrong consciousness (*log shes, mithyā-jñāna*)

yellow parchment (*shog ser tshigs*)

yoga (*rnal 'byor*)

yoga tantra (*rnal 'byor rgyud*)

yogic practice (*rnal 'byor spyod pa, yogācāra*)

yogi (*rnal 'byor pa*)

yoginī (*rnal 'byor ma*)

yoklu (*g.yog klu*)

Proper Names

Ajātaśatru (*Ma skyes dgra*)

Akṣobhya (*Mi bskyod pa*)

Amaravajradevī (*gSer chos 'chi med rdo rje lha mo*)

Amitābha (*'Od dpag med*)

Amitāyus (*Tshe dpag med*)

Amoghasiddhi (*Don yod grub pa*)

Ānanda (*Kun dga' bo*)

Ānandagarbha (*Kun dga' snying po*)

Ārāḍa Kālāma (*Ring 'phur*)

Āryadeva (*'Phags pa'i lha*)

Asaṅga (*Thogs med*)

Aśoka (*Chos rgyal Mya ngan med*)

Aśvaghoṣa (*rTa dbyangs*)

Atiśa [Dīpaṃkara Śrījñāna](*Jo bo rje*)

Avadhūtipa (*A ba dhu ti pa*)

Avalokiteśvara (*sPyan ras gzigs*)

Bagor Bairotsana (*Pa gor Bai ro tsa na*)

Baram Kagyu (*'Ba' ram bKa' rgyud*)

Baso Chögi Gyeltsen (*Ba so Chos kyi rGyal mtshan*)

Bé Jambel (*dBas 'Jams dpal*)

Belchen Kékhö (*dPal chen Ge khod*)

Belden Yéshé (*dPal ldan Ye shes*), Panchen Lama III

Belgyi Dorjé (*dPal gyi rDo rje*)

Belsa (*Bal bza'*)

Beltsek (*dPal brtsegs*)

Bé Ratna (*sBas Ratna*)

Bhaiṣajyaguru (*sMan gyi bla ma*)

Bhṛkutī (*Khro gnyer can ma*)

Bimbisāra (*gZugs can snying po*)

Bodhimitra (*Byang chub grogs po*)

Bön (*Bon*)

Brahmadatta (*Tshangs pas sbyin*)

Buddhaguhya (*Sangs rgyas gsang ba*)

Cakrasaṃvara (*'Khor lo bde mchog*)

Candrakīrti (*Zla ba grags pa*)

Channa (*'Dun pa*)

Chim Shakya Trawa (*mChims Sha kya Pra ba*)

Chöbar (*Chos 'bar*)

Chögi Lodrö (*Chos kyi bLo gros*) of Mar (*Mar pa*)

Chögi Wangchuk (*Chos kyi dBang phyug*)

Chögyel Pakpa (*Chos rgyal 'Phags pa*)

Chogyur Déchen (*mChog gyur bDe chen*)

Chöjé Töndrup Rinchen (*Chos rje Don grub Rin chen*)

Chokro Lügyeltsen (*Cog ro kLu'i rgyal mtshan*)

Chucham (*Chu lcam*)

Consequence School (*Thal 'gyur pa, Prāsaṅgika*)

Cunda (*sKul bye*)

Dakchen Lodrö Gyeltsen (*bDag chen bLo gros rGyal mtshan*)

Daktsépa (*sTag rtse pa*)

Dampa Déshek Shérap Senggé (*Dam pa bDe gshegs Shes rab Seng ge*)

Dānaśīla (*Dā na shi la*)

Daṇḍapāṇi (*Lag na be con*)

Dar (*'Dar*)

Darma Dodé (*Dar ma mDo sde*)

Darma Wangchuk (*Dar ma dBang phyug*)

Dédruk Khenchen Ngawang Rapden (*sDe drug mKhan chen Ngag dbang Rab brtan*)

Dharmabodhi (*Dhar ma bo dhi*)

Dharmakīrti (*Chos kyi grags pa*)

Dharmapāla (*Chos skyong*)

Doktséwa (*Tog rtse ba*)

Ḍombī Heruka (*Ḍombi He ru ka*)

Dongga (*gDong dga'*)

Dönpa Shenrap (*sTon pa gShen rab*)

Dorjé Chang (*rDo rje 'chang, Vajradhara*)

Dorjé Chörap (*rDo rje chos rab*)

Dorjé Drak (*rDo rje brag*)

Dorjé Gyelpo (*rDo rje rgyal po*)

Draba Ngönshé (*Gra ba mNgon shes*)

Dradi Géshé Rinchen Döndrup (*Bra sti dGe bshes Rin chen Don grub*)

Drakpa Gyeltsen (*Grags pa rGyal mtshan*)

Drenka mukti (*Bran ka Mukti*)

Drigum Tsenpo (*Gri gum bTsan po*)

Drikung Kagyu (*'Bri gung bKa' brgyud*)

Drobukpa (*sGro sbug pa*)

Drogön (*'Gro mgon*)

Drokmi (*'Brog mi Lo tsā Shākya Ye shes*)

Dromdön (*'Brom ston pa rGyal ba'i 'byung gnas*)

Druchen Yungdrung Lama (*Bru chen g.Yung drung bLa ma*)

Drukpa Kagyu (*'Brug pa bKa' brgyud*)

Dudjom Rinpoche (*bDud 'joms Rin po che*)

Durjayacandra (*Grub chen Mi thub zla ba*)

Düsong (*Dus srong*)

Dzogchen Péma Lingpa (*rDzogs chen Padma gLing pa*)

Gadong oracle (*dGa' gdong chos skyong*)

Gampopa (*sGam po pa*)

Gaṇapati (*Tshog bdag*)

Gangchen (*Kang chen*)

Garap Dorjé (*dGa' rab rDo rje, Surativajra*)

Garbhasuvarnasūtraśrī (*dPal mo sNying gi gser thag*)

Gawa Beltsek (*sKa ba dPal brtsegs*)

Gayadhara (*Ga ya dha ra*)

Gélukpa (*dGe lugs pa*)

Gendün Druba (*dGe 'dun Grub pa*), Dalai Lama I

Gendün Gyatso (*dGe 'dun rGya mtsho*), Dalai Lama II

Ghaṇṭāpāda (*Dril pu pa*)

Gö Khukpa Hlétsé (*'Gos Khug pa Lhas btsas*)

Gompo Namgyel (*mGon po rnam rgyal*)

Gönchok Gyelpo (*dKon mchog rGyal po*)

Gönchok Jikmé Ongpo (*dKon mchogs 'Jigs med dBang po*)

Gongchu (*Kong chu*)

Gongjo (*Kong jo*)

Gongpo (*Kong po*)

Gopā (*Sa 'tsho ma*)

Gorampa Sönam Senggé (*Go ram pa bSod rnams Seng ge*)

Great Exposition School (*Bye brag tu smra ba, Vaibhāṣika*)

Great Miracle (*Cho 'phrul chen mo*)

Great Vehicle (*Theg pa chen po, Mahāyāna*)

Guhyasamāja (*gSang ba 'dus pa*)

Guṇaprabha (*Yon tan 'od*)

Guṇeru (*Gu ne ru*)

Günga Gyeltsen Bel Sangpo (*Kun dga' rGyal mtshan dPal bZang po*)

Günga Nyingpo (*Kun dga' sNying po*)

Güntu Sangmo (*Kun tu bZang mo, Samtabhadrī*)

Güntu Sangpo (*Kun tu bZang po, Samantabhadra*)

Gyasa (*rGya bza'*)

Gyeltsap Darma Rinchen (*rGyal tshab Dar ma Rin chen*)

Gyelwa Karmapa (*rGyal dbang Kar ma pa*)

Gyodön Sönam Lama (*sKyo ston bSod nams bLa ma*)

Hashang Mahāyāna (*Hwa shang Ma ha ya na*; Chinese: *Heshang Moheyan*)

Hayagrīva (*rTa mgrin*)

Heruka (*Khrag thung*)

Heruka Cakrasaṃvara (*Khrag thung 'Khor lo bde mchog*)

Hevajra (*Kye rdo rje*)

Hīnayāna (*Theg pa dman pa*)

Hinudevī (*Lha mo hi nu*)

Hla Rik (*Lha rigs*)

Hlasang (*Lha bzang*)

Hūṃkāra (*Hūṃ mdzad*)

Indrabhūti (*Indra bhu ti*)

Indrabodhi (*rGyal po rā dza*)

Indrasena (*dBang po'i sde*)

Jambel Gyatso (*'Jam dpal rGya mtsho*), Dalai Lama VIII

Jambel Shé Nyen (*'Jam dpal bShes gnyen, Mañjuśrīmitra*)

Jamgön Kongtrül (*'Jam mgon Kong sprul bLo gros mTha' yas*)

Jamyang Gyeltsen (*'Jam dbyangs rGyal mtshan*)

Jamyang Kyentsé Ongpo (*'Jam dbyangs mKhyen brtse dBang po*)

Jamyang Khyentsé Wangchuk (*'Jam dbyangs mKhyen brtse'i dBang phyug*)

Jamyang Shéba (*'Jam dbyangs bZhad pa*)

Jangchup Gyeltsen (*Byang chub rGyal mtshan*)

Jangchup Ö (*Byang chub 'Od*)

Jang Gya (*lCang skya*)

Jetāri (*Dze ta ri*)

Jétsun Drakpa Gyeltsen (*rJe btsun Grags pa rGyal mtshan*)

Jétsunpa Chögi Gyeltsen (*rJe btsun pa Chos kyi rGyal mtshan*)

Jikmé Lingpa (*'Jigs med gLing pa*)

Jinamitra (*Dzi na mi tra*)

Jñānapāda (*Ye shes rkang pa*)

Jñānasūtra (*Ye shes mdo*)

Jñānendra (*Dznya na indra*)

Jomden Rikpé Sangyé (*bCom ldan Rigs pa'i Sangs rgyas*)

Jonangpa (*Jo nang pa*)

Jowo Rinpoché (*Jo bo Rin po che*)

Kadampa (*bKa' gdams pa*)

Kagyu (*bKa' brgyud*)

Kānha (*Nag po pa*)

Kālacakra (*Dus kyi 'khor lo*)

Kamalaśīla (*Ka ma la shi la*)

Kāmarāja (*'Dod rgyal*)

Kāṇha (*Ka ṇha*)

Karma Kagyu (*Karma bKa' brgyud*)

Karma Lingpa (*Kar ma gLing pa*)

Karmapa (*Karma pa*)

Katok Rigzin Tséwang Norbu (*Kaḥ thog Rigs 'dzin Tshe dbang Nor bu*)

Kauṇḍinya (*Kau ṇḍi nya*)

Kédrup Jé (*mKhas grub rJe*)

Kédrup Gyatso (*mKhas grub rGya mtsho*), Dalai Lama XI

Kékö (*Ge khod*)

Kelsang Gyatso (*bsKal bzang rGya mtsho*), Dalai Lama VII

Khön (*'Khon*)

Khön Bargyé (*'Khon Bar skyes*)

Khön Lüwangpo (*'Khon kLu'i dbang po*)

Khön Nāgarakṣita (*'Khon Nāgarakṣita*)

Kīrtibhadra (*sNyan grags bzang po*)

Kṛṣṇacārin (*Nag po spyod pa*)

Kṣāntivādin (*bZod pa smra ba*)

Küngtang (*Gung thang*)

Kurukullā (*Rig byed ma*)

Kutsang Rinpoché (*Ke'u tshang Rin po che*)

Kyungpo Nenjor (*Khyung po rNal 'byor*)

Lalitavajra (*Rol pa'i rdo rje*)

Lang (*rLangs*)

Lang Darma (*gLang Dar ma*)

Lekbé Shérap (*Legs pa'i Shes rab*)

Lha Totori Nyentsen (*Lha Tho tho ri gNyan btsan*)

Licchavi (*Li tsā bi*)

Līlavajra (*sGeg pa'i rdo rje*)

Lion of the Śākya (*Sa kya Seng ge*)

Lobön Sönam Tsémo (*sLob dpon bSod nams rTse mo*)

Lokakṣema (*'Jig rten bde ba*)

Lokeśvara (*'Jig rten dbang phyug*)

Longchen Rapjampa (*kLong chen Rab 'byams pa*)

Losang Belden Denbé Nyima (*bLo bzang dPal ldan bsTan pa'i Nyi ma*), Panchen Lama IV

Losang Tséwang (*bLo bzang Tshe dbang*)

Lūhipāda (*Lū'i pa*)

Lungdok Gyatso (*Lung rtogs rGya mtsho*), Dalai Lama IX

Machik Lapdrön (*Ma gcig Lab sgron*)

Madhyamaka (*dBu ma*)

Mahākāla (*Nag po chen po*)

Mahākāśyapa (*'Od srung chen po*)

Mahālakṣmī (*dPal lam shis pa chen*)

Mahāyāna (*Theg pa chen po*)

Maitreya (*Byams pa*)

Maitripa (*Me tri pa*)

Mandāravā (*Mandā ra bā*)

Mañjuśrī (*'Jam dpal*)

Mañjuśrīmitra (*'Jam dpal bshes gnyen*)

Māra (*bDud*)

Māratikā (*Ma ra ti ka*)

Ma Rinchen Chok (*rMa Rin chen mchog*)

Mar Kagyu (*dMar bKa' rgyud*)

Marpa (*Mar pa*)

Mayādevī (*sGyu 'phrul lha mo*)

Middle Way Consequence School (*dBu ma thal 'gyur pa, Prāsaṅgika-madhyamaka*)

Middle Way School (*dBu ma, Madhyamaka*)

Milarépa (*Mi la ras pa*)

Mind Only School (*Sems tsam pa, Citta-mātra*)

Mipam Gyatso (*Mi pham rGya mtsho*)

Mönlam Chenmo (*sMon lam Chen mo*)

Muchen Gönchok Gyeltsen (*Mus chen dKon mchog rGyal mtshan*)

Mūla-Sarvāstivāda (*gZhi thams cad yod par smra ba*)

Nāgārjuna (*kLu sgrub*)

Nāgeśvara (*kLu'i dbang phyug*)

Nairātmyā (*bDag med ma*)

Nakpo Utsita Chiwa Mépa (*Nag po U tsi ṭa 'Chi ba Med pa, Uciṭāmara*)

Nāropa (*Na ro pa, Naḍapāda*)

Néchung oracle (*gNas chung chos skyong*)

Nésar Jamyang Kyentsé Wangchuk (*gNas gsar 'Jam dbyangs mKhyen brtse'i dBang phyug*)

New Kadampa (*bKa' gdams gsar ma*)

Ngakchang Günga Rinchen (*sNgags 'chang Kun dga' Rin chen*)

Ngawang Belden (*Ngag dbang dPal ldan*)

Ngawang Losang Gyatso (*Ngag dbang bLo bzang rGya mtsho*), Dalai Lama V

Ngawang Yéshé Gyatso (*Ngag dbang Ye shes rGya mtsho*)

Ngenlam Gyelwa Chokyang (*Ngan lam rGyal ba mChog dbyangs*)

Ngödrup Drakpa (*dNgos grub Grags pa*)

Ngorchen Gönchok Hlündrup (*Ngor chen dKon mchog Lhun grub*)

Ngorchen Günga Sangpo (*Ngor chen Kun dga' bZang po*)

Niguma (*Ni gu ma*)

Nup Sangyé Yéshé (*gNubs Sangs rgyas Ye shes*)

Nyak Jñanākumara (*gNyags Jñānakumāra*)

Nyang Rel Nyima Öser (*Nyang ral Nyi ma 'Od zer*)

Nyarong Chikhyab (*Nyag rong sPyi khyab*)

Nyatri Tsenpo (*gNya' khri bTsan po*)

Nyel (*gNyal*)

Nyelwa Nakpo (*Myal ba Nag po*)

Nyima Drakpa (*Nyi ma Grags pa*)

Nyingma (*rNying ma*)

Orgyen Terdak Lingpa (*O rgyan gTer bdag gLing pa*)

Öserden (*'Od zer ldan*)

Pabongka (*Pha bong kha*)

Padampa Sangyé (*Pha dam pa Sangs rgyas*)

Padmasambhava (*Pad ma 'byung gnas*)

Padmavajra (*Padma ba dzra*)

Pakmodrupa (*Phag mo gru pa*)

Pakmodrupa Dorjé Gyelpo (*Phag mo gru pa rDo rje rGyal po*)

Pakmo Kagyu (*Phag mo bKa' brgyud*)

Pakpa (*'Phags pa*)

Panchen Lama (*Paṇ chen bla ma*)

Patrul Rinpoché (*dPal sprul Rin po che*)

Péma Lingpa (*Padma gLing pa*)

Péma Ösel Dongak Lingpa (*Padma 'Od gsal mDo sngags gLing pa*)

Pohla (*Pho lha*)

Prabhāhasti (*Pra bha ha sti*)

Prajāpatī (*sKye dgu'i bdag mo*)

Prajñā (*Shes rab*)

Prāṇasādhana (*Dzam dmar srog sgrub*)

Prasenajit (*gSal rgyal*)

Pudön (*Bu ston*)

Rāhula (*sGra gcan 'dzin*)

Rakṣitapāda (*bSrung ba'i zhabs*)

Rapjampa (*Rab 'byams pa*)

Ratna Lingpa (*Ratna gLing pa*)

Ratnasambhava (*Rin chen 'byung gnas*)

Réchungpa Dorjé Drakpa (*Ras chung pa rDo rje Grags pa*)

Relbachen (*Ral pa can*)

Rendawa (*Red mda' ba*)

Réting Rinpoché Jambel Yéshé (*Rva sgreng Rin po che 'Jam dpal Ye shes*)

Rikdzin Gödem (*Rig 'dzin rGod ldem*)

Rikdzin Ngagi Ongpo (*Rig 'dzin Ngag gi dbang po*)

Rinchen Sangpo (*Rin chen bZang po*)

Rolbé Dorjé (*Rol pa'i rDo rje*), Karmapa IV

Śabalagaruḍa (*Khyung khra*)

Sachen Günga Nyingpo (*Sa chen Kun dga' sNying po*)

Śākya (*Śā kya*)

Śākyamitra (*Śā kya bshes gnyen*)

Śākyamuni (*Śā kya thub pa*)

Sakya Paṇḍita Günga Gyeltsen Bel Sangpo (*Sa skya Paṇḍita Kun dga' rGyal mtshan dPal bzang po*)

Sakya Senggé (*Sa kya Seng ge*)

Śākyaśrībhadra (*Śā kya shri bha dra*)

Sakya Trizin (*Sa skya Khri 'dzin*)

Sakya Trizin Ngawang Günga (*Sa skya Khri 'dzin Ngag dbang Kun dga'*)

Samantabhadra (*Kun tu bzang po*)

Samantabhadrī (*Kun tu bzang mo*)

Sangyé Gyatso (*Sangs rgyas rGya mtsho*)

Sangyé Lama (*Sangs rgyas bLa ma*)

Sangyé Lingpa (*Sangs rgyas gLing pa*)

Śāntabhadra (*Śān ta bha dra*)

Śāntarakṣita (*Zhi ba 'tsho*)

Śāntideva (*Zhi ba lha*)

Śāntipa (*Śān ti pa*)

Saraha (*Sa ra ha*)

Śāriputra (*Sha ri'i bu*)

Saroruhavajra (*mTsho skye rdo rje*)

Sarvārthasiddha (*Don thams cad grub pa*)

Śavari (*Śā ba ri*)

Sékhar Chungwa (*Se mkhar Chung ba*)

Sénalek (*Sad na legs*)

Shakya Chokden (*Śā kya mchog ldan*)

Shangdön Chöbar (*Zhang ston Chos 'bar*)

Shangpa Kagyu (*Shangs pa bKa' brgyud*)

Shangpo (*Shangs po*)

Shang Tselpa (*Shangs mTshal pa*)

Shenrap (*gShen rab*)

Shérap Tsültrim (*Shes rab Tshul khrims*)

Shikpo Lingpa (*Zhig po gLing pa*)

Shudön Dorjé Gyap (*Zhu ston rDo rje skyabs*)

Shuksep Kagyu (*Shug seb bKa' rgyud*)

Siddhārtha Gautama (*Don grub Gau ta ma*)

Śīlendrabodhi (*Shi lendra bo dhi*)

Siṃhanāda (*Seng ge sgra*)

Siṃhavaktrā (*Seng ge gdong ma*)

Sönam Gyatso (*bSod nams rGya mtsho*), Dalai Lama III

Songtsen Gampo (*Srong btsan sGam po*)

So Yéshé Wangchuk (*So Ye shes dBang phyug*)

Śrī Siṃha (*Shri sing ha*)

Subhūti (*Rab 'byor*)

Śuddhodana (*Zas gtsang ma*)

Sumatikīrti (*bZang po'i blos gros grags pa*)

Sumpa Khenpo (*Sum pa mkhan po*)

Surativajra (*dGa' rab rdo rje*)

Surchung (*Zur chung*)

Surendrabodhi (*Su rendra bodhi*)

Surpoché (*Zur po che*)

Sūtra School (*mDo sde pa, Sautrāntika*)

Śvetaketu (*Dam pa tog dkar*)

Sugataśrī (*bDe gshegs dpal ldan*)

Taklung Kagyu (*sTag lung bKa' brgyud*)

Tangla (*Thang la*)

Tārā (*sGrol ma*)

Tarpa Lotsawa (*Thar pa Lo tsā ba*)

Tarthang Tulku (*Dar thang sPrul sku*)

Tenzin Gyatso (*bsTan 'dzin rGya mtsho*), Dalai Lama XIV

Terdak Lingpa (*gTer bdag gLing pa*)

Tilottamā (*Thig le mchog ma*)

Tönmi Sambhota (*Thon mi Sam bho ṭa*)

Töpa Bhadra (*Thod pa Bhadra*)

Totori Nyentsen (*Tho tho ri gNyan btsan*)

Tötreng (*Thod phreng*)

Translations of Teachings (*bKa' 'gyur*)

Translations of Treatises (*bsTan 'gyur*)

Tri Détsuktsen (*Khri lDe gtsug btsan*)

Trinlé Gyatso (*'Phrin las rGya mtsho*), Dalai Lama XII

Tri Songdétsen (*Khri Srong lde btsan*)

Tritsun (*Khri btsun*)

Tröma (*Khros ma*)

Tropu Kagyu (*Khro phu bKa' rgyud*)

Trülnang (*'Phrul snang*)

Tsang Lekdrup (*gTsang Legs grub*)

Tsangyang Gyatso (*Tshangs dbyangs rGya mtsho*), Dalai Lama VI

Tsarchen Losel Gyatso (*Tshar chen bLo gsal rGya mtsho*)

Tsarpa (*Tshar pa*)

Tselpa Kagyu (*mTshal pa bKa' brgyud*)

Tsenpo Khoré (*bTsan po 'Khor re*)

Tsong Khapa Losang Drakpa (*Tsong kha pa bLo bzang Grags pa*)

Tsultrim Gyatso (*Tshul khrims rGya mtsho*), Dalai Lama X

Tsur Shönnu Senggé (*mTshur gZhon nu Seng ge*)

Tugen Losang Chögi Nyima (*Thu'u bkwan bLo bzang Chos kyi nyi ma*)

Tupden Gyatso (*Thub bstan rGya mtsho*), Dalai Lama XIII

Tüsum Khyenpa (*Dus gsum mKhyen pa*)

Udraka Rāmaputra (*Rangs byed kyi bu lhag spyod*)

Upāli (*Nye bar 'khor*)

Vāgīśvarakīrti (*Ngag dbang grags pa*)

Vairocana (*rNam par snags mdzad, Bai ro tsa na*)

Vajradhara (*rDo rje 'chang*)

Vajrakīla (*rDo rje phur pa*)

Vajrapāṇi (*Phyag na rdo rje*)

Vajrasattva (*rDo rje sems dpa'*)

Vajravārāhī (*rDo rje phag mo*)

Vajrayoginī (*rDo rje rnal 'byor ma*)

Vasubandhu (*dByig gnyen*)

Vasudhara (*Ba su dha ra*)

Vasudharā (*Nor rgyun ma*)

Vimalamitra (*Dri med bshes gnyen*)

Virūpa (*Bi rū pa*)

Werma (*Wer ma*)

White Tārā (*sGrol dkar*)

White Yak of Being (*Srid kyi g.yag po dkar po*)

Yamāntaka (*gShin rje gshed*)

Yamāri (*gShin rje*)

Yamsang Kagyu (*g.Ya' bzang bKa' rgyud*)

Yangdak Gyelpo (*Yang dag rGyal po*)

Yaśodharā (*Grags 'dzin ma*)

Yerpa Kagyu (*Yer pa bKa' rgyud*)

Yeshe Dönden (*Ye shes Don ldan*)

Yéshédé (*Ye shes sde*)

Yéshédo (*Ye shes mdo, Jñānasūtra*)

Yéshé Ö (*Ye shes 'od*)

Yéshé Tsogyel (*Ye shes mTsho rgyal*)

Yönden Gyatso (*Yon tan rGya mtsho*), Dalai Lama IV

Titles of Works Mentioned

Ascertainment of Valid Cognition (*Tshad ma rnam par nges pa, Pramāṇa-viniścaya*), by Dharmakīrti

Associated Collection (*Saṃyuktāgama*; Pāli: *Saṃyutta-nikāya*)

Beyond Thought (*bSam mi khyab*), by Doktséwa (*Tog rtse ba*)

Blue Annals (*Deb ther sngnon po*), by Gö Lotsawa (*'Gos lo tsā ba*)

Cakrasaṃvara Tantra (*'Khor lo bde mchog rgyu*)

Collection Sūtra (*'Dus pa'i mdo*)

Compendium of Abhidharma (*Chos mngon pa kun btus, Abhidharma-samuccaya*), by Asaṅga

Compendium of All Knowledge (*Shes bya kun khyab*) by Jamgön Kongtrül

Compendium of Mahāyāna (*Theg pa chen po bsdus pa, Mahāyāna-saṃgraha*), by Asaṅga

Compendium of the Truth of All Tathāgatas (*De bzhin gshegs pa thams cad kyi de kho na nyid bsdus pa'i mdo, Sarva-thatāgata-tattva-saṃgraha*)

Compendium of Valid Cognition (*Tshad ma kun las btus pa, Pramāṇa-samuccaya*), by Dignāga

Commentary on the Compendium of Valid Cognition (*Tshad ma rnam 'grel gyi tshig le'ur byas pa, Pramāṇavārttika*), by Dharmakīrti

Complete Path of the Great Seal (*Phyag rgya chen po'i lam yongs su rdzogs pa*), by Indrabodhi

Diamond Sūtra (*rDo rje gcod pa'i mdo, Vajracchedikā-sūtra*)

Differentiation of the Middle Way and the Extremes (*dBu dang mtha' rnam par 'byed pa, Madhyānta-vibhāga*), by Vasubandhu

Differentiation of Phenomena and the Nature of Phenomena (*Chos dang chos nyid rnam par 'byed pa, Dharma-dharmatā-vibhāga*), by Vasubandhu

Differentiation of the Three Vows (*sDom gsum rab dbye*), by Sakya Paṇḍita (*Sa skya Paṇḍita*)

Entry Into the Bodhisattva Deeds (*Byang chub sems dpa'i spyod pa la 'jug pa, Bodhicaryāvatāra*), by Śāntideva

Entry Into the Middle Way (*dBu ma la 'jug pa, Madhyamakāvatāra*), by Candrakīrti

Enumerated Collection (*Ekottara-āgama*; Pāli: *Aṅguttara-nikāya*)

Essence of the Good Explanations, Treatise Differentiating the Interpretable and the Definitive (*Drang ba dang nges pa'i don rnam par phye ba'i bstan bcos legs bshad snying po*), by Tsong Khapa (*Tsong kha pa*)

Essential Drop of Wisdom Tantra (*rGyud ye shes thig le, Jñānatilaka-tantra*)

Extensive Sport Sūtra (*rGya cher rol pa'i mdo, Lalitavistara-sūtra*)

Fifty Stanzas on the Guru (*bLa ma lnga bcu pa, Gurupañcaśikā*), by Aśvaghoṣa

Flame Point of the Completion Stage (*rDzogs rim mar me'i rtse lta bu'i lam skor*), by Saroruhavajra

Fourfold Innermost Essence (*sNying thig ya bzhi*)

Four Hundred (*bsTan bcos bzhi brgya pa, Catuḥśataka*), by Āryadeva

Four Interwoven Commentaries on the Great Exposition of the Stages of the Path (*Lam rim mchan bzhi sbrags ma*) with the commentaries of Ba so Chos kyi rgyal mtshan, Sde drug mKhan chen, Ngag dbang Rab brtan, 'Jam dbyangs bzhad pa'i rdo rje, and Bra sti dge bshes Rin chen don grub

Fundamental Tantra of the Two Examinations (*rTsa rgyud brtag gnyis*)

Golden Rosary of the Good Explanations (*Legs bshad gser pheng*), by Tsong Khapa

Golden Tortoise (*gSer gyi rus sbal*), Bon po *gter ma* discovered by Ngödrup Drakpa (*dNgos grub Grags pa*)

Great Chronicle (*Mahāvastu*)

Great Exposition of Secret Mantra (*sNgags rim chen mo*), by Tsong Khapa

Great Exposition of Tenets (*Grub mtha' chen mo*), by Jamyang Shéba (*'Jam dbyangs bZhad pa*)

Great Exposition of the Stages of the Path (*Lam rim chen mo*), by Tsong Khapa

Great Jeweled Wishing Tree (*Rin po che'i ljon shing chen mo*)

Great Seal (*Phyag rgya chen po, Mahamudra*), by Vāgīśvarakīrti

Guhyamūlagarbha-tantra (*sGyu 'phrul gsang ba snying po'i rgyud*)

Guhyasamāja-tantra (*gSang ba 'dus pa'i rgyud*)

Heart Essence of Longchenpa (*kLong chen snying thig*)

Hevajra-tantra (*Kye rdo rje rgyud*)

History of Buddhism (*Chos 'byung*) by Pudön (*Bu ston*)

Illumination of the Thought, Extensive Explanation of [Candrakīrti's] 'Entry into the Middle Way' (*dBu ma la 'jug pa'i rgya cher bshad pa dgongs pa rab gsal*), by Tsong Khapa

Innermost Essence of the Great Expanse (*kLong chen snying thig*)

Instructions on Straightening the Crooked (*Yon po srong ba'i gdams ngag*), by Uciṭāmara

Kālacakra-tantra (*Dus kyi 'khor lo rgyud*)

Kiss Tantra (*rGyud kha sbyor*)

Lalitavistara-sūtra (*rGya cher rol pa'i mdo*)

Lamp for the Path to Awakening (*Byang chub lam gyi sgron ma, Bodhipathapradīpa*), by Atiśa

Lengthy Collection (*Dīrghāgama*; Pāli: *Dīgha-nikaya*)

Lives of the Eighty-Four Adepts (*Caturśīti-siddha-pravṛtti*)

Magical Net (*sGyu 'phrul drwa ba*)

Middle Length Collection (*Madhyama-āgama*; Pāli: *Majjhima-nikāya*)

Nine Profound Methods of the Generation Stage (*bsKyed rim zab pa'i tshul dgu*), by Saroruhavajra

Official Edict (*bKa' shog*)

Olapati, by Kṛṣṇacārin

Ornament for Clear Realizations (*mNgon par rtogs pa'i rgyan, Abhisamayālaṃkāra*), by Maitreya

Ornament for the Mahāyāna Sūtras (*Theg pa chen po'i mdo sde'i rgyan, Mahāyāna-sūtrālaṃkāra*), by Maitreya

Perfection of Wisdom in 8,000 Lines (*'Phags pa shes rab kyi pha rol tu phyin pa brgyad stong pa'i mdo, Aṣṭasāhasrikā-prajñāpāramitāsūtra*)

Precious Appearance of the Inseparability of Cyclic Existence and Nirvāṇa, The Essential View of All Tantras (*rGyud thams cad kyi snying po lta ba 'khor 'das dbyer med rin po che snang ba*)

Precious Garland (*Rin po che'i phreng ba, Ratnāvalī*), by Nāgārjuna

Precious Garland of Tenets (*Grub pa'i mtha'i rnam par bzhag pa rin po che'i phreng ba*), by Gönchok Jikmé Ongpo (*dKon mchog 'Jigs med dBang po*)

Presentation of the Grounds and Paths, Beautiful Ornament of the Three Vehicles (*Sa lam gyi rnam bzhag theg gsum mdzes rgyan*), by Gönchok Jikmé Ongpo (*dKon mchog 'Jigs med dBang po*)

Refutation of Errors Regarding Secret Mantra (*sNgags log sum 'byin*)

Root Verses on the Middle Way (*dBu ma rtsa ba'i tshig le'ur byas pa, Mūlamadhyamaka-kārikā*), by Nāgārjuna

Sampuṭa-tantra (*Sam pu ṭa rgyud, Yang dag pa sbyor ba'i rgyud*)

Saṃvara-tantra (*sDom pa'i rgyud*)

Secret Basic Essence Tantra (*sGyu 'phrul gsang ba snying po'i rgyud, Guhya-mūla-garbha-tantra*)

Secret Tantra of the General Precept of All Maṇḍalas (*gSang ba spyi rgyud, Sarvamaṇḍalasāmānya-vidhīnām-guhyatantra*)

Short Collection (*Kṣudraka-āgama*; Pāli: *Khuddaka-nikāya*)

Spontaneous Birth and Attainment (*Lhan cig skyes sgrub*), by Ḍoṃbī Heruka

Stages of Final Meditations (*bSam gtan phyi ma, Dhyānottara-paṭalakrama*)

Stages of Meditation (*sGom pa'i rim pa, Bhāvanā-krama*), by Kamalaśīla

Statement of Ba (*sBa bzhed*)

Sūtra Explaining the Thought (*dGongs pa nges par 'grel pa'i mdo, Saṃdhinirmocana-sūtra*)

Sūtra of the Fortunate Eon (*bsKal pa bzang po'i mdo, Bhadrakalpaka-sūtra*)

Sūtra of the Great Final Nirvāṇa (*Yongs su mya ngan las 'das pa chen po'i mdo, Mahāparinirvāṇa-sūtra*; Pāli: *Mahāparinibbana-sutta*)

Sūtra of the Meeting of Father and Son (*Yab dang sras mjal ba'i mdo, Pitāputrasamāgama-sūtra*)

Sūtra on Individual Liberation (*So sor thar pa'i mdo, Prātimokṣa-sūtra*)

Sūtra on Monastic Discipline (*'Dul ba'i mdo, Vinaya-sūtra*), by Guṇaprabha

Sūtra on the Ten Dharmas (*Chos bcu pa'i mdo, Daśa-dharma-sūtra*)

Sūtra on the Ten Levels (*mDo sde sa bcu pa, Daśabhūmika-sūtra*)

Sūtra Turning the Wheel of Dharma (*Chos kyi 'khor lo rab tu bskor ba'i mdo, Dharma cakrapravartana-sutra*)

Tantra Called 'Questions of the Superior Subāhu' (*dPung bzangs pa'i rgyud, Āryasubāhu-paripṛccha-nāma-tantra*)

Tantra of the Great Natural Arising of Awareness (*Rig pa rang shar chen po'i rgyud*)

Three Cycles of Fundamental Mind (*gNyug sems skor gsum*), by Mipam (*Mi pham*)

Three Cycles of Revelation (*bsGrags pa skor gsum*), a collection of Bon po *gter ma* texts

Three Principal Aspects of the Path (*Lam gtso rnam gsum*), by Tsong Khapa

Treasury of Abhidharma (*Chos mNgon pa'i mdzod, Abhidharmakośa*), by Vasubandhu

Treasury of the Knowledge of Valid Cognition (*Tshad ma rigs pa'i gter*), by Sakya Paṇḍita (*Sa skya Paṇḍita*)

Treasury of Well-Spoken Jewels (*Legs par bshad pa rin po che'i gter, Subhāsitaratnanidhi*), by Sakya Paṇḍita

Treatise on the Mind of Awakening (*Byang chub sems 'grel, Bodhicitta-vivaraṇa*), by Nāgārjuna

Vajra-pañjara-tantra (*rDo rje gur rgyu*)

Vajra Verses (*rDo rje tshig rkang, Vajra-gāthā*), by Virūpa

Locations

Abhasvara (*'Od gsal, Ābhāsvara*)

Achi (*A phyi*)

Amdo (*A mdo*)

Bodhgaya (*Bodhgayā*)

Bodhimanda (*Byang chub snying po, Bodhimaṇḍa*)

Bön Mountain (*Bon ri*)

Bugyel (*sPu rgyal*)

Bumla (*'Bum la*)

China (*rGya nag*)

Chong Gyé (*'Phyong rgyas*)

Circle of Awakening (*Byang chub snying po, Bodhimaṇḍa*)

Densatil (*gDan sa mthil*)

Desire Realm (*'Dod khams, Kāma-dhātu*)

Dhanakośa (*Da na ko sha'i mtsho gling*)

Do Dö (*mDo stod*)

Do Mé (*mDo smad*)

Drébung (*'Bras spungs*)

Drébung Déyang (*'Bras spungs bDe yangs*)

Drébung Gomang (*'Bras spungs sGo mang*)

Drébung Loséling (*'Bras spungs bLo gsal gling*)

Dri River (*'Bri chu*)

Drikung (*'Bri khung*)

Drokri (*'Brog ri*)

Drongmoché (*Grong mo che*)

Form Realm (*gZugs khams, Rūpa-dhātu*)

Formless Realm (*gZugs med khams, Ārūpya-dhātu*)

Ganden (*dGa' ldan, Tuṣita*) heaven

Ganden (*dGa' ldan, Tuṣita*) monastery

Ganden Jangtsé (*dGa' ldan Byang rtse*)

Ganden Puntsokling (*dGa' ldan Phun tshogs gling*)

Ganden Shardzé (*dGa' ldan Shar rtse*)

Golden Island (*gSer gling*)

Gongpo (*rKong po*)

Gugé (*Gu ge*)

Gurkha

Gyangdur (*rKyang 'dur*)

Gyantsé (*rGyal rtse*)

Hlamö Latso (*Lha mo'i bLa mtsho*)

Hlokha (*Lho kha*)

India (*rGya gar, 'Phags yul*)

Jambudvipa (*'Dzam bu'i gling, Jambudvīpa*)

Jokhang (*Jo khang*)

Kailasha (*Ti se, Kailāśa*)

Kamba Dzong (*Gam pa rDzong*)

Kangchen (*Gangs can*)

Kanyakubja (*Kānyakubja*)

Kapilavastu (*Ser skya'i gnas, Kapilavastu*)

Katok (*Kaḥ thog*)

Kham (*Khams*)

Korlochen (*'Khor lo can*)

Kumbum (*sKu 'bum*)

Kuśinagara (*Grong khyer rtsa can*)

Labrang (*bLa brang*)

Lang (*rLangs*)

Lari (*bLa ri*)

Légi Wangmoché (*Las kyi dbang mo che*)

Lhasa (*Lha sa*)

Litang (*Li thang*)

Lower Tantric College (*rGyud smad Grwa tsang*)

Lumbinī (*Lumb'i tshal*)

Machu (*Rma chu*)

Magadha (*Ma ga dha*)

Magical Temple of the North (*Byang phyogs sprul pa'i lha khang*)

Marpori (*dMar po ri*)

Mé (*sMad*)

Menri (*sMan ri*)

Mindroling (*sMin grol gling*)

Nālandā (*Nālendra*)

Nālendra (*Nā lendra*)

Nandavana (*dGa' ba'i tshal, Nandavana*)

Nartang (*sNar thang*)

Néchung (*gNas chung*)

Ngari (*mNga' ris*)

Ngari Gorsum (*mNga' ris skor gsum*)

Ngor Éwam Chöden (*Ngor E waṃ Chos ldan*)

Norbulingka (*Nor bu gling ka*)

Nyarong (*Nyag rong*)

Odantapurī (*Otantapuri'i gtsug lag khang*)

Oḍḍiyāna (*O rgyan*)

Ölmo Lungring (*'Ol mo lung ring*)

Pakmodru (*Phag mo gru*)

Paruṣakavana (*rTsub 'gyur tshal*)

Penyül (*'Phan yul*)

Pö (*Bod*)

Podrang (*Pho brang*)

Potala (*Po ta la*)

Rājagṛha (*rGyal po'i khab*)

Ramoché (*Ra mo che*)

Rasa (*Ra sa*)

Réting (*Rwa sgrengs*)

Rinbung (*Rin spungs*)

Riwotsé Nga (*Ri bo rtse lnga*)

Rumtek (*Rum bteg*)

Sahor (*Za hor, Sahor*)

Sakya (*Sa skya*)

Samyé (*bSam yas*)

Sangri Khangmar (*Zangs ri khang dmar*)

Sārnāth

Séra Monastery (*Se ra dGon pa*)

Séra Jé Monastery (*Se ra Byes dGon pa*)

Séra Mé Monastery (*Se ra sMad dGon pa*)

Shalu (*Zha lu*)

Shangshung (*Zhang zhung*)

Sharchenchok (*Shar chen lcog*) prison

Shédrupling (*bShad bsgrub gling*)

Shigatsé (*gZhis ka rtse*)

Śītavana (*bSil ba'i tshal*)

Śrāvastī (*Mnyan yod*)

Śrī Dhānyakaṭaka (*Shri dhana'i gling*)

Sokla Gyao (*Sog la skya bo*)

Sosadvīpa (*So sa gling gi dur khrod*)

Sur Ukpalung Monastery (*Zur 'ug pa lung dGon pa*)

Taksik (*rTag gzigs*)

Taktsé (*sTag 'tsher*)

Tangchu (*gTang chu*) river

Tangla (*Thang la*) mountains

Tashihlünpo (*bKra shis lhun po*)

Tashi Trigo (*bKra shis khrigs sgo*)

Three Provinces (*Chol kha gsum*)

Toling (*Tho ling*)

Tradruk (*Khra 'brug*)

Trang (*'Phrang*)

Trāyatriṃśa (*Sum cu rtsa gsum*)

Trochu (*Khro bcu*)

Tsang (*gTsang*)

Tsang Chumik (*gTsang Chu mig*)

Tsongkha (*Tsong kha*)

Tsuklakhang (*gTsug lag khang*)

Tsurphu (*mTshur phu*)

Tuna (*Dud sna*)

Tuṣita (*dGa' ldan*)

Ü (*dBus*)

Upper Tantric College (*rGyud stod Grwa tsang*)

Uru (*dBu ru*)

Varanasi (*Wā rā ṇa si, Chos skor gnas, Vārāṇasī*)

Vaiśālī (*Yangs pa can*)

Vajrāsana (*rDo rje gdan*)

Vikramaśīla (*Rnam gnon tshul*)

White Chöden (*mChod rten dkar po*)

Yarlung (*Yar lung*)

Yéru Ensa (*g.Yas ru dBen sa*)

Select Bibliography

Allione, Tsultrim. *Women of Wisdom.* London: Routledge & Kegan Paul, 1984; London: Arkana, 1984.

Amipa, Sherap Gyaltsen. *A Waterdrop from the Glorious Sea: A Concise Account of the Advent of Buddhism in General and the Teachings of the Sakyapa Tradition in Particular.* Rikon: Tibetan Institute, 1976.

Aris, Michael. *Hidden Treasures and Secret Lives: A Study of Pemalingpa (1450–1521) and the Sixth Dalai Lama (1683–1706).* Shimla: Indian Institute of Advanced Study and Delhi: Motilal Banarsidass, 1988.

______. "Jamyang Khyentse's Brief Discourse on the Essence of All the Ways." *Kailash* 5.3, 1977, pp. 205–28.

Aris, Michael, and Aung San Suu Kyi, eds. *Tibetan Studies in Honour of Hugh Richardson: Proceedings of the International Seminar on Tibetan Studies,* Oxford 1979. Warminster: Aris and Phillips, 1980.

Asanga. *Le Compendium de la Super-Doctrine d'Asanga (Abhidharma-samuccaya),* tr. Walpola Rahula (Paris: École Française d'Extrême-Orient, 1971)

Asia Watch. *Evading Scrutiny: Violations of Human Rights After the Closing of Tibet.* Washington, D.C.: Asia Watch, 1988.

______. *Human Rights in Tibet.* New York: Human Rights Watch, 1988.

______. *Merciless Repression: Human Rights in Tibet.* Washington, D.C.: Asia Watch, 1990.

Avedon, John F. *In Exile From the Land of Snows.* New York: Knopf, 1984.

______. *Tibet Today.* London: Wisdom, 1987.

Aziz, Barbara N. "Moving Towards a Sociology of Tibet." *Tibet Journal* 12.4, 1987, pp. 72–86.

______. "Women in Tibetan Society and Tibetology." Helga Uebach and Jampa L. Panglung, eds. *Tibetan Studies. Proceedings of the 4th Seminar of the International Association for Tibetan Studies.* Munich: Kommission für Zentralasiatische Studien, Bayerische Akademie der Wissenschaften, 1988, pp. 25–34.

Aziz, Barbara N., and Matthew Kapstein, eds. *Soundings in Tibetan Civilization.* New Delhi: Manohar, 1985.

Bacot, Jacques. *La Vie de Marpa le "Traducteur."* Paris: Librairie Orientaliste Paul Geuthner, 1937.

Bareau, André. *Recherches sur la biographie du Buddha dans les Sūtrapiṭaka et les Vinayapiṭaka anciens.* Paris: École française d'Etrême-Orient, 1963-1995.

Basak, Pradhagovinda, ed. *Mahāvastu Avadāna.* Calcutta: Sanskrit College, 1963.

Bays, Gwendolyn, tr. *The Voice of the Buddha.* Berkeley: Dharma Publishing, 1983. 2 vols.

Bechert, Heinz, ed. *The Dating of the Historical Buddha. Part 2.* Göttingen: Vandendoeck & Ruprecht, 1992.

Beckwith, Christopher I. *Silver on Lapis: Tibetan Literary Culture and History.* Bloomington, IN: Indiana University Press, 1987.

Beckwith, Christopher I. *The Tibetan Empire in Central Asia.* Princeton: Princeton University Press, 1987.

Bell, Sir Charles. *Tibet, Past and Present.* Oxford, 1924.

———. *Portrait of a Dalai Lama.* London: Collins, 1946.

Benson, Herbert. "Mind/Body Interactions including Tibetan Studies." In *Mind Science,* ed. H.H. the Dalai Lama et al. Boston: Wisdom, 1991, pp. 37–48.

Benson, Herbert, et al. "Body Temperature Changes During the Practice of gTum-mo Yoga." *Nature* 295, January 1982, pp. 234–36.

Berzin, Alexander, tr. *The Four-Themed Precious Garland: An Introduction to Dzogchen,* by Longchen Rabjampa. Dharamsala: Library of Tibetan Works and Archives, 1979.

Berzin, Alexander. *The Mahāmudrā Eliminating the Darkness of Ignorance* and *Aśvaghoṣa's Fifty Stanzas of Guru Devotion.* Dharamsala: Library of Tibetan Works and Archives, 1978.

Beyer, Stephan. *The Cult of Tārā: Magic and Ritual in Tibet.* Berkeley: University of California Press, 1978.

Buffertrille, Katia, and Hildegard Diemberger, eds. *Territory and Identity in Tibet and the Himalayas.* Leiden: E.J. Brill, 2002.

Bond, George. *The Word of the Buddha.* Colombo: M.D. Gunasena, 1982.

Bosson, James E. *A Treasury of Aphoristic Jewels: The Subhāṣitaratna-nidhi of Sa skya Paṇḍita.* Indiana University Uralic and Altaic Series, 92. Bloomington: Indiana University and The Hague: Mouton, 1969.

Brauen, Martin, and Per Kvaerne, eds. *Tibetan Studies Presented at the Seminar of Young Tibetologists, Zürich, June 26–July 1, 1977.* Zürich: Völkerkundemuseum der Universität Zürich, 1978.

Broido, Michael M. "Bshad thabs: Some Tibetan Methods of Explaining the Tantras." In Steinkellner, Ernst and Helmut Tauscher, eds., *Contributions on Tibetan and Buddhist Philosophy,* vol. 2. Vienna: Arbeitkreis für Tibetische und Buddhistische Studien, Universität Wien, 1983, pp. 15–45.

Bsod nams rgya mtsho. *Tibetan Mandalas, The Ngor Collection.* Tokyo: Kodansha, 1983.

Canzio, Ricardo O. "The Place of Music and Chant in Tibetan Religious Culture." *Tibetan Studies* (Zürich) 13-16, 1978, pp. 14–17.

Cassinelli, C.W., and Robert B. Ekvall. *A Tibetan Principality: The Political System of Sa sKya.* Ithaca. Cornell University Press, 1969.

Cech, Krystyna. *The History, Teaching and Practice of Dialectics according to the Bon Tradition.* P.O. Ochghat, via Solan, H.P.: Yungdrung Bon Monastic Centre, 1984.

Chandra, Lokesh. *Buddhist Iconography of Tibet.* 2 vols. Kyoto: Rinsen Book Co., 1986.

Chang, Garma Chen-chi. *The Hundred Thousand Songs of Milarepa.* 2 vols. Boulder and London: Shambhala, 1989.

Choephel, Gendun. *The White Annals.* Tr. Samten Norboo. Dharamsala: Library of Tibetan Works and Archives, 1978.

Chogay Trichen Rinpoche [Thubten Legshay Gyatsho]. *Gateway to the Temple: Manual of Tibetan Monastic Customs, Art, Building and Celebrations.* Tr. David Paul Jackson. Kathmandu: Ratna Pustak Bhandar, 1979.

———. *The History of the Sakya Tradition: A Feast for the Minds of the Fortunate.* Bristol: Ganesha Press, 1983.

Chokyi Nyima Rinpoche. *The Bardo Guidebook.* Hong Kong: Rangjung Yeshe, 1991.

———. *The Union of Mahamudra and Dzogchen.* Kathmandu: Rangjung Yeshe, 1989.

Conboy, Kenneth, and James Morrison. *The CIA's Secret War in Tibet.* Lawrence, KS: University of Kansas Press, 2002.

Conze, Edward. *The Large Sūtra on Perfect Wisdom.* London: Luzac & Co., 1961.

Corlin, Claes. *The Nation in Your Mind: Continuity and Change among Tibetan Refugees in Nepal.* Ph.D. dissertation, University of Göteborg, 1975.

Cozort, Daniel. *Highest Yoga Tantra. An Introduction to the Esoteric Buddhism of Tibet.* Ithaca: Snow Lion, 1986.

Davidson, Ronald. *Indian Esoteric Buddhism: A Social History of the Tantric Movement.* New York: Columbia University Press, 2002.

Davidson, Ronald. *Tibetan Renaissance: Tantric Buddhism in the Rebirth of Tibetan Culture.* New York: Columbia University Press, 2005.

Demiéville, Paul. *La Concile de Lhasa.* Paris: Imprimerie National de France, 1952.

Desio, Ardito. *Ascent of K2.* London: Elek Books, 1955.

Dhondup, K. *Songs of the Sixth Dalai Lama.* Dharamsala: Library of Tibetan Works and Archives, 1981.

Dilgo Khyentse, H.H. *The Wish-Fulfilling Jewel: The Practice of Guru Yoga According to the Longchen Nyingthig Tradition.* Boston: Shambhala, 1988.

Doctor, Andreas. *Tibetan Treasure Literature: Revelation, Tradition, and Accomplishment in Visionary Buddhism.* Ithaca: Snow Lion, 2005.

Dodin, Thierry, and Heinz Räther, eds. *Imagining Tibet: Perceptions, Projections, and Fantasies.* Boston: Wisdom Publications, 2001.

Donden, Dr. Yeshi. *Health Through Balance: An Introduction to Tibetan Medicine.* Tr. Jeffrey Hopkins. Ithaca: Snow Lion, 1986.

Devoe, Dorsh Marie. "Keeping Refugee Status: A Tibetan Perspective." Scott Morgan and Elizabeth Colson, eds. *People in Upheaval.* New York: Center for Migration Studies, 1987, pp. 54–65.

Douglas, Nik, and Meryl White. *Karmapa: The Black Hat Lama of Tibet.* London: Luzac, 1976.

Douglas, Kenneth, and Gwendolyn Bays, tr. *The Life and Liberation of Padmasambhava.* 2 vols. Emeryville, CA: Dharma Publishing, 1978.

Dowman, Keith. *Masters of Enchantment: The Lives and Legends of the Mahasiddhas.* Rochester, VT: Inner Traditions International, 1988.

______. *The Power-Places of Central Tibet: The Pilgrim's Guide.* London: Routledge & Kegan Paul, 1988.

______. *Sky Dancer: The Secret Life and Songs of the Lady Yeshe Tsogyel.* New York: Arkana, 1984; London: Routledge & Kegan Paul, 1984.

Dreyfus, Georges. *Recognizing Reality: Dharmakīrti's Philosophy and Its Tibetan Interpreters.* Albany: State University of New York Press, 1997.

Dreyfus, Georges. *The Sound of Two Hands Clapping: The Education of a Tibetan Buddhist Monk.* Berkeley: University of California Press, 2003.

Dudjom Rinpoche. *The Nyingma School of Tibetan Buddhism.* 2 vols. London: Wisdom, 1991.

Ekvall, Robert B. *Religious Observances in Tibet: Patterns and Function.* Chicago: University of Chicago Press, 1964.

Elchert, Carole, ed. *White Lotus: An Introduction to Tibetan Culture.* Ithaca: Snow Lion, 1990.

Eliade, Mircea. *Patterns of Comparative Religion.* Cleveland: World Publishing, 1963.

Ellingson, Ter. "'Don rta dbyangs gsum: Tibetan Chant and Melodic Categories." *Asian Music* 10-12, 1979, pp. 112–56.

Ellingson, Ter. *Maṇḍala of Sound: Concepts and Sound Structures in Tibetan Ritual Music.* Ann Arbor: University Microfilms, 1980. Ph.D. dissertation, University of Wisconsin, 1979.

Epstein, Lawrence, and Richard F. Sherburne, eds. *Reflections on Tibetan Culture. Essays in Memory of Turrell V. Wylie.* Studies in Asian Thought and Religion, 12. Lewiston and Queenston: The Edwin Mellen Press, 1990.

Evans-Wentz, W.Y. *The Tibetan Book of the Great Liberation.* London: Oxford University Press, 1968.

Evans-Wentz, W.Y. *Tibet's Great Yogi Milarepa: A Biography from the Tibetan.* London: Oxford University, 1928; reprint 1969, 1980.

Ferrari, Alfonsa. *Mk'yen Brtse's Guide to the Holy Places of Central Tibet.* Rome: IsMEO, 1958.

Fisher, James F., ed. *Himalayan Anthropology: The Indo-Tibetan Interface.* The Hague: Mouton, 1978.

Frauwallner, Erich. *The Earliest Vinaya and the Beginnings of Buddhist Literature*; Rome: Serie Orientale Roma, vol. VIII, 1956.

Garfield, Jay, tr. *The Fundamental Wisdom of the Middle Way: Nāgārjuna's Mūlamadhyamakakārikā.* New York: Oxford University Press, 1995.

Gelong, Tarchin, tr. *The Womb of Form: Pith Instructions in the Six Yogas of Naropa from the Teachings of Namgyal Rinpoche.* Ottawa: Crystal Word Publications, 1981.

Goldstein, Melvyn C. "The Balance between Centralization and Decentralization in the Traditional Tibetan Political System." *Central Asiatic Journal* 15, 1971, pp. 170–82.

______. *A History of Modern Tibet, 1913-1951: The Demise of the Lamaist State.* Berkeley: University of California Press, 1989.

Goldstein, Melvyn C., and Cynthia M. Beall. *Nomads of Western Tibet: The Survival of a Way of Life.* London: Serindia Publications, 1990; Berkeley: University of California Press, 1990.

Goodman, Steven D. "Mi-Pham rgya-mtsho: An Account of His Life, the Printing of His Works, and the Structure of His Treatise Entitled *mKhas-pa'i tshul la 'jug-pa'i sgo.*" *Wind Horse* 1, 1981, pp. 58–78.

Goodman, Steven D., and Ronald M. Davidson, eds. *Tibetan Buddhism: Reason and Revelation.* Albany: SUNY Press, 1992.

Gross, Rita M. *Buddhism After Patriarchy: A Feminist History, Analysis, and Reconstruction of Buddhism.* Albany: SUNY Press, 1992.

Guenther, Herbert V. *From Reductionism to Creativity: Rdzogs-chen and the New Sciences of Mind.* Boston: Shambhala, 1989.

______. *The Jewel Ornament of Liberation by sGam-po-pa.* London: Rider, 1963; reprint Berkeley: Shambhala, 1971; Boulder: Prajna Press, 1981.

______. *The Life and Teaching of Nāropa.* Oxford: Clarendon Press, 1963.

Gyaltsen, Khenpo Könchog. *The Garland of Mahamudra Practices: A Translation of Kunga Rinchen's "Clarifying the Jewel Rosary of the Profound Fivefold Path."* Ithaca: Snow Lion, 1986.

______. *The Great Kagyu Masters: The Golden Lineage Treasury.* Ithaca: Snow Lion, 1990.

______. *In Search of the Stainless Ambrosia.* Ithaca: Snow Lion, 1988.

Gyaltsen, Shardza Tashi. *Heart Drops of Dharmakaya: Dzogchen Practice of the Bön Tradition.* Ithaca: Snow Lion, 2002.

Gyatso, Geshe Kelsang. *Clear Light of Bliss: Mahamudra in Vajrayana Buddhism.* London: Wisdom, 1982.

______. *Meaningful to Behold: View, Meditation and Action in Mahayana Buddhism: An Oral Commentary to Shantideva's Bodhicaryavatara.* London: Wisdom, 1980.

Gyatso, Janet. *Apparitions of the Self: The Secret Autobiographies of a Tibetan Visionary.* Princeton: Princeton University Press, 1999.

______. "The Development of the gCod Tradition." In Aziz, Barbara N., and Matthew Kapstein, eds., *Soundings in Tibetan Civilization.* New Delhi: Manohar, 1985, pp. 320–41.

———. "Down with the Demoness: Reflections on a Feminine Ground in Tibet." *Tibet Journal* 12.4, 1987, pp. 38–53.

Gyatso, Janet and Hanna Havnevik, eds. *Women in Tibet.* New York: Columbia University Press, 2005.

Gyatso, Tenzin, Dalai Lama XIV. *The Buddhism of Tibet and The Key to the Middle Way.* Tr. Jeffrey Hopkins. London: George Allen & Unwin, 1975.

———. *Freedom in Exile.* New York: HarperPerennial, 1990.

———. *Kalachakra Tantra: Rite of Initiation.* Tr. Jeffrey Hopkins. London: Wisdom, 1985.

———. *Kindness, Clarity, and Insight.* Tr. Jeffrey Hopkins. Ithaca: Snow Lion, 1984.

———. *Path to Bliss: A Practical Guide to Stages of Meditation.* Ithaca: Snow Lion, 1991.

Gyatsho, Thubten Legshay. *Gateway to the Temple.* Kathmandu: Ratna Pustak Bhandar, 1979.

Haarh, Erik. *The Yarlung Dynasty.* Copenhagen: G.E.C. Gad's Forlag, 1969.

Harrer, Heinrich. *Seven Years in Tibet.* London: Reprint Society, 1955; Los Angeles: J.P. Tarcher, 1982.

Hookham, S.K. *The Buddha Within.* Albany: SUNY Press, 1991.

Hopkins, Jeffrey. *Compassion in Tibetan Buddhism.* London: Rider, 1980.

———. *Emptiness Yoga.* Ithaca: Snow Lion, 1987.

———. *Meditation on Emptiness.* London: Wisdom, 1983.

———. *Tantra in Tibet: The Great Exposition of Secret Mantra by Tsong-ka-pa. Part One.* London: Allen & Unwin, 1977.

———. *The Yoga of Tibet: The Great Exposition of Secret Mantra by Tsong-ka-pa. Parts Two and Three.* London: Allen & Unwin, 1981.

Horner, I. B., tr. *The Collection of the Middle Length Sayings.* 2 vols. London: Luzac & Co., 1967.

Houston, G.W. *Sources for a History of the Bsam yas Debate.* Sankt Augustin: VGH Wissenschaftsverlag, 1980.

Huber, Toni. "Introduction: A mdo and Its Modern Transition." In Toni Huber, ed., *Amdo Tibetans in Transition: Society and Culture in the Post-Mao Era.* Leiden: E.J. Brill, 2002, pp. xi–xxiii.

———. "Shangri-la in Exile: Representations of Tibetan Identity and Transnational Culture." In Thierry Dodin and Heinz Räther, eds., *Imagining Tibet: Perceptions, Projections, and Fantasies.* Boston: Wisdom Publications, 2001.

Inaba, Shoju. "The Lineage of the Sa skya pa. A Chapter of the Red Annals." *Memoirs of the Research Department of the Toyo Bunko* 22, 1963, pp. 106–23.

Ishihama, Yumiko. "On the Dissemination of the Belief in the Dalai Lama as a Manifestation of the Bodhisattva Avalokiteśvara," *Acta Asiatica* 64, 1993, pp. 3–56.

Jackson, David P. "Commentaries on the Writings of Sa-skya Paṇḍita: A Bibliographical Sketch." *Tibet Journal* 8.3, 1983, pp. 3–23.

______. *The Early Abbots of 'Phan-po Na-lendra: The Vicissitudes of a Great Tibetan Monastery in the 15th Century.* Wien: Arbeitskreis für Tibetische und Buddhistische Studien, Universität Wien, 1989.

______. *The Entrance Gate for the Wise: Sa-skya Paṇḍita on Indian and Tibetan Traditions of Pramāṇa and Philosophical Debate.* 2 vols. Wien: Arbeits-kreis für Tibetische und Buddhistische Studien Universität Wien, 1987.

Jackson, Roger. "Sa skya Paṇḍita's Account of the bSam yas Debate: History as Polemic." *Journal of the International Association for Buddhist Studies* 5.2, 1982, pp. 89–99.

______. "The Kalachakra in Context." In *The Wheel of Time: The Kalachakra in Context,* ed. Geshe Lhundub Sopa, Roger Jackson, and John Newman. Madison, WI: Deer Park Books, 1985, pp. 1–50.

Kalu Rinpoche. *The Dharma That Illuminates All Beings Like the Light of the Sun and the Moon.* Albany: SUNY Press, 1986.

______. *The Gem Ornament of Manifold Instructions Which Benefits Each and Everyone Appropriately.* Ithaca: Snow Lion, 1986.

Kapstein, Matthew. *Reason's Traces: Identity and Interpretation in Indian and Tibetan Buddhist Thought.* Boston: Wisdom Publications, 2001.

______. "Religious Syncretism in 13th Century Tibet: The Limitless Ocean Cycle." In Aziz, Barbara N., and Matthew Kapstein, eds., *Soundings in Tibetan Civilization.* New Delhi: Manohar, 1985, pp. 358–71.

______. "The Shangs-pa bKa'-brgyud: An Unknown Tradition of Tibetan Buddhism." In Aris, Michael, and Aung San Suu Kyi, eds., *Tibetan Studies in Honour of Hugh Richardson.* Warminster: Aris and Phillips, 1980, pp. 138–44.

______. *The Tibetan Assimilation of Buddhism: Conversion, Contestation, and Memory.* Oxford: Oxford University Press, 2000.

Karmay, Samten Gyaltsen. "A General Introduction to the History and Doctrines of Bon." *Memoirs of the Research Department of the Toyo Bunko* 33, 1975, pp. 171–218.

———. *The Great Perfection (Rdzogs Chen): A Philosophical and Meditative Training in Tibetan Buddhism.* Leiden: E.J. Brill, 1988.

———. *Secret Visions of the Fifth Dalai Lama: The Gold Manuscript in the Fournier Collection.* London: Serindia, 1988.

Khetsun Sangbo Rinbochay. *Tantric Practice in Nying-ma.* London: Rider, 1982.

Klieger, P. Christiaan. *Accomplishing Tibetan Identity: the Constitution of a National Consciousness.* Ph.D. dissertation, University of Hawai'i, 1989.

———. *Tibetan Nationalism: The Role of Patronage in the Accomplishment of a National Identity.* Meerut, India: Archana Publications, 1992.

Klein, Anne. *Meeting the Great Bliss Queen: Buddhists, Feminists, and the Art of Self.* Boston: Beacon Press, 1995.

———. "Primordial Purity and Everyday Life: Exalted Female Symbols and the Women of Tibet." In Clarissa W. Atkinson et al., *Immaculate and Powerful: The Female in Sacred Image and Social Reality.* London: Crucible, 1987, pp. 111–38.

Kværne, Per K. "Bonpo Studies, the A Khrid System of Meditation." Part I: *Kailash* 1.1, 1973, pp. 1–50; Part II: *Kailash* 1.4, 1973, pp. 247–332.

———. "'The Great Perfection' in the Tradition of the Bonpos." In Lai, Whalen, and Lewis R. Lancaster, eds., *Early Ch'an in China and Tibet.* Berkeley: Asian Humanities Press, 1983, pp. 367–92.

La Vallée Poussin, Louis de, tr. *Abhidharmakośa,* VI. Paris: Institut Belge des Hautes Études Chinoises, 1971.

Lama Yeshe. *Introduction to Tantra: A Vision of Totality.* London: Wisdom, 1987.

Lamotte, Étienne. *History of Indian Buddhism.* Louvain-la-Neuve: Université Catholique de Louvain, 1988.

Lamotte, Étienne, tr. *La Somme du Grand Véhicule d'Asaṅga (Mahāyāna-saṃgraha).* Louvain: Université de Louvain, 1973.

Lati Rinbochay and Denma Lochö Rinbochay, *Meditative States in Tibetan Buddhism.* London: Wisdom, 1983.

Lhalungpa, Lobsang P. *The Life of Milarepa: A New Translation from the Tibetan.* Boston: Shambhala, 1977; New York: Arkana, 1984.

———. *Mahāmudrā: The Quintessence of Mind and Meditation.* Boston: Shambhala, 1986.

Lhundrub, Ngorchen Konchog. *The Beautiful Ornament of the Three Visions.* Ithaca: Snow Lion, 1991.

Ling-pa, Jigme. *The Dzogchen Innermost Essence Preliminary Practice.* Dharamsala: Library of Tibetan Works and Archives, 1982.

Lodrö, Geshe Gendün. *Walking Through Walls.* Tr. Jeffrey Hopkins. Ithaca: Snow Lion, 1992.

Lopez, Donald S. *Prisoners of Shangri-La: Tibetan Buddhism and the West* Chicago: University of Chicago Press, 1998.

McLeod, Kenneth, tr. *The Chariot for Travelling the Path to Freedom: The Life Story of Kalu Rinpoche.* San Francisco: Kagyu Dharma, 1985.

______. *A Direct Path to Enlightenment by 'Jam-mGon Kong-sPrul the Great.* Vancouver: Kagyu Kunkhyab Choling, 1974.

Mimaki, Katsumi. *Blo gsal grub mtha'.* Kyoto: Université de Kyoto, 1982.

Mitra, Rajendralala, ed. *The Lalita Vistara.* Calcutta: C.R. Lewis, Baptist Mission Press, 1877.

Mkhas grub rje. *Introduction to the Buddhist Tantric Systems.* Tr. F.D. Lessing and Alex Wayman. Delhi: Motilal Banarsidass, 1978.

Morgan, Scott, and Elizabeth Colson, eds. *People in Upheaval.* New York: Center for Migration Studies, 1987.

Mullin, Glenn H. *Death and Dying: The Tibetan Tradition.* London: Arkana, 1987.

______. *Selected Works of the Dalai Lama II.* Ithaca: Snow Lion, 1985.

Nakamura, Hajime. *Indian Buddhism: A Survey with Bibliographical Notes.* Delhi: Motilal Banarsidass, 1987.

Nebesky-Wojkowitz, René de. *Oracles and Demons of Tibet: The Cult and Iconography of the Tibetan Protective Deities.* The Hague: Mouton, 1956; Taipei: SMC Publishing, 1956.

______. *Tibetan Religious Dances.* The Hague: Mouton, 1976.

Nietupski, Paul. "Sino-Tibetan Relations in Eighteenth-Century Labrang." In Katia Buffertrille and Hildegard Diemberger, eds., *Territory and Identity in Tibet and the Himalayas.* Leiden: E.J. Brill, 2002, pp. 121–134.

Norbu, Jamyang. *Warriors of Tibet: The Story of Aten and the Khampas' Fight for the Freedom of Their Country.* London: Wisdom Publications, 1979.

Norbu, Namkhai. *The Crystal and the Way of Light: Sūtra, Tantra and Dzogchen.* New York and London: Routledge & Kegan Paul, 1986.

———. *Dream Yoga and the Practice of Natural Light.* Ithaca: Snow Lion, 1992.

Norbu, Thinley. *Magic Dance: The Display of the Self-Nature of the Five Wisdom Dakinis.* New York: Jewel Publishing House, 1981.

Norbu, Thubten J. "Festivals of Tibet." *Journal of Popular Culture* 16.1, 1982, pp. 126–34.

Nowak, Margaret. *Tibetan Refugees: Youth and the New Generation of Meaning.* New Brunswick, NJ: Rutgers University Press, 1984.

Obermiller, Eugene. *History of Buddhism (Chos-ḥbyung by Bu-ston).* 2 vols. Heidelberg, 1931–33.

Pal, Pratapaditya. *Art of Tibet.* Berkeley: University of California, 1984.

Palmo, Anila Rinchen. *Cutting Through Ego-Clinging: Commentary on the Practice of Tchod.* Landrevie: Dzambala, 1988.

The Path of Purity (Buddhaghosa's Visuddhimagga). Tr. Pe Maung Tin. London: Pāli Text Society, 1971.

Petech, Luciano. *China and Tibet in the Early Eighteenth Century: The History of the Establishment of the Chinese Protectorate in Tibet.* T'oung Pao Monographs, 1. Leiden: E.J. Brill, 1972; Westport, CT: Hyperion Press, 1973.

Piburn, Sidney. *The Dalai Lama: A Policy of Kindness.* Ithaca, New York: Snow Lion, 1990.

Pott, P. H. "Some Remarks on the 'Terrific Deities' in Tibetan 'Devil Dances'." In Matsunaga, Yukei, ed., *Studies of Esoteric Buddhism and Tantrism in Commemoration of the 1150th Anniversary of the Founding of Koyasan.* Koyasan: Koyasan University Press, 1965, pp. 269–78.

Powers, John. "Conflict and Resolution in the Biography of Milarepa." *Tibet Journal* 17.1, Spring, 1992, pp. 68–77.

———. *History as Propaganda: Tibetan Exiles Versus the People's Republic of China.* New York: Oxford University Press, 2004.

Powers, John and Deane Curtin. "Mothering: Moral Cultivation in Buddhist and Feminist Ethics." *Philosophy East and West* 44.1, 1994, pp.1–18.

Ray, Reginald A. *Secret of the Vajra World: The Tantric Buddhism of Tibet.* Boston: Shambhala, 2001.

Rhie, Marylin and Robert Thurman. *Wisdom and Compassion: The Sacred Art of Tibet.* New York: Harry N. Abrams, 1991.

Rhys Davids, T.W. and C.A.F. tr. *Long Discourse Collection* (*Dīgha-nikāya*). London: Luzac & Co., 1959.

Richardson, Hugh E. *Tibet and Its History.* Boulder and London: Shambhala, 1984.

Lati Rinbochay and Denma Lochö Rinbochay, *Meditative States in Tibetan Buddhism* (London: Wisdom, 1983),

Roerich, George N. *The Blue Annals.* Delhi: Motilal Banarsidass, 1976.

______. "Mongol-Tibetan Relations in the 13th and 14th Centuries." *Tibet Society Bulletin* 6, 1973, pp. 40–55.

Ruegg, David Seyfort. *Buddha-Nature, Mind, and the Problem of Gradualism in a Comparative Perspective.* London: School of Oriental and African Studies, 1989.

______. *The Life of Bu ston Rin po che with the Tibetan Text of the Bu ston rNam thar.* Serie Orientale Roma, 34. Rome: IsMEO, 1966.

______. *Le Traité du Tathāgatagarbha de Bu Ston Rin Chen Grub.* Paris: École Française d'Extrême-Orient, 1973.

Sakya Pandita. *Illuminations.* Tr. Geshe Wangyal and Brian Cutillo. Novato, CA: Lotsawa, 1988.

Saṃdhinirmocana-sūtra (*'Phags pa dgongs pa nges par 'grel pa'i mdo*): *The Tog Palace Edition of the Tibetan Kanjur.* Leh: Smanrtsis Shesrig Dpemzod, 1975–1978.

Samuel, Geoffrey. *Civilized Shamans: Buddhism in Tibetan Societies.* Washington: Smithsonian Institution, 1995.

______. "Early Buddhism in Tibet: Some Anthropological Perspectives." In Aziz, Barbara N., and Matthew Kapstein, eds., *Soundings in Tibetan Civilization.* New Delhi: Manohar, 1985, pp. 383–97.

Sangay, Thubten. "Tibetan Rituals of the Dead." *Tibetan Medicine* 7, 1984, pp. 30–40.

Sautman, Barry, and June Teufel Dreyer, eds. *Contemporary Tibet: Politics, Development, and Society in a Disputed Region.* London: M.E. Sharpe, 2006.

Schopen, Gregory. *Buddhist Monks and Business Matters: Still More Papers on Monastic Buddhism in India.* Honolulu: University of Hawai'i Press, 2004.

______. *Figments and Fragments of Mahāyāna Buddhism in India: More Collected Papers.* Honolulu: University of Hawai'i Press, 2005.

Shakabpa, Tsepon W. D. *Tibet: A Political History.* New Haven: Yale University Press, 1967; reprint New York: Potala, 1984.

Shakya, Tsering. *The Dragon in the Land of Snows: A History of Modern Tibet Since 1947.* New York: Columbia University Press, 1999.

Shukla, Karunesha, ed. *Śrāvakabhūmi*. Patna: K.P. Jayaswal, 1973.

Silananda, Venerable U. *The Four Foundations of Mindfulness*. London: Wisdom, 1990.

Simmer-Brown, Judith. *Dakini's Warm Breath: The Feminine Principle in Tibetan Buddhism*. Boston: Shambhala Publications, 2001.

Skorupski, Tadeusz, ed. *Indo-Tibetan Studies: Papers in Honour and Appreciation of Professor David L. Snellgrove's Contribution to Indo-Tibetan Studies*. Tring: Institute of Buddhist Studies, 1990.

———. "Tibetan g-Yung Drung Monastery at Dolanji." *Kailash* 8.1–2, 1981, pp. 25–44.

Skorupski, Tadeusz, and Krystyna Cech. "Major Tibetan Life Cycle Events—Birth and Marriage Ceremonies." *Kailash* 11.1–2, 1984, pp. 5–32.

Snellgrove, David L. *Buddhist Himalaya*. Oxford: Bruno Cassirer, 1957; Oxford: Oxford University Press, 1975.

———. *Four Lamas of Dolpo*. 2 vols. Oxford: Bruno Cassirer, 1967.

———. *Indo-Tibetan Buddhism: Indian Buddhists and Their Tibetan Successors*. 2 vols. Boston: Shambhala, 1987.

———. *The Nine Ways of Bon: Excerpts from gZi brjid*. London Oriental Series, 18. London: Oxford University Press, 1967.

Snellgrove, David L., and Hugh E. Richardson. *A Cultural History of Tibet*. London: Weidenfeld and Nicolson, 1968; Boulder: Prajna Press, 1980.

Sobisch, Jan-Ulrich. *Three-Vow Theories in Tibetan Buddhism*. Wiesbaden: Dr. Ludwig Richert Verlag, 2002.

Sogyal Rinpoche. *The Tibetan Book of Living and Dying*. San Francisco: Harper, 1992.

Sopa, Geshe Lhundup. "*Śamathavipaśyanāyuganaddha*: The Two Leading Principles of Buddhist Meditation." In Minoru Kiyota, ed., *Mahāyāna Buddhist Meditation*. Honolulu: University Press of Hawaii, 1978, pp. 46–65.

Sopa, Geshe Lhundup, and Hopkins, Jeffrey. *Cutting Through Appearances*. Ithaca: Snow Lion, 1989.

Stearns, Cyrus. *Luminous Lives: The Story of the Early Masters of the Lam 'Bras Tradition in Tibet*. Boston: Wisdom Publications, 2001.

Steinkellner, Ernst, and Helmut Tauscher, eds. *Contributions on Tibetan Language, History and Culture. Proceedings of the Csoma de Körös Symposium held at Velm-Vienna, Austria, 13-19 September 1981*. 2 vols.

Vienna: Arbeitskreis für Tibetische und Buddhistische Studien, Universität Wien, 1983.

Studholme, Alexander. *The Origins of Oṃ Maṇi Padme Hūṃ: A Study of the Kāraṇḍavyūha Sūtra.* Albany: State University of New York Press, 2002.

Takpo Tashi Namgyal. *Mahāmudrā.* Boston: Shambhala, 1986.

Tarthang Tulku. *Mother of Knowledge: The Enlightenment of Ye-shes mTsho-rgyal.* Berkeley: Dharma Publishing, 1983.

Teichman, Eric. *Travels of a Consular Officer in North-West China* (Cambridge: Cambridge University Press, 1922.

Tharchin, Sermey Geshe Lobsang. *A Commentary on Guru Yoga and Offering of the Mandala.* Ithaca: Snow Lion, 1980.

Thondup, Tulku. *Buddha Mind: An Anthology of Longchen Rabjam's Writings on Dzogpa Chenpo.* Ithaca: Snow Lion, 1989.

———. *Hidden Teachings of Tibet: An Explanation of the Terma Tradition of the Nyingma School of Buddhism.* London: Wisdom, 1986.

Thurman, Robert A.F. *The Life and Teachings of Tsong Khapa.* Dharamsala: Library of Tibetan Works and Archives, 1982.

Trungpa, Chögyam. *Born in Tibet.* Harmondsworth: Penguin, 1971.

———. *The Rain of Wisdom: Vajra Songs of the Kagyü Gurus.* Tr. Nalanda Translation Committee. Boulder and London: Shambhala, 1980.

Tsering, Migmar. "Sakya Pandita: Glimpses of His Three Major Works." *Tibet Journal* 13.1, 1988, pp. 12–19.

Tsomo, Karma Lekshe. "Tibetan Nuns and Nunneries." *Tibet Journal* 12.4, 1987, pp. 87–99.

Tucci, Giuseppe. *Deb ther dmar po gsar ma: Tibetan Chronicles.* Rome: IsMEO, 1971.

———. *The Religions of Tibet.* London: Routledge & Kegan Paul, 1980; Berkeley: University of California Press, 1980.

———. *Stupa: Art, Architectonics, and Symbolism.* New Delhi: Aditya Prakashan, 1988.

———. *The Temples of Western Tibet and their Artistic Symbolism.* 2 vols. New Delhi: Aditya Prakashan, 1988.

———. *Tibetan Painted Scrolls.* 3 vols. Rome: La Libreria Dello Stato, 1949; reprint Kyoto: Rinsen Book Co., 1980.

Tuttle, Gray. *Tibetan Buddhists in the Making of Modern China.* New York: Columbia University Press, 2005.

Vasubandhu. *Treasury of Abhidharma (Abhidharmakośa)*. Tr. Louis de La Vallée Poussin; English tr. Leo Pruden; Berkeley: Asian Humanities Press, 1988.

van der Kuijp, Leonard W.J. *Contributions to the Development of Tibetan Buddhist Epistemology from the Eleventh to the Thirteenth Century*. Wiesbaden: Franz Steiner Verlag, 1983.

von Fürer-Haimendorf, Christoph. *The Renaissance of Tibetan Civilization*. Oracle, AZ: Synergetic Press, 1990.

Wangyal, Geshe. *The Door of Liberation: Essential Teachings of the Tibetan Buddhist Tradition*. Boulder: Shambhala, 1983.

Warder, A.K. *Indian Buddhism*. Delhi: Motilal Banarsidass, 1970.

Willis, Janice D. *Feminine Ground: Essays on Women and Tibet*. Ithaca: Snow Lion, 1987.

———. "On the Nature of Rnam-thar: Early Dge-lugs-pa Siddha Biographies." In Aziz, Barbara N., and Matthew Kapstein, eds., *Soundings in Tibetan Civilization*. New Delhi: Manohar, 1985, pp. 304–19.

———. "Tibetan Anis: The Nun's Life in Tibet." *Tibet Journal* 9.4, 1984, pp. 14–32.

Wylie, Turrell V. "The First Mongol Conquest of Tibet Reinterpreted." *Harvard Journal of Asiatic Studies* 37, 1977, pp. 103–33.

———. "Reincarnation: A Political Innovation in Tibetan Buddhism." In Ligeti, Louis, ed., *Proceedings of the Csoma de Körös Memorial Symposium, Hungary, 24–30 September 1976*. Budapest: Akadémiai Kiadó, 1978, pp. 579–86.

———. "A Standard System of Tibetan Transcription." *Harvard Journal of Asiatic Studies* 22, 1959, pp. 261–76.

Yuthok, Lama Choedak. *The Triple Tantra*. Canberra: Gorum Publications, 1997.

Indexes

Index of Technical Terms

INDEX OF PROPER NAMES

Titles of Works Mentioned

Index of Locations